Lecture Notes in Computer Science 14419

Services Science

Subline of Lecture Notes in Computer Science

More information about this series at https://link.springer.com/bookseries/558

Flavia Monti · Stefanie Rinderle-Ma ·
Antonio Ruiz Cortés · Zibin Zheng ·
Massimo Mecella
Editors

Service-Oriented Computing

21st International Conference, ICSOC 2023
Rome, Italy, November 28 – December 1, 2023
Proceedings, Part I

 Springer

Editors
Flavia Monti ⓘ
Sapienza University of Rome
Rome, Italy

Stefanie Rinderle-Ma ⓘ
Technical University of Munich
Garching, Germany

Antonio Ruiz Cortés ⓘ
University of Seville
Seville, Spain

Zibin Zheng ⓘ
Sun Yat-sen University
Guangzhou, China

Massimo Mecella ⓘ
Sapienza University of Rome
Rome, Italy

ISSN 0302-9743   ISSN 1611-3349 (electronic)
Lecture Notes in Computer Science
ISBN 978-3-031-48420-9   ISBN 978-3-031-48421-6 (eBook)
https://doi.org/10.1007/978-3-031-48421-6

This Springer imprint is published by the registered company Springer Nature Switzerland AG
The registered company address is: Gewerbestrasse 11, 6330 Cham, Switzerland

Paper in this product is recyclable.

Preface

The 21st International Conference on Service-Oriented Computing (ICSOC 2023) took place in Rome (Italy) from November 28 to December 1, 2023. ICSOC is the premier international forum aiming at bringing together academics, industry researchers, developers, and practitioners to report and share ground-breaking work in the area of Service-Oriented Computing. It offers a top-tier platform for unveiling results advancing our understanding of various aspects of the field. This includes everything from application and system considerations to cutting-edge topics like artificial intelligence, machine learning, big data analytics, the Internet of Things (IoT), and emerging technologies such as quantum computing, blockchain, chatbots, and sustainable green IT solutions. Reflecting upon the remarkable history of previous ICSOC editions, including Trento (Italy, 2003), New York (USA, 2004), Amsterdam (the Netherlands, 2005), Chicago (USA, 2006), Vienna (Austria, 2007), Sydney (Australia, 2008), Stockholm (Sweden, 2009), San Francisco (USA, 2010), Paphos (Cyprus, 2011), Shanghai (China, 2012), Berlin (Germany, 2013), Paris (France, 2014), Goa (India, 2015), Banff (Canada, 2016), Malaga (Spain, 2017), Hangzhou (China, 2018), Toulouse (France, 2019), Dubai (United Arab Emirates - virtual, 2020), Dubai (United Arab Emirates - virtual, 2021) and Sevilla (Spain, 2022), ICSOC 2023 continued to build for the next decade upon this rich tradition of excellence.

ICSOC 2023 followed the two-round submission and reviewing process introduced in the previous two editions. Other than a traditional research track, it included four tracks as they relate to service computing research: (1) Artificial Intelligence for Services and as-a-Service, (2) Big Data Analytics for Services and as-a-Service, (3) Novel Service Frameworks for IoT-based and Smart Environments, and (4) Emerging Technologies. Each track was managed by a track chair, hence enhancing the quality and rigor of the paper review process. The conference attracted 208 paper submissions (29 received in the first round) co-authored by researchers, practitioners, and academics from 30 countries across all continents. Three PC members carefully double-blindly reviewed each paper submission, except for a small minority of papers (5%) with two reviews. The reviews were followed by discussions moderated by a senior PC member who made a recommendation in the form of a meta-review to the track chairs and PC co-chairs. The PC consisted of 148 world-class experts in service-oriented computing and related areas (131 PC members and 17 senior PC members) from different countries across all continents. Based on the recommendations and the discussions, 35 papers (16.83%) were accepted as full papers. We also selected 10 short papers (4.81%). In total, 12 of the 29 papers submitted in the first round were recommended for resubmission with minor or major revisions, and 6 were accepted as full or short papers. In addition, 4 papers were submitted to the industry track and 3 of them were accepted as full papers.

The conference program also included three keynotes from distinguished researchers:

- IoTility: Unleashing the Utility of Internet of Things through Microservices Architectural Extensions, given by Abdelsalam (Sumi) Helal (University of Florida, USA)
- Service Governance in a Transforming World - Challenges Ahead, given by Pablo Fernandez (University of Seville, Spain)
- Logic, Automata, and Games in Service Composition, given by Giuseppe De Giacomo (University of Oxford, UK)

Finally, tutorials, a Ph.D. symposium, a demo session and six workshops were organized to broaden the scope of ICSOC 2023. The workshops were:

- The 7th Workshop on Adaptive Service-oriented and Cloud Applications (ASOCA 2023)
- The 3rd International Workshop on AI-enabled Process Automation (AIPA 2023)
- The 19th International Workshop on Engineering Service-Oriented Applications and Cloud Services (WESOACS 2023)
- The 1st International Workshop on Secure, Accountable and Privacy-Preserving Data-Driven Service-Oriented Computing (SAPD 2023)
- The 1st Services and Quantum Software Workshop (SQS 2023)
- The 1st International Workshop on Sustainable Service-Oriented Computing: Addressing Environmental, Social, and Economic Dimensions (SSCOPE 2023)

We would like to express our gratitude to all individuals, institutions, and sponsors that supported ICSOC 2023. We would like to thank all the authors and participants for their insightful work and discussions. We are grateful to the members of the Senior Program Committee, the international Program Committee, and the external reviewers for their rigorous and robust reviewing process. We would like to express our gratitude to the area chairs Fabio Patrizi, Dan Li, Francesco Leotta, and Juan Manuel Murillo Rodriguez, for their tremendous support throughout the review process. ICSOC 2023 paper management was performed through the Conftool Conference Management System.

We would like to thank the ICSOC Steering Committee for entrusting us with organizing the 21st edition of this prestigious conference. We are grateful to all the members of the Organizing Committee and to all who contributed to make ICSOC 2023 a successful event. We are indebted to the local arrangements team from Sapienza Università di Roma for the successful organization of all conference, social, and co-located events, and to Consulta Umbria who acted as organizing agency. We also acknowledge the prompt and professional support from Springer, who published these proceedings as part of the Lecture Notes in Computer Science series.

November 2023

Massimo Mecella
Stefanie Rinderle-Ma
Antonio Ruiz Cortés
Zibin Zheng

Organization

General Chair

Massimo Mecella   Sapienza Università di Roma, Italy

Program Committee Chairs

Stefanie Rinderle-Ma   Technical University of Munich, Germany
Antonio Ruiz Cortés   Universidad de Sevilla, Spain
Zibin Zheng   Sun Yat-sen University, China

Focus Area 1: Artificial Intelligence for Services and as-a-Service Chair

Fabio Patrizi   Sapienza Università di Roma, Italy

Focus Area 2: Big Data Analytics for Services and as-a-Service Chair

Dan Li   Sun Yat-sen University, China

Focus Area 3: Novel Service Frameworks for IoT-Based and Smart Environments Chair

Francesco Leotta   Sapienza Università di Roma, Italy

Focus Area 4: Emerging Technologies Chair

Juan Manuel Murillo Rodríguez   University of Extremadura, Spain

Demo Co-chairs

Devis Bianchini   Università di Brescia, Italy
Damian A. Tamburri   TU/e - JADS, The Netherlands and Politecnico di Milano, Italy

Workshop Co-chairs

Pierluigi Plebani   Politecnico di Milano, Italy
Naouel Moha   École de Technologie Supérieure de Montréal, Canada

Ph.D. Symposium Co-chairs

Gowri Ramachandran	Queensland University of Technology, Australia
Helen Paik	University of New South Wales, Australia
Johanna Barzen	University of Stuttgart, Germany

Proceedings and Conference Management System Chair

Flavia Monti	Sapienza Università di Roma, Italy

Local Organization, Finance and Sponsorship Chair

Massimo Mecella	Sapienza Università di Roma, Italy

Publicity, Web and Social Presence Co-chairs

Marco Calamo	Sapienza Università di Roma, Italy
Flavia Monti	Sapienza Università di Roma, Italy

Local Committee

Consulta Umbria	(Organizing Agency)
Filippo Bianchini	Sapienza Università di Roma, Italy
Marco Calamo	Sapienza Università di Roma, Italy
Francesca De Luzi	Sapienza Università di Roma, Italy
Mattia Macrí	Sapienza Università di Roma, Italy
Jerin George Mathew	Sapienza Università di Roma, Italy
Flavia Monti	Sapienza Università di Roma, Italy

Steering Committee

Boualem Benatallah	Dublin City University, Ireland
Athman Bouguettaya	University of Sydney, Australia
Fabio Casati	University of Trento, Italy
Bernd J. Krämer	FernUniversität in Hagen, Germany
Winfried Lamersdorf	University of Hamburg, Germany
Heiko Ludwig	IBM, USA
Mike Papazoglou	Tilburg University, The Netherlands
Jian Yang	Macquarie University, Australia
Liang Zhang	Fudan University, China

Senior Program Committee

Marco Aiello	University of Stuttgart, Germany
Boualem Benatallah	Dublin City University, Ireland

Athman Bouguettaya	University of Sydney, Australia
Carlos Canal	University of Malaga, Spain
Flavio De Paoli	Università di Milano-Bicocca, Italy
Schahram Dustdar	TU Wien, Austria
Hakim Hacid	Zayed University, United Arab Emirates
Brahim Medjahed	University of Michigan-Dearborn, USA
Cesare Pautasso	University of Lugano, Switzerland
Barbara Pernici	Politecnico di Milano, Italy
Manfred Reichert	University of Ulm, Germany
Manuel Resinas	University of Seville, Spain
Michael Q. Sheng	Macquarie University, Australia
Stefan Tai	TU Berlin, Germany
Mathias Weske	HPI / University of Potsdam, Germany
Jian Yang	Macquarie University, Australia
Liang Zhang	Fudan University, China

Program Committee

Alessandro Aldini	University of Urbino, Italy
Moayad M. Alshangiti	University of Jeddah, Saudi Arabia
Andreas Andreou	Cyprus University of Technology, Cyprus
Yacine Atif	University of Skövde, Sweden
Marcos Baez	Bielefeld University of Applied Sciences, Germany
Luciano Baresi	Politecnico di Milano, Italy
Khalid Belhajjame	Université Paris Dauphine, France
Salima Benbernou	Université de Paris, France
Javier Berrocal	University of Extremadura, Spain
Juan Boubeta-Puig	University of Cádiz, Spain
Omar Boucelma	Aix-Marseille University, France
Lars Braubach	Hochschule Bremen, Germany
Uwe Breitenbücher	University of Stuttgart, Germany
Antonio Brogi	University of Pisa, Italy
Antonio Bucchiarone	Fondazione Bruno Kessler, Italy
Christoph Bussler	Robert Bosch LLC, USA
Cristina Cabanillas	University of Seville, Spain
Wing-Kwong Chan	City University of Hong Kong, China
Francois Charoy	University of Lorraine, France
Sanjay Chaudhary	Ahmedabad University, India
Feifei Chen	Deakin University, Australia
Lawrence Chung	University of Texas at Dallas, USA
Marco Comuzzi	UNIST, South Korea
Hoa Khanh Dam	University of Wollongong, Australia
Valeria de Castro	University Rey Juan Carlos, Spain
Martina De Sanctis	Gran Sasso Science Institute, Italy
Bruno Defude	Télécom SudParis, France
Andrea Delgado	Universidad de la República, Uruguay

Shuiguang Deng	Zhejiang University, China
Francesco Di Cerbo	SAP, France
Claudio Di Ciccio	Sapienza Università di Roma, Italy
Gregorio Diaz Descalzo	Universidad de Castilla - La Mancha, Spain
Chen Ding	Toronto Metropolitan University, Canada
Hai Dong	RMIT University, Australia
Khalil Drira	LAAS-CNRS, France
Yucong Duan	Hainan University, China
Joyce El Haddad	Université Paris-Dauphine, France
Rik Eshuis	Eindhoven University of Technology, The Netherlands
Onyeka Ezenwoye	Augusta University, USA
Noura Faci	Université Lyon 1, CNRS, France
Marcelo Fantinato	University of São Paulo, Brazil
Sheik Mohammad Mostakim Fattah	University of Adelaide, Australia
Zhiyong Feng	Tianjin University, China
Pablo Fernandez	University of Seville, Spain
Afonso Ferreira	CNRS, France
Joao E. Ferreira	University of São Paulo, Brazil
George Feuerlicht	University of Technology, Australia
Marios-Eleftherios Fokaefs	École Polytechnique Montréal, Canada
Xiang Fu	Hofstra, USA
G. R. Gangadharan	NIT Tiruchirappalli, India
Felix Garcia	University of Castilla-La Mancha, Spain
José María García	Universidad de Sevilla, Spain
José Garcia-Alonso	University of Extremadura, Spain
Ilche Georgievski	University of Stuttgart, Germany
Mohamed Graiet	ISIMM, Tunisia
Daniela Grigori	Université Paris Dauphine, France
Georg Grossmann	University of South Australia, Australia
Nawal Guermouche	Université de Toulouse, France
Mohand-Saïd Hacid	Université Claude Bernard Lyon 1, France
Jun Han	Swinburne University of Technology, Australia
Chihab Hanachi	IRIT - Toulouse University, France
Qiang He	Swinburne University of Technology, Australia
Richard Hull	IBM Research, USA
Fuyuki Ishikawa	National Institute of Informatics, Japan
Hai Jin	HUST, China
Sokratis Katsikas	Norwegian University of Science and Technology, Norway
Gerald Kotonya	Lancaster University, UK
Hemza Labbaci	University of Tours, France
Philippe Lalanda	UGA, France
Alexander Lazovik	University of Groningen, Netherlands
Weiping Li	Peking University, China
Ying Li	Zhejiang University, China

Jiuyun Xu	China University of Petroleum, China
Sami Yangui	CNRS-LAAS, France
Sira Yongchareon	Auckland University of Technology, New Zealand
Tetsuya Yoshida	Nara Women's University, Japan
Jian Yu	Auckland University of Technology, New Zealand
Qi Yu	Rochester Institute of Technology, USA
Dong Yuan	University of Sydney, China
Gianluigi Zavattaro	University of Bologna, Italy
Uwe Zdun	University of Vienna, Austria
Wei Zhang	University of Adelaide, Australia
Xuyun Zhang	Macquarie University Australia
Weiliang Zhao	Macquarie University, Australia
Zhangbing Zhou	China University of Geosciences, China
Christian Zirpins	Karlsruhe University of Applied Sciences, Germany

Additional Reviewers

Roberto Cipollone
Leandro de Souza Rosa
Matthias Ehrendorfer
Ruibing Jin
Nataliia Klievtsova

Alessandro Trapasso
Silvestro Veneruso
Neng Zheng
Peilin Zheng
Zhijie Zhong

Keynotes

IoTility: Unleashing the Utility of Internet of Things Through Microservices Architectural Extensions

Abdelsalam (Sumi) Helal

Univerity of Florida, USA

While we all share the excitements of great IoT visions and impressive IoT scenarios and possibilities, we do not yet have a clear pathway to realizing this vision systematically and on a broad and large scale. In fact, it can be argued that the focus on vision and abstracting away many details, including about "things" themselves were intentional to productively bolster our imagination; but this approach has now run its course. Ignoring the details and staying abstract will be counterproductive at this stage. We view the success of the IoT to largely depend on how its main ingredient, the thing, is architected, prepared, and tooled to deliver on the high expectations of the blue-sky visions. In other words, we see no short cuts to having to walk before we run. Service-oriented device architecture (SODA) was a successful beginning in our research journey, where devices were made capable of generating and publishing their services to an edge node or as endpoints in the cloud. IoT programmability through traditional service composition was a tangible gain at the time, which was utilized in the Gator Tech Smart House – an assistive environment for graceful aging project. However, much remains to be needed to achieve an explicit thing architecture capable of delivering on the highly anticipated visions. For example, we still do not understand how to expressly program an IoT as we have programmed previous generations and forms of the computer. This is obviously an essential requirement for any meaningful proliferation and adoption of the IoT technology. Except for a few ideas and tools that exist today, the programmability view of IoT lacks clarity and, in fact, there are no clear boundaries that separate IoT as a distributed computer from IoT as applications. In this talk, after a brief introduction to SODA, we will present requisite requirements that we must satisfy to bolster the programmability and utility of IoT as an emerging industry and as an applications ecosystem. We will present our current/ongoing work on critical extensions to the microservices architecture, collectively referred to as IoTility. First, we will focus on self- and peer-conscious microservices, which enable the IoT to autonomically learn how its things may relate to one another and what opportunities can be collectively formed, even tentatively, to the IoT users and their smart spaces. Second, we will show how giving microservices consciousness promises to make them a first-class citizen and a capable actor in the development and operation lifecycles of IoT applications and systems. This "collaborative microservice programmability" extension brings disrupting changes to the well- and long-established roles of software development, making the IoT thing (and its vendor who created it in the first place), as well as the lay user, primary developers of the IoT applications. Third, we will present

IoTranx a "safety" framework that brings transactional extensions to microservices for the development of safe cyber-physical systems and applications using IoT. We will show how such "safety-oriented programming model" prevents or avoids harms, errors, and malfunctions in presence of several cyber-physical uncertainties or un-orchestrated multiple IoT deployments. Fourth, we will revisit programmability from a different angle, and that is the inequitable utility. Despite numerous advances in IoT, it remains the case that a lay user must be of the DIY type or a computer geek to combine and program a collection of IoT devices into a smart space. We will present some ideas to democratize the IoT technology and to overcome its inequitable utility. We will present these democratization ideas within an example in the personal health domain.

Service Governance in a Transforming World - Challenges Ahead

Pablo Fernandez

University of Sevilla, Spain

Service-oriented computing (SOC) has gained traction across various domains, offering a fertile ground for the emergence of new generations of service chains. These service chains are growing and evolving continuously, unlocking unparalleled integration and customization opportunities. This shift towards SOC has introduced an ecosystem of seamless interoperability; however, it doesn't come without governance challenges. As the intricacy of the service chains grows, issues related to agility, privacy, and capacity management become evident. In this talk, we will reflect on different challenges that should be faced to harness these opportunities.

Logic, Automata, and Games in Service Composition

Giuseppe De Giacomo

University of Oxford, UK

Temporal logics on finite traces (LTLf, LDLf, PPLTL, etc.) are increasingly attracting the interest of the scientific community. These logics are variants of temporal logics used for specifying dynamic properties in Formal Methods, but focussing on finite though unbounded traces. They are becoming popular in several areas, including AI planning for expressing temporally extended goals, reactive synthesis for automatically synthesizing interactive programs, reinforcement learning for expressing non-Markovian rewards and dynamics, and Business Process Modeling for declaratively specifying processes. These logics can express general safety and guarantee (reachability) properties, though they cannot talk about the behaviors at the infinitum as more traditional temporal logics on infinite traces. The key characteristic of these logics is that they can be reduced to equivalent regular automata, and in turn, automata, once determinized, into two-player games on graphs. This gives them unprecedented computational effectiveness and scalability. In this talk, we will look at these logics, their corresponding automata, and resulting games, and show their relevance in service composition. In particular, we show how they can be used for automatically synthesizing orchestrators for advanced forms of goal-oriented synthesis.

Contents – Part I

Architecture and System Aspects

Containers and Microservices

Emerging Technologies and Approaches

Contents – Part II

Service Frameworks for IoT, Mobile and Smart Environments

Industrial Papers

AI for Service Systems

Continuous Certification of Non-functional Properties Across System Changes

Marco Anisetti⬤, Claudio A. Ardagna⬤, and Nicola Bena^(✉)⬤

Department of Computer Science, Università degli Studi di Milano, Milan, Italy
`{marco.anisetti,claudio.ardagna,nicola.bena}@unimi.it`

Abstract. Existing certification schemes implement continuous verification techniques aiming to prove non-functional (e.g., security) properties of software systems over time. These schemes provide different re-certification techniques for managing the certificate life cycle, though their strong assumptions make them ineffective against modern service-based distributed systems. Re-certification techniques are in fact built on static system models, which do not properly represent the system evolution, and on static detection of system changes, which results in an inaccurate planning of re-certification activities. In this paper, we propose a continuous certification scheme that departs from a static certificate life cycle management and provides a dynamic approach built on the modeling of the system behavior that reduces the amount of unnecessary re-certification. The quality of the proposed scheme is experimentally evaluated using an ad hoc dataset built on publicly-available datasets.

Keywords: Assurance · Continuous Certification · Machine Learning · Security

1 Introduction

From service to cloud-edge computing, from big data to machine learning (ML), from mobile systems to 5G, we witnessed the birth of a new digital era where the physical environment is strictly blended with complex service-based systems. The huge benefits in terms of functionalities and efficiency in every domain of life collide with the need of trust, including guarantees on safety, security, and privacy, for the final users. This need for trust is the most important barrier to the wide adoption of modern service-based systems in safety-critical scenarios, requiring to redesign existing solutions for system non-functional verification.

Assurance is the accepted way to prove a specific non-functional behavior on a target system [5]. In this context, several certification schemes (e.g., [2, 8–10]) have been defined to support continuous verification of target systems' non-functional properties over time and across system changes [3,4,8,10]. These schemes support a continuous certificate life cycle management based on re-certification, implementing a verification process that aims to adapt a certificate according to system and contextual changes. Current approaches however fall

F. Monti et al. (Eds.): ICSOC 2023, LNCS 14419, pp. 3–18, 2023.
https://doi.org/10.1007/978-3-031-48421-6_1

short in supporting the peculiarities of modern dynamic, distributed systems [8, 10], building on strong assumptions that make them ineffective in the real world. More in detail, they are built on system models [2,18] that are not designed to tackle system evolution, and result in erroneous certification processes built on inaccurate (i.e., partial) evidence. In addition, life cycle management is built on static and predefined triggers, where re-certification is executed at fixed time instants, or when code changes and new vulnerabilities are observed [6,8,9]. These assumptions result in the proliferation of unnecessary re-certification, on one side, and inaccurate re-certification due to unpredictable and cascade effects of a system change [8], on the other side.

The solution in this paper aims to fill in the above gaps (Sect. 2) by defining a continuous certification scheme that departs from a static management of the certificate life cycle and provides a dynamic approach built on the modeling of the system behavior (Sect. 3). The certification scheme implements a new re-certification process that is triggered by changes to the system behavior. Dynamic triggering reduces the amount of unnecessary re-certification and considers the impact of cascading effects on re-certification.

The contribution of this paper is threefold: *i)* we first define a certification scheme built on a new definition of valid certificate, where system behavior modeling tracks system changes over time (Sect. 3); *ii)* we then design and implement a dynamic certificate life cycle management that monitors system executions to trigger re-certification (Sects. 4 and 5); *iii)* we finally extend a publicly-available dataset built on three service-based distributed systems in literature to generate a dataset suitable for the assessment of continuous assurance techniques (Sect. 6.1). The quality of our scheme is experimentally evaluated using such dataset and a system behavioral modeling built on ML (Sect. 6.2).

2   Background and Motivations

2.1   Continuous Certification in a Nutshell

A certification scheme awards a certificate to the target (service-based) system when enough evidence is collected to prove the support of a non-functional property [5]. A scheme is based on three pillars: *i)* non-functional property p; *ii)* target of certification ToC; and *iii)* certification model $\mathcal{CM}$ [2].

A non-functional property p models a system requirement as follows.

Definition 1. *A non-functional property is a pair $(\hat{p}, \{A_i\})$, where $\hat{p}$ is the name of the property and $\{A_i\}$ is a set of attributes refining it [2,4].*

Example 1. Let us consider a microservice written in Java managing applicable discounts in an e-commerce system. An important requirement for the system is to guarantee low response time to complete the checkout, for instance, at most 10ms with 1ms tolerance. Property performance can then be modeled as $p_p=(\hat{p}_p, \{lang=\text{Java}, max\text{-}time=10\text{ms}, tolerance=1\text{ms}\})$, with $\hat{p}_p=Performance$.

A target of certification ToC represents the system to be certified, modeled as a set of *components* $\{c_i\}$ grouped according to their functionalities (e.g., user authentication, database management) or code organization (e.g., packages of a Java program) [2].

Example 2. Following Example 1, the microservice is composed of the following components: c_{db} for database interaction, c_{api} for serving HTTP endpoints, and c_{cross} for horizontal functionalities such as logging and metrics.

A certification model $\mathcal{CM}=\langle p, ToC, \{\{tc_i\}_{c_j}\}\rangle$ specifies the activities to collect the evidence proving that p holds on ToC; it is defined by the Certification Authority (CA). It can be mapped to Evaluation Assurance Levels in Common Criteria modeling the strength of the evaluation, while maintaining the flexibility that is requested to properly evaluate dynamic service-based systems. Our approach is agnostic to the specific evidence collection technique and can be used with testing, monitoring, and formal methods [5]. With no lack of generality, we consider test-based evidence collected by an accredited lab on behalf of CA according to a set $\{\{tc_i\}_{c_j}\}$ of test cases in $\mathcal{CM}$; each test case tc_i insists on a component c_j of ToC, and specifies input and expected output. The collected evidence is used to award a certificate $\mathcal{C}=\langle \mathcal{CM}, \{ev\}\rangle$, with $\mathcal{CM}$ the corresponding certification model and $\{ev\}$ the set of collected evidence proving $\mathcal{CM}.p$ on $\mathcal{CM}.ToC$ [2]. Digital signatures on $\mathcal{CM}$ and $\mathcal{C}$ implement the chain of trust rooted at the CA [4].

Example 3. Following Example 2, test case tc_1 sends 50 concurrent requests to c_{api} with a varying interval. Collected evidence contains the measured response times and proves p_p *iff* the average response time is less than the threshold in p_p.

Continuous certification schemes extend the above process to track the evolution of the ToC over time by *i)* identifying changes occurred to the target, for instance by monitoring its source code [6], execution traces [3,10], metrics [18], or logs [12], and *ii)* updating certificate according to fixed rules [4].

2.2 Gaps of Continuous Certification

The fundamental assumptions underpinning the certification of modern systems [2,4] define their correctness, trustworthiness, and soundness as follows.

Definition 2. *Trust, correctness, and soundness of existing certification schemes build on the following three assumptions:*

A1) the certification model $\mathcal{CM}$ is created by a trusted CA, binding certificates on the chain of trust rooted at the CA [4] (**Trust**);

A2) $\mathcal{CM}.ToC$ correctly represents the target system components; $\mathcal{CM}.p$ correctly represents the property held by the system (**Correctness**);

A3) when sufficient evidence is collected according to $\mathcal{CM}$, a certificate $\mathcal{C}$ is awarded proving that $\mathcal{CM}.ToC$ supports $\mathcal{CM}.p$ (**Soundness**).

A certificate $\mathcal{C}$ (and the process that brought to its awarding) is valid *iff* ToC, $\mathcal{CM}$, and $\mathcal{C}$ itself satisfy A1, A2, and A3 as follows.

Definition 3 (Valid Certificate). *A certificate is valid iff the certification model prepared by a trusted CA (A1) correctly represents the target system and its property (A2), and the certificate is released by successfully collecting sufficient evidence from the target system represented in the certification model (A3).*

Existing approaches fail to preserve certificate validity in Definition 3, according to the following gaps.

Static Target of Certification. Existing certification schemes statically define the ToC [1–3, 17–19]. This approach assumes the CA to manually define the ToC, or the ability to derive it from the code and accompanying artifacts (e.g., BPEL workflow), which may not be available in modern systems. Also, it assumes the ToC to always be *valid* across system changes, resulting in certification schemes that provide an erroneous support for system evolution and continuous evaluation. Assumption A2 does not hold in these settings.

Lack of a Proper Certificate Life Cycle Management. Existing continuous certification schemes lack of a proper certificate life cycle management. Assumptions A2 and A3 do not hold in these settings.

- *Ineffective change detection.* Existing schemes monitor ToC and trigger re-certification mostly according to *i)* code changes [6,8] and *ii)* timers (i.e., expired evidence or certificate) [8,9]. Among them, Common Criteria builds on static and predefined triggers (e.g., new attack landscape) to monitor the system behavior, or involves developers in notifying such changes. Existing approaches fail to consider the dynamicity of system behavior introducing false positives and false negatives. A code change or an expired timer do not necessarily require re-certification (false positive); static monitoring cause environmental changes to go unnoticed (false negative).
- *Inaccurate planning and inefficient adaptation.* Detected changes trigger adaptive actions that *i)* involve the CA in preparing a novel certification model possibly based on information provided by the system developers [8], or *ii)* directly adapt the certificate according to fixed rules [4]. Both cases introduce inaccuracy, reducing the certificate validity. They consider detected changes only, ignoring the unpredictable and cascade effects that a change on a system component has on the other components [8]

Figure 1(a) shows existing continuous certification schemes [3,6,8,9] executing partial or full re-certification at each change. Figure 1(b) shows our certification scheme that supports certificate validity in Definition 3.

3 Our Approach

We extend the notions of certification model and certificate in Sect. 2 to manage the full chain of their releases, keeping track of ToC changes over time and implementing a continuous certification process preserving certificate validity in Definition 3. We define a certification model as a function of time as follows.

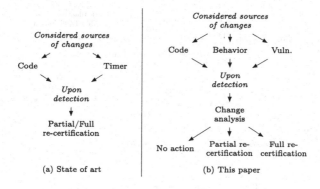

Fig. 1. Continuous certification schemes

Definition 4 ($\mathcal{CM}_t$). *A certificate model $\mathcal{CM}_t$ at time t is a tuple of the form $\langle p, ToC, \{\{tc_i\}_{c_j}\}, \mathcal{CM}_{t-1}\rangle$, where*

- *p, ToC, and $\{\{tc_i\}_{c_j}\}$ are described in Sect. 2.1 and defined at time t;*
- *$\mathcal{CM}_{t-1}$ is a reference to the certification model at time $t-1$ (if any).*

We then extend the definition of certificate as a function of time as follows.

Definition 5 ($\mathcal{C}_t$). *A certificate $\mathcal{C}_t$ at time t is a tuple of the form $\langle\mathcal{CM}_t, \{ev\}_t, \mathcal{B}, \mathcal{C}_{t-1}, st\rangle$, where*

- *$\mathcal{CM}_t$ is the certification model (Definition 4);*
- *$\{ev\}_t$ includes: i) the new evidence $\{\overline{ev}\}$ collected at time t and ii) the subset of evidence $\{ev\}_{t-1}$ in certificate $\mathcal{C}_{t-1}$ not superseded by evidence in $\{\overline{ev}\}$;*
- *$\mathcal{B}$ is the adaptive system model (system model in the following) modeling the system behavior. It originates from the first certificate release and is then updated during the continuous certification process;*
- *$\mathcal{C}_{t-1}$ is a reference to the certificate at time $t-1$ (if any);*
- *st is the certificate status retrieved using function $\mathtt{state}$: $\mathcal{C}_t \rightarrow$ {Valid, Suspended, Superseded, Revoked}.*

Building on industrial standards (e.g., CCRA [8]), our scheme considers 4 scenarios as follows.

- **S0: Certificate $\mathcal{C}_{t-1}$ is still valid,** when no changes are observed at time t. The certificate and, in turn, certification model are still up-to-date.
- **S1: Certification model $\mathcal{CM}_{t-1}$ is still valid,** the most frequent scenario, when most of the updates (code or deployment) at time t are minor, such that the certification model still correctly represents the system (A2). It is only necessary to re-collect some evidence (A3) to preserve certificate validity.
- **S2: Certification model $\mathcal{CM}_{t-1}$ needs revision,** when the system undergoes some not-negligible changes at time t, to the point that some portions of ToC and p in the certification model no longer represent the target of certification (A2). The certification model needs to be adjusted (A2) by the CA (A1) and drives the release of an updated certificate (A3).

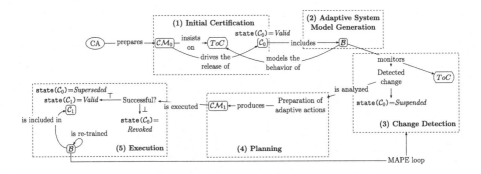

Fig. 2. Overview of our approach.

- **S3**: **Certification model** $\mathcal{CM}_{t-1}$ **cannot be repaired**, when the system undergoes a significant change at time t, such that the certification model does not correctly represent it (A2). A novel certification model should be defined by a trusted party (A1) to award a valid certificate (A3).

Figure 2 depicts our certification process that consists of 5 phases as follows.
Initial certification executes the standard certification process in Sect. 2 (step (1) in Fig. 2). Certification model $\mathcal{CM}_0=\langle p, ToC, \{\{tc_i\}_{c_j}\}, -\rangle$ is first defined. Evidence $\{ev\}_0$ is then collected according to $\mathcal{CM}_0$, resulting in the award of certificate $\mathcal{C}_0=\langle \mathcal{CM}_0, \{ev\}_0, \mathcal{B}, -, Valid\rangle$.
Adaptive system model generation completes certificate $\mathcal{C}_0$ with system model $\mathcal{B}$ (step (2) in Fig. 2). It models the normal system behavior and detects behavioral changes on the target components, using, for instance, a formal representation thereof (e.g., Petri nets, Abstract State Machines), or an ML model created by collecting *observable* data from the system execution.

Upon awarding $\mathcal{C}_0$, the continuous certification process, the focus of this paper, starts. It implements a *semi-automatic MAPE* (Monitoring, Analysis, Planning, Execute) *loop* preserving certificate validity in Definition 3 as described in the following three phases, and detailed in Sects. 4 and 5.
Change detection corresponds to phase Monitoring of the MAPE loop and monitors the target system, comparing its current behavior against behavior $\mathcal{B}$ in the certificate (step (3) in Fig. 2). Phase change detection detects several types of changes caused by, for instance, workload variations, code changes, new vulnerabilities [4]. If a change is detected, certificate status changes to *Suspended*. Contrary to [8], phase change detection strongly relies on dynamic system behavior, reducing the number of false positives. Observed changes are then analyzed in phase planning.
Planning corresponds to phases Analysis and Planning of the MAPE loop, and analyzes the observed changes using fine-grained rules (step (4) in Fig. 2). Phase planning first evaluates the impact of a change on the certification model $\mathcal{CM}_{t-1}$: *i)* no impact (scenarios *S0* and *S1*), *ii)* partial impact (scenario *S2*), *iii)* full

impact (scenario *S3*). It then produces the *adaptive actions* to define the new certification model $\mathcal{CM}_t$ that correctly represents the system.

Execution corresponds to phase Execution of the MAPE loop and integrates the adaptive actions in phase planning to collect evidence according to $\mathcal{CM}_t$ (step (5) in Fig. 2). If evidence collection is successful, an updated certificate $\mathcal{C}_t$ is released, including system model $\mathcal{B}$ updated according to the changes identified at phase change detection. The previous certificate $\mathcal{C}_{t-1}$ is either superseded ($\texttt{state}(\mathcal{C}_{t-1}) = Superseded$) in case $\mathcal{C}_t$ is successfully awarded ($\texttt{state}(\mathcal{C}_t) = Valid$), or revoked ($\texttt{state}(\mathcal{C}_{t-1}) = Revoked$), otherwise. The continuous process restarts at phase change detection.

4 Change Detection

Phase change detection continuously monitors ToC to retrieve system changes for later analysis. It considers system behavioral changes (Δ_b) according to system model $\mathcal{B}$ in $\mathcal{C}$, code changes (Δ_c), and vulnerabilities (Δ_v).

Behavioral change (Δ_b) detects anomalies in the system behavior at time t and is defined as $\Delta_b=(r, \{c_i\})$, where $r \in \{\top, \bot\}$ and $\{c_i\}$ is the set of components affected by behavioral changes. Our scheme continuously collects data that are fed into the system model $\mathcal{C}_{t-1}.\mathcal{B}$ to observe anomalies in the system behavior. If an anomaly is detected, that is, the behavior of the target system at time t differs from behavior $\mathcal{C}_{t-1}.\mathcal{B}$ at time $t-1$, $\Delta_b=(\top, \{c_i\})$; $\Delta_b=(\bot, \emptyset)$, otherwise.

Code change (Δ_c) detects variations in the code base, upon any releases, and is defined as $\Delta_c=(r, \{c_i\}, \mathcal{M})$, where $r \in \{\top, \bot\}$, $\{c_i\}$ is the set of components affected by the change, and $\mathcal{M}$ is a set of metrics M_i. A metric M_i, possibly taken from standard software engineering literature [7], is a function $\texttt{src}_{t-1} \times \texttt{src}_t \rightarrow [-1, 1]$, where a value <0 (≥ 0, resp.) indicates a *minor* change (*major* change, resp.) to source code $\texttt{src}$ at time t with respect to source code $\texttt{src}$ at time $t-1$. When a code change is detected, $\Delta_c=(r, \{c_i\}, \mathcal{M})$; $\Delta_c=(\bot, \emptyset, \emptyset)$, otherwise.

Vulnerability change (Δ_v) detects a new vulnerability and is in the form $\Delta_v=(r, \{(c, \texttt{vuln})\})$, where $r \in \{\top, \bot\}$, and pair $(c, \texttt{vuln})$ indicates the vulnerable component c and the corresponding vulnerability $\texttt{vuln}$. Our certification scheme monitors external databases for new vulnerabilities affecting ToC [8]. We adopt a conservative approach that collects all relevant vulnerabilities and, later in phase planning, filters out those not impacting on the property of interest (e.g., a bug on an encryption algorithm unlikely affects performance). When a new vulnerability is discovered, $\Delta_v=(\top, \{(c, \texttt{vuln})\})$; $\Delta_v=(\bot, \emptyset)$, otherwise.

Phase change detection can be defined according to Δ_b, Δ_c, Δ_v as follows.

Definition 6. *Phase change detection takes as input i) the system (e.g., its code, logs, traces) at time t, ii) certification model $\mathcal{CM}_{t-1}$, and iii) certificate $\mathcal{C}_{t-1}$; and returns as output a triple $\langle \Delta_b, \Delta_c, \Delta_v \rangle$, where i) $\Delta_b=(r, \{c_i\})$; ii) $\Delta_c=(r, \{c_i\}, \mathcal{M})$; iii) $\Delta_v=(r, \{(c, \textbf{vuln})\})$*

We recall that in case $r=\bot$, $\Delta_b=(\bot, \emptyset)$, $\Delta_c=(\bot, \emptyset, \emptyset)$, $\Delta_v=(\bot, \emptyset)$.

If at least one change has been detected, meaning that $\exists \Delta_i \in \{\Delta_b, \Delta_c, \Delta_v\}$, $\Delta_i.r = \top$, the status of current certificate $\mathcal{C}_t$ is $\texttt{state}(\mathcal{C}_t) = Suspended$, until the changes are analyzed and adaptive actions on the certification model or certificate are taken in phases planning and execution in Sect. 5. Otherwise, if $\forall \Delta_i \in \{\Delta_b, \Delta_c, \Delta_v\}$, $\Delta_i.r = \bot$, no changes are detected and $\texttt{state}(\mathcal{C}_t) = Valid$.

Example 4. Let us assume that certification model $\mathcal{CM}_{t-1}$ and corresponding certificate $\mathcal{C}_{t-1}$ have been released for ToC in Example 2. At time t, a new version of the service is released, where component c_{db} has been updated to improve its efficiency. As a consequence, the behavior of c_{db} and, as a cascading effect, the one of c_{api} are affected. Our system model identifies such changes, and phase change detection returns as output $\langle \Delta_b = (\top, \{c_{api}, c_{db}\}), \Delta_c = (\top, \{c_{db}\}, \{1\}), \Delta_v = (\bot, \emptyset) \rangle$, where $\{1\}$ is the metric value based on cyclomatic complexity of c_{db}. Given the detected changes, $\texttt{state}(\mathcal{C}_{t-1}) = Suspended$.

Phase change detection must account for change timing. For instance, a code change is detected as soon as a new version is released on the repository; however, it might take some time to observe its effects (if any) on the behavior of the running system. To ensure consistent results, we adopt a *buffering* strategy, where a time buffer is used to monitor for behavioral changes after any code changes. The buffer duration depends on the specific system.

5 Planning and Execution

Phase planning produces the adaptive actions by integrating changes Δ_b, Δ_c, and Δ_v retrieved in phase change detection (Sect. 5.1). Phase execution executes these actions (Sect. 5.2).

5.1 Planning

Phase planning analyzes the detected changes in $\langle \Delta_b, \Delta_c, \Delta_v \rangle$ (Sect. 4) and defines the adaptive actions according to the applicable scenario in Sect. 3. To this aim, each scenario is associated with a *precondition* as a Boolean formula that must be evaluated $\top$ (*true*) and a set of *conditions* as Boolean formulas expressed over $\langle \Delta_b, \Delta_c, \Delta_v \rangle$ chained with a logical or ($\vee$). The scenario identified at time t is the one whose precondition and conditions are evaluated $\top$ first, considering the evaluation order *S0, S1, S2, S3*.

Once the applicable scenario is selected, phase planning generates the pair $(\mathcal{CM}_t, \mathcal{T})$ as output, representing the adaptive actions to be executed in phase execution, where *i)* $\mathcal{CM}_t$ is the certification model correctly representing the system after changes at time t (see A2 in Definition 2); *ii)* $\mathcal{T} \in \mathcal{CM}_t$ is a subset of test cases in $\mathcal{CM}_t$ to be later executed in response to changes.

Table 1 summarizes, for each scenario, precondition, conditions, and corresponding output, which are detailed in the following.

Table 1. Summary of phases planning and execution (comp. stands for component).

S#	Precondition	Conditions	Output ($\mathcal{CM}_t$, $\{tc\}$)
S0	No behavioral changes No vulnerabilities	(2a) No code changes (2b) Minor code change on non-critical, existing comp.	$- \mathcal{CM}_t = \mathcal{CM}_{t-1}$ $- T = \emptyset$
S1	No vulnerabilities No critical comp. No new comp.	(4a) Behavioral change (environmental) (4b) Behavioral change (minor code change) (4c) Major code change without impact on behavior	$- \mathcal{CM}_t = \mathcal{CM}_{t-1}$ $- T =$ test cases on comp. affected by the change
S2	–	(6a) Vulnerability discovered (6b) Behavioral change (major code change) on non-critical, existing comp.	$- \mathcal{CM}_t = \mathcal{CM}_{t-1} \cup \{tc\}_{\text{new}}$ $- T =$ test cases on comp. affected by the change
S3	–	(8a) Behavioral change (environmental) on critical, existing comp. (8b) Major/minor code change on critical, existing comp. (8c) Code change adding a new comp.	$-$ New $\mathcal{CM}_t$ $-$ All test cases in $\mathcal{CM}_t$

S0: Certificate C_{t-1} is still valid.

Precondition: S0 does not involve any behavioral or vulnerability-related changes.

$$\neg \Delta_b.r \wedge \neg \Delta_v.r \tag{1}$$

Conditions: S0 is selected in case of (2a) no code change; or (2b) minor code change without impact on the behavior, critical components, and new components, as formalized in the following.

$$\neg \Delta_c.r \tag{2a}$$

$$\Delta_c.r \wedge \forall M_i \in \mathcal{M}, M_i(\mathtt{src}_{t-1}, \mathtt{src}_t) < 0 \wedge \tag{2b}$$
$$\forall c_i \in \Delta_c.\{c\}, (\neg \mathtt{critical}(c_i) \wedge c_i \in \mathtt{src}_{t-1})$$

where function $\mathtt{critical}$ is a Boolean function that identifies those components $c_i \in ToC$ that are critical for the non-functional property of interest (e.g., component c_{api} for property performance in Example 1).

Output: The code change does not have any observable effects on system behavior, and $\mathcal{CM}_{t-1}$ and $\mathcal{C}_{t-1}$ are valid (Definition 3). The continuous certification process can then restart from phase change detection in Sect. 4.

S1: Certification model $\mathcal{CM}_{t-1}$ is still valid.

Precondition: S1 does not involve vulnerability changes nor changes with impact on critical and new components, as formalized in the following.

$$\neg \Delta_v.r \wedge \left(\forall c_i \in \Delta_c.\{c\} \cup \Delta_b.\{c\}, (\neg \mathtt{critical}(c_i) \wedge c_i \in \mathtt{src}_{t-1}) \right) \tag{3}$$

Conditions: S1 is selected in case of (4a) a behavioral change caused by an environmental change; (4b) a behavioral change caused by a minor change in the code; or (4c) a major change in the code without impact on the behavior, as formalized in the following.

$$\Delta_b.r \tag{4a}$$

$$\Delta_b.r \wedge \Delta_c.r \wedge \forall M_i \in \mathcal{M}, M_i(\mathtt{src}_{t-1}, \mathtt{src}_t) < 0 \tag{4b}$$

$$\neg \Delta_b.r \wedge \Delta_c.r \wedge \exists M_i \in \mathcal{M}, M_i(\mathtt{src}_{t-1}, \mathtt{src}_t) \geq 0 \tag{4c}$$

A minor or major change on components $\Delta_c.\{c\}$ does not imply that only test cases insisting on $\Delta_c.\{c\}$ should be considered, due to the unpredictable cascading effects introduced by code changes. Our scheme exploits system model $\mathcal{B}$ as the main source of actual changes, therefore retrieving *all* the components $\Delta_c.\{c\} \cup \Delta_b.\{c\}$ involved in the change.

Output: $\mathcal{CM}_{t-1}$, which is still valid, and existing test cases insisting on the components whose code or behavior changed (i.e., $\Delta_c.\{c\} \cup \Delta_b.\{c\}$), as follows.

$$\mathcal{CM}_t \leftarrow \langle \mathcal{CM}_{t-1}.p, \mathcal{CM}_{t-1}.ToC, \mathcal{CM}_{t-1}.\{tc\}, \mathcal{CM}_{t-1} \rangle \tag{5a}$$

$$\mathcal{T} \leftarrow \forall c_i \in \Delta_c.\{c\} \cup \Delta_b.\{c\}, \ \mathcal{CM}_t.\{\{tc_j\}_{c_k}\} \mid c_k = c_i \tag{5b}$$

S2: Certification model $\mathcal{CM}_{t-1}$ needs revision.
Precondition: S2 does not have any preconditions.
Conditions: S2 is selected in case of (6a) a vulnerability retrieved from external databases; or (6b) behavioral change caused by major code change not involving critical and new components, as formalized in the following.

$$\Delta_v.r \tag{6a}$$

$$\begin{gathered} \Delta_b.r \wedge \Delta_c.r \wedge \exists M_i \in \mathcal{M}, M_i(\mathtt{src}_{t-1}, \mathtt{src}_t) \geq 0 \wedge \\ \forall c_i \in \Delta_c.\{c\} \cup \Delta_b.\{c\}, (\neg \mathtt{critical}(c_i) \wedge c_i \in \mathtt{src}_{t-1}) \end{gathered} \tag{6b}$$

S2 involves the accredited lab in the addition or modification of test cases insisting on the components involved in the change (i.e., $\Delta_c.\{c\} \cup \Delta_b.\{c\} \cup \Delta_v.\{c\}$). As in S1, our scheme relies on $\mathcal{B}$ to identify such components.
Output: An updated certification model $\mathcal{CM}_t$ with novel test cases $\{tc\}_{\mathrm{new}}$, and test cases insisting on all changed components, as follows.

$$\mathcal{CM}_t \leftarrow \langle \mathcal{CM}_{t-1}.p, \mathcal{CM}_{t-1}.ToC, \mathcal{CM}_{t-1}.\{tc\} \cup \{tc\}_{\mathrm{new}}, \mathcal{CM}_{t-1} \rangle \tag{7a}$$

$$\mathcal{T} \leftarrow \forall c_i \in \Delta_c.\{c\} \cup \Delta_b.\{c\} \cup \Delta_v.\{c\}, \ \mathcal{CM}_t.\{\{tc_j\}_{c_k}\} \mid c_k = c_i \tag{7b}$$

S3: Certification model $\mathcal{CM}_{t-1}$ cannot be repaired.
Precondition: S3 does not have any preconditions.
Conditions: S3 is selected in case of (8a) a behavioral change on a critical, existing component caused by an environmental change (e.g., an increased rate of requests under property performance in Example 1); (8b) a code change of any extents affects a critical, existing component; or (8c) a code change due to a new component, as formalized in the following.

$$\Delta_b.r \wedge \exists c_i \in \Delta_b.\{c\}, \mathtt{critical}(c_i) = \top \ \wedge \ c_i \in \mathtt{src}_{t-1} \tag{8a}$$

$$\Delta_c.r \wedge \exists c_i \in \Delta_c.\{c\}, \mathtt{critical}(c_i) = \top \ \wedge \ c_i \in \mathtt{src}_{t-1} \tag{8b}$$

$$\Delta_c.r \wedge \exists c_i \in \Delta_c.\{c\}, c_i \notin \mathtt{src}_{t-1} \tag{8c}$$

S3 involves the accredited lab in the definition of a new certification model including new test cases or updating existing ones. Certification model $\mathcal{CM}_{t-1}$, in fact, cannot be repaired and re-certification from scratch is needed. The above conditions specify that *i)* any critical components impacted by a change require re-certification, *ii)* the addition of a new component cannot fall under *S1* or *S2* because $\mathcal{B}$ does not model the new version of the system yet. Therefore it cannot identify all the components involved in the cascading effect as in *S1* and *S2*. *Output:* A new certification model $\mathcal{CM}_t$ (function **new**) and new test cases, as formalized in the following.

$$\mathcal{CM}_t \leftarrow \textbf{new}(previous = \mathcal{CM}_{t-1}) \tag{9a}$$
$$\mathcal{T} \leftarrow \mathcal{CM}_t.\{tc\} \tag{9b}$$

Example 5. Let us consider detected changes $\langle \Delta_b=(\top, \{c_{api}, c_{db}\}), \Delta_c=(\top, \{c_{db}\}, \{1\}), \Delta_v=(\bot, \emptyset)\rangle$ in Example 4. Phase planning identifies *S3* as the applicable scenario according to the corresponding conditions (8a)∨(8b)∨(8c). It then returns as output *i)* a novel certification model $\mathcal{CM}_t$ where the maximum allowed response time in property performance in Example 1 is reduced to 7ms thanks to the code changes on c_{db}, and *ii)* the set $\mathcal{T}$ of all test cases in $\mathcal{CM}_t$.

The result $(\mathcal{CM}_t, \mathcal{T})$ of phase planning is used in phase execution to collect additional evidence maintaining the certificate validity in Definition 3. We recall that, at the end of phase planning, certification model $\mathcal{CM}_t$ correctly represents the target system as defined in Assumption A2 in Definition 2.

5.2 Execution

Phase execution, performed by the accredited lab, applies the adaptive actions retrieved in phase planning to possibly restore certificate validity. It takes as input the result $(\mathcal{CM}_t, \mathcal{T})$ of phase planning and certificate $\mathcal{C}_{t-1}$, and executes test cases $\mathcal{T}$ against $\mathcal{CM}_t.ToC$ to award a new $\mathcal{C}_t$. It consists of three steps as follows.
Evidence collection executes the test cases in $\mathcal{T}$ to collect fresh evidence $\{\overline{ev}\}\in\{ev\}_t$ from the system at time t.
System model re-training updates system model $\mathcal{B}$ according to the identified changes, to model the evolved behavior of the target system (see Assumption A2 in Definition 2).
Certificate release awards a valid certificate $\mathcal{C}_t=\langle\mathcal{CM}_t, \{ev\}_t, \mathcal{B}, \mathcal{C}_{t-1}, Valid\rangle$ according to Definition 3. Certificate $\mathcal{C}_{t-1}$ is *Superseded* ($\texttt{state}(\mathcal{C}_{t-1})=Superseded$). We note that evidence collected at time $t-i$ with $i>0$ can be obtained from the certificate $\mathcal{C}_{t-i}$ in the chain of certificate release. We also note that, if evidence collection or system model updating fails, the entire process stops, requiring to fix the system or the certification model. Certificate $\mathcal{C}_{t-1}$ becomes invalid and is *Revoked* ($\texttt{state}(\mathcal{C}_{t-1})=Revoked$), and a re-certification from scratch is needed.

Example 6. Let us assume that the test cases $\mathcal{T}$ in Example 5 are executed by the accredited lab and evidence is collected proving p_p. $\mathcal{B}$ is updated according to the new system behavior and $\mathcal{C}_t$ awarded with $\texttt{state}(\mathcal{C}_t) = Valid$.

6   Experiments

We experimentally compared the quality of our approach with the state of the art (SOTA) in Fig. 1(a) measuring *i)* the recall of phase change detection in retrieving changes and the components affected by (cascading) changes; *ii)* the precision of phase planning in the identification of adaptive actions (avoiding unnecessary re-certification) and selection of scenario *S0–S3*. Additional paper artifacts and a detailed walkthrough of our approach are available at https:// doi.org/10.13130/RD_UNIMI/9WXZRC.

6.1   A Dataset for Continuous Assurance Techniques Evaluation

We built our experimental datasets on three publicly-available datasets D_{MS}, D_{SN}, D_{TT}, providing normal and anomalous execution traces of three microservice-based distributed systems [15,16]: *i) media service (MS)*, a system comprising $N{=}38$ microservices for streaming and reviewing movies [11]; *ii) social network (SN)*, a system comprising $N{=}36$ microservices for a social network application [11]; *iii) train ticket (TT)*, a system comprising $N{=}41$ microservices for train tickets management [20]. The dataset D_{MS}, D_{SN}, D_{TT} of each system contained $1,000$ data points (after random filtering) with the response time of each microservice according to an execution path in normal/anomalous traces. Each distributed system was mapped to a *ToC* and each microservice to a component $c{\in}ToC$. We then extended the above three datasets, which only consider code and behavioral changes, to probabilistically generate datasets D'_{MS}, D'_{SN}, and D'_{TT} maximizing the coverage of all scenarios *S0–S3* of a system evolution (see Sect. 3) The generated datasets fill in a major gap in literature, supporting the evaluation of continuous assurance techniques in all their facets.

Table 2 shows the probabilities that drove the generation of datasets D'_{MS}, D'_{SN}, D'_{TT}, where each row is an experimental setting. Each point in the dataset was annotated with probability 0.4 of representing a system change. Anomalous data points were used to represent environmental changes (Δ_b) or code changes with impact on the behavior (Δ_c with cascading), normal data points to represent no changes or code changes without impact on the behavior (Δ_c), according to the specific experimental setting, which are detailed in the following.

We divided the experimental settings in four groups *P1.*–P4.** varying the probability of a specific change in Δ_b, Δ_c, Δ_c with cascading occurs. Group *P1.** assigned uniform probabilities to Δ_b, Δ_c, Δ_c with cascading. Groups *P2.*–P4.** assigned a larger probability (0.5) to environmental changes in *P2.**, code changes in *P3.**, and code changes with cascading in *P4.**, respectively, while assigning uniform probability (0.25) to the remaining changes. We note that

Table 2. Probabilities for the experimental datasets

Name	Δ_b	Δ_c	Δ_b with cascad.	critical	minor	$n(comp)_b$	$n(comp)_{min}$	$n(comp)_{maj}$
P1.1	0.3$\overline{3}$	0.3$\overline{3}$	0.3$\overline{3}$	0.75	0.25	0.25	0.25	0.25
P1.2	0.3$\overline{3}$	0.3$\overline{3}$	0.3$\overline{3}$	0.5	0.5	0.5	0.5	0.5
P1.3	0.3$\overline{3}$	0.3$\overline{3}$	0.3$\overline{3}$	0.25	0.75	0.75	0.75	0.75
P2.1	0.5	0.25	0.25	0.75	0.25	0.25	0.25	0.25
P2.2	0.5	0.25	0.25	0.5	0.5	0.5	0.5	0.5
P2.3	0.5	0.25	0.25	0.25	0.75	0.75	0.75	0.75
P3.1	0.25	0.5	0.25	0.75	0.25	0.25	0.25	0.25
P3.2	0.25	0.5	0.25	0.5	0.5	0.5	0.5	0.5
P3.3	0.25	0.5	0.25	0.25	0.75	0.75	0.75	0.75
P4.1	0.25	0.25	0.5	0.75	0.25	0.25	0.25	0.25
P4.2	0.25	0.25	0.5	0.5	0.5	0.5	0.5	0.5
P4.3	0.25	0.25	0.5	0.25	0.75	0.75	0.75	0.75

changes caused by vulnerabilities were not included because both our scheme and SOTA can correctly detect them.

We finally defined the probabilities that determine the profile of the components involved in the change, modeling *i)* the probability *critical* that a component is critical (probability $(1-critical)$ that is not critical, resp.); *ii)* the probability *minor* of a minor change Δ_c and Δ_c with cascading (probability $(1-minor)$ of a major change, resp.); *iii)* the probability $n(comp)_b$ that a component is involved in an environmental change, $n(comp)_{min}$ is involved in a *minor* code change, and $n(comp)_{maj}$ is involved in a *major* code change. We note that the probability that more than one component is involved linearly decreases. We also note that, in case of a code change with impact on the behavior, additional affected components are extracted at random among the remaining components. In other words, we defined three probability sets that properly represent the life cycle of modern distributed systems (e.g., based on DevOps). The first probability set models the scenario of major changes with critical impact (i.e., with impact on critical components) on a low number of components; it is applied to experimental settings *P*.1*. The second probability set models an average scenario balancing minor and major changes, as well as critical and non-critical impact, on a medium number of components; it is applied to experimental settings *P*.2*. The third probability set models the scenario of minor changes with non-critical impact on a high number of components; it is applied to experimental settings *P*.3*. These settings jointly allow to measure the ability to detect the correct scenario *Si* in representative system life cycles. For instance, the criticality of a component is needed to distinguish between *S1* and *S3*, and the extent of the code change between *S1* and *S2*.

Table 3. Comparisons of our scheme and SOTA

Name	REC(changes)		PREC(no action)		REC(comp)		ACC(scenarios)			
	Our	SOTA	Our	SOTA	Our	SOTA	ACC(S0)	ACC(S1)	ACC(S2)	ACC(S3)
P1.1	0.9948	0.6693	0.993	0.8179	0.8622	0.5727	0.8464	0.8716	0.9996	0.8622
P1.2	0.9894	0.6892	0.9882	0.8289	0.8769	0.5205	0.8397	0.8789	1	0.826
P1.3	0.9858	0.6741	0.9846	0.8242	0.8808	0.4215	0.8397	0.8456	0.9995	0.8402
P2.1	0.9958	0.6751	0.9946	0.8153	0.8633	0.5664	0.8445	0.8744	0.9998	0.8579
P2.2	0.9933	0.6738	0.9927	0.8203	0.8718	0.4968	0.844	0.8761	0.9998	0.8133
P2.3	0.9835	0.6645	0.9822	0.8218	0.8857	0.3874	0.835	0.8577	1	0.8072
P3.1	0.9948	0.6733	0.994	0.821	0.8676	0.5838	0.8469	0.9059	0.9998	0.8229
P3.2	0.9912	0.6761	0.9893	0.8184	0.8724	0.5129	0.8434	0.8621	1	0.8355
P3.3	0.9856	0.6726	0.9844	0.8157	0.8808	0.4037	0.8402	0.8549	0.9998	0.8172
P4.1	0.9949	0.6822	0.9947	0.8266	0.8707	0.5914	0.8439	0.8834	0.9998	0.8684
P4.2	0.9911	0.6821	0.9911	0.8373	0.8723	0.5325	0.8373	0.8404	0.9998	0.8802
P4.3	0.9875	0.6943	0.9858	0.8246	0.883	0.4238	0.8434	0.8494	0.9995	0.8391
AVG	0.9906	0.6772	0.9895	0.8227	0.874	0.5011	0.842	0.8667	0.9998	0.8392

6.2 Quality Evaluation

We comparatively evaluated the quality of SOTA and our scheme according to datasets D'_{MS}, D'_{SN}, D'_{TT} in Sect. 6.1. Adaptive system model is implemented as a set of *isolation forests* [13,14]. Each forest in the set was responsible for detecting behavioral changes in a specific component of the considered system. Results have been averaged on 10 executions over the three datasets.

Table 3 shows our results averaging the results on D'_{MS}, D'_{SN}, D'_{TT}, since negligible variations were observed across the three datasets.

We first measured the recall of phase change detection in terms of detected changes ($REC(changes)$). Our scheme detected $\approx$99% of changes, compared to only $\approx$68% of SOTA.

We then measured the ability of our scheme (phase planning) and SOTA of correctly classifying a change reducing unnecessary re-certification (scenario $S0$). Column $PREC(no\ action)$ shows the precision of our scheme and SOTA when a change does not require any adaptive actions according to the certification scheme. Our scheme exhibits a precision of $\approx$99%, compared to $\approx$82% of SOTA.

Furthermore, when adaptive actions are needed, existing solutions may target a subset of ToC due to the inability of detecting cascading effects in code changes. Column $REC(comp)$ shows the recall of phase change detection in terms of the ability of detecting the components affected by a change. Our scheme detects $\approx$87% of affected components, compared to $\approx$50% of SOTA, meaning that the adaptive actions miss half of the affected components according to SOTA.

Columns $ACC(S0)$–$ACC(S3)$ show the accuracy of phase planning in retrieving the correct scenario. Our scheme achieved $\approx$84% for $S0$, $\approx$87% for $S1$, $\approx$99% for $S2$, and $\approx$84% for $S3$, respectively, meaning that the detected scenario, and corresponding adaptive actions, are correct in 90% of the cases.

We also evaluated the quality of our system model $\mathcal{B}$ in terms of accuracy (ACC), precision ($PREC$), and recall (REC). On average on the three datasets, precision is $\geq$99% (i.e., no risk of false positives), while accuracy and recall are

$\geq 81\%$ and $\geq 75\%$, respectively. Interested readers can access detailed results and their motivations in our online supplement.

7   Discussion and Future Work

We designed a continuous certification scheme for modern service-based distributed systems, implementing a dynamic certificate lifecycle management built on the modeling of the system behavior. Fine-grained planning of adaptive actions based on system behavior permits to reduce the amount of unnecessary re-certification, especially in scenarios (e.g., DevOps) with high frequency of minor system changes. While our solution cannot guarantee to detect all changes, we empirically demonstrated that it clearly outperforms the state of the art also in cases where the system behavior is modeled with a standard ML algorithm (i.e., isolation forest). The paper leaves space for future work. First, we will study the impact of ML techniques for system behavior modeling on our continuous certification. Then, we will provide a taxonomy of code metrics for continuous certification. Finally, we will extend our solution to approach continuous certification of composite service-based systems.

Acknowledgements. The work was partially supported by the projects *i)* MUSA – Multilayered Urban Sustainability Action – project, funded by the European Union – NextGenerationEU, under the National Recovery and Resilience Plan (NRRP) Mission 4 Component 2 Investment Line 1.5: Strengthening of research structures and creation of R&D "innovation ecosystems", set up of "territorial leaders in R&D" (CUP G43C22001370007, Code ECS00000037); *ii)* SERICS (PE00000014) under the NRRP MUR program funded by the EU – NextGenerationEU; *iii)* 1H-HUB and SOV-EDGE-HUB funded by Università degli Studi di Milano – PSR 2021/2022 – GSA – Linea 6; and *iv)* program "piano sostegno alla ricerca" funded by Università degli Studi di Milano.

References

1. Anisetti, M., Ardagna, C.A., Damiani, E., El Ioini, N., Gaudenzi, F.: Modeling time, probability, and configuration constraints for continuous cloud service certification. In: COSE, vol. 72 (2018)
2. Anisetti, M., Ardagna, C.A., Bena, N.: Multi-dimensional certification of modern distributed systems. IEEE TSC **16**(3), 1999–2012 (2023)
3. Anisetti, M., Ardagna, C.A., Damiani, E., El Ioini, N.: Trustworthy cloud certification: a model-based approach. In: Proceedings of SIMPDA 2014. Milan, Italy, November 2014
4. Anisetti, M., Ardagna, C.A., Damiani, E., Gaudenzi, F.: A semi-automatic and trustworthy scheme for continuous cloud service certification. IEEE TSC **13**(1), 30–43 (2020)
5. Ardagna, C., Asal, R., Damiani, E., Vu, Q.: From security to assurance in the cloud: a survey. ACM CSUR **48**(1), 1–50 (2015)
6. Baron, C., Louis, V.: Towards a continuous certification of safety-critical avionics software. Comput. Ind. **125**, 103382 (2021)

7. Bogner, J., Wagner, S., Zimmermann, A.: Automatically measuring the maintainability of service- and microservice-based systems: a literature review. In: Proceedings of IWSM Mensura 2017. Gothenburg, Sweden, October 2017

8. Criteria, C.: Assurance continuity: CCRA requirements. Technical Report, Common Criteria (2021)

9. Egea, M., Mahbub, K., Spanoudakis, G., Vieira, M.R.: A certification framework for cloud security properties: the monitoring path. In: Proceedings of A4Cloud 2014, Malaga, Spain, June 2014

10. Faqeh, R., et al.: Towards dynamic dependable systems through evidence-based continuous certification. In: Proceedings of ISoLA 2020. Rhodes, Greece, October 2020

11. Gan, Y., et al.: An open-source benchmark suite for microservices and their hardware-software implications for cloud & edge systems. In: Proceedings of ASPLOS 2019. Providence, RI, USA, April 2019

12. Lins, S., Schneider, S., Sunyaev, A.: Trust is good, control is better: creating secure clouds by continuous auditing. IEEE TCC **6**(3), 890–903 (2018)

13. Liu, F.T., Ting, K.M., Zhou, Z.H.: Isolation forest. In: Proceedings of IEEE ICDM 2008, Pisa, Italy, December 2008

14. Liu, F.T., Ting, K.M., Zhou, Z.H.: Isolation-based anomaly detection. ACM TKDD **6**(1), 1–39 (2012)

15. Qiu, H., Banerjee, S.S., Jha, S., Kalbarczyk, Z.T., Iyer, R.K.: FIRM: an intelligent fine-grained resource management framework for SLO-oriented microservices. In: Proceedings of USENIX OSDI 2020. Virtual, November 2020

16. Qiu, H., Banerjee, S.S., Jha, S., Kalbarczyk, Z.T., Iyer, R.K.: Pre-processed tracing data for popular microservice benchmarks (2020)

17. Simons, A.J.H., Lefticaru, R.: A verified and optimized stream x-machine testing method, with application to cloud service certification. STVR **30**(3), e1729 (2020)

18. Stephanow, P., Fallenbeck, N.: Towards continuous certification of infrastructure-as-a-service using low-level metrics. In: Proceedings of IEEE UIC-ATC-ScalCom. Beijing, China, August 2015

19. Stephanow, P., Srivastava, G., Schütte, J.: Test-based cloud service certification of opportunistic providers. In: Proceedings of IEEE CLOUD 2016. San Francisco, CA, USA, June-July 2016

20. Zhou, X., et al.: Benchmarking microservice systems for software engineering research. In: Proceedings of IEEE/ACM ICSE 2018. Gothenburg, Sweden, May, June 2018

Deep Learning Model for Personalized Web Service Recommendations Using Attention Mechanism

Marwa Boulakbech[✉], Nizar Messai, Yacine Sam, and Thomas Devogele

LIFAT, Tours University, Tours, France
{marwa.boulakbech,nizar.messai,yacine.sam,thomas.devogele}@univ-tours.fr

Abstract. The big volume of candidate Web services and their differences make it hard for developers to discover a set of appropriate ones for mashup creation. Thus, recommending suitable services is a vital problem. Service recommendation methods should not only meet the functional needs of users but also consider contextual features like application domain and service performances to provide more personalized recommendations. In this paper, we propose an attention-based deep learning model for service recommendation. It makes service recommendation based on service characteristics and user feed-backs. Specifically, we build a service network, which learns to intelligently discover services with two attention mechanisms - a functional attention mechanism that takes tags as functional prior to mine the function-related features of services and mashups, and a non-functional attention mechanism that considers service qualities to guide the selection of the most appropriate ones and improves user satisfaction. Experiments are carried out on a real-world web API dataset crawled from ProgrammeableWeb.com.

Keywords: Web services recommendation · Mashups · Deep Learning · Attention mechanism · QoS and QoE

1 Introduction

With the wide adoption of Service-Oriented Architectures (SOA) and Cloud Computing, Web services, usually in the form of Web APIs (Application Programming Interface), have grown rapidly both in quantity and diversity. They become first-class citizens and the core functionality of any Web application. Developers can create value-added Mashup applications by integrating existing Web resources to meet complex business requirements [1]. Typically they browse and evaluate potentially useful Web services from a repository, and then "centrally" leverage mashup tools to quickly include selected Web APIs, or services, in their applications. Due to the overwhelming number of available services, it is often hard and time-consuming for developers to find their desired ones from a sea of resources. To speed up the mashup creation, recommending suitable services for developers is a vital problem.

F. Monti et al. (Eds.): ICSOC 2023, LNCS 14419, pp. 19–33, 2023.
https://doi.org/10.1007/978-3-031-48421-6_2

In recent years, many service recommendation methods have been proposed by researchers in various fields [2–4]. Generally, they can be classified into three classes: (1) content-based service recommendation, (2) QoS-based service recommendation, and (3) service recommendation using deep learning techniques.

First, most of the content-based service recommendation approaches match by analyzing the functionality provided by services and mashups. Since the content of services and mashups can be learned from their descriptions, natural language processing techniques are often used to infer similarities between service descriptions and mashup requirements. Such methods suffer from the intention gap issue. All learned features from service descriptions corresponding to different intentions are considered equally important when generating recommendations. For example, suppose we represent the description of a mashup m as *"A French Web Application that sends the best health insurance offers using your GMail account"*, a service s1 described as *"Find best health insurance offers in North America"*, and a service s2 described as *"It is a Web API that allows users to get ideal protection for cars registered in The City of Paris"* will be recommended for the mashup M by traditional methods based on functional context. However, they should not be matched together in practice since they are describing two different application scenarios. To select a suitable service, context information like application scenario should be considered. In addition, non-functional context information like service quality from user feed-backs can be exploited to improve recommendation performance and boost user satisfaction.

Second, QoS-based methods primarily evaluate service quality and recommend the best service based on service quality, response time and consistency. Collaborative filtering is often used in QoS-based predictions, where services are recommended considering a user's past ratings for similar services or similar users.

Third, service recommendation using deep learning techniques uses a variety of deep learning technologies to process descriptions of services and mashups and their invocation history, such as: RNN (Recurrent Neural Networks), DNN (Deep Neural Networks). Deep learning technology helps developing more efficient service recommendation models. For instance, the attention mechanisms have been widely used in various fields, such as recommender systems [5,6]. The core of the attention mechanisms is to assign different weights to inputs, paying more attention to relevant information and ignoring irrelevant information. Recently, the transform based entirely on the attention mechanisms has been proposed, which completely eliminated recurrence and convolutions, and has achieved very good performance.

Although many methods of the above three classes have been very successful, there are still two problems that hinder their practical use:

(i) *How to accurately capture user requirements for mashup creation?* Service descriptions usually correspond to different intentions. To select relevant features from descriptions, feature extraction engineering can be used. However, it is a manual process and requires domain expertise.

(ii) *How to combine QoS and user perception to reach high satisfactory user experience?* Most of existing QoS-based recommendation techniques [4,7] ignore user's perception of the service quality. However, there are close relationships between QoS and user satisfaction. Different users may have different concerns and personalized experiences on the same service.

To address the above issues, this paper proposes a personalized Web services recommendations approach based on a deep learning model that fully mines functional and non-functional service features from useful information using attention mechanism to capture user needs and satisfaction. We first intelligently discover mashups with similar functionalities. Afterward, we build a composite service network that learns function-related features of services based on tags and description information. In parallel, based on user feedback, we learn the non function-related features of services. Then, the recommendation module uses attention aggregation to couple the two service representations and generate the final recommendation result. Our contributions are summarized as follows:

- We use a deep learning model that employs embedding techniques to represent features of Web services without using explicit feature engineering techniques.
- We use attention mechanism that considers contextual information to capture user satisfaction and provide personalized recommendations.
- We implement the proposed approach and evaluate it on a real-world dataset. Results show that the proposed approach outperforms the state-of-the-art ones.

The rest of the paper is organized as follows. Section 2 provides preliminaries and formal definitions. Section 3 details the architecture and main components of the proposed deep learning model for personalized service recommendation. Section 4 describes the implementation and the evaluation settings and discusses the experimentation results. Section 5 surveys related work. Finally, Sect. 6 concludes the paper and gives insights on future work directions.

2 Preliminaries

In this section, the symbolic representation and the problem definition are given.

The set of service, mashup, user feed-backs are expressed as $S = \{s_1, s_2, ...s_S\}$, $M = \{m_1, m_2, ...m_M\}$, $U = \{u_1, u_2, ...u_U\}$, $F = \{f_1, f_2, ...f_F\}$ respectively.

Service. A service s is a collection of functions, denoted as a 3-tuple, $s = (ns, ds, < t_1, t_2, ..., t_n >)$ where n is the name of s, d represents the description of s and $< t_1, t_2, ..., t_n >$ represents the set of tags associated to s.

Mashup. A mashup m represents the composition of one or more Web services into one single application, making it available as a composite service. A mashup can be denoted as a 3-tuple, $m = (nm, dm, < s_1, s_2, ..., s_n >, < t_1, t_2, ..., t_m >$ where nm represents the name of m, dm represents the description of m, $< s_1, s_2, ..., s_n >$ denotes the set of service invoked by m and $< t_1, t_2, ..., t_m >$ represents the set of tags associated to m.

User Feedback. A Feedback rating is the perception of each user about invoked services representing an overall perception. For the ith invoked service, a user provides a feedback rating that indicates the level of satisfaction with the service after each interaction with the service. Then users maintain n feedback ratings which represent their perception of s_i's performance. $r_{u,i}$ is the feedback ratings of web service s_i rated by user u.

Personalized Web Service Recommendation. Given a user requirement description of a new mashup, find the top-k services that best match functional and non-functional requirements.

3   A Deep Learning Model for Personalized Web Service Recommendation

In this section, we detail the Personalized Service Recommendation Deep Learning model (PSRDL) for mashup creation. The architecture of the PSRDL model is shown in Fig. 1. First, it finds the neighbor mashups that are most similar to the new mashup according to their description through the neighbor finding module. Then, representation module builds a deep neural network to learn service representation using attention mechanism to capture functional and non-functional representation learning. Finally, the top-k selected services for the new mashup can be calculated, by the recommendation module, using the attention matching from the representation of its neighbor mashups for each service.

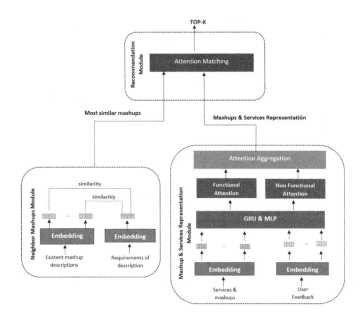

Fig. 1. Architecture of PSRDL Model

3.1   Neighbor Mashups Module

The mashup or service is typically represented by a description of its functionality. For each description in mashup m, we convert it into an l-dimensional vector denoted as VD_m. For the new mashup $m\prime$ to be created, the developer needs to enter the mashup requirements or description, $m\prime_{dm}$, consisting of a set of phrases, sentences, or even paragraphs as the developer's initial query for similar mashups. This module searches for its neighbor mashups that meet the requirement of $m\prime$ based on their similarity as follow:

$$sim_{m\prime, Nm\prime} = cosine(vD_m\prime, vD_{Nm\prime})$$

where Nm is the neighbor of the new mashup $m\prime$.

3.2   Mashup and Service Representation Module

This module aims to learn a service and a mashup representation based on a three layer architecture.

A- Embedding Layer. The embedding layer generates the dense representations of services and mashups based on their descriptions $d_i \in D_*$ where $1 < i < |D_*|$, $D_* = [D_s, D_m]$ and their tags $t_j \in T_*$ where $1 < j < |T_*|$, $T_* = [T_s, T_m]$. We use the Word2vec [8] technique, which is a shallow neural language model that can process text data and generate word vectors. Latent vectors $VD_s \in R^l$, $VD_m \in R^l$, $VT_s \in R^l$, $VT_m \in R^l$, represent the l-dimensional descriptions and tags features of service and mashup respectively. For each service $s \in S$ and each mashup $m \in M$, the embedding layer generates the latent vectors V_s and V_m as: $V_s = VD_s + VT_s$ and $V_m = VD_m + VT_m$.

B- MLP & GRU Layer. This layer allows learning deep features of services, mashups and user-feed-backs using their compressed representations generated from the embedding layer. Since words in tags are usually discrete and semantic independent, we choose MLP technique [9] to learn the tag representations $h(t_i)$ as:

$$h(t_i) = sigmoid(W_t.VT(t_i) + b_t)$$

where $VT(t_i)$ is the input vector of the ith tag and W_t, b_t are parameters to be learned.

To generate the final tag representation $v(t)$ we mean-pooling all tags vectors:

$$v(t) = \frac{1}{|T|} \times \sum_{i=1}^{T} h(t_i)$$

where $|T|$ represents the number of tags associated with a service or a mashup.

Different from tags, words in service or mashup description are interdependent and semantic-correlated, thus we use the GRU technique [10] to capture their semantic dependencies. The description representation $h(d_i)$ is formulated as follows:

$$\overrightarrow{z_t} = sigmoid\ (W_z.X_t + b_z)$$

$$\overrightarrow{r_t} = sigmoid\ (W_r.X_t + b_r)$$

$$\overrightarrow{\tilde{h_t}} = tanh\ (W_h.(\overrightarrow{r_t} \times X_t) + b_h)$$

$$\overrightarrow{h_t} = (1 - \overrightarrow{z_t}) \times \overrightarrow{h_{t-1}} + \overrightarrow{z_t} \times \overrightarrow{\tilde{h_t}}$$

$$h(d_i) = \overrightarrow{h_t}$$

and

$$W_* = \{W_z, W_r, W_h\};\ X_t = \{VW(d_i), h_{t-1}\}$$

C- Attention Layer. This layer aims to allocate more attention to the important input regarding functional and non-functional features.

1) Functional Attention Mechanism

In the services and mashups network, tags are used to abstract the functional features of services and the words related to the functional properties in descriptions are semantically similar to the corresponding tags and should be stressed. However, different words in descriptions have different importance for the overall functional intention, some of them can be decisive while others are irrelevant to the service's recommendation. Therefore, we introduce a functional attention layer that can detect pertinent function-oriented features and learns to assign an attention score a_i to each one in descriptions as follows:

$$a_i = sigmoid(v(t_x)\ h(d_i))$$

where $v(t_x) = \{v(t_s), v(t_m)\}$ is the tag representation, $v(t_s)$ is the tag representation of services and $v(t_m)$ is the tag representation of mashups.

2) Non-functional Attention Mechanism

This step aims to learn non functional features like reputation of service and mashups to provide more personalized and accurate recommendation services. We focus on QoS and QoE. Four QoS metrics are considered including availability, reliability, latency, and response time. There are two types of considered QoS parameters in this paper, including positive parameters, and negative parameters. The positive parameters (q^+) infer to the QoS parameters such as reliability and availability that should be maximized. On the contrary, the negative parameters (q^-) refer to QoS parameters that should be minimized, like latency and response time. Equation 1 is for negative parameters and Eq. 2 is for positive parameters. In these equations, $s.q_i$ refers to the ith QoS parameter (q_i) of the service s that is being normalized, and $min\ (q_i)$ and $max\ (q_i)$ represent the minimum and maximum values of the corresponding QoS parameter in the dataset.

$$\begin{cases} \frac{s.q_i - min\ (q_i)}{max\ (q_i) - min\ (q_i)} & if\ max\ (q_i) \neq min\ (q_i) \\ 1 & if\ max\ (q_i) = min\ (q_i) \end{cases} \quad (1)$$

$$\begin{cases} \frac{max\ (q_i) - s.q_i}{max\ (q_i) - min\ (q_i)} & if\ max\ (q_i) \neq min\ (q_i) \\ 1 & if\ max\ (q_i) = min\ (q_i) \end{cases} \quad (2)$$

Then, we generate K random QoE values (K denotes the number of subjective tests. It means that for each service, K persons give their feedback in a number value format). Afterward, based on Pearson equation [11], we calculate Q coefficient values (weights) for each service corresponding to its QoS values. We have considered $K = 100$, and $Q = 4$ since we have four QoS parameters. Finally, utilizing the calculated weights c_{ij} and QoS values given in the dataset, we can calculate the final QoE value. To this end, we have used the following equations, which linearly correlate QoE and QoS values [12,13]

$$c_{ij} = \left| \frac{\sum_{k=1}^{K}(q_{ij} - \bar{q}_i)(qoe_k - q\bar{o}e)}{\sqrt{\sum_{k=1}^{K}(q_{ij} - \bar{q}_i)^2}\sqrt{\sum_{k=1}^{K}(qoe_k - q\bar{o}e)^2}} \right| \quad (3)$$

$$QoE(s_j) = \sum_{i=1}^{Q} c_{ij}(s_j) * q_{ij}(s_j) \quad (4)$$

where q_{ij} is the current QoS value for jth service (s_j), for which we calculate the weight. $\bar{q}_i$ is the mean value for the ith QoS parameter, and qoe_k is the kth user feedback value among K users.

We consider the QoE value as a positive QoS parameter. The final service rating value $R(s_i)$ is calculated as follows:

$$R(s_i) = \sum_{i=1}^{2} w_i * s.q_i^- + \sum_{i=3}^{5} w_i * \frac{1}{s.q_i^+}$$

We use the simple additive weight (SAW) method to linearly combine the objectives. w_i are weights/coefficients for each of the QoS parameters and they should sum up to 1 $\sum_{i=1}^{5} w_i = 1$. These weights can be defined by the service requester. Since we focus on reliability, its coefficient is considered as $w_{rel} = 0.5$ and for the rest of parameters (availability, response time, latency, and QoE) the coefficients are considered as $w_i = 0,125$. For mashups, the rating value is calculated using the several composed services each of which has its own QoS and QoE values. The QoS values of the composite service is the aggregation values of its sub-services.

We use MLP network to learn deeper and high-order features from rating patterns as follows: $h(r_{s_i}) = sigmoid(W_{ra}.R(s_i) + b_{ra})$

where $R(s_i)$ is the rating value of the ith service, W_{ra}, b_{ra} are parameters to be learned. The output $h(r_{s_i})$ will be the rating-based representation of the service i. We calculate the rating-based representation of the mashup $h(r_{m_i})$ using the same equation. Afterward, we mean-pooling all service rating representations to generate the final representation $v(r_{s_i})$

$$v(r_{s_i}) = \frac{1}{Rs} \times \sum_{i=1}^{Rs} h(r_{s_i})$$

where Rs represents the number of ratings associated with a service s_i.

The final mashup rating representation $v(r_{m_i})$ is as follow:

$$v(r_{m_i}) = \frac{1}{Rm} \times \sum_{i=1}^{Rm} h(r_{m_i})$$

where Rm represents the number of ratings associated with a mashup m_i.

3) Attention aggregation

This module combines both the functional attention and the non functional attention mechanisms. The representation of service $v(s_i)$ and the mashup representation $v(m_i)$ can finally be calculated as an aggregation process by adding all weighted word representations, the mean-pooled tag representations, and the rating representations as follow:

$$v(s_i) = v(t_{s_i}) \oplus \sum_{j}^{|D_{s_i}|} \frac{h(d_j) * a_j}{|D_{s_i}|} \oplus v(r_{s_i})$$

$$v(m_i) = v(t_{m_i}) \oplus \sum_{j}^{|D_{m_i}|} \frac{h(d_j) * a_j}{|D_{m_i}|} \oplus v(r_{m_i})$$

3.3   Recommendation Module

This module aims to generate the top-k services using an attention matching operation as follow:

$$P(m\prime) = Matchning(N, V) = Sum(softmax\left(\frac{NV}{\sqrt{d}}\right))$$

We use the scaled dot product [14] to calculate the similarity between the mashup neighbor set and service representation. Here, the neighbor set can be expressed as $N = \{n_1, n_2, ...n_N\} \in R^{N*d}$ and the service representation can be expressed as $V = \{v_1, v_2, ..., v_V\}$. Calculate the attention score of N and V by scaling the dot product, and use softmax on it to get the attention weight. Finally, the Sum operation computes the weighted sum of the last dimension of the attention weights to generate $P(m\prime)$. It represents the probabilities that services in candidate set will form the new mashup $m\prime$.

4   Evaluation

4.1   Parameter Learning

We minimize the recommendation ranking loss similar to [15] based on the triplet Ranking Loss method. The triple contains a query q_i (called the anchor instance), a satisfying service s_i^+ (called the positive instance) and a non-satisfying service s_i^- (called the negative instance) randomly sampled from the dataset. The objective is that the distance between the anchor sample and the negative sample representations is greater (and bigger than a margin ma) than the distance between the anchor and positive representations. Therefore, the loss function can be defined as:

$$L(q_i, s_i^+, s_i^-) = \max(0, \ Ma \ + \ d(q_i, s_i^+) \ - \ d(q_i, s_i^-)$$
$$= \max(0, \ Ma \ - \ cos(v(q_i), v(s_i^+)) \ + \ cos(v(q_i), v(s_i^-)))$$

where Ma is a constant margin. Since the query can be satisfied with more than one service (a mashup), it can hence be treated as multiple training samples. Then, with all positive and negative triple training samples $T = (q_i, s_i^+, s_i^-), 1 \leq i \leq N$; N the size of training samples. Then, our goal is to minimize the cumulative loss:

$$J = \arg\min_{W,b} \sum_i^N L(q_i, s_i^+, s_i^-)$$

where $W = \{W_t, W_q, W_z, W_r, W_h, W_r a\}$ is a set of weight parameters and $b = \{b_t, b_q, b_z, b_r, b_h, b_r a\}$ is a set of biases that are to be learned.

We use Stochastic Gradient Descent (SGD) We use Stochastic Gradient Descent (SGD) with mini-batches as the optimization strategy which minimizes the above objective and updates the model parameters through back-propagation process. Mini-batch gradient descent is typically the algorithm of choice when training a neural network. It reduces the variance of the parameter updates, which can lead to more stable convergence and make use of highly optimized matrix that make computing the gradient efficient. We consider two cases:

1. if $f(q_i, s) \geqslant Ma$

$$\frac{\partial L}{\partial \omega} = 0, \ \frac{\partial L}{\partial \theta} = 0, \ \forall \omega \in W, \ \theta \in b$$

2. if $f(q_i, s) \geqslant Ma$

$$\frac{\partial L}{\partial \omega} = -\frac{\partial f(q_i, s)}{\partial \omega}, \ \omega' = \omega - \eta.\frac{\partial L}{\partial \omega}, \forall \omega \in W,$$

$$\frac{\partial L}{\partial \theta} =, -\frac{\partial f(q_i, s)}{\partial \theta} \ \theta' = \theta - \eta.\frac{\partial L}{\partial \theta}, \ \forall \theta \in b$$

where $f(q_i, s) = 2 \ y \ cos(v(q_i), v(s_i))$ $y = \begin{cases} 1, & s_i^+, \\ -1, & s_i^- \end{cases}$ and η is the learning rate of SGD.

4.2   Experimentation

Dataset Description: We use a real-world dataset crawled from programmableweb.com, which has been widely used in many tasks like API service recommendation. We report in Table 1 statistics about the dataset. We collected 6417 Mashups, 19380 APIs and other information such as API category and API rating. Before the model validation, we preprocessed the dataset as follows:

- Pruning and tokenization: We built a stop word list and discarded all the meaningless words like "the", "API", "Mashup", etc. We then used the StandardAnalyzer and PosterStemFilter tools from Lucene Package to transform all terms into tokens with the prefix and suffix removed.
- Description segmentation and Repository construction: We split all service and Mashup descriptions into sentences according to the separator. All terms and sentences are properly numbered. We then constructed a service repository and a Mashup repository.

Table 1. xx

Item	Value
Number of APIs	19380
Number of Mashups	6417
Number of APIs categories	384
Average number of API per category	50.46
Average number of member API per Mashup	2.2

As it is hard to determine the number of services recommended for a given user query, we set this number based on the statistical results, where is approximately exponentially distributed, and more than 99% Mashups invoke 1–10 Web APIs. Thus, we report experimental results obtained by recommending up to 10 Web APIs. All the Mashups in the dataset have been divided into 10 equal subsets, and each fold in the subsets is used as a testing set (i.e., we manually removed all their linked Web APIs and used them as relevant Web APIs when evaluating), while the other remaining subsets are combined as a training dataset. Then the results of each fold are summed up and their averages are reported.

Evaluation Metrics: We evaluate the recommendation accuracy based on the following metrics:

$$Recall@N = \frac{|CR(m_i) \bigcap Rec(m_i)|}{|CR(m_i)|}$$

$$Precision@N = \frac{|CR(m_i) \bigcap Rec(m_i)|}{|Rec(m_i)|}$$

$$F - measure@N = \frac{2 * Recall * Precision}{Recall + Precision}$$

where $CR(m_i)$ is the relevant APIs of Mashup m_i, and $Rec(m_i)$ represents the recommended APIs. $|CR(m_i)|$ and $|Rec(m_i)|$ are the numbers of APIs in $CR(m_i)$ and $Rec(m_i)$ respectively. The higher values of these metrics mean better recommendation accuracy.

Approaches Comparison: We take these baselines to evaluate our method, which are shown as follows:

- TF-IDF: It recommends Web APIs whose descriptions are similar to that of the target Mashup based on the vector space model. The term frequency and inverse document frequency are used to calculate the similarity between Web APIs and the target Mashup based on the cosine similarity calculation method.
- BLSTM: This method jointly learns two embeddings representing the functional features of Web APIs and the functional requirements of Mashups based on BLSTM. The cosine similarity is adopted and the top ranked Web APIs are finally selected.
- TA-BLSTM [16]: This method introduces an attention mechanism to reveal the functional information of Mashup and API descriptions. It also uses the cosine method to calculate the closeness between Mashups and APIs.
- FC-LSTM [17]: this method is similar to TA-BLSTM but incorporates Mashup requirements as an application scenario to help select the most appropriate services.
- ICNC-CF [18]: this method clusters Mashups based on the latent topics learned by a two-level topic model with considering the relationships between Mashups. Then, it explores item-based collaborative filtering algorithm to rank and recommend Web services using historical invocation history between Mashups clusters and Web services.
- PSRDL: our method combines a functional and non-functional attention-based model for service recommendation using MLP and GRU techniques.

For parameters setting in the baselines, we experimented multiple times and chose the following settings. For baseline method BLSTM and TA-BLSTM, we learned the word embeddings based on the Skip-Gram algorithm in Word2vec tool implemented in Java, and the dimension of learned embeddings is fixed as 100. We implemented the proposed model based on the TensorFlow platform. During the model training, SGD is the optimization strategy with setting the learning rate η and margin Ma as 0.01 and 0.1 respectively. In addition, a recommended candidate API pool with size P is required for each training Mashup. We put all positive services into the pool then randomly sample negative services from the entire service repository until the pool size reaches P. To choose the best value, we design extensive experiments.

Experimental Results: Figure 2 illustrates the performance of the baseline methods. We can observe that the Recall values increase gradually with the increase of recommended services, while the Precision values follow the opposite trend since more and more non-member services appear in the recommendation results. The performance of our method PSRDL greatly exceeds that of other state-of-the-art methods.

RNN-based methods, including BLSTM, TagBLSTM and TA-BLSTM, demonstrate better performance compared with the keyword matching-based method TF-IDF. This is because that deep RNN-based model can automatically extract features that are helpful in the service recommendation task, while other methods usually demand great human effort to mine features that are sometimes meaningless.

Figure 2(c) shows the comprehensive metric F-measure which trade-offs the Recall and Precision results. We can note that the proposed method outperforms LSTM methods with an average F-measure improvement of 7.8% over FC-LSTM, 23.7% over TA-BLSTM and 48.4% over BLSTM. This demonstrates the GRU model is superior to the LSTM model. In addition, we can also observe that PRSDL performs better than methods without an attention mechanism (TF-IDF, BLSTM and ICNC-CF) and the reason is that attention mechanism focuses on more important properties of Mashups and services. Furthermore, PSRDL is superior to FC-LSTM which means the QoE has a positive effect on the recommendation accuracy since it contains rich information that can be useful complementary to the recommendation.

During the training of the proposed recommendation model, each trained Mashup is attached with a training pool size P. Figure 2(d) presents its influence on the recommendation results measured by F-measure. We can observe that the larger pool size is beneficial for obtaining better accuracy. However, although the larger setting of P means larger training data, it also means that more training time is required to complete an epoch over the whole training instance. Note that after 10 epochs of training, PSRDL converges to the best recommendation results.

5   Related Work

5.1   Content-Based Web Service Recommendation

Content-based service recommendation methods focus on mining the relationship between mashups and web service requirements, and directly recommend those web services that are close to the mashup using functional description of services [19,20]. Service topic features are extracted from the topic model, and service recommendation is made by service topic feature matching. For example, [21] proposed a method based on mashup description to discover the important word characteristics of the service and bridge the vocabulary gap between mashup developers and service providers. However, much efforts are required for manual semantic annotation witch may lead to the loss of information and intention gap. [22] used the factorization machine to model the information of multiple dimensions, such as the similarity between mashups and services, the popularity of services, etc., to predict and recommend the services corresponding to the target mashups. Compared with the above works, we use a deep neural network as the modeling basis to build a complete end-to-end service recommendation framework.

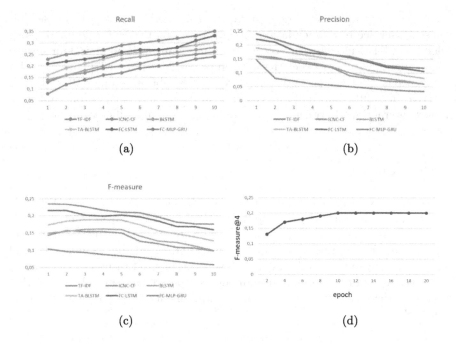

Fig. 2. Performance comparisons of the baseline methods (a) Recall results (b) Precision results (c) F-measure results (d) Influence of pool size on F-measure

5.2 QoS-Based Web Service Recommendation

[23] presented a location-aware collaborative filtering method for QoS-based Web service which combines users' location and services' location to find similar users and similar services. [24] proposed a session level representation method based on multidimensional attention mechanism to enhance the matching degree between user interaction sequences and user intentions, and reduce the impact of noise interaction. However, because QoS is dynamic and changes over time, QoS-aware methods may encounter uncertainty. Thus, inject user's perception in the service quality using QoE can deliver satisfactory user experience. [25] proposed a general collaborative filtering (GCF) method based on a neural network to model the user-service interactions. [26] presented a framework that leverages learning-to-rank and active learning techniques to boost recommendation performance by exploiting user feedback. In this paper, we combine QoS and QoE to provide more personalized Web service recommendations.

5.3 Web Service Recommendation with Deep Learning Technology

In recent years, the adoption of deep learning technology for service recommendation has become very popular. Different from the traditional method, it can automatically learn representative features from the original data and mine the hidden information, like the context and the word order. For example, [17] proposed a service recommendation method based on text extension and depth model, and LSTM model with two attention mechanisms is employed for service recommendation to help select the most appropriate service. [27] constructed a heterogeneous information network (HIN) to describe mashup, API and their respective attribute information. Existing methods rely heavily on capturing complex interactions between mashups and services and suffer from cold start service.

6   Conclusion

In this paper, we propose a deep Learning Model for Personalized Web Service Recommendations. Using Attention Mechanism we learn functional and non-functional service features to provide more personalized and accurate recommendation. We propose a neighbor mashup finding module to deal with cold start problem in recommender system. The experimental results demonstrated the effectiveness of the proposed deep model compared with several state-of-the-art ones. In the future we plan to do more experiments to qualitatively evaluate our model.

References

1. Yu, J., Benatallah, B., Casati, F., Daniel, F.: Understanding mashup development. IEEE Internet Comput. **12**(5), 44–52 (2008)
2. Wang, X., Zhu, J., Zheng, Z., Song, W., Shen, Y., Lyu, M.R.: A spatial-temporal qos prediction approach for time-aware web service recommendation. ACM Trans. Web (TWEB) **10**(1), 1–25 (2016)
3. Yin, Y., Xu, H., Liang, T., Chen, M., Gao, H., Longo, A.: Leveraging data augmentation for service qos prediction in cyber-physical systems. ACM Trans. Internet Technol. (TOIT) **21**(2), 1–25 (2021)
4. Yu, T., Yu, D., Wang, D., Hu, X.: Web service recommendation for mashup creation based on graph network. J. Supercomput., 1–28 (2023)
5. Wang, X., He, X., Cao, Y., Liu, M., Chua, T.-S.: Kgat: knowledge graph attention network for recommendation. In: Proceedings of the 25th ACM SIGKDD International Conference on Knowledge Discovery & Data Mining, pp. 950–958 (2019)
6. Li, X., Zhang, X., Wang, P., Cao, Z.: Web services recommendation based on metapath-guided graph attention network. J. Supercomput. **78**(10), 12 621–12 647 (2022)
7. Cao, B., Zhang, L., Peng, M., Qing, Y., Kang, G., Liu, J.: Web service recommendation via combining bilinear graph representation and xdeepfm quality prediction. IEEE Trans. Network Serv. Manage. (2023)
8. Mikolov, T., Chen, K., Corrado, G., Dean, J.: Efficient estimation of word representations in vector space. arXiv preprint arXiv:1301.3781 (2013)
9. Ramchoun, H., Ghanou, Y., Ettaouil, M., Janati Idrissi, M.A.: Multilayer perceptron: architecture optimization and training (2016)
10. Chung, J., Gulcehre, C., Cho, K., Bengio, Y.: Empirical evaluation of gated recurrent neural networks on sequence modeling. arXiv preprint arXiv:1412.3555

11. Lalanne, F., Cavalli, A., Maag, S.: Quality of experience as a selection criterion for web services. In: 2012 Eighth International Conference on Signal Image Technology and Internet Based Systems, pp. 519–526. IEEE (2012)
12. Lai, P., et al.: Qoe-aware user allocation in edge computing systems with dynamic qos. Futur. Gener. Comput. Syst. **112**, 684–694 (2020)
13. Li, M., Xu, H., Tu, Z., Su, T., Xu, X., Wang, Z.: A deep learning based personalized qoe/qos correlation model for composite services. In: 2022 IEEE International Conference on Web Services (ICWS), pp. 312–321. IEEE (2022)
14. Vaswani, A., et al.: Attention is all you need. In: Advances in Neural Information Processing Systems, vol. 30 (2017)
15. Wei, J., He, J., Chen, K., Zhou, Y., Tang, Z.: Collaborative filtering and deep learning based recommendation system for cold start items. Expert Syst. Appl. **69**, 29–39 (2017)
16. Shi, M., Tang, Y., Liu, J.: Ta-blstm: tag attention-based bidirectional long short-term memory for service recommendation in mashup creation. In: 2019 International Joint Conference on Neural Networks (IJCNN), pp. 1–8. IEEE (2019)
17. Shi, M., Liu, J., et al.: Functional and contextual attention-based lstm for service recommendation in mashup creation. IEEE Trans. Parallel Distrib. Syst. **30**(5), 1077–1090 (2018)
18. Cao, B., Liu, X.F., Rahman, M.M., Li, B., Liu, J., Tang, M.: Integrated content and network-based service clustering and web apis recommendation for mashup development. IEEE Trans. Serv. Comput. **13**, 99–113 (2017)
19. Lian, S., Tang, M.: Api recommendation for mashup creation based on neural graph collaborative filtering. Connect. Sci. **34**(1), 124–138 (2022)
20. Yao, L., Wang, X., Sheng, Q.Z., Benatallah, B., Huang, C.: Mashup recommendation by regularizing matrix factorization with api co-invocations. IEEE Trans. Serv. Comput. **14**(2), 502–515 (2018)
21. Shi, M., Liu, J., Zhou, D., Tang, Y.: A topic-sensitive method for mashup tag recommendation utilizing multi-relational service data. IEEE Trans. Serv. Comput. **14**, 342–355 (2018)
22. Kang, G., Liu, J., Xiao, Y., Cao, B., Xu, Y., Cao, M.: Neural and attentional factorization machine-based web api recommendation for mashup development. IEEE Trans. Network Serv. Manage. **18**, 4183–4196 (2021)
23. Liu, J., Tang, M., Zheng, Z., Liu, X., Lyu, S.: Location-aware and personalized collaborative filtering for web service recommendation. IEEE Trans. Serv. Comput. **9**(5), 686–699 (2015)
24. Kwapong, B.A., Anarfi, R., Fletcher, K.K.: Personalized service recommendation based on user dynamic preferences. In: Ferreira, J.E., Musaev, A., Zhang, L.-J. (eds.) SCC 2019. LNCS, vol. 11515, pp. 77–91. Springer, Cham (2019). https://doi.org/10.1007/978-3-030-23554-3_6
25. Ma, W., Shan, R., Qi, M.: General collaborative filtering for web service qos prediction. Math. Probl. Eng. **2018**, 1–18 (2018)
26. Zhou, Y., Yang, X., Chen, T., Huang, Z., Ma, X., Gall, H.C.: Boosting api recommendation with implicit feedback. IEEE Trans. Softw. Eng. **48**, 2157–2172 (2021)
27. Liang, T., et al.: Mobile app recommendation via heterogeneous graph neural network in edge computing. Appl. Soft Comput. **103**, 107162 (2021)

Deep Reinforcement Learning-Based Scheduling for Same Day Delivery with a Dynamic Number of Drones

Boyang Zhou[1,2(✉)] and Liang Cheng[1,2]

[1] Lehigh University, Bethlehem, USA
boz319@lehigh.edu
[2] University of Toledo, Toledo, USA

Abstract. Same-Day Delivery (SDD) has emerged as a popular trend in the retail market, relieving workers from repetitive and monotonous tasks. Despite these advantages, SDD scheduling is challenging as there is no prior information available for upcoming tasks. Existing research has attempted to address this problem using local heuristic search, approximate dynamic programming, and reinforcement learning algorithms. However, none of these approaches has considered a dynamic number of drones, which can change due to unforeseen crashes or employing new drones due to the heavy workload. In this paper, we propose a Same-Day Delivery with a Dynamic Number of Drones (SD4) problem. To address this problem, we present a reinforcement learning model using Double Deep-Q Network (DDQN) to handle both task scheduling with a dynamic number of drones and drone employment simultaneously.

Keywords: Unmanned Aerial Vehicles (UAV) · Double Deep-Q Networks (DDQN)

1 Introduction

The advancement of battery technology and control theory has made Unmanned Aerial Vehicles (UAVs), or drones, more applicable to commercial settings. Same-day delivery (SDD) is one of the most important applications of UAVs. Although SDD is widely investigated by researchers in logistics [1–4,6], existing research lacks the consideration of a changing number of vehicles (e.g., drones) during the delivery. Drones are vulnerable to crashes in harsh and uncertain environments and can be shared by different depots causing a changing number of drones. Thus, it is necessary to develop scheduling algorithms that deal with the dynamic number of drones. We propose a Same-Day Delivery with a Dynamic number of Drones (SD4) problem, specifically targeting same-day meal delivery.

This work is supported by NSF Award No. 2146968. Any opinions, findings, and conclusions or recommendations expressed in this paper are those of the author(s) and do not necessarily reflect the views of the sponsors of the research.

© The Author(s), under exclusive license to Springer Nature Switzerland AG 2023
F. Monti et al. (Eds.): ICSOC 2023, LNCS 14419, pp. 34–41, 2023.
https://doi.org/10.1007/978-3-031-48421-6_3

The SD4 problem involves two main novelties: The first novelty is scheduling tasks for a dynamic number of drones, while the second novelty involves coordinating drones, including their deployment and release, to enable more efficient drone utilization, particularly when depots experience peak periods in different time periods. The main contributions of the paper are as follows:

1. We propose the SD4 problem, which considers the dynamic number of drones and drone coordination during delivery for more realistic delivery scenarios.
2. We use a reinforcement learning model that employs Double Deep-Q Networks (DDQN [5]) to solve the SD4 problem. This model is evaluated in terms of convergence, solution quality, and real-time performance.

The rest of the paper is organized as follows. Section 2 proposes the SD4 system for same-day meal delivery. Section 3 and Sect. 4 demonstrate the reinforcement learning model and environment setup. Section 5 evaluates our solution.

2   System Description for Meal Delivery with SD4

This section provides an overview of the SD4 system. We take same-day meal delivery as the application scenario of SD4. Figure 1 illustrates the architecture of the SD4 system for meal delivery.

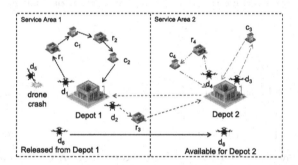

Fig. 1. The system architecture for the same-day meal delivery

A meal delivery task t_j in the SD4 system consists of two components: the restaurant and the customer, denoted as r_j and c_j, respectively, in Fig. 1. There are two types of delivery in the system: individual delivery and collaborative delivery. Individual delivery occurs when a task can be assigned to a single drone. For instance, in Fig. 1, tasks t_1 and t_2 are assigned to drone d_1 as individual deliveries. Collaborative delivery, on the other hand, is necessary when the restaurant and the customer of a task are located in different service areas of depots. Task t_3 is an example of collaborative delivery. Drones may crash during delivery. Moreover, depots may release their drones (i.e., d_6). Depot 2 must estimate whether employing d_6 would improve overall system performance after it is released by depot 1.

3   Environment Setup for SDD Task Scheduling

Environment setup plays a crucial role in reinforcement learning. The environment of a reinforcement learning model consists of state, action, and reward. In this section, we introduce the environment setup for SDD task scheduling. We make the following assumptions for the SD4 problem:

1. Drones have a fixed maximum flight time regardless of the payload of a task.
2. Each drone can only deliver a single meal at a time.
3. Depots can reject any request without penalty, except in the case of a collaborative delivery where a drone has already picked up the meal.
4. Drones switch their batteries in depots and the switching time is negligible.

3.1   Task and State

Task t_j can be described by a five-tuple $(arr_j, r_j, c_j, dl_j, p_j)$. arr_j is the arrival time of task t_j. r_j and c_j are 2D coordinates for the restaurant and the customer, respectively. dl_j is the deadline for finishing this task. p_j is the penalty for t_j. State S_j for task t_j in the task scheduling environment is a vector that contains the following elements:

1. $Avl = [avl_1, avl_2, ..., avl_n]$ indicating the ready time for the next departure of each drone, where n is the number of drones in the system.
2. p_j and dl_j, representing the penalty and deadline for task t_j, respectively, which are appended to S_j.
3. $F_j = [f_{1j}, f_{2j}, ..., f_{nj}]$, where f_{ij} is the time for the drone i to execute t_j.

3.2   Action and Reward

Action a_j needs to be taken for task t_j. a_j can take one of the following values:

$$a_j = \begin{cases} 0 & \text{if } t_j \text{ is rejected} \\ k & t_j \text{ is assigned to the } k \text{ th drone, } 1 \le k \le n \end{cases} \quad (1)$$

The immediate reward $R(S_j, a_j)$ is designed to provide feedback action a_j under the current state S_j. It is defined by Eq. 2.

$$R(S_j, a_j) = \begin{cases} p_j & \text{if } t_j \text{ is rejected} \\ 1 & tf_{a_j} <= dl_j \\ 1 - \frac{tf_{a_j} - dl_j}{t_{max}} & \text{Otherwise} \end{cases} \quad (2)$$

4   Reinforcement Learning Model and Environment Setup for Drone Employment

This section discusses the reinforcement learning model and the environment setup for the admission of drones. Figure 2 depicts the model for drone employment, where the shared environment can adaptively choose the agent and provide states and rewards based on the task type. The $DDQN_2$ set contains trained DDQN models for scheduling with different numbers of drones.

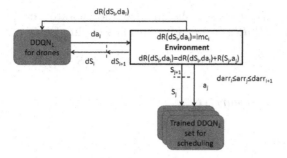

Fig. 2. Reinforcement learning model for drone employment

4.1 Task and State

A two-tuple $(darr_i,\ davl_i)$ describes employable drone dt_i, where $darr_i$ is the time when the depot is notified of the availability of dt_i, and $davl_i$ is the time when dt_i will be ready for the next task. dS_i is the state for drone employment at $darr_i$. It includes the following elements:

1. $Avl' = [avl_1,...,avl_{maxN}]$, where $maxN$ is the maximum number of drones accommodated by the depot. When $i > n$, then $avl_i = t_{max}$ so that no work can be assigned to the ith drone since it is absent.
2. $davl_i$ notifies the agent of the time when dt_i will be ready for meal delivery.
3. $End = [end_1,...,end_{maxN}]$ indicates the off-work time for each drone. Drone i will stop working and leave the depot at end_i. N represents the number of non-employed drones belonging to the depot. Drones belonging to the depot are not allowed to leave the depot unless they crash.

4.2 Action and Reward

Two decisions must be made for each employable drone: whether to accept it and the corresponding release time if accepted. Hence, da_i is designed to make these two simultaneous decisions. The values of da_i are as follows:

$$da_i = \begin{cases} 0 & dt_i \text{ is rejected} \\ k & dt_i \text{ is accepted and it needs to work} \\ & \text{for } \frac{t_{max}*k}{l}, 1 \le k \le l \end{cases} \qquad (3)$$

The parameter l is used to divide the time horizon t_{max} into l equal-length time intervals. $dR(dS_i, da_i)$ is the reward when action da_i is taken under state dS_i. $dR(dS_i, da_i)$ contains a immediate cost imc_i of employing drone dt_i. imc_i is calculated using dp, $davl_i$, and da_i in Eq. 4.

$$imc_i = \begin{cases} 0 & \text{if } da_i = 0 \\ (\min(t_{max}, davl_i + \frac{t_{max}*da_i}{l}) \\ -davl_i) * \frac{dp}{t_{max}} & \text{Otherwise} \end{cases} \qquad (4)$$

Besides imc_i, $dR(dS_i, da_i)$ should also incorporate the reward for task scheduling. Thus, $dR(dS_i, da_i)$ can be calculated using Eq. 5.

$$dR(dS_i, da_i) = imc_i + \sum_j R(S_j, a_j) \tag{5}$$

, where $darr_i < arr_j < darr_{i+1}$.

5 Evaluation

This section presents the evaluation of our reinforcement learning-based approach for SD4, which is divided into two parts: (i) evaluation for SDD task scheduling, and (ii) evaluation for the model for drone employment.

5.1 Evaluation of DDQN for SDD Task Scheduling

We use simulations to evaluate the performance of our proposed model. Here is the setup. The service area of a depot is a 30 by 30 plane, where each unit distance takes one minute for a drone to travel. Euclidean distance is used for the calculation. The maximum shift duration (t_{max}) is set to 600 min, and the maximum flight time $maxF$ of a drone is 60 min. The r_j and c_j coordinates are randomly generated, ensuring that the drone can complete tasks in an individual way or a collaborative way within $maxF$. The penalty p_j is set to 0 for individual delivery tasks and -1 for collaborative ones with food picked up.

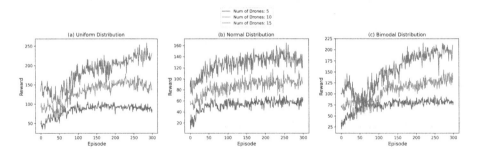

Fig. 3. Plots for the rewards vs. training episodes using 5, 10, 15 drones under different distributions

Convergence Evaluation. To investigate how the workload distribution affects the performance of DDQN, we generated workload using uniform, normal, and bimodal distributions. Figure 3 shows the variation of SDD meal delivery rewards with trained episodes for 5, 10, and 15 drones under the three workload distributions. Each episode represents a shift in the system. As we can see, the model converges well in all scenarios.

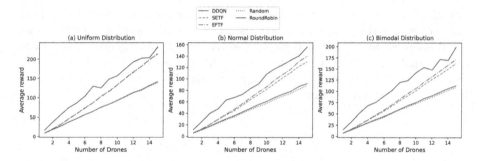

Fig. 4. The average rewards and the average number of scheduled tasks achieved by DDQN, greedy algorithm 1, and greedy algorithm 2 with different numbers of drones under the three workload distributions

Solution Quality Evaluation. To evaluate the quality of solutions of our DDQN, we compare our DDQN model with some traditional scheduling algorithms, including the Shortest Execution Time First (SETF), the Earliest Finish Time First (EFTF), round-robin, and random selection.

SETF: The depot greedily assigns task t_j to the drone that has the shortest task completion time (i.e., $a_j = \underset{i}{argmin}\, f_{ij}$).

EFTF: In EFTF, instead of greedily choosing the shortest execution time, the depot assigns the task t_j to the drone, which has the smallest avl_i after tasking the task (i.e., $a_j = \underset{i}{argmin}\,(avl_i + f_{ij})$).

The evaluation for solution quality was conducted by running 100 episodes for each scenario, and then calculating the average rewards of five algorithms. Figure 4 (a), (b), and (c) shows the average rewards versus different numbers of drones achieved by the five algorithms under different workload distributions.

Three workload distributions were used in the evaluation, and all three distributions have the same workload expectation. DDQN can increase the average reward by a range from 2.5% to 104.1% compared with the best result from the four traditional real-time scheduling algorithms.

5.2 Evaluation for the Drone Employment Model

In this section, we mainly evaluate the model for drone employment. The service area and task generation are inherited from Sect. 5.1. A depot is assumed to have 4 drones initially, and $maxN$ is 8. We evaluate the performance of DDQN for employable drones under normal and bimodal distributions. The uniform distribution is not included as it cannot benefit from employing drones. There will be 20 employable drone requests uniformly distributed in each shift. l is set to 10 for the selection of da_i and the calculation of end_i.

Convergence Evaluation. The first part of the evaluation focuses on the convergence of the DDQN model for employable drones. We set dp to -20 in this example. The rewards vs. training episodes for normal and bimodal workload distributions are shown in Fig. 5, with the mean rewards calculated for the closest 50 episodes to provide a better measurement of convergence. The results indicate that the DDQN model for employable drones converges well in both distributions. It takes fewer than 200 episodes for the model to converge under the two workload distributions.

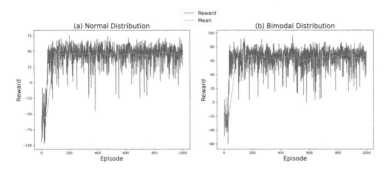

Fig. 5. Plots for the rewards vs. training episodes of DDQN for employable drones under different distributions

Solution Quality Evaluation. The solution quality evaluation involves comparing the performance of the drone employment model to that of DDQN models designed solely for SDD task scheduling under different dp values. We use five DDQN models that can schedule tasks using 4 to 8 drones as baselines. To ensure a fair comparison, we adjust the reward for the DDQN models for task scheduling by adding $dp * (n - 4)$, where n is the number of drones. We then compare the gap between the reward obtained from the drone employment model and the best-adjusted reward derived from the five DDQN models under different dp values to evaluate the solution quality.

Figure 6 presents the reward achieved by the drone employment model and the reward gap in different scenarios. As $|dp|$ increases, the reward gap and reward tend to decrease. There is an outlier of the reward gap when $|dp|$ is 5 under the normal workload distribution. In this case, an additional drone can always produce a positive effect because $|dp|$ is small. However, the decrement stops when $|dp|$ reaches a threshold in both distributions since employing a drone with a high cost will always cause a negative effect. Thus, the model stops employing any drone in these scenarios, causing a 0 reward gap and a constant reward. Drone employment in SD4 will not cause a negative effect no matter how large $|dp|$ is and can increase the reward by up to 21.0% compared with the best-adjusted reward from DDQN models for static numbers of drones.

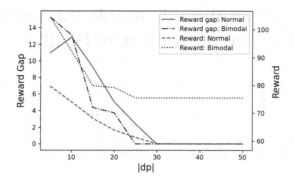

Fig. 6. Reward gap between the drone employment model and DDQN models

5.3 Real-Time Performance Evaluation

The evaluation is conducted on a machine equipped with an i9-13900k CPU and an Nvidia RTX 4080 GPU. The average inference time is less than 50 μs for both models in all scenarios.

6 Conclusion

This paper introduces a novel approach to solving the SD4 problem using a reinforcement learning model. The proposed model is capable of dynamic task scheduling and employment of drones by depots, which can increase the overall system efficiency. The model is evaluated in terms of convergence, solution quality, and real-time performance. The results show that the DDQN model for task scheduling outperforms traditional greedy algorithms under different workload distributions and numbers of drones, while the drone employment model further enhances the system efficiency.

References

1. Dayarian, I., Savelsbergh, M.: Crowdshipping and same-day delivery: employing in-store customers to deliver online orders. Prod. Oper. Manag. **29**(9), 2153–2174 (2020)
2. Dayarian, I., Savelsbergh, M., Clarke, J.P.: Same-day delivery with drone resupply. Transp. Sci. **54**(1), 229–249 (2020)
3. Klapp, M.A., Erera, A.L., Toriello, A.: The dynamic dispatch waves problem for same-day delivery. Eur. J. Oper. Res. **271**, 519–534 (2018)
4. Schubert, D., Kuhn, H., Holzapfel, A.: Same-day deliveries in omnichannel retail: integrated order picking and vehicle routing with vehicle-site dependencies. Naval Res. Logist. (NRL) **68**(6), 721–744 (2021)
5. Van Hasselt, H., Guez, A., Silver, D.: Deep reinforcement learning with double Q-learning. In: Proceedings of the AAAI Conference on Artificial Intelligence (2016)
6. Voccia, S.A., Campbell, A.M., Thomas, B.W.: The same-day delivery problem for online purchases. Transp. Sci. **53**(1), 167–184 (2019)

Designing Reconfigurable Intelligent Systems with Markov Blankets

Boris Sedlak$^{(\boxtimes)}$ ⓘ, Victor Casamayor Pujol ⓘ, Praveen Kumar Donta ⓘ, and Schahram Dustdar ⓘ

Distributed Systems Group, TU Wien, 1040 Vienna, Austria
{b.sedlak,v.casamayor,pdonta,dustdar}@dsg.tuwien.ac.at

Abstract. Compute Continuum (CC) systems comprise a vast number of devices distributed over computational tiers. Evaluating business requirements, i.e., Service Level Objectives (SLOs), requires collecting data from all those devices; if SLOs are violated, devices must be reconfigured to ensure correct operation. If done centrally, this dramatically increases the number of devices and variables that must be considered, while creating an enormous communication overhead. To address this, we (1) introduce a causality filter based on Markov blankets (MB) that limits the number of variables that each device must track, (2) evaluate SLOs decentralized on a device basis, and (3) infer optimal device configuration for fulfilling SLOs. We evaluated our methodology by analyzing video stream transformations and providing device configurations that ensure the Quality of Service (QoS). The devices thus perceived their environment and acted accordingly – a form of decentralized intelligence.

Keywords: Intelligent Systems · Computing Continuum · Markov Blankets · Sensory State · Service Level Objectives · Exact Inference

1 Introduction

Computing Continuum (CC) systems as envisioned in [2,5] are large-scale distributed systems composed of a wide variety of devices. Applications running in the CC pose ambitious requirements, e.g., near real-time latency while dealing with huge volumes of data. Additionally, requirements may change over time; to provide the best possible service, the CC system must adapt. However, given the highly distributed nature of the CC, it is a challenging task to dynamically reconfigure all contained devices, while ensuring high-level system objectives.

In this regard, we envision CC systems employing decentralized intelligence, which allows system parts to make decisions independently, in favor of the application running on top. Smaller units in the CC (e.g., edge devices) would thus obtain the ability to evaluate their own state to ensure requirements are fulfilled. One promising option to model this, is the behavioral concept introduced

Funded by the European Union (TEADAL, 101070186).

F. Monti et al. (Eds.): ICSOC 2023, LNCS 14419, pp. 42–50, 2023.
https://doi.org/10.1007/978-3-031-48421-6_4

by Friston et al. [6,8]. Essentially, it comprises sensory information and actions within a Markov blanket (MB) [10], through which a *thing* interacts with its environment. The MB shields the *thing* from all the variables it is conditionally independent of. Therefore, to determine the state of the *thing*, only the variables in the MB must be considered. Transferring this concept to the CC, you could model each device's behavior through MBs [11] and evaluate device requirements by considering a limited amount of variables. Existing work [7,9,11], however, assumes prior knowledge of how metrics are related to the system state; this approach is not scalable if requirements change during operation or metric correlations are unknown at design time. Thus, existing approaches would fail to ensure the intricate requirements of CC systems.

Each tier in the CC poses its own requirements, which must be fulfilled to create a composable and unified service. To model requirements, Cloud Computing introduced Service Level Objectives (SLOs) as a means to achieve business agreements between infrastructure provider and application developer. However, we propose to expand SLOs to requirements that directly influence the system behavior and the application performance. Inspired by the work of Friston et al., and continuing the research agenda set in [3,5], we aim to leverage the behavioral concept of MBs to represent SLOs throughout the CC. The causality filter of the MB reduces the scope of variables that each device must analyze; thus, decreasing the computational effort of analysis. This empowers resource-constrained devices along the Edge to evaluate SLOs themselves.

In this paper, we propose to evaluate application requirements through MB-based SLOs. The method constrains each SLO to a set of metrics and infers configurations that fulfill them. Further, the output is explainable due to the graphical model used. Hence, the contributions of this article are the following:

- A statistical reasoning model for analyzing conditional dependencies between metrics in distributed systems. Whenever requirements change, the model may thus itself answer which metrics are related to their fulfillment.
- The graphical representation of the device state as MB, which allows interpreting the device behavior. The state can be broken down into several SLOs; in case any of them is violated, it can be explained why.
- A mechanism to infer optimal configurations from MBs given mutable system requirements. It was evaluated under two scenarios in which our approach provided the only configuration that did not violate any SLO.

2   Methodology

From a high-level perspective, we plan to analyze the device state, map selected variables to the SLO fulfillment, and provide adaptive device configurations. Our three-step methodology to achieve this is visualized in Fig. 1: Edge devices produce metrics about ongoing processing; then Bayesian Network Learning (#1) is used to identify correlations between metrics and reflect the impact of environmental changes (e.g., increased incoming requests). Next, we introduce system

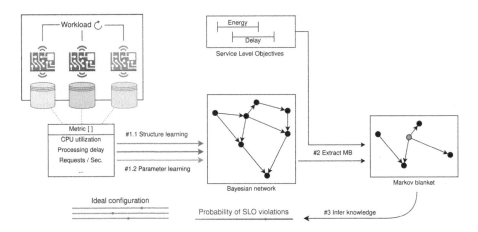

Fig. 1. Methodology for training Bayesian networks and extracting knowledge

requirements (i.e., SLOs) and extract a minimum subset of metrics for SLO fulfillment (#2). Ultimately, we use these MBs to estimate the probability of SLO violations and (#3) infer the configuration with the highest compliance level.

While the proposed methodology describes a sequence of actions, the tools themselves (e.g., algorithms for structure learning) can be optimized depending on the data. This three-step methodology will be our main mechanism for predicting the probabilities of SLO violations given a device configuration. If an SLO is violated due to an environmental change, e.g., a high request count and thus exceeded application delay, we compare possible configurations and provide the one with the highest probability of fulfilling the SLO. This matches our envisioned level of intelligence, i.e., "understanding a situation and reacting according to needs", and neatly fits the principles of elastic computing [4].

3   Case Study

The following case study will be used to evaluate our methodology. In particular, we present two video streaming scenarios that require privacy-preserving transformations. We analyze device metrics to build a Bayesian Network (BN), specify SLOs that characterize the QoS, extract the MB around each SLO, and finally, infer system configurations that have the lowest chance of violating SLOs.

3.1   Setup

Training a BN requires data; therefore, we use the framework introduced in [12], which allows edge devices to detect privacy-violating patterns (e.g., screen, face, or voice) in a stream and transform it continuously to resolve possible privacy violations. As a workload, it fits our methodology because it (1) provides an ample set of metrics reflecting the QoS of ongoing processing, (2) can be

Table 1. (Parameterizable) Metrics captured during workload execution

Name	Unit	Description	Param
delay	ms	processing time per frame	No
CPU	%	utilization of the CPU	No
memory	%	utilization of the system memory	No
pixel	num	number of pixel contained in a frame	Yes
fps	num	number of frames received per second	Yes
bitrate	num	number of pixels transferred per second	No
distance	px	relative distance of object between frames	No
transformed	T/F	if the model detected a pattern (i.e., face)	No
GPU	T/F	if the device employs a GPU	No
config	nominal	mode in which the device operates	Yes
consumption	W	energy pulled by the device	No

parameterized, and (3) can be executed on edge devices. Using the framework, we specify a privacy model that detects faces within a video stream and blurs the respective region, a scenario useful for office monitoring or AR setups [1, 12]. During execution, 11 metrics are captured, which we introduce in Table 1. Each row contains a short description, the measurement unit, and if it can be parameterized. For example, *pixel* and *fps* are video stream properties; however, the producer can adapt them to create a variable *bitrate*. *Config* determines the device operation mode; devices such as Nvidia Jetson Xavier NX[1] can thus limit their energy consumption and the number of active CPU cores. It is worth mentioning the metric *distance*, which tracks the relative position of a detected face between frames, indicating how fluent/sluggish an object is tracked.

To explore correlations between metrics, we simulate an adaptive bitrate; precisely, the producer periodically switches between different *fps* (12, 16, 20, 26, 30) and *pixel* (120p, 180p, 240p, 360p, 480p, 720p), while the edge device moves through *config* modes. Current parameter assignments are part of the metrics set, which is persisted with every processed frame. Metrics are directly observable by the device; except for *consumption*, which is captured through an external power plug[2] over a telemetry period of 10 s. Metrics are accumulated in a CSV file, which will contain 756,000 rows, captured within 2.5 h.

We identified five SLOs that describe the system state in terms of QoS and Quality of Experience (QoE); however, each applicable scenario can have its own subset of relevant SLOs. We assign a name to each SLO and highlight the metrics from Table 1 (e.g., *bitrate*) that are used to evaluate the state of the SLO. Some SLOs are constructed by combining metrics (i.e., **within_time**), others are com-

---

[1] https://docs.nvidia.com/jetson/archives/r34.1/DeveloperGuide/text/SO/
JetsonXavierNxSeries.html, accessed June 13th 2023.

[2] https://www.delock.com/produkt/11827/merkmale.html, accessed June 13th 2023.

pared against a customizable threshold (e.g., **pixel_distance**), while other SLOs directly mimic the value (True/False) of the metric (i.e., **transform_success**).

network_usage Edge devices have limited network interfaces, and in some cases, limited network bandwidth. Since video streams are transferred over the network, *bitrate* is important to control network congestion.

energy_cons Edge devices are restricted in terms of resources and thus must economize or limit their energy *consumption* while ensuring compliance with the remaining system requirements (i.e., other SLOs).

within_time Video processing introduces a considerable streaming *delay*, which can lead to dropping frames and consequently poorer QoE. Hence, the stream's *fps* can be adjusted to limit/avoid dropping frames.

pixel_distance Measures the quality of the object tracking capacity; we expect the tracked object not to jump, but to have a smooth trajectory. Hence, we define a range for the acceptable *distance*.

transf_success Private or confidential information must not be disclosed; therefore, it must maximize the number of transformed faces in the stream.

The workload was executed on the Jetson Xavier NX, which supports GPU-accelerated video processing over NVIDIA CUDA. To explore correlations between *GPU* and other metrics, we execute the entire workload twice on the Xavier NX – once with and once without CUDA acceleration enabled.

3.2   Model Construction

For constructing the BN, we leverage *pgmpy*[3], a Python-based framework that supports an ample set of algorithms for structure and parameter learning, e.g., Hill-Climb Search (HCS) and Maximum Likelihood Estimation (MLE). We train the BN with HCS and MLE on all captured metrics, which takes roughly 30 s on the Xavier NX. After training the BN, we extract the MB for each SLO; the resulting MBs are visualized in Figs. 2: The first three graphics show simple SLOs, i.e., such that require exactly one metric for evaluation. For example, **energy_cons** must evaluate *consumption* to determine the state of the SLO. Metrics that have an edge pointing to *consumption* (i.e., *bitrate*, *config*, and *GPU*) causally influence the variable and thus the SLO fulfillment. On the other hand, **within_time**, is composed of two metrics and thus features two MBs. Complex SLOs [9] (i.e., such that consist of n metrics) would produce n MBs; therefore, increasingly complex SLOs will require a sophisticated mechanism to merge and compress MBs.

We argue that the MBs extracted for each SLO are plausible because contained edges can be rationally explained. Further, all MB SLOs contain at least one parameterizable metric within their sensory state, i.e., among the variables that influence the SLO outcome. From a requirements perspective, this is essential because it allows a device to adapt dynamically to fulfill given SLOs.

---

[3] https://pgmpy.org/, accessed June 14th, 2023.

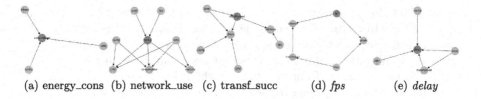

(a) energy_cons (b) network_use (c) transf_succ   (d) *fps*   (e) *delay*

Fig. 2. Markov blankets of the SLOs extracted from the Bayesian network

3.3 Device Configuration Inference

To infer device configurations that comply with the SLOs, we extract information from the BN with Variable Elimination (VE). Instead of querying the entire BN, we execute the queries on the minimum subset of relevant variables, i.e., the MB of each SLO. Since the MBs of the SLOs contained all three parameterizable metrics (i.e., *fps*, *pixel*, and *config*), a device must include these parameters in an inferred configuration; otherwise, there is no full control over the SLOs. However, suppose we would only trace a subset of the SLOs (e.g., **network_usage** & **transf_success**), a configuration must only include the respective parameters contained in the MBs, e.g., *fps* & *pixel*, but not *config*.

VE computes the probability of SLO violations for exactly one parameter assignment; we repeatedly apply this approach for all assignments. To be precise, the parameter space for (*pixel* : *fps* : *config*) consists of (5 : 6 : 3) possible assignments. Iterating over $5 * 6 * 3 = 90$ combinations and 5 SLO-MBs produces $5 * 90 = 450$ inference queries, which require roughly 700ms on the Jetson Xavier NX. The result is a list of configurations that fulfill the given SLOs, e.g., one could be (240p : 20fps : 4C_20W). To deal with changing requirements and heterogeneous characteristics of CC devices, it is possible to provide additional constraints to the VE (e.g., *GPU*=False), or customize SLOs to rank a metric rather than limiting it (e.g. minimize *consumption*).

3.4 Evaluation

To evaluate the quality of inferred configurations, we compare the number of SLO violations between devices that apply inferred or arbitrary configurations. We envision two scenarios that are based on the workload for face blurring. The scenarios are described below, while the corresponding SLO thresholds are presented in Table 2. We intend to minimize **energy_cons** for both scenarios regardless of whether the energy supply would be constrained:

Scenario A: To create a virtual map (like Google Street View[4]), a camera-equipped car captures street videos. The car has an edge device installed to transform the stream; the result is directly rendered to a local map and only accessed remotely in case of inspection, so **network_usage** is of less importance. We assume the rendering process to run in the background; therefore, the GPU

---

[4] https://www.google.com/streetview/, accessed June 18th 2023.

is not available for processing. To create a detailed map, **pixel_distance** must be low, and **within_time** fulfilled in most cases. However, the stream can be re-rendered to blur undetected faces, thus **transf_success** is less critical.

Scenario B: Within a smart factory, employees equipped with head-mounted cameras conduct an audit. To protect privacy, the video stream is transformed on an edge device before streaming to remote consumers. Video content is intended for live inspection only; therefore, **pixel_distance** and **within_time** are less important, while high **transf_success** prevents privacy breaches. However, since audits involve various providers and consumers, low **network_usage** is desired.

Table 2. SLO thresholds that reflect the scenarios' requirements

Scenario	transf_success	distance	network_usage	within_time	energy_cons	GPU
A	$\geq 90\%$	≤ 35	$\leq 8.2\ Mio.\ px/s$	$\geq 95\%$	$min(x)$	No
B	$\geq 98\%$	≤ 60	$\leq 1.6\ Mio.\ px/s$	$\geq 75\%$	$min(x)$	Yes

Table 3. List of configurations generated by exact inference or picked naively

Scenario	Source	Resolution	FPS	Mode	GPU
A	inferred	240p	20	4C_15W	No
	naive	360p	30	6C_20W	
	random #1	120p	16	6C_20W	
	random #2	720p	12	2C_10W	
B	inferred	240p	16	2C_10W	Yes
	naive	180p	26	4C_15W	
	random #1	360p	20	2C_15W	
	random #2	480p	30	6C_20W	

We supply the SLO thresholds to the inference mechanism; the resulting configurations are presented in Table 3: The first line contains the inferred configuration, and the second line the naive assumption; the third and fourth lines are randomly generated. To evaluate the number of SLO violations, we measured each configuration's performance over 10 min; results are presented in Table 4. Over the measurement course, the inferred configurations fulfilled the SLOs for both scenarios. The naive assumption, on the other hand, violated one SLO within each scenario (red cell), i.e., in Scenario A it failed to fulfill **within_time**, while in Scenario B **transf_success** was violated. The randomly generated configurations committed two SLO violations in Scenario A and one in Scenario B each. The results show that our inferred configurations fulfilled all given SLOs while also consuming the least energy.

Table 4. Fulfillment of SLOs depending on scenario and configuration

Scenario	Source	transf_success	distance	network_usage	within_time	energy_cons
A	inferred	98%	15 (97%)	2.0 Mio.	100%	6.0W
	naive	100%	10 (100%)	6.9 Mio.	92%	8.0W
	random #1	4%	127 (2%)	0.4 Mio.	100%	7.0W
	random #2	100%	28 (89%)	11 Mio.	100%	6.0W
B	inferred	98%	18(98%)	1.6 Mio.	100%	6.0W
	naive	92%	11(99 %)	1.5 Mio.	100%	6.5W
	random #1	99%	15 (100%)	4.6 Mio.	100%	6.0W
	random #2	100%	10 (100%)	12.3 Mio.	97%	7.5W

4   Conclusion and Future Work

This paper proposed a statistical reasoning model for explaining causal relations between metrics and the system state, which is reflected by a set of SLOs and their MBs. Essentially, this provides individual edge devices with decentralized intelligence, which helps to cope with the scale and complexity of CC systems. Our methodology was able to provide configurations that would not commit SLO violations; however, the scale of CC systems makes it necessary to assess the impacts of increasingly large Bayesian networks in terms of performance and precision. Furthermore, to cover heterogeneity among CC devices, we aim to infer configurations for arbitrary devices.

References

1. Baniya, P., et al.: Towards policy-aware edge computing architectures. In: 2020 IEEE International Conference on Big Data (Big Data), December 2020
2. Beckman, P., et al.: Harnessing the computing continuum for programming our world. In: Fog Computing, pp. 215–230. John Wiley & Sons, Ltd., April 2020
3. Casamayor Pujol, V., Raith, P., Dustdar, S.: Towards a new paradigm for managing computing continuum applications. In: IEEE 3rd International Conference on Cognitive Machine Intelligence, CogMI 2021, pp. 180–188 (2021)
4. Dustdar, S., Guo, Y., Satzger, B., Truong, H.L.: Principles of elastic processes. Internet Comput. IEEE **15**, 66–71 (2011)
5. Dustdar, S., Pujol, V.C., Donta, P.K.: On distributed computing continuum systems. IEEE Trans. Knowl. Data Eng. **35**(4), 4092–4105 (2023). https://doi.org/10.1109/TKDE.2022.3142856
6. Friston, K.: Life as we know it. J. R. Soc. Inter. **10**(86), 20130475 (2013). https://doi.org/10.1098/rsif.2013.0475
7. Fürst, J., Fadel Argerich, M., Cheng, B., Papageorgiou, A.: Elastic services for edge computing. In: 2018 14th International Conference on Network and Service Management (CNSM), pp. 358–362, November 2018
8. Kirchhoff, M., Parr, T., Palacios, E., Friston, K., Kiverstein, J.: The Markov blankets of life: autonomy, active inference and the free energy principle. J. R. Soc. Inter. **15**(138), 20170792 (2018)

9. Nastic, S., et al.: SLOC: service level objectives for next generation cloud computing. IEEE Internet Comput. **24**(3) (2020). https://doi.org/10.1109/MIC.2020.2987739
10. Pearl, J.: Probabilistic Reasoning in Intelligent Systems : Networks of Plausible Inference. Morgan Kaufmann, San Mateo, California (1988)
11. Sedlak, B., Casamayor Pujol, V., Donta, P.K., Dustdar, S.: Controlling data gravity and data friction: from metrics to multidimensional elasticity strategies. In: IEEE SSE 2023, Chicago, IL, USA, July 2023
12. Sedlak, B., Murturi, I., Donta, P.K., Dustdar, S.: A privacy enforcing framework for transforming data streams on the edge. IEEE Trans. Emerg. Top. Comput. (2023). https://doi.org/10.1109/TETC.2023.3315131

Exploiting Category Information in Sequential Recommendation

Shuxiang Xu[1,2], Qibu Xiang[1,2], Yushun Fan[1,2(✉)], Ruyu Yan[1,2],
and Jia Zhang[3]

[1] Beijing National Research Center for Information Science and Technology, Beijing,
China
[2] Department of Automation, Tsinghua University, Beijing, China
{xsx22,xqb22,yanry18}@mails.tsinghua.edu.cn, fanyus@tsinghua.edu.cn
[3] Department of Computer Science, Southern Methodist University, Dallas, TX, USA
jiazhang@smu.edu

Abstract. In recent years, sequential recommender systems have been
widely applied for service recommendations. However, most existing solutions do not take full advantage of one key factor that usually influences
user behaviors: the category of services. It is necessary yet challenging to
capture users' category preferences. Firstly, the complex inherent relationships that exist among categories are vital but difficult to mine and
encode. Secondly, since interest preferences and category preferences are
closely related, their dynamic evolution has to be studied simultaneously.
To tackle the above challenges, we propose a novel Reciprocal Dual-
Channel Network (RDCN) to capture users' comprehensive dynamic
characteristics toward more accurate recommendations. For the former
challenge, we devise a novel strategy to obtain the co-occurrence information of services and categories and jointly pre-train their embeddings.
For the latter challenge, we design a Co-Guided Attention module and
a Co-Guided GRU module to extract interest preferences and category
preferences, respectively. Experimental results on three public datasets
have demonstrated the necessity of exploiting the category information
and the effectiveness of the proposed RDCN model.

Keywords: Sequential Service Recommendation · Category
Preference · Dual-Channel Learning

1 Introduction

To provide satisfactory user experiences, many online service platforms, such
as E-commerce sites, video sites, and news sites, need to predict the content
in which users are interested. Sequential recommender systems (SRSs) emerge
to solve this problem by modeling users' sequential behaviors to capture the
evolution of their preferences, and thus providing personalized recommendations.

The key to SRSs is how to accurately capture users' interests from their historical behaviors. In recent years, RNN-based models and attention mechanisms

F. Monti et al. (Eds.): ICSOC 2023, LNCS 14419, pp. 51–66, 2023.
https://doi.org/10.1007/978-3-031-48421-6_5

have shown their effectiveness in capturing users' general interests based upon their ability to model sequential information [5,8]. In addition, some SRSs solutions further leverage certain attributes of users and services (e.g., users' age and gender, or category and price of services) as well as contextual information for preference extraction to obtain high-quality recommendations [19,20].

Despite the success of those solutions, they do not take full advantage of one important factor that influences user behaviors: the category of services. Although some methods realize the importance of category information [11], they position category as one item in the attribute list among price, brand, and so on. Economics reveals that the category factor is a key factor affecting user behaviors [1]. Users typically target on a category first, before hunting for a specific service as one instance of the selected category. Modeling inherent relationships among categories may help to determine users' category preferences, and consequently narrow down the scope of recommendations. Therefore, we argue that category should be considered as a first-class citizen when modeling user preference.

How to effectively represent category deserves careful examination, though. Two major challenges arise. The first challenge is how to integrate the intrinsic relationships of categories into their embeddings. The concepts of complement and substitute in economics [1] have taught us that different categories are intrinsically related. Most of the existing solutions simply use an embedding lookup table to encode categories. For instance, Li et al. [9] adopt Word2vec [10] to embed the text descriptions of categories into latent vectors with semantic information, which ignores the relations of categories in the user-service interactions. For example, cosmetics and makeup removers are not strongly semantically related categories, but they are tightly related good categories. The second challenge is how to capture the dynamic evolution of users' category preferences, while simultaneously capturing their interest preferences. A user's category preference keeps evolving and his/her recent behaviors significantly influence the next behavior. For example, after buying a mouse, a user is likely to purchase a matching keyboard. This scenario implies that users' interest preferences and category preferences are not only closely related, but also evolve dynamically.

To tackle the aforementioned two challenges, in this paper, we propose a novel **R**eciprocal **D**ual-**C**hannel **N**etwork (RDCN). For the first challenge, we devise a two-phase mechanism. We first construct a co-occurrence matrix of categories based on category sequences. Considering that bundling relationships also exist in services, we adopt the same way to create a co-occurrence matrix of services. We then design an extended Structural Deep Network Embedding (SDNE) [16] model to simultaneously train the embedding matrices of service and category, which ensures that the embeddings contain holistic correlations of service-service, category-category, and service-category. For the second challenge, we devise an improved multi-head attention module [15] and gated recurrent unit (GRU) [2] module to mutually capture users' interest preferences and category preferences, respectively. Specifically, we introduce category embeddings to affect the allocation of attention values when capturing interest preferences, and apply service embeddings to control the information flow of the gated unit when capturing category preferences. During the actual prediction phase, both preferences are combined to jointly score candidate services to obtain more comprehensive recommendation results. The contributions of this paper are summarized as follows:

- We devise a novel strategy to mine the complex intrinsic associations of services and categories and fuse them into corresponding embedding matrices.
- We develop RDCN to simultaneously model users' interest and category preferences, which learns more precise profile-level features and enables more interpretable prediction.
- Extensive experimental results on three public datasets demonstrate that RDCN outperforms the state-of-the-art models.

2 Related Work

2.1 Sequential Recommendation

Sequential recommender systems (SRSs) focus on modeling users' dynamic preferences. Early studies on SRSs assume that a user's next behavior only depends on recent interactions, so Markov Chain (MC) is typically adopted to predict the next service of interest to the user [4]. However, MC-based models perform poorly in complex scenarios because of their incapacity to capture collective dependencies over user-service interactions. In recent years, RNN-based models have been adopted for sequential recommendation due to their superiority in modeling sequential patterns [5,19]. Hidasi et al. [5] propose GRU4Rec that exploits Gated Recurrent Units to improve recommendation performance. In addition, some methods leverage the attention mechanism to obtain the collective preferences of a user [3,20]. SASRec [8] uses a self-attention block for sequential recommendation; and LightSANs [3] maps a user's behaviors into latent interests with low complexity. To solve the inconsistent prediction issue, CORE [7] unifies the representation space and generates consistent latent representations.

2.2 Attribute Enhanced Recommendation

In addition to user-service interactions, the information carried by users and services can be utilized to improve the quality of recommendations. Some methods integrate the attribute data into a user's representation to enrich user characteristics [9,11,19,22], while some other methods extract attribute preferences separately to construct a user's multi-faceted preferences [20,21]. MLP4Rec [9] embeds some service-related attributes, such as brand and category, into latent vectors and adopts MLP to learn cross-channel and cross-feature relations. FDSA [20] is relatively similar to our work, applying two multi-head attention channels to extract user preferences separately, but it does not introduce information gain between channels. Zhang et al. [21] argue that the price factor plays an important role in determining user purchase behaviors, and design a co-guided heterogeneous hypergraph network to extract user price preferences.

In contrast, we argue that the category factor is more essential and interpretable than other attributes. Moreover, capturing user category preferences may greatly help to interpret the motivation of user behaviors. Therefore, we consider category as a first-class citizen instead of an attribute.

3   Methodology

3.1   Problem Statement

Let $\mathcal{U} = \{u_1, u_2, ..., u_{|\mathcal{U}|}\}$ and $\mathcal{S} = \{s_1, s_2, ..., s_{|\mathcal{S}|}\}$ denote the set of users and the set of services, where $|\mathcal{U}|$ and $|\mathcal{S}|$ are the number of users and services, respectively. Each user u has sequential interactions $\mathcal{I}^u = \{s_1^u, ..., s_t^u, ..., s_{|\mathcal{I}^u|}^u\}$, where $s_t^u \in \mathcal{S}$ denotes the service invoked by user u at time step t. Each service has a category attribute $c \in \mathcal{C}$, where $\mathcal{C} = \{c_1, c_2, ..., c_{|\mathcal{C}|}\}$ is the set of all the categories and $|\mathcal{C}|$ denotes the number of categories. Given the interaction history $\mathcal{I}^u$, the target of the sequential recommendation is to identify the services from $\mathcal{S}$ that user u may interact with at the next time step, i.e., $s_{|\mathcal{I}^u|+1}^u$.

3.2   Framework Overview

Figure 1 illustrates the blueprint of our proposed method, which comprises two stages. In the embeddings pre-training stage shown on the lower half, based on user-service interactions, we calculate the co-occurrence frequency to construct the similarity matrix, and then perform sparsification and graph embedding to obtain the embeddings of services and categories.

In the second stage shown on the upper half, we encode user behaviors with the pre-trained embeddings and adopt dual-channel, namely Co-Guided Attention and Co-Guided GRU, to extract the users' interest preference and category preference respectively, and then combine both preferences to jointly score candidate services.

3.3   Graph Construction

A common service graph construction method is to connect services in the same interaction sequence in a pairwise manner. For long interactions, however, many services at both ends may be weakly related. Therefore, we adopt the sliding window method to filter the services with correlation in the same sequence and take the co-occurrence frequency as the connection strength between service vertices. We then sparse the service graph, using an adaptive dual-threshold method to ensure the sparsity and connectivity of the graph structure.

Co-Occurrence Calculation. To calculate co-occurrence frequency, the conventional sliding window method only considers the relative position interval between services, but the real interaction time interval also affects the correlation between services. Two services are weakly related if they have a large distance

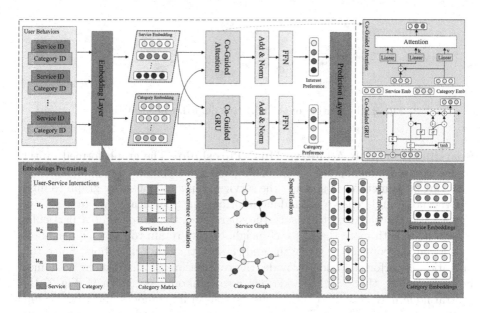

Fig. 1. Illustration of the RDCN model, mainly comprising two parts: embeddings pre-training and preference extraction.

in terms of position or time. Therefore, we integrate the sequence position and the real interaction time to calculate the interval between services. Specifically, we set the size of the sliding window to L. Taking service i as the center, service j co-occurs with i if their sequence positions pos_i and pos_j and real interaction time t_i and t_j satisfy:

$$|pos_i - pos_j| + \log(\frac{|t_i - t_j|}{\delta}) \leq \frac{L}{2}, \tag{1}$$

where δ is the time scale factor. Let cnt_i denote the occurrence times of service i, and $num_{i,j}$ denote the co-occurrence times of service i and service j. We traverse all the user-service interaction sequences and obtain their co-occurrence frequency via an average operation:

$$f(i,j) = f(j,i) = \frac{2 * num_{i,j}}{cnt_i + cnt_j}. \tag{2}$$

The co-occurrence between services implies certain bundles and similarities, so we apply the co-occurrence frequency to form the similarity matrix of services: $A \in \mathbb{R}^{|\mathcal{S}| \times |\mathcal{S}|}$, where $A_{i,j} = f(i,j)$. Similarly, we map the service sequence to the category sequence and obtain the similarity matrix of categories: $B \in \mathbb{R}^{|\mathcal{C}| \times |\mathcal{C}|}$. The similarity matrix can be viewed as the adjacency matrix of a graph with weighted connections. Different weights represent different influences, which models the bundling relationship between services and between categories.

Fig. 2. Illustration of the adaptive dual-threshold method.

Sparsification with Adaptive Dual-Threshold. The graph formed by the co-occurrence frequency has a high connection density, so we devise an adaptive dual-threshold method to sparsify the service graph and category graph to filter out the noise and remove redundant information. Specifically, we first set the upper ratio threshold γ_1 to ensure the sparsity of the graph. For a particular service node with more than $\gamma_1 * |\mathcal{S}|$ neighbors, we retain top $\gamma_1 * |\mathcal{S}|$ neighbors by sorting the connection strengths and remove the other neighbors. Since this operation is performed node by node, the connections of a particular node may be all removed; that is, this node has no neighbors. As shown in Fig. 2, the central node may close its connections with several neighbors and thus leading to the appearance of isolated nodes. Therefore, we set the lower ratio threshold γ_2 to ensure the connectivity of the graph. If a service node originally with more than $\gamma_2 * |\mathcal{S}|$ neighbors has less than $\gamma_2 * |\mathcal{S}|$ neighbors due to the sparsification operation, we restore its top $\gamma_2 * |\mathcal{S}|$ neighbors. A similar operation is performed on the category graph. Using the ratio threshold makes the number of neighbors dynamically adjust with the number of vertices, and setting the dual-threshold can ensure the sparsity and connectivity of the graph simultaneously.

3.4   Graph Embedding

After obtaining the similarity matrices of services and categories, we build an extended Structural Deep Network Embedding (SDNE) [16] model to train their embedding matrices simultaneously. The original SDNE model can embed homogeneous graphs, that is, it can only embed service-service graphs or category-category graphs. Although services and categories are heterogeneous data, they are closely related. If services and categories are embedded separately, their latent representation will lack correlation. Thus, we adopt two autoencoders to embed both services and categories by modifying the loss function.

An SDNE model comprises an encoder and a decoder, which first encodes the similarity matrix into the embeddings and then decodes the embeddings to reconstruct the similarity matrix. Taking the service similarity matrix $\mathbf{A} = \{\mathbf{a}_1, \mathbf{a}_2, ..., \mathbf{a}_{|\mathcal{S}|}\}$ as an example, given the similarity vector $\mathbf{a}_i = \{a_{i,j}\}_{j=1}^{|\mathcal{S}|}$, we represent the encoding and decoding process as follows:

$$\mathbf{v}_i = \sigma(\mathbf{W}_e \mathbf{a}_i + \mathbf{b}_e), \qquad (3)$$

$$\hat{\mathbf{a}}_i = \sigma(\mathbf{W}_d \mathbf{v}_i + \mathbf{b}_d), \qquad (4)$$

where $\sigma(\cdot)$ is the sigmoid function, $\mathbf{W}_e$, $\mathbf{b}_e$, $\mathbf{W}_d$, $\mathbf{b}_d$ are trainable model parameters, $\mathbf{v}_i$ is the embedded vector of $\mathbf{a}_i$, and $\hat{\mathbf{a}}_i$ is the reconstructed similarity vector. The loss function of the SDNE is as follows:

$$\mathcal{L}_\mathcal{S} = \mathcal{L}_{1st} + \mathcal{L}_{2nd} = \sum_{i,j=1}^{|\mathcal{S}|} a_{i,j} \| \mathbf{v}_i - \mathbf{v}_j \|_2^2 + \lambda \sum_{i=1}^{|\mathcal{S}|} \| (\hat{\mathbf{a}}_i - \mathbf{a}_i) \odot \mu \|_2^2, \qquad (5)$$

where μ is the penalty vector, and $\mathcal{L}_{1st}$ and $\mathcal{L}_{2nd}$ describes the first-order and the second-order proximity between services, respectively. This loss function ensures both the local pairwise similarity and global neighborhood structure similarity of services. Similarly, given the similarity vector $\mathbf{b}_i$ of category i, the encoded embedding $\mathbf{q}_i$ and the decoded vector $\hat{\mathbf{b}}_i$, the loss function of training the category embedding is as follows:

$$\mathcal{L}_\mathcal{C} = \sum_{i,j=1}^{|\mathcal{C}|} b_{i,j} \| \mathbf{q}_i - \mathbf{q}_j \|_2^2 + \lambda \sum_{i=1}^{|\mathcal{C}|} \| (\hat{\mathbf{b}}_i - \mathbf{b}_i) \odot \mu \|_2^2. \qquad (6)$$

The above two loss functions ensure the similarity within categories and services, respectively. To introduce the similarity between categories and services, we design the following service-category proximity cost function:

$$\mathcal{L}_{\mathcal{S},\mathcal{C}} = \sum_{i=1}^{|\mathcal{S}|} \| \mathbf{a}_i - \mathbf{b}_{c(i)} \|_2^2, \qquad (7)$$

where $c(i)$ represents the category of service i. Therefore, the loss function of our extended SNDE model becomes:

$$\mathcal{L}_{emb} = \mathcal{L}_\mathcal{S} + \mathcal{L}_\mathcal{C} + \mathcal{L}_{\mathcal{S},\mathcal{C}}. \qquad (8)$$

After sufficient training, we can get the embeddings of services and categories: $\mathbf{M} \in \mathbb{R}^{|\mathcal{S}| \times d}$ and $\mathbf{N} \in \mathbb{R}^{|\mathcal{C}| \times d}$, where d denotes the dimensionality. These embeddings maintain not only internal relations but also external relations.

3.5 Preferences Extraction Block

After the pre-training process, we need to extract the user's interest and category preferences. It is worth noting that both preferences are closely related to each other. For example, a user's preference for a particular category depends not only on the category but also on the specific service. Therefore, we design a way to jointly capture either preference, as shown in the upper half of Fig. 1. When capturing interest preferences, the category is used as auxiliary information; when capturing category preferences, the service is used as auxiliary information. This approach brings an information gain between the two preference extraction processes and enhances personalized features of the user.

Embedding Layer. Given the maximum length m of sequences that the model can handle, the user-service interactions $\mathcal{I}^u$ can be truncated into $\{s_1^u, s_2^u, ..., s_m^u\}$. We use the pre-trained embedding matrices $\mathbf{M}$ and $\mathbf{N}$ to obtain the service sequence embeddings $\mathbf{E}^{\mathcal{S}} := \{\mathbf{e}_1^{\mathcal{S}}, \mathbf{e}_2^{\mathcal{S}}, ..., \mathbf{e}_m^{\mathcal{S}}\} \in \mathbb{R}^{m \times d}$ and corresponding category sequence embeddings $\mathbf{E}^{\mathcal{C}} := \{\mathbf{e}_1^{\mathcal{C}}, \mathbf{e}_2^{\mathcal{C}}, ..., \mathbf{e}_m^{\mathcal{C}}\} \in \mathbb{R}^{m \times d}$.

Category Preference Extraction. Since users' demand for a category mostly originates from the influence of their recent behaviors, it is necessary to adopt a temporal sequence model to capture the evolution pattern of category preferences. Specifically, we adopt the gated recurrent unit (GRU) [2] model, which controls the propagation of information by an update gate and a reset gate, to extract the sequential features. Considering that the service sequence also affects users' category preferences, we introduce the service information to control the value of both gates and name this model variant as Co-Guided GRU. The extraction process of category preferences is as follows:

$$\mathbf{z}_t = \sigma(\mathbf{W}_z \cdot [\mathbf{h}_{t-1}, \mathbf{e}_t^{\mathcal{C}} + \alpha * \mathbf{e}_t^{\mathcal{S}}]), \tag{9}$$

$$\mathbf{r}_t = \sigma(\mathbf{W}_r \cdot [\mathbf{h}_{t-1}, \mathbf{e}_t^{\mathcal{C}} + \alpha * \mathbf{e}_t^{\mathcal{S}}]), \tag{10}$$

$$\widetilde{\mathbf{h}}_t = \tanh(\mathbf{W} \cdot [\mathbf{r}_t \odot \mathbf{h}_{t-1}, \mathbf{e}_t^{\mathcal{C}}]), \tag{11}$$

$$\mathbf{h}_t = (1 - \mathbf{z}_t) \odot \mathbf{h}_{t-1} + \mathbf{z}_t \odot \widetilde{\mathbf{h}}_t, \tag{12}$$

where $\mathbf{h}_t$ denotes the representation of the user's category preference at time step t, $\sigma(\cdot)$ denotes the sigmoid function, $\odot$ denotes the element-wise product, and $\mathbf{W}_z, \mathbf{W}_r, \mathbf{W} \in \mathbb{R}^{d \times 2d}$ are trainable parameters. In this process, service features can control the update gate $\mathbf{r}_t$ and the reset gate $\mathbf{z}_t$, and further influence the evolution of the category preference. Considering that service features play only a minor role, we set the influence coefficient $\alpha \in [0, 1]$ to control the influence of service features. It is worth noting that the representations of interest and category preferences are not mixed, because the interest preference is only used to control the flow of information. Moreover, since different service sequences may correspond to the same category sequence, the service features can enhance the personalized features of user category preference. For simplicity, the process of category preference extraction with a residual structure can be defined as:

$$\mathbf{O}^{\mathcal{C}} = \mathbf{E}^{\mathcal{C}} + \text{Co-GRU}(\mathbf{E}^{\mathcal{C}}, \alpha * \mathbf{E}^{\mathcal{S}}). \tag{13}$$

Interest Preference Extraction. In the phase of extracting the interest preference, we use a self-attention layer, which is defined as:

$$\text{Attn}(\mathbf{Q}, \mathbf{K}, \mathbf{V}) = \text{Softmax}(\frac{\mathbf{Q}\mathbf{K}^{\mathbf{T}}}{\sqrt{d/h}})\mathbf{V}, \tag{14}$$

where $\mathbf{Q}$, $\mathbf{K}$, and $\mathbf{V}$ represent queries, keys, and values, respectively, h denotes the total number of heads, and $\sqrt{d/h}$ is the scale factor. The basic idea of the self-attention mechanism is to assign weights and integrate information by calculating the similarity between service representations. Since the self-attention model does not contain position information, we first introduce the trainable position embeddings $\mathbf{P} := \{\mathbf{p}_1, \mathbf{p}_2, ..., \mathbf{p}_m\} \in \mathbb{R}^{m \times d}$ to the service embeddings:

$$\widetilde{\mathbf{E}}^{\mathcal{S}} = \mathbf{E}^{\mathcal{S}} + \mathbf{P}. \tag{15}$$

Considering that the user's interest preference is also influenced by the category information, it is necessary to introduce category features when assigning attention weights. Therefore, we combine the service vector and the category vector as the service's query and key, and take the service vector as the value. We name this new method as Co-Guided Attention. Similar to the category preference extraction process, we also introduce the influence coefficient $\alpha \in [0, 1]$ to control the influence of category features. The multi-head attention operation can be represented as follows:

$$\mathbf{O}^{\mathcal{S}} = \widetilde{\mathbf{E}}^{\mathcal{S}} + \text{Co-Attn}(\widetilde{\mathbf{E}}^{\mathcal{S}}, \alpha * \mathbf{E}^{\mathcal{C}}), \tag{16}$$

$$\text{Co-Attn}(\widetilde{\mathbf{E}}^{\mathcal{S}}, \alpha * \mathbf{E}^{\mathcal{C}}) = [\text{head}_1, \text{head}_2, ..., \text{head}_h]\mathbf{W}^{O}, \tag{17}$$

$$\text{head}_i = \text{Attn}((\widetilde{\mathbf{E}}^{\mathcal{S}} + \alpha * \mathbf{E}^{\mathcal{C}})\mathbf{W}_i^{Q}, (\widetilde{\mathbf{E}}^{\mathcal{S}} + \alpha * \mathbf{E}^{\mathcal{C}})\mathbf{W}_i^{K}, \widetilde{\mathbf{E}}^{\mathcal{S}}\mathbf{W}_i^{V}), \tag{18}$$

where $\mathbf{W}_i^{Q}$, $\mathbf{W}_i^{K}$, $\mathbf{W}_i^{V} \in \mathbb{R}^{d \times d/h}$, $\mathbf{W}^{O} \in \mathbb{R}^{d \times d}$ are model parameters, and h denotes the total number of heads. With the introduction of category information, services with strong category relevance have high attention scores. This approach provides the possibility to reveal the real reason why a user is interested in a service, i.e., preference for a certain category. Specifically, some users' behaviors may be strongly influenced by category, so the introduction of category information can assign high weights to services with similar categories and thus expose key services that affect users' decisions.

Fully-Connected Layer. We use two two-layer fully-connected networks with residual connections for the final interest and category preferences extraction:

$$\mathbf{O}^{\mathcal{C}} = \text{LayerNorm}(\mathbf{O}^{\mathcal{C}} + \text{ReLU}(\mathbf{O}^{\mathcal{C}}\mathbf{W}_1 + \mathbf{b}_1)\mathbf{W}_2 + \mathbf{b}_2), \tag{19}$$

$$\mathbf{O}^{\mathcal{S}} = \text{LayerNorm}(\mathbf{O}^{\mathcal{S}} + \text{ReLU}(\mathbf{O}^{\mathcal{S}}\mathbf{W}_3 + \mathbf{b}_3)\mathbf{W}_4 + \mathbf{b}_4), \tag{20}$$

where $\mathbf{W}_*$, $\mathbf{b}_*$ are learnable parameters.

3.6   Prediction and Optimization

After obtaining the user's interest preference $\mathbf{O}_t^{\mathcal{S}}$ and category preference $\mathbf{O}_t^{\mathcal{C}}$ at time step t, we integrate both preferences to score each candidate service s:

$$y_{t,s} = \mathbf{O}_t^{\mathcal{S}}\mathbf{M}_s^{T} + \beta * \mathbf{O}_t^{\mathcal{C}}\mathbf{N}_{c(s)}^{T}, \tag{21}$$

where $\mathbf{M}_s^{T}$ and $\mathbf{N}_{c(s)}^{T}$ represent the embeddings of service s and its category $c(s)$, respectively. To flexibly adjust the influence of category preference on prediction, we introduce a category importance coefficient β ($\beta \geq 0$). In the training phase, we apply the Binary Cross-Entropy loss function to train the model:

$$\mathcal{L} = - \sum_{\mathcal{I}^u \in \mathcal{I}} \sum_{t \in [1,\dots,m]} [\log(\sigma(y_{t,s_t})) + \sum_{j \notin \mathcal{I}^u} \log(1 - \sigma(y_{t,j}))], \qquad (22)$$

where $\mathcal{I}$ is the set of user-service interactions, $\sigma(\cdot)$ denotes the sigmoid function, s_t is the ground truth service, and j is the negative sampling service at time step t. In the training phase, we drift the interaction sequence one step to the right as the expected outputs of the previous interactions, and sample one negative service for each positive service.

4   Experiments

We designed and conducted extensive experiments on public datasets to answer the following questions: 1) Does RDCN perform better than baselines? 2) What is the effect of the pre-trained embeddings? 3) What is the effect of the category information? 4) What is the effect of the dual-channel preference extraction?

4.1   Experimental Setup

Datasets. To evaluate the performance of our RDCN and baseline models, we selected three publicly available datasets: Jewelry[1], Cosmetics[2] and Taobao[3]. The characteristics of three datasets after pre-processing are described in Table 1. As for the interaction sequence, we set the maximum length as 50 and used the last service for testing, the penultimate service for validation, and the rest of the sequence for training.

Table 1. Statistics of the datasets.

Statistics	Jewelry	Cosmetics	Taobao
#user	1,937	3,515	1,026
#service	2,147	4,122	2,308
#category	7	125	305
#interaction	33,194	58,967	7,415
avg.length	17.14	16.78	7.23

Baselines and Evaluation Metrics. To evaluate performance, we compared our proposed RDCN with 14 competitive baseline methods, which are RNN-based or Attention-based models: GRU4Rec [5], GRU4Rec+ [6], SASRec [8], SASRec+, SHAN [18], BERT4Rec [13], FDSA [20], RepeatNet [12], GC-SAN [17], S3Rec [22], LightSANs [3], SINE [14], CORE [7], MLP4Rec [9]. SASRec+ is an improved version of SASRec, combining category embeddings and item embeddings to enrich item representations. For the evaluation, we randomly sampled 100 negative services for each positive service in the testing set. Following [8,11], we adopted HR@K and NDCG@K to evaluate the performance of all the models and set $K = \{5, 10\}$ for both metrics.

---

[1] https://www.kaggle.com/datasets/mkechinov/ecommerce-purchase-history-from-jewelry-store.

[2] https://www.kaggle.com/datasets/mkechinov/ecommerce-events-history-in-cosmetics-shop.

[3] https://tianchi.aliyun.com/dataset/649.

Hyper-parameters and Other Settings. In the phase of graph construction, we set the size of the sliding window as 20 for Jewelry and Cosmetics and 10 for Taobao, and set the time scale factor as 20 days for Jewelry and 1 day for Cosmetics and Taobao. For the service graph and the category graph on the three datasets, we set the adaptive dual-threshold as $\{0.2, 0.1\}$ and $\{0.3, 0.15\}$, respectively. In the phase of graph embedding, we set the hidden size as 256 for Jewelry and Taobao and 128 for Cosmetics. As for the hyper-parameter settings, we set the learning rate as 0.002 and the batch size as 64 for the three datasets, the influence coefficient α as 0.2 for Jewelry and Cosmetics and 0.5 for Taobao, the category importance coefficient β as 0.5 for Jewelry and 1.0 for Cosmetics and Taobao, and the number of heads h as 4 for Jewelry and Taobao and 2 for Cosmetics. For a fair comparison, we implemented all the models by PyTorch.

4.2 Overall Performance

We divided all the models into two categories based on whether they use category information or not. The comparison results of the models are summarized in Table 2, where the models above the dashed line only capture users' interest preferences and the models below introduce category information to enrich profile-level features. From the results, we have the following observations:

Table 2. Performance comparison between different models on the three datasets. In terms of each indicator, the best performance of all models is boldfaced and the best performance of baselines is underlined. "*" indicates the significant improvement against the best baseline by the two-sided t-test ($p < 0.01$).

Model	Jewelry				Cosmetics				Taobao			
	HR@5	NDCG@5	HR@10	NDCG@10	HR@5	NDCG@5	HR@10	NDCG@10	HR@5	NDCG@5	HR@10	NDCG@10
GRU4Rec [5]	0.2984	0.2265	0.4037	0.2606	0.4575	0.3459	0.5838	0.3868	0.1947	0.1446	0.2619	0.1661
SASRec [8]	0.3810	0.3072	0.4641	0.3338	0.4905	0.3795	0.6074	0.4172	0.2808	0.2564	0.3578	0.2810
SHAN [18]	0.4218	0.3519	0.4874	0.3728	0.4706	0.3606	0.5829	0.3971	0.3219	0.2784	0.3852	0.2988
RepeatNet [12]	0.3856	0.3303	0.4631	0.3552	0.4407	0.3533	0.5621	0.3924	0.2902	0.2586	0.3508	0.2775
BERT4Rec [13]	0.3989	0.3393	0.4779	0.3625	0.4358	0.3525	0.5550	0.3909	0.2855	0.2447	0.3461	0.2639
GC-SAN [17]	0.4027	0.3272	0.4858	0.3541	0.4728	0.3731	0.5696	0.4056	0.2734	0.2393	0.3280	0.2567
LightSANs [3]	0.4166	0.3509	0.5028	0.3787	0.4982	0.3989	0.6125	0.4357	0.3090	0.2671	0.3577	0.2827
SINE [14]	0.3774	0.2982	0.4662	0.3268	0.4912	0.3656	0.5913	0.4001	0.3095	0.2719	0.3592	0.2878
CORE [7]	0.4140	0.3401	0.5049	0.3693	0.4817	0.3837	0.5995	0.4218	0.3311	0.2990	0.3682	0.3109
GRU4Rec+ [6]	0.3277	0.2546	0.4366	0.2903	0.4813	0.3770	0.5991	0.4150	0.2525	0.2075	0.3219	0.2267
SASRec+	0.4325	0.3602	0.5007	0.3822	0.5164	0.4049	0.6165	0.4370	0.3143	0.2848	0.3738	0.3039
FDSA [20]	0.4259	0.3514	0.5137	0.3783	0.5098	0.4005	0.6179	0.4354	<u>0.3415</u>	<u>0.3047</u>	<u>0.4010</u>	<u>0.3236</u>
S3Rec [22]	<u>0.4356</u>	<u>0.3585</u>	<u>0.5172</u>	<u>0.3846</u>	<u>0.5212</u>	<u>0.4054</u>	<u>0.6360</u>	<u>0.4419</u>	0.3300	0.2991	0.3836	0.3163
MLP4Rec [9]	0.4036	0.3440	0.4913	0.3722	0.4902	0.3747	0.6105	0.4138	0.3102	0.2653	0.3541	0.2794
Ours	**0.4423**	**0.3737***	**0.5331***	**0.4028***	**0.5442***	**0.4264***	**0.6640***	**0.4642***	**0.3740***	**0.3286***	**0.4335***	**0.3463***
Improv.	1.54%	4.24%	3.07%	4.73%	4.41%	5.18%	4.40%	5.05%	9.52%	7.84%	8.10%	7.01%

(1) Models that leverage category information usually outperform those who only use service embeddings, e.g., GRU+ outperforms GRU and SASRec+ outperforms SASRec, which demonstrates the importance of category information.

(2) In the baseline models, S3Rec and FDSA show competitive performance. S3Rec exploits the association between services and categories by pretraining, while FDSA uses a separate multi-head attention module to capture feature-level transition patterns. This suggests that exploiting association information, as well as extracting category preferences, can effectively improve model performance.
(3) On the three datasets, our proposed RDCN outperforms all the baseline models in terms of all the evaluation metrics. The reasons may be two-fold for the performance improvement. The first is that we model and encode complex relationships between services and categories, which facilitates the process of capturing sequential transition patterns. The second is that we design a dual-channel preference extraction block to extract users' preferences, and the introduction of the category information enhances the user's personalized characteristics to accurately identify the services of interest.

4.3   The Effect of the Pre-trained Embeddings

Recall that we adopt the graph embedding model to jointly pre-train the embeddings of services and categories. To validate the effectiveness of this approach, we first observed the impact of this approach on the embeddings. As shown in Fig. 3, we selected five categories in Jewelry and adopted the t-SNE algorithm to map the embeddings into a two-dimensional plane, where the dots represent services and the pentagrams represent categories. From the results, we can infer that using the joint graph embedding method can obtain high spatial similarity between services of the same category. At the same time, vectors of the service and its category also have high spatial similarity. In general, the method we devised can fuse the complex relationship between services and categories into their embeddings, which lays the foundation for the process of preference extraction.

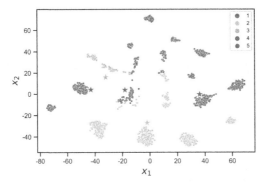

Fig. 3. Service and category vectors of Jewelry after dimensionality reduction.

To verify that the pre-trained embeddings can enhance the model performance, we set up ablation experiments and denoted the original model and the model without pre-trained embeddings as **w/ emb** and **w/o emb**, respectively. From Fig. 4, we can see that **w/ emb** outperforms **w/o emb**, which indicates that after encoding the intrinsic association between services and categories, the model can accurately capture their transition pattern and get precise predictions.

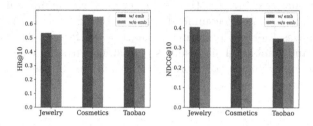

Fig. 4. Performance with/without pre-trained embeddings on the three datasets.

4.4   The Effect of the Category Information

To explore the role of the category information in predicting user behavior, we conducted ablation experiments and denoted the original model and the model without category information as **w/ category** and **w/o category**, respectively. For **w/o category**, we pre-trained the service embeddings and used the multi-head attention module to extract users' interest preferences. As shown in Table 3, **w/ category** outperforms **w/o category** over three datasets. We argue that the introduction of category information can enhance the personalized characteristics of users. In addition, the improvement is the smallest on Jewelry and the largest on Taobao. From Table 1, with a similar number of services, Jewelry and Taobao contain 7 and 305 categories, respectively. Therefore, when the number of categories is relatively large, the category information becomes more important to identify services of interest to users.

Table 3. Performance with/without category information on the three datasets.

Model	Jewelry		Cosmetics		Taobao	
	HR@10	NDCG@10	HR@10	NDCG@10	HR@10	NDCG@10
w/o category	0.5124	0.3911	0.6290	0.4420	0.3908	0.3145
w/ category	**0.5331**	**0.4028**	**0.6640**	**0.4642**	**0.4335**	**0.3463**
Improv.	4.04%	2.99%	5.56%	5.02%	10.93%	10.11%

Recall that we combine interest and category preferences to score the candidate services and set β to control the weight of category preferences. We tested the effect of β on the model performance, which can present the effect of the category factor on the prediction. As shown in Fig. 5 (d)–(f), if $\beta = 0$, which means we only use the user's interest preferences to score the candidates, the model performance is much worse than introducing the category information. As β increases, the metrics first rise and then fall. The reason may be that each category has multiple services, and if we overemphasize the importance of categories, the personality characteristics of the services will be difficult to capture, and thus the model cannot recommend accurate services for users. In addition, the model achieves the best performance at $\beta = 0.5$ for Jewelry and $\beta = 1.0$ for Cosmetics and Taobao. This result is consistent with the conclusion of the previous experiment, that is the more categories in the dataset, the higher the importance of category information.

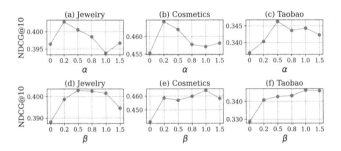

Fig. 5. Performance with different α and β values on three datasets.

In general, we can draw a meaningful conclusion that with a fixed number of services, if the dataset contains many categories, we should appropriately increase the influence of categories in filtering candidate services; on the contrary, if there are few categories, we should reduce the influence of the category.

4.5   The Effect of the Dual-Channel Preference Extraction

Recall that in the dual-channel preference extraction module, we set the influence coefficient α to adjust the weight of the auxiliary information. We tested the effect of α on model performance. As shown in Fig. 5 (a)–(c), when $\alpha = 0$, that is, there is no information exchange between two preference extraction channels, the performance of the model is poor. As α increases, the performance of the model improves, but too large α also leads to poor performance. We speculate that the auxiliary information with a large proportion covers the original preference information, and thus leads to inaccurate user preferences.

5   Conclusions

To further enrich personalized characteristics of users, this paper presents a novel Reciprocal Dual-Channel Network (RDCN) to extract users' category preferences. Specifically, we devise a novel strategy to construct service and category graphs and encode intrinsic associations among services and categories into their embeddings. Two designed modules, a Co-Guided Attention module and a Co-Guided GRU module, jointly mine users' interest and category preferences. Extensive experiments prove the effectiveness and scalability of the proposed model. In the future, we plan to enhance the preference extraction process by introducing more information such as item attributes and contextual information. In addition, we plan to analyze social relationship between items by studying the co-occurrence information between them.

References

1. Carbaugh, R.: Contemporary Economics: an Applications Approach. Routledge, Oxfordshire, UK (2016)
2. Cho, K., et al.: Learning phrase representations using RNN encoder-decoder for statistical machine translation. arXiv preprint arXiv:1406.1078 (2014)
3. Fan, X., Liu, Z., Lian, J., Zhao, W.X., Xie, X., Wen, J.R.: Lighter and better: low-rank decomposed self-attention networks for next-item recommendation. In: Proceedings of The 44th International ACM SIGIR Conference on Research and Development in Information Retrieval, pp. 1733–1737 (2021)
4. Garcin, F., Dimitrakakis, C., Faltings, B.: Personalized news recommendation with context trees. In: Proceedings of The 7th ACM Conference on Recommender Systems, pp. 105–112 (2013)
5. Hidasi, B., Karatzoglou, A., Baltrunas, L., Tikk, D.: Session-based recommendations with recurrent neural networks. arXiv preprint arXiv:1511.06939 (2015)
6. Hidasi, B., Quadrana, M., Karatzoglou, A., Tikk, D.: Parallel recurrent neural network architectures for feature-rich session-based recommendations. In: Proceedings of The 10th ACM Conference on Recommender Systems, pp. 241–248 (2016)
7. Hou, Y., Hu, B., Zhang, Z., Zhao, W.X.: Core: Simple and effective session-based recommendation within consistent representation space. arXiv preprint arXiv:2204.11067 (2022)
8. Kang, W.C., McAuley, J.: Self-attentive sequential recommendation. In: Proceedings of IEEE International Conference on Data Mining (ICDM), pp. 197–206. IEEE (2018)
9. Li, M., Zhao, X., Lyu, C., Zhao, M., Wu, R., Guo, R.: Mlp4rec: A pure MLP architecture for sequential recommendations. arXiv preprint arXiv:2204.11510 (2022)
10. Mikolov, T., Chen, K., Corrado, G., Dean, J.: Efficient estimation of word representations in vector space. arXiv preprint arXiv:1301.3781 (2013)
11. Rashed, A., Elsayed, S., Schmidt-Thieme, L.: CARCA: context and attribute-aware next-item recommendation via cross-attention. arXiv preprint arXiv:2204.06519 (2022)
12. Ren, P., Chen, Z., Li, J., Ren, Z., Ma, J., De Rijke, M.: RepeatNet: a repeat aware neural recommendation machine for session-based recommendation. In: Proceedings of the AAAI Conference on Artificial Intelligence, vol. 33, pp. 4806–4813 (2019)
13. Sun, F., et al.: Bert4rec: sequential recommendation with bidirectional encoder representations from transformer. In: Proceedings of The 28th ACM International Conference on Information and Knowledge Management, pp. 1441–1450 (2019)
14. Tan, Q., et al.: Sparse-interest network for sequential recommendation. In: Proceedings of The 14th ACM International Conference on Web Search and Data Mining, pp. 598–606 (2021)

15. Vaswani, A., et al.: Attention is all you need. In: Advances in Neural Information Processing Systems, vol. 30 (2017)
16. Wang, D., Cui, P., Zhu, W.: Structural deep network embedding. In: Proceedings of The 22nd ACM SIGKDD International Conference on Knowledge Discovery and Data Mining, pp. 1225–1234 (2016)
17. Xu, C., et al.: Graph contextualized self-attention network for session-based recommendation. In: IJCAI, vol. 19, pp. 3940–3946 (2019)
18. Ying, H., et al.: Sequential recommender system based on hierarchical attention network. In: Proceedings of International Joint Conference on Artificial Intelligence (2018)
19. Zhang, M., Liu, J., Zhang, W., Deng, K., Dong, H., Liu, Y.: CSSR: a context-aware sequential software service recommendation model. In: Hacid, H., Kao, O., Mecella, M., Moha, N., Paik, H. (eds.) ICSOC 2021. LNCS, vol. 13121, pp. 691–699. Springer, Cham (2021). https://doi.org/10.1007/978-3-030-91431-8_45
20. Zhang, T., et al.: Feature-level deeper self-attention network for sequential recommendation. In: Proceedings of International Joint Conferences on Artificial Intelligence, pp. 4320–4326 (2019)
21. Zhang, X., et al.: Price does matter! modeling price and interest preferences in session-based recommendation. arXiv preprint arXiv:2205.04181 (2022)
22. Zhou, K., et al.: S3-rec: self-supervised learning for sequential recommendation with mutual information maximization. In: Proceedings of The 29th ACM International Conference on Information & Knowledge Management, pp. 1893–1902 (2020)

Niagara: Scheduling DNN Inference Services on Heterogeneous Edge Processors

Daliang Xu[1], Qing Li[1], Mengwei Xu[2(✉)], Kang Huang[3],
Gang Huang[1,5], Shangguang Wang[2], Xin Jin[1(✉)], Yun Ma[4(✉)],
and Xuanzhe Liu[1]

[1] Key Laboratory of High Confidence Software Technologies (Peking University),
Ministry of Education, School of Computer Science, Peking University, Beijing, China
{xudaliang,liqingpostdoc,hg,xinjinpku,liuxuanzhe}@pku.edu.cn
[2] State Key Laboratory of Networking and Switching Technology, Beijing University
of Posts and Telecommunications, Beijing, China
{mwx,sgwang}@bupt.edu.cn
[3] Linggui Tech Company, Beijing, China
kang.huang@nlptech.com
[4] Institute for Artificial Intelligence, Peking University, Beijing, China
mayun@pku.edu.cn
[5] National Key Laboratory of Data Space Technology and System, Beijing, China

Abstract. Intelligent applications heavily rely on deep neural network (DNN) inference services executed on edge devices to fulfill functional prerequisites while safeguarding user data privacy. However, the execution of such DNN services on resource-constrained edge devices poses a significant challenge: low throughput of inference tasks. To this end, this paper proposes `Niagara`, a novel system designed to maximize system throughput by judiciously scheduling DNN inference services on heterogeneous processors available on edge devices. `Niagara` faces two critical challenges: uncertain workload dynamics and high scheduling complexity. To effectively address these challenges, `Niagara` employs a predictive model to anticipate incoming workload patterns and orchestrates the allocation of services across heterogeneous processors through a combination of offline scheduling optimization and online service dispatching strategies. We have implemented `Niagara` and conducted thorough experiments. The results demonstrate that `Niagara` surpasses state-of-the-art approaches by elevating DNN inference throughput by up to 4.67×, all while satisfying the same stringent inference latency requirements. Furthermore, `Niagara` has been successfully deployed in real-world power supply substations to detect violations, ensuring uninterrupted, accident-free operation during its six-month deployment period.

Keywords: Edge Computing · Heterogeneous Processors · DNN Inference Service

F. Monti et al. (Eds.): ICSOC 2023, LNCS 14419, pp. 67–85, 2023.
https://doi.org/10.1007/978-3-031-48421-6_6

1 Introduction

Recent years have witnessed various intelligent edge applications (e.g., healthcare, entertainment, and smart home applications) becoming integral components of our daily lives [13]. These applications often rely on deep neural networks (DNNs) for sophisticated sensory interpretation, such as user context and physical surroundings. To ensure a seamless user experience, these edge applications, such as violation operation detection [39], immersive online shopping [41] and AR emoji [38], typically prefer to employ a set of flexible and reliable edge DNN inference services [22,28,35,38]. For instance, violation operation detection, which determines whether operators in a state grid corporation wear valid helmets and gloves during operations, necessitates at least four DNN inference services: human detection, pose estimation, and helmet/gloves classification.

However, executing DNN inference services on resource-constraint edge devices often encounters the low throughput problem [22,35,38,39]. Previous studies have primarily focused on optimizing the execution of *individual* DNN services [23,30,31,37], which limits their effectiveness in addressing performance bottlenecks within a multi-service environment.

To tackle this issue, we have observed that various types of heterogeneous processors on edge devices [3,5–7,12] (e.g., ARM A57 cores [1] and the NVIDIA Pascal GPU on Jetson TX2 [3]) can be harnessed to deliver high-throughput DNN services. To this end, we present Niagara, the first scheduling engine for DNN inference services on edge devices. The core idea behind Niagara is to monitor processor status, predict incoming workload dynamics, and efficiently schedule DNN inference services across heterogeneous processors. Niagara faces two primary challenges:

• **High complexity in scheduling design.** As will be elaborated in Sect. 2, optimizing DNN-inference-service-to-processor affinity, enabling parallel execution, and efficiently batching inputs have the potential to significantly enhance DNN inference services execution. However, the multiple interdependent optimization choices render the scheduling of DNN services to processors a challenging task.

• **Unknown and mutative DNN inference service workload.** The design of Niagara grapples with a dilemma between the need for global knowledge and timely decision-making. Theoretically, having advanced knowledge of upcoming requests could offer more scheduling opportunities. However, services depend on future input, which is only accessible when the corresponding DNN inference service (e.g., person detection) has been executed.

To address the above two challenges, we incorporate two novel techniques: (1) *Offline optimizer and online service scheduler*. We have identified that DNN service request patterns can be abstracted into several typical **service graph templates**. Based on that, Niagara optimizes the service-to-processor scheduling strategy for each service graph template offline, caches the strategy, and matches the appropriate strategy to user requests belonging to specific templates online. The offline optimizer accounts for inter-service dependency, batch/parallel execution, and resource constraints. (2) *Dynamic input predictor*. We have found that the service graph tends to be more stable than the content, providing an opportunity for prediction. Consequently, we construct a time series model [16,33] of the DNN service graph based on the latest and global historical data and employ a combined prediction algorithm to forecast the future DNN service graphs.

Implementation and Evaluation. We implement an end-to-end prototype of `Niagara` on the Android OS. Our evaluation comprises 8 types of DNN inference service combinations, including 11 distinct DNN services, 3 real-world video stream requests, and 3 different edge devices. These experiments have been conducted in real-world settings. Compared to the state-of-the-art baselines, `Niagara` can enhance overall processing throughput by up to 4.67× while maintaining the same response requirements on identical hardware.

In-the-Wild Deployment. `Niagara` has been integrated into a custom-made IP camera on a Snapdragon 865 development board and deployed in several power supply substations that serve millions of people in a large Chinese city. This deployment aims to enhance the safety of operators working on electric switching operations. During the 6-month pilot run, which included over 18,000 maintenance jobs, zero accidents were reported, representing a significant improvement over traditional human-based supervision. In the near future, `Niagara` will be extended to thousands of substations, showcasing how edge intelligence can contribute to society.

The key contributions of this paper are summarized as follows.

- We quantitatively analyze the challenges and opportunities of DNN inference service execution on edge devices.
- We propose `Niagara`, the first DNN inference services scheduling engine on heterogeneous edge processors. It incorporates two key techniques, including a service graph predictor and a template-based optimizer that judiciously schedules DNN services across processors.
- We evaluate our scheduling strategy and system on popular CNN services with real-world datasets. The results show that `Niagara` and its scheduling solution can effectively improve the overall processing throughput.

2 Background and Related Work

To enhance the quality of edge services, numerous prior studies [14,19,21,24–26,34,36,40] have centered their efforts on augmenting the scheduling efficiency of offloading tasks in the realm of mobile-edge computing, considering factors such as service caching, service dependencies, and multiple application scenarios. For instance, some of these investigations have concentrated on scheduling offloading tasks while simultaneously taking service caching into account [14,24,34,40]. Their objective is to harness caching mechanisms for storing and retrieving frequently used services at the edge, thereby diminishing the necessity for task offloading and mitigating latency. Other studies have underscored the scheduling of dependent services on fog or edge nodes, considering service priorities or catering to multiple applications [19,25,26]. These works

Table 1. Latency and utilization of DNN services on SnapDragon 865 SoC.

DNN service	DNN model	Latency			Utilization		
		CPU	GPU	DSP	CPU	GPU	DSP
Person detection	SSD-quant	112.1 ms	**79.9 ms**	103.1 ms	361%	56%	77%
Pose estimation	CenterNet	**22.9 ms**	31.7 ms	-	287%	30%	-
Helmet detection	SSD-helmet-quant	25.6 ms	8.4 ms	**5.9 ms**	195%	58%	85%
Gloves detection	pole-gloves	6.7 ms	**3.2 ms**	-	198%	34%	-
Text recognition	OCR-recognition	**30.8 ms**	38.1 ms	-	295%	35%	-

meticulously address the dependencies between services and prioritize their execution to meet application requirements and bolster overall performance. However, our work, `Niagara`, focuses specifically on maximizing the utilization of heterogeneous processors available on edge devices for efficient and high-throughput service scheduling.

Another critical issue in DNN services scheduling pertains to the unanticipated dynamic inputs. Several studies have endeavored to forecast future requests by harnessing deep learning methodologies [20,32]. Meanwhile, other research endeavors [18,27] have taken it a step further by jointly addressing scheduling challenges alongside input prediction. However, these undertakings often prove excessively intricate for practical application in online DNN services prediction scenarios.

In summary, the distinctive hardware specifications of edge devices and the unique computing paradigm associated with DNN model inference render the scheduling of edge services notably distinct from conventional web services and offloading tasks. For instance, the Snapdragon 865 SoC, commonly deployed as the main board for IP cameras [5], includes CPU, GPU, and DSP, whereas other edge devices may feature an Edge TPU or NPU instead. Typically, different DNN models executed on such heterogeneous processors exhibit divergent behaviors. To gain a comprehensive understanding of these distinctive features, we conducted preliminary offline experiments on the Snapdragon 865 SoC, as summarized in Table 1.

• **Service-processor affinity and hardware support.** Our preliminary offline experiments (Table 1) have yielded a crucial insight: a discernible service-processor affinity exists. In other words, there is no one-size-fits-all processor to which all services can be indiscriminately scheduled. For instance, the person detection service achieves its optimal performance on the GPU, while the pose estimation service exhibits superior execution on the CPU. This affinity arises from the highly varied characteristics inherent in modern DNNs, including network architecture, layer shapes, and input sizes [29]. Additionally, certain processors, such as the Hexagon DSP, lack support for floating-point arithmetic, thereby rendering services reliant on quantized models, like helmet detection, more compatible with specific hardware compared to their floating-point counterparts, which can be executed on a wider array of hardware platforms.

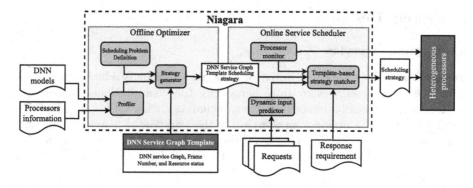

Fig. 1. System workflow of Niagara.

- **Parallel or sequence execution.** Different processors boast distinct capabilities when concurrently executing multiple services (parallel execution), thus maximizing hardware utilization. For instance, the CPU can achieve a maximum utilization of 400% in the Snapdragon 865 SoC, while the GPU and DSP are capped at 100%. To ensure optimal performance, the resource consumption by parallel execution on the same processor must not exceed the processor's capacity. Otherwise, processor contention can severely hamper inference performance. Edge CPUs and GPUs typically support parallel execution, whereas edge DSPs/NPUs do not.

- **Batch execution** is a common strategy to group several identical services for simultaneous execution. This approach yields a longer instruction queue and greater instruction parallelism, mitigating stalls in memory access. However, since all these batched services end simultaneously, their output cannot be obtained until all services have completed their execution. Consequently, batch execution can bolster processor utilization and throughput while simultaneously introducing longer per-service latency. For instance, in the case of pose estimation and helmet detection, employing batching can achieve a throughput improvement by 33–68%, albeit at the cost of incurring a 45–51% increase in latency on the GPU. To that end, Niagara should meticulously design batch execution strategies to mitigate these drawbacks.

Summary and Implications. All the above factors must be carefully considered when optimizing DNN inference service scheduling for heterogeneous edge processors. Furthermore, the dynamic nature of hardware contexts in multi-tenant devices necessitates continuous monitoring and real-time adaptation of scheduling decisions by our system.

3   System Design

3.1   System Overview

Design Goal. The primary objective of `Niagara` is to achieve a high throughput of DNN inference services by fully harnessing the computational capacity of heterogeneous processors on edge devices, including CPUs, GPUs, and DSPs.

Workflow. Figure 1 provides an overview of the workflow of `Niagara`. The fundamental concept underlying `Niagara` is the utilization of *DNN inference service graph templates*. These templates consist of a set of elements: <a service graph $\mathcal{G}$, the number of requested services $\mathcal{RN}$, the resource status $\mathcal{S}$, and a maximum latency requirement Lat_{max}^{RQ} >. Specifically, it signifies that each of the $\mathcal{RN}$ subsequent service requests will follow the same service graph $\mathcal{G}$. Furthermore, these service graphs are executed on heterogeneous processors, taking into account the current processor status $\mathcal{S}$, which could indicate the availability of idle CPUs or the utilization of busy GPUs. Each inference service within $\mathcal{G}$ must respond within the latency requirement Lat_{max}^{RQ}.

`Niagara` employs these service graph templates to generate feasible strategies offline for various scenarios. These strategies subsequently schedule real-time online services onto the heterogeneous processors.

The input to `Niagara` consist of user-initiated service requests and the corresponding response requirements. Once deployed on an edge device, `Niagara` operates in two distinct stages:

Algorithm 1: Online service scheduling algorithm

    Input   : Cached template strategies *cached_strategies_map*
    Output: Scheduling strategy *strategy*
1 Current_service_graph_template *template*
2 **while** *True* **do**
3   Input *data* = user.request.Get() // `Receive input data from users`
4   *service_graph* = *Dynamic_input_predictor(data)* // `Section 3.5`
5   *states* = *Processor_monitor()* // `Section 3.6`
6   **if** *temple* == *NULL* or *Euclidean_distance(service_graph, template)* < *threshold* **then**
          /* `Section 3.4 Template-based strategy matcher`   */
7   **for** *t, s* ∈ *cached_strategies_map* **do**
8   **if** *states* < *t.S* and *Euclidean_distance(service_graph, t.G)* > *Euclidean_distance(service_graph, template.G)* **then**
9   *template* = *t*, *strategy* = *s*
10   **end**
11   **end**
12   *strategy* = *Strategy_adapter(strategy)* // `Section 3.4`
13   **return** *strategy*
14   **end**
15 **end**

- *Offline optimizer (Sect.* 3.2 and *Sect.* 3.3) In the offline stage, `Niagara` formulates the DNN inference services serving problem as a scheduling problem. The inputs for this scheduling problem encompass the service graph template and profiling data related to the services and the heterogeneous processors. A solver is employed to identify feasible solutions for each template.
- *Online service scheduler.* When the request data is received, *Dynamic Input Predictor* (Sect. 3.5) predicts the service graph within the data frame, while the *Processor Monitor* (Sect. 3.6) continuously monitors the status of the processors. Based on response requirements, processors status, and service graph, the *Template-based strategy matcher* (Sect. 3.4) selects the most suitable strategy from the precomputed offline strategies and adapts it to accommodate the real service graph. This allows services to be dispatched effectively to heterogeneous processors. The scheduling algorithm is illustrated in Algorithm 1.

3.2   Problem Formulation

Preliminaries. `Niagara` considers how to schedule various DNN inference services onto heterogeneous processors. Notably, `Niagara` does not modify the structural aspects of the DNN models within these services, in order to maintain accuracy and performance. As a result, it is incumbent upon the developers of each DNN inference service to provide configurations that specify essential details about the DNN model and the processors. These configurations include information about the processors on which the DNN models can potentially execute and the utilization of processors by each model. Users, in turn, are only required to invoke the DNN inference services and supply their input data.

DNN Inference Service Graph Model. Within `Niagara`, it is assumed that an edge device needs to process RN continuous requests, producing a total of N services, denoted by $\mathcal{V} = \{v_1, v_2, \cdots, v_N\}$ which belong to L ($L \leq N$) types. `Niagara` employs a directed acyclic graph (DAG) $\mathcal{G} = (\mathcal{V}, \mathcal{E})$ to represent the dependent relationships among DNN inference services, where $\mathcal{V}$ signifies the service set and $\mathcal{E}$ represents the set of edges symbolizing the dependencies among these services. If there exists an edge $e_{i,k}$ between any two services i and k, it implies that the output of service i serves as input to service k, signifying that service k cannot commence execution until service i has completed its tasks.

Batch Execution Latency Model. `Niagara` employs a linear model [28] to characterize batch execution latency:

$$batch\_lat(b) = a(b-1) + lat\_single \tag{1}$$

where b signifies the batch size and a represents the additional latency incurred when a new service input is appended to an existing batch execution. Notably, due to the diversity in services and processors, the parameter a is a two-dimensional matrix with dimensions equal to the number of service types and the number of processor types. Determining these parameters can be accomplished through linear fitting, utilizing profiling results.

Table 2. Notation table of problem definition in `Niagara`.

Variable	Notation	Description
Placement	$x_{i,j}$	Whether service $v_i \in \mathcal{V}$ executes on the processor $r_j \in \mathcal{R}$.
Batch	$B_{i,k,j}$	Whether services $v_i, v_k \in \mathcal{V}$ are batched on processor $r_j \in \mathcal{R}$.
Parallel	$PL_{i,k,j}$	Whether services $v_i, v_k \in \mathcal{V}$ execute in parallel on processor $r_j \in \mathcal{R}$.
Starting time	t_i	Starting time of service i.
Execution time intermediate variable	$T_{i,j}$	The i-th service's latency when running on the j-th type processor. If the i-th service executes separately, the value equals $L_{i,j}$. When the i-th service executes in batch, based on Eq. (1), the value is formulated as $T_{i,j} = a_{i,j}^T \sum_{k=1}^{N} B_{i,k,j} + L_{i,j}$

Heterogeneous Processors Execution Model. `Niagara` posits the existence of M types of heterogeneous processors, denoted as $\mathcal{R} = \{r_1, r_2, \cdots, r_M\}$. Each processor $r_j \in \mathcal{R}$ possesses its unique processing capacity denoted by E_j. Service v_i has the flexibility to execute on any processor $r_j \in \mathcal{R}_i$ in various modes such as sequential, batch, or parallel. However, it is essential to emphasize that service execution is exclusive to a single processor at any given time. Regardless of the execution mode, services must not be interrupted or preempted, and they must complete their execution within the user-defined real-time threshold $Lat^{RQ}max$. When multiple services execute in parallel, their combined hardware utilization must not exceed the capacity of the processor.

Scheduling Problem Definition. Given the service graph $\mathcal{G}$ and associated profiler information, including latency ($L_{i,j}$) and hardware utilization ($U_{i,j}$) for each service, processor capacity (E_j), and user-defined response requirement (Lat_{max}^{RQ}), `Niagara` considers DNN service-to-processor selection, batch execution, and parallel execution simultaneously. This entails the introduction of four primary decision variables and one intermediate variable are summarized in Table 2.

Our solution should satisfy the following constraints:

• *DNN service-to-processor selection constraint.* Any service should execute on exactly one supported processor. `Niagara` does not allow multiple processors to cooperate to complete single DNN service inference.

$$\sum_{j \in \mathcal{R}_i} x_{i,j} = 1, \forall i \in N \qquad (2)$$

• *Dependency constraint:* Any service can start iff all precedent services are completed, formulated as for any edge $< i, k > \in \mathcal{E}$, v_k can start iff v_i finishes.

$$t_i + \sum_{j=1}^{M} x_{i,j} T_{i,j} \leq t_k \tag{3}$$

• *Sequence execution constraint:* Any service's execution cannot be interrupted. For any service i and k, if they execute on the same processor j in sequence and $t_i < t_k$, then the service v_k must wait until v_i completes.

$$\frac{t_k - t_i}{x_{i,j} x_{k,j} (1 - PL_{i,k,j})(1 - B_{i,k,j})} \geq T_{k,j} \tag{4}$$

• *Parallel constraint:* Paralleling services' execution times must overlap, meaning when services i and j both execute on the resource j and execute in parallel, their start time distance must be less than or equal to their execution time.

$$x_{i,j} * x_{k,j} * PL_{i,k,j} * abs(t_k - t_i) \leq min(T_k, T_i) \tag{5}$$

• *Batch constraint:* Batch services must begin simultaneously, meaning when services i and j execute on the resource j and are batched, their start time distance must be zero.

$$x_{i,j} * x_{k,j} * B_{i,k,j} * (t_k - t_i) \leq 0 \tag{6}$$

• *Request real-time constraint:* Any services within a request $\mathcal{RQ}$ should complete before users' requirement Lat_{max}^{RQ} to guarantee a real-time response.

$$\forall v_i, v_k \in \mathcal{RQ}, t_k - t_i \leq Lat_{max}^{RQ} \tag{7}$$

• *Capacity constraint:* When several services execute in parallel, their hardware utilization cannot exceed the processor's capacity. The overall hardware utilization will be nearly equal to the combined hardware utilization of individual services running independently.

$$\sum_{k=1}^{N} PL_{i,k,j} U_{k,j} + U_{i,j} \leq E_j \tag{8}$$

• *Objective and optimization model.* Our goal is to find a feasible solution with a maximum throughput which is denoted by $C = 1/\max\{t_i + \sum_{j=1}^{M} x_{i,j} T_{i,j}, \forall i \in N, \forall j \in M\}$. Thus, the problem can be formulated as the following model:

$$\max C \quad s.t. \ Eq. \ (2) - (8) \tag{9}$$

NP-Hard Problem. It is important to note that the scheduling problem within Niagara is an instance of a classical NP-Hard problem, the Traveling Salesman Problem (TSP) [17]. Consequently, determining the optimal scheduling strategy for this problem is also NP-hard.

3.3   Template-Based Scheduling Strategy Generator

In addressing our scheduling problem, we have found success in leveraging the cutting-edge GUROBI solver [2]. This solver yields solutions with an optimality loss of less than 10% since our service decision variables remain relatively small, numbering around 100. Nevertheless, it is imperative to acknowledge that obtaining an approximately optimal solution through this method may entail several hours of computational effort, rendering it impractical for online scheduling.

To circumvent this challenge, `Niagara` introduces an innovative offline-online hybrid heuristic algorithm. Our insight stems from the observation that the majority of service request patterns exhibit remarkable stability over time. For instance, tasks such as face recognition consistently involve sub-tasks such as person detection, face detection, and face recognition. In response to this observation, we introduce the concept of *service graph templates*, which encapsulate common service patterns frequently encountered in real-world scenarios. For exceptional and unexpected cases, we also offer an adaptation mechanism designed to modify the scheduling strategy in real-time, aligning it with the specific requirements of dispatching online DNN cascades to heterogeneous processors (as detailed in Sect. 3.4).

Each service graph template comprises four essential components: service graph $\mathcal{G}$, request number $\mathcal{RN}$, resource status $\mathcal{S}$, latency requirement Lat_{max}^{RQ}. Through the analysis of existing request data, we endeavor to identify as many request patterns for services within a single frame as possible. For the second parameter, request number, the range is 1-N, with N representing the maximum number of frames that can be processed within a single second. In addition, `Niagara` conducts a comprehensive exploration of the status of heterogeneous processors, as elaborated in Sect. 3.6. Taking the Snapdragon 865 SoC as an exemplar, `Niagara` systematically considers all feasible combinations of CPU cores, GPUs, and DSPs, encompassing various resource-status scenar-

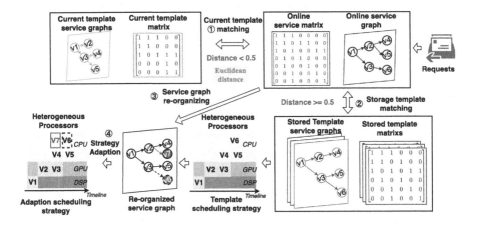

Fig. 2. The workflow of strategy matcher.

ios, thereby ensuring adaptability to the underlying hardware configurations. Regarding the final parameter, the response requirement, `Niagara` endeavors to generate scheduling strategies for all possible scenarios within intervals of 50 ms, ranging from 50 ms to 1000 ms. In practice, `Niagara` has the capacity to generate a multitude of service graph templates and their corresponding feasible scheduling strategies, all of which are stored locally on edge devices. This storage incurs a minimal overhead of less than 10 MB.

3.4   Template-Based Strategy Matcher

The matcher takes into account two primary inputs: the real-time service graph and the processor's status. We outline its workflow as illustrated in Fig. 2.

The service graph is stored in a two-dimensional matrix format, with a value of 1 indicating the presence of a dependency between services. The Matcher, guided by the processor's status, is responsible for selecting appropriate template strategies under conditions that are no worse than the input circumstances. To achieve this, `Niagara` utilizes the Euclidean distance metric [15] to quantify the disparity between the online service graph (derived from the current image) and the service graph template, ultimately identifying the most suitable strategy.

The matcher includes the following steps:

- Step ①: When the distance between the online service graph and the current service graph template falls below a predefined threshold (e.g., 0.5), `Niagara` continues to employ the current template. This process is depicted in Fig. 2①.
- Step ②: If the distance exceeds the threshold, `Niagara` discontinues the current scheduling strategy and selects a new one that closely matches the online

---

Algorithm 2: Dynamic predictor algorithm

    Input : First_order_exponential_predictor A, Holt_Winters_predictor B
1 CSGP = NULL // CSGP: `current_service_graph_prediction`
2 **while** $True$ **do**
3   Input $data$ = user.request.Get() // Receive request data from user
4      $image\_info = Main\_DNN\_inference(data)$
5      $service\_graph = Graph\_generator(image\_info)$
6   **if** $CSGP.service\_graph\ != service\_graph$ **then**
7          $CSGP.service\_graph = service\_graph$
8   **if** $A.history\_accuracy > B.history\_accuracy$ **then**
9             $CSGP.last\_number = A.Predict(service\_graph)$
10   **else**
11            $CSGP.last\_number = B.Predict(service\_graph)$
12   **end**
13   **end**
14      $CSGP.service\_graph.Execute()$
15      $A.Update(number), B.Update(number)$
16 **end**

service graph. For instance, in Fig. 2②, the blue template is chosen due to its minimal distance, and it corresponds to a scheduling strategy.

- Step ③: Recognizing that the online service graph may not always align perfectly with the template, `Niagara` incorporates an adaptation mechanism to accommodate unexpected variations. As demonstrated in Fig. 2③, `Niagara` first reorganizes the current service graph. It endeavors to match online graph services with template services as closely as possible. Services that do not find a match, such as v6 and v7 in Fig. 2, are flagged, while the scheduling positions of matching services remain consistent with the template's corresponding strategy. Notably, v6 represents an extra service, while v7 is a newly added service.
- Step ④: `Niagara` selects the first unmatching newly added service (e.g., v7) and places it within the earliest available idle period, as depicted in Fig. 2④. In cases where the template scheduling strategy includes extraneous, redundant services, such services are eliminated (e.g., v6). Other services commence as early as possible while adhering to any applicable constraints.

3.5   Dynamic Input Predictor

The predictor is a crucial component in forecasting future service graphs, denoted as pairs of $<service\ graph,\ request\ number>$. Algorithm 2 shows its functionality.

Different scenarios often exhibit distinct recurring patterns in their service graphs. For instance, in the context of a parking system, events such as license plate recognition at an entrance gate may occur at regular intervals, while violation operation detection is more likely to follow a pattern similar to the most recent historical data. To address these diverse scenarios, `Niagara` employs a combined prediction approach, encompassing first-order prediction and triple exponential smoothing (Holt-Winters method), to capture both the latest and global historical patterns. It operates as follows:

- The predictor initiates the first DNN service inference in accordance with the ongoing scheduling strategy or its affinity processor, should no active strategy exist. After execution, the predictor obtains essential information such as the count of people or cars, which forms the basis for predicting the service graph within the current request.
- If the newly predicted service graph diverges from the current one, `Niagara` proceeds to compare the historical accuracy of the predictors and selects the more precise one. This selection informs the prediction of how many frames the service graph will remain constant.

3.6   Processor Monitor

In this section, we discuss the processor monitoring mechanism implemented in our system. The monitor leverages system files such as *`/proc/stat`* and *`/sys/class/kgsl/kgsl-3d0/gpu_busy_ percentage`* to acquire real-time utilization data for the CPU and GPU, and utilizes a benchmarking tool from the Hexagon DSP SDK to obtain information about DSP utilization.

Our monitoring system continuously inspects the status of these processors at intervals of 100 ms. This monitoring frequency is deliberately set to be smaller than the service inference time to ensure the precision of our measurements while avoiding any adverse impact on the quality of service delivery.

4   Implementation and Evaluation

We have developed an end-to-end prototype of our system, comprising over 3,800 lines of code, built on the Android OS 10.0 platform. For DNN inference, we have employed TFLite, a runtime environment capable of supporting on-device CPU, GPU, and DSP inference. To ensure smooth execution of DNN inference while preserving the desired strategy order, we have implemented a ThreadPool and an InferenceFinishListener, enabling asynchronous processing.

4.1   Experiment Settings and Methodology

Hardware and OS. In order to assess the versatility of our scheduling strategy across diverse heterogeneous processor platforms, we executed `Niagara` on three SoCs configurations detailed in Table 4. These SoCs are widely employed in IP cameras, as indicated by [5]. Each of these SoCs encompasses three heterogeneous processors with varying capabilities. To maintain uniformity, all these devices operated on the Android 10 system.
Baselines. To highlight the advantages of our approach, we conducted a comparative analysis of `Niagara` against the following existing methods:

Table 3. Experimental combinations of 3 scenarios and their corresponding datasets.

DNN service combination	Name	Complexity	DNN1	DNN2	DNN3	Video Input	Video Description
Violation Operation Detector (VOD)	VOD	High	SSD-Main	CenterNet- Keypoint	Pole-gloves/ SSD-helmet-quant	Power grid site 1 week, 1 camera	Resolution: 960*540 FPS:30
	VOD-Y	Low	Tiny-yolov3-quant				
	VOD-FH	Middle	SSD-Main		Pole-gloves/ SSD-helmet		
	VOD-FR	Low	Fast-RCNN-quant		Pole-gloves/ SSD-helmet-quant		
	VOD-P	Low	SSD-Main	Posenet			
Vehicle License Plate Detector (LPR)	LPR	Low	Tiny-yolov3-quant	Wpod	OCR-recognizer	Traffic cameras 1 week, 20 cameras [28]	Resolution: : 960*540 FPS:30
Nameplate Identification (NI)	NI	Middle	SSD-Main	Text detector	OCR-recognizer	Power grid site 1 week, 3 cameras	Resolution: 416*416 FPS:30
	NI-FR	Middle	Fast-RCNN-quant				

- *TFLite* employs unmodified TensorFlow Lite 2.4.0 [11]. When a service request for a model is received, TFLite immediately invokes a new runtime instance for execution, consistently dispatching the service to its affinity processor.
- *Greedy Algorithm* consistently schedules the service to its affinity processor, ensuring assignment until the processor becomes idle and can accommodate it.
- *FIFO-algortihm* will transform the task graph into a FIFO queue according to its topological sort. Whenever a processor can accommodate the first task in the queue, it should execute immediately. If several processors can accommodate it, this algorithm will always select the processor with the minimum latency.
- *ODTSC Algorithm.* Originally designed to optimize the scheduling of a DNN service graph on heterogeneous edge nodes while minimizing total latency under resource constraints, we have modified this algorithm to suit the on-device heterogeneous processors' environment [40].
- *LSTM-Niagara algorithm* uses the LSTM model as the dynamic predictor, and other parts are the same as `Niagara`. We LSTM-Niagara to evaluate our dynamic predictor efficiency.

Evaluation Scenarios. The assessment of `Niagara` encompasses 3 real application (video surveillance) scenarios encompassing 8 distinct service combination patterns, as outlined in Table 3. These scenarios make use of a range of pre-trained DNN models, including publicly available models and those developed by the authors, such as SSD-Helmet and pole-gloves.

Table 4. Experimental platforms.

SoC	Description	capacity
SnapDragon 865 [10]	CPU: 4*Kryo 585(A77)	400%
	GPU: Adreno 650	100%
	DSP: Hexagon 698	100%
SnapDragon 855 [9]	CPU: 4*Kryo 485(A76)	400%
	GPU: Adreno 640	100%
	DSP: Hexagon 690	100%
SnapDragon 750G [8]	CPU: 2*Kryo 570(A76)	200%
	GPU: Adreno 619	100%
	DSP: Hexagon 694	100%

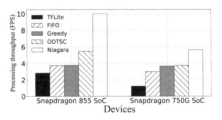

Fig. 3. Processing throughput of VOD atop two different devices.

Evaluation Datasets. The evaluation dataset comprises three video streams, with two of them collected from real-world environments where `Niagara` has been deployed, and one sourced from open repositories commonly utilized in edge service benchmarks, as meticulously delineated in Table 3. All videos have undergone uniform preprocessing to attain a frame rate of 30 frames per second (fps), thus ensuring evaluation consistency.

The complexity classification, as presented in Table 3, elucidates the number of services encompassed within a given request. Here, "high", "middle", and "low" denote the presence of more than 10 services, 7–10 services, and less than 7 services, respectively.

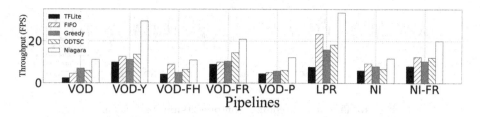

Fig. 4. Processing throughput of all eight experimental combinations.

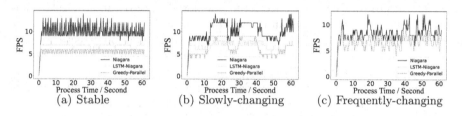

(a) Stable   (b) Slowly-changing   (c) Frequently-changing

Fig. 5. Throughput of one-minute real videos in three different situations.

4.2   Experiment Results

Different Combinations. We evaluate 8 combinations in Table 3 in three real scenarios, as shown in Fig. 4. Each pipeline's result is averaged over 100 same requests. Overall, `Niagara` achieves a 3.0×, 1.9×, 2.0×, and 1.8× throughput improvement compared with TFLite, FIFO, Greedy, and ODTSC on average, respectively. That is because our strategy jointly considers batch and parallel execution with DNN inference service-to-hardware selection. As the scenario is more complex, the benefits `Niagara` obtains are more. VOD-Y is one of the best examples. It uses a tiny-yolov3-quant model for person detection service, which consumes the least hardware utilization. Thus, this service can be parallelized with any other DNN services on the CPU, significantly reducing the critical path length. On the contrary, the nameplate identification (NI) pipeline's performance improvement is not so obvious because the person detection service consumes lots of hardware resources, and no one can be parallelized with it

Different Edge Devices. We also evaluate `Niagara` on different edge devices, as shown in Table 4. From Fig. 3, `Niagara` always achieves the lowest delay compared with the other four baselines. For instance, `Niagara`'s throughput is 10 FPS on Snapdragon 855 SoC development board, while 5.46 FPS, 3.78 FPS, 3.74 FPS, and 2.84 FPS under ODTSC, Greedy, FIFO, and TFLite baselines, respectively. On Snapdragon 750G SoC development board, `Niagara` can achieve 4.56×, 1.87×, 1.52×, and 1.50× higher throughput, respectively.

Besides, comparing the two figures, Snapdragon 855 SoC achieves better performance improvement than Snapdragon 750G SoC. That is because 855 SoC has a higher-performance SoC with a four-core CPU, while 750G SoC only has two, providing more scheduling space for `Niagara` to exploit.

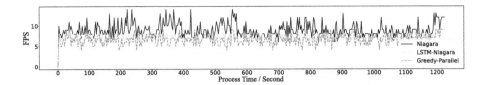

Fig. 6. Throughput comparison of a 20-min real video.

Real Deployment. We have successfully deployed `Niagara` in an electric station and conducted evaluations in three typical situations: stable, slowly changing, and frequently changing, with a focus on violation operation detection (VOD in Table 3). Additionally, we also analyzed `Niagara`'s performance over a 20-min work period to assess its efficiency.

The evaluation results, shown in Fig. 5 and 6, demonstrate the effectiveness of `Niagara` compared to state-of-the-art baselines. `Niagara` achieves throughput improvements ranging from 1.26 to 2.33 ×. Particularly, in scenarios with more stable content, `Niagara` provides greater benefits, e.g., Fig. 5(a) and Fig. 6 200–250 s. This can be attributed to `Niagara` accurately predicting unforeseen service graphs, providing more scheduling space, which enables better utilization of its offline strategies.

5   Discussion

Applicability of NPU in Edge Devices. Many contemporary edge devices are furnished with Neural Processing Units (NPUs), such as the Kirin 9000 [4]. Since `Niagara` is a hardware-agnostic framework, the integration of support for new NPUs entails minimal alterations to existing algorithms and system design. This integration process primarily involves the addition of NPU-specific support implementations, encompassing profiling, hardware configurations, and hardware status monitoring. Actually, `Niagara` already extends its support to NPUs, with experimental deployments showcasing its compatibility with a particular NPU architecture (Hexagon DSP) developed by Qualcomm.

6   Conclusion

This work proposed `Niagara` to achieve high throughput for serving DNN inference services on edge devices. `Niagara` proposes an offline algorithm for the on-edge-device DNN inference service scheduling problem. It then applies the template scheduling strategies to the variable unforeseen DNN cascades application with the help of an input predictor, processor monitor, and strategy matcher. We have implemented a prototype of `Niagara` on commodity edge devices and comprehensively evaluate its effectiveness via a set of experiments on typical DNN inference service scenarios.

Acknowledgement. This work was supported by the National Key Research and Development Program of China under the grant number 2022YFB4500700, the National Natural Science Foundation of China under the grant numbers 62325201, 62172008, 62102009, and 62102045, the National Natural Science Fund for the Excellent Young Scientists Fund Program (Overseas), the China Postdoctoral Science Foundation 8206300713, the Beijing Outstanding Young Scientist Program under the grant number BJJWZYJH01201910001004, and Center for Data Space Technology and System, Peking University.

References

1. Cortex A57. https://en.wikipedia.org/wiki/ARM_Cortex-A57
2. Gurobi solver. http://www.gurobi.com
3. Jetson TX2. https://www.nvidia.com/en-us/autonomous-machines/embedded-systems/jetson-tx2/
4. Kirin 9000. https://www.hisilicon.com/cn/products/Kirin/Kirin-flagship-chips/Kirin-9000
5. Powerful 64-bit heterogeneous processing, advanced analytics and 4G LTE redefine the IP camera. https://www.edge-ai-vision.com/2015/11/qualcomm-announces-ip-camera-reference-platform-with-high-end-processing-imaging-and-analytics-capabilities-to-advance-security-cameras/
6. Qualcomm snapdragon 625 IP camera. https://anyconnect.com/recommended-sbcs/thundercomm/thundercomm-qualcomm-snapdragon-625-ip-camera
7. Snapdragon 650 IP camera brings consciousness to camera security. https://www.qualcomm.com/news/onq/2016/02/snapdragon-650-ip-camera-brings-consciousness-camera-security
8. Snapdragon 750G SOC. https://www.qualcomm.com/products/mobile/snapdragon/smartphones/snapdragon-7-series-mobile-platforms/snapdragon-750g-5g-mobile-platform
9. Snapdragon 855 SOC. https://www.qualcomm.com/products/mobile/snapdragon/smartphones/snapdragon-8-series-mobile-platforms/snapdragon-855-mobile-platform
10. Snapdragon 865 SOC. https://www.qualcomm.com/products/mobile/snapdragon/smartphones/snapdragon-8-series-mobile-platforms/snapdragon-865-plus-5g-mobile-platform
11. Tflite. https://www.tensorflow.org/lite/
12. Edge TPU (2021). https://github.com/XiaoMi/mace
13. Almeida, M., Laskaridis, S., Mehrotra, A., Dudziak, L., Leontiadis, I., Lane, N.D.: Smart at what cost? Characterising mobile deep neural networks in the wild. In: ACM IMC, pp. 658–672 (2021)
14. Chai, F., Zhang, Q., Yao, H., Xin, X., Gao, R., Guizani, M.: Joint multi-task offloading and resource allocation for mobile edge computing systems in satellite IoT. IEEE Trans. Veh. Technol. **72**(6), 7783–7795 (2023)
15. Danielsson, P.E.: Euclidean distance mapping. Comput. Graphics Image Process. **14**(3), 227–248 (1980)
16. Diggle, P., Al-Wasel, I.: Time series (1990)
17. Dorigo, M., Gambardella, L.M.: Ant colonies for the travelling salesman problem. Biosystems **43**(2), 73–81 (1997)
18. Eshraghi, N., Liang, B.: Joint offloading decision and resource allocation with uncertain task computing requirement. In: IEEE INFOCOM, pp. 1414–1422 (2019)

19. Fu, X., Tang, B., Guo, F., Kang, L.: Priority and dependency-based DAG tasks offloading in fog/edge collaborative environment. In: CSCWD, pp. 440–445 (2021)
20. Hu, S., et al.: Temporal-aware qos prediction via dynamic graph neural collaborative learning. In: Troya, J., Medjahed, B., Piattini, M., Yao, L., Fernández, P., Ruiz-Cortés, A. (eds.) ICSOC, vol. 13740, pp. 125–133. Springer, Cham (2022). https://doi.org/10.1007/978-3-031-20984-0_8
21. Huang, V., Wang, C., Ma, H., Chen, G., Christopher, K.: Cost-aware dynamic multi-workflow scheduling in cloud data center using evolutionary reinforcement learning. In: Troya, J., Medjahed, B., Piattini, M., Yao, L., Fernández, P., Ruiz-Cortés, A. (eds.) ICSOC, vol. 13740, pp. 449–464. Springer, Cham (2022). https://doi.org/10.1007/978-3-031-20984-0_32
22. Jeong, J.S., et al.: Band: coordinated multi-DNN inference on heterogeneous mobile processors. In: ACM MobiSys, pp. 235–247 (2022)
23. Kim, Y., Kim, J., Chae, D., Kim, D., Kim, J.: μlayer: low latency on-device inference using cooperative single-layer acceleration and processor-friendly quantization. In: EuroSys, pp. 1–15 (2019)
24. Li, Z., Yang, C., Huang, X., Zeng, W., Xie, S.: CoOR: collaborative task offloading and service caching replacement for vehicular edge computing networks. IEEE Trans. Veh. Technol., 1–6 (2023)
25. Liao, H., Li, X., Guo, D., Kang, W., Li, J.: Dependency-aware application assigning and scheduling in edge computing. IEEE IoT (2021)
26. Liu, J., Ren, J., Zhang, Y., Peng, X., Zhang, Y., Yang, Y.: Efficient dependent task offloading for multiple applications in MEC-cloud system. IEEE TMC (2021)
27. Meng, Z., Xu, H., Huang, L., Xi, P., Yang, S.: Achieving energy efficiency through dynamic computing offloading in mobile edge-clouds. In: IEEE MASS, pp. 175–183. IEEE (2018)
28. Shen, H., et al.: Nexus: a GPU cluster engine for accelerating DNN-based video analysis. In: ACM SOSP, pp. 322–337 (2019)
29. Sze, V., Chen, Y.H., Yang, T.J., Emer, J.S.: Efficient processing of deep neural networks: a tutorial and survey. Proc. IEEE 105(12), 2295–2329 (2017)
30. Tan, T., Cao, G.: FastVA: deep learning video analytics through edge processing and NPU in mobile. In: IEEE INFOCOM, pp. 1947–1956. IEEE (2020)
31. Wang, M., Ding, S., Cao, T., Liu, Y., Xu, F.: AsyMo: scalable and efficient deep-learning inference on asymmetric mobile CPUs. In: ACM MobiCom, pp. 215–228 (2021)
32. Wei, T., Zhang, P., Dong, H., Jin, H., Bouguettaya, A.: Mobility-aware proactive QoS monitoring for mobile edge computing. In: Troya, J., Medjahed, B., Piattini, M., Yao, L., Fernández, P., Ruiz-Cortés, A. (eds.) ICSOC, vol. 13740, pp. 134–142. Springer, Cham (2022). https://doi.org/10.1007/978-3-031-20984-0_9
33. Wei, W.W.: Time series analysis. In: The Oxford Handbook of Quantitative Methods in Psychology, vol. 2 (2006)
34. Xiao, H., Xu, C., Ma, Y., Yang, S., Zhong, L., Muntean, G.M.: Edge intelligence: a computational task offloading scheme for dependent IoT application. IEEE Wirel. Commun. 21(9), 7222–7237 (2022)
35. Xu, M., Zhang, X., Liu, Y., Huang, G., Liu, X., Lin, F.X.: Approximate query service on autonomous IoT cameras. In: ACM MobiSys, pp. 191–205 (2020)
36. Yang, Y., Chen, G., Ma, H., Zhang, M.: Dual-tree genetic programming for deadline-constrained dynamic workflow scheduling in cloud. In: Troya, J., Medjahed, B., Piattini, M., Yao, L., Fernández, P., Ruiz-Cortés, A. (eds.) ICSOC, vol. 13740, pp. 433–448. Springer, Cham (2022). https://doi.org/10.1007/978-3-031-20984-0_31

37. Yeo, H., Chong, C.J., Jung, Y., Ye, J., Han, D.: NEMO: enabling neural-enhanced video streaming on commodity mobile devices. In: ACM MobiCom, pp. 1–14 (2020)
38. Yi, J., Lee, Y.: Heimdall: mobile GPU coordination platform for augmented reality applications. In: ACM MobiCom, pp. 1–14 (2020)
39. Zhang, J., et al.: MobiPose: real-time multi-person pose estimation on mobile devices. In: ACM SenSys, pp. 136–149 (2020)
40. Zhao, G., Xu, H., Zhao, Y., Qiao, C., Huang, L.: Offloading tasks with dependency and service caching in mobile edge computing. IEEE Trans. Parallel Distrib. Syst. **32**(11), 2777–2792 (2021)
41. Zhao, Z., Luo, H., Chu, S.C., Shang, Y., Wu, X.: An immersive online shopping system based on virtual reality. J. Netw. Intell. **3**(4), 235–246 (2018)

Plan, Generate and Match: Scientific Workflow Recommendation with Large Language Models

Yang Gu, Jian Cao$^{(\boxtimes)}$, Yuan Guo, Shiyou Qian, and Wei Guan

Shanghai Jiao Tong University, Shanghai, China
{gu_yang,cao-jian,gy2022,qshiyou,guan-wei}@sjtu.edu.cn

Abstract. The recommendation of scientific workflows from public repositories that meet users' natural language requirements is becoming increasingly essential in the scientific community. Nevertheless, existing methods that rely on direct text matching encounter difficulties when it comes to handling complex queries, which ultimately results in poor performance. Large language models (LLMs) have recently exhibited exceptional ability in planning and reasoning. We propose "Plan, Generate and Match" (**PGM**), a scientific workflow recommendation method leveraging LLMs. PGM consists of three stages: utilizing LLMs to conduct planning upon receiving a user query, generating a structured workflow specification guided by the solution steps, and using these plans and specifications to match with candidate workflows. By incorporating the planning mechanism, PGM leverages few-shot prompting to automatically generate well-considered steps for instructing the recommendation of reliable workflows. This method represents the first exploration of incorporating LLMs into the scientific workflow domain. Experimental results on real-world benchmarks demonstrate that PGM outperforms state-of-the-art methods with statistical significance, highlighting its immense potential in addressing complex requirements.

Keywords: Scientific Workflow Recommendation · Large Language Models · Planning · Prompting

1 Introduction

Scientific workflows, often depicted as directed acyclic graphs (DAGs), serve as a formal representation of data processing services and their associated data flow. These workflows are utilized to automate the handling and analysis of extensive scientific data [1,2], thus accelerating scientific discovery. Nowadays, an increasing number of scientific workflows are being shared in online repositories such as *myExperiment* [3], *Galaxy* [4], and *WorkflowHub* [5]. For instance, *Galaxy* contains over 18,000 workflows from diverse scientific domains, each with metadata like title, annotations, tags.

© The Author(s), under exclusive license to Springer Nature Switzerland AG 2023
F. Monti et al. (Eds.): ICSOC 2023, LNCS 14419, pp. 86–102, 2023.
https://doi.org/10.1007/978-3-031-48421-6_7

The recommendation of scientific workflows from those repositories, utilizing either textual [6] or structural queries [7], has emerged as an efficient and effective approach for researchers to reuse and repurpose existing workflows. Users find it more convenient and easier to express their requirements using natural language descriptions, rather than structural features such as intended workflow drafts [8]. Therefore, the research of recommending suitable scientific workflows that precisely align with users' textual requirements holds significant importance.

Existing workflow recommendation methods mainly rely on text matching techniques [9], like bag-of-words approach [6], to calculate the text similarity between user queries and candidate workflows. However, these methods are limited to handling simple and straightforward queries. As the complexity and scale of user intents increase [10], recommending appropriate workflows becomes challenging for both human experts and computational models.

Actually, scientific workflow recommendation can be modeled as a complex reasoning task, involving understanding user intents, extracting key information, and matching it with candidate workflows. To tackle complex problems, humans often employ planning to break down intricate problems and schedule solution steps before implementation. Planning has been successful in various reasoning tasks like arithmetic computation [11] and code generation [12]. Motivated by these, we aim to integrate planning into recommendation, specifically focusing on transforming user requirements into a plan that aligns them with the process representation of workflows and facilitates the extraction of key information.

However, the realization of plan-guided recommendation relies on the approach to generate plans from user requirements. Developing such an algorithm from scratch necessitates a substantial amount of labeled requirement-plan data for training, which can be time-consuming and knowledge-intensive. On the other hand, large language models (LLMs) have recently exhibited remarkable reasoning capabilities without explicit training [13]. By incorporating auxiliary reasoning prompts [14] or a series of exemplary prompts (e.g., chain of thought (CoT)) [15,16], known as zero-shot and few-shot prompting respectively, LLMs have demonstrated significant improvements in planning to solve reasoning tasks [11]. While some studies have found limitations in the planning abilities of LLMs [17], these limitations are typically observed in classical planning problems with constrained domains and action states.

Consequently, we propose "Plan, Generate, and Match" (**PGM**), an innovative scientific workflow recommendation approach that harnesses the robust planning and reasoning abilities of LLMs. PGM comprises three stages: 1) **Planning**: where LLMs are employed to parse user queries and conduct logical planning; 2) **Specification Generation**: which involves extracting and generating a structured specification of the user's intended workflow, guided step by step by the plan; 3) **Matching**: where workflows are matched and recommended based on the degree of matching with the user queries, determined by utilizing the generated plan and specification. Benefiting from this **planning mechanism**, PGM leverages few-shot prompting to autonomously generate plans without requiring annotated plan corpora or additional training, thereby facilitating a better understanding of user intents and instructing subsequent generation and matching processes. In summary, this paper presents the following contributions:

- We develop a novel three-stage framework for recommending scientific workflows according to user queries, which marks the milestone of the first exploration of introducing LLMs into the domain of scientific workflows.
- Utilizing LLMs as the brain for planning and generating, PGM can automatically yield well-considered steps that guide the recommendation of reliable workflows.
- Extensive experiments on real-world expert-rated benchmarks demonstrate that PGM significantly surpasses state-of-the-art approaches across various metrics, highlighting the remarkable capability and immense potential of PGM in comprehending and addressing complex requirements.

2   Related Work

2.1   Scientific Workflow Recommendation

For simple textual queries, keyword-based search methods compute text similarity between keywords and metadata (e.g., titles and tags) of candidate workflows [1]. When users provide paragraph descriptions, topic modeling and TF-IDF (Term Frequency-Inverse Document Frequency) algorithms are employed to match query features with workflows [8]. To enhance semantic relevance [18], a hierarchical semantic similarity algorithm is proposed [19]. Graph matching and activity knowledge graphs are used when users provide preliminary sketches [7], which is yet less user-friendly and inconvenient for various users.

In this paper, we focus on user needs expressed in natural language paragraphs. Unlike traditional methods relying on direct text matching, the emergence of LLMs has created new possibilities for planning-based recommendation.

2.2   Prompting Methods

Prompting is a technique used to elicit reasoning capabilities and desired outputs from LLMs. It can be achieved through zero-shot prompting, where instructions are provided, or few-shot prompting, where a few input-output examples are given. Zero-shot CoT prompting, proposed by Kojima et al. [14], adds a *"Let's think step by step"* prompt to facilitate coherent reasoning. Few-shot CoT prompting, introduced by Wei et al. [15], achieves superior performance by providing human-crafted reasoning examples. Subsequent studies [11,20] have further expanded on few-shot prompting, such as task decomposition and prompt ensemble. For example, Lu et al. [20] develop Chameleon, an AI system based on LLMs like GPT-4 [21], which employs a planner prompted by module sequence examples to decompose complex problems into solvable sub-tasks.

Apart from Chameleon, several other methods have utilized LLMs for plan generation in embodied fields. Wang et al. [16] develop DEPS, an interactive planning approach to enable multi-task agents via a LLM-aided explainer and planner. Jiang et al. [12] propose a two-phase self-planning code generation method that outperforms direct LLM-based approaches. However, these methods are tailored to domain-specific tasks with relatively fixed solving patterns, rendering them unsuitable for scientific workflow recommendation problem. Our plan-aided approach leverages LLMs prompted by a few samples to comprehend user intents, devise plans and generate specifications for subsequent matching.

3 Preliminaries

Definition 1 (Scientific Workflow). *A scientific workflow **sw** is a tuple* (***Title, Desc, Input, Output, Act, Link***), *where **Title** is the title of sw, **Desc** is the textual description of sw in short-document, **Input** is a set of input data of sw, **Output** is a set of output data of sw, **Act** is a set of activities belonging to sw, and **Link** is a set of datalinks connecting activities in Act.*

Definition 2 (User Query). *A user query **q** is a natural language paragraph.*
For more intuition, we employ the workflow card to report comprehensive details of workflows in the repository. As shown in Fig. 1, the workflow card comprises a workflow preview and attribute information demonstrated in Definition 1, some of which are used for matching in our PGM.

Fig. 1. Workflow card of a sample workflow sw_{233} (http://www.myexperiment.org/workflows/233.html) in myExperiment.

4 Plan, Generate and Match (PGM)

PGM is an LLMs-aided scientific workflow recommendation framework, which is comprised of three stages: planning, specification generation and matching, as shown in Fig. 2. Given a user query, the first stage involves adopting an LLM, prompted by a few planning examples, to devise action plans. In the second stage, the LLM utilizes spec-generation prompting to generate a structured specification of the intended workflow, following the step-by-step guidance of the plan. Finally, the structured specification and plan are used to compute the matching degree between the user query and candidate workflows in the repository.

4.1   Stage I: Planning

In real-world scenarios, user queries often involve complex intents that require orchestrating multiple sub-tasks to recommend the desired workflows. To address this, we introduce **planning** as the initial step in PGM. The objective of this stage is to utilize LLMs to analyze the user query and devise a step-by-step plan that guides the subsequent generation process.

To accomplish this, we leverage the planning capabilities of LLMs through a **few-shot planning prompting** approach. The inputs for the planning stage consist of a user query q_0, a planning task instruction I_1, and a few demonstration examples $D_1 = \langle (q_1, p_1) \oplus (q_2, p_2) \oplus \cdots \oplus (q_{t_1}, p_{t_1}) \rangle$, where each (q_i, p_i) denotes a hand-crafted query-plan example pair, t_1 is a relatively low number denoting the number of examples, and $\oplus$ signifies the concatenation operation between two samples. Prompted by the above natural language content, the LLMs-based planner $\mathcal{P}$ is to output an action plan p_0. That is to say,

$$p_0 \leftarrow \mathcal{P}(q_0; I_1, D_1) \tag{1}$$

The prompt that includes I_1 and D_1 plays a crucial role in effectively eliciting LLMs for planning. To ensure the efficient and logical generation of plans, we invite some domain experts to design prompts adhering to specific principles:

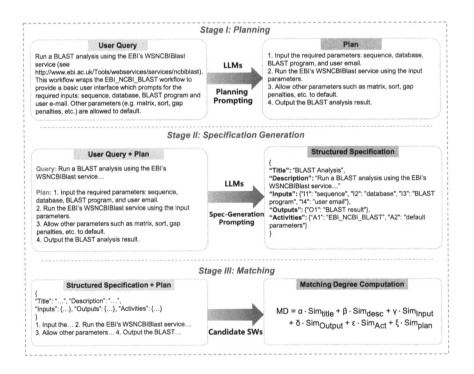

Fig. 2. Overview of the proposed PGM framework.

1. To enable LLMs to gain a clear understanding of the task, we draw inspiration from the successful application of Plan-and-Solve (PS) prompting [11]. The instruction I_1 is specified as *"Your task is to first **understand the user query** and **devise a plan** for generating a structured specification of the user's intended scientific workflow."*, as shown in Fig. 3.
2. To enhance the LLMs' comprehending of planning intention and criteria, it is important that the demonstrations D_1 comprise representative examples. These examples should contain essential steps without excessive details [12], while maintaining logical connections between the steps to guide the correct execution order. It is crucial to select typical examples of average length that encompass various workflow structures, including pipelines, trees and DAGs. Atypical or marginal examples should be avoided to ensure the model's generalizability.
3. In addition, a prompt *"Let's think step by step"* [12,15] is introduced between the user query and plan to trigger LLMs to devise a logical plan. Furthermore, to ensure consistency in the prompt examples, we strive to use a uniform expression, such as starting with a verb like *"Input"*, *"Output"*, *"Use"*, or a conjunction like *"If"*, as illustrated in the example in Fig. 3.

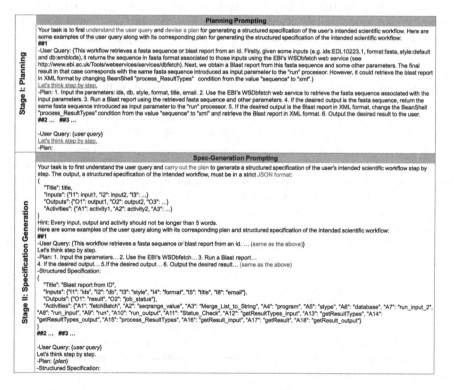

Fig. 3. Exemplary prompts for the planning and specification generation stages of PGM. These prompts contain injectable slots, such as *user query* and *plan*, which are replaced with the corresponding text before being inputted into the LLM.

4.2   Stage II: Specification Generation

In the specification generation stage, the goal is to generate a structured specification of the user's intended workflow based on the action plan. To achieve this, we still employ LLMs with a **few-shot spec-generation prompting**. The inputs for **specification generation** stage consist of a user query q_0 appended with an action plan p_0, along with a generation task instruction I_2 and a few demonstration examples $D_2 = \langle (q_1, p_1, s_1) \oplus (q_2, p_2, s_2) \oplus \cdots \oplus (q_{t_2}, p_{t_2}, s_{t_2}) \rangle$, where each (q_i, p_i, s_i) denotes a hand-crafted query-plan-specification example triplet, and t_2 denotes the number of examples. Note that t_2 is lower than t_1 due to context length limitations. These natural language demonstrations are given to an LLM generator $\mathcal{G}$ to produce a structured specification $spec_0$:

$$spec_0 \leftarrow \mathcal{G}(q_0, p_0; I_2, D_2) \tag{2}$$

To better generate $spec_0$ that accurately represents user-desired workflows and facilitate its use in the subsequent stage, LLMs should extract key information of workflows by following a structured specification (e.g., JSON format). Therefore, we provide a standardized template for intended workflows and instruct the LLM to conduct information extraction guided by the plan through slot filling. As depicted in Fig. 3, this template includes four slots ("Title", "Inputs", "Outputs", and "Activities") to capture the intended workflow's key information. Moreover, to enhance practicality and simplify the problem, we incorporate a hint *"Every input, output and activity should not be longer than 5 words"* based on real workflow statistics. Domain experts fill in these fields according to the query, plan, their expertise, and workflow information, creating demonstration examples D_2. These examples trigger LLMs to automatically analyze user queries and extract key information accordingly [20].

It is worth noting that the "Desc" attribute and "Link" attribute in the definition of sw are not included in the output template. The "Desc" attribute, representing the description of the expected workflow, is naturally filled with the user query q_0 and incorporated into the final structured specification without a separate slot to preserve resources, as illustrated in Fig. 2. As for the "Link" attribute, determining the appropriate links is on the basis of activity generation that may be unstable, which is more complex and uncertain for LLMs-based approach. Therefore, introducing low-quality link information in the subsequent matching process may have adverse effects.

4.3   Stage III: Matching

In the last **matching** stage, PGM leverages the generated plan and structured specification to match with workflows in the repository. Just as shown in Fig. 2, we aim to compute the matching degree MD between the user query and candidate scientific workflows.

4.3.1   Embedding Model.   This part first briefly introduces the embedding models used for the subsequent similarity computation. Since the majority users

of scientific workflows are from the biomedical and bioinformatics fields [6], we employ BioLinkBERT[1] [22], achieving SOTA performance on several biomedical NLP benchmarks like BLURB [2], as our basic embedding model. Furthermore, to enhance its adaptability across multiple domains, we perform unsupervised fine-tuning on the original BioLinkBERT using the workflow descriptions in experimental datasets. This fine-tuning process enables us to effectively embed different objects, facilitating the subsequent calculating of semantic similarity.

4.3.2 Similarity Computation. Given five key attributes (Title, Description, Inputs, Outputs and Activities) of the user's intended workflow extracted from the query, we compute semantic similarity between them and the corresponding attributes of candidate workflows. Moreover, since plans characterize workflows in a more formalized and logical manner, we additionally use the LLM-aided planning approach described earlier to generate a plan based on the description of the candidate workflow. This results in six attributes considered for similarity computation, which can be categorized into text-based and set-based approaches.

A. Text-Based Computation

The **Title, Description and Plan** attributes are represented as pure strings, allowing for direct similarity calculation. We employ the fine-tuned BioLinkBERT model to embed each attribute of both the intended workflow and candidate workflow. The semantic similarity between them, denoted as Sim_{title}, Sim_{desc}, and Sim_{plan} respectively, is measured using cosine similarity.

B. Set-Based Computation

The **Inputs, Outputs and Activities** attributes are sets containing multiple elements. To compute their similarity, we formulate it as a matching optimization problem between sets [8]. Given two sets U_1 and U_2 (representing Inputs, Outputs or Activities), and the similarities $sim(u_1, u_2)$ between their respective elements (computed using cosine similarity of their name embeddings obtained from the fine-tuned BioLinkBERT model), our objective is to find a matching $M \subseteq U_1 \times U_2$ that maximizes the sum of similarities, denoted as sum:

$$\mathbf{max} \quad sum = \sum_{(u_1, u_2) \in M} sim(u_1, u_2)$$

$$\mathbf{s.t.} \quad u_1 \in U_1, u_2 \in U_2; \ \forall v \in U_1 \cup U_2, \text{ at most one edge in } M \text{ is incident upon } v.$$

$$(3)$$

The *maximum weight matching (mw)* algorithm [23] can be used to solve this problem. Then, the similarity between U_1 and U_2 is normalized by $Sim(U_1, U_2) = \frac{sum}{|U_1|+|U_2|-sum}$, where $|\cdot|$ signifies the set size. In this way, we can obtain the semantic similarity of these three attributes, Sim_{Input}, Sim_{Output} and Sim_{Act}.

4.3.3 Matching Degree Computation. Finally, the semantic matching degree between the user query and candidate workflow is determined by the weighted average of six similarities:

---

[1] https://huggingface.co/michiyasunaga.
[2] https://microsoft.github.io/BLURB/leaderboard.html.

$$MD = \alpha \cdot Sim_{title} + \beta \cdot Sim_{desc} + \gamma \cdot Sim_{Input}$$
$$+ \delta \cdot Sim_{Output} + \varepsilon \cdot Sim_{Act} + \xi \cdot Sim_{plan} \tag{4}$$

where the values of six weights are assigned using a combination weighting method of analytic hierarchy process (AHP) and factor analysis such that $\alpha + \beta + \gamma + \delta + \varepsilon + \xi = 1$. This method effectively integrates subjective expert experience with objective data characteristics, ensuring the rationality and consistency of the comprehensive evaluation metric MD [24].

5 Experiments

5.1 Experimental Settings

5.1.1 Benchmarks. The proposed method is evaluated on a widely-used expert-generated benchmark [8], which consists of two datasets: the myExperiment dataset and the Galaxy dataset. The former contains 1,483 Taverna workflows from myExperiment, while the latter contains 139 Galaxy workflows. The benchmark includes over 2,000 matching degree ratings assigned by domain experts.

Within the myExperiment dataset, there are two subsets. The first subset includes 24 query workflows, each accompanied by a **ranking list** of 10 randomly selected comparison workflows. The matching degree between the query workflow and the comparison workflows was rated by experts with the options *well-matched*, *matched*, *related*, and *unmatched*. The second subset includes 8 query workflows, each accompanied by 21–68 candidate workflows (not ranked), with matching degrees rated by experts as before. The Galaxy dataset comprises a single subset, which follows the same structure as the first subset of the myExperiment dataset, including 8 query workflows.

Before evaluation, we collected various attributes of these workflows. The majority of experiments were conducted using myExperiment dataset due to its larger and more comprehensive nature. The Galaxy dataset was utilized to investigate the impact of dataset-specific properties on the algorithm performance.

5.1.2 Evaluation Metrics. We use the descriptions of query workflows in the datasets as sample queries, which are derived from actual users, thus closely resembling real scenarios. Following [8], we evaluate the performance of **matching degree computation** using *Correctness* and *Completeness* on the first subset of both datasets. Additionally, we assess the **recommendation** performance using *Precision* and *Recall* on the second subset of the myExperiment dataset.

A. Correctness and Completeness: Using these two metrics, we aim to compare the algorithms' matching degree-based rankings against the experts' rankings. For each sample query, we would like to compute each comparison workflow's matching degree with the query and produce a new ranking list of comparison workflows sorted in descending order. If in both rankings the element-pair are not tied [6] and their order is the same, the pair's order is called *concordant*. If their orders differ, the pair is *discordant*. *Correctness* measures the correlation between the algorithm ranking and the expert ranking, and *Completeness* measures the completion of the algorithm ranking relative to the expert ranking:

$$Correctness = \frac{\#concordant - \#discordant}{\#concordant + \#discordant} \tag{5}$$

$$Completeness = \frac{\#concordant + \#discordant}{\#pairs\_ranked\_by\_experts} \tag{6}$$

where $\#pairs\_ranked\_by\_experts$ denotes the number of ranked element-pairs that are not tied in the expert ranking.

B. Precision and Recall: On the second subset of the myExperiment dataset, we recommend top-k workflows from the candidate list for each query and evaluate the performance by:

$$Precision@k = \frac{\sum_i^k match(sw_i)}{k} \tag{7}$$

$$Recall@k = \frac{\sum_i^k match(sw_i)}{\#Match} \tag{8}$$

where $1 \leq k \leq 10$, $match(sw_i) \in \{0,1\}$ indicates the matching status of i_{th} workflow in the recommendation list, and $\#Match$ denotes the total number of matched workflows in the candidate list. Since the expert ratings for whether a workflow is considered a match are quaternary, we consider different matching thresholds: *well-matched* or *matched*. For example, when the threshold is *matched*, only workflows with a rating of *well-matched* or *matched* are considered matches. Moreover, it is difficult to adopt rank-related metrics because expert ratings are discrete while algorithm ratings are continuous in this work.

5.1.3 Implementations. In our experiments, we employ the GPT-3.5-turbo and GPT-4 as the main LLMs, accessed through the OpenAI API[3]. To ensure more stable outputs from LLMs, we set *temperature* to 0. The number of few-shot exemplars, t_1, t_2, are set to 8 and 4 as suggested in the paper [15]. Figure 3 shows the exemplary prompts in two stages. Additional prompts and the source code of PGM can be found at https://github.com/t-harden/PGM. Moreover, $\alpha, \beta, \gamma, \delta, \varepsilon, \xi$ are set to 0.178, 0.211, 0.118, 0.113, 0.171, 0.209, respectively.

Furthermore, we compare four state-of-the-art baselines without using LLMs: (1) Description-based Method (**DM**), which recommends workflows based on the similarity between user queries and workflow descriptions using TF-IDF model [6]. (2) Activity-based Method (**AM**), an extension of DM that incorporates activity names from workflows in the similarity calculation [1]. (3) Workflow Embedding-based Method (**WFER**), which employs the SDNE graph

---

[3] https://platform.openai.com/.

embedding model to represent workflows based on their textual descriptions, retrieving workflows with high vector similarity [9]. (4) Heterogeneous Information Network-based Method (**HDSWR**), which represents workflows and their objects as a heterogeneous information network (HIN) graph and utilizes metapath-based similarity algorithms for recommendation [18]. The statistical significance between them and our approach is tested using a Wilcoxon signed-rank test [25].

5.2 Main Results

5.2.1 Evaluation of Matching Degree Computation. Figure 4 shows the mean correctness and completeness over all query workflows by different methods on the first subset of both datasets. Here are the key findings from our analysis:

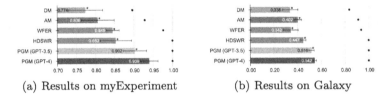

(a) Results on myExperiment   (b) Results on Galaxy

Fig. 4. The overall ranking performance on two datasets. Mean correctness (bars) with standard deviation (errorbars), and mean completeness (black spots) for algorithms against expert ratings. Numerical values denote mean correctness. * denotes statistical significance ($p < 0.05$) between the comparative method and PGM (GPT-4).

(1) Experimental results suggest that PGM achieves state-of-the-art ranking performance in matching degree computation with statistical significance on both datasets. With the benefits of LLMs' exceptional planning and reasoning abilities, PGM (GPT-3.5) outperforms the strongest competitor, HDSWR, by 5.7% and 15.4% w.r.t Correctness metric on two datasets. When employing GPT-4, PGM gains an additional 4.1% and 5.0% improvement.

(2) The decrease in correctness observed for all algorithms on the Galaxy dataset can be attributed to the limited availability of textual information, such as descriptions, in Galaxy workflows. This limitation hinders the extraction and matching of semantics. However, PGM consistently achieves a mean completeness of 1.0, surpassing the first three baselines. This emphasizes the importance of employing more fine-grained similarity assessment methods.

5.2.2 Evaluation of Recommendation. In this part, we investigate the algorithms' recommendation performance in terms of *Precision@k* and *Recall@k* over the top-k results, considering different matching thresholds as discussed in Sect. 5.1. From Fig. 5, we can observe that:

(1) Across all thresholds and metrics, PGM is nearly superior to other comparative methods and this competitive superiority continues for different k. Particularly, PGM (GPT-4) is able to find almost all the *well-matched* workflows as the recall of that is close to 1.0 when $k \geq 8$. The results verify that the plan-guided approach enables accurate understanding and logical decomposition of complex user intents, thereby facilitating effective workflow recommendation.

(2) In general, pure text-based methods (DM and AM) underperform those considering structural features (other four). Although DM and AM yield relatively comparable results to WFER and HDSWR for the *matched* threshold, they perform much worse than PGM when looking for *well-matched* workflows. This is because structural information, such as activity dependencies, is implicitly captured through the specification generation guided by the plan. This additional knowledge enhances the recommendation of top matched workflows, complementing the explicit textual features.

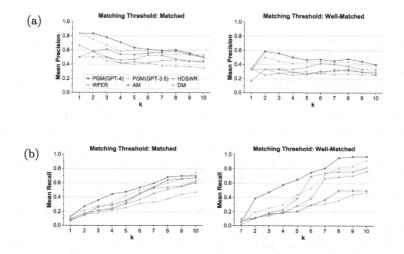

Fig. 5. The overall recommendation performance on the myExperiment dataset.

5.3 Ablation Study

We conduct ablation studies to examine the contributions of the main stages or mechanisms in the framework. The following variants are evaluated:

- **PGM-Light.** We merge the generation of plans and specifications into one stage in this variant and use the almost same few-shot examples of spec-generation prompting as in PGM's Stage II.
- **PGM\Plan.** We remove the planning mechanism from PGM and instead use a few-shot prompting to trigger LLMs to directly generate a structured specification from user queries ($\alpha = 0.217, \beta = 0.288, \gamma = 0.142, \delta = 0.138, \varepsilon = 0.215$).

- **PGM\Spec.** We remove the specification generation stage from PGM and utilize the generated plans and user queries to perform matching degree computation ($\beta = 0.557, \xi = 0.443$).

Table 1. Ablation studies on main stages/mechanisms of our approach. \ denotes the removing operation. "Cor", "Com", "Pre" and "Rec" represent mean Correctness, Completeness, Precision and Recall. All methods are equipped with GPT-4. * denotes statistical significance ($p < 0.05$) between the variant and PGM.

Method	Cor	Com	Pre@5	Rec@5	Pre@10	Rec@10	Avg. Δ
PGM	**0.939**	**1.000**	**0.467**	**0.648**	**0.400**	**0.972**	-
PGM-Light	0.912_*	1.000	0.437_*	0.597_*	0.381_*	0.936_*	4.3%↓
PGM\Plan	0.863_*	1.000	0.372_*	0.402_*	0.342_*	0.816_*	16.2%↓
PGM\Spec	0.808_*	0.967	0.311_*	0.295_*	0.274_*	0.498_*	30.9%↓

The mean results on two subsets of the myExperiment dataset, using the *well-matched* threshold, are reported in Table 1.

(1) It can be seen that PGM-Light is slightly inferior to PGM. We speculate that this may be attributed to the reduced number of few-shot exemplars for planning in PGM-Light, which could result in lower-quality of devised plans and further impact the specification generation. Nevertheless, this one-stage generation approach can save more time and resources in demonstration construction and model inferring. Thus, PGM-Light constitutes a trade-off between saved resources and dropping performance.

(2) Note that removing planning mechanism causes severe performance degradation, with an average decrease of [8.1%, 20.3%, 38.0%] in terms of Correctness, Precision@5 and Recall@5 metrics, respectively. These noticeable differences provide compelling evidence that LLMs-aided planning plays a vital role in understanding user intents and aligning them with workflow processes by abstracting step-by-step instructions.

(3) Among the three variants, leaving out specification generation stage leads to the most pronounced performance drop. This is due to the absence of extracting fine-grained and structured information that is mixed within the complex queries, which increases the risk of overlooking critical elements.

5.4   Robustness Analysis

In this part, we analyze the robustness of planning mechanism by examining performance under different prompt configurations using GPT-4, *well-matched* threshold and the myExperiment dataset.

Table 2. Robustness results for different annotators and different order of exemplars.

	Cor	Com	Pre@5	Rec@5
PGM(annotator A)	$0.94_{\pm0.02}$	$1.00_{\pm0.00}$	$0.47_{\pm0.03}$	$0.65_{\pm0.03}$
different annotator B	$0.93_{\pm0.02}$	$1.00_{\pm0.00}$	$0.45_{\pm0.02}$	$0.63_{\pm0.01}$
different annotator C	$0.95_{\pm0.04}$	$1.00_{\pm0.00}$	$0.47_{\pm0.05}$	$0.66_{\pm0.05}$

* Standard deviation shown is for different order of exemplars, with five different random seeds.

• **Different annotators.** We first investigate robustness to three different annotators. In addition to the results above, which use planning prompting written by an annotator A, two other experts (annotators B and C) independently wrote plans for the same few-shot exemplars. Table 2 showcases no notable difference among three annotations, which implies that the success of the planning mechanism is not dependent on a specific linguistic style.

• **Different order of exemplars.** Following [15], we analyze the standard deviation of performance when considering different exemplar orders in the prompt. The results in Table 2 show relatively small standard deviations in all cases, indicating that the order of prompts does not significantly affect the performance.

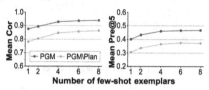

Fig. 6. Robustness results for different number of exemplars.

• **Different number of exemplars.** From Fig. 6, we also find that the improvement of planning prompting over direct spec-generation prompting remains consistent when varying the number of few-shot exemplars in the prompt. This again confirms the robustness and effectiveness of the planning mechanism.

5.5   Case Study

To further validate the effectiveness of our approach, we conduct case studies with qualitative analysis. Figure 7 illustrates the recommendation process and results for the user query depicted in Fig. 2 when the threshold is *well-matched*. PGM generates a four-step plan to guide the specification generation, computes the matching degree of candidates, and recommends the top-k workflows.

Note that the query in this case is derived from the description of the query workflow with id *202* in the myExperiment dataset. Hence, the golden standard workflow sw_{202} is not included in the final recommendation list. However, we still compute the matching degree between the query and sw_{202}, which yields a result of 0.871 (Rank #0) that is higher than all the other candidates. This confirms the correctness of our computation method. Moreover, among the top-3 workflows recommended by PGM, two are rated as *well-matched* by experts, and one is rated as *matched*. These workflows can fulfill user requirements and provide

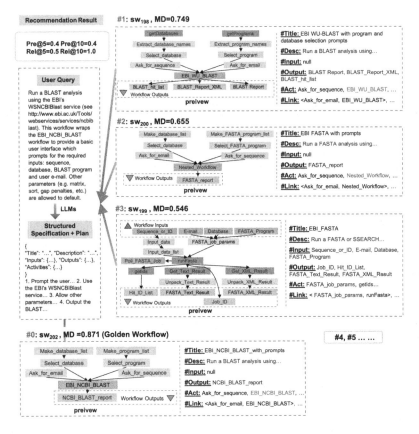

Fig. 7. Case study on the recommendation of PGM (GPT-4) for the user query in Fig. 2. Please refer to the corresponding website, similar to sw_{233} in Fig. 1, for complete information of workflow attributes that are not shown here due to space constraints.

valuable references for reuse and repurposing. For example, as shown in the work-flow cards in Fig. 7, the textual information and graph structure of recommended sw_{198} (Rank #1), sw_{200} (Rank #2) and the golden workflow sw_{202} are generally identical, with the main difference being the substitution of individual activities, such as *EBI_WU_BLAST*, *Nested_Workflow* and *EBI_NCBI_BLAST*, depending on user needs. To sum up, our LLMs-based approach demonstrates its powerful capability in comprehending and addressing intricate queries, thereby providing users with appropriate and reliable workflows.

6   Limitations and Discussions

As the pioneering work exploring the utilization of LLMs in the scientific work-flow domain, PGM has introduced a novel paradigm for workflow recommenda-tion. However, it is important to acknowledge that there are still some limitations and areas for improvement in our approach: **1)** Although the results in Sect. 5.4 are relatively robust to the prompt for planning, the generated plans may not always be optimal because the performance of LLMs could be unpredictable and unstable. Addressing the challenge of reducing uncertainties and enabling robust learning of plan patterns from prompts is an important area for further investigation. **2)** General-purpose LLMs, such as the GPT series used in PGM, have limitations in learning domain-specific semantics due to their training data. There is significant potential for enhancing the performance of PGM by fine-tuning these general LLMs using domain-specific workflow data in future work. **3)** Plan-aided recommendation methods are not exclusive to scientific workflows. We believe that it is valuable and promising to explore the application of the planning mechanism with LLMs in other process-oriented service compositions, such as business processes and ML/AI workflows.

7   Conclusion

In this paper, we put forward PGM, a three-stage scientific workflow recommendation method based on LLMs, to address users' text queries. Leveraging the inherent capabilities of LLMs in comprehension and reasoning, PGM effectively handles complex problems by first parsing the query and devising a plan. Subsequently, PGM generates a structured specification of the intended workflow through few-shot prompting, guided by the plan. Finally, PGM computes the matching degree between the query and candidate workflows using the plan and specification, enabling recommendation. The core of PGM lies in LLMs-aided planning mechanism, which facilitates a deep understanding of user intents and provides guidance for subsequent generation and matching. Experimental results validate the superior performance of PGM compared to alternative methods. Furthermore, through extensive ablation studies, robustness analysis and case studies, we provide compelling evidence of the effectiveness of our approach.

Acknowledgements. This work is supported by China National Science Foundation (No. 62072301) and the Program of Technology Innovation of the Science and Technology Commission of Shanghai Municipality (No. 21511104700).

References

1. Djaffardjy, M., et al.: Developing and reusing bioinformatics data analysis pipelines using scientific workflow systems. Comput. Struct. Biotechnol. J. (2023)
2. Gu, Y., Cao, J., Qian, S., Zhu, N., Guan, W.: MANSOR: a module alignment method based on neighbor information for scientific workflow. Concurrency Comput. Pract. Exp., e7736 (2023)
3. De Roure, D., Goble, C., Stevens, R.: The design and realisation of the myExperiment Virtual Research Environment for social sharing of workflows. Futur. Gener. Comput. Syst. **25**(5), 561–567 (2009)
4. Blanchi, C., Gebre, B., Wittenburg, P.: Canonical workflow for machine learning tasks. Data Intell. **4**(2), 173–185 (2022)

5. da Silva, R.F., Pottier, L., Coleman, T., Deelman, E., Casanova, H.: WorkflowHub: community framework for enabling scientific workflow research and development. In: 2020 IEEE/ACM Workflows in Support of Large-Scale Science (WORKS), pp. 49–56. IEEE (2020)

6. Starlinger, J.: Similarity measures for scientific workflows. Ph.D. thesis, Humboldt-Universität zu Berlin, Mathematisch-Naturwissenschaftliche Fakultät (2016). https://doi.org/10.18452/17406

7. Zhou, Z., Wen, J., Wang, Y., Xue, X., Hung, P.C., Nguyen, L.D.: Topic-based crossing-workflow fragment discovery. Futur. Gener. Comput. Syst. **112**, 1141–1155 (2020)

8. Starlinger, J., Brancotte, B., Cohen-Boulakia, S., Leser, U.: Similarity search for scientific workflows. Proc. VLDB Endowment (PVLDB) **7**(12), 1143–1154 (2014)

9. Yu, X., Wu, W., Liao, X.: Workflow recommendation based on graph embedding. In: 2020 IEEE World Congress on Services (SERVICES), pp. 89–94. IEEE (2020)

10. Gu, Y., Cao, J., Qian, S., Guan, W.: SWORTS: a scientific workflow retrieval approach by learning textual and structural semantics. IEEE Trans. Serv. Comput. (2023)

11. Wang, L., et al.: Plan-and-solve prompting: improving zero-shot chain-of-thought reasoning by large language models. arXiv preprint arXiv:2305.04091 (2023)

12. Jiang, X., Dong, Y., Wang, L., Shang, Q., Li, G.: Self-planning code generation with large language model. arXiv preprint arXiv:2303.06689 (2023)

13. Yao, Y., Li, Z., Zhao, H.: Beyond chain-of-thought, effective graph-of-thought reasoning in large language models. arXiv preprint arXiv:2305.16582 (2023)

14. Kojima, T., Gu, S.S., Reid, M., Matsuo, Y., Iwasawa, Y.: Large language models are zero-shot reasoners. arXiv preprint arXiv:2205.11916 (2022)

15. Wei, J., et al.: Chain of thought prompting elicits reasoning in large language models. arXiv preprint arXiv:2201.11903 (2022)

16. Wang, Z., Cai, S., Liu, A., Ma, X., Liang, Y.: Describe, explain, plan and select: interactive planning with large language models enables open-world multi-task agents. arXiv preprint arXiv:2302.01560 (2023)

17. Pallagani, V., et al.: Understanding the capabilities of large language models for automated planning. arXiv preprint arXiv:2305.16151 (2023)

18. Wen, Y., Hou, J., Yuan, Z., Zhou, D.: Heterogeneous information network-based scientific workflow recommendation for complex applications. Complexity **2020** (2020)

19. Zhou, Z., Cheng, Z., Zhang, L.J., Gaaloul, W., Ning, K.: Scientific workflow clustering and recommendation leveraging layer hierarchical analysis. IEEE Trans. Serv. Comput. **11**(1), 169–183 (2016)

20. Lu, P., et al.: Chameleon: plug-and-play compositional reasoning with large language models. arXiv preprint arXiv:2304.09842 (2023)

21. OpenAI: GPT-4 Technical report (2023)

22. Yasunaga, M., Leskovec, J., Liang, P.: LinkBERT: pretraining language models with document links. arXiv preprint arXiv:2203.15827 (2022)

23. Kuhn, H.W.: The Hungarian method for the assignment problem. Nav. Res. Logist. Q. **2**(1–2), 83–97 (1955)

24. Li, H.: Research progress on evaluation methods and factors influencing shale brittleness: a review. Energy Rep. **8**, 4344–4358 (2022)

25. Woolson, R.F.: Wilcoxon signed-rank test. Wiley Encycl. Clin. Trials, 1–3 (2007)

Predicting Effect and Cost of Microservice System Evolution Using Graph Neural Network

Xiang He[✉], Zihao Shao, Teng Wang, Haomai Shi, Yin Chen,
and Zhongjie Wang

Faculty of Computing, Harbin Institute of Technology, Harbin, China
{hexiang,chenyin,rainy}@hit.edu.cn

Abstract. With the increasing prevalence of microservice technology, the architectural flexibility and scalability of software systems have witnessed notable advancements. However, this progress has also brought about a challenge in meeting the frequent changes in user requirements, thereby adversely affecting the quality of the system. It is crucial for microservice systems to undergo evolution through the modification of system configurations to adapt to changing requirements, and various methods for system evolution have been proposed. However, the evolution schemes generated by these methods vary in terms of the degree of improvement in quality and the cost required for evolution, such as time and money, i.e., different evolution effect and evolution cost. Considering the above, it is necessary to predict effect and cost before applying these schemes to real systems. Existing physical methods possess drawbacks such as high expenses and time-consuming setup procedures. Conversely, simulation methods, which are based on mathematical models, necessitate certain simplifications, resulting in disparities between the outcomes and the actual results. To overcome these challenges, this paper introduces a prediction method for microservice system evolution. By employing Graph Neural Network techniques to learn from historical data, this method enables precise prediction of the effects and costs associated with various microservice evolution schemes. And based on the above algorithm, an online prediction system is implemented, independent of the microservice system for long-term prediction. Experimental results validate the accuracy and robustness of the proposed prediction method.

Keywords: Microservice system · Evolution Effect · Evolution Cost · Prediction

1 Introduction

With the rapid growth of the digital economy, software services have become crucial infrastructures. Cloud-native technologies, particularly microservices, have gained prominence due to their ability to handle complex requirements,

F. Monti et al. (Eds.): ICSOC 2023, LNCS 14419, pp. 103–118, 2023.
https://doi.org/10.1007/978-3-031-48421-6_8

diverse technologies, and high concurrency [13]. The decentralized and deconcentrated nature of microservices architecture enhances scalability and flexibility but also introduces increased system complexity. However, the frequent changes in microservice system requirements pose challenges for meeting system demands and can lead to performance degradation. Therefore, it is essential to adapt the system to changing requirements during runtime, known as microservice system evolution, while ensuring maintainability, scalability, and reliability.

There are different methods for microservice system evolution to improve performance and scalability. These methods vary in terms of the quality improvement they provide and the cost they incur, known as the evolution effect and evolution cost, respectively. Evolution methods like service placement and offloading change how microservices are deployed to meet new requirements, affecting the resource cost of the system and other evolution effects such as response time.

In order to assist developers in comprehending microservice system evolution, managing and maintaining the system, it is imperative to measure the effects and costs of microservice evolution, such as average response time, energy consumption, resources required for deployment. Figure 1 illustrates the importance of these measurements, as they provide valuable insights for developers to make informed decisions and achieve better outcomes in the evolution process of microservice systems.

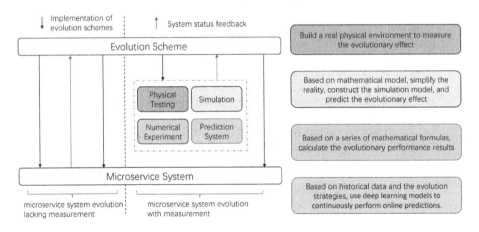

Fig. 1. Comparison of Various Measurement Methods

As shown in Figure 1, the existing methods for evaluating the evolution effect and cost include physical testing, simulation, and numerical experiment methods [1,2,17], which are evaluated prior to the implementation of the evolution scheme. Physical testing involves conducting tests in a real hardware environment to verify system performance and indicators. While it provides a realistic simulation of the production environment, it has drawbacks such as high cost, time consumption, and setup difficulties. Simulation testing uses tools to mimic system behavior on computers, while numerical experiments rely on mathematical equations to calculate results without simulations or real systems. Both methods allow for repeated testing without affecting the production environment, but their accuracy in representing reality is limited due to simplifications in modeling.

To overcome the constraints of existing evaluation methods and to achieve more accurate outcomes, this study introduces a novel prediction approach utilizing Graph Neural Network (GNN). Our goal is to develop an online prediction system for long-term evolution forecasting in microservice systems. By leveraging historical data, our method enables more precise estimation of the impact and cost of microservice evolution. The following major contributions have been achieved:

1. Drawing from the definitions of evolution effect and cost, this paper introduces a prediction method that is applicable to diverse evolution metrics in microservice systems. Leveraging Deep Learning, the proposed method comprises two steps: feature dimensionality reduction for single instance and overall microservice system prediction based on GNN.
2. Based on the proposed prediction method, this paper implements a online prediction system that is focused on evolution effect and evolution cost. The prediction system operates independently of the running microservice system, collects historical logs online to predict the evolution effect and cost of the microservice system and can adapt to microservice collection additions and deletions during long-term operation.
3. To validate the effectiveness of the proposed prediction method and system, this paper conducts multiple experiments using an open-source service collection in a real physical environment. The experimental results obtained from these experiments showcase the accuracy and reliability of the prediction method and system.

The remainder of this paper is structured as follows. Section 2 provides a summary of the relevant literature. Section 3 elaborates on the model of the microservice system. Section 4 concentrates on the proposed prediction method and prediction system. Section 5 outlines the experiments conducted in detail. Finally, Sect. 6 concludes the paper and discusses potential future work.

2   Related Work

Existing studies provide a comprehensive investigation into the performance prediction of microservice systems and serve as a valuable source of inspiration for this paper. Service system evolution [16] refers to the continuous change and development of a service system over time in response to changing business needs, technological advancements. In a microservice system, the MAPE-K framework [8] can be employed to achieve self-adaptation, which enables the system to automatically adjust its configuration and behavior based on real-time system status and environmental changes, thus in turn leading to changes in evolution effects and costs.

There are many studies on measures of evolution effects and costs [1,2,4,11, 17] nowadays. The traditional simulation tool, CloudSim [2], is widely utilized in the simulation of large-scale cloud computing systems due to its high scalability. Mahmud et al. [11] proposed a simulation of applications relied on the simulation of energy consumption in CloudSim 3.0 to model the entire fog computing infrastructure environment. In the numerical experiment method, Deng [4] et al. discussed the problem of realizing optimal application deployment in a resource-constrained distributed edge environment and mathematically modeled the average response time of the environment as the optimization goal. Xiang [17] and others discussed the allocation of computing resources and traffic scheduling in the edge computing environment. The article defined the system model and the corresponding response time in detail. The physical method is limited by the high cost and the difficulty of setting up the physical environment. Simulation and numerical methods may deviate from reality to some extent due to the simplification of multiple factors that exist in reality.

Furthermore, there have been some studies conducted on QoS prediction [3,6,12,15]. Wang et al. [15] proposed a deep learning-based QoS prediction method in mobile edge computing. Luo et al. [10] introduced a tensor-based non-negative latent factor decomposition method for solving the temporal pattern problem in quality of service prediction. The method improves the accuracy and scalability of QoS prediction by modeling the time-dependent effects. Zou et al. [18] introduces a method called NDMF for solving the sparse and missing data problem in quality of service prediction. The method improves the accuracy and robustness of QoS prediction by integrating neighborhood information and depth matrix decomposition. Courageux-Sudan et al. [3] proposed a simulation-based approach to automatically predict the performance of microservice applications. However, these studies primarily emphasize the interaction between services, service requests, and services, while overlooking the impact of external evolution schemes.

3   Microservice System Evolution Modeling

This section outlines the modeling of the problem in the context of microservice systems, system evolution methods, and system evolution metrics.

3.1   Microservice System

In this paper, MSS can be represented as $MSS =< U, G(V, E), MS >$. They are described separately below.

Definition 1 (Microservice). *There is a set of microservices in a microservices system, defined as $MS = \{ms_1, ms_2, ...\}$. A microservice is defined as $ms_i =< api_i, r_i >$.*

- api_i represents the set of functional interfaces provided by ms_i
- r_i represents the computational resources required by ms_i, including the CPU and memory resources.

Definition 2 (Service Instance). *Based on user requests and resources, the administrator deploys specific service instances S on $Server_i$. Each microservice instance $s^i_j \in S$ indicates that ms_j is deployed on $Server_i$. A service instance s^i_j is defined as a tuple $s^i_j =< r'_j, num_i >$.*

- r'_j denotes the computing resources allocated by the instance to $Server_i$
- num_i denotes the number of deployed instances.

Definition 3 (Server). *The microservices system is deployed on a set of servers, which is defined as $Server = \{server_1, server_2, ...\}$. A Server is defined as $server_i =< R_i, S_i >$.*

- R_i represents the computing and storage resources available on the server, including CPU and memory. It is important to note that this article does not currently consider other types of resources, hence $R_i =< CPU_i, MEMORY_i >$.
- S_i represents the set of microservice instances.

Definition 4 (Service Chain). *Service chains are utilized to delineate the interdependencies amidst microservices ms, defined as $chain_i = \{ms_i, ..., ms_j\}$.*

Circular dependencies are not considered in this paper as they are generally regarded as poor practice in microservice architectures, and in such cases, achieving microservice independence and isolation from one another is difficult.

Definition 5 (Network Topology). *The network topology among the servers is graphically depicted by a denoted graph, referred to as $G(V, E)$.*

- $V = \{Server_1, ..., Server_N\}$
- $E = \{edge_{ij}, i \neq j, 0 \leq i, j \leq |V|\}$, $edge_{ij}$ represents the data dependency between Servers due to chain.

Definition 6 (User Request). *Continuous user requests are divided into multiple time periods denoted as $U =< u_1, ..., u_t >$.*

Within these time periods, user requests are represented as $u_t = \{u^{ij}_t\}^{N,m}_{i=0,j=0}$, where u^{ij}_t represents the user requests that reach the ms_j instance on $Server_i$ at time t.

3.2   Microservice System Evolution

The system evolution acquires and analyzes runtime information from the Microservice System MSS and generates a viable evolution scheme based on the analysis. The scheme is then executed in the MSS to bring about a new state of the system.

The evolution scheme comprises a range of evolution operation. In this paper, we focus on three types of widely used and more important evolution operation. These three are the most common and are widely used in placement, offloading and other problems.

Definition 7 (Evolution Scheme). *The evolution scheme generated can be considered as a fusion of the aforementioned three types of evolution methods, namely, scheme* $=< F_d, F_u, F_t >$.

- Evolution operation of deployment plan F_d. Deployment plan $\theta = \{\theta_{ij}\}_{i=0,j=0}^{n,m}$, where θ_{ij} represents the number of ms_j deployed on $Server_i$. F_d changes the original θ to θ'.
- Evolution operation related to user requests F_u. The operation include authentication, traffic control, etc. At time point t, the microservices system efficiently and stably processes u_t by performing various operations and filtering out any that do not meet the requirements.
- Evolution operation related to request forwarding F_t. This action makes changes to the current system's routing and load balancing policies. Different policies correspond to different user distributions, which in turn affect the performance of the whole system.

3.3   Evolution Metrics

To ensure the scalability and versatility of our method and system, we have selected four particularly valuable and widely utilized metrics. These encompass two types of effect metrics e: average response time and throughput rate, as well as two cost metrics c: CPU requirements for deployment and MEMORY resources. While our method is not limited to a specific metric but can be applied to a range of effect and cost metrics.

Average Response Time. Response time refers to the cumulative duration between the user's request transmission and the receipt of a corresponding response. It is typically quantified in milliseconds (ms) and represents the mean duration expended on all requests.

Throughput Rate. Throughput rate pertains to the efficiency of a service in processing requests and is computed as the ratio of the total number of processed requests to the total processing time..

CPU and Memory. Microservices rely on CPU and memory resources during runtime to effectively carry out their tasks. CPU resources are used to process computational tasks and execute code and algorithms, while memory resources are used to store data and temporary computational results.

4   Proposed Method

Our proposed method consists of a prediction algorithm and a prediction system. In which this paper introduces a GNN-based *predicitonmethod* for predicting the evolution effects and costs, which is utilized to develop a comprehensive *predictionsystem* that can be integrated into existing microservices systems.

4.1   Prediction Algorithm

As illustrated in Fig. 2, the prediction algorithm employed in this study can be delineated into two main components: feature reduction for an individual instance and graph neural network (GNN) prediction for the comprehensive microservice system. The features f of a single instance are amalgamated with MSS and *scheme*, serving as the input for the GNN model. Subsequently, the GNN model predicts the evolution $effect$ and $cost$ of the overall microservice system.

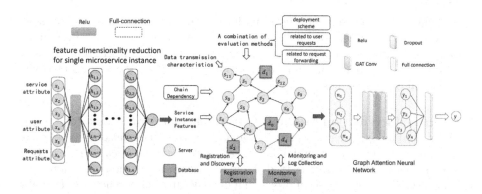

Fig. 2. Proposed Prediction Algorithm

Feature Dimensionality Reduction for Single Microservice Instance. For $MS = \{ms_1, ms_2, ...\}$, where different ms_i correspond to different features f_i, and the same ms_i will have multiple feature choices f_i^j under different $metrics_j$. Thus the feature $F = \{f_1, f_2, ...\}$ of MS varies significantly among different f_i, and the overall feature space is particularly large. So it is challenging to identify a feature engineering approach that is applicable to all types of microservices. At the same time, in a large collection of microservices MS, it is not a wise choice to input all the features of all services into the deep model, both in terms of time, resources and prediction effectiveness. Therefore, the prediction method proposed in this paper initially conducts feature dimensionality reduction on a single microservice instance. Reducing the original $m-dimension$ features to $m-n$ dimension features reduces the original complexity $O(m)$ to $O'(m) + O(m-n)$ at a smaller cost, where the complexity $O'(m)$ of the feature reduction work is much smaller than the complexity $O(m-n)$ of the graph neural network.

This approach is fundamentally equivalent to the QoS prediction of a single microservice instance, and it maps various microservice feature types from the original space to the same new feature space to ensure the task independence of node features.

Based on existing literature [6,15] and microservice modeling, selected following features f. These features contain a rich amount of information and can provide better predictive power for the target variables.

- Resource allocation: The performance of the program is based on the resources it occupies. $r = < Cpu, Memory >$, here this article uses the CPU and Memory resources required for the deployment
- Bandwidth: Indicates the available bandwidth of the network connection.
- Service attributes: Microservice performance is related to its own service attributes. Different features can be used for each type of microservice to achieve better prediction results.

As shown on the left in Fig. 2, multilayer perceptron (MLP) is utilized to reduce feature dimensionality and predict relevant indicators for individual instances. Comprised of interconnected nodes or neurons, MLP represents a nonlinear mapping between input and output vectors. Nodes are connected via weights and output signals.

GNN-Based Prediction Method. Considering that MSS consists of a series of distributed independent $Servers$ as well as MS while the relationship between services in MSS exhibits complex nonlinear characteristics, it can be viewed as a graph structure. In contrast to traditional deep learning methods, graph neural networks (GNNs) are capable of processing unstructured data in network formats and disseminating information and parameter updates between nodes. Among them GAT stands out by incorporating an attention mechanism to learn the weight distribution of neighboring nodes. It also excels in tasks by applying the message passing mechanism to dynamic graphs. As such, this paper leverages the GAT [14] approach to predict overall performance metrics.

As depicted in Fig. 2, the prediction process consists of three steps. Firstly, the initial features of microservices, denoted as f_i, are dimensionally reduced to obtain f'_i. Secondly, the features of a single instance, f'_i, along with the information of MS, $Servers$, and three evolution operations (F_d, F_t, F_u), are combined to construct a graph-structured data denoted as $G(V, E)$. Finally, the graph G is fed into the GAT to obtain the final prediction result.

The prediction model presented in this paper employs a two-layer GAT architecture, integrating the relu activation function and a dropout layer. It is crucial to strike a balance in the depth of GAT layers as excessively deep networks can adversely impact training stability. The dropout layer is incorporated to mitigate overfitting in the neural network. Specifically, the two-layer GAT network is responsible for node-level prediction, yielding a node feature vector obtained through weighted aggregation. In order to aggregate the node features into the entire graph's features, a fully connected layer is utilized.

4.2 Prediction System

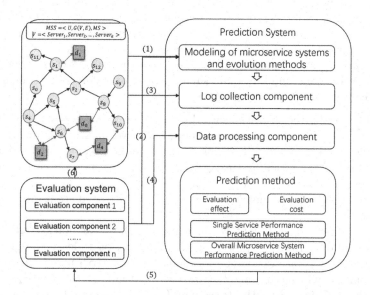

Fig. 3. Prediction System

Predictive system P offers support for various functions, including information collection, log collection, and data processing within MSS. Its purpose is to establish a connection between the MSS, evolution methods, and prediction algorithms. By decoupling the predictive system from the original MSS, it becomes capable of operating independently. Furthermore, it can be adaptively updated to accommodate long-running microservice systems that undergo frequent evolution.

As depicted in Fig. 3, prediction system P can be partitioned into six distinct steps that are involved in the interaction with MSS and the evolution methods:

(1) MSS is required to transmit certain properties to P, which include MSS, interface information of all ms, and the intricate invocation relationship between ms, among other things. Armed with this information, the prediction system can engage in modeling activities pertaining to MSS.

(2) P necessitates specific evolution operations, which may include, but are not limited to, instance deployment plan, routing strategy, load balancing strategy, and the like.

(3) P necessitate the log output of MSS over a period of time denoted by T. Present-day microservice systems are predominantly based on container technologies like K8s and docker. Drawing upon them, a diverse array of performance metrics can be extracted from MSS, which forms the foundation of the predictive methodology expounded in this paper.

(4) The data processing component of P filters and processes raw log information into the data format that is requisite for the prediction methodology.

(5) Drawing upon the logs from the past time period T, the prediction capability is acquired from the data by amalgamating the information pertaining to MSS and the evolution scheme. Consequently, the evolution effect and cost within t are predicted. This iterative process, depicted in equations (4) and (5), continues until a superior evolution scheme is attained.

(6) Refining evolution methods for implementation on real-world MSS can result in significant time and economic savings, prevent unforeseen incidents, and enhance the overall quality of MSS.

Simultaneously, the operation of a long-running MSS is susceptible to significant changes, including hardware upgrades, server migrations, failures, and microservice version updates. These changes can impact the performance of individual microservices, which, in turn, affects the overall evolution performance of the system. Consequently, existing prediction models must be retrained to reflect the updated performance metrics and generate precise predictions about future performance.

In the long-term operation of MSS, at time T_i, the prediction system P leverages historical data from the preceding $T_i - T_{i-k}$ period to learn the prediction capabilities and forecast various performance metrics MSS under the influence of the evolution scheme at time T_i. Similarly, at the next moment T_{i+1}, based on the historical data from the preceding $T_i - T_{i-k+1}$ period, the system predicts the metrics at T_{i+1}. Here, k represents the parameter set by the forecasting system, which can be flexibly adjusted based on the actual scenario.

During the initial phase of MSS, when there is a lack of data required for training, a cold start phase occurs. To address this issue during phase T_0, a warm-up mechanism can be employed. The warm-up mechanism initializes the service by simulating traffic and utilizing virtual users. During this warm-up period, diverse performance metrics of the service, such as response time, throughput, and error rate, are recorded to generate data for the prediction system.

5   Experiment and Analysis

In this section, experiments were conducted in a real-world environment to demonstrate the prediction system P's accuracy and reliability. Additionally, the experiment simulated typical microservice addition and deletion scenarios, and the results indicate that the prediction system P can maintain a relatively good health under such conditions.

5.1 Experimental Setup

Experimental Environment and Metrics. In this paper, experiments were conducted on a server cluster comprising five servers running the Linux operating system, including a master node and four work nodes. The version of Kubernetes (K8s) used was 1.17, and the version of Docker was 17.03.

The microservice set utilized in the experiment is the open-source benchmark microservice system RescureService [7], which consists of over 20 services. The user simulation was implemented using the Python thread pool, where a specific type of user input was manually designed, and the number of users was generated based on mathematical distribution. This paper conducted nearly one hundred hours of experiments under different evolution methods and user distributions, resulting in the collection of almost 8000 time periods of data. Relevant information was then extracted from the data to organize the relevant experiments.

In this paper, we have selected RMSE (Root Mean Squared Error), MAE (Mean Absolute Error), and Spearman's correlation coefficient as the evolution indicators for the experiment. RMSE is a commonly used indicator in regression analysis to evaluate the accuracy of the prediction model. MAE measures the mean absolute difference between the actual and predicted values in a regression analysis.

The significance test of Spearman's correlation coefficient is employed to assess the statistical significance of the correlation between two variables. Its purpose is to verify whether our predicted results align with the observed trends in the actual results. The significance level, typically set at 0.05, serves as a critical threshold to determine the significance of the correlation. If the resulting p-value is below 0.05, it indicates a significant correlation between our predicted results and the actual results.

Experimental Strategy. To evaluate the evolution of prediction effectiveness, this paper compares four baseline methods.

- Math-Method [4]: A mathematical modeling-based approach is employed to calculate response time and throughput rate. Regarding the determination of resource requirements for deployment, they are calculated based on the specific configuration at the time of deployment.
- Single-Step: The single-step instance prediction step is removed, and all features are input into the GNN model without dimensionality reduction mapping.
- GCN [9]: The GNN method in the prediction algorithm chooses the GCN model instead of the GAT model.
- GraphSage [5]: As above, choose the GraphSage model.

To enhance the reliability of the experimental outcomes and minimize errors, we conducted three experiments for each experimental method. Each experiment involved a distinct combination of evolution methods and user distributions, leading to varying evolution effects and costs. We collected three distinct datasets by conducting experiments in physical environments based on different user distributions and evolution methods. Each set of experiments corresponded to a different time period $[1,2,\ldots,t_0,t_0+1,\ldots,t_0+t_1]$. We trained the prediction model using past data from 1-t_0, subsequently generating predictions for MSS from t_0 to t_1. The obtained results, denoted as y', for the time period from t_0 to t_0+t_1, are compared against the ground truth results y. Various indicators, including MAE, RMSE, and correlation coefficients, are then calculated to assess the performance of the predictions.

Table 1. Experimental Results for Evolution Effects

evolution Effect		Average Response Time			Throughput Rate		
		Exp.1	Exp.2	Exp.3	Exp.1	Exp.2	Exp.3
RMSE	Our	**83.07**	**67.18**	**75.55**	**18.61**	**19.79**	**18.54**
	Math-Method	123.01	104.14	108.9	27.19	26.10	26.54
	Single-Step	92.07	71.93	76.37	19.47	22.25	20.73
	GCN	83.57	82.36	81.20	18.88	20.42	22.10
	GraphSage	84.4475	75.8141	80.5187	19.2119	21.0231	19.9201
MAE	Our	**60.82**	**48.82**	**56.69**	**14.27**	**14.57**	**12.75**
	Math-Method	85.84	75.51	81.15	21.31	20.91	20.66
	Single-Step	70.48	52.68	57.50	14.43	15.97	15.11
	GCN	63.34	60.67	62.43	14.78	15.09	16.27
	GraphSage	63.08	55.07	62.17	15.55	15.74	14.85
Spearman	Our	4.84e-13	**4.60e-17**	**5.00e-09**	5.10e-16	**8.93e-25**	**3.54e-33**
	Math-Method	0.23	0.33	0.25	0.1528	0.17	0.1865
	Single-Step	9.94e-07	6.77e-16	2.47e-08	2.24e-15	1.46e-12	1.46e-09
	GCN	**5.57e-15**	2.56e-08	1.60e-06	2.64e-16	7.01e-14	3.95e-11
	GraphSage	1.30e-14	4.63e-11	7.17e-06	**4.44e-18**	1.52e-13	9.61e-16

Meanwhile, with respect to the prediction of microservices evolution, this study conducts simulations on the addition and deletion of diverse microservices, and compares the results with prior experimental findings. Specifically, we devise four comparative experiments involving the absence of certain services [7], namely: a singular material management service (Management 1), a singular sensor service (Sensor), a singular image recognition service (Image), and two material management classes (Management 2). Among them, Management1, 2 are mainly for interaction with the database, Sensor is mainly for request sending, and Image is a computationally intensive service. They better represent the different kinds of microservices.

5.2   Experiments for Evolution Effect and Cost

The experimental outcomes on evolution effect metrics are presented in Table 1. The unit of RMSE and MAE for the average response time is in milliseconds, while the unit of throughput rate is the number of requests per second, signifying the average number of user requests processed by the microservice system in one second.

Furthermore, the experimental findings on evolution cost metrics are displayed in Table 2. The numerical unit of CPU resources required for evolution is millicore, which serves as a measure of CPU resources. In terms of the unit of memory required for evolution, Kubernetes employs the unit of memory (Memory) in bytes, and Mi (Mebi) is utilized to denote 2^{20} (1048576) bytes.

Table 2. Experimental Results of Evolution Cost

evolution Cost		CPU			Memory		
		Exp.1	Exp.2	Exp.3	Exp.1	Exp.2	Exp.3
RMSE	Our	**12.66**	**12.70**	**12.65**	22.75	**22.67**	**19.76**
	Math-Method	47.12	43.84	46.25	123.10	112.02	105.14
	Single-Step	13.12	13.15	12.98	**22.12**	25.73	24.34
	GCN	13.53	14.12	13.48	23.14	24.14	22.20
	GraphSage	12.97	13.82	11.17	24.14	25.83	20.51
MAE	Our	**9.89**	**9.70**	9.80	20.13	19.99	**16.59**
	Math-Method	35.12	31.73	34.69	112.26	102.33	85.84
	Single-Step	9.94	10.1277	**9.57**	20.17	22.11	22.70
	GCN	10.12	11.34	10.63	**14.78**	**15.09**	17.27
	GraphSage	10.13	10.29	11.17	21.19	23.93	18.12
Spearman	Our	**3.23e-17**	**1.36e-16**	**5.13e-15**	**5.27e-23**	**4.21e-19**	**5.07e-19**
	Math-Method	0.31	0.21	0.25	0.19	0.21	0.15
	Single-Step	7.42e-08	3.73e-13	2.32e-09	4.94e-17	8.71e-16	3.47e-18
	GCN	5.78e-08	5.85e-15	1.01e-07	7.37e-16	2.36e-13	6.61e-16
	GraphSage	9.14e-13	7.31e-11	3.02e-08	2.14e-14	5.31e-17	3.12e-06

Based on the aforementioned results, it is evident that our proposed method, GCN, and GraphSage, which utilize graph neural network methods, demonstrate superior performance compared to traditional mathematical approaches. These methods excel in extracting higher-level features from historical data to provide more accurate predictions. Among the various GNN methods, GAT has demonstrated superior performance. The unique attention mechanism of GAT can capture the nonlinear interactions between nodes, thereby enhancing the network's expressive ability.

Moreover, the feature dimensionality reduction for single microservice instance also improves the prediction accuracy to a certain extent. This process compresses complex features and attributes into low-dimensional vectors, facilitating better understanding and processing of the data by the prediction system.

5.3 Experiments for Microservice Additions and Deletions

During the operation of MSS_0, various scenarios may occur that go beyond the proposed evolution scheme, such as the addition, deletion, and reconfiguration of microservices, which lead to changes in graph topology of $G(V, E)$ and result in the emergence of MSS_1. Although the prediction system developed in this paper is capable of making predictions for MSS_1, during the early stage of its evolution, the system can only rely on data from MSS_0 due to the lack of new data. To assess the impact of this on our prediction performance, we conducted experiments to evaluate the effectiveness of the prediction system during this transitional phase. The experimental results for microservice additions and deletions are presented in Table 3.

As can be observed from the experimental results, the absence of microservices has varying impacts on different metrics and different microservices. The impact of the absence of different services on the same metrics is influenced by the inherent nature of the service.

Table 3. Experiments for Microservice Additions and Deletions

Microservice Missing		Evolution Effect		Evolution Cost	
		Response Time	Throughout Rate	CPU	Memory
RMSE	Management 1	101.05	20.01	12.14	22.25
	Sensor	80.12	19.13	12.05	23.15
	Image	874.56	18.73	13.56	25.35
	Management 2	105.80	20.17	13.15	24.17
MAE	Management 1	67.18	16.10	10.10	19.75
	Sensor	60.84	16.17	10.15	21.84
	Image	599.72	15.99	11.72	22.13
	Management 2	85.91	16.87	10.89	21.10
Spearman	Management 1	3.89e-16	2.10e-11	1.12e-17	1.87e-17
	Sensor	5.79e-13	1.56e-14	2.15e-15	3.70e-15
	Image	4.04e-08	7.10e-09	7.15e-08	4.04e-11
	Management 2	4.22e-11	3.42e-12	9.35e-12	7.12e-14

Through comparison with the experimental results presented in Tables 1 and 2, it is evident that even in the absence of one or two service data, the proposed prediction system can still perform performance prediction with reasonable accuracy, as indicated by the acceptable range of loss accuracy.

6   Conclusion and Future Work

This paper presents a prediction method that is applicable to various metrics pertaining to microservice system evolution. Using this method, a prediction system for microservice evolution is developed to forecast the performance of a long-running microservice system, which can guide the evolution of the system. The accuracy and robustness of the proposed prediction method and system are validated through long-term experiments conducted in a real-world environment.

Potential future research endeavors may involve optimizing the evolution scheme based on the proposed prediction approach and extending the prediction capabilities to multiple microservice systems, instead of being limited to a single system. Additionally, the experimental program aims to collaborate with companies to obtain larger-scale datasets, thereby providing more robust evidence of the benefits of deep learning methods.

Acknowledgements. Research in this paper is supported by the National Key Research and Development Program of China (2022ZD0115404) and the National Natural Science Foundation of China (62372140, 61832014, 61832004).

References

1. Aslanpour, M.S., Toosi, A.N., Taheri, J., Gaire, R.: AutoScalesim: a simulation toolkit for auto-scaling web applications in clouds. Simul. Model. Pract. Theory **108**, 102245 (2021)
2. Calheiros, R.N., Ranjan, R., Beloglazov, A., De Rose, C.A., Buyya, R.: CloudSim: a toolkit for modeling and simulation of cloud computing environments and evaluation of resource provisioning algorithms. Softw. Pract. Exp. **41**(1), 23–50 (2011)
3. Courageux-Sudan, C., Orgerie, A.C., Quinson, M.: Automated performance prediction of microservice applications using simulation. In: 2021 29th International Symposium on Modeling, Analysis, and Simulation of Computer and Telecommunication Systems (MASCOTS), pp. 1–8. IEEE (2021)
4. Deng, S., et al.: Optimal application deployment in resource constrained distributed edges. IEEE Trans. Mob. Comput. **20**(5), 1907–1923 (2020)
5. Hamilton, W., Ying, Z., Leskovec, J.: Inductive representation learning on large graphs. Adv. Neural. Inf. Process. Syst. **30**, 1–11 (2017)
6. He, X., Tu, Z., Wagner, M., Xu, X., Wang, Z.: Online deployment algorithms for microservice systems with complex dependencies. IEEE Trans. Cloud Comput. **11**, 1746–1763 (2022)
7. He, X., et al.: Rescureservice: a benchmark microservice system for the research of mobile edge and cloud computing. arXiv preprint arXiv:2212.11758 (2022)
8. Kephart, J.O., Chess, D.M.: The vision of autonomic computing. Computer **36**(1), 41–50 (2003)
9. Kipf, T.N., Welling, M.: Semi-supervised classification with graph convolutional networks. arXiv preprint arXiv:1609.02907 (2016)

10. Luo, X., Wu, H., Yuan, H., Zhou, M.: Temporal pattern-aware QoS prediction via biased non-negative latent factorization of tensors. IEEE Trans. Cybern. **50**(5), 1798–1809 (2019)
11. Mahmud, R., Pallewatta, S., Goudarzi, M., Buyya, R.: iFogSim2: An extended iFogSim simulator for mobility, clustering, and microservice management in edge and fog computing environments. J. Syst. Softw. **190**, 111351 (2022)
12. Ren, X., et al.: DeepQSC: a GNN and attention mechanism-based framework for QoS-aware service composition. In: 2021 International Conference on Service Science (ICSS), pp. 76–83. IEEE (2021)
13. Stine, M.: Migrating to Cloud-native Application Architectures. O'Reilly Media (2015)
14. Velickovic, P., Cucurull, G., Casanova, A., Romero, A., Lio, P., Bengio, Y., et al.: Graph attention networks. STAT **1050**(20), 10–48550 (2017)
15. Wang, S., Zhao, Y., Huang, L., Xu, J., Hsu, C.H.: Qos prediction for service recommendations in mobile edge computing. J. Parallel Distrib. Comput. **127**, 134–144 (2019)
16. Wang, Z., He, X., Liu, L., Tu, Z., Xu, H.: Survey on requirement-driven microservice system evolution. In: 2020 IEEE International Conference on Services Computing (SCC), pp. 186–193. IEEE (2020)
17. Xiang, Z., Deng, S., Jiang, F., Gao, H., Tehari, J., Yin, J.: Computing power allocation and traffic scheduling for edge service provisioning. In: 2020 IEEE International Conference on Web Services (ICWS), pp. 394–403. IEEE (2020)
18. Zou, G., Chen, J., He, Q., Li, K.C., Zhang, B., Gan, Y.: NDMF: Neighborhood-integrated deep matrix factorization for service QoS prediction. IEEE Trans. Netw. Serv. Manage. **17**(4), 2717–2730 (2020)

QoS Prediction via Multi-scale Feature Fusion Based on Convolutional Neural Network

Hanzhi Xu, Yanjun Shu, Zhan Zhang, and Decheng Zuo[✉]

Harbin Institute of Technology, Harbin, Heilongjiang, China
hzxu@stu.hit.edu.cn, {yjshu,zhangzhan,zuodc}@hit.edu.cn

Abstract. Quality of Service (QoS) prediction is a crucial aspect in service management. However, the existing QoS prediction methods face several limitations, such as loss of information during encoding, incomplete feature extraction and neglect of the interaction between features. To this end, this paper proposes a new **Q**oS **PR**ediction method based on a **M**ulti-**S**cale convolutional neural **N**etwork, i.e., QPRMSN. For each service invocation, we build a feature matrix that encodes invocation context and QoS characteristics by using status codes with degrees of membership. Then, a multi-scale convolutional neural network is employed to extract features that keep detailed information during deep global features mining. Moreover, we introduce attention mechanism to learn the intrinsic relationships between features to strengthen key features. Finally, QPRMSN completes the QoS prediction based on a multi-level feature matrix. Extensive experiments are conducted on a real-world dataset to evaluate the performance of QPRMSN. The experimental results demonstrate that QPRMSN outperforms the state-of-the-art QoS prediction models and is better at QoS context encoding.

Keywords: QoS prediction · Convolutional neural network · multi-scale

1 Introduction

Services have been widely used in our daily life, such as e-learning, e-commerce, and e-shopping [1,2]. Quality of Service (QoS) is the non-functionality attributes of service, including throughput, response time, availability, and reliability. It expresses the quantitative performance of services invoked by users [3]. As an intuitive and basic indicator, QoS plays a curial role in service selection [4]. Due to the heterogeneous and dynamic network status, a service QoS is varied for the same user in different invocations. However, monitoring QoS of each invocation requires additional time and expense for cloud facilities and leads to a lot of unknown QoS values. When many QoS values are unknown, users are difficult to select a suitable service to fulfill their QoS requirements. Therefore, accurate QoS prediction is necessary for effective service selection.

F. Monti et al. (Eds.): ICSOC 2023, LNCS 14419, pp. 119–134, 2023.
https://doi.org/10.1007/978-3-031-48421-6_9

QoS prediction is a hot topic in service computing and a huge number of QoS prediction methods have been developed. Collaborative filtering is widely employed in QoS prediction, which can be roughly divided into memory-based algorithms [6–8] and model-based algorithms [12,16,21]. The Memory-based filtering method is simple to understand and implement. But its accuracy is low, especially when the data is sparse. With the rise of deep-learning techniques, the model-based filtering methods attract more and more attentions, such as CNN (Convolutional Neural Network) [11,12] and MLP (MultiLayer Perceptron) [23]. However, the performance of these techniques in the field of QoS prediction is still not perfect. There are three key limitations that need to be addressed.

Firstly, the QoS matrix data and environmental context information cannot be directly utilized by deep neural networks [5]. Existing data preprocessing methods suffer from significant loss of accuracy, especially when dealing with numeric QoS attributes due to a lack of effective coding methods. Secondly, the intrinsic relationship between adjacent data in the QoS matrix greatly contributes to the QoS prediction, but it is difficult to reflect in the feature matrix of the deep network. Thirdly, the interactions between feature vectors of different attributes in QoS data are not fully learned and exploited. The interaction between features is a critical aspect of QoS prediction information. However, the existing model lacks a useful component to extract this important factor.

To address these limitations, this paper proposes a new QoS prediction method based on multi-scale convolutional neural network, i.e., **QPRMSN**. The method consists of two parts: data encoding and multi-scale convolutional neural network. For the first limitation, the data encoding of QPRMSN maps original QoS attribute values to discrete intervals with their membership degrees by fuzzy logic, which ensures the rich semantic information of the input and avoids the loss of precision caused by rounding of numeric information. To solve the second limitation, QPRMSN employs a convolutional neural network with multi-scale receptive fields [9]. The network reduces the size of the original feature matrix to multiple scales by downsampling and then extracts features through convolution operations on different scale feature matrices. To deal with the interaction between different features and their importance in the total features, i.e., the third limitation, QPRMSN introduces the vector level attention mechanism [10]. The weights of receptive fields with different scales are obtained through the channel-level attention mechanism during receptive field fusion to improve prediction accuracy. In the end, the multi-scale fused feature matrix is processed by a fully connected layer to obtain the predicted QoS value.

In summary, the main contributions of this paper are as follows:

- A new encoding method is proposed to extract the characteristics of user/service and environmental context. QoS feature data is mapped to discrete intervals and their membership degrees of the intervals are encoded as state codes to construct feature vectors with rich semantic information.
- We employ both vector-level and channel-level attention mechanisms to learn the interaction between different feature vectors and the importance of different scale feature matrices.

– We propose a QoS prediction method QPRMSN by integrating feature encoding, multi-scale CNN, and attention mechanism. It accurately expresses the information related to QoS and extracts rich features with correlations between them. Extensive experiments on the real-world data show that QPRMSN achieves superior accuracy than traditional filter and deep learning methods. We will share our code on Github[1].

2   The Framework of QPRMSN

Figure 1 shows the overall architecture of QPRMSN, which consists of two parts: an encoding layer and a multi-scale convolutional neural network. The information about QoS is primarily from two aspects: the QoS matrix and the environment of network invocations. In QPRMSN, both two types of information are considered, and the encoding step transforms them into digital features. The vector-level attention mechanism is introduced in the encoding layer to learn the interaction between different feature vectors and their respective importance. The deep features of these attributes are extracted by assembling them into the feature matrix and passing them through a multi-scale convolution neural network. The channel-level attention mechanism gives appropriate importance degrees of feature matrices from different scale receptive fields.

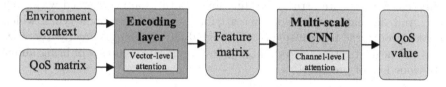

Fig. 1. The architecture of QPRMSN.

3   Methodology of Forming the Feature Matrix

3.1   Features Within the Environment Context

The environment context comprises various relevant information about the network conditions, such as regions and IP addresses, which significantly impact QoS. The environment context features are divided into user context feature matrix P_u^e and service context feature matrix P_s^e. The data in these two matrices are directly referenced from the service and user respectively in service invocation records. There is a WSDL document in service context, which records important information about the service invocation. To make full use of the information in the WSDL document, it is converted into the feature vector of the service through the word2vec method after parsing it according to the important fields.

---

[1] https://github.com/bearflying/QPRMSN

3.2   Features within the QoS Matrix

Suppose a service invocation scenario with M users and N services. Define the QoS matrix as $Q \in \mathbb{R}^{M \times N}$ ($\mathbb{R}$ is the set of real numbers), then the QoS of user i to service j is $q_{ij} \in Q$. QoS prediction can be clearly abstracted to fill in the vacant positions of a sparse QoS matrix in a reasonable way. The problem is that such a QoS matrix implies few and confusing mathematical laws. Matrix factorization is a technique that decomposes a matrix into the product of two matrices. This approach separates the user-implicit features from the service-implicit features, thereby increasing the expressiveness of the features. In QPRMSN, the probability matrix factorization (PMF) is applied to split the user-service QoS matrix into a user feature matrix $P_u^i = \{u_1, u_2, ..., u_i, ..., u_M\}$ and a service feature matrix $P_s^i = \{s_1, s_2, ..., s_i, ..., s_N\}$, where u_i is the feature vector of user i, s_j is the feature vector of service j, and $Q \approx P_u^i P_s^i$.

3.3   Encoding of Features

In QPRMSN, two encoding methods are used. For non-numeric data, we directly use one-hot encoding [24]. It consists of several placeholders representing the state space of attributes. Only the higher placeholder takes effect when encoding, which represents the attribute in this state. However, such encoding in practical applications causes some semantic deficiencies because the encoding results of different features are orthogonal, but some features are correlated with each other. And the feature values of some attributes are floating point types, which cannot be converted to activated bits through direct mapping. Directly discretizing to the nearest integer or retaining a few significant figures will bring about an obvious loss of precision.

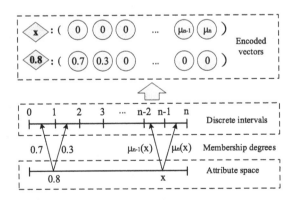

Fig. 2. Examples of encoding method of series numeric data.

We employ fuzzy logic to address this problem by discretizing the attribute space into n intervals of equal width, as shown in Fig. 2., where the midpoint of the i-th interval I_i is denoted as m_i. The interval length equals the distance between adjacent interval midpoints, i.e., $len(I_i) = m_{i+1} - m_i = d$. Each attribute value is mapped into two adjacent discrete intervals, and the degree of membership $\mu_i(x)$ to I_i is computed as:

$$\mathcal{D} \leftarrow \{I_1 \cup I_2 \cup ... \cup I_i \cup ... \cup I_n | I_1 \cap I_2 \cap ... \cap I_i \cap ... \cap I_n = \phi\} \tag{1}$$

$$\mu_i(x) = \begin{cases} 1 - \dfrac{|m_i - x|}{d}, & x \in I_i \\ \dfrac{|m_{i\pm1} - x|}{d}, & x \in I_{i\pm1}, x \mp \dfrac{d}{2} \in I_i \\ 0 & , \text{ else} \end{cases} \tag{2}$$

where x is the value to be encoded. This discretization approach guarantees that the same degree of membership holds equivalent meaning within the vector.

In some cases, the feature values of certain attributes exhibit large variation ranges, leading to excessive intervals in their discretization results with few valid intervals and scattered distribution. QPRMSN uses a preprocessing step that utilizes the logarithmic function to increase the uniformity and density of the data distribution. With the preprocessing step, the semantic expression effect is improved from sparse data I to dense data $\widetilde{I}$. The logarithmic function is applied to both the feature values and memberships, as shown below:

$$\widetilde{I} = lnI \tag{3}$$

$$\widetilde{\mu}_i(x) = \mu_i(lnx) \tag{4}$$

The final encoding result $A_\mathcal{D}(x)$ is represented as a vector composed of the membership degrees of the attribute value within each interval group, as follows:

$$A_\mathcal{D}(x) = (\mu_1(x), \mu_2(x), ..., \mu_i(x), ..., \mu_n(x)) \tag{5}$$

$A_\mathcal{D}(x)$ can be deblurred and accurately reconstructed into the original data through a linear transformation, which is supported by an ample number of parameters in the subsequent embedding layer. In other words, our encoding method maximally preserves the information contained in the original data. After encoding, the features of the user and service from QoS matrix, as well as the user and service environmental context features, exhibit sparsity and differ in size. Therefore, an embedding layer is required to transform these four types of feature matrices or vectors into a unified size and concatenate them together to form a dense feature matrix for one network invocation case, which serves as the input to the neural network.

4   Neural Network with Multi-scale Receptive Fields

Figure 3 is the multi-scale convolutional neural network architecture, which mainly consists of an embedding layer, feature fusing layers, attention mechanism and fully connected layer. The embedding layer converts the sparse encoded feature vectors into dense uniform ones and concatenates them to matrices with weights by vector-level attention mechanism. Then, the feature matrices are resized into three scales and extracted deep features through convolutional operations. The small-sized feature matrix contains more global and structural information, while the large-sized feature matrix contains more shallow detail information. Here, as a down-sampling process, the pooling layer functions flexibly adjust the size of the feature matrix. After upsampling to the same size, feature matrices of multiple scales are fused. To account for the interactions between different channels and their contributions to the overall feature matrix, the channel-level attention mechanism is introduced to obtain the most appropriate weights for them through network learning. The roles of key components in the network are elaborated in the following sections.

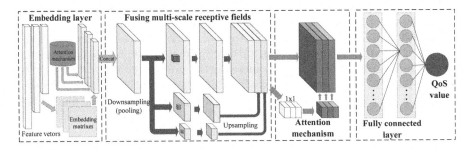

Fig. 3. Network architecture of multi-scale convolutional neural network.

4.1   Embedding Layer

To transform sparse vectors into information-rich dense vectors and standardize the sizes of vectors, we introduce an embedding layer at the beginning of the network, as shown in Fig. 3.

Assume that $e = (e_1, e_2, ..., e_t)^T \in \mathbb{R}^{t \times 1}$ is a t-dimensional sparse feature vector encoded by an attribute. That is, the state space of this attribute has t states, or the total number of discrete intervals mapped to is t. We introduce the embedding matrix $X = (x_1, x_2, ..., x_t) \in \mathbb{R}^{r \times t}$ and compute the intermediate matrix $E_X = Xe = (e_1 x_1, e_2 x_2, ..., e_t x_t)$. So the embedded dense vector can be calculated as follows:

$$e^E = e_1 x_1 + e_2 x_2 + ... + e_t x_t \in \mathbb{R}^{r \times 1} \tag{6}$$

The t-dimensional feature vector is converted to r-dimensional through the embedding layer. Since this layer is a linear transformation, it can largely retain the original features. The representation of correlations between features are strengthened after converting to a dense matrix, laying the foundation for the effective feature extraction by multi-scale convolution.

4.2   Fusing Multi-scale Receptive Fields

In QPRMSN, average pooling plays a crucial role in implementing multi-scale receptive field variations, as it can modify the size of the output matrix by adjusting the stride of the sliding window. The mathematical principle is illustrated as follows:

$$p_{i,j} = \sum_{z=ia}^{(i+1)a-1} \sum_{v=ja}^{(j+1)a-1} x_{z,\,v} + b \tag{7}$$

where $p_{i,j}$ is the value of the feature matrix to be pooled at position (i, j), a is the step size of the pooling sliding window, b is the bias and $x_{z,v}$ is the value of position (z, v) in the feature matrix. It can be seen that the height and width of each pooled feature matrix become $\frac{1}{a}$ of the original. The embedded dense feature matrix is first passed through three pooling layers of different scales, reducing its size by $a = 1, 2, 4$, respectively. As the compression size becomes smaller, it implies that a new matrix of the same unit contains more original information. Consequently, this is equivalent to a larger receptive field for the subsequent convolutional feature extraction.

Convolutional layers extract the features at the three scales. By analyzing the multi-scale network structure from the perspective of network backpropagation and incorporating the pooling process into the neural network model $Z^{(l+1)} = W^{(l+1)} f(Z^{(l)}) + b^{(l+1)}$, we can deduce the gradient of the multi-scale fusion matrix respect to the original feature matrix as follows:

$$\frac{\partial Z^F}{\partial Z^O} = \sum_{i=1}^{3} \frac{1}{a_i} (W_i^F)^T \odot f'(Z^O) \tag{8}$$

where Z^F and Z^O are the fused and original matrix, W_i^F is the weight matrix at the i-th scale, $\odot$ denotes Hadamard product and f is the activate function.

As shown in Eq. 8, the feature matrices at different scales incur varying losses to the previous layer. Matrices with larger receptive fields contribute to the loss of original features at a proportion of $\frac{1}{a}$, indicating that the global features of the QoS information matrix are utilized to correct the original feature with the ratio of $\frac{1}{a}$. Moreover, the information within the encoded feature matrix of QPRMSN is implicit and structured, containing numerous potential logical correlations that may not be directly perceptible to humans. Ordinary convolutional layers pay more attention to the correlation between adjacent elements in the feature matrix while ignoring the correlation between elements that are far apart. The multi-scale network can address this issue. High-receptive-field convolutions can learn patterns among globally distributed information, whereas low-receptive-field convolutions focus on patterns among closely distributed information.

In order to effectively fuse multi-scale feature matrices and retain more original details, the deep small-size feature matrices need to be enlarged to the same size. The upsampling process is realized by the deconvolution method. It increases the size of the feature matrix by inserting 0 between the rows and columns. After the convolution operation, a new large-size feature matrix is obtained.

4.3 Attention Mechanism

The attention mechanism can provide weights for the information in the network so that the feature extraction and learning of the network can be directed in a better direction. QPRMSN incorporates the attention mechanism twice. The first usage is when concatenating feature vectors as shown in the leading of Fig. 3. The weight calculation principle is illustrated as follows:

$$E_{weighted} = softmax\left(EW_K(EW_O)^T\right)W_V E \qquad (9)$$

W_O, W_K and W_V are three parameter matrices. W_O and W_K map the original feature matrix E to a higher-level linear space. In the new space, the interaction between different vectors in the matrix is calculated by matrix multiplication to generate a weight matrix. Finally, the elements in the feature matrix E are assigned weights. The weights are normalized by the $Softmax()$ function so that the sum of the weights is 1.

The attention mechanism is introduced for the second time to assign different weights to multi-scale information as shown in Fig. 3. The contributions of global features at high receptive fields and detailed features at low receptive fields to the overall representation are distinct. Thus, they require respective weights to strike a balance. The channel-level attention mechanism here is implemented by a parallel 1×1 scale convolutional layer with its network parameters. Specifically, each channel of the feature matrix is compressed into a value by average pooling, and this value has the receptive field of this channel. The relationship between the compressed values of different channels is established using two matrix multiplication operations, and their parameters are updated to generate the weight value of each channel, as follows:

$$w = sigmoid(W_2^{d \times \frac{d}{s}} ReLU(W_1^{\frac{d}{s} \times d} z^d)) \qquad (10)$$

$W_1^{\frac{d}{s} \times d}$ and $W_2^{d \times \frac{d}{s}}$ are parameter matrices. They update parameters for compressed d-dimensional vectors z^d to become weight vectors. The dimensional transformation of $W_1^{\frac{d}{s} \times d}$ and $W_2^{d \times \frac{d}{s}}$ is for the consideration of enhancing the generalization ability of the matrix. After the vector is operated with $W_1^{\frac{d}{s} \times d}$, it is activated by ReLU to enhance the discrimination of its role as weight. The weights are limited to the range $(0,1)$ by the $sigmoid$ function. Finally, the previous feature matrix is weighted channel-wise by multiplication.

4.4 Fully Connected Layer

The fully connected layer serves two purposes. Firstly, it enhances the network's fitting ability by introducing learnable parameters. Secondly, it flattens the three-dimensional feature matrix into a final prediction value.

QPRMSN uses the absolute value error as the loss function, which has strong robustness and can resist the influence of some outliers in service invocation data. Its mathematical formula is as follows:

$$loss = \sum_{i=1}^{M} \sum_{j=1}^{N} |y_{i,j} - \hat{y}_{i,j}| \tag{11}$$

where $\hat{y}_{i,j}$ is the true QoS value of service j invoked by user i and $y_{i,j}$ is the result of the network output.

5 Experiments

5.1 Data Set

We validate the effectiveness of our method on a real QoS dataset, i.e., the WS-Dream dataset, which is one of the commonly used datasets in the field of QoS prediction [12,23,24]. This dataset focuses on two QoS attributions, i.e., response time and throughput. Statistics of the dataset are shown in Table 1.

5.2 Metrics

To assess the effectiveness of QPRMSN, we use the mean absolute error (MAE) and the root mean square error (RMSE) compared to other QoS prediction methods. The MAE and RMSE are defined as follows:

$$MAE = \frac{1}{n} \sum_{i=1}^{n} |y_i - \hat{y}_i| \tag{12}$$

$$RMSE = \sqrt{\frac{1}{n} \sum_{i=1}^{n} (y_i - \hat{y}_i)^2} \tag{13}$$

where $\hat{y}_i$ is the ith true QoS value and y_i is the ith result of the network. The MAE can intuitively reflect the overall accuracy on this batch of data. The RMSE is to highlight the weight of the larger error in the total error by the operation of squaring.

Table 1. Statistics of Dataset

Statistics	Values	Statistics	Values
Users	339	Services	4,107
Users' Regions(UR)	31	Services' Regions(SR)	71
Users' Autonomous Systems(UAS)	137	Services' Autonomous Systems(SAS)	822
Users' Subnets(USN)	178	Services' Subnets(SSN)	1,317
Users' IP Addresses(UIP)	339	Services' IP Addresses(SIP)	1,710
Service Invocations	1,392,951	Services' Documents(WSDL)	4,107
Range of response-time(RT)	0–20 s	Range of throughput(TP)	0–1000 kbps

5.3 Baselines

The following classic algorithms with superior performance on the QoS prediction task as baselines to compare with QPRMSN. They cover several basic ideas in the field, namely, memory-based filtering, model-based filtering, matrix factorization, and heuristic-based filtering.

- UPCC [17], IPCC [18], UIPCC [19]: These three methods are based on memory filtering, which focus on the users and services most similar to the users to be predicted by calculating the Pearson coefficient.
- PMF [20], CSMF [21]: These two methods are based on model-based filtering. They decompose the user-service QoS matrix through the probability matrix, so as to predict QoS by obtaining more hidden information.
- FM [22]: It is a factorization machine, which is often used in the field of feature combine.
- DNM [23]: It is a filtering method based on neural network. It uses deep learning technology to mine the features between users, services and their contextual information, so as to obtain accurate prediction results.
- MGCCF [12]: It is a filtering method based on neural network. It uses a graph convolutional collaborative filtering with multi-component and deep factorization machine for QoS prediction.

The experimental platform is a lightweight application server equipped with a 26-core 3.9 GHz CPU with the highest frequency and 256 G memory, running the Ubuntu 14.04 operating system.

5.4 Performance Comparison

In order to show the prediction accuracy of QPRMSN under real conditions, it is necessary to construct sparse QoS data to verify the prediction accuracy. We randomly delete the corresponding proportion of the original data set according to different degrees of density. We compare the prediction performance of QPRMSN and other baselines at four levels of density from 2.5% to 10%. The environment context is combined of {UR, UAS, USN} and {SR, SAS, SSN, SIP}. Among the parameters that may affect the accuracy of the network, we initialize the network weights with random decimals in the interval $(0,1)$. The network uses MSGD as the optimizer. The learning rate gradually decreases until the network converges, and its variation range is $(10^{-6}, 10^{-2})$. Other parameters that have no effect on the accuracy of the network are obtained through adjustments. The memory-based filtering methods calculate the prediction values by finding several neighboring users/services with high similarity. The number of neighbors for the user is set to 10 and the number of neighbors for the service is set to 50. The regularization parameters of the matrix factorization algorithm are set to 0.1 for response time and 10 for throughput. Table 2 shows the response time and throughput prediction results of QPRMSN and other baselines under different data densities. The optimal data at each density is bolded.

Table 2. Performance Comparison For Response Time and Throughput Prediction

QoS Attributes	Methods	Density = 2.5%		Density = 5%		Density = 7.5%		Density = 10%	
		RMSE	MAE	RMSE	MAE	RMSE	MAE	RMSE	MAE
Response Time	UPCC	1.5178	0.7216	1.4115	0.6512	1.3717	0.6012	1.3469	0.5886
	IPCC	1.6634	0.7592	1.4228	0.6461	1.3857	0.6148	1.3542	0.5934
	UIPCC	1.5106	0.7132	1.4106	0.6384	1.3619	0.5896	1.3427	0.5835
	PMF	1.6993	0.6510	1.5395	0.5982	1.4594	0.5614	1.4268	0.5449
	CSMF	1.5618	0.6925	1.4337	0.6008	1.3832	0.5723	1.3476	0.5443
	FM	1.5122	0.7124	1.4126	0.6356	**1.3653**	0.5963	1.3490	0.5698
	DNM	1.4829	0.4777	1.4274	0.4147	1.3745	0.3843	1.3567	0.3628
	MGCCF	1.4783	0.5116	1.3950	0.5010	1.3723	0.4202	1.3527	0.4008
	QPRMSN	**1.4652**	**0.4656**	**1.3790**	**0.3854**	1.3701	**0.3802**	**1.3464**	**0.3506**
Throughput	UPCC	64.26	28.03	56.63	25.43	52.16	21.88	51.52	20.32
	IPCC	66.07	27.44	56.72	25.09	52.91	22.78	52.41	21.54
	UIPCC	64.15	26.87	**55.90**	23.80	**51.78**	21.37	**50.63**	20.04
	PMF	72.89	26.08	66.41	22.54	62.67	21.64	60.74	21.49
	CSMF	68.80	24.26	60.53	21.26	58.24	19.24	56.76	18.41
	FM	68.75	26.39	59.24	22.95	57.45	21.91	55.48	21.07
	DNM	65.65	18.29	59.33	14.85	56.55	13.82	54.50	12.92
	MGCCF	65.38	18.53	58.78	14.53	56.41	13.46	54.32	12.78
	QPRMSN	**64.08**	**16.63**	57.96	**14.15**	55.85	**13.06**	54.16	**12.54**

QPRMSN outperforms all other baselines in terms of MAE. The most significant improvement in terms of response time is observed at a density of 5%, where the MAE decreases by 0.293, equivalent to a reduction of 7.06% in accuracy loss compared to the best performance of other baselines. QPRMSN achieves the minimum RMSE in most cases in terms of response time prediction. The most significant improvement in throughput prediction is at the data density of 2.5%, where the MAE reduces by 9.07%. But in RMSE about throughput prediction, memory-based filtering methods perform better. This could be attributed to the fact that the feature extraction process is incomplete when the data is too sparse, making inferential prediction methods less effective than searching for similar users or services. On the other hand, the large range of values for throughput makes individual cases with large errors more impactful on RMSE, indicating that neural network models tend to deviate more from the correct value when the data range is large.

6   Discussion

We conduct a series of experiments to investigate the performance of QPRMSN in-depth. In the hyperparameter study, the data density is set to 10%, and the QoS attribute selected is response time.

6.1   Ablation Study for Encoding Method

To evaluate the encoding method of QPRMSN, we conducted a comparative experiment using the one-hot attribute encoding, which controls different numbers of digits after the decimal point. We choose the response time as the QoS attribute and the range of decimal places is set from 1 to 5, with all other conditions being optimal and identical. The experimental results are shown in Table 3. Although the number of decimal places increases to 5, the accuracy gradually improves but still remains below the performance of QPRMSN. This is because that the one-hot encoding generates an excessive number of categories, which leads to overly sparse encoded vectors and the loss of correlation among them.

Table 3. Ablation Study for Encoding Method

Methods	Number	Density = 2.5%		Density = 5%		Density = 7.5%		Density = 10%	
		RMSE	MAE	RMSE	MAE	RMSE	MAE	RMSE	MAE
Controlling Digitals	1	1.6124	0.7529	1.5445	0.6574	1.5210	0.6257	1.4823	0.5856
	2	1.5676	0.6534	1.5268	0.5360	1.4709	0.5241	1.4547	0.5156
	3	1.5123	0.5975	1.4654	0.4765	1.4402	0.4683	1.3896	0.4426
	4	1.4965	0.5112	1.4188	0.4223	1.4085	0.4168	1.3852	0.4082
	5	1.4937	0.4954	1.4525	0.4552	1.4232	0.4512	1.3895	0.4130
QPRMSN		**1.4652**	**0.4656**	**1.3790**	**0.3854**	**1.3701**	**0.3802**	**1.3464**	**0.3506**

6.2   Effect of Embedding Dimension

The output dimension of the embedding layer is an important hyperparameter of QPRMSN. It determines the distribution of features in the feature matrix before entering the multi-scale CNN. Insufficient dimensions in the embeddings may lead to inadequate feature expression, while excessive dimensions may result in sparse features that carry little information and hinder feature extraction. To conduct a comparative experiment, the dimensions of the embedding layer are set to 16, 32, 64, 128, 192 and 256 respectively. The experimental results are shown in Fig. 4 (a). Before the dimension reaches 128, the accuracy rate increases with an increasing embedding dimension. When the dimension size continues to increase and reaches 256, the accuracy rate drops due to the reasons previously analyzed.

6.3   Effect of the Number of Convolution Kernels

As the number of convolution kernels increases, more levels of features can be extracted. However, the increase in the number of convolution kernels also means an increase in network parameters, which can lead to over-fitting and reduced accuracy of the network. To validate the trend of accuracy as the number of convolution kernels increases, we first maintain the same number of kernels at each scale in the complex network structure proposed in QPRMSN. The number of convolution kernels changes from 32 to 128 with a step size of 16. The experimental results are shown in Fig. 4 (b). The accuracy rate reaches the highest in the range of 64–80 convolution kernels, and the end of 80 is slightly higher than 64. However, beyond 80 convolution kernels, the network accuracy tends to decline as the number of convolution kernels continues to increase.

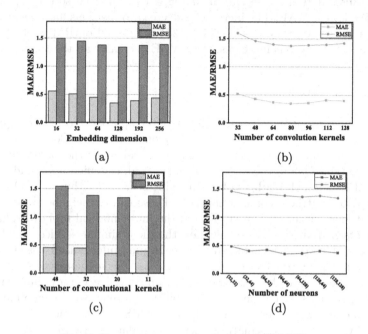

Fig. 4. Hyperparameter Analysis of QPRMSN.

Based on the current research on CNNs, deeper feature matrices require more convolution kernels to extract more implicit information. We set the number of convolution kernels in the three-scale convolutional layer according to the four types of ratios {1:2:2, 1:2:4, 1:4:8, 1:4:16}. In order to maintain consistency in the total number of convolution kernels across different ratios, we set the number of kernels in the convolutional layer with the largest size to {48, 32, 20, 11} respectively for each ratio. In this way, the total number of convolution kernels can also maintain a high accuracy rate known from previous experiments. The experimental results are shown in Fig. 4 (c). The ratio of {1:4:8} has achieved the lowest MAE and RMSE.

6.4   Effect of the Number of Neurons in the Fully Connected Layers

The fully connected layer considers global information comprehensively and serves as the final feature expression before calculating the predicted value. However, an excessive number of neurons in the fully connected layer not only waste computational resources, but can also lead to over-fitting. In order to study the impact of the number of neurons in the fully connected layer on the accuracy rate, the number of the first two fully connected layers is set to {{32, 32},{32, 64},{64,32},{64,64},{64,128},{128,64},{128,128}}. The third fully connected layer consisted of only one neuron to calculate a unique prediction value. The experimental results are shown in Fig. 4 (d), and the setting of {64,64} achieves the lowest MAE. The increase or decrease of neurons has a tendency to reduce the accuracy rate on MAE. {128,128} is optimal on RMSE. In general, as the number of neurons increases, the RMSE decreases all the time.

7   Related Work

Shao et al. first proposed a memory-based filter approach to predict QoS values of Web services [17]. They use the Pearson Correlation Coefficient (PCC) to search users similar to the target, so as to calculate the prediction value according to their QoS in the same service. He et al. classified users and services by physical location through the k-means clustering algorithm. The QoS value is predicted by matrix decomposition [13]. These similar neighbor-based methods exhibit lower accuracy. Xu et al. used the mathematical tool of Probability Matrix Factorization (PMF) to calculate the most similar services [14,15]. He et al. proposed HMF, which introduces geographic information based on user and service latent matrix factorization to increase the semantics of information [26]. The model-based filtering method has improved accuracy and can cope with data sparseness, but it has poor flexibility and relies too much on artificial hyperparameters. Moreover, compared to QPRMSN, these methods only utilize partial QoS-related information, such as singular geographic or QoS matrix information.

Recently, deep-learning-based QoS prediction models have been mainstream due to their superior feature extraction ability. Wu et al. propose DNM (Deep Neural Model) [23] for multiple attributes QoS prediction with contexts. In this model, they map contextual features into semantical space through the embedding layer. The dot product of feature vectors is used to extract interaction information between them. Their model ignores the implicit digital patterns in the QoS matrix. Xia et al. propose a joint deep networks based multi-source feature learning for QoS prediction (JDNMFL) [11]. They use the one-hot encoding to express the QoS information, which causes the loss of precision by rounding of numeric information. Ding et al. propose a graph convolutional collaborative filtering (MGCCF) with multi-component and deep factorization machine for QoS prediction [12]. They introduce node-level attention to identify latent components and component-level attention to obtain the importance of components. But they do not take full advantage of the QoS information in the context of network invocations. Therefore, existing QoS prediction methods based on DNN have limitations in model design and employ simplistic network architectures. QPRMSN can effectively extract QoS-related information by exploring multi-level features. Additionally, compared to QPRMSN, the existing methods lack precise and efficient encoding schemes when utilizing various QoS-related information as input to the network, leading to information loss.

8 Conclusion

In this paper, we propose a QoS prediction method based on a multi-scale convolutional neural network which is named QPRMSN. Our method fuses the global and detailed features of QoS by a multi-scale neural network. First, we introduce a membership-based discretization method to encode the implicit information within the QoS matrix of users and services, as well as the explicit information of their context. Then, the sparse feature matrix is transformed into a dense matrix through the embedding layer. Features are extracted through a multi-scale convolutional neural network, and features of different scales are fused. Finally, the QoS value is predicted by the fully connected layer. The multi-scale convolutional neural network can extract deep features of the QoS matrix, and the new encoding method is effective. Extensive experiments demonstrate that QPRMSN achieves superior prediction accuracy compared to existing methods. In future, we will focus on the matrix factorization step to find more efficient and interpretable methods for improving the accuracy of QoS prediction.

Acknowledgements. This work is partially supported by China NSF (No. 61202091) and China NSF (No. 62171155).

References

1. Tang, M., Zheng, Z., Kang, G., Liu, J., Yang, Y., Zhang, T.: Collaborative web service quality prediction via exploiting matrix factorization and network map. IEEE Trans. Netw. Service Manage. **13**(1), 126–137 (2016)
2. Xu, L.D., He, W., Li, S.: Internet of things in industries: a survey. IEEE Trans. Ind. Informat. **10**(4), 2233–2243 (2014)
3. Kritikos, K., Plexousakis, D.: Requirements for QoS-based web service description and discovery. IEEE Trans. Serv. Comput. **2**, 320–337 (2009)
4. Zheng, X., Da Xu, L., Chai, S.: QoS recommendation in cloud services. IEEE Access **5**, 5171–5177 (2017)
5. Xu, Y.: Context-aware QoS prediction for web service recommendation and selection. Expert Syst. Appl. **53**, 75–86 (2016)
6. Zheng, Z., Ma, H., Lyu, M.R., King, I.: Collaborative web service QoS prediction via neighborhood integrated matrix factorization. IEEE Trans. Serv. Comput. **6**(3), 289–299 (2013)
7. Fletcher, K.K., Liu, X.F.: A collaborative filtering method for personalized preference-based service recommendation. In: IEEE International Conference on Web Services (ICWS), pp. 400–407 (2015)
8. Yu, Z., Wong, R.K., Chi, C.: Efficient role mining for context-aware service recommendation using a high-performance cluster. IEEE Trans. Serv. Comput. **10**(6), 914–926 (2017)
9. Hu, J., et al.: Squeeze-and-excitation networks. In: IEEE Transactions on Pattern Analysis and Machine Intelligence (2019)

10. Vaswani, A., et al.: Attention is all you need. In: The 31st International Conference on Neural Information Processing Systems (NIPS). Curran Associates Inc., Red Hook, NY, USA (2017)

11. Xia, Y., et al.: Joint deep networks based multi-source feature learning for QoS prediction. IEEE Trans. Serv. Comput. **PP**(99), 1–1 (2021)

12. Ding, L., et al.: QoS prediction for web services via combining multi-component graph convolutional collaborative filtering and deep factorization machine. In: 2021 IEEE International Conference on Web Services (ICWS), Chicago, USA (2021)

13. He, P., Zhu, J., Zheng, Z., Xu, J., Lyu, M.R.: Location-based hierarchical matrix factorization for web service recommendation. In: 2014 IEEE International Conference on Web Services (ICWS), pp. 297–304. IEEE (2014)

14. Xu, Y., Yin, J., Lo, W.: A unified framework of QoS-based web service recommendation with neighborhood-extended matrix factorization. In: Proceedings of the IEEE 6th International Conference on Service-Oriented Computing and Applications, pp. 198–205 (2013)

15. Xu, Y., Yin, J., Lo, W., Wu, Z.: Personalized location-aware QoS prediction for web services using probabilistic matrix factorization. In: Lin, X., Manolopoulos, Y., Srivastava, D., Huang, G. (eds.) WISE 2013. LNCS, vol. 8180, pp. 229–242. Springer, Heidelberg (2013). https://doi.org/10.1007/978-3-642-41230-1_20

16. Yin, Y., et al.: QoS prediction for service recommendation with deep feature learning in edge computing environment. Mob. Netw. Appl. **25**, 1–11 (2019)

17. Shao, L., et al.: Personalized QoS prediction for web services via collaborative filtering. In: Proceedings of the IEEE International Conference on Web Services, pp. 439–446 (2007)

18. Sarwar, B.M., et al.: Item-based collaborative filtering recommendation algorithms. In: Proceedings of the 10th International Conference on World Wide Web, pp. 285–295 (2001)

19. Zheng, Z., Ma, H., Lyu, M.R., King, I.: QoS-aware web service recommendation by collaborative filtering. IEEE Trans. Serv. Comput. **4**, 140–152 (2011)

20. Mnih, A., Salakhutdinov, R.R.: Probabilistic matrix factorization. In: Proceedings of the 20th International Conference Neural Information Processing Systems, pp. 1257–1264 (2008)

21. Wu, H., Yue, K., et al.: Collaborative QoS prediction with context-sensitive matrix factorization. Future Gener. Comput. Syst. **82**, 669–678 (2018)

22. Rendle, S.: Factorization machines with libFM. ACM Trans. Intell. Syst. Technol. **3**(3) (2012) Art. no. 57

23. Wu, H., et al.: Multiple attributes QoS prediction via deep neural model with contexts. IEEE Trans. Serv. Comput. **14**(4), 1084–1096 (2018)

24. Zheng, Z., Zhang, Y., Lyu, M.R.: Distributed QoS evaluation for real-world web services. In: Proceedings of the IEEE International Conference on Web Services, pp. 83–90 (2010)

25. Lin, T.Y., Dollár, P., Girshick, R., He, K., Hariharan, B., Belongie, S.: Feature pyramid networks for object detection. In: 2017 IEEE Conference on Computer Vision and Pattern Recognition (CVPR), pp. 936–944, Honolulu, HI, USA (2017)

26. He, P., et al.: A Hierarchical matrix factorization approach for location-based web service QoS Prediction. In: IEEE International Symposium on Service Oriented System Engineering. IEEE Computer Society (2014)

27. Su, K., et al.: Web service QoS prediction by neighbor information combined nonnegative matrix factorization. J. Int. Fuzzy Syst. **30**, 3593–3604 (2016)

Architecture and System Aspects

Decision-Making Support for Data Integration in Cyber-Physical-System Architectures

Evangelos Ntentos[1]([✉]), Amirali Amiri[1], Stephen Warnett[1], and Uwe Zdun[2]

[1] University of Vienna, Faculty of Computer Science, Software Architecture Group,
Doctoral School Computer Science, Vienna, Austria
{evangelos.ntentos,amirali.amiri,stephen.warnett}@univie.ac.at
[2] University of Vienna, Faculty of Computer Science, Software Architecture Group,
Vienna, Austria
uwe.zdun@univie.ac.at

Abstract. Cyber-Physical Systems (CPS) design is a complex challenge involving physical and digital components working together to accomplish a specific goal. Integrating such systems involves combining data from various distributed Internet of Things (IoT) devices and cloud services to create meaningful insights and actions. Service-based IoT data integration involves several steps: collection, processing, analysis, and visualization. Adopting a holistic approach that considers physical and digital aspects is crucial when designing data integration in distributed CPS. Architectural design decisions are vital in shaping a CPS' functionality and system qualities, such as performance, security, and reliability. Although several patterns and practices for CPS architecture have been proposed, much of the knowledge in this area is informally discussed in the grey literature, e.g., in practitioner blogs and system documentation. As a result, this architectural knowledge is dispersed across many sources that are often inconsistent and based on personal experience. In this study, we present the results of a qualitative, in-depth study of the best practices and patterns of distributed CPS architecture as described by practitioners. We have developed a formal architecture decision model using a model-based qualitative research method. We aim to bridge the science-practice gap, enhance comprehension of practitioners' CPS approaches, and provide decision-making support.

Keywords: Architectural Design Decisions · Cyber-Physical Systems · Data Integration · Software Architecture · Grounded Theory

1 Introduction

Several authors have attempted to document patterns and best practices related to distributed CPS [6,8,10,14]. However, these works focus on applying published patterns or scientific results. In contrast, established industry practices are primarily found in grey literature like blogs, experience reports, and system

© The Author(s), under exclusive license to Springer Nature Switzerland AG 2023
F. Monti et al. (Eds.): ICSOC 2023, LNCS 14419, pp. 137–152, 2023.
https://doi.org/10.1007/978-3-031-48421-6_10

documentation. While these sources offer some understanding of existing practices, they lack systematic architectural guidance. The reported practices vary and rely on personal experience, creating uncertainty and risk in CPS design. One needs extensive experience or a comprehensive study of knowledge sources to address this. We aim to provide a more complete and consistent view of current industrial practices, complementing existing knowledge.

We conducted an in-depth qualitative study of CPS descriptions provided by practitioners. These descriptions contain informal information about established practices and patterns in distributed CPS. Following a model-based qualitative research method [18], we systematically analyzed the practitioner sources using coding and constant comparison methods [3], followed by precise software modeling. This allowed us to develop a detailed software model of established practices, patterns, and their relationships. This paper aims to study the following research questions:

- **RQ1** What are the patterns and practices currently used by practitioners for supporting data integration in CPS architectures?
- **RQ2** How are the current data integration patterns and practices related? In particular, which architectural design decisions (ADDs) are relevant when architecting data integration in CPS?
- **RQ3** What are the influencing factors (i.e., decision drivers) in architecting data integration in CPS in the eye of the practitioner today?

This paper has three key contributions. Firstly, we conducted a qualitative study on CPS architectures, analyzing 37 knowledge sources to identify established industrial practices, patterns, relationships, and decision drivers. Secondly, we created a formal architectural design decision (ADD) model. The model encompasses 7 decisions, 31 decision options, and 22 decision drivers. Lastly, we evaluated the model's level of detail and completeness, demonstrating that our research method provides a more comprehensive examination of established practices than informal pattern mining. Our approach, derived from practitioners' perspectives, offers valuable insights into distributed CPS design.

The rest of this paper is structured as follows: In Sect. 2, we compare our work to the related work. Section 3 explains the research methods we have applied in our study and summarizes the knowledge sources. Section 4 describes our reusable ADD model on CPS. Section 5 evaluates and Sect. 6 discusses our results. Finally, Sect. 7 considers the threats to the validity of our study, and Sect. 8 summarizes our findings.

2   Related Work

Several approaches that study CPS patterns and practices exist: Jamaludin et al. [8] present a comprehensive overview of CPS state of the art and highlight the importance of understanding CPS characteristics and architectures. This knowledge is crucial for designing and implementing CPS systems that can meet the requirements of various applications and ensure their reliability and adaptability. Henneke et al. [6] focus on analyzing communication patterns for CPS, such as discovery, request-response, and publish/subscribe. Reinfurt et al. [13] present five patterns that address various problems derived by examining numerous production-ready IoT offerings to identify recurring proven solution principles. Washizaki et al. [16] conducted a systematic literature review, identifying 32 papers from which 143 IoT architecture and design patterns were extracted. These patterns were analyzed based on various characteristics, and directions for improvements in publishing and adopting IoT patterns were outlined. Pontes et al. [12] introduced the Pattern-Based IoT Testing approach to simplify and organize the testing process for IoT ecosystems. This approach uses testing tactics that target common behavior patterns in the system, referred to as "IoT Test Patterns." Ghosh et al. [2] evaluated the current state of IoT research and discovered that existing studies were limited, biased, and subjective. Their study utilized a thorough qualitative approach to systematically analyze the grey literature on CPS to tackle this issue, providing the first comprehensive analysis.

There are several decision documentation-related approaches (e.g., for service-oriented solutions [19], service-based platform integration [9], REST vs. SOAP [11], and big data repositories [4]). However, this kind of research does not yet encompass CPS architectures. Warnett and Zdun [15] present a Grounded Theory-based approach to current practitioner understanding and architectural concepts of ML solution deployment. They formulated seven ADDs along with various relations between them. In particular, they modeled twenty-six decision options and forty-four decision drivers in ML deployment. Other authors have combined decision models with formal view models [5]. We improve these techniques with a formal modeling approach derived from qualitative research methodology.

Our study analyzes practitioner methods and techniques to bridge the gap between theory and practice in CPS data integration. Our formal model includes ADDs, decision options, practices, drivers, and relationships and aims to provide insights to help practitioners make informed data integration decisions in CPS.

3   Research Method

This section discusses the research method followed in this study and the modeling tool we used to create and visualize the decision model.

This paper aims to systematically study established practices in data integration architecture within CPS architectures. We utilize a model-based qualitative research method described in [18], which combines Grounded Theory (GT) [3] with pattern mining techniques (e.g., [1]) and their integration with GT [7]. This approach involves iterative steps of data interpretation to construct a theory based on the collected data. Data analysis is performed concurrently with data collection rather than afterward.

Constant comparison is a crucial aspect of GT, where researchers continuously compare existing and new data, identifying abstract concepts. These concepts are organized into categories and linked with properties and relationships. This iterative process guides subsequent research iterations.

Our knowledge-mining procedure involved searching for new sources, applying coding techniques to identify model elements and decision drivers, and continuously comparing codes with the existing model to improve it. We stopped the analysis using the concept of theoretical saturation, where additional sources did not contribute anything new. Our study had already converged after twenty-five sources. The sources used are summarized in Table 1, and our search relied on our experience with relevant tools, methods, patterns, and practices.

We employed three types of coding in our methodology:

- Open coding, which involves developing concepts based on the data, asking specific and consistent questions, precise and consistent coding, and memo writing with minimal assumptions.
- Axial coding, which entails developing categories and linking data, concepts, categories, and properties.
- Selective coding, which focuses on integrating developed categories and grouping them around a central core category.

Fig. 1 illustrates our research method steps. To gather practitioner sources, we used popular search engines like Google, StartPage, and DuckDuckGo, along with topic portals like InfoQ and DZone. Initial search terms aligned with our focus, such as "CPS data integration." GT coding practices and constant comparison were employed iteratively to identify concepts, categories, properties, and relationships. The decision model was developed using the CodeableModels tool, a Python-based modeling tool[1] that enabled precise definition of meta-models, models, and instances in code.

Subsequent iterations involved searches using relevant terms based on identified topics from previous iterations, focusing on areas requiring coding and their potential contributions to the model. Practitioner articles were selected based on relevance to the topic and not primarily promotional in nature, with both authors reviewing and approving the source selection.

During the coding process, open coding transformed conceptual details into labels, while axial coding identified recurring and related concepts. Each source was carefully examined line by line, with memos documenting thought processes, interpretations, and reasoning for traceability. Selective coding extracted main ideas and refined previous sources. Formal UML-based modeling was employed for axial and selective coding, resulting in a precise and consistent theory represented as a UML model. Theoretical saturation was reached when approximately twelve additional sources no longer significantly contributed to our model. A summary of our knowledge sources can be found in Table 1.

---

[1] https://github.com/uzdun/CodeableModels.

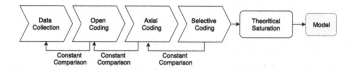

Fig. 1. Research Method Steps

4   Reusable ADD Model for Data Integration in CPS Architectures

This section presents the reusable ADD model we derived based on our study (see the data[2]). Figure 2 depicts the meta-model for the ADD models. This model encompasses the Decisions within an ADD model. Each Decision is associated with a Context, represented by a domain object that signifies the specific system part or aspect to which the decision applies. Decisions consist of Options and all options are categorized as Solutions. Each option is accompanied by Forces, which may have an impact on the decision. Furthermore, Decisions, Solutions, and Options can have Relations among them. A Solution can be linked to another Solution, with the condition that either the source or target of the relation must be an Option. It is essential for all Solutions in the model to be directly linked to a Decision, either through the Decision itself or through other Options. Decisions and Options can also have next-decision relations, indicating their sequential order or dependency.

The reusable ADD model consists of a single decision category, the *Data Integration in CPS Category*, which comprises seven top-level decisions, as depicted in Fig. 3. It is worth noting that all elements of our model are instances of a meta-model, with meta-classes such as *Decision, Category*, etc., which are also included in the model descriptions below. Also note that our model consists of concepts representing decisions, decision options, practices, patterns, and forces arising from our sources while applying our research methodology. These emergent concepts, appropriately named in our model, may be traced back to the referenced sources.

IoT Data Stream Integration and IoT Data Stream Integration Tasks (Fig. 4). *IoT data stream integration* combines and processes data from multiple devices or sensors to extract meaningful insights and enable better decision-making [S2, S3, S4, S33, S34, S35, S37]. It involves several steps, including data acquisition, prepossessing, analysis, and visualization. Several practices and patterns exist. *Edge-based IoT Data Stream Integration* is a decentralized practice for processing and analyzing IoT data. The data is processed closer to the source rather than transmitted to a central server or cloud-based service [S22, S3, S33]. Alternatively, *Cloud-based IoT Data Stream Integration* is a centralized option for processing and analyzing IoT data, where the data is transmitted to a remote server or cloud-based service for processing and analysis [S2, S26, S3,

---

[2] https://doi.org/10.5281/zenodo.8367400.

Table 1. Knowledge Sources Included in the Study

ID	Description	Reference
S1	How to Build an Industrial IoT Project Without the Cloud	https://bit.ly/3KqLsYd
S2	Understand the Azure IoT Edge runtime and its architecture	https://bit.ly/3XTSJ5C
S3	Connecting IoT devices to the cloud	https://thght.works/3KvnivM
S4	Real-time Data Streaming in IoT: Why and How	https://bit.ly/3kek9Wp
S5	Edge to Twin: A scalable edge to cloud architecture for digital twins	https://go.aws/3xIhSFR
S6	Understanding edge computing for manufacturing	https://red.ht/3XTy2qw
S7	Husarnet: Connected Things Without a Cloud	https://bit.ly/3XN0hHu
S8	How to use digital twins for IoT device configurations	https://bit.ly/3kodBEz
S9	Mainflux 0.11 — Digital Twin, MQTT Proxy And More	https://bit.ly/3xLbEoU
S10	Connecting OPC UA Publisher to Amazon AWS IoT with MQTT	https://bit.ly/3klcDJi
S11	IoT Telemetry Collection using Google Protocol Buffers, Google Cloud Functions, Cloud Pub/Sub, and MongoDB Atlas	https://bit.ly/3Zb1h9A
S12	Gathering system health telemetry data from AWS IoT Greengrass core devices	https://go.aws/3YZBmlC
S13	Digital Twins: Components, Use Cases, and Implementation Tips	https://bit.ly/3lZNyUH
S14	If You Build Products, You Should Be Using Digital Twins	https://bit.ly/3Sj8r9v
S15	Choose a device communication protocol	https://bit.ly/3SnEqW2
S16	Through edge-to-cloud integration framework	https://bit.ly/3Zs1iFI
S17	Send cloud-to-device messages from an IoT hub	https://bit.ly/3lSGRU1
S18	Stream Processing with IoT Data: Challenges, Best Practices, and Techniques	https://bit.ly/3ILxtLd
S19	Intelligence at the Edge Part 3: Edge Node Communication	https://bit.ly/3ZesxUI
S20	7 patterns for IoT data ingestion and visualization- How to decide what works best for your use case	https://go.aws/3YUNMLg
S21	How does a digital twin work?	https://ibm.co/3ZaZxgy
S22	Cloud Edge Computing: Beyond the Data Center	https://bit.ly/3Inl92j
S23	Understand Azure IoT Edge modules	https://bit.ly/3Ew9sFz
S24	Understand and use device twins in IoT Hub	https://bit.ly/3KqHWwU
S25	Understand and use module twins in IoT Hub	https://bit.ly/3xJCYDP
S26	How a Cloud Integration Platform Can Help Your Business	https://bit.ly/3nmHwy1
S27	Edge-to-cloud communication	https://bit.ly/3khYPiL
S28	Device connectivity	https://ibm.co/41vHgfZ
S29	How the IoT is creating today's hottest tech job: Edge analytics	https://bit.ly/3lZe8xh
S30	Edge Computing Architecture	https://bit.ly/3xTdwvz
S31	The Hark Platform	https://bit.ly/3xKFfik
S32	IoT Gateway User Guide	https://bit.ly/3InyJTx
S33	How to structure data ingestion and aggregation pipelines	https://bit.ly/3StSSMb
S34	What Is Streaming Data Integration?	https://bit.ly/3IIFPDp
S35	Plan your IoT real-time data streaming process	https://bit.ly/3EumGSZ
S36	What Is an Integration Platform? Do I Need One?	https://ibm.co/3kU52Sh
S37	What is Data Streaming?	https://bit.ly/3yrJrDI

S33]. Another option is *Peer-to-peer (P2P) based IoT Integration*, which is a decentralized practice of connecting IoT devices and integrating their data [S2,

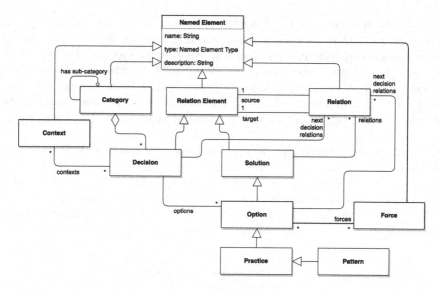

Fig. 2. Meta-model for ADD Models

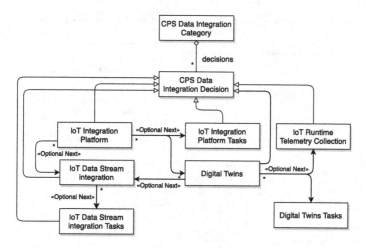

Fig. 3. Reusable ADD Model on Data Integration in CPS Architectures: Overview

S3, S4, S33, S34, S35]. In a P2P network, devices communicate directly with each other without the need for a central server or cloud-based service. Finally, some systems require *No IoT Data Stream Integration.*

Integrating the copious amounts of data IoT devices generate into a larger system can prove daunting [S1, S3, S4, S18, S33, S34, S35, S37]. Data stream integration involves several essential tasks, including *Data Gathering*, which involves collecting data from various sources to gain insights, make informed decisions, or optimize business operations [S1, S3, S4, S18, S20, S35]. *Data Normalization* arranges data in a database to reduce redundancy and enhance consistency [S1, S3, S4, S18, S20]. *Data Filtering* involves selecting a subset of data from a larger dataset based on specific criteria. *Data Aggregation* merges data from multiple sources or groups into a concise summary view [S1, S3, S4, S18, S20]. Lastly, *Data Anomaly Detection* entails identifying patterns or data points within a dataset that deviates from expected behavior [S18, S4, S20]. The decision context is the *IoT Data Stream*, i.e., the decision has to be taken for every IoT data stream separately.

Several factors influence the decision outcome. For instance, P2P and edge-based IoT data stream integration offer advantages such as shorter *development time, resilience,* as well as increased *data security* and *privacy* [S33, S34, S35]. Cloud-based IoT data stream integration may have higher network *latency* and may be more susceptible to *data security, integrity* and *privacy* concerns. However, *scalability* is an advantage of this practice [S2, S3, S4, S34, S35, S37].

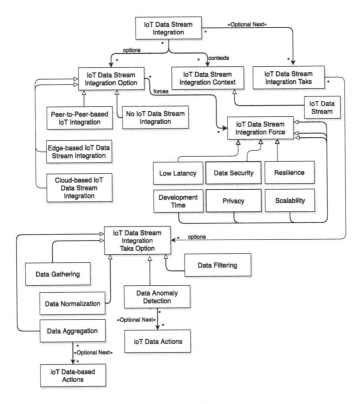

Fig. 4. IoT Data Stream Integration and IoT Data Stream Integration Tasks Decision

IoT Integration Platform and IoT Integration Platform Tasks (Fig. 5).

An *IoT integration platform* is a software solution enabling connecting and communicating between different devices and systems in an IoT ecosystem [S1, S16,

S20, S26, S30, S36]. It provides a central hub for managing and controlling IoT devices, data, and applications [S16, S20, S21, S26, S30, S36]. IoT integration platforms typically offer a range of features and functionalities, such as device management, data analytics, security and authentication, communication protocols, and integration with third-party systems and applications [S36, S20]. Different patterns and practices are used for connecting and integrating systems, applications, and services. One option is to use a *Cloud Integration Platform From Cloud Vendor* that seamlessly connects cloud-based applications and services [S1, S26, S30, S36]. Alternatively, *Edge Integration Platform from a Cloud Vendor* can integrate edge devices and systems with their cloud-based applications and services [S2, S30, S23]. Another practice is *Open/Standardized Cloud Integration Platform* that provides standard protocols, interfaces, and tools to connect and integrate different systems, applications, and services [S2, S30, S26]. Similarly, the *Open/Standardized Edge Integration Platform* simplifies the integration process by offering a common framework that can be used across edge devices, vendors, and domains [S1, S2, S23, S26, S30, S36].

When deciding on an *IoT integration platform*, the following tasks should be considered. One possible platform task is *Install and Update Device Workloads*, which involves deploying new software or updates to devices in a system [S20, S23, S26, S30, S36]. Additionally, updating device workloads requires careful planning and testing to ensure that updates are applied smoothly and do not cause downtime. *Establish Security* is another practice that involves implementing measures to protect against unauthorized access, data breaches, and other potential security threats [S36, S20]. Another practice is *Monitoring* referring to the ongoing observation and analysis of a system's performance and behavior. *Health Checking* evaluates the health status of a system, service, or application [S2, S20, S23]. The practice *Managing Device Communication* involves ensuring that devices can communicate with each other effectively and securely [S23, S3, S28]. *Edge/Cloud Platform Integration* involves integrating edge devices with cloud platforms to enable seamless data exchange, processing, and analysis between edge and cloud [S6, S9, S23]. Both decisions are made in the context of *IoT Edge* and *Cloud Computing*.

According to sources [S26, S30, S36], the Cloud Integration Platform and Edge Integration Platform provided by the cloud vendor affect system *evolvability*. They also impact *vendor lock-in* [S2, S23, S30]. Conversely, Open/Standardized Cloud Integration Platform and Open/Standardized Edge Integration Platform have a positive influence on *interoperability* [S1, S16, S26] and *configuration effect*, ensuring effective implementation of system configuration changes without negatively affecting performance or stability [S16, S26, S30, S36]. Moreover, Installing and Updating Device Workloads and Edge/Cloud Platform Integration contribute to *compatibility*. Monitoring and health checking ensure data *integrity* [S30, S31, S36]. Lastly, Managing Device Communication can impact the *security*.

Digital Twins and Digital Twins Tasks (Fig. 6). *Digital Twins* refer to virtual representations of physical objects, systems, or processes [S9, S21]. They

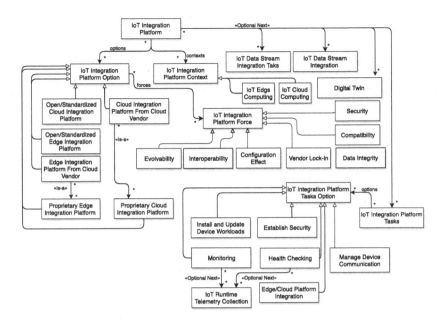

Fig. 5. IoT Integration Platform and IoT Integration Platform Taks Decision

are created using data from sensors, IoT devices, and other sources that collect data on the object or system in question [S21]. The digital twin mimics the physical object or system in real-time, allowing for better monitoring, analysis, and optimization [S5, S8, S9, S13, S14, S21, S24, S25]. Digital Twins enable remote monitoring, predictive maintenance, and provide insights into performance. The relation between digital twins and CPS data integration is that digital twins are an integral part of the data integration process in CPS. There are two options regarding this decision; one is to use *Digital Twin* and *No Digital Twin*. This decision can be decided in each *IoT Data Stream* context. If *Digital Twin* is chosen, the *Digital Twin Tasks* decision is an important follow-up decision on the tasks the twin shall fulfill [S5, S8, S9, S13, S14, S20, S21]. A *Device Metadata Twin* is a type of digital twin that reflects a physical device's metadata and configuration information, providing a virtual representation of the device for monitoring, management, and maintenance purposes [S5, S14, S21]. The *IoT Module Data Twin* practice involves creating a digital twin that mimics the behavior and data of an IoT module [S13, S14, S21]. *Device Visualization* transforms physical devices into digital representations displayed on dashboards for easier monitoring, management, and interaction [S14, S20, S21]. *Device Control* enables remote management and operation of physical devices through a digital interface, including functions like power control, settings adjustment, and other necessary operations [S14, S24, S25]. *Device Configuration* involves the setup and customization of physical devices [S21, S24, S25]. This decision can be made for each *IoT Data Stream* where a digital twin is applied.

Device Metadata Twin and IoT Module Data Twin benefit the *flexibility* for adapting and changing in response to new requirements or changes in the physical system it represents, as well as *automation* for automating tasks and processes [S5, S8, S9, S14, S20, S21]. Device Visualization positively impacts *visibility* for monitoring and visualizing the performance and behavior of physical systems in a digital form [S20, S21]. Device Configuration and Device Control practices benefits *Configurability*.

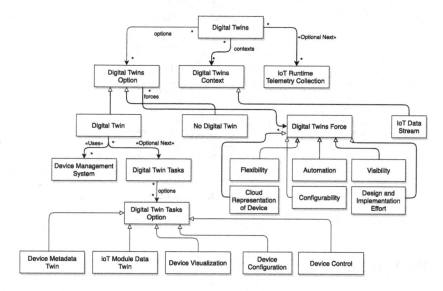

Fig. 6. Digital Twins and Digital Twins Tasks Decision

IoT Runtime Telemetry Collection (Fig. 7). IoT runtime telemetry collection involves collecting and analyzing data related to the performance and behavior of IoT devices and systems while in operation [S2, S11, S12, S15, S17, S19, S27, S28]. The telemetry data includes device status, network connectivity, sensor readings, and other performance indicators. Options for implementation include not collecting telemetry, using cloud-based or edge-based runtime telemetry collection. The option *No Runtime Telemetry Collection* is the most straightforward. *Cloud-based Runtime Telemetry Collection* gathers data and metrics from cloud-based applications and systems for analysis, collected in a central platform [S2, S11, S12, S15, S27]. On the other hand, *Edge-based Runtime Telemetry Collection* [S2, S11, S12, S15, S27] is a practice that involves the collection of runtime data from various devices and systems located at the edge of a network. This practice can use *Device Configuration* to set up and customize a device's settings to meet specific requirements [S21, S24, S25]. This decision can be made for each *IoT Data Stream*.

Cloud-based Runtime Telemetry Collection and Edge-based Runtime Telemetry Collection can benefit *product quality improvement* [S12, S15, S27]. Furthermore, it enables *monitoring* of connected devices to detect anomalies and prevent downtime while providing insights into device performance and usage to optimize operations and improve *efficiency*. Additionally, by analyzing telemetry data, organizations can predict when maintenance is needed to improve *reliability*.

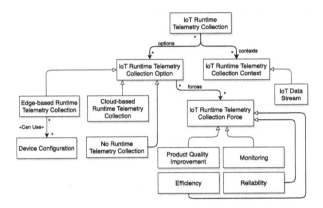

Fig. 7. IoT Runtime Telemetry Collection

5   Evaluation

We meticulously constructed an ADD model based on the chosen sources following the sequence presented in Table 1. We named the ADD model elements using the terminology from the respective sources and generated generic type names based on these element names. Whenever a new type name arose, we compared it against the existing names and determined whether the new type name was required. As illustrated in Fig. 8, the theoretical saturation point was attained after incorporating twenty-five sources. In the initial thirteen sources, we had to modify the designated type names frequently. However, in the following twelve sources, such changes were less frequent. No further modifications and additions were necessary for the remaining sources.

6   Discussion

This section discusses our findings for the research questions from Sect. 1.

RQ1: After analyzing *37* practitioner knowledge sources, we discovered evidence for *31* patterns and practices currently used by practitioners for supporting data integration in CPS architectures, which we modeled as ADD decision options. These patterns and practices are associated with ADDs and were found to be largely independent of each other. An exception is the *Edge-based Runtime*

Telemetry Collection practice, which can use the *Device Configuration* practice. Another commonality is that the *IoT Data Stream Integration, IoT Integration Platform, IoT Integration Platform Tasks* and *IoT Runtime Telemetry Collection* decisions all offer decision edge-based and cloud-based decision options. Depending on the specific needs, the practitioner may wish to mix and match these edge and cloud-based practices.

During our research, we discovered a subtle aspect that the practitioner should take note of. Both the decisions for *Digital Twins Tasks* and *IoT Runtime Telemetry Collection* include *Device Configuration* as an option, while the decision for *IoT Data Stream Integration* offers *P2P-based IoT Integration*. It is important to highlight that the latter decision option, despite its different description, may still involve device configuration implicitly. Therefore, when designing CPS, the practitioner should consider this potential overlap.

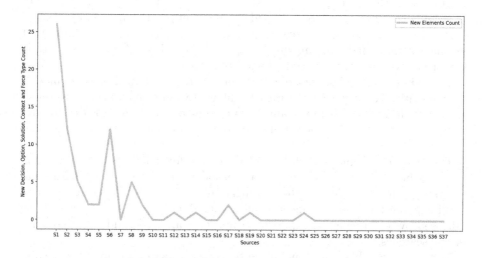

Fig. 8. Number of Elements of Newly-Added Sources

RQ2: Given the central *CPS Data Integration* decision, we identified *7* top-level ADDs for supporting data integration in CPS architectures. Our research revealed subtle relations between ADDs and decision options, which may not be immediately apparent. For instance, the seemingly loosely-related *Data Anomaly Detection, Digital Twins, IoT Runtime Telemetry Collection, Cloud-based IoT Data Stream Integration* decisions all are applied in the *IoT Data Stream* context, which is an important consideration during the planning of a CPS architecture.

RQ3: Our research helped us discover *22* influencing factors (forces) when architecting CPS in the context of data integration from the practitioners' perspective. We found that these forces were generally fairly specific to the individual ADDs and decision options but identified some common to multiple ADDs and their options. For example, *Flexibility, Automation, Visibility* apply to the *Digital*

Twins decision and, assuming the *Digital Twin* decision option is selected, then also the decision options for the *Digital Twin Tasks* decision; *Device Configuration* applies to decision options for both the *Digital Twins Tasks* decision and the *IoT Runtime Telemetry Collection* decision; *Security* applies especially to decision options associated with *IoT Data Stream Integration, IoT Data Stream Integration Tasks* and *IoT Integration Platform Tasks* decisions, but must be considered throughout.

Since the above forces are central to multiple ADDs and their respective decision options, the practitioner may wish to consider the significance of these forces early in the architectural planning of a system and be guided accordingly.

7 Threats to Validity

We discuss the threats to validity based on the threat types by Wohlin et al. [17].

To enhance internal validity, we used independent practitioner reports instead of interviews to avoid bias. However, interviews could have revealed important information that might be missing in reports. To address this, we extensively examined diverse sources, exceeding what was necessary.

To minimize researcher bias, different team members cross-checked all models independently. Yet, a potential threat to internal validity remains due to possible biases within the research team. This applies to our coding procedure and formal modeling as well, where different researchers might have used different approaches.

The experience and search-based procedure for knowledge sources may introduce bias. However, our research method primarily relied on additional sources adhering to specific criteria, mitigating this threat. Nonetheless, there is still a potential threat of unconsciously excluding certain sources, which we addressed by assembling an experienced author team and conducting comprehensive searches.

Our results can likely be generalized to various types of architectures involving data integration in CPS. However, there is a threat to external validity, indicating that our findings are applicable only to similar CPS architectures. Generalizing to novel or unconventional architectures may require modifications to our models.

8 Conclusion

We conducted a GT-based grey literature study to create a model for data integration in CPS architectures that included ADDs, decision options, relations, and decision drivers. Our research focused on supporting data integration in CPS architectures and addressed three research questions. For RQ1, we analyzed 37 practitioner knowledge sources and identified 31 patterns and practices used by practitioners in data integration. These patterns and practices were modeled as ADD decision options and were found to be largely independent. We also highlighted the relationships between certain practices and the flexibility of mixing edge-based and cloud-based approaches. RQ2 explored the top-level ADDs for data integration in CPS architectures. Based on the central CPS Data Integration decision, we identified seven top-level ADDs and revealed subtle relationships between them. Understanding the shared contexts and dependencies among these ADDs is crucial during CPS architectural planning. In RQ3, we identified 22 influencing factors (forces) that impact CPS architecture design in the context of data integration. These forces varied across individual ADDs and their options.

This paper proposes a promising approach that systematically and impartially studies multiple sources and integrates findings through formal modeling. By following this methodology, potential issues can be mitigated, and a rigorous and unbiased understanding of current practices in specific fields, like data integration in CSP architecture, can be obtained.

Acknowledgements. This work was supported by the FFG (Austrian Research Promotion Agency) project MODIS (no. FO999895431).

References

1. Coplien, J.: Software Patterns: Management Briefings. SIGS, New York (1996)
2. Ghosh, A., Edwards, D., Hosseini, M.R.: Patterns and trends in internet of things (IoT) research: future applications in the construction industry. Eng., Constr. Architect. Manage. **28**, 457–481 (2020)
3. Glaser, B.G., Strauss, A.L.: The discovery of grounded theory: strategies for qualitative research. de Gruyter (1967)
4. Gorton, I., Klein, J., Nurgaliev, A.: Architecture knowledge for evaluating scalable databases. In: Proceedings of the 12th Working IEEE/IFIP Conference on Software Architecture, pp. 95–104 (2015)
5. van Heesch, U., Avgeriou, P., Hilliard, R.: A documentation framework for architecture decisions. J. Syst. Softw. **85**(4), 795–820 (2012)
6. Henneke, D., Elattar, M., Jasperneite, J.: Communication patterns for cyber-physical systems. In: 2015 IEEE 20th Conference on Emerging Technologies and Factory Automation (ETFA), pp. 1–4 (2015)
7. Hentrich, C., Zdun, U., Hlupic, V., Dotsika, F.: An approach for pattern mining through grounded theory techniques and its applications to process-driven SOA patterns. In: Proceedings of the 18th European Conference on Pattern Languages of Program, pp. 1–16 (2015)
8. Jamaludin, J., Rohani, J.M.: Cyber-physical system (CPS): state of the art. In: 2018 International Conference on Computing, Electronic and Electrical Engineering (ICE Cube), pp. 1–5 (2018). https://doi.org/10.1109/ICECUBE.2018.8610996
9. Lytra, I., Sobernig, S., Zdun, U.: Architectural decision making for service-based platform integration: a qualitative multi-method study. In: Proceedings of WICSA/ECSA (2012)
10. Musil, A., Musil, J., Weyns, D., Bures, T., Muccini, H., Sharaf, M.: Patterns for self-adaptation in cyber-physical systems. In: Biffl, S., Lüder, A., Gerhard, D. (eds.) Multi-Disciplinary Engineering for Cyber-Physical Production Systems, pp. 331–368. Springer, Cham (2017). https://doi.org/10.1007/978-3-319-56345-9_13

11. Pautasso, C., Zimmermann, O., Leymann, F.: RESTful web services vs. big web services: making the right architectural decision. In: Proceedings of the 17th World Wide Web Conference, pp. 805–814 (2008)
12. Pontes, P., Lima, B., Faria, J.: Test patterns for IoT, pp. 63–66 (2018)
13. Reinfurt, L., Breitenbücher, U., Falkenthal, M., Leymann, F., Riegg, A.: Internet of things patterns, pp. 1–21 (2016). https://doi.org/10.1145/3011784.3011789
14. Sha, L., Meseguer, J.: Design of complex cyber physical systems with formalized architectural patterns. In: Wirsing, M., Banâtre, J.-P., Hölzl, M., Rauschmayer, A. (eds.) Software-Intensive Systems and New Computing Paradigms. LNCS, vol. 5380, pp. 92–100. Springer, Heidelberg (2008). https://doi.org/10.1007/978-3-540-89437-7_5
15. Warnett, S.J., Zdun, U.: Architectural design decisions for machine learning deployment. In: 19th IEEE International Conference on Software Architecture (ICSA 2022) (2022). http://eprints.cs.univie.ac.at/7270/
16. Washizaki, H., Ogata, S., Hazeyama, A., Okubo, T., Fernández, E., Yoshioka, N.: Landscape of architecture and design patterns for IoT systems. IEEE Internet Things J. **7**, 10091–10101 (2020). https://doi.org/10.1109/JIOT.2020.3003528
17. Wohlin, C., Runeson, P., Hoest, M., Ohlsson, M.C., Regnell, B., Wesslen, A.: Experimentation in Software Engineering. Springer, Cham (2012)
18. Zdun, U., Stocker, M., Zimmermann, O., Pautasso, C., Lübke, D.: Guiding architectural decision making on quality aspects in microservice APIs. In: Pahl, C., Vukovic, M., Yin, J., Yu, Q. (eds.) ICSOC 2018. LNCS, vol. 11236, pp. 73–89. Springer, Cham (2018). https://doi.org/10.1007/978-3-030-03596-9_5
19. Zimmermann, O., Koehler, J., Leymann, F., Polley, R., Schuster, N.: Managing architectural decision models with dependency relations, integrity constraints, and production rules. J. Syst. Softw. **82**(8), 1249–1267 (2009)

IDLGen: Automated Code Generation for Inter-parameter Dependencies in Web APIs

Saman Barakat[✉][ID], Ana Belén Sánchez[ID], and Sergio Segura[ID]

SCORE Lab, I3US Institute, Universidad de Sevilla, Seville, Spain
{salias,anabsanchez,sergiosegura}@us.es

Abstract. The generation of code templates from web API specifications is a common practice in industry. However, existing tools neglect the dependencies among input parameters (so-called inter-parameter dependencies), extremely common in practice and usually described in natural language. As a result, developers are responsible for implementing the corresponding validation logic manually, a tedious and error-prone process. In this paper, we present IDLGen, an approach for the automated generation of validation code for inter-parameter dependencies in web APIs. Specifically, we exploit the IDL4OAS extension for specifying inter-parameter dependencies as a part of OpenAPI Specification (OAS) files. To make our approach applicable in practice, we present an extension of the popular OpenAPI Generator tool ecosystem, automating the generation of Java and Python code for the management of inter-parameter dependencies in web APIs. Evaluation results show the effectiveness of the approach in accelerating the development of APIs, generating up to 9.4 times more lines of Java code than the current generator. This leads to average time savings ranging from 16 to 24 min when implementing API operations including between one and three dependencies, when compared to manual coding. More importantly, the generated code mitigates human errors, making web APIs significantly more reliable.

Keywords: Web APIs · Open API and Scaffolding · Code generation

1   Introduction

Web Application Programming Interfaces (APIs) enable communication between heterogeneous devices and systems over the Web. They have gained significant interest in the software industry as the *de-facto* standard for software integration. API directories such as Rapid [32] index over 40K web APIs from different domains such as shopping, finance, and social networks. Web APIs can be categorized into various types based on application designs and the communication protocols they use. Hypertext Transfer Protocol (HTTP) APIs, arguably the de-facto standard, use the HTTP protocol to interact—typically through CRUD

F. Monti et al. (Eds.): ICSOC 2023, LNCS 14419, pp. 153–168, 2023.
https://doi.org/10.1007/978-3-031-48421-6_11

(Create, Read, Update, and Delete) operations—with resources (e.g., a *video* in
the YouTube API [40] or an *invoice* in the PayPal API [30]). HTTP APIs often
implement the principles of the REST architectural style for distributed systems,
being referred to as RESTful APIs [10]. Henceforth, we will use the term web
API to refer to RESTful web APIs or, more generally, to HTTP APIs.

Web APIs are commonly described using the OpenAPI Specification (OAS)
format [12,29]. An OAS document describes a web API in terms of the operations supported, as well as their input parameters and the possible responses.
OAS documents are heavily used nowadays for automating certain tasks in the
API lifecycle. One of these applications is *scaffolding*: generating code templates
for both API servers and clients from the OAS specification of the API. There are
multiple tools available for code generation, including AutoRest [2], Codegen [6],
NSwag [25], and OpenAPI Generator [28], among others. OpenAPI Generator
Ais a popular open-source code generation tool ecosystem for OAS. It is developed in Java and offers over 50 generators for clients and servers in different
programming languages.

Web APIs typically include inter-parameter dependencies. These are constraints that restrict the way in which two or more input parameters can be
combined to form a valid call to the service [20,21]. For example, when searching
for businesses in the Yelp API[1], the parameter `location` is "required if either
`latitude` or `longitude` is not provided", and both parameters are "required
if `location` is not provided". A recent study revealed that dependencies are
extremely common and pervasive in industrial web APIs: they appear in 4 out
of every 5 APIs across all application domains and types of operations [21]. However, the current version of OAS provides no support for the formal description of
these types of dependencies, despite being a highly demanded feature by practitioners[2]. Instead, users are encouraged to describe them informally using natural
language[3]. As a result, current scaffolding tools do not support the generation
of validation code for inter-parameter dependencies, as these are not specified
in OAS documents. Therefore, the validation code associated to these dependencies must be manually implemented. In the previous example, for instance,
developers should write the required assertions to make sure that `latitude` and
`longitude` parameters are used together when the `location` parameter is not
provided in an API call, both in clients and servers. This is not only tedious,
but also error-prone, making validation failures very common in practice [22].

In this paper, we present IDLGen, an approach for the automated generation
of code for validating inter-parameter dependencies in web API servers. For this,
we leverage IDL4OAS, an OAS extension for specifying *inter-parameter dependencies* as a part of OAS documents using the Inter-parameter Dependency
Language (IDL) [17,20]. To make our approach readily applicable in practice,
we present an extension of the OpenAPI Generator tool ecosystem, enabling
the automated generation of Java and Python code for the validation of inter-

[1] https://docs.developer.yelp.com/reference/v3_business_search.
[2] https://github.com/OAI/OpenAPI-Specification/issues/256.
[3] https://swagger.io/docs/specification/describing-parameters.

parameter dependencies in API servers. Evaluation results show that our approach generates up to 940% more lines of code (LoC) for Java, 491% on average. This improvement is even more noticeable for Python, where the OpenAPI Generator generates an empty method for each API operation, whereas IDLGen generates up to 68 LoC, 37.2 on average, Additionally, the results of an empirical study with 81 participants revealed that IDLGen saves, on average, between 16 and 24 min per API operation (including between one and three dependencies) when compared to manual coding. More importantly, our results show that IDLGen effectively avoids human mistakes, common in practice, making web APIs significantly more reliable.

A very preliminary version of this work, restricted to code generation for Java, was presented in [3]. This paper extends our previous work in several directions, including a significantly larger evaluation with 14 industrial API operations, code generation for Java and Python, and an empirical study with 81 participants.

2   Background

This section introduces key concepts to contextualize our proposal, namely, IDL, the IDL4OAS extension, and the OpenAPI Generator tool ecosystem.

2.1   Inter-parameter Dependency Language (IDL)

The Inter-parameter Dependency Language (IDL) is a textual domain-specific language used to describe dependencies among input parameters in web APIs [20]. IDL was created based on the results of a study of more than 2.5K operations of 40 real-world APIs. Specifically, IDL supports expressing seven types of inter-parameter dependencies widely used in practice. As an example, Listing 1 shows a fragment of an IDL document describing the inter-parameter dependencies found in the Google Maps Places API [13]. In what follows, we briefly introduce the types of dependencies supported by IDL including references to Listing 1:

```
1   // Operation: Search for places within specified area:
2   ZeroOrOne(radius, rankby=='distance');
3   IF rankby=='distance' THEN keyword OR name OR type;
4   maxprice >= minprice;
5
6   // Operation: Query information about places:
7   AllOrNone(location, radius);
8   Or(query, type);
9   maxprice >= minprice;
10
11  // Operation: Get photo of place:
12  OnlyOne(maxheight, maxwidth);
13
14  // Operation: Automcomplete place name:
15  IF strictbounds THEN location AND radius;
```

Listing 1. IDL specification of Google Maps Places API.

– **Requires.** This type of dependency emerges when the presence of a parameter *p1* in a request requires the presence of another parameter *p2*. For example, line 3 indicates that if the parameter *rankby* of the search operation in

Google Maps is set to 'distance', then at least one of the following parameters must be present: *keyword, name* or *type.*

- **Or.** Given a set of parameters, one or more of them must be included in the request. As an example, in the Google Maps Places API, when searching for places (line 8), both *query* and *type* parameters are optional, but at least one of them must be used.
- **OnlyOne.** Given a set of parameters, one and only one of them must be included in the request. For example, line 12 indicates that only one of the parameters *maxheight* and *maxwidth* must be used.
- **AllOrNone.** Given a set of parameters, either all of them must be included in the request, or none of them. For example, as expressed in line 7, either both *location* and *radius* are used, or none of them.
- **ZeroOrOne.** Given a set of parameters, zero or at most one must be included in the request. For example, line 2 indicates that if the parameter *radius* is used, then *rankby* cannot be set to 'distance' and vice versa.
- **Arithmetic/Relational.** Relational and arithmetic dependencies relate two or more parameters using standard relational and arithmetic operators. For example, as stated in line 4, the parameter *maxprice* must be greater than or equal to *minprice.*
- **Complex.** These dependencies are specified as a combination of the previous ones.

We refer the reader to [17,20] for a detailed description of the language, including its grammar.

2.2   IDL4OAS

Web APIs are commonly described using the OAS [29] format, arguably the industry standard. OAS documents describe web APIs in terms of the elements it comprises, namely, paths, operations, resources, request parameters, and responses. IDL4OAS [20] is an OAS extension for describing inter-parameter dependencies within OAS using the IDL language. This makes it possible to process dependencies automatically and leverage them, for example, for automated test case generation [22].

IDL4OAS supports specifying inter-parameter dependencies at the operation level. As an example, Listing 2 shows an excerpt of an OAS document in YAML format extended with IDL4OAS, corresponding to the Get Bussiness operation of the Yelp API [38]. As illustrated, the property "x-dependencies" has been added to the "GET /businesses/search" operation. This property is an array of elements, where each element—preceded by a hyphen— represents a single dependency following the syntax of IDL.

```
1  paths:
2    /businesses/search:
3      get:
4        parameters:
5          - name: location [...]
6          - name: latitude [...]
7          - name: longitude [...]
```

```
 8        - name: open_now [...]
 9        - name: open_at [...]
10        - name: limit [...]
11        - name: offset [...]
12        - [...]
13      [...]
14      x-dependencies:
15        - Or(location, latitude AND longitude);
16        - ZeroOrOne(open_now, open_at);
17        - offset + limit <= 1000;
18        - IF offset AND NOT limit THEN offset <= 980;
```

Listing 2. OAS document of the Get Businesses operation from the Yelp API extended with IDL4OAS

2.3 OpenAPI Generator

OpenAPI Generator is a set of tools that automatically generate API clients library, server stubs, configuration, and documentation files based on a given OAS definition of the API [28]. It is developed in Java, with over 50 generators for clients and servers that generate code for different programming languages.

OpenAPI Generator has transforming logic as well as templates for each generation of code. Built-in templates are written in Mustache [24], which is a template system with multiple implementations for different languages and technologies. The templates contain common code, independent of the specific API, and have variables that are replaced with the parsed data from the OAS file. As an example, Listing 3 (Lines 1, 18–28), shows the code generated when running OpenAPI Generator on the *Search Business* operation within the Yelp API, as shown in Listing 2. It basically consists of a method including some media type checks and returning an HTTP error (501 -"Not implemented") to let the developer know that (s)he must implement the functionality of the operation.

3 Approach: IDLGen

We propose IDLGen, an approach for the automated generation of validation code for inter-parameter dependencies in Web APIs. Given an API request, the generated code automatically checks its conformance to the inter-parameter dependencies of the API, returning an informative error in case a violation is detected. By automating this process, our approach not only saves development time but also eliminates potential bugs caused by programming mistakes, which are prevalent in the validation code of web APIs [21,23].

Figure 1 depicts an overview of the approach. IDLGen generates code from the API specification in OAS format, arguably the industry standard. This makes our approach readily applicable and language-independent. Specifically, we leverage the IDL4OAS extension for extending OAS files with a rigorous specification of inter-parameter dependencies using the IDL language. Hence, given an input OAS file enriched with IDL4OAS, we propose transforming each dependency into a fragment of executable code that checks whether the incoming API request satisfies it or not, returning an informative message and an HTTP error status code in case it is violated. We propose using code templates for the generation of code, making our approach easily customizable.

```
 1  default ResponseEntity<BusinessesResult> getBusinesses(. . .) {
 2  +   // Check dependency: Or(location, latitude AND longitude);
 3  +   if(DependencyUtil.doNotSatisfyOrDependency((location != null),(latitude != null) &&
        (longitude != null))){
 4  +       return new ResponseEntity("Dependency not satisfied: Or(location, latitude AND
            longitude);", HttpStatus.BAD_REQUEST);
 5  +   }
 6  +   // Check dependency: ZeroOrOne(open_now, open_at);
 7  +   if(DependencyUtil.doNotSatisfyZeroOrOneDependency((openNow != null),(openAt != null))){
 8  +       return new ResponseEntity("Dependency not satisfied: ZeroOrOne(open_now, open_at);",
            HttpStatus.BAD_REQUEST);
 9  +   }
10  +   // Check dependency: offset + limit <= 1000;
11  +   if(!(!(offset != null && limit != null) || (offset+limit<=1000.0))){
12  +       return new ResponseEntity("Dependency not satisfied: offset + limit <= 1000;",
            HttpStatus.BAD_REQUEST);
13  +   }
14  +   // Check dependency: IF (offset AND NOT limit) THEN offset <= 980;
15  +   if(!(!((offset != null) && !(limit != null)) || (offset != null && offset<=980.0))){
16  +       return new ResponseEntity("Dependency not satisfied: IF (offset AND NOT limit) THEN
            offset <= 980;", HttpStatus.BAD_REQUEST);
17  +   }
18    getRequest().ifPresent(request -> {
19      for (MediaType mediaType: MediaType.parseMediaTypes(request.getHeader("Accept"))) {
20        if (mediaType.isCompatibleWith(MediaType.valueOf("application/json"))) {
21          String exampleString = ". . .";
22          ApiUtil.setExampleResponse(request, "application/json", exampleString);
23          break;
24        }
25      }
26    });
27    return new ResponseEntity<>(HttpStatus.NOT_IMPLEMENTED);
28  }
29  +   public static boolean doNotSatisfyOrDependency(boolean... assertions){
30  +       boolean result = false;
31  +       for (int i=0;i<assertions.length;i++){
32  +           result = result || assertions[i];
33  +           if (result)
34  +               return false;
35  +       }
36  +       return true;
37  +   }
38  +   public static boolean doNotSatisfyZeroOrOneDependency(boolean... assertions){
39  +       boolean result = true;
40  +       for (int i=0;i<assertions.length;i++){
41  +           result = result && ZeroOrOneAllOrNoneElement(i,assertions,false,true);
42  +           if (!result)
43  +               break;
44  +       }
45  +       return !result;
46  +   }
47  +   private static boolean ZeroOrOneAllOrNoneElement(int i,boolean[] allElements,
        boolean negateElement, boolean negateRemainingElements){
48  +       boolean element = negateElement ? allElements[i]:!allElements[i];
49  +       if (element)
50  +           return true;
51  +       boolean result = true;
52  +       for (int j=0;j<allElements.length;j++){
53  +           if (i!=j){
54  +               boolean otherElement = negateRemainingElements ? !allElements[j]:allElements[j];
55  +               result = result && otherElement;
56  +               if (!result)
57  +                   return false;
58  +           }
59  +       }
60  +       return true;
61  +   }
```

Listing 3. Code generated by IDLGen for the Get Businesses operation (Yelp API)

To make our approach applicable in practice, we have developed IDLGen, an extension of the widely recognized OpenAPI Generator tool suite [28], complementing its functionalities to generate Java and Python code to deal with dependencies in web API servers. To achieve our objectives, we created a fork of the OpenAPI Generator project on GitHub [15]. Within this fork, we extended the functionality of two generators, responsible for generating projects for "Spring" and "FastAPI" frameworks. Additionally, we developed a Mustache template that incorporates the necessary logic for different types of dependencies, including *Or, OnlyOne, AllOrNone*, and *ZeroOrOne*. Leveraging the extended classes, the IDL parser [16], and the Mustache template, we translated dependencies expressed using IDL4OAS [20] into conditional blocks for each assertion within an operation. If the condition specified by the dependency is not met, the code returns a bad request HTTP status code (400), accompanied by descriptive error messages.

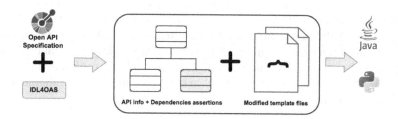

Fig. 1. IDLGen overview

As an example, Listings 3 depicts the Java server code generated by IDLGen for the Get Bussiness operation of the Yelp API. The tool receives as input the specification of the API operation, shown in Listing 2, including the description of dependencies in an IDL4OAS block. Lines of code generated by IDLGen are highlighted in green and preceded by the symbol '+' for illustrative purposes. Lines not highlighted are those generated by the original OpenAPI Generator. As illustrated, the code generated by IDLGen consists of conditional statements checking whether or not each dependency is violated (lines 2–17), plus some auxiliary methods for checking non-trivial dependencies (lines 29–61). Overall, IDLGen generates 55 LoC without counting comments, whereas the original OpenAPI Generator generates 10 LoC. This means an improvement of 450% on the amount of generated code.

4 Evaluation

We aim to answer the following research questions:

- **RQ1**: *What are the gains of using* IDLGen *in terms of the amount of generated code?* We aim to quantify the gains of our approach in terms of the lines of code automatically generated in comparison with standard code generators.

– **RQ2**: *What are the benefits of* IDLGen *in terms of development time and ratio of failures?* We aim to study the benefit of using our approach in reducing development time and faults in the validation code of inter-parameter dependencies compared to manual implementation.

4.1 Subject APIs

We used a dataset of 14 API operations from 10 real-world APIs previously used in the context of web API testing [33]. These operations represent a diverse set in terms of domains, sizes, and dependencies, including all the types of inter-parameter dependencies identified in [21] (c.f. Sect. 2.1). Table 1 shows the web API operations used in this study. For each operation, the table shows the name and reference of the API it belongs to, name, number of parameters, number of dependencies, and number (and percentage) of parameters involved in its dependencies (column PD(%)). For each API, we used the OAS specification file provided in [33], which includes the specification of IDL dependencies using IDL4OAS. Since the experiments were run locally, we slightly modified each OAS file changing the server URL and removing security-related configuration details, e.g. OAuth. The resulting OAS files used in our experiments are available as part of the supplementary material [4].

4.2 Experiment 1: Code Generation

In this experiment, we aim to answer RQ1 by evaluating the amount of code generated by our approach in comparison to standard specification-driven tools.

Experimental Setup. We used IDLGen—our extension of the OpenAPI Generator tool—to generate Java server code (Spring) and Python server code (FastAPI) for the API operations listed in Table 1. Specifically, for each operation, we generated code using the standard OAS specification files—with no information about inter-parameter dependencies—and the OAS files enriched with IDL4OAS—describing inter-parameter dependencies using IDL. Then, we computed the number of generated lines of code on each scenario, with and without dependencies. To make the results more accurate, we restricted the counting of LoC to the method implementing the API operation (and corresponding auxiliary methods), excluding imports and class definitions code, since it is common in both cases. The generated projects are available as part of the supplementary material of the paper [4].

Experimental Results. Table 1 shows the result of our experiment on 14 real-world API operations. On the one hand, the original OpenAPI Generator tool—with no support for dependencies—generated exactly 10 LoC of Java for each API operation. This is because the code generated is always the same: a method template with some basic media type checks (see lines 18–28 from the example in Listing 3). Analogously, it generated an empty method in Python for each API operation. On the other hand, IDLGen—including support for dependencies–generated between 13 and 104 LoC of Java (59.1 LoC on average) and between 2 and 68 LoC of Python (37.2 on average). This means IDLGen generated between 30% and 940% more Java code (491% on average) than the popular OpenAPI Generator tool (recall that the tool generates a method with 10 LoC for all API operations). The improvement is even more noticeable in Python, where OpenAPI Generator generated an empty method for each API operation, whereas IDLGen generated up to 68 LoC. As expected, this improvement seems to be proportional to the number of dependencies of the operation. As an example, the largest portion of code (94 LoC for Java, 68 LoC for Python) was generated for the API operation with more dependencies, YouTube Search, with 31 parameters and 15 dependencies (c.f. Table 1).

Table 1. Java and Python #LoC generated by IDLGen. Deps = Dependencies. PD(%) = Number and percentage of parameters involved in the dependencies.

API Operation	Parameters	Deps	PD(%)	Java	Python
Amadeus - HotelOffers [1]	27	8	11 (41%)	**93**	**62**
Box - FoldersItems [5]	9	3	5 (56%)	**43**	**25**
DHL - FindByAddress [8]	10	1	2 (20%)	**22**	**9**
Foursquare - VenuesSearch [11]	17	3	7 (41%)	**53**	**32**
Ohsome - ElementArea [26]	11	3	7 (64%)	**86**	**59**
Ohsome - ElementAreaRatio [26]	15	4	9 (60%)	**89**	**61**
OMDb - Search [27]	9	1	3 (33%)	**47**	**29**
Travels - TripsUser [35]	6	1	2 (33%)	**13**	**2**
Tumblr - BlogLikes [36]	5	1	3 (60%)	**37**	**21**
Yelp - BusinessesSearch [38]	14	4	7 (50%)	**55**	**34**
Yelp - TransactionsSearch [38]	3	1	3 (100%)	**22**	**9**
YouTube - Comments [40]	6	3	4 (67%)	**77**	**52**
YouTube - CommentThreads [40]	11	6	9 (82%)	**86**	**58**
YouTube - Search [40]	31	15	26 (84%)	**104**	**68**
Mean				**59.1**	**37.2**

To check the correctness of the generated code we performed a sanity check as follows. We used the open-source framework RESTest [22,33] for automatically generating test cases for the API operations under test. Specifically, for each subject API operation, we used RESTest to generate 1000 valid test cases— satisfying all the dependencies described in the OAS file—and 1000 invalid test cases—API requests violating one or more inter-parameter dependencies. Then, we ran the test cases against the validation code generated and confirmed that they were correctly processed. Specifically, valid calls were handled returning a

200 HTTP status code[4], whereas invalid calls were correctly identified, returning proper 400 HTTP status codes and descriptive error messages. This supports the validity of the generated code. The generated test cases are also available as a part of the supplementary material [4].

> **Response to RQ1**
>
> IDLGen generates between 1.3 and 9.4 times more Java code than a standard code generator. The improvement is even more noticeable in Python, where OpenAPI Generator generates no code (empty method), and IDLGen generates between 2 and 68 LoC.

4.3   Experiment 2: Implementation Time and Faults

In this experiment, we aim to address RQ2 by evaluating the time required by developers to implement the validation code for checking inter-parameter dependencies, as well as the failure rate of the produced code.

Experimental Setup. We conducted an experiment with 81 s-year students of the Software Engineering Bachelor Degree at *University of Seville*. Specifically, the experiment was conducted in the course on Software Architecture and Integration. The experiment took place at the end of the course when students had gained experience consuming and implementing REST APIs using the Spring framework. Participants were tasked with implementing inter-parameter dependencies for two API operations, keeping a record of the invested time. Then, the resulting code was analyzed by the authors, who ran a thorough test suite on each participant project to identify failures.

The 81 participants were divided into four groups, who attended a session of 1 h and 50 min each. The authors of the paper conducted each session. At the beginning of each session, the instructors briefly introduced inter-parameter dependencies and IDL. Then, participants were asked to download two template Java projects (Spring Boot) from GitHub, where they had to implement the inter-parameter dependencies of two API operations: a mock version of the search business transactions operation in the Yelp Fusion API, and a mock version of the folder listing operation in the Box API. The Yelp Fusion API project featured a single dependency, whereas the Box API project had three dependencies, depicted in IDL format in Listings 4 and 5, respectively. Participants were asked to implement and test their code and then submit it through the university virtual platform, indicating the starting and ending time for each project as a part of the submission. In a later step, each submission was thoroughly analyzed by the authors, running a test suite on each participant project. These

---

[4] We configured the tool such that the generated code returns a 200 status code (rather than 501 - "Not implemented") when all dependencies are satisfied.

test suites were carefully crafted by the authors trying to cover the most relevant input combinations and including both valid and invalid API requests. As a sanity check, we used IDLGen for generating code for both API operations and confirmed that the generated code passed both test suites.

Among the 162 submissions received (two projects per participant), five of them were empty and were discarded, resulting in 77 projects for the Yelp API, and 80 for the Box API. All submissions, duly anonymized, are included in the supplementary material [4], as well as the test suites used.

```
1  - Or(location, latitude AND longitude);
```

Listing 4. IDL specification of the Search Business Transactions operation (Yelp API)

```
1  - IF marker THEN usemarker == true;
2  - IF (usemarker == true AND folder_id == '0') THEN NOT sort;
3  - ZeroOrOne(usemarker == true, offset);
```

Listing 5. IDL specification of the Folder Listing operation (Box API)

Experimental Results. As summarized in Table 2, participants took between 2 and 42 min (15.6 min on overage) to implement the validation code for the Yelp API operation (one dependency), and between 8 and 62 min (24.3 min on average) for the Box API operation (three dependencies). In sharp contrast, IDLGen took less than one second to automatically generate the validation code of both API operations.

Table 2. Average implementation time (min) and percentage of projects with failures

API operation	Projects	Time			Failures (%)
		Min	Max	Avg	
Box - FoldersItems	80	8	62	24.3	92.5
Yelp - TransactionsSearch	77	2	42	15.6	51.9

In terms of faults, more than half (51.9%) of the Yelp API projects did not pass one or more of the test cases created by the authors. On the other hand, a significantly higher percentage (92.5%) of the Box API projects failed at least one test case. Upon analyzing the test results, it was observed that 44.3% of Yelp API projects failed when making a valid request that included the *location* parameter. It appears that the participants either misunderstood the logic behind the *Or* dependency or did not adequately test their code for valid requests. This is because when the *location* dependency is passed, the request should be valid regardless of the *latitude* and *longitude* values. In the case of the Box API, we found that a significant portion of the failures (78%) were due to a null value not properly checked (dependency *(IF marker THEN usemarker==true;)*) throwing a Null Pointer Exception. These results support previous findings revealing that many of the failures revealed in Web APIs are due to faults in the input validation logic [23]. Again, this is in sharp contrast with our approach, where valid code is automatically generated, discarding potential human mistakes.

As expected, the time and percentage of failures observed in manual coding seem to increase with the number and complexity of dependencies. This suggests that the benefits of IDLGen would be significantly more noticeable in highly-constrained API operations, e.g., 25 out of the 31 input parameters of the search operation in the YouTube API are involved in at least one dependency [20].

The results also revealed the potential of IDLGen to improving code maintainability. For example, we observed that some of the participants tried to check all the dependencies in a single long if statement, making the code error-prone and hard to understand. In contrast, code generated by IDLGen addresses each dependency independently, showing descriptive error messages for each of them.

> Response to RQ2
>
> IDLGen saves, on average, between 16 and 24 minutes in API operations with between one and three dependencies. More importantly, the generated code mitigates human error, making Web APIs substantially more reliable. Savings are expected to be more noticeable as the number and complexity of dependencies increases.

5   Related Work

Several papers have addressed the problem of automated code generation of web APIs. Ed-douibi et al. presented an approach called EMF-REST that takes Eclipse Modeling Framework (EMF) data models as input to generate REST APIs [9]. GÃşmez et al. introduced a proposal called CRUDyLeaf based on Domain-Specific Languages (DSL). The tool takes an entity with CRUD operations (Create, Read, Update, Delete) to generate Spring Boot REST APIs [14].

QueirÃşs presented Kaang, an automatic generator of REST Web applications. Its goal is to reduce the impact of creating a REST service by automating all its workflow, such as creating file structuring, code generation, dependencies management, etc. [31]. This tool is based on Yeoman [39], an open-source, client-side development stack consisting of tools and frameworks intended to help developers build web applications.

Deljouyi et al. introduced MDD4REST [7], a model-driven methodology that uses Domain-Driven Design (DDD) to produce a rich domain model for web services. Also, it designs REST web services using modeling languages and supports automatic code generation through a transformation of models. The authors in [37] used UML class diagrams to model a set of NoSQL database collections, and then automate the generation of common database access functions and the wrapping of these functions within a set of REST APIs.

Li et al. proposed a Navigation-First Design approach to make a REST API navigable before implementing any service actions [19]. This approach is based on REST Chart [18], which is a model and language to design and describe REST

APIs without violating the REST constraints. Rossi [34] proposed a model-driven approach to develop a REST API. First, they used modeling of the API with specific profiles. Then, a model transformation exploited REST API Modeling Language (RAML) as an intermediate notation that could be used to produce documentation and code for various languages automatically.

In contrast to related papers, this is the first work addressing code generation for inter-parameter dependencies in web APIs. Evaluation results show that this leads to important gains in terms of productivity and reliability. Our work is based on exploiting an enriched version of the OAS specification— arguably the de-facto standard in the industry—making it easy to integrate our approach into related tools.

6   Threats to Validity

In this section, we discuss the potential validity threats that may have influenced our work and how these were mitigated.

Internal Validity. *Are there factors that might affect the results of our evaluation?* A potential threat is the possibility of implementation errors within the IDLGen extension, which could compromise the accuracy and reliability of the generated code. To mitigate this threat, we conducted extensive testing and validation throughout the development process. More importantly, we ran 28K automatically generated test cases (2K test cases per API operation) on the code generated for the 14 subject API operations revealing no failures.

The validity of the experiment with people may be compromised due to the lack of experience of the students who participated in the study. To mitigate this threat, we conducted the experiment at the end of the course, when students had gained extensive experience in consuming and implementing REST APIs. We also simplified the examples by excluding parameters unrelated to dependencies, which allowed students to focus exclusively on the implementation process. In addition, we provided thorough explanations of the dependencies for both examples to ensure that students understood the tasks effectively. Overall, the results show that implementing the validation code for inter-parameter dependencies is time-consuming and error-prone, supporting the value of IDLGen to generate error-free code in a matter of seconds.

External Validity. *To what extent can we generalize the findings of our investigation?* The generalizability of our findings may be limited due to the specific set of API operations evaluated. To mitigate this threat, we carefully selected a diverse sample of 14 operations from 10 industrial APIs with millions of users worldwide. Similarly, we focused on a specific and highly popular code generator, OpenAPI Generator, and therefore our results may not be generalized further. To the best of our knowledge, however, none of the state-of-the-art generators for web APIs supports the generation of validation code for inter-parameter dependencies, and therefore the gain reported in our paper should be analogous when considering similar tools.

7   Conclusions and Future Work

This paper presents IDLGen, an approach for the automated generation of validation code for inter-parameter dependencies in web APIs. Specifically, our approach leverages the IDL4OAS extension for describing dependencies as a part of OAS files. The generated code can automatically detect whether or not incoming API calls satisfy the dependencies among input parameters, returning informative errors in case they are violated. To implement our approach, we extended the well-known OpenAPI Generator tool ecosystem to automate the generation of Java and Python code for inter-parameter dependencies in web APIs. The evaluation results show that IDLGen generates up to 9.4 times more LoC for Java servers than a state-of-the-art code generator (5 times more LoC on average), with similarly noticeable savings in Python. The results of an empirical study with 81 participants revealed that IDLGen saves an average of between 16 min (one dependency) and 24 min (three dependencies) per API operation. More importantly, the code generated minimizes the possibility of making mistakes, making APIs significantly more robust and reliable.

Several challenges remain for future work. We plan to address the automated generation of documentation for inter-parameter dependencies. Also, we aim to obtain feedback from the core team of the OpenAPI Generator project for eventually merging our approach into the official tool ecosystem.

Acknowledgements. This work has been partially supported by grants PID2021-126227NB-C22 and TED2021-131023B-C21, funded by MCIN/AEI/10.13039/5011 00011033 and by European Union "NextGenerationEU"/PRTR». Ana B. Sánchez was supported by the VI Plan Propio de Investigación y Transferencia of Universidad de Sevilla 2021 [VI PPIT-US].

References

1. Amadeus Hotel Search API. https://developers.amadeus.com/self-service/category/hotel/api-doc/hotel-search/api-reference. Accessed July 2023
2. AutoRest. https://github.com/Azure/autorest. Accessed June 2023
3. Barakat, S., Roque, E.B., Sánchez, A.B., Segura, S.: Specification-driven code generation for inter-parameter dependencies in web APIs. In: Troya, J., et al. (eds.) ICSOC 2022. LNCS, pp. 261–273. Springer, Cham (2023). https://doi.org/10.1007/978-3-031-26507-5_21
4. Barakat, S., Sánchez, A.B., Segura, S.: [Supplementary material] IDLGen: Automated Code Generation for Inter-parameter Dependencies in Web APIs, July 2023. https://doi.org/10.5281/zenodo.8138633
5. Box API. https://developer.box.com/reference/. Accessed July 2023

6. Swagger Codegen. https://swagger.io/tools/swagger-codegen/. Accessed June 2023

7. Deljouyi, A., Ramsin, R.: MDD4REST: model-driven methodology for developing RESTful web services. In: MODELSWARD, pp. 93–104. Scitepress (2022)

8. DHL Location Finder API. https://developer.dhl.com/api-reference/location-finder. Accessed July 2023

9. Ed-Douibi, H., Izquierdo, J.L.C., GÃşmez, A., Tisi, M., Cabot, J.: EMF-REST: generation of RESTful APIs from models. In: Proceedings of the 31st Annual ACM Symposium on Applied Computing, vol. 04–08-April-2016, pp. 1446–1453. Association for Computing Machinery (2016)

10. Fielding, R.T.: REST: Architectural Styles and the Design of Network-Based Software Architectures. Doctoral dissertation, University of California (2000)

11. Foursquare Search for Venues API. https://developer.foursquare.com/reference/v2-venues-search. Accessed July 2023

12. Gamez-Diaz, A., Fernandez, P., Ruiz-Cortes, A.: Automating SLA-driven API development with SLA4OAI. In: Yangui, S., Bouassida Rodriguez, I., Drira, K., Tari, Z. (eds.) ICSOC 2019. LNCS, vol. 11895, pp. 20–35. Springer, Cham (2019). https://doi.org/10.1007/978-3-030-33702-5_2

13. Google Maps API. https://developers.google.com/maps/documentation/places/web-service/search. Accessed July 2023

14. Gómez, O.S., Rosero, R.H., Cortés-Verdín, K.: CRUDyLeaf: a DSL for generating spring boot REST APIs from entity CRUD operations. Cybern. Inf. Technol. **20**(3), 3–14 (2020)

15. IDLGen. https://github.com/ssegura/openapi-generator/tree/IDLGen-extension. Accessed July 2023

16. IDL Parser. https://github.com/isa-group/IDL-mvn-dep. Accessed July 2023

17. Inter-parameter Dependency Language (IDL). https://github.com/isa-group/IDL. Accessed July 2023

18. Li, L., Chou, W.: Design and describe REST API without violating REST: a petri net based approach. In: 2011 IEEE International Conference on Web Services, pp. 508–515 (2011)

19. Li, L., Tang, T., Chou, W.: Automated creation of navigable REST services based on REST chart. J. Adv. Manage. Sci., 385–392 (2016)

20. Martin-Lopez, A., Segura, S., Muller, C., Ruiz-Cortes, A.: Specification and automated analysis of inter-parameter dependencies in web APIs. IEEE Trans. Serv. Comput., 1–14 (2021)

21. Martin-Lopez, A., Segura, S., Ruiz-Cortés, A.: A catalogue of inter-parameter dependencies in RESTful web APIs. In: Yangui, S., Bouassida Rodriguez, I., Drira, K., Tari, Z. (eds.) ICSOC 2019. LNCS, vol. 11895, pp. 399–414. Springer, Cham (2019). https://doi.org/10.1007/978-3-030-33702-5_31

22. Martin-Lopez, A., Segura, S., Ruiz-Cortés, A.: RESTest: black-box constraint-based testing of RESTful Web APIs. In: Kafeza, E., Benatallah, B., Martinelli, F., Hacid, H., Bouguettaya, A., Motahari, H. (eds.) Service-Oriented Computing, pp. 459–475. Springer, Cham (2020)

23. Martin-Lopez, A., Segura, S., Ruiz-Cortés, A.: Online testing of RESTful APIs: promises and challenges. In: Proceedings of the 30th ACM Joint European Software Engineering Conference and Symposium on the Foundations of Software Engineering, pp. 408–420. ESEC/FSE 2022. Association for Computing Machinery, New York (2022)

24. Logic-less templates. https://mustache.github.io/. Accessed July 2023

25. NSwag toolchain. https://github.com/RicoSuter/NSwag. Accessed June 2023
26. Ohsome API. https://docs.ohsome.org/ohsome-api/v1/. Accessed July 2023
27. OMDb API. https://www.omdbapi.com/. Accessed July 2023
28. OpenAPI Generator. https://openapi-generator.tech/. Accessed July 2023
29. OpenAPI Specification. https://www.openapis.org/. Accessed July 2023
30. PayPal Invoicing API. https://developer.paypal.com/docs/api/invoicing/v1/#invoices. Accessed July 2023
31. Queirós, R.: Kaang: A RESTful API Generator for the Modern Web. In: 7th Symposium on Languages, Applications and Technologies SLATE 2018. vol. 62, pp. 1:1–1:15. Schloss Dagstuhl-Leibniz-Zentrum für Informatik (2018)
32. RapidAPI Hub. https://rapidapi.com/hub. Accessed March 2022
33. RESTest: Automated Black-Box Testing of RESTful Web APIs. https://github.com/isa-group/RESTest. Accessed July 2023
34. Rossi, D.: UML-based model-driven REST API development. In: WEBIST 2016 - Proceedings of the 12th International Conference on Web Information Systems and Technologies, pp. 194–201 (2016)
35. Travel   API.   https://github.com/isa-group/RESTest/tree/master/src/test/resources/Travel. Accessed July 2023
36. Tumblr API. https://www.tumblr.com/docs/en/api. Accessed July 2023
37. Wang, B., Rosenberg, D., Boehm, B.W.: Rapid realization of executable domain models via automatic code generation. In: 2017 IEEE 28th Annual Software Technology Conference (STC), pp. 1–6 (2017)
38. Yelp API. https://docs.developer.yelp.com/reference. Accessed July 2023
39. Yeoman. https://yeoman.io/. Accessed July 2023
40. YouTube Data API. https://developers.google.com/youtube/v3/docs. Accessed July 2023

Time-Aware Log Anomaly Detection Based on Growing Self-organizing Map

Daniil Fedotov$^{(\boxtimes)}$, Jaroslav Kuchar, and Tomas Vitvar

Czech Technical University in Prague, Prague, Czech Republic
{daniil.fedotov,jaroslav.kuchar,tomas.vitvar}@fit.cvut.cz

Abstract. A software system generates extensive log data, reflecting its workload and potential failures during operation. Log anomaly detection algorithms use this data to identify deviations in system behavior, especially when errors occur. Workload patterns can vary with time, depending on factors like the time of day or day of the week, affecting log entry volumes. Thus, it's essential for log anomaly detection to consider temporal information that captures workload variations. This paper introduces a novel log anomaly detection method that incorporates such time information and demonstrates how smaller models enhance anomaly detection precision. We evaluate this method on a high-throughput production workload of a software system, showcasing its superior performance over conventional log anomaly detection methods.

Keywords: anomaly detection · GSOM · clustering

1 Introduction

A software system generates a vast amount of structured and semi-structured data written to log files. These files contain various information types, such as garbage collector logs, diagnostic logs, or component-specific logs. In a production environment, the system's workload typically fluctuates throughout the day or experiences seasonal variations, like increased activity on Black Fridays or during Christmas. Incidents may trigger specific error types that occur more frequently, accompanied by new error messages not seen during standard operations. Log files serve as a tool for operations teams to monitor system behavior changes that might signal an incident. Early detection enables rapid response to mitigate business impact.

In this paper we define a novel method for log anomaly detection with temporal information based on Growing Self-Organizing Map (GSOM) [1]. GSOM is an artificial neural network based on unsupervised competitive learning and we use it to produce spatially organized low-dimensional representation of high-dimensional data. We define a sliding window that we use to split log data into a

This research was supported by the Student Summer Research Program 2021 of FIT CTU in Prague and the Grant Agency of the Czech Technical University in Prague, grant No. SGS20/209/OHK3/3T/18.

F. Monti et al. (Eds.): ICSOC 2023, LNCS 14419, pp. 169–177, 2023.
https://doi.org/10.1007/978-3-031-48421-6_12

number of overlapping time intervals that represent various workloads. We train models for each window and use the models to detect anomalies in log data during runtime. We evaluate the method on a system that handles a production workload of several hundreds of requests per second.

2   Related Work

There are several research approaches used in log anomaly detection. Wurzenberger et al. [8] defines an incremental clustering method and semi-supervised anomaly detection method. Such an approach leads to loosing semantic and temporal information. Liang at al. [4] use Rule-based classifier, Support Vector Machines and Nearest Neighbor classifiers. The downside of these approaches is that they are difficult to use in real-world settings as they require a retraining of models anytime when changes occur in log files. Vinayakumar et al. [7] proposes methods based on Long-Short Term Memory neural network. Meng et al. [5] present their own word representation method called *template2vec* inspired by *word2vec* [6]. LSTM neural networks can provide powerful methods for analyzing logs, however, since they use supervised learning algorithms, they require labeled data for training.

3   Time-Aware Log Anomaly Detection

Sliding Window. We use timestamps to assign entries to specific windows, defining a sliding window technique. Normal system operation involves fluctuations in request volumes, as well as occasional restarts or updates, impacting workload and log generation. Log entries considered "normal" during one time period may be anomalous at another time, like higher server workloads on Monday mornings compared to weekends which is driven by increased user activity. Existing approaches typically train models on the entire dataset. Such larger models may struggle with identifying narrower anomalies specific to certain time intervals, influenced by biased training data favoring frequently occurring log messages.

Figure 1 illustrates the sliding window technique that helps to collect the most detailed training set for the GSOM models. A white stripe in the figure represents the log data, the gray rectangle is the sliding window, where parameter T defines the size of the window, the dashed line rectangle shows the starting position of the sliding window which corresponds to the first recorded log entry, and δt parameter defines a step the window slides through the log data. In Sect. 4 we define the parameters on a specific dataset.

Log Parsing. We extract information from the created windows. For each log entry, we process the text using NLP techniques. This involves filtering out redundant information like file paths, numbers, and punctuation, converting messages to lowercase, and tokenizing them into words. We also remove stopwords, which are common words with little meaning.

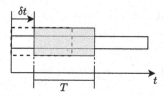

Fig. 1. Sliding window over log data

Feature Extraction. After we parse log entries, we use Doc2Vec model [3] to transform entries to their numeric vector representation. Each vector is a feature representing attributes and properties of its corresponding log entry. The vectors represent points in a high-dimensional semantic space.

Training of GSOM Models. We use GSOM method to compute a set of models that we use to evaluate logs during runtime to detect anomalies in the log data. In the GSOM training algorithm neurons compete among themselves for the opportunity to best represent an input vector with a dimension *dim* from a training dataset. Formally, in a training step t, a neuron i with a weight vector w_i that is the closest in Euclidean distance to an input vector x_t wins the competition. The winner is called Best Matching Unit (BMU):

$$d(x_t, w_i) = \sum_{k=1}^{dim} \sqrt{(x_{t,k} - w_{i,k})^2}. \tag{1}$$

The BMU further adjusts its weights and weights of neighbor neurons towards the input vector:

$$w_i(t+1) = w_i(t) + \theta(i, v, t) \cdot \eta(t) \cdot (x_t - w_i(t)) \tag{2}$$

where $\theta(i, v, t)$ is a neighborhood function for the BMU i to a neuron v on a training step t and $\eta(t)$ is a learning rate on the training step t.

The training of the GSOM network consists of one *training (growing) phase* and a number of so called *smoothing phases*. During smoothing phases, the method adjusts weights of existing neurons to minimize the quantization error.

Anomaly Detection. We define two approaches to detect anomalies, namely *Clustering* and *GSOM model structure*.

Clustering. As a result of the GSOM algorithm, similar input vectors are close to each other in the GSOM model which in turn form clusters. In order to identify such clusters and their *centroids* in the model, we apply K-means algorithm. We run K-means partitioning on a trained GSOM model's weights several times with different values of k parameter ranging from 2 to $\sqrt{N}$, where N is a number of neurons in the GSOM model. We then identify the best cluster partition as the one with the lowest Davies-Bouldin index (DB index), which measures the within-cluster variation and between-cluster variation for the resulting clusters (see Formula 3).

$$DB = \frac{1}{n} \sum_{i=1, i \neq j}^{n} \max\left(\frac{S_i + S_j}{d(c_i, c_j)}\right), \tag{3}$$

where

- n – number of clusters,
- S_i, S_j – within cluster variations,
- $d(c_i, c_j)$ – between cluster variation.

GSOM model structure. We compute Euclidean distances from each input vector to neurons' weight vectors of GSOM models.

When log entries are anomalous, they tend to deviate significantly from the corresponding GSOM model's neurons in Euclidean space. Therefore, it is crucial to establish a maximum allowable distance, referred to as a *threshold*, to determine whether log entries are anomalous or not. In the first approach, we calculate the average Euclidean distance from each input vector in the training dataset to the nearest cluster centroid within the GSOM model. In the second approach, we directly compute the Euclidean distance to the weight vectors of GSOM neurons. These distances are calculated using a training dataset that contains vectors representing the baseline behavior of the server.

For both approaches, we gather statistical data on these distances, which serves as the basis for subsequent threshold computation. Using Formula 4, we determine the threshold as a k-sigma upper limit of the distances from the baseline vectors to the GSOM models (further details on how we determine the value of k for calculating the threshold are provided in Sect. 4).

$$threshold = \mu + k\sigma, \tag{4}$$

where

- k – number of standard deviations from the mean,
- μ – mean Euclidean distance from baseline vectors to trained GSOM,
- σ – standard deviation for Euclidean distances from baseline vectors to trained GSOM.

Finally, according to Formula 5 we say that log entries from a testing dataset are anomalous if their distance of vectors to corresponding model's neurons is greater than the threshold value.

$$GSOM(x) = \begin{cases} d(x, c) \geq threshold, & \text{anomaly} \\ d(x, c) < threshold, & \text{normal} \end{cases} \tag{5}$$

4   Experiments and Evaluation

Model Training. In order to establish a baseline, we use logs from multiple server instances running production workloads for 7 days. During the training phase, we divide daily log data into 24 overlapping intervals using a sliding window technique. We configure parameters as $T = 75$ min and $\delta t = 60$ min. Figure 2 illustrates log trends for these intervals. These parameter choices align with our knowledge of data and workload patterns. For instance, there are message peaks from around 11:50 to 12:00 and message dips at approximately 11:45. The chosen sliding window parameters ensure that workload patterns are covered at most once for each interval, making intervals "equivalent" in terms of pattern coverage.

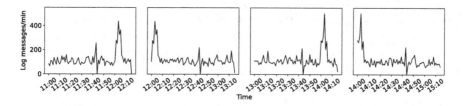

Fig. 2. Baseline log data partitioned into overlapping intervals

We extract features for each window using a 120-component Doc2Vec embedding enriched with timestamps, resulting in 123-component feature vectors for every log entry. Pre-trained embedding models on general text data are unsuitable for our domain-specific log data. Consequently, we trained a custom Doc2Vec model on server log data to compute these embeddings. We then normalize the data within each window using MinMax scaling (see Formula 6) to make sure all values are positive, aligning with the GSOM model's weight initialization in the $0; 1$ interval.

$$X_{scaled} = \frac{X - min(X)}{max(X) - min(X)}, \tag{6}$$

For each window we then train a GSOM model with uniform hyperparameters and iterations to maintain consistency across all models. Table 1 lists the hyperparameter values and iteration counts.

Table 1. GSOM training and smoothing parameters

	Training	Smoothing 1.	Smoothing 2.
Iterations	400	50	50
Learning rate	0.9	0.6	0.6
Spread factor	0.6	0.6	0.6
Neighborhood	6	2	1
Max neurons	5000	5000	5000

Anomaly Detection Evaluation. We use log data from a separate time period and a single server instance within the server cluster, distinct from the training data. This period corresponds to incidents on the server instance, resulting in behavior different from the baseline servers used during training. We use log data from 8:00 to 16:00 when the system experienced high workloads.

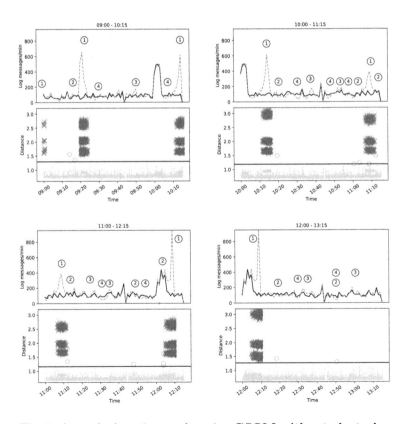

Fig. 3. Anomaly detection results using **GSOM without clustering**

In Fig. 3, we show 4 plots that correspond to 4 time intervals with high work-loads. The upper charts represent a frequency of log messages per minute where the solid line shows the baseline trend we use in the training phase and the dashed line represents the testing log trend that contains anomalies. The bottom charts show the anomaly detection results. The straight solid lines represent the threshold value, the points below the threshold line represent log entries as true negatives, the circles represent log entries as false positives, and finally the crosses represent log entries that are true positives. We identify 4 types of server behavior that we mark in charts as 1,2,3 and 4:

Type 1: Correctly detected log entries as anomalies (the crosses above the threshold line).

Type 2: Log entries detected as anomalies, but they actually correspond to normal server's behavior (circles). There are anomalies of this type due to the imbalance in the training datasets and the same hyperparameters' preset for the models (types of log entries in the training dataset are not equal from the quantitative point of view).

Type 3: The trend of the baseline server's behavior and the trend of messages in the testing dataset do not match while there are no anomalies detected. Such differences in the two trends are normal due to the dynamic nature of receiving and processing requests and the generation of corresponding log entries.

Type 4: The trend of the baseline server's behavior shows dynamics in generation of log entries, however, there is no such dynamics in the testing trend. We call this type the "gap". This behavior is caused by a temporary suspension of the server. In our work, we focus on detection of anomalous log entries by using the content of log entries and we do not consider the gap anomalies to be critical to be detected.

Evaluation Details. We compared our method with two widely used anomaly detection techniques: PCA and Isolation Forest from Loglizer [2]. PCA represents a basic approach, while Isolation Forests are a commonly adopted method in anomaly detection. We fine-tune method parameters to optimize precision, recall, and F-measure metrics and assess their performance on the same datasets. The evaluation results, presented in Table 2, include "Pr" (precision), "Rec" (recall), and "F1" (F-measure). The columns "GSOM w/o cl." and "GSOM w/ cl." show results with and without clustering applied to GSOM models, respectively.

During the evaluation we experimentally found that our method achieves the best performance when the value of k parameter in anomaly threshold computation is set to 10 for GSOM w/o cl. and set to 2 for GSOM w/ cl.

In the evaluation results, both GSOM methods perform well on our test dataset, surpassing PCA and outperforming Isolation Forest in terms of precision and recall. Comparing the two GSOM methods, GSOM without clustering and GSOM with clustering yield similar results for precision, recall, and F-measure, with the latter showing slightly lower precision only in the 11:00–12:15 interval (0.89 for GSOM with clustering and 0.99 for GSOM without clustering), but

Table 2. Evaluation results

Time	Metric											
	GSOM w/o cl.			GSOM w/ cl.			PCA			Isolation Forest		
	Pr	Rec	F1	Pr	Rec	F1	Pr	Rec	F1	Pr	Rec	F1
08:00–09:15	0.99	0.74	0.85	0.99	0.74	0.85	0.63	0.24	0.35	0.33	0.78	0.47
09:00–10:15	0.99	0.75	0.86	0.99	0.75	0.86	0.65	0.26	0.37	0.42	0.76	0.54
10:00–11:15	0.98	0.74	0.85	0.99	0.74	0.85	0.59	0.23	0.33	0.39	0.75	0.51
11:00–12:15	0.99	0.74	0.85	0.89	0.78	0.83	0.67	0.23	0.35	0.41	0.87	0.56
12:00–13:15	0.99	0.74	0.85	0.99	0.74	0.85	0.41	0.25	0.31	0.23	0.70	0.35
13:00–14:15	0.99	0.78	0.87	0.99	0.76	0.86	0.58	0.25	0.35	0.29	0.76	0.43
14:00–15:15	0.99	0.77	0.86	0.99	0.77	0.86	0.53	0.24	0.33	0.38	0.79	0.51
15:00–16:15	0.98	0.76	0.86	0.99	0.76	0.86	0.54	0.25	0.34	0.39	0.81	0.53
Average	0.99	0.75	0.86	0.98	0.75	0.85	0.57	0.24	0.34	0.35	0.78	0.49

better recall (0.78 for GSOM with clustering and 0.74 for GSOM without clustering). Despite their similar performance, applying clustering to GSOM weight vectors reduces problem dimensionality and the time complexity of the method.

5   Conclusion and Future Work

Log anomaly detection is crucial for operations teams to identify potential incident triggers within log data. One approach involves using unsupervised machine learning algorithms to train models on log data representing standard system behavior, enabling real-time anomaly detection. We've developed a method utilizing Growing Self-Organizing Map and time information in log data. Time is significant in enterprise environments, as log data generation varies with system workloads and operational events.

In our future research we plan to expand our GSOM model with a Knowledge Graph, providing background knowledge of service architecture. This integration will help uncover data links and incident patterns during server operation, enhancing model explainability and interpretability.

References

1. Alahakoon, D., Halgamuge, S., Bala, S.: Dynamic self-organizing maps with controlled growth for knowledge discovery. IEEE Trans. Neural Netw. **11**(3), 601–614 (2000). https://doi.org/10.1109/72.846732
2. He, S., Zhu, J., He, P., Lyu, M.R.: Experience report: System log analysis for anomaly detection. In: 2016 IEEE 27th International Symposium on Software Reliability Engineering (ISSRE), pp. 207–218 (2016). https://doi.org/10.1109/ISSRE. 2016.21

3. Le, Q., Mikolov, T.: Distributed representations of sentences and documents. In: Xing, E.P., Jebara, T. (eds.) Proceedings of the 31st International Conference on Machine Learning. Proceedings of Machine Learning Research, vol. 32, pp. 1188–1196. PMLR, Beijing (2014). https://proceedings.mlr.press/v32/le14.html
4. Liang, Y., Zhang, Y., Xiong, H., Sahoo, R.: Failure prediction in IBM BlueGene/L event logs, pp. 583–588 (2007). https://doi.org/10.1109/ICDM.2007.46
5. Meng, W., et al.: LogAnomaly: unsupervised detection of sequential and quantitative anomalies in unstructured logs (2019)
6. Mikolov, T., Yih, W.T., Zweig, G.: Linguistic regularities in continuous space word representations. In: Proceedings of the 2013 Conference of the North American Chapter of the Association for Computational Linguistics: Human Language Technologies, pp. 746–751. Association for Computational Linguistics, Atlanta (2013). https://aclanthology.org/N13-1090
7. Vinayakumar, R., Soman, K.P., Poornachandran, P.: Long short-term memory based operation log anomaly detection. In: 2017 International Conference on Advances in Computing, Communications and Informatics (ICACCI), pp. 236–242 (2017). https://doi.org/10.1109/ICACCI.2017.8125846
8. Wurzenberger, M., Skopik, F., Landauer, M., Greitbauer, P., Fiedler, R., Kstner, W.: Incremental clustering for semi-supervised anomaly detection applied on log data (2017)

Containers and Microservices

An Empirical Evaluation of the Energy and Performance Overhead of Monitoring Tools on Docker-Based Systems

Madalina Dinga[1], Ivano Malavolta[1], Luca Giamattei[2(✉)],
Antonio Guerriero[2], and Roberto Pietrantuono[2]

[1] Vrije Universiteit Amsterdam, Amsterdam, The Netherlands
`m.dinga@student.vu.nl`, `i.malavolta@vu.nl`
[2] University of Naples Federico II, Naples, Italy
{`luca.giamattei`,`antonio.guerriero`,`roberto.pietrantuono`}`@unina.it`

Abstract. *Context.* Energy efficiency is gaining importance in the design of software systems, but is still marginally addressed in the area of microservice-based systems. Energy-related aspects often get neglected in favor of other software quality attributes, such as performance, service composition, maintainability, and security.

Goal. The aim of this study is to identify, synthesize and empirically evaluate the energy and performance overhead of monitoring tools employed in the microservices and DevOps context.

Method. We selected four representative monitoring tools in the microservices and DevOps context. These were evaluated via a controlled experiment on an open-source Docker-based microservice benchmark system.

Results. The results highlight: *i)* the specific frequency and workload conditions under which energy consumption and performance metrics are impacted by the tools; *ii)* the differences between the tools; *iii)* the relation between energy and performance overhead.

1 Introduction

In recent years, the motivation to reduce energy consumption by conservation and efficient use has grown significantly. It has become not only a means for gaining control over costs but, most importantly, a way of reducing the carbon footprint of economic and human activity. This is reflected across all industries, including software development [16]. Nevertheless, energy consumption has only recently come to attention in literature [5]. With the advent of microservice-based systems coupled with agile (specifically DevOps) practices, a great focus is put on continuous monitoring: teams need feedback from the system running in the field, in order to get measures about systems performance, security, reliability, to track the status of microservices, to timely detect issues, and act consequently. However, this requires the deployment and operation of (sometimes complex) monitoring tools running alongside the microservices, which in turn might contribute to the overall energy consumed by the system.

F. Monti et al. (Eds.): ICSOC 2023, LNCS 14419, pp. 181–196, 2023.
https://doi.org/10.1007/978-3-031-48421-6_13

This study aims to raise awareness on this matter by assessing the impact on energy consumption and performance overhead of monitoring tools employed in microservice-based systems. We limit the scope to systems running in Docker containers since energy is highly dependent on the platform. This helps to separate its effect from the main factor (i.e., the tools). Docker was chosen because it is one of the most popular container-based virtualization solutions [11].

To achieve our goal, we answer the following research questions. **RQ1**: What is the impact of using different monitoring tools on energy efficiency of Docker-based systems? **RQ2**: What is the impact of using different monitoring tools on performance of Docker-based systems?

We set up an extensive empirical study in which we select 4 monitoring tools run alongside a Docker-based system, and we measure energy consumption at machine level and several performance indicators (CPU, RAM, network, execution time). We then statistically analyze the results to understand the impact of the monitoring tools on both aspects under different conditions.

The contribution and results of this study are relevant to *i)* Docker-based systems developers, as they offer a better understanding on how to integrate monitoring tools within their applications in an energy-efficient manner; *ii)* the tools' maintainers, as they highlighting the impact of their monitoring systems on energy and performance, and showing potential improvements; *iii)* researchers working on microservices and DevOps, as they push toward addressing the problem of an efficient monitoring that has to trade off energy consumption for the need of gathering as much relevant information as possible to ensure quality.

The full replication package of the study is available at https://github.com/ S2-group/icsoc-2023-energy-perf-monitoring-docker-rep-pkg.

2   Background

As defined by Fowler and Lewis, the **microservices** architectural style is "an approach for developing a single application as a suite of small services, each running in its own process and communicating with lightweight mechanisms, often an HTTP resource API" [1]. **Docker** [11] is one of the most recurrent technologies for implementing microservices [4]. It is a lightweight virtualization platform for packaging software solutions into self-contained and independently-deployed units (i.e., containers). Among others, with Docker, teams can develop and deploy their (loosely-coupled) microservices independently from each other, make faster and more frequent releases, and test their microservices in autonomy.

Being inherently distributed, microservice-based systems require specialized **monitoring tools**, such as Netdata[1], Prometheus[2], etc. Without losing generality, a monitoring tool is typically composed of one or more DBs for storing the collected metrics (e.g., the Time Series Database in Prometheus), a dashboarding platform for querying the DBs and/or showing the collected metrics to the user (e.g., Grafana), an alerting subsystem for sending notifications to the

---

[1] https://www.netadata.cloud.
[2] https://prometheus.io.

user (e.g., the rule-based Alert Manager component in Prometheus), and a set of **monitoring components** (e.g., Prometheus exporters) – typically one for each microservice – that collect metrics about their associated microservice (e.g., average CPU usage) and make those metrics available to the DBs. Despite their undoubted usefulness for the observability of the system, the just-mentioned monitoring components do not contribute directly to the functionalities of the system; still, they are deployed together with the microservices being monitored and compete for the same hardware resources. In this study, we are interested in quantifying the overhead that the just-mentioned monitoring components produce in terms of performance and energy consumption of the monitored system.

The collection of performance-related measures (e.g., CPU load, memory utilization, network requests) is relatively straightforward for Docker-based systems, primarily thanks to already-existing monitoring components wrapping Linux utilities such as SAR[3]. Differently, **the measurement of power consumption** (and thus energy) requires extra effort and technical skills. Some well-known tools for monitoring energy are PowerPack (physical measurement), RAPL (software-based measurement), or PowerAPI (software library). In this study, we favour accuracy and measure the power consumption at machine-level using a well-known physical power meter called *Watts Up Pro* [8].

3   Related Work

To our knowledge, there is no comprehensive study about the energy consumption of monitoring tools in the context of microservices.

Heward et al. [7] look into the performance impact of service monitoring for web applications. They explore various architecture designs for monitoring the web traffic. One conclusion is that a colocated proxy used for monitoring is much more efficient than a proxy located on a different machine. Similar to our study, this paper assesses the impact of monitoring tools, however it does not consider their impact on energy efficiency.

Foutse et al. [9] assess the impact of cloud patterns on performance and energy consumption and provide a series of guidelines for implementing energy-efficient cloud-based applications. Their results focus around the environmental impact of microservice-based systems, showing that migration to a microservices architecture can improve performance, while reducing energy consumption. The study does not take into account monitoring.

A related study [10] investigates the use of SmartNIC's, a low-power processor, for improving server energy-efficiency without latency loss, in the context of microservices. They propose E1, an execution platform for SmartNIC-accelerated servers, which, according to the authors, can significantly improve cluster energy-efficiency up to 3×, with minimal latency cost, for common microservices. The paper focuses on improving the energy efficiency of microservice-based systems, however it does not take into account the potential overhead of monitoring tools.

---

[3] https://linux.die.net/man/1/sar.

Santos et al. [14] compare the energy consumption of applications running in Docker containers to those running bare-metal. The authors demonstrate that Docker increases the energy consumption even if the system under test is idle. The effect is caused by the activity of the Docker daemon (dockerd), a service that permanently runs on the host and orchestrates the containers. While this paper focuses on the energy footprint of Docker, our study explores how various monitoring tools running alongside Docker-based systems impact energy.

4 Study Design

4.1 Experimental Subjects: *Monitoring Tools*

Tools Selection. We searched for open-source monitoring tools on GitHub, looking at the ones reporting DevOps as topics in their description. The tools have been selected according to the following requirements:

– Compatible with microservices applications running in Docker containers.
– Do not require integration at the application level (i.e. code instrumentation), and in general aiming to:
  • avoid introducing unnecessary confounding variables, such as communication overhead due to interaction between additional components,
  • avoid increasing the deployment of the integrated applications,
  • aid replication of the experiments.
– Capable to collect metrics at container level.

Table 1. Monitoring tools

Monitoring Tool		
ELK Stack	Website	https://www.elastic.co/elastic-stack/
	Github	https://github.com/elastic/elasticsearch
	First and last release*	2/8/2010 and 07/29/2022
	Stars on Github*	60,700
Netdata	Website	https://www.netdata.cloud/
	Github	https://github.com/netdata/netdata
	First and last release*	9/26/2015 and 08/11/2022
	Stars on Github*	60,300
Prometheus	Website	https://prometheus.io/
	Github	https://github.com/prometheus/prometheus
	First and last release*	2/25/2015 and 08/13/2022
	Stars on Github*	43,800
Zipkin	Website	https://zipkin.io/
	Github	https://github.com/openzipkin/zipkin
	First and last release*	6/3/2016 and 1/27/2022
	Stars on Github*	15,600

*The date of access for the most recent release and for the number of stars on Github is 8/15/2022.

With these requirements, we aim to aid the replicability of the experiments and facilitate the interpretation of the results avoiding biases. Then, we ranked the tools in terms of stars and selected the top four, reported in Table 1. Specifically, the ranking included three metric-based tools (ELK Stack, Netdata, and Prometheus) and one tracing-based tool (Zipkin).

Benchmark System. As part of the setup, we select a well-known Docker-based microservice application, TrainTicket[4] (TTS) [17], and integrated it with the monitoring tools. TTS is a medium-size benchmark system containing 24 microservices related to business logic, out of 41 in total, implemented in different languages. It has been previously used in several experimental studies and is representative for industrial multi-container Docker applications through to its size, granularity, and variety of microservices [3].

Integration. The integration of TTS with the monitoring tools follows the most basic configuration and deployment described in the documentation of the tools. ELK stack is integrated using Metricbeat[5], a lightweight shipper for host and service metrics. Metricbeat is deployed directly on the host and it monitors all of the deployed Docker containers. Metrics are stored in Elasticsearch and can be visualised in Kibana - both running in separate Docker containers. Frequency is the time interval (in seconds) at which metrics are sent to the Elasticsearch cluster. A snapshot of Metricbeat metrics is generated every second for high level, 5 s for medium level and 10 s for low level.

Netdata, similar to Metricbeat, has an agent that discovers all available control groups (cgroups) on the host system and collects their metrics. The collection frequency has the same progression as for ELK stack (1/5/10 s).

Prometheus is integrated with cAdvisor (Container Advisor)[6] to monitor the running containers. cAdvisor has the same approach as Metricbeat and Netdata – it gathers container metrics, such as CPU and memory through cgroups. Frequency is configured the same way (1/5/10 s) as the previous two tools.

As for Zipkin[7], the integration with the TTS is made with Java Sleuth[8]. It is configured using the *PercentageBasedSampler*, i.e., only a given proportion of traces are stored. The frequency is changed using probabilistic sampling: only a configurable percent of the traces are processed and stored. The setting for high is 100%, for medium 50%, and for low 25%. Further details about the integration are in the replication package: each integration has its own *Compose* file defining the services, networks, and volumes required to run the tools alongside the TTS.

4.2 Goal and Research Questions

The goal of the experiment is expressed via the Goal-Question-Metric approach [2]: to *analyze monitoring tools, for the purpose of evaluation, with respect*

---

[4] https://github.com/FudanSELab/train-ticket.
[5] https://www.elastic.co/beats/metricbeat.
[6] https://github.com/google/cadvisor.
[7] https://zipkin.io/.
[8] https://spring.io/projects/spring-cloud-sleuth.

to their energy and performance overhead, from the point of view of developers and tool maintainers, in the context of Docker-based systems. The RQs are:

RQ1: What is the impact of using different monitoring tools on the energy efficiency of Docker-based systems?

RQ2: What is the impact of using different monitoring tools on the performance of Docker-based systems?

Several performance indicators are considered pertaining to resource consumption and execution time, which will be analyzed individually. These are: *percentage of CPU utilization* while running at user level; *load average*, computed as the average number of runnable or running tasks (R state), and the number of tasks in uninterruptible sleep (D state) over the last minute; *percentage of used memory (RAM)*; *number of input datagrams successfully delivered per second* to IP user-protocols, and *total number of input datagrams received per second*, including those received in error; *execution time* in seconds.

4.3 Experiment Variables

To mitigate the mono-operation bias and to accurately represent the runtime overhead of the tools, we consider the following **independent variables**.

Monitoring Tool, five levels: the *baseline*, where we run the TTS deployed without any monitoring tool, plus the above-mentioned tools, Elasticsearch, Netdata, Prometheus, and Zipkin. The tool is deployed along with the TTS.

Frequency: the scrape interval, in the case of tools that collect metrics (Elasticsearch, Netdata, Prometheus), and the sampling interval, in the case of the tracing tool (Zipkin). It is treated as a blocking factor with three levels (high, medium, low). Ratio measures are transformed to ordinal ones based on the minimum allowed scrape interval and maximum allowed sampling rate among the tools. Based on this, level "high" corresponds to 1 s for metric collection tools and 100% sampling rate for tracing tools, level "medium" is 5 s and 50% and level "low" is 10 s and 25%, respectively.

Workload: the number of virtual users that stress the system during the test. It is treated as a blocking factor with three levels (high, medium, low). The mapping to ordinal scale considers the capabilities of the system as follows: level high corresponds to the highest number of users supported such that the tests are completed successfully (Table 2).

Deployment: the strategy used for deploying the system. This factor is fixed, in order to separate its effect from the main factor. The monitoring tools, next to the TTS are deployed on a single Ubuntu machine using Docker Compose V2 for running the containers on Docker platform.

The **dependent variables** are: **Energy efficiency** (total energy consumed (Joules) by TTS during a load test), and the above-defined performance metrics (**CPU usage, CPU load, RAM usage, Network traffic, Execution time**). The null hypotheses for RQ1 and RQ2 state that a dependent variable does not significantly differ when using different monitoring tools. The proper hypothesis tests will be used depending on the data characteristics. Table 2 shows the ratio values for the co-factors (frequency and workload).

Table 2. Ratio values corresponding to treatments for every monitoring tool

Tool	Frequency			Workload		
	Low	Medium	High	Low	Medium	High
ELK Stack	10 s	5 s	1 s	10	20	40
Netdata	10 s	5 s	1 s	10	20	40
Prometheus	10 s	5 s	1 s	10	20	40
Zipkin	25%	50%	100%	10	20	40

4.4   Experiment Design

We alternate every possible combination (4 monitoring tools plus the baseline, 3 frequency levels, and 3 workload levels) of all of the levels across all independent variables, following a $5 \times 3 \times 3$ full factorial design. We do not consider frequency in the case of the baseline treatment, since it does not apply in that case. This means we only have 3 runs for the baseline, for 3 levels of workload, leading to 39 trials in total, i.e., $(5 \times 3 \times 3)$-6. We aim to keep the monitoring tool effect at the core of the experiment, while also considering frequency and workload as factors that might influence energy efficiency. In order to mitigate their effect and to ensure an unbiased assignment, we analyze each combination of the co-factors separately, resulting in 9 different blocks. The results might differ depending on how energy and performance are affected at runtime when running the experiment under different frequency and workload conditions.

Each of the 39 runs is repeated 10 times and in randomized execution order, to mitigate the potential bias caused by the order in which tools are run.

4.5   Experiment Execution

Testbed. The experiment is performed on a machine with a 64-bit Intel(R) Xeon(R) CPU E3-1231 v3 @ 3.40 GHz octa-core processor, 32 GB RAM, running Ubuntu Server 18.04 as operating system, which runs TTS and the monitoring tool. The server is fully dedicated to this experiment to reduce the chances of external factors contributing to the energy and performance measurements. The scripts orchestrating and running the experiments and the results of the energy measurements are run on two further separate machines to avoid bias.

Metrics Collection. For energy measurements collection, we opted for measuring energy at machine level using a physical power meter. Specifically, the *Watts Up Pro* power meter is used to collect power measures from the monitored server, in watts (W), at one second intervals, then used to compute energy (J). For performance measurements, we use SAR, a system utility allowing for monitoring the resources of a Linux system, again with a one-second interval.

Experiment Execution. Each run has a profiling time of 13.7 min on average, which may vary depending on the execution time of the load test. We add 3 min idle time between consecutive runs to guards against carryover effects (consecutive runs influencing each other) [15] and 10 min, for system initialization, which leads to 26.7 min to complete one run. We perform 10 runs for every trial (39 tri- als), resulting in 390 runs in total, executing for 10,413 min (more than 7 d). We set the execution time for a run to be at least 10 min, taking into account the fre- quency of 1 s at which Watts Up Pro collects energy measurements. This results in at least 600 measurements for a run, which allows to accurately compute the energy efficiency.

We orchestrated the experiment using Experiment Runner[9], a Python-based framework for automatically executing experiments targeting software systems. For each run, these steps are performed: (i) deploy of TTS along with the chosen monitoring tool, (ii) start monitoring energy and performance (with Watts Up Pro and SAR), (iii) interact with the system by triggering a load test script, (iv) stop monitoring once the load test has completed, (v) stop all processes related to TTS, or to the monitoring tool running alongside, (vi) clean up the system by removing all unused local volumes and restarting Docker Engine.

Workload. The load test script was obtained by merging together a set of scripts generated with K6[10], an open-source load testing tool. K6 can generate scripts for performance testing starting from the Swagger/OpenAPI specification of the REST APIs. We obtain 34 scripts for each of the 34 microservices which are integrated with Swagger. The scripts are included in the replication package of the study. Each of the scripts is stressing a different microservice by interacting with its API. Since the requests propagate through the entire system, the 7 remaining microservices which are not directly tested are also interacted with.

The 34 scripts are merged together into a single load test script which will be used during a run to stress the entire system. We perform multiple itera- tions of this script, with several virtual users (10, 20 and 40), to ensure that the duration of a run is at least 10 min. On average, each user performs the same amount of work (i.e., 34.5 iterations of the load test script in one run). The replication package contains: (i) the raw measures, (ii) the scripts for data pro- cessing and analysis and (iii) the scripts to automate the experiment execution.

5   Results

5.1   Results on Energy Efficiency (RQ1)

Figure 1 reports the energy consumed by the compared tools, with values ranging from 38,552 to 88,516 J. The coefficient of variation is between 21.3% and 26.8% and the standard deviation shows that the data is relatively disperse (13,453 globally), which most probably comes from the difference among the frequency- workload blocks. Considering the mean values (the diamond in the box plot), there is a visible difference between the baseline (53,755 J) and running a tool alongside the TTS (54,543 J, 55,046 J, 56,760 J, 60,668 J, respectively for Net- data, Prometheus, ELK Stack, Zipkin). As expected, the tools have a footprint on energy, with Netdata being the most energy-efficient tool and Zipkin the

---

[9] https://github.com/S2-group/experiment-runner.
[10] https://k6.io/.

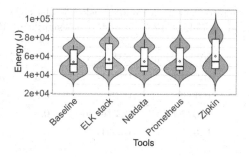

Fig. 1. Energy efficiency across monitoring tools

least one. Median values (the bars in the plot) are slightly lower but confirm the ranking. The distributions are similar to each other, with Zipkin having the highest variance (ranging from 38,552 J to 88,516 J). All the distributions are highly bimodal, with two separate groups, suggesting an impact of the blocking factors, frequency and workload. Figure 2 reports the results by block, showing that Zipkin consumes more than other monitoring tools when the workload is high.

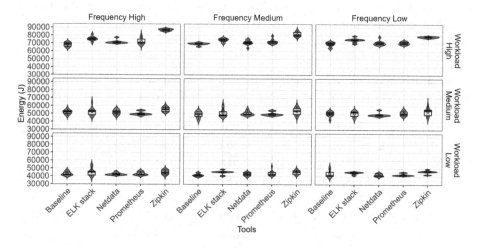

Fig. 2. Energy efficiency across all frequency and workload level combinations

To statistically analyze the data, we first run Shapiro-Wilks test to check for normality for each of the 9 blocks. Results are in Table 3, SW column, with significance level $\alpha = 0.05$. The p-value for testing the null hypothesis, stating that the energy sample is drawn from a normal distribution, is lower than 0.05 for 7 blocks out of 9, even after applying various data transformations (logarithmic, reciprocal, square root and exponential). We conclude that data are mostly not normally distributed for energy, hence we proceed with non-parametric statistical

Table 3. Results of Shapiro-Wilk (SW) and Kruskal-Wallis (KW) tests for each frequency (F) and workload (W) block. Bold text denotes a significant difference ($\alpha = .05$)

Block	SW (p-value)	KW (p-value)	η^2	η^2 interpretation
F Low, W Low	**0.00113**	**0.00156**	0.3	large
F Low, W Medium	0.0939	0.21	0.0413	small
F Low, W High	**0.0157**	**3.77e-06**	0.59	large
F Medium, W Low	**0.0172**	**0.00157**	0.299	large
F Medium, W Medium	**0.019**	0.303	0.0189	small
F Medium, W High	**0.00228**	**1.17e-06**	0.645	large
F High, W Low	**9.25e-05**	0.154	0.0594	small
F High, W Medium	0.0826	**0.022**	0.165	large
F High, W High	**9.52e-05**	**4.58e-07**	0.69	large

tests. Specifically, we apply the Kruskal-Wallis test to determine if at least one of the monitoring tools differ from the others. The p-values are lower than the $\alpha = 0.05$ (Table 3, column KW) for 6 out of 9 blokcs. It means that for those blocks a significant difference in energy efficiency among monitoring tools is detected. The magnitude of variability in energy efficiency attributable to the monitoring tools, computed as the eta-squared statistic [12], η^2, is generally large, for all the statistically significant results (Table 3, last two columns).

Table 4. Results of the Wilcoxon test - frequency (F) and workload (W) combination of treatments (block). Bold text denotes a significant difference ($\alpha = .05$)

Tool	Block	p-value	Cliff's δ	δ interpretation
ELK stack	F Low, W High	**0.002**	-0.86	large
	F Medium, W Low	**0.015**	-0.72	large
	F Medium, W High	**0.733e-03**	-0.94	large
	F High, W High	**0.825e-03**	-0.96	large
Netdata	F High, W High	**0.014**	-0.68	large
Prometheus	F Medium, W Low	**0.015**	-0.70	large
	F High, W High	**0.026**	-0.60	large
Zipkin	F Low, W High	**0.458e-03**	-1.00	large
	F Medium, W Low	**0.009**	-0.84	large
	F Medium, W High	**0.458e-03**	-1.00	large
	F High, W High	**0.825e-03**	-1.00	large

Table 5. Dunn test ($\alpha = 0.05$) per block. **grey**: not significant, **green**: significant

vs		Netdata									Prometheus									ELK stack							
Prometheus																											
ELK stack																											
Zipkin																											
Config. Workload	L	M	H	L	M	H	L	M	H	L	M	H	L	M	H	L	M	H	L	M	H	L	M	H	L	M	H
Frequency	L	L	L	M	M	M	H	H	H	L	L	L	M	M	M	H	H	H	L	L	L	M	M	M	H	H	H

As a significant difference between the tools exists, we perform a pairwise comparison between each monitoring tool and the baseline, by applying the Wilcoxon test across all blocks with Benjamini-Hochberg (B-H) correction for multiple-comparison protection. There is significant difference for every tool for at least one block (Table 4). The Cliff's delta for those blocks shows a large effect according to the interpretation by Romano [13]. Also, Table 5 reports the Dunn's test comparing each tool with each other. Both these tests confirm that Zipkin is the most-consuming tool, followed by ELK stack.

> **Result 1** - Monitoring tools significantly impact the energy efficiency of Docker-based systems, under several (6 out of 9) frequency and workload conditions. Not all tools have the same impact; Zipkin has the largest negative impact. A high workload contributes markedly to high consumption of all the tools, and exacerbates the difference between the tools.

5.2 Results on Performance (RQ2)

Figure 3 reports performance. The replication package contains Tables with summary statistics of these results. The CPU usage percentage is 52.4% on average globally, with the lowest recorded values for ELK stack (49.0%) and the highest for Zipkin (57.6%). Apart from Zipkin, there seems to be a negligible difference between the baseline and the tools. For the CPU load average, Zipkin still shows the highest value, 18.4, while Netdata and Prometheus show the lower ones (16.6). RAM usage has a very low standard deviation. The mean is 70.7%, with the minimum average value for the baseline (65.1%) and the highest for ELK stack (99.2%). This means that ELK stack has a very high memory footprint, keeping the RAM usage close to the maximum capacity throughout the execution of the load test. This phenomenon might be an indication of the high energy consumption of ELK stack, where we obtained a significant difference for 4 out of 9 blocks (Table 4). Also, Zipkin tends to be more memory- and CPU-intensive than other monitoring tools like Netdata and Prometheus, and also in this case Zipking was shown to consume more energy than the baseline for 4 out of 9 blocks. In terms of execution time, looking at the mean values, it is not highly impacted by tools such as Netdata and Prometheus. ELK stack and Zipkin however have the highest execution time on average. A run has a duration of 13.7 min on average, with the minimum being 10 min (for Prometheus) and a maximum of 18 min (for Zipkin).

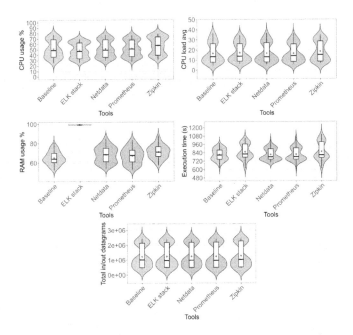

Fig. 3. Dependent variables across monitoring tools

Table 6. Results of the Shapiro-Wilk test for each frequency (F) and workload (W) block. Bold text denotes a significant difference ($\alpha = .05$)

Block	CPU	Memory	Network	Load	Exec. time
F Low, W Low	**0.000412**	**1.07e-05**	**0.0015**	0.178	**2.81e-05**
F Low, W Medium	**0.000864**	**9.09e-06**	0.298	**3.88e-06**	0.585
F Low, W High	**0.014**	**1.95e-05**	0.323	0.575	0.0807
F Medium, W Low	0.435	**1.02e-05**	**1.94e-05**	0.212	**7.77e-05**
F Medium, W Medium	**0.00248**	**1.01e-05**	0.114	**3.68e-07**	**0.00395**
F Medium, W High	0.388	**8.72e-05**	0.533	0.639	0.59
F High, W Low	0.693	**5.94e-06**	**0.00158**	0.657	**0.000204**
F High, W Medium	**0.0466**	**1.71e-05**	0.066	**0.000453**	0.518
F High, W High	0.183	**5.43e-05**	**0.0041**	0.111	0.0317

Result 2 - Monitoring tools like Zipkin (for CPU) and ELK Stack (for RAM) increase the resources' usage and affect the execution times more than other tools. The same result was observed with total energy consumed.

The mean network traffic is similar for all the tools. This is expected, since the same amount of traffic is likely generated while running the load test. The distributions in all the cases except for RAM are bimodal, highlighting the variability among the different blocks.

The Shapiro-Wilk normality tests (Table 6) show that in most cases data are not normally distributed for any of the dependent variables.

As before, we run the Kruskal-Wallis test for each variables to detect a possible difference between the monitoring tools on performance. For CPU usage, CPU load, and RAM usage, the obtained p-values are significant forall the blocks. The magnitude of the difference attributable to the tool (eta-squared statistic) is *large* in 9 out 9, 2 out of 9, and 9 out 9 cases for CPU usage, CPU load, and RAM usage, respectively. For network traffic and execution time, the difference is significant only in 2 and 4 cases, respectively. The Tables per variable with KW p-values and η^2 results are in the replication package.

The Wilcoxon test across all blocks, with the B-H correction, compares each tool against the baseline. Results are hereafter summarized:

- **CPU Usage:** In general, for ELK stack and Zipkin there is a significant impact of monitoring tools on CPU usage. The trend is more pronounced under a high workload. The p-values for 3 blocks allow to reject the null hypothesis that the median difference between the baseline and ELK stack is zero. The same stands for 6 blocks regarding Zipkin. This confirms the previous observations. Also, the Cliff's delta reveal always a large effect when the p-values are significant.
- **CPU Load:** For Zipkin and Netdata there is at least one block where the impact on CPU load is significant. This means that these tools can influence CPU load under specific frequency and workload conditions.
- **RAM Usage:** Except for Netdata, there is statistical significance for every tool, for at least one block. The Cliff's delta effect size is large for all these blocks but one (on Prometheus). The results for ELK stack further confirm the previous observations that ELK stack has a very high memory footprint (under all workload-frequency conditions, RAM usage is close to 100%).
- **Network Traffic:** In general, there is no statistical significance for network traffic (only in one block for Netdata, Prometheus and Zipkin the difference is significant). This is expected, as running a monitoring tool should not influence the network traffic generated by running the load test.
- **Execution Time:** In case of ELK stack and Zipkin there is statistical significance and Cliff's delta estimates show large effect size. Again, a high workload increases the impact and exacerbates the differences: the longest execution time is for Zipkin under the high workload-high frequency configuration (more details in the replication package plots). For Netdata and Prometheus, there are no statistically significant results.

> **Result 3** - Monitoring tools influence the CPU usage, CPU load, RAM usage and execution time, under specific frequency and workload conditions. Zipkin and ELK stack have the largest impact, exacerbated when running under high workload conditions.

Table 7. Correlation coefficients

	CPU usage	CPU load	RAM usage	Execution time	Network
Pearson	0.859	0.899	0.187	0.867	0.961
Spearman	0.829	0.851	0.290	0.796	0.954

Finally, we analyze each dependent variable in relation to energy efficiency (Table 7). CPU usage, load average and execution time are strongly correlated with energy efficiency. Although this does not imply causation, their reduction can potentially improve energy efficiency. However, there is a relatively small correlation between RAM usage and energy efficiency. This also explains why ELK stack is not worse than Zipkin in terms of energy consumption, despite its intensive use of RAM. The correlation between network traffic and energy efficiency is also high, primarily due to the presence of 3 groups each corresponding to a level of workload – high network traffic leads to the highest energy values, while low network traffic leads to the lowest values.

> **Result 4** - CPU usage, CPU load average and execution time are strongly correlated with energy efficiency.

6   Threats to Validity

Internal Validity. To mitigate the *history* threat, where events occurring at the same time a treatment is applied could produce the effect, we repeat each run 10 times. Also, to avoid order effects, execution order is randomized. To avoid *carryover effects* (i.e., consecutive treatments influencing each other), we stop the running systems and wait for 3 min before starting the next run. We also alternate the baseline with the other treatments, as a best practice to be able to verify any noticeable changes in absence of intervention. We address the *ambiguous temporal precedence* threat by ensuring replication of the exact sequence of independent variables manipulation, thanks to the Experiment Runner tool.

External Validity. We select well-known monitoring tools for microservices, considering their popularity on GitHub. Clearly, different tools might impact energy and performance differently. To mitigate this risk, we applied a minimalistic setup, following the documentation to avoid introducing unnecessary confounding variables (due to additional components, for instance). We compared the tools on a widely used microservice benchmark application, Train Ticket; though, using another application would lead to different results. Future replications of this experiment will help in mitigating this potential source of bias.

Construct Validity. We are confident about the integration of the monitoring tools, as we carefully tested each of them running alongside the system before running the experiment. The implementation is publicly available. Also, hardware power meters, like the one we used, are known to have high accuracy and do not influence the measured system [6].

7   Conclusions and Future Work

In this study we conducted an empirical assessment of the energy and performance overhead of monitoring tools on Docker-based systems. We obtained significant results in terms of energy and performance (CPU usage, CPU load, RAM usage, network traffic and execution time), under specific frequency and workload conditions. Not all the tools impact energy efficiency and performance in the same way, but we observed a high energy consumption and a high CPU, RAM and execution time for the same tools. The correlation analysis confirms the association for CPU and execution time, but not for memory, hence the latter is likely to have a smaller impact on energy. For a more granular analysis, to be able to detect energy hotspots in monitoring tools, we plan to deploy a software power meter in a future iteration, such as SmartWatts[11], that measures energy at container level.

Acknowledgements. This project has received funding from the European Union's Horizon 2020 research and innovation programme under the Marie Skło- dowska-Curie grant agreement No 871342 "uDEVOPS".

References

1. Microservices (2023). https://martinfowler.com/articles/microservices.html
2. Basili, V.R.: Software Modeling and Measurement: The Goal Question Metric Paradigm. Computer Science Technical Report Series, CS-TR-2956 (1992)
3. Cortellessa, V., Di Pompeo, D., Eramo, R., Tucci, M.: A model-driven approach for continuous performance engineering in microservice-based systems. J. Syst. Softw. **183**, 111084 (2022)
4. Di Francesco, P., Lago, P., Malavolta, I.: Architecting with microservices: a systematic mapping study. J. Syst. Softw. **150**, 77–97 (2019)
5. Ergasheva, S., Khomyakov, I., Kruglov, A., Succi, G.: Metrics of energy consumption in software systems: a systematic literature review. IOP Conf. Ser. Earth Environ. Sci. **431**, 012051 (2020)
6. Fahad, M., Shahid, A., Manumachu, R.R., Lastovetsky, A.: A comparative study of methods for measurement of energy of computing. Energies **12**(11), 2204 (2019)
7. Heward, G., Müller, I., Han, J., Schneider, J.G., Versteeg, S.: Assessing the performance impact of service monitoring. In: ASWEC 2010, pp. 192–201. IEEE (2010)

---

[11] https://powerapi-ng.github.io/smartwatts.html.

8. Hirst, J.M., Miller, J.R., Kaplan, B.A., Reed, D.D.: Watts up? pro ac power meter for automated energy recording (2013)
9. Khomh, F., Abtahizadeh, S.A.: Understanding the impact of cloud patterns on performance and energy consumption. J. Syst. Softw. **141**, 151–170 (2018)
10. Liu, M., Peter, S., Krishnamurthy, A., Phothilimthana, P.M.: E3: energy-efficient microservices on smartnic-accelerated servers. In: USENIX, pp. 363–378 (2019)
11. Merkel, D., et al.: Docker: lightweight linux containers for consistent development and deployment. Linux j **239**(2), 2 (2014)
12. Pierce, C.A., Block, R.A., Aguinis, H.: Cautionary note on reporting eta-squared values from multifactor ANOVA designs. Educ. Psychol. Meas. **64**(6), 916–924 (2004)
13. Romano, J., Kromrey, J.D., Coraggio, J., Skowronek, J.: Appropriate statistics for ordinal level data: Should we really be using t-test and cohen'sd for evaluating group differences on the NSSE and other surveys. In: FAIR, vol. 177, p. 34 (2006)
14. Santos, E.A., McLean, C., Solinas, C., Hindle, A.: How does docker affect energy consumption? evaluating workloads in and out of docker containers. J. Syst. Softw. **146**, 14–25 (2018)
15. Vegas, S., Apa, C., Juristo, N.: Crossover designs in software engineering experiments: benefits and perils. IEEE Trans. Softw. Eng. **42**(2), 120–135 (2015)
16. Verdecchia, R., Lago, P., Ebert, C., de Vries, C.: Green it and green software. IEEE Softw. **38**(6), 7–15 (2021)
17. Zhou, X., et al.: Benchmarking microservice systems for software engineering research. In: 40th ACM/IEEE International Conference on Software Engineering (ICSE) (2018)

ChainsFormer: A Chain Latency-Aware Resource Provisioning Approach for Microservices Cluster

Chenghao Song[1] , Minxian Xu[1(✉)] , Kejiang Ye[1] , Huaming Wu[2] ,
Sukhpal Singh Gill[3] , Rajkumar Buyya[4] , and Chengzhong Xu[5]

[1] Shenzhen Institute of Advanced Technology, Chinese Academy of Sciences,
Shenzhen, China
{ch.song,mx.xu,kj.ye}@siat.ac.cn
[2] Tianjin University, Tianjin, China
whming@tju.edu.cn
[3] Queen Mary University of London, London, UK
s.s.gill@qmul.ac.uk
[4] Cloud Computing and Distributed Systems (CLOUDS) Lab, School of Computing
and Information Systems, The University of Melbourne, Melbourne, Australia
rbuyya@unimelb.edu.au
[5] State Key Lab of IoTSC, University of Macau, Macau, China
czxu@um.edu.mo

Abstract. The trend towards transitioning from monolithic applications to microservices has been widely embraced in modern distributed systems and applications. This shift has resulted in the creation of lightweight, fine-grained, and self-contained microservices. Multiple microservices can be linked together via calls and inter-dependencies to form complex functions. One of the challenges in managing microservices is provisioning the optimal amount of resources for microservices in the chain to ensure application performance while improving resource usage efficiency. This paper presents *ChainsFormer*, a framework that analyzes microservice inter-dependencies to identify critical chains and nodes, and provision resources based on reinforcement learning. To analyze chains, ChainsFormer utilizes light-weight machine learning techniques to address the dynamic nature of microservice chains and workloads. For resource provisioning, a reinforcement learning approach is used that combines vertical and horizontal scaling to determine the amount of allocated resources and the number of replicas. We evaluate the effectiveness of *ChainsFormer* using realistic applications and traces on a real testbed based on Kubernetes. Our experimental results demonstrate that *ChainsFormer* can reduce response time by up to 26% and improve processed requests per second by 8% compared with state-of-the-art techniques.

Keywords: Microservice · Chain · Reinforcement learning · Kubernetes · Scaling

© The Author(s), under exclusive license to Springer Nature Switzerland AG 2023
F. Monti et al. (Eds.): ICSOC 2023, LNCS 14419, pp. 197–211, 2023.
https://doi.org/10.1007/978-3-031-48421-6_14

1   Introduction

Microservice architecture is a popular approach for designing and developing modern applications. It involves breaking down monolithic applications into smaller, fine-grained components that can work together to provide services for users [15]. This approach allows development teams to focus on implementing different microservices, thereby speeding up the development process. Additionally, microservices can be updated or upgraded independently, making maintenance efforts more manageable. To ensure reliability and performance, microservices can be scaled and operated individually, depending on workload fluctuations and environmental variance.

Despite their independence, microservices are not entirely self-contained. Communication-based dependencies, such as remote procedure calls, exist between different microservices [7]. These dependencies can represent how requests are processed among different microservices. Based on these dependencies, microservices can be combined into chains to fulfill complex services. The length of a chain can vary from several nodes to tens of nodes. A single microservice, such as a database-related service, can also be shared by multiple chains to support the formation of different services. Additionally, microservice chains can be dynamic, scaling in or out as needed to accommodate new microservices. Given these features of microservices and the resource usage fluctuations, it is challenging to precisely pre-configure the amount of resources, provision and scale resources when deploying microservices in clusters.

Traditional approaches for improving application performance often rely on over-provisioning and autoscaling, which involve allocating more CPU and memory resources to microservices. These approaches typically use performance models, simple heuristics, static thresholds, or machine learning algorithms. However, these approaches have several limitations. Firstly, accurate performance models and efficient heuristic-based scheduling policies require significant manual efforts and training, which are infeasible for large-scale microservices with a large number of configurable parameters. Secondly, machine learning (ML) based approaches, such as support vector machines, rely on centralized graph databases, which can lead to scalability issues and inefficient scheduling when microservice chains are updated. Therefore, alternative approaches are needed to address these limitations and enable effective management of microservices.

This paper presents a solution to the limitations of traditional approaches with *ChainsFormer*, a chain latency-aware resource provisioning framework for microservices cluster based on chain feature analysis. *ChainsFormer* dynamically scales CPU and memory resources to microservices to ensure high-quality service. This framework utilizes online telemetry data, including requests information, application running data, and hardware resource usage, to capture the system state. By leveraging ML and reinforcement learning (RL) models, *ChainsFormer* can adapt to variances in the system and reduce the need for manual efforts. Overall, *ChainsFormer* provides an effective solution for managing microservices with a high degree of automation and accuracy.

Table 1. Comparison of related work

Approach	Autoscaling	Workloads Prediction	Machine Learning based Resource Provisioning	Chain Analysis	Quick Adaption to Dynamic Chains	SLO-awareness
Sage [2]		✓	✓	Partial		✓
Firm [9]	✓		✓	✓		✓
Parslo [8]	✓			✓		✓
PEMA [4]	✓					✓
Autopilot [10]	✓	✓	✓			✓
Sinan [14]	✓		✓	✓		✓
Seer [3]			✓	✓	✓	✓
CoScal [12]	✓	✓	✓			✓
ChainsFormer (ours)	✓	✓	✓	✓	✓	✓

To efficiently manage the dynamic nature of microservice chains and adapt to changes quickly, *ChainsFormer* employs various techniques. It first identifies the critical chain using the calling graph and utilizes a decision tree to find the critical node that has a significant influence on microservice performance. This approach avoids the limitations of heavy machine learning techniques and centralized graph databases, which struggle with dynamic changes. Additionally, *ChainsFormer* utilizes RL to make efficient and optimized decisions regarding vertical and horizontal scaling. These decisions include when to conduct scaling actions, which microservice should be scaled with resources, and how many resources of each type should be scaled. Furthermore, these decisions can be further optimized through RL with updated decisions, resulting in even more efficient resource provisioning.

To evaluate the effectiveness of *ChainsFormer*, we deployed representative microservice applications on Kubernetes, which is the state-of-the-art container orchestration platform. We compared *ChainsFormer* with three state-of-the-art baselines and used realistic traces from Alibaba to measure application performance and response time. Our results show that *ChainsFormer* outperforms the baselines in terms of application performance and response time. These findings demonstrate the effectiveness of *ChainsFormer* in providing efficient resource provisioning and management for microservice chains.

In summary, we make the following key **contributions**:

- We present the design of a framework that aims to handle the dynamic changes in microservice applications by identifying critical chains and nodes.
- We propose an RL-based approach for combining vertical and horizontal scaling to make decisions on efficient resource provisioning, which uses historical data for offline training and makes online decisions based on system states.
- We develop the designed framework on top of Kubernetes platform. Using realistic workload traces and real-world microservice, we demonstrate the efficiency of *ChainsFormer* compared to the state-of-the-art baselines.

2   Related Work

In this section, we will discuss the current state-of-the-art techniques that are designed to address the challenges of resource provisioning and autoscaling in microservices, in order to meet the desired quality of service levels.

Resource Provisioning for Microservices. Sage [2] aims to perform root cause analysis in microservice-based systems by utilizing causal Bayesian networks to identify the underlying reason for service level objective (SLO) violations. After identifying the root cause, Sage initiates autoscaling actions to mitigate the issue. One of the advantages of Sage is that it only requires lightweight tracking and is suitable for large-scale deployments. However, a major limitation of Sage is its heavy reliance on pre-trained machine learning models. Seer [3] employs deep learning models to predict quality of service (QoS) violations and dynamically adjusts allocated resources to each microservice to prevent such violations. It is particularly suitable for scenarios with frequent service updates and requires a large amount of tracking data. However, the accuracy of detection can be affected by significant application changes. Parslo [8] is a gradient descent-based approach that assigns partial SLOs to nodes in a microservice to provide resource configuration solutions quickly. One of Parslo's main advantages is its ability to achieve a globally optimal solution for large-scale services that have already been deployed. However, Parslo is limited in its support for only certain types of Directed Acyclic Graphs, and its performance may not be guaranteed in all circumstances. PEMA [4] uses iterative feedback-based tuning to optimize resource allocation to meet SLO requirements. Compared to other approaches, PEMA is lightweight and does not require any offline experiments or pre-training. However, PEMA's performance may be poor during resource update intervals, and its inability to capture the dependencies between microservices due to the lack of pre-training may limit its effectiveness. The fundamental limitation of this line of work is that they do not consider features of microservice chain, which can lead to inefficient actions and performance degradation.

Micoservice Autoscaling. Autopilot [10] utilizes ML algorithms to analyze historical data on prior executions and performs a set of finely-tuned heuristics to adjust a job's resource requirements while it is running. The benefit of Autopilot is its ability to modify resource requirements on-the-fly, allowing it to adapt to changing workload demands. However, Autopilot's conservative approach can lead to overprovisioning and resource wastage. Sinan [3] leverages a set of machine learning models to determine the performance impacts of microservice dependencies and allocate appropriate resources for each tier. Sinan is an explainable approach and can be used for complex microservices, while it only monitors CPU resources and does not provide auto-tuning capabilities. CoScal [12] leverages data-driven decisions and enables multi-faceted scaling based on reinforcement learning. CoScal utilizes gradient recurrent units to accurately predict workloads, which assists in achieving efficient scaling. However, one limitation is that the model re-training required for adapting to new applications can be costly. FIRM [9] is a system that utilizes online telemetry data and machine learning methods to adaptively detect and locate microservices that lead to SLO violations. It can make decisions based on reinforcement learning to mitigate SLO violations via fine-grained and dynamic resource provisioning. FIRM proposes a two-level ML framework to locate critical microservice paths and nodes. However, FIRM has certain limitations. The scalability of centralized

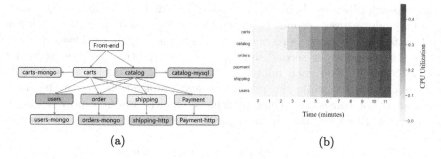

Fig. 1. (a) Microservice graph structure of Sock Shop application. (b) CPU utilization of each microservice from top tier to bottom tier. When workloads increase, the CPU utilization of all microservices increases.

graph databases is limited, and it cannot handle transient SLO violations that occur within an interval shorter than the minimum interval due to the heavy ML techniques.

The comparisons between *ChainsFormer* and other relevant work are presented in Table 1. Our work is most similar to CoScal and FIRM. However, there are notable differences between them. Firstly, CoScal is deployed on Docker Swarm, while *ChainsFormer* is designed specifically for Kubernetes. Secondly, CoScal does not incorporate chain analysis for resource management, whereas *ChainsFormer* leverages chain analysis techniques to optimize resource allocation within microservice chains. Thirdly, both CoScal and *ChainsFormer* employ reinforcement learning, but *ChainsFormer* utilizes the SARSA algorithm, which allows for faster convergence by updating Q-values based on the current policy. In comparison to FIRM, *ChainsFormer* employs lightweight ML techniques to handle transient SLO violations in microservice chains, a task that FIRM does not address due to its heavy ML models and the associated high costs of model re-training. Additionally, *ChainsFormer* does not require a centralized graph database like FIRM, which enhances its scalability by avoiding a central bottleneck caused by large amounts of data. In *ChainsFormer*, runtime data is stored on worker nodes and only fetched by the central node when model training or retraining is required, significantly reducing the overhead on the central node.

3   The ChainsFormer Framework

To motivate our design, we deployed the Sock Shop application[1] to observe how different microservices react to changes in workloads by monitoring utilization usage. As shown in Fig. 1a, a request sent to the Sock Shop application can be distributed to different microservices from front-end to back-end tiers. The processing of a request can form different calling chains, for example, a request

---

[1] Sock Shop: A Microservices Demo Application. https://microservices-demo.github.io/.

can go through different chains to complete different functionalities, e.g. checking items under a user account (front-end → carts → users), or paying for an item (front-end → catalog → payment). As shown in Fig. 1b, workloads increase from 0–110 requests per second during 0–11 minutes (requests per second is increased with 10 after each minute), and the CPU utilization also increases for all microservices, while the resource usage propagation among the nodes in a chain is not consistent. Thus, to achieve efficient resource provisioning of microservices, the scheduler should consider the features of the microservice chain properly.

To address the above observations, we propose the overview architecture design of *ChainsFormer* as shown in Fig. 2 and the key designs are as below:

- *ChainsFormer* first processes the incoming requests from users via Workload Generator by recording the number of requests and extracting the tracing data and performance counters.
- To make the resource provisioning more efficient, *ChainsFormer* applies the neural network-based prediction algorithm to estimate future workloads.
- *ChainsFormer* detects SLO violations and utilizes real-time data to dynamically identify critical chains and locate critical nodes that result in SLO violations. To support the quick adaption to the dynamic changes in chains, *ChainsFormer* includes an auto-adaptor that can quickly detect the changes.
- *ChainsFormer* analyzes the telemetry data collected by Workload Generator and node information identified by Chains Analyzer, and makes scaling decisions to provision resources for critical nodes. The decision is made automatically on the Kubernetes cluster by an RL-based resource scaler, which considers resource utilization, performance metrics, and future workloads.

3.1   Workload Generator

Workload Generator module in *ChainsFormer* is responsible for processing the raw workload trace to make fit with other modules, e.g. extracting the key information of workloads (e.g. timestamp and user id) and providing initial analyses for the workloads. Based on the required functionalities, workloads are distributed to different microservices that are deployed on different work nodes in the microservices cluster. For example, we have observed that the workloads of the Sock Shop application are distributed to Front-end (45.5%), Order (22.7%), Carts (22.7%), Catalog (5.7%) and Random item (3.4%) with different percentages. The processed workloads are also regularly stored in log files for workloads prediction, and the performance counters that indicate system performance are provided to resource scalers for autoscaling microservices.

To reduce the state space of our RL model, we process the workloads by dividing the workloads into a number of levels, e.g. using CPU utilization levels to represent the number of workloads, where the same scaling actions can be applied to the same level to reduce action space. For example, Fig. 3 shows the original continuous Alibaba's workloads converted to 10 discrete CPU utilization levels at per-day and per-minute intervals, and each level represents 10% utilization, e.g. level 0 represents utilization ranges from 0% to 10%.

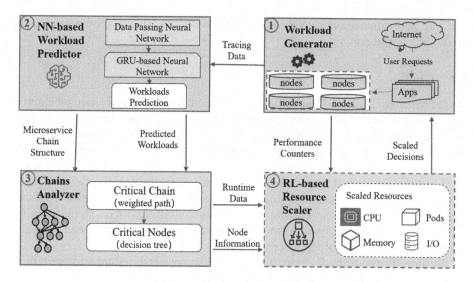

Fig. 2. Framework of *ChainsFormer*

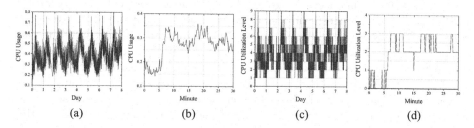

(a)   (b)   (c)   (d)

Fig. 3. (a) Original Alibaba per-day workloads. (b) Original Alibaba per-minute workloads. (c) Converted Alibaba per-day workloads. (d) Converted Alibaba per-minute workloads.

3.2 Neural Network-Based Workload Predictor

The Workload Predictor aims to accurately forecast the future workloads in system, and provides information for the RL-based Resource Scaler module to dynamically scale the number of pod replicas. The Workload Predictor module can be realized via different prediction approaches, such as ML-based prediction algorithms. *ChainsFormer* considers the workloads prediction as a category of multi-variate time series forecast problem, where the workloads are time-relevant and multiple variables (e.g. CPU usage, memory usage, network throughput, and hard disk read/write) can influence the final prediction results.

ChainsFormer utilizes a GRU-based neural network validated in [13], named esDNN, to predict future workloads, which can overcome the limitations of gradient explosion and disappearance when conducting long-term prediction. The esDNN can extract the key features of workloads, and convert multivariate time series forecasting into supervised learning to keep as much information as possible. The performance of esDNN has been validated to achieve good accuracy in predicting workloads.

3.3 Chains Analyzer

One of the main goals of *ChainsFormer* is to identify the critical chain efficiently and accurately based on tracing data and inter-dependencies, along with identifying the critical nodes that impact the latency of the critical chain. We define the critical chain as the one with the longest end-to-end latency, which represents the total time taken by a request to traverse the entire microservice chain, starting from the moment it enters the system until the user receives the response. Furthermore, the critical nodes (highlighted in Fig. 4a for Train-Ticket application) are defined as the nodes that have a substantial impact on the latency of the critical chain, and any performance degradation in these nodes can severely affect the performance of the microservices.

To identify the critical chain, *ChainsFormer* uses tracing data to construct an execution graph that shows the processing sequence of a user request. The graph includes all the microservices involved in processing the request. We then apply a weighted longest path algorithm [5] to find the critical chain, which is the chain with the longest end-to-end latency. The weight of each edge is the processing time between different nodes. This algorithm is lightweight and can adapt to changes in chains quickly. For example, if the blue chain in Fig. 4a has the highest latency, it can be identified as the critical chain. The critical chain will be changed to the red chain when its latency becomes to be the longest. We also identify critical nodes in the critical chain, which are the nodes that have a significant impact on latency. These critical nodes can significantly degrade the performance of microservices.

The critical nodes are identified based on a decision tree, as shown in Fig. 4b. This tree classifies the nodes into critical and non-critical based on real-time data from the selected critical microservice chain and a trained model using historical running data. To reduce the overhead on the central node, the runtime data is stored on worker nodes and only fetched by the central node when model training or retraining is required. Nodes with high latency, CPU, and memory usage are more likely to be classified as critical nodes. In case the identification has a high error rate (e.g. 5%), a model updating mechanism is triggered to update the decision tree.

3.4 RL-Based Resource Scaling

The resource scaler uses RL techniques to determine the optimal scaling actions. Compared to static and meta-heuristic approaches, the RL-based approach can effectively explore a larger solution space and respond to dynamic status changes. The RL-based resource scaler employs a hybrid scaling approach that includes both vertical scaling and horizontal scaling. Vertical scaling is used to quickly adjust resources such as CPU, memory, and network on the local machine, while horizontal scaling adds or removes active nodes in the system.

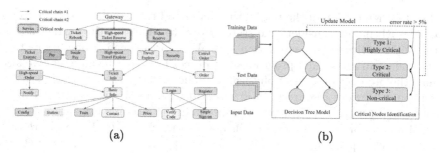

Fig. 4. (a) Train-Ticket application with critical chain (https://github.com/Fudan SELab/train-ticket). (b) Decision tree model for critical node identification

In *ChainsFormer*, the problem of RL-based resource scaling is modeled as a Markov Decision Process [11]. At each time interval t, the system state is represented by $s_t \in S$, and an action $a_t \in A$ can be taken to transition the state to s_{t+1}, yielding a reward of R_{t+1} based on the policy π_θ, which has configurable parameters θ. The state space S is associated with an action space A, and a transition matrix captures the probability of taking different actions during state transitions. The goal of RL is to optimize the policy to maximize the expected cumulative reward.

To achieve this, *ChainsFormer* employs the SARSA algorithm [6] to learn the policy for the Markov decision process and estimate the expected cumulative reward of state-action pairs using the action-value function $Q_t(s, a)$. When action a_t is taken at time interval t, the value of Q_{t+1} is updated using the reward R_{t+1} and propagated to the next time interval as:

$$Q_{t+1}(s_t, a_t) = Q_t(s_t, a_t) + \alpha[R_{t+1} + \gamma max_{a'} Q_t(s_{t+1}, a') - Q_t(s_t, a_t)], \qquad (1)$$

where $\alpha \in (0, 1]$ is the learning rate and $\gamma \in [0, 1]$ is the discount factor. To address the curse of dimensionality associated with updating the Q Table with a large solution space, we train the model offline to minimize the loss function and reduce training time. Online training is used to make decisions and update actions with rewards. We also employed the divided load levels to reduce the state space, as discussed in Sect. 3.1. In addition, we use the SARSA algorithm to further reduce computational costs by using $R_{t+1} + \gamma max_{a'} Q_t(s_{t+1}, a')$ as the update target to guide the estimate of the true action-value function. This approach considers only the sampling of successive s_{t+1}, a_{t+1}, and immediate reward R_{t+1}. The estimation of the action-value function at the time interval $t + 1$ is given by:

$$Q_{t+1}(s_t, a_t) = Q_t(s_t, a_t) + \alpha[R_{t+1} + \gamma Q_t(s_{t+1}, a_{t+1}) - Q_t(s_t, a_t)], \qquad (2)$$

where the $Q_t(s_{t+1}, a_{a+1})$ and each update can be obtained via one-step transition $(s_t, a_t, R_{t+1}, s_{t+1}, a_{t+1})$ of the state-action-reward-state-action pair.

To implement the RL-based resource scaler module, we utilize various parameters of the current pod as inputs to the RL model. These parameters include the load state, the position of the pod in the chain, and the latency of the microservice. The RL model considers the state $s_t \in S$ to represent the current status of the microservice chain, and action $a_t \in A$ comprises scaling operations that adjust the chain status and provisioned resources by a specific amount. We also assume the presence of a set of physical machines $P = (M_1, M_2, \ldots, M_K)$ in the system that provides resources. Each physical machine M_k is represented by a tuple $U_k = (u_k^1, u_k^2, \ldots, u_k^I)$, where u_k^i represents the resource utilization of type i out of a total of I resource types on physical machine M_k. For each M_k, we denote the set of possible actions as $a_k^i = \{h_k, v_k^i\}$, where $h_k \in [-n, n]$ represents the number of horizontal replicates that can be added or removed, $v_k^i \in [-m, m]$ represents the amount of vertical scaling that can be applied to resource type i. A positive value of h_k or v_k^i indicates that more resources are added, whereas negative values indicate resource removal. Given K as the total number of physical machines, the final set of actions is represented as the Cartesian product of the sub-action sets: $A = \prod_{k=1}^{K} \prod_{i=1}^{I} a_k^i$.

The main objective of the *ChainsFormer* system is to enhance resource utilization while ensuring QoS requirements are met. Therefore, the reward function is designed to consider two key metrics: resource utilization and response time. The reward for resource utilization is formulated in Eq. (3).

$$R_u(u_k) = \begin{cases} \frac{\sum_{k=1}^{K} U_k^{max} - u_k}{K} + 1, & u_k \leq U_k^{max}, \\ \frac{\sum_{k=1}^{K} u_k - U_k^{max}}{K} + 1, & u_k > U_k^{max}, \end{cases} \tag{3}$$

where U_k^{max} represents the highest utilization threshold of all resource types for physical machine M_k, and u_k is the current utilization of M_k. The system receives a positive reward when the utilization is below the threshold, and the reward decreases when the utilization is higher or significantly lower than the predefined threshold.

The reward for response time, denoted as $R_q(rt)$, is modeled based on the maximum acceptable response time RT_{max}.

$$R_q(rt) = \begin{cases} e^{-\left(\frac{rt - RT_{max}}{RT_{max}}\right)^2}, & rt > RT_{max}, \\ 1, & rt \leq RT_{max}, \end{cases} \tag{4}$$

which shows that when the system is operating normally, the reward is 1. However, as the system's performance degrades and violates the RT_{max}, the reward gradually decreases and converges to 0.

The final reward value is based on the resource utilization R_u and response time R_q at time interval t, which is formulated as follows:

$$r(s_t, a_t) = \frac{R_q^t}{R_u^t}, \tag{5}$$

where higher values of R_q^t and lower values of R_u^t can increase the total reward.

Algorithm 1 outlines the overall procedure of *ChainsFormer*. Initially, the algorithm collects the system status to enable the RL process (line 1), which

---

Algorithm 1: *ChainsFormer*: Overall Procedure

Input : Table $Q(s, a)$ contains all state/action pairs from experience pool by offline training, time intervals T, probability of random action ϵ, learning rate α, discount factor γ

1 Initialize system status, and monitoring model;
2 **for** t *from* 1 *to* T **do**
3      $U_t^k \leftarrow$ Resource utilization of M_k at time interval t;
4      $W_{t-1} \leftarrow$ Workloads level at time interval $t - 1$;
5      $\hat{W}_t \leftarrow$ Predicted workload level;
6   **if** $\hat{W}_t \neq W_{t-1}$ **then**
7   Choose a action from action set A with ϵ probability, or select an action with the $\max(Q_t(s_t, a_t))$;
8   Conduct $a_t = \{h_k(t), v_k^i(t)\}$ with horizontal scaling and vertical scaling
9   **if** *online training is triggered* **then**
10             $s_{t+1} \leftarrow$ system state at time interval $t + 1$;
11             $R_{t+1} \leftarrow$ reward calculation by Eq. (5);
12   Update Q value:
                $Q_{t+1}(s_t, a_t) = Q_t(s_t, a_t) + \alpha[R_{t+1} + \gamma Q_t(s_{t+1}, a_{t+1}) - Q_t(s_t, a_t)]$;
13   **end**
14   Store transition $(s_t, a_t, R_{t+1}, s_{t+1}, a_{t+1})$in experience pool;
15   **end**
16 **end**

---

includes monitoring the workloads level, resource utilization, and metrics at each time interval to construct the complete system states (lines 3-5). Upon a change in workload level (line 6), resources are dynamically scaled to optimize resource usage while maintaining the required QoS. The SARSA algorithm commences by selecting actions randomly with a probability of ϵ from the experience pool and transitions to another state (line 7). The chosen actions entail vertical and horizontal scaling to allocate resources effectively (line 8). *ChainsFormer* facilitates online training by storing the transition $(s_t, a_t, R_{t+1}, s_{t+1}, a_{t+1})$ in the experience pool and subsequently updating the decisions based on rewards with better outcomes (lines 9–14).

4   Performance Evaluations

4.1   Experimental Settings

We use the workload dataset provided by Alibaba[2] as demonstrated in Sect. 3.1, which includes 8-day data traces from homogeneous 4,034 servers. We utilize the Locust toolkit to generate resource usage based on profiled data of machines. We evaluate the performance of the Train-Ticket application (a larger application

---

[2] Alibaba Cluster Trace Program: https://github.com/alibaba/clusterdata/tree/v2018.

than the Sock Shop used for motivation in Sect. 3) and use the Jaeger monitoring toolkit to track the distribution of requests. The application is deployed on a Kubernetes-based cluster consisting of five nodes, each with an Intel Xeon E5-2660 processor and 64 GB of RAM. One physical machine serves as the master of the cluster, while the others serve as workers.

4.2 Baselines and Metrics

We have compared *ChainsFormer* (**CF**) with 3 state-of-the-art baselines implemented by us.

KS [1]: it is employed by native Kubernetes and mainly relies on horizontal scaling, which involves dynamically adding or removing the number of replicas. It follows a threshold-based approach based on resource usage metrics such as CPU and memory, where more replicas are added when the pre-defined resource threshold is exceeded (e.g. CPU utilization > 0.7) and vice versa.

AUTO [10]: it is derived from Google Autopilot and uses a hybrid approach to scale resources based on workloads. The approach combines horizontal scaling and vertical scaling to dynamically adjust the allocated resources to tasks based on historical data.

FIRM [9]: it utilizes machine learning techniques, specifically support vector machine and reinforcement learning, to identify and mitigate microservices responsible for SLO violations.

We have adopted three widely used metrics to evaluate the performance: *1) Requests per second (RPS)* represents the system's ability to process requests within a specific time period, and a higher value shows better performance. *2) Number of failures* indicates the number of requests that were not processed or did not receive a response due to an overloaded situation. A lower value for this metric represents a more reliable system. *3) Average response time:* is a dominant metric to measure performance, and a good autoscaling algorithm should aim to reduce it.

4.3 Experiment Analyses

Due to page limitations, we present key results. Figure 5a compares the average requests per second over different time periods. To highlight differences among periods, we analyze results over 5 periods (e.g. 1,000 minutes, 2,000 minutes, and 5,000 minutes), covering short-term and long-term comparisons. It is noteworthy that the loads significantly vary during different time periods. For instance, the highest loads were observed during the first 2,000 minutes, and the average load during the 5,000 minutes period was much lower. It is observed that the KS approach performs the worst in terms of RPS compared to other baselines. This could be due to the limited capability of the threshold-based approach. The AUTO approach, which leverages ML-based techniques, can process larger RPS compared to KS. The FIRM approach can obtain better RPS during the first 3,000 minutes, but during the 4,000-5,000 minutes, it performs worse than AUTO. Our proposed approach, *ChainsFormer*, can achieve the best RPS in the long-term, i.e., when the time period is larger than 3,000 minutes. This optimization comes from our more accurate identification of critical chains and nodes. At the early stage of request processing, FIRM performs well when the critical path is identified. However, after load changes, the identified critical path may not be critical anymore. Additionally, it is reasonable to note that FIRM with a static critical path does not fit workloads with high variances well. In conclusion, CF optimized the requests per second up to 8.1% compared to the baselines.

Figure 5b illustrates the comparison of the number of failures, presenting the average results in five different time periods. It is observed that KS has the highest number of failures compared to other baselines due to its static policy, which shows that it struggles to handle high-variant workloads. AUTO significantly reduces the number of failures. For instance, during the first 1,000 minutes, AUTO reduces the failures from 350 to 80 by leveraging historical data. FIRM and CF further optimize the failures by utilizing critical chains and nodes, where the results are quite close. Overall, CF can reduce the number of failures by 8.3% compared to FIRM.

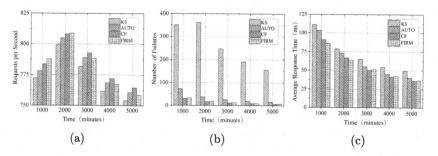

(a) (b) (c)

Fig. 5. Comparison of (a) requests per second, (b) number of failures, and (c) average response time.

Figure 5c depicts the comparison of average response time. Among all five time periods, the average response time of KS is at the highest value, which we consider as a benchmark test to analyze the performance of the other three algorithms. AUTO is optimized compared to KS and maintains the second-highest response time. It optimizes around 10% of response time, for example, decreasing from 110 ms to 100 ms during the first 1,000 minutes. The results of CF and FIRM are consistent with the analyses of RPS. In the early stage, FIRM slightly outperforms CF, while in the long run (e.g. 3,000 to 5,000 minutes), CF achieves a lower response time than FIRM. Overall, *ChainsFormer* optimizes response time by 1.4% to 26.6% compared to the baselines.

To evaluate the scalability of *ChainsFormer*, we conducted experiments comparing it with FIRM under different numbers of requests as shown in Fig. 6. We gradually increased the number of requests (from 400 to 1200 per second)

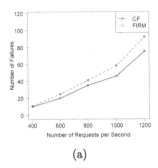 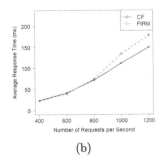

(a)   (b)

Fig. 6. Scalability comparison of (a) number of failures, and (b) average response time when the number of requests increase.

and monitored the system's performance. The number of failures in *Chains-Former* exhibited a slower rate of increase compared to FIRM as the number of requests grew. Similarly, the average response time in *ChainsFormer* remained relatively stable as the number of requests grew. In contrast, FIRM experienced a more pronounced increase in average response time under the same conditions. These findings validate the scalability of *ChainsFormer* and its ability to handle larger workloads while maintaining good performance. The results suggest that *ChainsFormer* is a promising solution for scaling microservice-based systems in scenarios with dynamic and growing request loads.

5   Conclusions

In this paper, we propose *ChainsFormer*, a microservice scaling approach that combines deep learning and reinforcement learning techniques to dynamically adjust resource allocation based on workload predictions and critical chain identification. By leveraging decision trees for rapid identification of critical chains and nodes, and using reinforcement learning to make real-time scaling decisions, *ChainsFormer* optimizes resource usage while maintaining high-quality of service in terms of response time, number of failures, and requests per second. Our experiments, conducted on a representative microservices application, show that *ChainsFormer* outperforms state-of-the-art algorithms from research and industry in terms of QoS optimization. Our approach has the potential to significantly improve the efficiency and reliability of microservices-based applications in cloud computing environments.

Acknowledgments. This work is supported by National Key R & D Program of China (No.2021YFB3300200), the National Natural Science Foundation of China (No. 62072451, 62102408), Shenzhen Industrial Application Projects of undertaking the National key R & D Program of China (No. CJGJZD20210408091600002), Shenzhen Science and Technology Program (No. RCBS20210609104609044), and Alibaba Group through Alibaba Innovative Research Program.

References

1. Burns, B., Beda, J., Hightower, K.: Kubernetes: up and running: dive into the future of infrastructure. O'Reilly Media (2019)
2. Gan, Y., Liang, M., Dev, S., et al.: Sage: practical and scalable ml-driven performance debugging in microservices. In: Proceedings of the 26th ACM International Conference on Architectural Support for Programming Languages and Operating Systems, ASPLOS 2021, pp. 135–151 (2021)
3. Gan, Y., Zhang, Y., Hu, K., et al.: Seer: leveraging big data to navigate the complexity of performance debugging in cloud microservices. In: Proceedings of the 24th International Conference on Architectural Support for Programming Languages and Operating Systemsm ASPLOS 2019, pp. 19–33 (2019)
4. Hossen, M.R., Islam, M.A., Ahmed, K.: Practical efficient microservice autoscaling with qos assurance. In: Proceedings of the 31st International Symposium on High-Performance Parallel and Distributed Computing, HPDC 2022, pp. 240–52 (2022)
5. Ioannidou, K., Nikolopoulos, S.D.: The longest path problem is polynomial on cocomparability graphs. Algorithmica **65**, 177–205 (2013)
6. Kardani-Moghaddam, S., Buyya, R., Ramamohanarao, K.: Adrl: a hybrid anomaly-aware deep reinforcement learning-based resource scaling in clouds. IEEE Trans. Parallel Distrib. Syst. **32**(3), 514–526 (2021)
7. Luo, S., Xu, H., Lu, C., et al.: An in-depth study of microservice call graph and runtime performance. IEEE Trans. Parallel Distrib. Syst. **33**(12), 3901–3914 (2022)
8. Mirhosseini, A., Elnikety, S., Wenisch, T.F.: Parslo: a gradient descent-based approach for near-optimal partial slo allotment in microservices. In: Proceedings of the ACM Symposium on Cloud Computing, SoCC 2021, pp. 442–457 (2021)
9. Qiu, H., Banerjee, S.S., Jha, S., et al.: {FIRM}: an intelligent fine-grained resource management framework for {SLO-Oriented} microservices. In: 14th USENIX Symposium on Operating Systems Design and Implementation (OSDI 20), pp. 805–825 (2020)
10. Rzadca, K., Findeisen, P., Swiderski, J., et al.: Autopilot: workload autoscaling at google. In: Proceedings of the Fifteenth European Conference on Computer Systems. EuroSys 2020 (2020)
11. Wang, S., Guo, Y., Zhang, N., et al.: Delay-aware microservice coordination in mobile edge computing: a reinforcement learning approach. IEEE Trans. Mob. Comput. **20**(3), 939–951 (2021)
12. Xu, M., Song, C., Ilager, S., et al.: Coscal: multifaceted scaling of microservices with reinforcement learning. IEEE Trans. Netw. Serv. Manage. **19**(4), 3995–4009 (2022)
13. Xu, M., Song, C., Wu, H., et al.: Esdnn: deep neural network based multivariate workload prediction in cloud computing environments. ACM Trans. Internet Technol. **22**(3) (2022)
14. Zhang, Y., Hua, W., Zhou, Z., et al.: Sinan: Ml-based and qos-aware resource management for cloud microservices. In: Proceedings of the 26th ACM International Conference on Architectural Support for Programming Languages and Operating Systems, ASPLOS 2021, pp. 167–181 (2021)
15. Zhong, Z., Xu, M., Rodriguez, M., et al.: Machine learning-based orchestration of containers: A taxonomy and future directions. ACM Comput. Surv. **54**(10s) (2022)

Energy-Efficient and Communication-Aware Resource Allocation in Container-Based Cloud with Group Genetic Algorithm

Zhengxin Fang[1]([✉]), Hui Ma[1], Gang Chen[1], and Sven Hartmann[2]

[1] Centre for Data Science and Artificial Intelligence & School of Engineering and Computer Science, Victoria University of Wellington, Wellington, New Zealand
{zhengxin.fang,hui.ma,aaron.chen}@ecs.vuw.ac.nz
[2] Department of Informatics, Clausthal University of Technology, Clausthal-Zellerfeld, Germany
sven.hartmann@tu-clausthal.de

Abstract. Microservice is a new architecture for application development that makes applications more flexible to deploy, extend and update compared to monolithic architectures. As container-based clouds rapidly gained popularity in recent years, more microservices are deployed in containers and composed of complex and elaborated applications for users. The challenges of microservices deployment in a container-based clouds arise from two-level resource allocations to not only minimize the overall energy consumption but also to reduce the communication data volume between microservices in physical networks to improve application performance. However, there is still a lack of research that considers these two important challenges jointly during microservice composition and resource allocation. Motivated by this, in this work, we propose a genetic algorithm-based algorithm, namely EC-GGA, to not only minimize the energy consumption in cloud data centers but also minimize the communication data volume of applications. We compare EC-GGA with several state-of-the-art algorithms to demonstrate the effectiveness of our proposed algorithm.

Keywords: Microservice · Container · Cloud Computing · Group Genetic Algorithm · Resource Allocation

1 Introduction

Service oriented architecture (SOA) in software development has the advantage of loose coupling compared to monolithic architectures, allowing to develop and extend applications with high flexibility [10]. Microservices [10], an essential architecture in SOA, are widely deployed in cloud data centers with virtualization technologies such as containers, and are composed of complex and elaborated applications for users. Container-based cloud becomes a new trend in the

F. Monti et al. (Eds.): ICSOC 2023, LNCS 14419, pp. 212–226, 2023.
https://doi.org/10.1007/978-3-031-48421-6_15

cloud computing environment since it is lightweight and easy to scale up, which significantly reduces the computation overheads compared to Virtual Machines (VMs) based cloud [12]. Deploying applications composed of microservices gives rise to *Energy-efficient and Communication-aware Resource Allocation problem in Container-based cloud* (ECRAC), which allocates proper resources to microservices with the objectives of minimizing energy consumption of applications while minimizing communications between microservices.

Currently, there are two main challenges of resource allocation in the container-based cloud environment. Firstly, resource allocation in container-based cloud is an NP-hard problem due to its complex and large search space [20]. Container-based clouds involve resource allocation at two levels, that is containers should be allocated to VMs (Container-VM level) and VMs should be allocated to Physical Machine (VM-PM level), which makes it more difficult than resource allocation in VM-based cloud. On the container-VM level, containers are allocated to VMs via *VM selection* or *VM creation*, to either select currently leased VM instances or new VM instances with selected VM types. Similarly, at the VM-PM level, VMs are allocated via PM selection or PM creation to allocate VMs to existing PMs or new PMs with selected PM types. Each level of resource allocation should satisfy constraints regarding CPU and memory resource capacity. Moreover, the selection and creation of VMs at the first level have a significant impact on the selection and creation of PMs at the second level. Therefore, to find resource allocation with minimal energy consumption, multiple VM and PM selection and VM and PM creation decisions must be made simultaneously.

The second challenge is that microservices deployed in different VMs and PMs frequently exchange high volumes of data, creating communication affinities [14]. In this paper, affinity is defined as the data volumes exchanged between two containers [4]. If containers with affinity are deployed to different PMs, it brings communication overhead, which depends on the communication data volumes transmitted by the physical network between different PMs in the cloud data center. Physical network overhead is incurred by the communication overhead, which ultimately affects the network latency, application request/response time, and causes extra energy consumption in the cloud data center. To minimize communication overhead, it is desirable to allocate containers with affinities into the same PM. However, placing all containers with affinity together may lead to inefficient usage of resources, i.e., VMs and PMs, resulting in energy inefficiency. In line with the above analysis, it is important to develop effective new approaches for resource allocation to strike a desirable trade-off between two contradicting objectives, i.e., energy consumption and communication overhead.

Existing research works on two-level resource allocation problems in container-based clouds mainly focus on optimizing energy consumption. In [17,18], a genetic algorithm is proposed to allocate applications with minimal energy consumption, with no consideration of communication overhead. Other works such as [4,7,11] aim to reduce the communication data volume in a cloud data center but only consider one-level resource allocation. As the above reviews, existing works consider either energy consumption or communication overhead alone. There is a lack of effective approaches that consider both the two objectives jointly.

Motivated by the above, in this paper, we aim to propose a Group Genetic Algorithm (GGA) based algorithm, namely EC-GGA, to solve ECRAC. To the best of our knowledge, our proposed algorithm is the first work to consider energy consumption and communication overhead jointly in the resource allocation problem of cloud data centers. The novelties of our proposed approach are the following:

- We develop a novel Energy-efficient and Communication-aware Crossover (EC-Crossover) for GGA to consider energy consumption and communication overhead jointly during the crossover operator;
- We propose a Best-Fit-Decreasing Insert (BFDI) method for re-arranging *free containers* (will be introduced in Sect. 4) that are generated by crossover according to both resource utilization and communication overhead; and
- We introduce a novel mutation operator to explore better solutions with less energy consumption and less communication data across PMs.

Organization. This paper is organized as follows. In Sect. 2 the related work is discussed. In Sect. 3 the energy-efficient communication-aware resource allocation problem in container-based cloud is defined. In Sect. 4 we present our new proposed algorithm to tackle this problem. In Sect. 5 we report on the experiments that we have conducted to evaluate our new algorithm. Finally, in Sect. 6 conclusions are given.

2   Related Work

Existing research works on resource allocation either consider two-level *Resource Allocation in Container-based cloud* (RAC) without paying attention to data communications between containers or consider communication cost but only focusing on one level resource allocation as in [8]. In this section, we first review algorithms for resource allocation problems in RAC in recent years and then review existing communication-aware algorithms for resource allocation.

Approaches for RAC. Heuristics is often used for RAC, which is treated as a bin packing problem. Best-Fit [1] is used to allocate containers/VMs to VMs/PMs with the highest resource utilization. Three heuristics are used in [20] to perform resource allocations on two levels simultaneously. First-Fit is used for both VM selection and PM selection. If no existing VMs can be used to host a given container, Best-Fit is used to select a VM type for a new VM instance. However, these heuristics often lead to local optima rather than global optimal solutions.

Due the the global search capacity, various evolutionary algorithms have been proposed to solve RAC. In [17], a vector-based GA method with a dual-chromosome representation is proposed to solve the RAC. The chromosomes at the first level encodes the solutions that allocate containers to VMs; while the chromosome at the second level encodes the solutions that allocate VMs to PMs. To get the allocation solutions, the chromosomes need to be decoded using the Next-Fit heuristic [15]. The decoding heuristic may not lead to the best final solutions.

To directly represent the two-level allocation solutions, [18] proposed a GA-based approach with a group-based representation, [18]. To evolve solutions in group-based solutions, several operators, including gene-level crossover, rearrangement, and merge, are proposed to search for the best solution of the RAC. To encourage evolved solutions to use a small number of PMs, [2] proposes a GGA-based approach with a group-based representation that constrains the length of the representation to solve the RAC.

Communication-Aware Resource Allocation. To reduce the communication overhead, [4] clusters VM with data communication into affinity groups. Within a group, all the items have affinity with at least one of the other items in the same group. If the affinity group is too large to be allocated into one single PM, [4] applies the min-cut heuristic to divide the affinity group into several smaller affinity groups, which are then allocated to PMs using the First-Fit-Decreasing method. Similarly, [7] also applies min-cut to partition an application into several microservice groups to minimize the communication data volume between each group. Partition ensures that each group can be allocated to at least one VM. Each group is allocated to the machine that has the highest communication data volumes within the group. When the communication data volumes are the same, the group chooses the most-loaded machine to host it.

As aforementioned algorithms place containers or VMs one by one, but the order of the placement also affects the outcomes. [8] proposed a concurrent container scheduling algorithm to allocate a batch of containers at the same time. They model the container scheduling problem as the minimum cost flow problem (MCFP) and represent the container requirement by a flow network. Each node of this flow network represents a container or a machine and the weight of this flow network implies the mapping quality between containers and machines. The containers with dependencies will be merged into an aggregator node that will be allocated into the same VM. Based on MCFP, the shortest path algorithm is used to find the best mapping between container nodes and VM nodes. However, this algorithm cannot deal with the situation when a group of containers cannot be allocated into one machine due to the resource capacity limit.

3   Energy-Efficient Communication-Aware MAC

An application is composed of a list of microservices $M = [m_1, ..., m_k]$, and each microservice is exclusive to a container. In a container-based cloud, given a list of containers $C = [c_1, ..., c_k]$, a range of VM types, and a range of PM types, containers are allocated to VM instances, which are further allocated to PMs. Each container c_i has a CPU occupation $\zeta^{cpu}(c_i)$ and a memory occupation $\zeta^{mem}(c_i)$. A VM type is defined as a tuple $\gamma_t = (\Omega^{cpu}(\gamma_t), \Omega^{mem}(\gamma_t), \pi^{cpu}(\gamma_t), \pi^{mem}(\gamma_t))$, where Ω is the capacity and π is the overhead. A VM instance v_i is of a VM type

γ_t. A PM type is defined as a tuple $\tau_t = (\Omega^{cpu}(\tau_t), \Omega^{mem}(\tau_t), E^{idle}(\tau_t), E^{full}(\tau_t))$, capturing its CPU and memory capacities, as well as the energy consumption when it is idle or under full workload, respectively. A PM instance p_i is of a PM type τ_t.

Energy Model. Eq. (1) quantifies the energy consumption for a given PM instance p_i, based on the popular non-linear energy model proposed in [5].

$$E(p_i) = E^{idle}(p_i) + (E^{full}(p_i) - E^{idle}(p_i)) \times (2\mu^{cpu}(p_i) - (\mu^{cpu}(p_i))^{1.4}) \quad (1)$$

where $E^{idle}(p_i)$ and $E^{full}(p_i)$ are the energy consumption of the PM instance p_i when it is idle or fully loaded, respectively. $\mu^{cpu}(p_i)$ is the CPU utilization level of the PM instance p_i, which is calculated by:

$$\mu^{cpu}(p_i) = \frac{\sum_{l=1}^{L}(\sum_{j=1}^{m} \pi^{cpu}(\gamma_j) * z_{j,l} + \sum_{i=1}^{n} \zeta^{cpu}(c_i) * x_{i,l}) * y_{l,p}}{\sum_{k=1}^{|\Pi|} \Omega^{cpu}(\tau_t) * w_{p,k}} \quad (2)$$

where $x_{i,l}$, $y_{l,p}$, $z_{j,l}$ and $w_{p,k}$ are binary decision variables, and L is the number of created VMs. $x_{i,l}$ takes 1 if c_i is allocated to the l-th created VM, and 0 otherwise. $y_{l,p}$ takes 1 if the l-th created VM instance is allocated to the p-th PM, and 0 otherwise. $z_{j,l}$ is 1 if the l-th created VM is of type j, and 0 otherwise. $w_{p,k}$ is 1 if the p-th created PM is of type k, 0 otherwise. And τ_t is the type of p_i.

Let $s = [p_1, p_2, ..., p_i]$ denote a solution, which is a list of PM instances. The total energy consumption with respect to a solution s is calculated as follows:

$$TEC(s) = \sum_{p_i \in s} E(p_i) \quad (3)$$

Communication Model. Let s denote a solution of ECRAC and X_s be an n-by-m binary matrix, where $x_{i,j}$ equals to 1 when container c_i is allocated to PM instance p_j in solution s, and 0 otherwise. Since there is data communication between microservices in the same application, we define an n-by-n affinity matrix A, where $a_{i,j}$ represents the affinity between container c_i and container c_j. It quantifies the total communication data volumes between container c_i and container c_j.

The total communication overhead can be computed as follows:

$$D(X_s) = \sum_{i=1}^{n} \sum_{j=1}^{n} a_{i,j} \cdot (1 - \sum_{k=1}^{m} x_{i,k} \cdot x_{j,k}) \quad (4)$$

where $(1 - \sum_{k=1}^{m} x_{i,k} \cdot x_{j,k})$ equals to 1 when container c_i and container c_j are on different PMs, otherwise it is 0. As a result, $D(X_s)$ indicates the total communication data volume between microservices that are placed on different PMs.

Optimization Objective. The objective of ECRAC is to jointly minimize the cloud data center energy consumption as well as the communication overhead. Let $S = \{s_1, s_2, ..., s_l\}$ denote the set of all possible solutions. The optimization objective of the ECRAC is defined as:

$$\min_{s_i \in S} \omega \cdot TEC(s_i) + (1 - \omega) \cdot D(X_{s_i}) \tag{5}$$

where $0 < \omega < 1$ indicates the importance of energy consumption while $1 - \omega$ indicates the importance of the communication overhead. Both $TEC(s_i)$ and $D(X_{s_i})$ in Eq. (5) are normalized by using the common min-max normalization technique [6].

4   Proposed Algorithm

In this section, we describe our proposed Energy-efficient and Communication-aware Group Genetic Algorithm (EC-GGA). The algorithm flowchart is shown in Fig. 1 (a), where the novel contributions of the algorithm are highlighted in green. It starts by generating an initial population of solutions using newly designed initialization, which are then evolved using a novel crossover operator, a rearrangement method, a mutation operator. Our new developments realize several key advantages. Firstly, the operators of EC-GGA are designed to improve resource utilization, which has a big impact on overall energy consumption. Meanwhile, EC-GGA tends to co-locate containers with affinity to reduce the communication overhead. Moreover, each operator considers two-dimensional resources (e.g., CPU and memory) jointly, which balances the utilization of these resources.

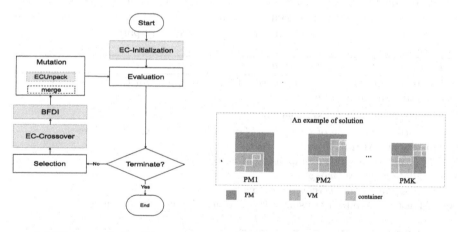

(a) The overall algorithm   (b) Representation of a chromosome

Fig. 1. Overall algorithm and representation of a chromosome in EC-GGA

4.1   Representation

EC-GGA employs a direct representation that represents the candidate solutions as a combination of PMs, VMs and containers. Figure 1 (b) shows an example solution that highlights PMs, VMs and containers with different colors, which includes a list of PMs, while every item in the list of PMs is a list of VMs. Similarly, every item in the list of VMs is a list of containers. This direct representation is a variable-length representation since the length of a solution depends on the number of used PMs. Such a variable-length representation has the advantage that it is flexible to permit the exploration of different solutions using well-designed evolution operators.

4.2   EC-Initialization

Algorithm 1 presents our proposed EC-Initialization algorithm. To generate a full population of initial solutions for the first generation, EC-GGA first checks whether each application (a group of containers with affinity) can be allocated to at least one of the existing VMs or a new VM instance. If not, the application will be partitioned by *binaryCut* into two affinity groups, which have the least communication data volumes between each other (lines 2 to 4). Each affinity group or application will be allocated through the First-Fit (FF) heuristic into VM, and similarly, VMs are also allocated to PMs with FF heuristic. Upon VM/PM creation, EC-Initialization creates VM/PM instances randomly when the existing VM/PM instances have insufficient resources. By using the First-Fit heuristic to allocate applications and VMs, EC-GGA ensures that the majority of VMs and PMs can enjoy high resource utilization to reduce the number of VMs and PMs in the initial solution. Meanwhile, the *binaryCut* can divide an application into two partitions and ensure that different partitions have the minimum communication between each other. Consequently, all initial solutions tend to enjoy low communication overhead between any pair of PMs.

Algorithm 1: EC-Initialization

Input   : A list of applications, a set of VM types, a set of PM types
Output: An initial solution

1 *affinityGroupList* ← *application* ;
2 **while** the occupation of *group* in *affinityGroupList* exceed the largest capacity of VM **do**
3   Split *group* into two groups using *binerayCut*;
4   Update *affinityGroupList*;
5 **for** *group* in *affinityGroupList* **do**
6   Allocate *group* to VM using *FF* or *RandomlyCreation* heuristic;
7   Allocate *newVm* to PM using *FF* or *RandomlyCreation* heuristic;

4.3   EC-Crossover

Our proposed Energy-efficient and Communication-aware Crossover operator, named EC-Crossover, is illustrated in Fig. 2. Each offspring solution is generated by preserving PMs from parent solutions. For example, in Fig. 2, two-parent solutions are sorted by the criterion introduced below. Afterward, PM1 is compared with PM1', PM2 is compared with PM2', and so on. The winning PM is the one with a higher criterion value, which is preserved in the offspring solution by copying the PM type and all of the VM types hosted in it. After copying, the crossover operator checks whether each container in VMs has been allocated. If so, the allocated containers will not be reallocated; otherwise, containers will be allocated to the corresponding VMs. Finally, the crossover operator will further remove PMs and VMs that do not have any workload.

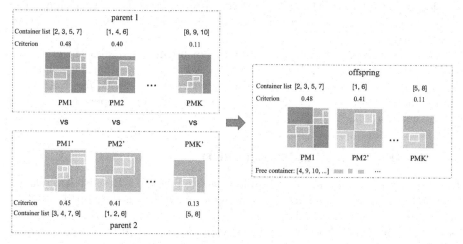

Fig. 2. An example of EC-Crossover

To maintain the population diversity, we propose to use two different preservation criteria, i.e., the *normalized resource* criterion in Eq. (6), and the *inner affinity* criterion in Eq. (7), to generate two offspring solutions from two-parent solutions. The *normalized resource* considers the CPU and memory utilization together, and the *inner affinity* indicates the communication data volumes inside the PM. The first offspring solution is generated by sorting the PMs according to the *normalized resource* and preserving PMs with high *normalized resource*; while the other offspring solution is generated by sorting the PMs in each parent solution according to the *inner affinity* and preserving PMs with high *inner affinity*.

$$NOR = \frac{\zeta^{cpu}(c_i))}{\Omega^{cpu}(p_k)} \times \frac{\zeta^{mem}(c_i)}{\Omega^{mem}(p_k)} \tag{6}$$

$$IA = \sum_{c_i, c_j \in p_k} A(i,j) \tag{7}$$

Since ECRAC is a two-dimensional bin packing problem, we should consider both CPU and memory capacity utilization when preserving PMs for the next generation. Otherwise, the resource utilization of VMs and PMs may not be balanced. For example, only considering memory utilization may result in PMs with high memory utilization but low CPU utilization, which leads to CPU resource wastage, as evidenced in [18]. To avoid such a situation, in our crossover operator, we preserve PMs for the next generation according to the *normalized resource*, which considers both CPU and memory utilization. It is expected to generate offsprings with balanced resource utilization and low resource wastage. By preserving PMs with high *normalized resource*, EC-Crossover improves the resource utilization of each PM to reduce the total number of used PMs, which further reduces the overhead energy consumption. Meanwhile, to reduce the communication data between PMs, EC-Crossover also preserves PMs with high *inner affinity* into the offspring solution, which helps to reduce data communication between PMs.

As shown in Fig. 2, some containers may not be allocated after the crossover operator since their hosting PMs are not selected to preserve offspring solutions. We refer to these unallocated containers as *free containers*. The *free containers* will be allocated subsequently through a new rearrangement operator proposed in Sect. 4.4.

4.4   Best-Fit-Decreasing Insert (BFDI)

To reallocate *free containers* to suitable PMs, we propose a Best-Fit-Decreasing Insert (BFDI) method. Our BFDI rearrangement method is developed based on the Best-Fit-Decreasing (BFD) heuristic [9]. Meanwhile, to find a suitable PM for a newly created VM, we propose a concept *Between Affinity BA* to calculate the affinity of the new VM v_{new} with each p_k of the PMs, see Eq.(8):

$$BA_k = \sum_{c_j \in p_k} \sum_{c_i \in v_{new}} A(i,j) \tag{8}$$

Algorithm 2 shows the process of our proposed BFDI algorithm. BFDI first groups *free containers* with affinity into *free affinity groups* (lines 3 to 8) that can be allocated into one single VM instance. After grouping, BFDI inserts the *free affinity groups* from the largest to the smallest into the most packed VM with sufficient resources. If there are no existing VM instances that can host the *free affinity group*, a new VM instance is created using *LargestVM* heuristic that selects a VM type not only can load the *free affinity group* but also has the largest remaining resource after hosting the *free affinity group*. In this way, the number of VMs and the overall VM overhead can be reduced. Once a new VM instance is created it should be placed into a PM instance. BFDI places the new VM into the PM with the largest *BA* and also enough capacity to host the new VM (*LargestBA* heuristic). If no existing PM instance has enough remaining resources to host the new VM, a new PM will be created randomly.

BFDI inserts the largest group first to the most packed VM and PM to improve resource utilization. Subsequently, smaller groups are allocated to reduce resource fragmentation. It considers the resource utilization and affinity together when re-arranging *free containers*, in order to balance the CPU and memory utilization and reduce resource wastage. Meanwhile, during the process of allocating newly created VMs to PMs, BFDI tends to place the new VM in the PM that has the largest affinity between the containers in the new VM and the containers in the PM, which helps to reduce the communication overhead.

Algorithm 2: BFDI Algorithm

Input   : A set of free containers, a set of PMs
Output: A set of allocated PMs

1 $freeContainerList \leftarrow free\ containers$;
2 $freeAffinityGroup \leftarrow \emptyset$;
3 **for** C **in** $freeContainerList$ **do** /*group free containers with affinity into affinity group*/
4     $affinityGroup \leftarrow \emptyset$;
5     $affinityGroup.$add(C);
6     $affinityGroup.$add(the container that have affinity with C);
7     $freeContainerList.$remove(containers in $affinityGroup$);
8     $freeAffinityGroup.$add($affinityGroup$);
9 **for** $group$ **in** $freeAffinityGroup$ **do** /*allocating affinity group*/
10   Allocate $group$ into a VM using BFD or $LargestVM$ heuristic;
11   Allocate $newVm$ into PM using $LargestBA$ or $RandomlyCreation$ heuristic;

4.5 Mutation

The mutation operation in EC-GGA consists of two steps, *Energy-efficient and Communication-aware Unpack (ECUnpack)* and *Merge*.

ECUnpack aims to remove PMs with low resource utilization or low inner communication. The ECUnpack operator first sorts the PMs in a solution according to either the *normalized resource* or the *inner affinity* in ascending order. One of the two criteria is randomly chosen with equal probability for sorting. Then the ECUnpack operator unpacks PMs in a roulette wheel style. That is, the probability of unpacking a PM is proportional to its rank in the sorted PM list.

Merge aims to reduce the overhead consumption of VMs. It repeatedly checks whether the total resource requirements of the two smallest VMs are in excess of the resource capacity of a larger VM, If not, all the containers in the two smallest VMs are reallocated to the larger VM so that the two small VMs can be released.

5   Experimental Evaluation

This section presents the experiment design and the experiment results to evaluate the performance of EC-GGA. We evaluate the performance of all competing algorithms in terms of fitness, overall energy consumption and communication overhead based on the resource allocation solutions found by the respective algorithms.

Dataset and Test Instance. There are 6 test instances in our experiments that cover four different sizes of containers (500, 1000, 1500) with two sets of VM types (real-world VM types and synthetic VM types) [18]. These test instances are shown in Table 1. We consider 20 different real-world VM types from Amazon EC2[1]. Additionally, 10 synthetic VM types are generated randomly. These irregular VM types bring additional challenges for the problem [2], which reflect the performance of our algorithm in an environment with irregular VM configurations. There are 12 types of PMs with different CPU and memory capacities, following [19].

Table 1. Six test instances in the experiment, size indicates the number of containers to be allocated in each test instance.

Instance	VM types	Sizes	Instance	VM types	Sizes
1	Real-world	500	4	Synthetic	500
2	Real-world	1000	5	Synthetic	1000
3	Real-world	1500	6	Synthetic	1500

Eight business application structures from [16] are considered as the patterns for composing microservices in this paper, corresponding to diverse online activities such as travel planning services and online shopping and so on. An example of such a business application structure is shown in Fig. 3. For any business application, the communication data volume between any pair of microservices of the application is generated randomly following a log-normal distribution, as recommended in [3].

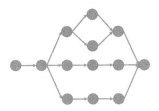

Fig. 3. An example of application structure in [16]

Baselines. We compare EC-GAA to four state-of-the-art algorithms: GGA [18], Docker Swarm (DS) [1], KP-HP [7], and ECSched [8]. GGA, DS, KP-HP and ECSched have been introduced in Sect. 2.

Experiment Setting. The parameter settings of EC-GGA are as follows: the crossover rate is 70%, the mutation rate is 20%, the elite size is 5, the tournament size is 7, and the population size is 100. The terminal condition of EC-GGA is the number of evolutionary generations reaching 100 [18]. The parameter settings of GGA are the same as EC-GGA.

---

[1] https://aws.amazon.com/ec2/pricing/on-demand/.

5.1 Experiment Results

We report the experiment results of EC-GGA and GGA based on their aver-age performance across 30 independent runs. EC-GGA are compared with each baseline algorithm by the Wilcoxon rank-sum test with a significance level of 0.05. The criteria used to compare are the fitness (Eq. (5)), energy consumption (Eq. (3)) and communication overhead (Eq. (4)), and the results are shown in Table 2, where "+", "−" and "=" imply that the performance is significantly better than, significantly worse than or equal to the algorithm is compared.

Table 2. Fitness (Eq. (5)), E (Energy consumption (kWh)) and C (Communication overhead (Mbps)) of 6 test instances with different numbers of containers and two sets of VM types for the baseline algorithms and EC-GGA (*Note: the lower values in the table the better performance*)

Instance	Criteria	GGA [18]	DS [1]	KP-HP [7]	ECSched [8]	EC-GGA
1	Fitness	0.4193	0.3733	0.2398	0.2618	0.1917 (+)(+)(+)(+)
	E	439.10 ± 33	548.76	604.30	651.19	479.85 ± 12 (−)(+)(+)(+)
	C	2408 ± 278	1533.00	15	49	15 ± 3 (+)(+)(=)(+)
2	Fitness	0.6679	0.6702	0.4411	0.4280	0.2983 (+)(+)(+)(+)
	E	952.25 ± 25	1385.00	1566.38	1516.84	1060.72 ± 47 (−)(+)(+)(+)
	C	7582 ± 610	5410	72	87	47 ± 14 (+)(+)(+)(+)
3	Fitness	0.7346	0.7682	0.4822	0.4679	0.4055 (+)(+)(+)(+)
	E	1417.42 ± 50	2016.51	2129.18	2043.32	1643.81 ± 61 (−)(+)(+)(+)
	C	12090 ± 1252	9095	99	244	100 ± 12 (+)(−)(+)(+)
4	Fitness	0.2516	0.2604	0.1786	0.1621	0.1204 (+)(+)(+)(+)
	E	470.85 ± 7	628.36	748.06	659.79	501.19 ± 32 (−)(+)(+)(+)
	C	2526 ± 267	2023	63	138	53 ± 16 (+)(+)(+)(+)
5	Fitness	0.6298	0.6591	0.4060	0.3427	0.2697 (+)(+)(+)(+)
	E	947.82 ± 7	1525.12	1696.56	1397.90	1113.10 ± 51 (−)(+)(+)(+)
	C	8257 ± 285	6113	181	315	191 ± 17 (+)(+)(−)(+)
6	Fitness	0.7441	0.7584	0.4814	0.4435	0.3690 (+)(+)(+)(+)
	E	1406.43 ± 21	2026.24	2170.50	1952.91	1641.64 ± 92 (−)(+)(+)(+)
	C	13739.93 ± 608	9925	236	538	335 ± 30 (+)(+)(−)(+)

We can observe from the results in Table 2 that EC-GGA significantly outper-forms all other four baseline algorithms in terms of fitness. This demonstrates that our proposed EC-GGA can find the best trade-off solutions to minimize both energy consumption and communication overhead.

In terms of energy consumption, EC-GGA reduces around 20% of energy consumption in test instances 3 and 6 compared with DS, KP-HP and ECSched. As for communication overhead, EC-GGA achieves the least communication overhead in three test instances (instances 1, 2 and 4) and is competitive in the other three instances (instances 3, 5 and 6) with KP-HP. Though EC-GGA consumes a small amount more energy (up to about 200 kWh) than GGA, it results in significantly less communication overhead (up to about 13300 Mbps) than GGA, and therefore much better application performance [13].

5.2 Further Analysis

Number of the Used VMs and PMs. Figure 4 presents the comparison of the baseline algorithms, and our proposed EC-GGA regarding the number of used VMs and PMs in the solutions of three test instances with real-world VM types (e.g., test instances 1, 2 and 3). As evidenced in this figure, EC-GGA significantly reduces the number of used VMs and PMs so as to reduce the overhead of VMs and PMs, which can save energy consumption.

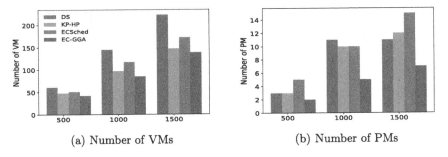

(a) Number of VMs   (b) Number of PMs

Fig. 4. The number of used VMs and PMs in test instances 1, 2 and 3 for the baseline algorithms and EC-GGA (*Note: the lower number the better*)

Resource Utilization of PMs. Figure 5 presents the comparison of CPU and memory utilization between baseline algorithms and EC-GGA. The comparison results show that EC-GGA achieves high-level utilization on both CPU and memory utilization in each test instance; while the CPU utilization of baseline algorithms in test instances with 1000 and 1500 containers are just around 30% to 40%, which causes resource wastage.

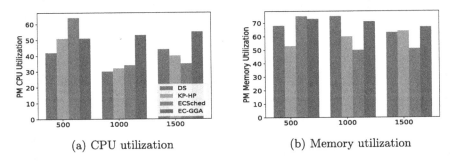

(a) CPU utilization   (b) Memory utilization

Fig. 5. The CPU and memory utilization of PMs in test instances 1, 2 and 3 for the baseline algorithms and EC-GGA.

Ablation Study. To analyze the effectiveness of our proposed operators (e.g. EC-Crossover, BFDI, ECUnpack), we conduct experiments to compare the

fitness of EC-GGA with GGA and EC-GGA without our newly designed operators. Table 3 presents the ablation study results, where all the results are tested
by the Wilcoxon rank-sum test and the meanings of "+", "−" and "=" are the
same as defined above. The result shows that each of our proposed operators is
effective since after removing one of these operators, the performance is worse
than the EC-GGA but still better than GGA.

Table 3. Ablation experiment for our proposed operators. The fitness (Eq. (5)) of EC-
GGA are compared with GGA [18], and EC-GGA without EC-Crossover, BFDI and
ECUnpack respectively. (*Note: the lower values in the table, the better performance*)

Instance	GGA	EC-GGA without EC-Crossover	EC-GGA without BFDI	EC-GGA without ECUn-pack	EC-GGA
1	0.4119	0.1901(+)	0.1877(+)	0.2068(+)	0.1835(+)(+)(+)(+)
2	0.6550	0.3010(+)	0.3159(+)	0.3184(+)	0.2900(+)(+)(+)(+)
3	0.7105	0.3562(+)	0.3759(+)	0.3742(+)	0.3422(+)(+)(+)(+)
4	0.4037	0.1498(+)	0.1627(+)	0.1655(+)	0.1422(+)(+)(+)(+)
5	0.6357	0.2608(+)	0.2881(+)	0.2903(+)	0.2574(+)(+)(+)(+)
6	0.7352	0.3669(+)	0.4078(+)	0.3985(+)	0.3588(+)(+)(+)(+)

6 Conclusion

In this paper, we propose a group genetic algorithm-based algorithm (EC-GGA)
for resource allocation in container-based cloud, which jointly considers the
energy consumption of data center and communication overhead. The experiment results show that EC-GGA reduces energy consumption and communication overhead when compared to the baseline algorithms. Meanwhile, EC-GGA
reduces the number of used VMs and PMs, and also balances the CPU and memory utilization which reduce wastage of resource. An ablation study is conducted
to show the effectiveness of our newly designed operators for the algorithm.

References

1. Docker swarm. https://docs.docker.com/engine/swarm/
2. Akindele, T., Tan, B., Mei, Y., Ma, H.: Hybrid grouping genetic algorithm for
   large-scale two-level resource allocation of containers in the cloud. In: Long, G.,
   Yu, X., Wang, S. (eds.) AI 2022. LNCS (LNAI), vol. 13151, pp. 519–530. Springer,
   Cham (2022). https://doi.org/10.1007/978-3-030-97546-3_42
3. Benson, T., Anand, A., Akella, A., Zhang, M.: Understanding data center traffic
   characteristics. ACM SIGCOMM Comput. Commun. Rev. **40**(1), 92–99 (2010)
4. Chen, J., et al.: Joint affinity aware grouping and virtual machine placement.
   Microprocess. Microsyst. **52**, 365–380 (2017)

5. Dayarathna, M., Wen, Y., Fan, R.: Data center energy consumption modeling: a survey. IEEE Commun. Surv. Tutorials **18**(1), 732–794 (2015)
6. Gajera, V., et al.: An effective multi-objective task scheduling algorithm using min-max normalization in cloud computing. In: 2016 2nd International Conference on Applied and Theoretical Computing and Communication Technology (iCATccT), pp. 812–816. IEEE (2016)
7. Hu, Y., de Laat, C., Zhao, Z.: Optimizing service placement for microservice architecture in clouds. Appl. Sci. **9**(21), 4663 (2019)
8. Hu, Y., Zhou, H., de Laat, C., Zhao, Z.: Concurrent container scheduling on heterogeneous clusters with multi-resource constraints. Futur. Gener. Comput. Syst. **102**, 562–573 (2020)
9. Kaaouache, M.A., Bouamama, S.: Solving bin packing problem with a hybrid genetic algorithm for VM placement in cloud. Procedia Comput. Sci. **60**, 1061–1069 (2015)
10. Nadareishvili, I., Mitra, R., McLarty, M., Amundsen, M.: Microservice architecture: aligning principles, practices, and culture. O'Reilly Media, Inc. (2016)
11. Narantuya, J., Ha, T., Bae, J., Lim, H.: Dependency analysis based approach for virtual machine placement in software-defined data center. Appl. Sci. **9**(16), 3223 (2019)
12. Piraghaj, S.F., Dastjerdi, A.V., Calheiros, R.N., Buyya, R.: A framework and algorithm for energy efficient container consolidation in cloud data centers. In: IEEE International Conference on Data Science and Data Intensive Systems, pp. 368–375. IEEE (2015)
13. Rong, H., Zhang, H., Xiao, S., Li, C., Hu, C.: Optimizing energy consumption for data centers. Renew. Sustain. Energy Rev. **58**, 674–691 (2016)
14. Sampaio, A.R., Rubin, J., Beschastnikh, I., Rosa, N.S.: Improving microservice-based applications with runtime placement adaptation. J. Internet Serv. Appl. **10**(1), 1–30 (2019)
15. Sengupta, J., Singh, P., Suri, P.K.: Energy aware next fit allocation approach for placement of VMs in cloud computing environment. In: Arai, K., Kapoor, S., Bhatia, R. (eds.) FICC 2020. AISC, vol. 1130, pp. 436–453. Springer, Cham (2020). https://doi.org/10.1007/978-3-030-39442-4_33
16. Shi, T., Ma, H., Chen, G., Hartmann, S.: Location-aware and budget-constrained service deployment for composite applications in multi-cloud environment. IEEE Trans. Parallel Distrib. Syst. **31**(8), 1954–1969 (2020)
17. Tan, B., Ma, H., Mei, Y.: Novel genetic algorithm with dual chromosome representation for resource allocation in container-based clouds. In: IEEE International Conference on Cloud Computing (CLOUD), pp. 452–456. IEEE (2019)
18. Tan, B., Ma, H., Mei, Y.: A group genetic algorithm for resource allocation in container-based clouds. In: Paquete, L., Zarges, C. (eds.) EvoCOP 2020. LNCS, vol. 12102, pp. 180–196. Springer, Cham (2020). https://doi.org/10.1007/978-3-030-43680-3_12
19. Wang, C., Ma, H., Chen, G., Huang, V., Yu, Y., Christopher, K.: Energy-aware dynamic resource allocation in container-based clouds via cooperative coevolution genetic programming. In: International Conference on the Applications of Evolutionary Computation (Part of EvoStar), pp. 539–555. Springer (2023). https://doi.org/10.1007/978-3-031-30229-9_35
20. Zhang, R., Zhong, A., Dong, B., Tian, F., Li, R.: Container-VM-PM architecture: a novel architecture for docker container placement. In: Luo, M., Zhang, L.-J. (eds.) CLOUD 2018. LNCS, vol. 10967, pp. 128–140. Springer, Cham (2018). https://doi.org/10.1007/978-3-319-94295-7_9

Engineering Self-adaptive Microservice Applications: An Experience Report

Vincenzo Riccio[1], Giancarlo Sorrentino[1], Matteo Camilli[1],
Raffaela Mirandola[2]([✉]), and Patrizia Scandurra[3]

[1] Politecnico di Milano, Milano, Italy
{vincenzo.riccio,giancarlo.sorrentino,matteo.camilli}@polimi.it
[2] Karlsruhe Institute of Technology (KIT), Karlsruhe, Germany
raffaela.mirandola@kit.edu
[3] University of Bergamo, Bergamo, Italy
patrizia.scandurra@unibg.it

Abstract. This paper reports our experience in engineering RAMSES, a Reusable Autonomic Manager for microServicES that conforms to the well-known MAPE-K *feedback control loop* model to realize self-adaptive microservices. The goal of RAMSES is to enforce the satisfaction of user-defined QoS attributes (e.g., availability, performance) of a microservice application at runtime. RAMSES's control loop components themselves are microservices. RAMSES is designed to ease its reuse across microservice applications. To illustrate RAMSES, we describe how we used it for making self-adaptive an e-food microservice application. We report the results of an experimental evaluation we conducted to validate the capability of RAMSES. Finally, we discuss our experience in facing existing challenges as well as the main lessons learned.

Keywords: Microservice applications · self-adaptation · MAPE-K

1 Introduction

The microservice architectural style is nowadays the de-facto standard to achieve scalable, flexible, and maintainable applications. Microservice frameworks (e.g., SPRING, GoMICRO, FLASK) allow practitioners to speed up microservices development and realize production-ready applications. These frameworks provide some self-adaptation means, mainly limited to autoscaling and circuit-breaking. However, there is a lack of frameworks supporting the seamless integration of control loops to realize the self-* properties for microservices. For this reason, developing microservice applications that can enact self-adaptation strategies to achieve arbitrary adaptation goals and, therefore realizing more resilient systems, is still challenging for practitioners.

To bridge the existing gap and investigate the challenges related to the development of microservice-based self-adapting systems, we developed RAMSES[1] a

---

[1] Source code and documentation publicly available at https://doi.org/10.5281/zenodo.8169049.

© The Author(s), under exclusive license to Springer Nature Switzerland AG 2023
F. Monti et al. (Eds.): ICSOC 2023, LNCS 14419, pp. 227–242, 2023.
https://doi.org/10.1007/978-3-031-48421-6_16

Reusable Autonomic Manager for microServicES, and here we report our experience in this engineering process. RAMSES conforms to the well-known feedback control loop model MAPE-K (Monitor-Analyse-Plan-Execute over a Knowledge base) [8] and wraps a microservice application for realizing self-adaptation. The goal of RAMSES is to enforce the satisfaction of user-defined QoS attributes (e.g., availability and response time) of a microservice application at runtime. RAMSES's control loop components themselves are microservices. We developed RAMSES using the Java-based SPRING BOOT and SPRING CLOUD frameworks[2] for building microservices systems. RAMSES has been designed for reusability; it can be used for adapting a preexisting microservice application built with any microservice framework, given that the target application provides an implementation for the probing and effecting interfaces required by RAMSES as *API-led integration* with the target microservice application.

In this experience report, we illustrate RAMSES describing how we used it to make a standalone e-food microservice application self-adaptive with user-defined QoS-driven adaptation goals. We also report the results of an experimental evaluation conducted to evaluate RAMSES, faced challenges, and lessons learned. Our main contributions are as follows: (i) the RAMSES framework and approach to engineering self-adaptive microservice applications, which is publicly available and ready for reuse; (ii) the application and evaluation of the RAMSES approach on a target microservice application; (iii) the results of an experimental campaign conducted with appropriate research questions to analyse how RAMSES behaves in specific scenarios that synthetically reproduce relevant operating conditions; and finally (iv) lessons learned and reflections gained from the engineering experience with RAMSES.

This paper is organized as follows. In Sect. 2, we present the e-food microservice application used to illustrate RAMSES. In Sect. 3, we describe the RAMSES framework. In Sect. 4, we report the results of the experimental evaluation of RAMSES. In Sect. 5, we discuss the faced challenges and lessons learned, while in Sect. 6 we discuss related work. Finally, we conclude the paper in Sect. 7.

2   Running Example

We introduce here SEFA (SErvice-based eFood Application), an open-source microservice application that we use as a running example throughout the paper. SEFA allows customers to browse a list of restaurants and their respective menus, choose some dishes, and finally place orders, paying for them by credit card and getting them delivered to a specific address. In architecture-based self-adaptation [5,8], we typically have a managed and a managing system. The former provides the domain functionality, while the latter realizes a (centralized or decentralized) MAPE-K feedback control loop that wraps the managing system to carry out adaptation goals. In our case, SEFA is the managed microservice application and RAMSES is the managing microservice layer that adapts SEFA.

---

[2] https://spring.io/microservices.

Table 1. supported adaptation scenarios in RAMSES

Scenario	Observable Properties	Examples of Adaptation strategies
S1: Violation of QoS specifications	Values of the QoS indicators of the service over time (e.g., availability, average response time)	- Change the current service implementation - Add instances in parallel - Shutdown of an instance with low performance - Change configuration properties
S2: Service unavailable	Success or failure of each service invocation	- Change the current service implementation - Add instances in parallel
S3: Better implementation available	Properties of the service implementations	- Change the current service implementation

SEFA is composed of domain-specific microservices, a gateway to expose RESTful APIs, and the infrastructure services EUREKA for service discovery and a *configuration server* for storing and serving distributed configurations to microservices at runtime. The set of domain-specific microservices include: `restaurant` service (handles restaurants and menus); `ordering` service (handles the customers' carts, and allows them to place their orders); `payment` proxy service (mediates with a third-party payment service; and `delivery` proxy service (mediates with a third-party delivery service at the end of an order).

SEFA is built using a modern technology stack including SPRING BOOT, SPRING CLOUD, and DOCKER containers. Furthermore, it adopts state-of-practice architectural patterns such as *API gateway* to handle incoming requests, *load balancer* to allocate requests to service instances according to a *roulette wheel selection* policy [11], and *circuit breaker* natively supported by SPRING CLOUD.

3   RAMSES Framework

RAMSES is a managing system that conforms to the MAPE-K feedback control loop. Each stage of the feedback loop is implemented as a standalone microservice implemented in Java using SPRING BOOT and SPRING CLOUD. The design of RAMSES was driven by the common adaptation scenarios Self-Adaptive Systems (SASs) listed in Table 1. These scenarios describe adaptation goals commonly found in microservices applications.

We designed RAMSES to be reusable accross different microservices applications. To this end, RAMSES is completely decoupled from the managed systems and interacts with it via two components: the *probe* allows RAMSES to retrieve all the relevant data from the managed microservice application, while the *actuator* allows RAMSES to change the configuration of the managed system. These probe/actuator components must be provided by the managed application following specific *probing/actuating* APIs. Once the managed application is connected to RAMSES via these APIs, RAMSES shows all configuration parameters of the MAPE-K loop and the current state of the knowledge (through an interactive web-based dashboard), including current QoS values, and the history of the actuated adaptations. In the following, we describe the probing and actuating APIs of RAMSES as well as the MAPE-K components in more detail.

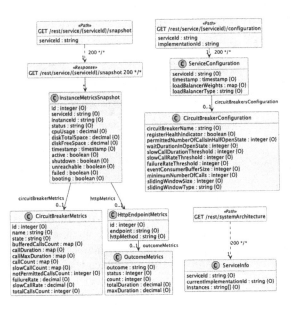

Fig. 1. Probing API

Knowledge and probing/actuating API. The `Knowledge` component maintains an up-to-date runtime model that abstracts relevant information about managed microservices either provided by the probing API or computed by other MAPE components. The `Service` is the main entity of this model. Each service has one or more `Service Implementations`. This latter entity includes attributes related to the operational profile of a specific service implementation, such as *trust* attributes (i.e., level of trust in a service implementation based on its ability to keep QoS requirements satisfied), and *shutdown threshold* (i.e., minimum number of requests that the service should be able to process). Each service is also associated with a `Service Configuration` that includes properties of the load balancer and the circuit breaker. Each service implementation yields one or more running instances, reified by the entity `Service Instance`.

We defined the probing/actuating interfaces as RESTful APIs. Figure 1 shows an example of PLANTUML class diagram generated from the APIs in the standard format OpenAPI[3]. The diagram shows available probing endpoints in terms of HTTP methods, their paths, and request/response parameters. The focus of monitoring is to gather metrics from all the instances of each service and store them in the knowledge as a collection of objects `Instance Metrics Snapshot` (or simply *snapshot*). Each snapshot includes a timestamp, the status of the instance, metrics related to the resource usage (e.g., CPU usage), metrics related to HTTP requests (e.g., number of server errors), and to circuit breakers (see the attributes of the classes `InstanceMetricsSnapshot`, `CircuitBreakerMetrics`, and `OutcomeMetrics` in Fig. 1). The metrics collected by RAMSES are used to

---

[3] https://spec.openapis.org/.

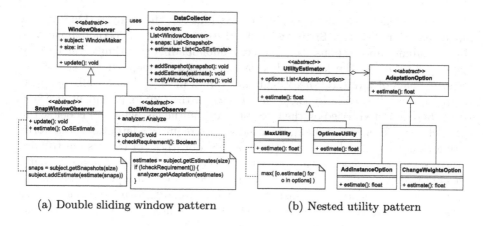

(a) Double sliding window pattern   (b) Nested utility pattern

Fig. 2. Design patterns adopted in RAMSES.

extract QoS indicators. At the current stage, the implementation of RAMSES focuses on availability and response time.

The actuating API of RAMSES exposes low-level operations to be applied to the managed microservices. These operations are, for instance, adding or removing service instances, and changing service configuration, such as the weights of the load balancer or the circuit breaker.

Monitor. This component is responsible for collecting data from the managed microservices. It periodically invokes the probe API to receive a snapshot of all the running instances (i.e., a collection of `InstanceMetricsSnapshot` objects). The `Monitor` is asynchronous w.r.t. the rest of the loop. It stores the snapshots in the knowledge, and then triggers the `Analyze` component to start a new asynchronous adaptation loop. The sampling period of the `Monitor` (*monitor scheduling*) can be dynamically configured via the RAMSES API or dashboard.

Analize. The `Analyze` component is in charge of (i) *QoS values computation* from incoming snapshots and (ii) *adaptation proposal*. In the first phase (i), the latest snapshots of each instance *i* for a service *s* are analyzed to compute the metrics of interest for each QoS indicator. To realize this phase we developed the so-called *double sliding window* pattern shown in Fig. 2a. The pattern represents a general solution that can be reused to customize RAMSES according to the specific QoS indicators. The `DataCollector` component is used to keep track of two collections: incoming snapshots and computed QoS estimates. Whenever a new snapshot or new QoS estimate is available, the component notifies all the `WindowObservers` in charge of analyzing the last window of interest with a given `size`. The observer components can be either of type `SnapWindowObserver` or `QoSWindowObserver`, for snapshots and QoS estimates, respectively. According to Fig. 2a, a `SnapWindowObserver` retrieves the last snapshot window and then computes a QoS estimate. The last estimate is then collected and, as a consequence, `QoSWindowObservers` are notified. A `QoSWindowObserver` retrieves the last QoS estimate window, checks a

QoS requirement, and then triggers the next phase of the analysis. Our current implementation has two `SnapWindowObservers` and two `QoSWindowObserver` (for availability and response time). `SnapWindowObservers` estimate the QoS by aggregating data in the last window by computing a weighted average of the measurements of interest. The weights are values in $[0, 1]$ dynamically assigned to microservice instances by the *load balancer*. If the QoS requirement *satisfaction rate* (computed based on the QoS estimates in the last window) is below the user-defined reference threshold, then the service requires adaptation. It is worth noting that, large window `size` increases the robustness of the system to false positives and outlier QoS estimates, while it decreases the adaptation reactivity. This parameter may be even changed at runtime given that a proper adaptation strategy is implemented. For instance, when the managed microservices enter a steady state the size can be increased. On the contrary, in case of transient states (e.g., due to bursts of users) the size shall decrease.

When a requirement is not satisfied, phase (ii) proposes a set of adaptation options with different priority levels. Options are compared by the `Plan` to select the one associated with the highest expected benefit. The current implementation of RAMSES includes the following extensible set of adaptation options that can be applied to each service s: `addInstance` to add a new instance i for s; `removeInstance` to shut an instance i of s down; `changeImplementation` to replace all n instances of s with n instances of another service implementation; and `changeWeights` to change the weights of the load balancer that handles the requests directed to the instances of a service s. The proposed adaptation options are stored in the shared knowledge before triggering the `Plan` component.

Plan. The `Plan` component determines the best adaptation option for each priority level. To estimate and compare the expected benefit of alternative options, we make use of the so-called *nested utility* pattern represented in Fig. 2b. This pattern represents a reusable solution we adopt to realize the notion of composite *utility function* through a hierarchical structure. Due to the heterogeneity of adaptation options and QoS indicators, we realized this general structure that can be customized to meet the needs of the managed system. According to Fig. 2b, `AdaptationOption` can be extended to represent the actions to be actuated. Selected examples follow: `AddInstanceOption` to resize the weight w of all instances in a uniform way using w equal to $(\#instances)^{-1}$; `ChangeWeightsOption` to recompute the weights all by solving an optimization problem using Mixed Integer Linear Programming (M-ILP) [18] maximizing the expected QoS for all services.

The method `estimate()` of each `AdaptationOption` computes the expected benefit by estimating the QoS values after applying the corresponding actions. For example, if the availability of a service does not satisfy the requirement, a `ChangeWeightsOption` instance estimates the availability of the service by calculating the weighted average availability of the current instances using the new weights. Ultimately, an `UtilityEstimator` instance computes, for a specific service, the best adaptation option depending on the selected strategy. As an example, `MaxUtility` selects the option associated with the highest estimated

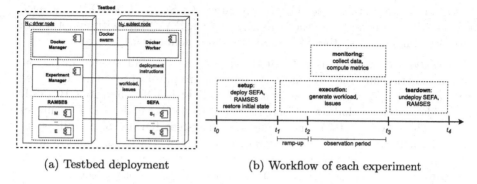

(a) Testbed deployment   (b) Workflow of each experiment

Fig. 3. Design of the experiments.

benefit. `OptimizeUtility` selects the option by maximizing multiple objectives (i.e., multiple QoS indicators). Then the chosen option for each service is referred to as *adaptation plan*. The plan is stored in the knowledge and the `Execute` component is triggered.

Execute. The `Execute` component retrieves from the knowledge the adaptation plan. Then, for each adaptation action, it invokes the actuator API as exposed by the managed microservice application to apply the changes required by the plan and update the knowledge for all the changes made to the services configuration. After processing the plan, the `Execute` component notifies the `Monitor` that the current MAPE-K loop is terminated in order to start a new loop execution.

4 Evaluation

In this section, we describe the evaluation of the managing system RAMSES using SEFA as managed microservice application benchmark. The evaluation aims at answering the following research questions:

RQ1: How does RAMSES perform regarding the achievement of QoS requirements?

RQ2: Does RAMSES achieve the self-healing property in case of unavailable services?

RQ3: Does RAMSES achieve the self-optimizing property in case better microservice instances are available?

We addressed these questions by conducting an experimental campaign composed of multiple experiments where the behavior of RAMSES has been assessed considering the three adaptation scenarios of interest introduced in Sect. 3. The adaptation scenarios were synthetically reproduced by controlling relevant operating conditions of the managed application SEFA. The effects of adaptations applied by RAMSES have been measured over the observation period of 20 minutes for all experiments. Each experiment includes the following two runs to assess our framework in the selected scenarios: (i) SEFA+RAMSES: managed system SEFA controlled by the managing system RAMSES (with adaptation); (ii) SEFA: managed system SEFA only (without adaptation).

Testbed Infrastructure. Our in-house developed testbed is illustrated in Fig. 3a. In our experiments, the two nodes N_1 and N_2 are physical machines equipped with an Apple M1 (8-core) processor, 16GB RAM LPDDR4, and 256GB NVMe SSD. The testbed includes two compute nodes N_1 (driver node) and N_2 (subject node). The driver contains the managing subsystem RAMSES as well as the ExperimentManager and DockerManager components. The ExperimentManager takes as input the definition of the experimental campaign and then it runs all the experiments following the workflow in Fig. 3b for each one of them.

The *setup* phase deploys two fresh instances of SEFA and RAMSES following a given configuration. We rely on DockerManager and DockerWorker components for the deployment/undeployment of the containerized microservices of the managed subsystem onto the subject node N_2. The database images are then loaded onto SEFA, and the initial state of the loop's knowledge is restored to make sure decisions are not influenced by past experiments. During the *execution* phase, the ExperimentManager replicates the desired operating conditions in N_2 by generating a workload for SEFA and by injecting specific issues/failures into microservices, as specified in the experimental campaign. After the ramp-up (from t_1 to t_2), the *monitoring* phase starts. Here, the ExperimentManager computes the metrics to quantify the effectiveness of RAMSES in achieving the adaptation goals. After the observation period T (from t_2 to t_3), the *teardown* phase terminates and undeploys both SEFA and RAMSES.

Table 2 lists all the factors we can control including the issues that can be synthetically injected into our testbed to realize the adaptation scenarios of interest. Concerning the configuration of the managing system, we adopted the following parameters: metric and analysis window size equal to 5, shutdown threshold 40%, monitor scheduling 5 seconds.

4.1   Results

RQ1 (Achievement of QoS Requirements). To address this RQ, we created and executed the adaptation scenario S1 by injecting degraded QoS as shown in Table 3. To measure the performance of RAMSES in achieving the QoS requirements we define the *QoS Degradation Area* (QoSDA) quantitative metric. Given an adaptation goal in terms of QoS requirement (e.g., target availability level) and an observation period T, the QoSDA measures the area between the QoS threshold and the actual QoS, for all time intervals in T such that the operating mode is degraded, that is, the actual QoS value is worse than the corresponding QoS requirement. Since the QoSDA measures the overall level of degradation, we compare this quantity collected from the two runs (with and without adaptation). Indeed, the adaptation actions actuated by RAMSES shall reduce the QoSDA as much as possible compared to no adaptation (the smaller the better).

Figure 4a shows an extract of our experimental results considering the two runs (SEFA and RAMSES+SEFA) under a uniform workload intensity of 100

Table 2. Controllable factors to realize the adaptation scenarios in our testbed.

Type	Factor	Description	Arguments
configuration (managed)	instances	N. of instances per microservice	target microservice, #instances
	boot time	Boot time required by each microservice instance.	target microservice instances, time (sec)
configuration (managing)	metric window size	N. of metric snapshots collected from each microservice instance buffered before triggering the analysis	#snapshots
	analysis window size	N. of metric values used to estimate the QoS level of each microservice instance	#values
	shutdown threshold	Minimum amount of requests that each microservice instance must be able to process to stay alive	rate (%)
	monitor scheduling	Sampling period of the monitor service.	period (sec)
environment	workload	Requests per second issued to the managed subsystem.	target microservice instances, #requests
issues	failures	Synthetic exceptions occur in the interval $[t, t']$ following a given failure rate	target microservice instances, t, t' (min:sec), rate (%)
	delays	Synthetic delay in the time interval $[t, t']$ following a given Normal distribution $\mathcal{N}(\mu, \sigma)$	target microservice instances, t, t' (min:sec), μ (millisec), σ (millisec)
	network issues	Microservice instances become unreachable in the time interval $[t, t']$ due to synthetic network issues.	microservice instances, t, t' (min:sec)

requests per second generated by 50 concurrent users. The plot shows the microservice **restaurant** and its QoS requirement *availability* > 0.9. RAMSES plans and then actuates two adaptations to satisfy the QoS requirement ($t = 2$ and $t = 3$ adaptation points). At the beginning of the run ($t < 2$) the availability is equal to ~ 0.7. RAMSES changes the weights of the load balancer to penalize the bad-performing instances. Indeed, as shown in Table 3, **restaurant**$_1$ has 80% failure rate. The changes actuated by RAMSES improve the availability up to ~ 0.8 at time $t = 3$. Since the target requirement is still not satisfied, RAMSES plans another change: two instances out of three are shut down, due to their poor performances. The microservice finally achieves a stable and desired QoS value from $t = 4$ on. The QoSDA is 4.28×10^2 when adaptation is performed

Table 3. Issues injected in the adaptation scenarios.

Scenario	Factor	Arguments
S1	instances	(restaurant, 3), (ordering, 2), (payment, 1), (delivery, 1)
	failures	(restaurant$_1$, [0:00–20:00], 80%), (restaurant$_2$, [0:00–20:00], 15%), (restaurant$_3$, [0:00–20:00], 5%), (ordering$_1$, [0:00–20:00], 5%), (ordering$_2$, [0:00–20:00], 7%), (payment$_1$, [0:00–20:00], 1%)
	delays	(ordering$_1$, [11:00–11:15, 13:00–15:00], 500 ms, 50 ms)
		(ordering$_2$, [11:00–11:15, 13:00–15:00], 400 ms, 100 ms)
S2	instances	(restaurant, 3), (ordering, 2), (payment, 1), (delivery, 1)
	failures	(payment$_1$, [0:35–20:00], 100%)
S3	instances	(restaurant, 2), (ordering, 2), (payment, 1), (delivery, 1)
	failures	(payment$_1$, [0:00–20:00], 14%)
	delays	(payment$_1$, [00:00–20:00], 19 ms, 1 ms)

(red area), while it is equal to 3.65×10^3 when no adaptation is performed. The adaptation options executed by RAMSES reduce the QoSDA by 88%. Figure 4b shows another extract considering the ordering service and the QoS requirement *response time* < 800 milliseconds. At the beginning of the experiment, the QoS requirement is not satisfied. It is worth noting that the first short-lasting delay injected at time $t = 11$ does not cause an adaptation since the analysis service recognizes the QoS level goes back to nominal. The second delay injected at time $t = 13$ triggers instead the adaptation process. Since both instances exhibit degraded performance, a new instance is added to the pool. This choice improves the service that satisfies again the QoS requirement from $t = 16$. QoSDA is equal to 6.39×10^3 and 8.22×10^3 with and without adaptation, respectively. In this case, RAMSES reduces the QoSDA by 22%.

RQ2 (Self-healing Property). This RQ focuses on the self-healing capability of the system when one or more services are *fully* unavailable. This means that from the point of view of a client, there are no instances that can process the client's requests. We consider here S2 in Table 3. In particular, the service instance payment fails at $t = 35$ seconds. Figure 4c shows the number of instances of the payment service over time (seconds) during the execution of this scenario. The plot shows the external point of view (i.e., client perception of the issues) and the internal one (i.e., RAMSES perspective). RAMSES takes around 25 seconds to react to the failure. In this period, the metrics window of the instance is filled

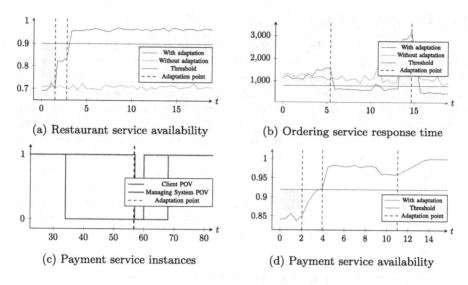

Fig. 4. Achievement of QoS requirements using RAMSES.

up with unreachable status. RAMSES identifies the current best adaptation strategy at $t = 57$: it shuts the faulty instance down and starts a new one. From the external perspective, the service goes back to operation and is ready to process new requests at $t = 68$.

RQ3 (Self-optimizing Property). In this RQ we study the self-optimizing capability of RAMSES when better instances of the managed services are available. We consider the adaptation scenario S3 in Table 3 and we specifically focus on the availability of payment service. In particular, the option changeImplementation considered by the managing system occurs when the *trust* level of the current implementation of a service decreases below the one associated with other available implementations. S3 starts with a single implementation of payment with a trust level equal to 2.0. Due to the injected failures in Table 3, the service does not satisfy the availability requirement 0.92 as illustrated by the QoS over time (minutes) in Fig. 4d. RAMSES executes addInstance at $t = 2$ and then changeWeights to favor the fresh service instance with higher availability. The two applied adaptations are enough to satisfy the target QoS from $t = 4$. However, the current implementation is penalized twice reducing the level of trust to zero. At time instant $t = 11$ a new service implementation becomes available (with new trust level 2.0). Since the trust is higher, RAMSES executes changeImplementatio to optimize the managing system further even if the requirements are satisfied. After this latter adaptation, the availability of payment reaches the maximum 1.0 from $t = 13$.

4.2   Threats to Validity

We limited *external* validity threats by selecting common technology stacks adopted by practitioners to develop microservices. Furthermore, our testbed allows us to control the environment and carry out common practices such as automated and continuous deployment and testing of the selected scenarios. Additional generalization of RAMSES may require experimental activities with a diverse set of managed microservice applications. To reduce threats to *internal* validity, we designed a scenario-based evaluation by detailing the independent variables of interest (Table 2) and how we control them to reproduce selected scenarios (Table 3). Direct manipulation has been crucial to assess cause-effect relations between external factors and observed results. We addressed *construct* validity threats by assessing the metrics used during our experiments. In particular, QoSDA is a monotonically increasing function of the relative distance between actual and required QoS level. Thus, a valid measure of the degradation.

5   Challenges and Lessons Learned

We identify the following key challenges from two main perspectives, namely *design space* and *control loop deployment* [9].

C1: Definition of adaptation goals. How to identify adaptation goals for microservices and balance contradictory requirements (e.g., quality properties trade-off) from the beginning? How to reconcile the proposed adaptation requirements with those pursued by the native self-adaptation capabilities of the underlying infrastructure-management framework?

C2: Design of probing/actuating interfaces. How to endow the managed microservices with probes/actuators components to make it observable and adaptable at runtime according to the adaptation goals? How to exploit the native support of diverse infrastructure-management frameworks, in which the managed microservices are realized to further extend these last with probing/actuating functions?

C3: Design of the control loop. How to design control loop components for monitoring and adapting microservice applications? How to exploit the native support to self-adaption of the underlying infrastructure-management framework to realize the MAPE-K control functions?

C4: Deployment of the control loop. How to distribute and allocate activities of the control loop components? Should the control loop components be deployed as a single monolithic service or decomposed into a collection of independently developed and deployed microservices?

C5: Reusability of the control loop. How to reuse the control loop components for diverse microservice applications to manage?

Concerning C1, we target adaptation goals that are commonly required in service-based applications, namely QoS-based reactive adaptation. To avoid any dependency to vendor-specific and version-specific external frameworks, this self-adaptation capability is fully implemented in RAMSES. This choice was also made to avoid possible issues emerging from conflicting user-defined goals in RAMSES and internal goals of the underlying layers.

To address C2, we exploited some mechanisms offered by Spring and other external tools (e.g., the Spring Boot module *Actuator* combined with Prometheus for collecting metrics). Observability features include auditing, health logging (e.g. for liveness and readiness states of an application), and metrics gathering, such as statistics on the HTTP requests made to the exposed endpoints and on the resource usage (e.g., CPU usage, memory usage). The actuation of adaptations is also delegated to the Spring *Config Server* module. Indeed, we found this approach useful to speed up the development of the probing/actuating APIs.

To address C3, the adaptation mechanism in RAMSES is implemented from scratch by microservices that reflect a MAPE-K control loop architecture, without using the native support for self-adaptation of the infrastructure. As a result, we developed reusable design patterns for the analysis and plan phases, namely the *double sliding window* and the *Nested utility* patterns. According to our experience, further managing *meta-layers* are needed to reconcile conflicting adaptation decisions made by RAMSES and infrastructure adaptation means.

To face C4, one can consider a spectrum of levels of granularity in the deployment of the control loop components [9]. In our solution, the control loop components are independently deployed as microservices that compose a single control loop for the managed microservices. An alternative is having multiple independent microservice-based control loops, one for each managed microservice (or quality aspect). In this case, control loops must coordinate their adaptation actions at the application level to resolve potential conflicts in their goals.

To address C5, we decided to adopt an *API-led* integration approach to connect to a target microservice application. Conforming to the MAPE-K architecture style, we defined probing and actuating interfaces in terms of RESTful APIs. The APIs allow RAMSES to be reusable given that the managed microservices implement such APIs to be monitored and adapted by RAMSES. In our current evaluation, we used a small-scale subject (SEFA). Thus, we do not generalize our results to other microservice applications, possibly based on different execution infrastructures. To mitigate this issue, we experimented RAMSES also with another microservice application RANDINT[4] still using Spring Boot and Spring Cloud. RANDINT is composed of a small set of microservices running in Docker containers, an API gateway acts as a single entry point, while service discovery and load balancing are implemented by using the Spring Cloud, Netflix Eureka, and the weighted load balancer. In this second benchmark, we could reuse the existing probe/actuator components realizing the APIs required by RAMSES. We plan to further investigate the extent to which RAMSES is reusable considering more heterogenous microservice applications and frameworks.

---

[4] Available in the supporting material.

6   Related Work

As highlighted by the research community of self-adaptive systems, the development of realistic exemplars is a challenging task [16]. Their development process is costly and time demanding. Even if some works have proposed reusable self-adaptation frameworks to ease the engineering of self-adaptive systems (e.g., the RAINBOW framework [4] and its extension REFRACT [15], and Activ-FORMS [6], to name a few), they are not ready-to-use, due to their complexity of use (mainly for the formal runtime models used in the decision making) and low generality (being experimented in specific domains and for exploratory research prototypes). Another research line in this community has been the development of *exemplars* that support comparing and evaluating the research on software engineering for adaptive and self-managing systems[5]. Similar exemplars related to our work are *Hogna* [1], *TAS* [17] and *SEAByTE* [13], which, however, focus on specific aspects (like deployment on cloud platform such as *Amazon EC2* [1], or A/B testing for [13]) or provide a simulated environment [17].

On the other hand, with the increasing popularity, of microservices technologies and frameworks, the need has arisen for approaches able to monitor the microservices' status (and the containers where they execute) at runtime to provide autoscaling and resilience capabilities management [12]. As already stated in Sect. 1, some of the existing platforms provide basic autoscaling and self-healing abilities. In [2], the authors present the results of a systematic mapping study where the use of self-adaptation techniques has been explored. They highlight the presence of philosophical papers setting the stage for the research in this direction [9], and the presence of several papers proposing theoretical solutions or models based on feedback loops. Only few of them are accompanied by the development of tools that are devoted to the solution of specific challenges. In [14], the authors address the challenge of finding an optimal allocation of microservices among the available servers. [7] focuses on cloud-native applications and defines a prototype allowing scalable applications on the cloud. In [3] the authors propose a framework that implements automatic container sizing and self-healing features for a microservice-based application deployed in Docker containers exploiting MAPE-K loops. In [19], an extension of Kubernetes has been developed to monitor microservices data and manage aspects of scalability. Towards the direction of reusing existing self-adaptation services and frameworks, of particular interest is the so-called *service mesh* technology, a dedicated infrastructure layer for handling service-to-service communication through well-established reliable libraries[6]. In [10] the authors envision the *Microservices and Service Mesh MAPE pattern*, where the system's containerized microservices communicate via a service mesh, and both the microservices and the service mesh are managed by MAPE services provided by the infrastructure.

The development of RAMSES stands at the confluence of these two research directions: the need to develop ready-to-use exemplars to share and facilitate

---

[5] https://www.hpi.uni-potsdam.de/giese/public/selfadapt/category/exemplar/.

[6] https://philcalcado.com/2017/08/03/pattern_service_mesh.html.

the adoption of self-adaptive systems, and the need to empower microservice-based applications with self-adaptation capabilities. RAMSES is a publicly available reusable managing system with an API-led integration with the managed microservice application. Besides, the development of RAMSES brings with it a set of lessons learned that can be useful to the research community.

7 Conclusion and Future Work

RAMSES is a microservice-based autonomic manager tailored to microservice applications. RAMSES is reusable given that the managed system implements the probing/actuating APIs. We discussed our experience in dealing with existing challenges to realize self-* properties with user-defined QoS indicators. We also defined design patterns that can be used to analyze and plan service adaptations.

We plan to extend the RAMSES's analysis task and its set of adaptation options. We want to consider other metrics (e.g., resource usage and circuit breakers metrics) to build more reliable indicators of the managed services. As a further improvement, the decision-making process could consider the costs and the risks derived from the application of an adaptation option. Moreover, the estimation could analyse the history of actuated adaptations using ML techniques. to quantify the actual benefits they brought.

Acknowledgment. This work has been partially founded by the topic Engineering Secure Systems of the Helmholtz Association (HGF) and by KASTEL Security Research Labs.

References

1. Barna, C., Ghanbari, H., Litoiu, M., Shtern, M.: Hogna: a platform for self-adaptive applications in cloud environments. In: SEAMS, pp. 83–87 (2015)
2. Filho, M., Pimentel, E., Pereira, W., Maia, P., Cortes, M.: Self-adaptive microservice-based systems - landscape and research opportunities. In: SEAMS, pp. 167–178 (2021)
3. Florio, L., Nitto, E.D.: Gru: an approach to introduce decentralized autonomic behavior in microservices architectures. In: IEEE ICAC, pp. 357–362 (2016)
4. Garlan, D., Cheng, S.W., Huang, A.C., Schmerl, B., Steenkiste, P.: Rainbow: architecture-based self-adaptation with reusable infrastructure. Computer **37**(10), 46–54 (2004)
5. Garlan, D., Schmerl, B.R., Cheng, S.: Software architecture-based self-adaptation. In: Zhang, Y., Yang, L., Denko, M. (eds.) Autonomic Computing and Networking, pp. 31–55. Springer, Boston (2009). https://doi.org/10.1007/978-0-387-89828-5_2
6. Iftikhar, M.U., Weyns, D.: ActivFORMS: active formal models for self-adaptation. In: SEAMS 2014, pp. 125–134. ACM, New York (2014)
7. Kehrer, S., Blochinger, W.: Model-based generation of self-adaptive cloud services. In: Muñoz, V.M., Ferguson, D., Helfert, M., Pahl, C. (eds.) CLOSER 2018. CCIS, vol. 1073, pp. 40–63. Springer, Cham (2019). https://doi.org/10.1007/978-3-030-29193-8_3

8. Kephart, J.O., Chess, D.M.: The vision of autonomic computing. IEEE Comput. **36**(1), 41–50 (2003)
9. Mendonca, N.C., Jamshidi, P., Garlan, D., Pahl, C.: Developing self-adaptive microservice systems: challenges and directions. IEEE Softw. **38**(2), 70–79 (2021)
10. Mendonça, N.C., Garlan, D., Schmerl, B., Cámara, J.: Generality vs. reusability in architecture-based self-adaptation: the case for self-adaptive microservices. In: ECSA '18. ACM (2018)
11. Mitchell, M.: An Introduction to Genetic Algorithms, pp. 124–125. The MIT Press, Cambridge (1999)
12. Ntentos, E., Zdun, U., Plakidas, K., Geiger, S.: Evaluating and improving microservice architecture conformance to architectural design decisions. In: Hacid, H., Kao, O., Mecella, M., Moha, N., Paik, H. (eds.) ICSOC 2021. LNCS, vol. 13121, pp. 188–203. Springer, Cham (2021). https://doi.org/10.1007/978-3-030-91431-8_12
13. Quin, F., Weyns, D.: SEABYTE: a self-adaptive micro-service system artifact for automating a/b testing. In: SEAMS, pp. 77–83 (2022)
14. Sampaio, A.R., Rubin, J., Beschastnikh, I., Rosa, N.S.: Improving microservice-based applications with runtime placement adaptation. J. Internet Serv. Appl. **10**, 1–30 (2019)
15. Swanson, J., Cohen, M.B., Dwyer, M.B., Garvin, B.J., Firestone, J.: Beyond the rainbow: self-adaptive failure avoidance in configurable systems. In: FSE 2014, pp. 377–388. ACM, New York (2014)
16. Weyns, D.: An Introduction to Self-adaptive Systems: A Contemporary Software Engineering Perspective. Wiley, Hoboken (2020)
17. Weyns, D., Calinescu, R.: Tele assistance: a self-adaptive service-based system exemplar. In: SEAMS, pp. 88–92 (2015)
18. Wolsey, L.A., Nemhauser, G.L.: Integer and Combinatorial Optimization, vol. 55. John Wiley & Sons, Hoboken (1999)
19. Zhang, S., Zhang, M., Ni, L., Liu, P.: A multi-level self-adaptation approach for microservice systems. In: 2019 IEEE 4th International Conference on Cloud Computing and Big Data Analysis (ICCCBDA), pp. 498–502 (2019)

FUSE: Fault Diagnosis and Suppression with eBPF for Microservices

Gowri Sankar Ramachandran$^{(\boxtimes)}$ (ID), Lewyn McDonald, and Raja Jurdak (ID)

Trusted Networks Lab, Queensland University of Technology, Brisbane, Australia
g.ramachandran@qut.edu.au

Abstract. Contemporary applications harness microservices architecture to attain scalability, loose coupling, and abstraction advantages. This approach involves breaking down applications into smaller, composable services, which are hosted in the cloud. Cloud deployment offers advantages like elastic load balancing, cost-efficiency, and ease of management. However, it raises two issues: trusting third-party providers and limited fault diagnosis due to generic logs. Deep runtime introspection of microservices on third-party clouds can enhance the resilience of cloud-native microservice-based applications.

This paper introduces *FUSE*, a novel framework based on eBPF technology that enables deep introspection of microservices' runtime behavior. FUSE observes microservices at the kernel level, tracing system calls, function invocations, and disk accesses to create a unique hash-based digest for each microservice invocation. This digest is then used to verify runtime correctness: correct microservices consistently produce a known, deterministic digest, while faulty services generate random traces. FUSE provides real-time fault detection and suppression, preventing cascading failures. Additionally, it introduces a *stability* score for succinctly capturing runtime consistencies in microservices. In our evaluation with four representative microservices on AWS EC2 instances, FUSE successfully detected 53 *runtime faults*.

Keywords: eBPF · Resilient Microservice · Fault Diagnosis

1 Introduction

Contemporary applications adopt microservices architecture to achieve scalability, load balancing, continuous integration and loose coupling for large-scale enterprise applications [7]. Some of the largest tech companies, including Amazon [8] and Microsoft [12], serve millions of customers following microservices architecture. The emergence of cloud computing platforms further accelerates the growth of microservices, allowing the service owners to deploy their applications on the cloud without needing to invest in hardware, software, and tooling resources, as existing cloud platforms offer many built-in services, including elastic load balancing, security, and remote management, for an affordable cost, making them attractive for the deployment of microservices [21].

© The Author(s), under exclusive license to Springer Nature Switzerland AG 2023
F. Monti et al. (Eds.): ICSOC 2023, LNCS 14419, pp. 243–257, 2023.
https://doi.org/10.1007/978-3-031-48421-6_17

As the applications switch from the "monolithic" to the "microservices" model, the end system consists of a set of independent services running on different cloud instances in a virtualised environment. Although cloud providers strive to provide reliable services to the service owners, there is still a possibility of service failures and faults at runtime [1,5,6]. Service meshes have been developed to make microservices resilient against communication failures, as the failure of a single service could impact other inter-connected services through the cascading effect [11]. Figure 1 (left) shows how a single faulty service can disrupt other interconnected services due to fault propagation. Sidecars monitor individual services and relay the information to the service mesh control plane to make dynamic decisions at runtime. Existing features of sidecars include traffic monitoring, load balancing, and fault-tolerant networking, but there is no support to *deeply* observe the "execution" of microservice at runtime to ensure consistency [4,14].

Existing literature highlights the benefits of observing microservices at the kernel level using the extended Berkeley Packet Filter (eBPF) [3,4,10,13,18,22]. eBPF offers a rich set of functionalities to monitor the runtime behaviour of microservices. It enables the service owners to develop *kernel probes*, which are user-defined programs with kernel privileges to deeply introspect the behaviour of applications running in the user space. eBPF provides several functionalities, including support for network observation, disk monitoring, and system call tracing to get fine-grained activity logs of user-level programs such as microservices. Extant literature proposes eBPF-based frameworks to classify microservices in data centres [3,4] and for monitoring network and performance [13,18,22], lacking a solution to detect and suppress runtime faults in microservice-based applications, which is the focus of this work.

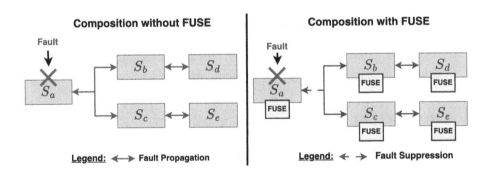

Fig. 1. Composing Microservices using FUSE to suppress fault.

This paper introduces *FUSE*, an eBPF-based fault-diagnosis and suppression framework for microservices architecture. FUSE differs from other works in the following ways:

- FUSE observes the runtime behaviour of microservices by monitoring system calls, function invocations, and disk accesses, including memory allocations, to create a *unique signature* (or digest) from traces for each invocation.
- FUSE categories microservices as an idempotent or non-idempotent service based on the signature.
- FUSE detects runtime faults by checking the signature of each invocation against the expected signatures. Upon fault detection, it promptly alerts the service administrator and the circuit-breaker to suppress cascading failures, as shown in Fig. 1 (right).
- FUSE also helps the service owners and developers quantify the runtime consistency of microservices through a novel *stability score* for microservices. A microservice composition with a high stability score is good for resiliency.

FUSE is implemented in a Linux environment with eBPF and evaluated on AWS EC2 instances running the Ubuntu operating system. The performance and effectiveness of FUSE are validated using four representative microservices that 1) register a user into a MySQL database, 2) query the system to retrieve the list of users, 3) test the strength of a password, and 4) add the numbers in a list. During the evaluation, FUSE successfully detected 53 runtime faults, highlighting its ability to prevent cascading failures by alerting service administrators and circuit breakers. Lastly, the stability score is a valuable feature for service administrators and software developers to improve the microservices' resiliency.

2 Background

2.1 extended Berkeley Packet Filter (eBPF)

The extended Berkeley Packet Filter, commonly known as eBPF, is a special type of virtual machine within the Linux kernel [15]. It was introduced in 1992 with a register-based filter for evaluating the network packets deep inside the kernel. *tcpdump* is one of the popular tools from the eBPF family. Although network monitoring is one of the popular use cases of eBPF, it does provide multiple hooks to trace and monitor various subsystems inside the Linux kernel. Some of the other hooks include Filetop (for tracking the file reads and writes), Opensnoop (attempts to track the files accessed by a specific process), and syscount (counts the number of system calls) [9]. The user-level programs can attach to these kernel hooks through eBPF probes such as kprobe, uprobe, tracepoint, and socket [9]. Depending on the type of selected hooks, the probes deliver detailed information to the user for deep introspection of application activities, including microservices.

2.2 Faults in Microservices

Microservices use a software framework such as Apache and Spring and run on a hardware infrastructure provided by the cloud provider in the case of cloud-native deployments. As discussed in [1], the microservices could be exposed to intermittent hardware faults due to cosmic radiation or impure packaging material. Facebook's data centres that serve a multitude of apps, such as Facebook, WhatsApp, and Instagram, experienced *silent data corruptions*, causing inaccurate computations [6]. Such runtime silent faults occur as a result of manufacturing defects at the silicon level [5]. The aging of microservices also introduces faults, which are undetected by Kubernetes probes, according to [17]. BROFY [10] explains the need to develop approaches for microservices' integrity validation as the attackers or faulty hardware could introduce *bitflip errors* (one or more of the bits gets flipped, changing the runtime behaviour) to the computation infrastructure, causing silent and undetectable failures. Additionally, services may fail to access the desired resource, including the database, to fulfil the functional requirements, resulting in run-time faults. These problems underscore the importance of developing approaches to detect runtime faults in microservices, which is the focus of this work.

3   Related Work

Existing works have studied approaches to enhance the monitoring capabilities of microservices to detect performance issues [3,4,13,18,22]. These works leverage eBPF to observe microservices' runtime behaviour by focusing on the networking activities [13], including TCP traffic [22] and latency [18], CPU activations [3, 4,22], Block I/O performance [22] to understand the performance bottlenecks. Although these works aim to improve microservices' performance, they don't propose fault diagnosis or suppression.

MAGNet [3] is similar to FUSE in the aspect of application-focused eBPF tracing, but it aims to generate identities for workloads in data centres without detecting faults using the eBPF traces. Hyunseok *et al.* [4] introduced a microservices fingerprinting technique by tracing the system calls used by microservices and trained a machine learning model to classify services. FUSE classifies the microservices based on eBPF trace, but it uses system calls, disk I/O activities, and function invocations to generate a unique digest per invocation without employing machine learning. Furthermore, FUSE contributes a fault detection and suppression framework and a stability scoring mechanism to tackle runtime faults.

The stability of microservices is studied using eBPF in [20], which leverages variable autoencoders to detect unstable or compromised containers based on eBPF traces. It monitors a pre-configured set of 72 Linux system calls to capture specific security incidents and application faults. This work is similar to ours in the aspect of the eBPF-based approach for stability analysis, but we focus on application-level or microservices fingerprinting using system calls, function invocation, and disk accesses without involving any machine learning. Areeg and Claus [19] detect anomalies in containerised microservices using Markov Models, wherein the key performance indicators such as *mpstat* and *vmstat* are collected at the application level to learn a model using Hierarchical Hidden Markov Models, which detect abnormal microservice behaviours with 97% accuracy. Unlike this paper, FUSE generates microservice-specific eBPF traces and detects stability and abnormality through a hash-based signature without applying machine learning algorithms. Many other works tackle anomalies or eBPF-based observability for microservices, but they don't focus on fault detection using eBPF-based tracing by combining system calls, function invocations, and disk accesses. Besides, none of the existing works introduces a stability scorecard for microservices, which is another novel contribution of our work.

4   FUSE: Fault Diagnosis and Suppression with eBPF for Microservices

4.1   System Model

Modern applications are composed of interconnected microservices, wherein each service $s_x \in \mathcal{S}$ could be connected with one or more services. In such circumstances, whenever the end user issues a request to a service, it may trigger a series of services to generate a response to the user. Upon receiving a request req_x, the service s_x processes the request by running computations exe_x and produces a response res_x. Here, exe_x may involve contacting other services, meaning the response could be generated with the help of other dependent services. Each service in $\mathcal{S}$ gets invoked numerous times in deployment, depending on the application's popularity and the customer base. Each service gets invoked $\mathcal{K}$ ($\mathcal{K} \in \mathbb{N}$) times in deployment, and the ith invocation of a service s_x can be denoted by I_x^i. Each invocation includes the execution phase (exe_x^i), which will use the hardware and software resources, including the Linux kernel. eBPF provides tools to introspect the behaviour of a service s_x at the execution phase (also called "runtime") by capturing kernel-level traces for exe_x^i, which is denoted by $trace_x^i$. In summary, i^{th} invocation of a service s_x can be represented by a tuple $\langle req_x^i, exe_x^i, res_x^i, trace_x^i \rangle$. This work builds on some key concepts, such as idempotency and stability, which are defined below.

Definition 1. *Idempotency* *The system's state remains the same when an operation is executed any number of times [16].*

GET and *HEAD* are examples of idempotent HTTP operations because they don't change the server's state on the request' successful completion. Besides, even the same request can be issued many times without altering the server's state. On the other hand, the *POST* operation of HTTP changes the server's state, meaning it may add a new item to a database; hence, it is *non-idempotent*.

Definition 2. *Idempotent Microservice* *A microservice is considered idempotent if it doesn't alter the system's state when a request is processed any number of times.*

A microservice that reads an employee's data from a database is an example of an idempotent microservice. In contrast, the service that registers a new employee's data is non-idempotent as it changes the server's state.

Definition 3. *Trace* *A trace of a microservice corresponds to the* low-level activities *that the service carries out inside the kernel to process a request req_x. $\mathcal{T}_x$ denotes a set of **unique** traces of service s_x and $\mathcal{L}_x$ denotes the length of $\mathcal{T}_x$.*

Software applications access the CPU, memory, and network by invoking schedulers, I/O management modules, and network managers to fulfil the desired functionalities. Here, the low-level activities correspond to all activities that happen within the kernel as part of the application's or microservice's execution. This work assumes microservices perform single functions upon receiving requests (req_x) with deterministic, bounded input sizes. For instance, the *register user to a database* service limits 'user name' input to 20 characters.

Definition 4. *Idempotent Trace* *A microservice's trace is idempotent if it doesn't change when the same or different requests are processed any number of times.*

Considering three invocations, p, q, and r, of service s_x the trace is said to be idempotent if and only if:

$$trace_x^p = trace_x^q = trace_x^r = \alpha, \ where \ \mathcal{T}_x = \{\alpha\} \ and \ \mathcal{L}_x = 1 \qquad (1)$$

Definition 5. *Stability of a Microservice:* *A microservice is said to be stable if its traces are idempotent for a given request req. The stability of a service in percentage is calculated using traces generated from $\mathcal{E}$ invocations. The stability of a microservice, sm_x, is:*

$$sm_x^{req} = (1 \div \mathcal{L}_x) * 100 \qquad (2)$$

Figure 2 (top) shows an example of an idempotent service with a stability score of 100% for $\mathcal{E}$ of 4 because it produces one unique trace. But, some services may produce more than one trace for $\mathcal{E}$ ($\mathcal{E} \in \mathbb{N}$) invocations. Figure 2 (bottom) illustrates an idempotent service with a stability score of 50% for $\mathcal{E}$ of 4, with two unique traces α and β. The higher stability score indicates runtime consistency, helping developers and administrators to build highly stable services.

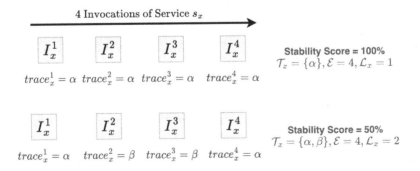

Fig. 2. Stability Score of Idempotent Service based on 4 Invocations.

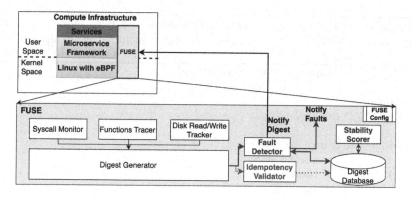

Fig. 3. FUSE Architecture: The dotted line indicates operations in idempotency validation mode, while normal line denotes fault detection and suppression operations.

4.2 Architecture of FUSE

At a high level, FUSE is a cross-layer architecture running at user and kernel spaces, as shown in Fig. 3. Microservices run in a computing environment, including a cloud instance. Typically, services are hosted on a framework such as Spring Boot. An operating system such as Ubuntu manages the resources for the application-level services. In this model, the operating system functions within the kernel space without offering much visibility to the users. In contrast, the services sit in the user space, leveraging the operating system to function correctly. FUSE leverages eBPF to monitor and extract kernel space activities of services to generate signatures and suppress faults. The user space activities for eBPF include setting up the necessary hooks and the configurations to generate, process, store, and validate traces. In contrast, the kernel space intercepts the traces required for the target microservices. The fundamental building blocks of FUSE are discussed in the rest of the section.

FUSE Configurations. FUSE can operate in two modes, including *idempotency validation* and *fault detection and suppression* modes, based on the configurations set by the microservices administrator. In the *idempotency validation mode*, FUSE runs the same microservice $\mathcal{E}$ times and collects the traces in a database. Subsequently, the traces are analysed to determine whether the microservice is *idempotent or not*. This mode must be activated for each microservice before production for fault diagnosis and suppression. The *fault detection and suppression mode* is activated at runtime to validate the microservices' trace for each invocation against the database. As shown in Fig. 3, this mode uses a different set of building blocks for detecting and suppressing faults based on the runtime traces.

Syscall Monitor tracks the system calls used by the microservice. At each microservice's invocation, this building block intercepts the system calls and generates a list, including the counts for each system call. For example, read is one of

---

Algorithm 1: FUSE in idempotency validation and fault detection and suppression modes: Stability score calculation is included in idempotency validation mode.

FUSE in idempotency validation mode

Require: S_x, $\mathcal{E}$
  $\mathcal{T} \leftarrow \{\}$ /* Empty $\mathcal{T}$ */

  for i = 1 to $\mathcal{E}$ **do**
     $trace_i$ = generateDigest(S_x)
     if $trace_i \notin \mathcal{T}$ **then**
        $\mathcal{T} = \mathcal{T} \cup trace_i$
     end if
  end for
  storeTraceinDatabase(S_x,$\mathcal{T}$)
  return

FUSE Stability Score Calculation

Require: S_x, $\mathcal{T}$
  $\mathcal{L} \leftarrow 0$ /* Length of $\mathcal{T}$ is 0 */
  $sm \leftarrow 0$ /* Stability score is initialised 0 */
  $\mathcal{L} = |\mathcal{T}|$ /* Length of $\mathcal{T}$ */
  $sm = (1 \div \mathcal{L})*100$ /* Stability score is calculated */
  storeStabilityScoreinDatabase(S_x,sm)
  return

FUSE in fault detection and suppression mode

  $trace_j$ = generateDigest(S_x) /* j^{th} invocation of a service */
  if $trace_j \notin \mathcal{T}$ **then**
     notifyFault()
  end if

---

the widespread system calls, and it opens a file or a resource. **Functions Tracer** traces the functions and libraries invoked by the microservice. For each invocation, this captures the list of files and libraries accessed by the microservice. **Disk Read/Write Tracker** tracks the number of reads and writes, including memory allocations, that happen during the execution of microservice along with a pointer to a file, indicating the files that were read from or written to.

Digest (or Signature) Generator processes the traces generated by the syscall monitor, functions tracer, and disk read/write tracker to create a digest or signature for each invocation. The digest is made by counting the number of calls, the list of functions invoked, the amount of data read from or written to, and *malloc* allocations. A cryptographic hash function such as sha256 creates a unique signature per invocation.

Idempotency Validator processes the digests during the *idempotency validation mode* by studying the consistency of digests. Each microservice is executed $\mathcal{E}$ times to perform idempotency validation. Therefore, this process is data intensive as multiple traces must be generated to determine whether a given microservice is *idempotent* or not. An idempotent microservice would always produce the known cryptographic hash for a given request type req_x because such a microservice always executes the same system calls, accesses the same list of functions, has the same data read from or written to, and allocates the same amount of memory. Algorithm 1 explains FUSE's operations.

Digest Database stores and manages digests associated with a microservice-based application. It is important to note that each microservice need not have its database; instead, a single database can be used to manage the digests.

Fault Detector gets activated in *fault detection and suppression mode*, and it is responsible for checking whether a digest of a recent microservice's invocation produces the known and expected digests. Recall that an idempotent microservice will have the known digest unless there is a fault. This module checks the digest and generates an alert to the service admin. Besides, the digest is also notified to the circuit breaker for fault suppression.

4.3   Fault Diagnosis and Suppression

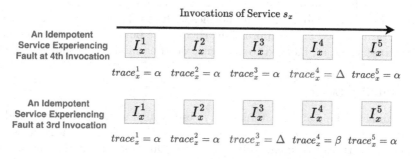

Fig. 4. Fault breaks the idempotency of an idempotent service.

Definition 6. *Faulty Microservice* *A microservice is said to be faulty when its traces are **intermittently** non-idempotent. An idempotent microservice can experience faults at runtime, breaking idempotency.*

Figure 4 elucidates how an idempotent microservice can experience an unexpected fault at runtime due to hardware or software failures, breaking the trace consistency. Note that any trace other than α is considered faulty for the first idempotent service in Fig. 4 (top). On the other hand, Fig. 4 (bottom) shows an idempotent service with more than one known trace to be considered non-faulty;

however, the 3rd invocation (see) produces an unexpected trace of Δ, denoting a runtime fault.

Figure 1 (left) shows that a single faulty service could impact other interconnected services if left untreated. Circuit breakers are recommended to increase the resiliency and availability of microservices in the event of cascading failures. A circuit breaker relies on *fault event* to open the circuit to prevent cascading failures. Network-related issues, server failures, and overloads are considered fault events in circuit breakers, allowing microservices to overcome major and obvious faults. Our approach complements existing techniques and further strengthens the circuit breakers by tackling less-obvious faults, which could arise due to hardware abnormalities or any unexpected behaviour only noticeable at runtime, including the involvement of an adversary. Our fault suppression technique is presented in the next section.

4.4 Fault Suppression

FUSE digests (or signatures) provide a stable reference for fault diagnosis, as a service could be *idempotent or non-idempotent*. Our fault suppression technique is proxy-based [2], meaning that the service interacts with other dependent services if and only if the digest of the current invocation satisfies the idempotency property (see Definitions 4). Any variations to the digest (or trace) indicate a fault (see Definition 6), suppressing outbound communications with dependent services, as shown in Fig. 1 (right). The circuit breaker opens the connection to prevent cascading failures. The *fault detection and suppression* mode monitors the trace following Algorithm 1 and notifies faults to the appropriate agent. Following a proxy-based fault suppression scheme, the outgoing requests to dependent microservices are blocked to prevent cascading failures, as shown in Fig. 1.

4.5 Stability Score

FUSE validates the stability of microservices through a stability scorer module, as shown in Fig. 3. As discussed in Definition 5, the stability of a microservice depends on its trace (or signature) consistency. Our stability scoring mechanism provides a score between 0% and 100% for microservices. A score closer to 100% indicates high stability, while any score close to 0% indicates poor stability. An idempotent service has a high stability score, while non-idempotent services have a low stability score. The stability scorer module takes the digests from the database and counts the unique digests per microservice in the *idempotency validation mode*, as shown in Algorithm 1.

This score is beneficial for system administrators and microservice architects. From the service management and resilience viewpoint, having an idempotent microservice with a stability score of 100% maximises the determinism and fault detection capabilities. In contrast, any score close to 0% shows the non-determinism of the microservice. Besides, when designing a microservice, the developers can aim to compose a *strictly idempotent microservice* by using

FUSE's stability score as it helps the developers understand hidden uncertainties in the code, which is only noticeable at runtime. Figure 2 shows how the stability score is calculated for an idempotent microservice.

5   Proof-of-Concept Implementation and Evaluation

FUSE is implemented using eBPF and tested on AWS EC2 instances running the Ubuntu operating system. To validate the practicality of FUSE, we have developed POST and GET services using Python Flask with the following functionalities: **1) New user registration service (S1):** receives a POST request with the user details, including the name, address, and country, and stores them in a *MySQL* database. **2) Users data retriever service (S2):** handles a GET request to gather the users' data from a *MySQL* database and sends it back to the requester. **3) Password strength checker service (S3):** receives a POST request to check the strength of a password the user selects. It receives a password string and checks its strength by assessing the lower and upper cases, digits, and length, and returns the password strength as *Strong* or *Weak*. **4) Addition service (S4):** adds the numbers in the request and returns the sum as a response. Our proof-of-concept implementation used a proxy that generates and validates the trace (or signature) for each POST or GET request. We evaluate the performance and stability of the example representative services and report the results. Each service was executed more than 1000 times in *idempotency validation* mode, i.e. $\mathcal{E} > 1000$.

5.1   Idempotency of Example Services

For $\mathcal{E} > 1000$, services S1, S2, S3, and S4 have $\mathcal{T}$ of 2, 4, 3, and 10, respectively, of which a single trace is dominant, making them idempotent. The sha256 hash is shortened to four characters in Table 1 for brevity. However, the real digest is 64 characters long. The amount of memory used, the number of functions accessed, and system calls invoked changes depend on the microservices, resulting in unique hashes per service. Figure 5 shows the distribution of hashes for S1, S2, S3, and S4 - it is clear that each microservice has a dominating hash that appears more than 97% of the time. Besides, S1, S2, S3, and S4 have stability scores of 50, 25, 33.3, and 10, respectively. The higher stability score corresponds to high determinism and stability. S1 is the most stable among the example services, while S4 is the least stable. Figure 6 shows how the stability score evolved with each invocation and stabilised. The instability of S4 and the high stability of S1 are apparent in Fig. 6.

Table 1. Stability Score of Services based on Traces.

Service	$\mathcal{T}$	$\mathcal{L}$	$\mathcal{E}$	Stability Score (in %)
S1	{'8507':7, 'f8ec':998}	2	1005	50
S2	{'3173':2, '7eb0':1015, '913b':1, '51a7':4}	4	1022	25
S3	{'075d':1094, '4532':11, '6947':1}	3	1106	33.3
S4	{'05db':1, '23e2':3, '4d6b':6, '6398':1163, '68c0':1, '735d':4, '8801':2, 'e280':2, 'f541':7, 'd447':1}	10	1190	10

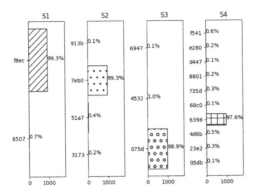

Fig. 5. Distribution of FUSE Traces for Services S1, S2, S3, and S4.

5.2   Overhead of FUSE

Traditional microservices don't rely on kernel-level traces for fault suppression. Thus, they don't incur any overhead within the request-response cycle. When a request is sent to a microservice, it gets processed, and the response is sent back. However, FUSE introduces an overhead in storage and latency. The **Storage Overhead of FUSE** originates from the storage of traces generated. FUSE produces multiple eBPF trace files to store file accesses, system call statistics, memory allocations, and disk operations. The storage overhead of FUSE per microservice execution is presented in Table 2, wherein the disk IO trace file takes up the most space while the system calls take up the least space, but these can be deleted periodically or immediately based on the requirements.

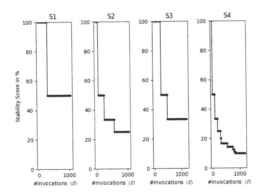

Fig. 6. Stability Score vs. Number of Invocations for S1, S2, S3, and S4.

Table 2. Storage Overhead for Trace Files

Service	Syscall Trace (Bytes)	Function Trace (Bytes)	Disk I/O Trace (Bytes)
S1	751	1710	16380
S2	751	1710	16379
S3	751	1647	16380
S4	1039	1647	16385

The **Latency of FUSE** differs from traditional microservices as the digest is generated immediately after the completion of each invocation. Without FUSE, S1, S2, S3, and S4 have an average latency of 13 milliseconds (ms), 14 ms, 5 ms, and 6 ms, respectively. In contrast, the average latency of S1, S2, S3, and S4 increases to 235 ms, 204 ms, 168 ms, and 276 ms with FUSE. The increased latency comes from processing the traces and the generation and notification of digest, which will be optimised in future work.

5.3   Faults Detected by FUSE

FUSE detected 53 faults at runtime for services S1 and S2 while S3 and S4 did not experience any faults, meaning all the traces for S3 and S4 came from T listed in Table 1. In contrast, for S1 and S2, FUSE detected faults with random traces that are unfound in T in Table 1. These 53 faults are because S1 and S2 rely on a MySQL database, which crashed due to being out of memory as *OOM killer* terminated the MySQL process, generating faulty traces. These traces indicated early signs of memory issues as they had additional system calls. The services ran correctly as long as there was enough memory, and then it started to experience faults, resulting in random and unknown traces, triggering faults. For S1, the observed trace during fault includes (8507), while for S2, the faulty traces include (3173, 913b, 51a7). These faults underscore FUSE's effectiveness in capturing runtime faults.

6   Discussion

Tool Selection for Digest Generation: eBPF offers a robust toolkit for generating traces of user-level programs, including microservices. This study has selected specific tools focused on system calls, function invocations, and disk operations, as highlighted in Table 1. The resulting unique digests at the kernel level attest to the effectiveness of these chosen tools. Nevertheless, there remains untapped potential in expanding FUSE's trace generation capabilities to uncover hidden faults and runtime inconsistencies, representing an exciting avenue for future research. **Impact of Inputs on the Digest:** Each service invocation's uniqueness arises from varying input characteristics. Many microservices validate inputs for error prevention prior to processing. Our evaluation has primarily considered microservices with typical inputs. However, there is room for more in-depth analysis by drastically altering input parameters, offering a promising area for future exploration. **Platform-Agnostic Traces:** This evaluation employed AWS EC2 instances running an Ubuntu operating system to validate FUSE. A valuable opportunity exists to execute the same microservices on diverse eBPF-compatible Linux systems, such as Amazon Linux, to assess the platform-agnostic nature of FUSE's traces. This paper assumes FUSE traces are generated in 'idempotency validation' mode on the production platform. However, testing how digests evolve when introducing a new platform could enhance FUSE's flexibility for platform migration, which we consider for future work.

7 Conclusion

Microservices frequently encounter runtime faults stemming from hardware issues, software bugs, and network disruptions. Detecting these faults is crucial for preempting failures and preventing cascading issues. FUSE, an innovative fault diagnosis and suppression tool built on eBPF, distinguishes microservices as idempotent or non-idempotent based on runtime traces. It dynamically identifies runtime faults by comparing actual traces with expected ones and blocks external requests to other services upon fault detection. FUSE introduces a unique stability scoring mechanism, evaluating microservices based on trace consistency and idempotency. A proof-of-concept implementation using eBPF and Flask, deployed on AWS EC2 instances, validates FUSE's practicality. Performance evaluations involving four representative microservices demonstrate FUSE's capacity to detect 53 runtime faults, albeit with some latency and storage overhead. Future work includes optimizing FUSE's performance through customized eBPF probes, confirming platform agnosticism across various eBPF-compatible Linux platforms, and enhancing its capabilities to analyze input impact on digests by varying inputs significantly in test services.

References

1. Cerveira, F., Oliveira, R.A., Barbosa, R., Madeira, H.: Evaluation of restful frameworks under soft errors. In: 2020 IEEE 31st International Symposium on Software Reliability Engineering (ISSRE), pp. 369–379. IEEE (2020)
2. Chandramouli, R.: Microservices-based application systems. NIST Spec. Publ. **800**(204), 800–204 (2019)
3. Chang, H., Kodialam, M., Lakshman, T.V., Mukherjee, S., Van der Merwe, J., Zaheer, Z.: MAGNet: machine learning guided application-aware networking for data centers. IEEE Trans. Cloud Comput. **11**(1), 291–307 (2023)
4. Chang, H., Kodialam, M., Lakshman, T., Mukherjee, S.: Microservice fingerprinting and classification using machine learning. In: 2019 IEEE 27th International Conference on Network Protocols (ICNP), pp. 1–11 (2019)
5. Constantinescu, C.: Intermittent faults and effects on reliability of integrated circuits. In: 2008 Annual Reliability and Maintainability Symposium, pp. 370–374. IEEE (2008)

6. Dixit, H.D., et al.: Silent data corruptions at scale. arXiv preprint arXiv:2102.11245 (2021)

7. Dragoni, N., et al.: Microservices: Yesterday, Today, and Tomorrow, pp. 195–216. Springer, Cham (2017)

8. Fulton III, S.M.: What led amazon to its own microservices architecture. The New Stack (2015)

9. Goldshtein, S.: The Next Linux Superpower: eBPF Primer. USENIX Association, Dublin (2016)

10. Hartono, A.P.P., Fetzer, C.: BROFY: towards essential integrity protection for microservices. In: 2021 40th International Symposium on Reliable Distributed Systems (SRDS), pp. 154–163. IEEE (2021)

11. Jagadeesan, L.J., Mendiratta, V.B.: When failure is (not) an option: reliability models for microservices architectures. In: 2020 IEEE International Symposium on Software Reliability Engineering Workshops (ISSREW), pp. 19–24. IEEE (2020)

12. Kakivaya, G., et al.: Service fabric: a distributed platform for building microservices in the cloud. In: Proceedings of the Thirteenth EuroSys Conference, pp. 1–15 (2018)

13. Levin, J., Benson, T.A.: ViperProbe: rethinking microservice observability with eBPF. In: 2020 IEEE 9th International Conference on Cloud Networking (CloudNet), pp. 1–8 (2020)

14. Li, W., Lemieux, Y., Gao, J., Zhao, Z., Han, Y.: Service mesh: challenges, state of the art, and future research opportunities. In: 2019 IEEE International Conference on Service-Oriented System Engineering (SOSE), pp. 122–1225 (2019)

15. McCanne, S., Jacobson, V.: The BSD packet filter: a new architecture for user-level packet capture. In: USENIX Winter, vol. 46 (1993)

16. Microservices, B.J., Varanasi, B., Bartkov, M.: Spring REST. Springer, Berkeley (2021). https://doi.org/10.1007/978-1-4842-0823-6

17. Power, A., Kotonya, G.: A microservices architecture for reactive and proactive fault tolerance in IoT systems. In: 2018 IEEE 19th International Symposium on "A World of Wireless, Mobile and Multimedia Networks" (WoWMoM), pp. 588–599 (2018)

18. Ranjitha, K., Tammana, P., Kannan, P.G., Naik, P.: A case for cross-domain observability to debug performance issues in microservices. In: 2022 IEEE 15th International Conference on Cloud Computing (CLOUD), pp. 244–246. IEEE (2022)

19. Samir, A., Pahl, C.: DLA: detecting and localizing anomalies in containerized microservice architectures using Markov models. In: 2019 7th International Conference on Future Internet of Things and Cloud (FiCloud), pp. 205–213 (2019)

20. Sharma, P., Porras, P., Cheung, S., Carpenter, J., Yegneswaran, V.: Scalable microservice forensics and stability assessment using variational autoencoders (2021)

21. Singleton, A.: The economics of microservices. IEEE Cloud Comput. 3(5), 16–20 (2016)

22. Weng, T., Yang, W., Yu, G., Chen, P., Cui, J., Zhang, C.: Kmon: an in-kernel transparent monitoring system for microservice systems with eBPF. In: 2021 IEEE/ACM International Workshop on Cloud Intelligence (CloudIntelligence), pp. 25–30 (2021)

ServiceSim: A Modelling and Simulation Toolkit of Microservice Systems in Cloud-Edge Environment

Haomai Shi, Xiang He, Teng Wang, and Zhongjie Wang[✉]

Faculty of Computing, Harbin Institute of Technology, Harbin, China
{hexiang,rainy}@hit.edu.cn, willtynn@outlook.com

Abstract. With the utilization of edge servers, cloud-native microservice systems are gradually evolving to the network edge, and large-scale distributed microservice systems in cloud-edge environments are emerging. Due to the limited resources of edge servers and dynamic end-user requests, service providers have to continuously propose optimized resource allocation, scheduling, and microservice system configuration policies to balance cost and quality of services. In the early stages of policy proposal, there is an urgent need for service providers to know how well the policy is working and to use this to rapidly iterate and optimize it. However, policy validation in such large-scale real cloud-edge environment is time-consuming and high resource cost. We propose ServiceSim, a simulation toolkit to simulate microservice systems in large scale cloud-edge environment to support policy validation. By comparing with real microservice system, it is show that ServiceSim can correctly reflect the trend of response time of service chains in a microservice system under dynamic end-user requests. Meanwhile, experiments validating edge collaboration and service deployment policies in traffic scenarios reflecting temporal and spatial preferences further illustrate that ServiceSim can effectively help the analysis of microservice system configuration policies and sensitively perceive cloud-edge network changes and the service structure of microservice system.

Keywords: Simulation · Microservice systems · Cloud-edge computing environment

1 Introduction

The low-latency service requirements of end-users drive computing resources down to the network edge [14], thus the centralized cloud computing paradigm is further extended with the emergence of distributed fog computing and edge computing paradigms, and the three together constitute a multi-layer cloud-edge computing environment [6,10,11]. Cloud-native microservice architecture with its characteristics of flexibility, high scalability, high resilience, and agile service delivery [12] successfully is used in such distributed environment. Applications are deployed as microservices on cloud and edge servers, constituting a distributed microservice system across multiple computing environments.

ⓒ The Author(s), under exclusive license to Springer Nature Switzerland AG 2023
F. Monti et al. (Eds.): ICSOC 2023, LNCS 14419, pp. 258–272, 2023.
https://doi.org/10.1007/978-3-031-48421-6_18

However, due to the limitation of computing, storage and other resources of edge servers, service providers have to optimize the use of network, computing, storage and other resources to meet diverse quality-of-service (QoS) requirements of users [19] and offer low-latency, resource-efficient services. A series of resource allocation policies (including user allocation [5], service placement, task offloading, data caching [18], etc.) and microservice system configuration policies (including load balancing, auto-scaling, etc.) were proposed, verified, and ultimately utilized to achieve these goals.

Notably, the headache-inducing policy validation process consumes a lot of effort and cost for service providers. Firstly, it is difficult and costly to build or rent a large-scale cloud-edge real experiment platform; secondly, the experiment results in the real environment cannot be reproduced; finally, the validation cycle on the real experiment platform is long, policies need to be realistically implemented and deployed in the platform. In fact, at this early stage of policy formulation, as it needs to be constantly optimized, there is an urgent need for a tool that can quickly validate the policy to help iterate it quickly.

For this purpose, simulation emerged. In particular, CloudSim [2] and a series of simulation tools based on it, such as EdgeCloudSim [16] and iFogSim [4], have been designed to support experimental verification of cloud, edge, and fog computing systems for various purposes. However, to the best of our knowledge, there is no simulation tool that supports both configuration policies verification of cloud-edge computing system and microservice system running on it. iFogSim2 [9], which most closely resembles what we are trying to achieve, also only supports the study of infrastructure configuration-related policies validation, such as application module migration from the perspective of infrastructure providers. While they modeled microservices on a multi-tier fog infrastructure, they did not consider the management of microservices. A set of configuration policies related to the running of the microservice system, such as service deployment, routing, load balancing, load admission are also need to be validated.

To address these limitations, we have developed a simulation toolkit called ServiceSim. This toolkit, built on the CloudSim simulation framework [2], is designed to simulate the running of microservice systems in large-scale, distributed cloud-edge environments. It takes into account the intricate relationship between services and provides a more flexible configuration interface for microservice systems. Our contributions are as follows:

- To support the simulation of large-scale microservice systems, we designed ServiceSim based on CloudSim with the capability to model heterogeneous network topology and flexible data transfer. Additionally, a more efficient simulation event update mechanism is implemented to effectively handle large-scale requests.
- We modeled the intricate invocation relationship between microservices in ServiceSim, enabling it to support not only the commonly used asynchronous service invocations in the form of directed acyclic graphs but also synchronous service invocations. At the same time, in addition to providing common microservice system components such as service discovery and load balancing

for modeling and simulation, load admission and request dispatching components are also designed to support more complex and flexible microservice system configurations.
– Based on the above two advantages, it can support various configuration policies verification of microservice system in large-scale cloud-edge environment. Comparison experiments with real microservices system validate the simulation effect of ServiceSim. Two sets of use cases on service deployment and edge collaboration illustrate the functionality of ServiceSim.

2   Related Work

Currently, CloudSim [2] and its derivatives are the most mainstream simulation tools for cloud-edge computing systems. CloudSim [2] was initially developed for the purpose of verifying task scheduling policies in cloud computing systems, and has been gradually improved, with the emergence of ContainerCloudSim [13] for container layer simulation, Cloudsimsdn [15] for software-defined network simulation, and NetworkCloudSim [3] for dependent tasks simulation. Later, various derivatives emerged for different purposes, such as Cloudanalyst [17] for verifying multi-cloud collaboration policies, and AutoScaleSim [1] for verifying resource scaling policies.

Table 1. The comparison in simulation objects and simulation goals between ServiceSim and other simulation tools.

Simulation tools	Simulation Objects	
CloudSim	Cloud computing system	Task
AutoScaleSim	Cloud computing system	Task
NetworkCloudSim	Cloud computing system	Parallel tasks
EdgeNetworkCloudSim	Edge computing system	Dependent tasks
EdgeCloudSim	Edge computing system	Task
iFogSim	Fog computing system	Application
iFogSim2	Fog computing system	Microservice based application
ServiceSim	Cloud-edge computing system	Microservice system

Gradually, with the emergence of edge computing systems, CloudSim [2] has been transformed again and applied to the verification of task scheduling policies under edge computing systems. Among them, the most famous are EdgeCloudSim [16] and iFogSim [4]. EdgeCloudSim [16] models each phase of a task from its entry into the edge computing system to the end of execution, and multiple models interact with each other to simulate the whole lifecycle of a task in the edge computing system. iFogSim [4] divides the cloud-edge computing system into multiple layers, which can well simulate the process of tasks scheduling from the edge to the cloud. Its biggest advantage is that it can fully and flexibly model cloud-edge computing systems with different structures.

However, as shown in Table 1, all the above simulation tools do not consider microservice systems. In real applications, services are mostly deployed as microservices in cloud-edge computing systems and provided to end-users. iFogSim2 [9] takes this into account by using directed acyclic graphs to model the relationships between services. Although it introduces the concept of microservices and provides the simulation of basic components such as service discovery and load balancing, as it is an extension of iFogSim [4], it still mainly focuses on the policies validation of sensor-driven task generation, task offloading, and task scheduling.

As can be seen, the simulation of microservice systems in a cloud-edge environment is still an urgent matter to be addressed. We aim to inherit CloudSim's good modeling of cloud-edge computing systems and add simulation of microservice systems on top of it.

3   Architecture and Implementation

To realize the simulation of microservice systems in the large-scale cloud-edge environment, as shown in Fig. 1, ServiceSim extends CloudSim "vertically upward" with three layers: the Infrastructure Layer, the Microservice Layer, and the User Request Layer. The following subsections describe the design and implementation of these key components in detail.

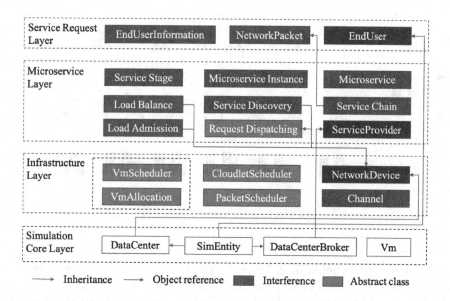

Fig. 1. ServiceSim architecture overview.

3.1   Infrastructure Layer

This layer is used to model and simulate the running environment of the entire microservice system, i.e., the distributed cloud-edge computing system. It consists of two main components: NetworkDevice and Channel, and four policies: VmAllocation, VmScheduler, CloudletSchedulet, and PacketScheduler.

NetworkDevice and Channel. ServiceSim divide the cloud-edge computing system into multiple levels based on the network distance from the end-user devices. As shown in Fig. 2, the levels range from Level 0 (end-user devices) to Level n (cloud), with intermediate levels including edge servers, base stations, fog devices, and network routers. The devices in each level and the connections between them are modeled using the components NetworkDevice and Channel, respectively. In this structure, each NetworkDevice may have multiple Same Level Devices, Parent Devices, and Children Devices.

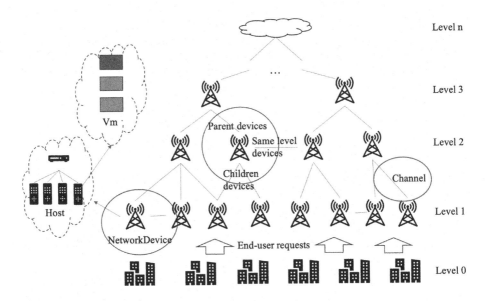

Fig. 2. Cloud-edge infrastructure architecture.

VmAllocation Policies and VmScheduler Policies. ServiceSim specifies that the smallest virtual computing unit in NetworkDevice is Vm, and each Vm will be assigned to run on a Host according to the VmAllocation Policy. As in the first phase of Fig. 3, each Host runs more than one Vm, and the Host manages its own compute resources according to the VmScheduler Policy to determine the compute capacity of each Vm on it. Both types of policies inherit from CloudSim, and each has a simple implementation.

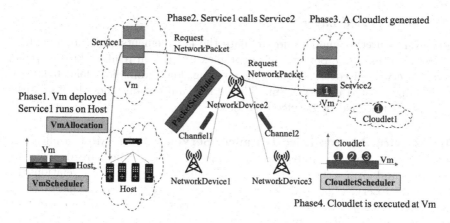

Fig. 3. Four resource allocation and task scheduling policies for Infrastructure Layer.

PacketScheduler Policies. When there is a network transmission between two NetworkDevices, the Channel manages its own network bandwidth and other resources to determine the transmission process of each packet according to the PacketScheduler Policy. As shown in the second phase of Fig. 3, Service1 deployed in NetworkDevice1 needs to call Service2 deployed in NetworkDevice3. Both Channel1 and Channel2, through which the data passes, need to be managed by PacketScheduler. PacketSchedulerTimeShared, a packet scheduler with a time-sharing policy, is implemented in ServiceSim, in which packets transmitted simultaneously share the bandwidth resources of a channel. ServiceSim users can also customize the scheduling policy for data transmission based on the interface defined in this policy.

CloudletScheduler Policies. After the request is transmitted over the network to the destination, the destination microservice instance receives the request, generates the task and executes it, as shown in phases 3 and 4 of Fig. 3. Tasks are executed on Vm according to the resources allocated by the CloudletScheduler Policy. In microservice systems, services may invoke other services during the execution, so the CloudletScheduler Policy in the infrastructure layer must be able to accurately identify such tasks with invocation dependencies. For this purpose, we draw on the modeling of dependency tasks in NetworkCloudSim [3] to complete this part of the CloudletScheduler Policy design. Unlike NetworkCloudSim, tasks in the microservice system are generated based on microservice invocations, and only when a service invocation occurs will a new task be generated on the corresponding microservice instance.

State Update Mechanism. Some redundant updates will be avoided in ServiceSim. A task's state will be updated when its own state changes, when the state of other tasks in the same service instance changes, and when the service it calls responds to its request.

3.2   Microservice Layer

This layer is used to model and simulate the key elements and components in a microservice system. Services with complex invocation relationships, gateway services, service discovery, request dispatching, load admission, load balancing are all implemented in ServiceSim. The arrival and response details of end-user requests are recorded by Service Provider.

Microservice, Microservice Instance, Service Chain. Most applications in the cloud-edge environment exist as microservices, which are deployed as containers and form service instances [8]. Because of the invocation relationships between microservices, an end-user request may trigger a series of requests within the microservice system, i.e., between microservice instances. A service chain commences at the entry gateway service and terminates at the atomic services (that do not call any other services). In ServiceSim, the invocation relationships between microservices is depicted by Service Stage, which is similar to the Task Stage in NetworkCloudSim [3]. As shown in Fig. 5(b), the request for a call between services is represented by *WAIT_SEND* and the response is represented by *WAIT_RECV*.

Load Admission and Load Balance. In the cloud-edge environment, each cloud or edge node is a cluster with multiple microservice instances deployed on it. As shown in Fig. 4, Service1 and Service2 are deployed on NetworkDevice1, and Service3 is deployed on NetworkDevice2. When an end-user request or a request for a call between services within the microservice system reaches the cluster, it first passes through the Load Admission component, and if the request is admitted, the request is forwarded to a specific microservice instance through the Load Balance component. ServiceSim users can design and implement their own load admission and load balancing algorithms.

Service Discovery and Request Dispatching. As microservices are deployed as multiple microservice instances, the service discovery mechanism is designed in ServiceSim to record the access addresses of the microservice instances. It is worth noting that each edge device maintains its own service discovery information in ServiceSim. If there is a collaborative relationship between multiple edge devices, they exchange their service discovery information with each other. As shown in step 4 of Fig. 4, Service2 needs to invoke Service3, and the deployment information of Service3 cannot be found in this device. Due to the collaborative relationship between NetworkDevice1 and NetworkDevice2, NetworkDevice1 has the service deployment information in NetworkDevice2, and the request will be dispatched based on the information. When there are multiple devices in the service discovery information that all contain microservice instances of Service 3, the Request Dispatching component will come into play, selecting a device and sending the request to it according to its defined priority rules. The collaboration mechanism between edge devices is controlled by these two components, the functionality of which is verified by the cases in Sect. 4.

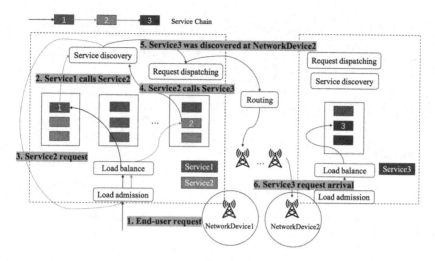

Fig. 4. The simulation components of microservice system.

3.3   Service Request Layer

End-user requests arriving at each edge device [7] and service invocation requests within the microservice system hold the end-user's personal data information. We use EndUserInformation to simulate this information, EndUser to model different distributions of end-user requests and NetworkPacket to simulate service requests or responses sent or received by end-users or between service instances. If it carries service request data, then a new task will be created in the corresponding microservice instance. If it carries response data, then the state of the relevant task in the corresponding microservice instance will be updated.

4   Use Case and Performance Evaluation

In this section, we utilize four sets of comparison experiments with real microservice systems to evaluate the simulation effect of ServiceSim. Meanwhile, two sets of policy validation case studies are constructed to illustrate the effectiveness of ServiceSim in helping microservice systems in cloud-edge environment to perform policy validation.

4.1   Simulation Effect Evaluation

We deployed a microservice system containing 10 services on a Kubernetes cluster with a node count of 4. Kubernetes cluster nodes have 56, 16, 56, 20 cpu threads and 160G, 160G, 256G, 32G of memory respectively. The invocation relationships between the microservices are shown in Fig. 5(a). The whole microservice system contains six service chains, and the entry services of Service Chain 0 (SC0) to Service Chain 5 (SC5) are Service 1 to Service 6, respectively.

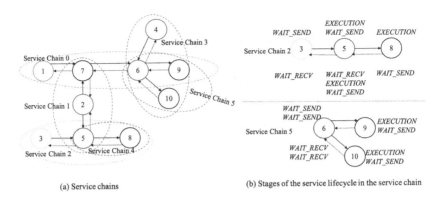

(a) Service chains   (b) Stages of the service lifecycle in the service chain

Fig. 5. Service chains and service lifecycle example.

We designed four sets of end-user request sequences and observed the response time of these four sets of end-user requests to compare them with the real physical experiment. The four sets of end-user request sequence are shown in Fig. 6. Request sequence 1 obeys Poisson distribution. SC3 and SC4 in Request sequence 2 are periodic requests and SC2 is burst requests. SC2 in Request sequence 3 is periodic requests and SC5 is burst requests. SC5, SC2, and SC3 in Request sequence 4 are periodic requests, burst requests, and sudden reduction requests, respectively. (Note: Because end-user requests obey Poisson distribution, the number of end-user requests per second in Fig. 6 shows the average value every 7 s in order to present the fluctuation of requests more clearly.)

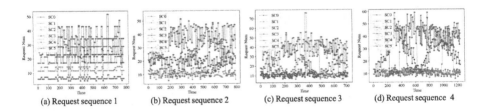

(a) Request sequence 1   (b) Request sequence 2   (c) Request sequence 3   (d) Request sequence 4

Fig. 6. Four groups of end-user request sequences.

Due to the limited length of the paper, we only show the simulation effect of Request sequence 4. The simulation results of Request sequence 1, Request sequence 2 and Request sequence 3 will be presented by ADF test (see below for details). The results are shown in Fig. 7, the six subplots in each of these figures show the comparison of response time of SC0 to SC5 under ServiceSim (SIM) and real microservices system (PHY).

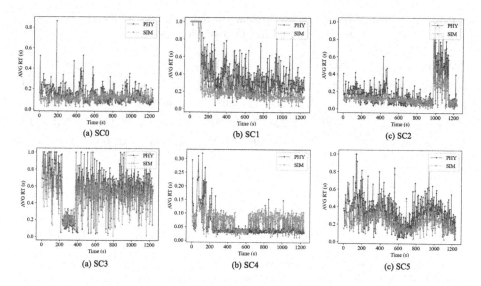

Fig. 7. Simulation effect under request sequence 4.

It can be seen that ServiceSim can correctly reflect the different distribution of end-user requests, and the response time is numerically similar to the real microservice system. In particular, the response time of SC4 in the PHY always fluctuates little and is almost lower than the simulated value. We have obtained from the link analysis of the PHY that there is a request exception when Service 5 in SC4 goes to request Service 8, and the request reception time of Service 8 is smaller than the request completion time of Service 8, which indirectly causes the response time of SC4 to depend only on Service 5. This fact tells us that one of the next optimization directions for ServiceSim is the generation of random exceptions. We further use the ADF test to check whether the sequence of response time differences between SIM and PHY of each service chain is smooth to determine whether ServiceSim presents results consistent with the trend of the real microservice system. The results of the ADF test are shown in Table 2, where values less than 0.05 are considered smooth.

The test results of most experiments are normal except the SC2 in Request sequence 3 and SC2 and SC5 in Request sequence 2. We use Fig. 8 to show more visually the comparison of the response time of these three service chains. It can be seen that ServiceSim can correctly simulate the trend of response time changes. It is possible that the response time of the real microservice system fluctuates more dramatically due to network conditions, etc.

Table 2. ADF test results for the sequence of response time differences between ServiceSim and real microservice system.

ADF test result	SC0	SC1	SC2	SC3	SC4	SC5
Request sequence 1	0.0024	2.66e−10	9.40e−6	5.87e−19	2.48e−6	4.52e−30
Request sequence 2	3.18e−5	1.29e−12	0.0877	0.0072	1.75e−7	0.3691
Request sequence 3	0.0003	2.22e−5	0.1426	2.15e−5	1.11e−5	4.98e−15
Request sequence 4	0.0074	3.99e−9	0.0099	0.0003	0.0007	0.0003

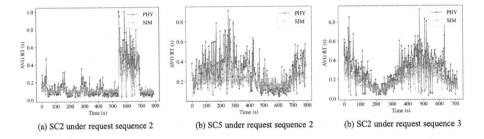

(a) SC2 under request sequence 2   (b) SC5 under request sequence 2   (b) SC2 under request sequence 3

Fig. 8. Simulation effect of ADF numerical anomaly service chains.

4.2   Case Study

Based on the design of the muti-level cloud-edge infrastructure in Sect. 3, in this experiment, We built a four-level cloud edge environment consisting of 32 edge clusters, one cloud data center (edge clusters and clouds are connected by two layers of routers). The network delay between edge clusters and routers in level 2 is set to 0.5 ms, while the network delay between routers in level 2 and level 3 is set to 2 ms. The network delay between router in level 3 and the cloud will be varied in subsequent experiments. The microservice structure is the same as in Sect. 4.1, as shown in Fig. 5. The number of microservice instances across the entire edge clusters is set to 200.

Case 1: Study on Edge Collaboration Policies Under Different Network Delay Characteristics. In this case, we observe the average response time (RT) of end-user requests corresponding to each service chain and the final completion time (FCT) of all requests in 10 s under two policies of global edge collaboration (GEC) and local edge collaboration (LEC) with an average of 600 end-user requests per second (100 requests per second for each service chain).

- Global edge collaboration policy (GEC): All 32 edge nodes work together to handle all requests.
- Local edge collaboration policy (LEC): Each of the 4 routers in level 2 acts as the center, connecting to 8 edge nodes. Requests can be passed between these 8 edge nodes and if the required service is not available, the request will be redirected to the cloud.

The edge collaboration policies are compared under different network conditions by flexibly configuring the network latency between edge and cloud. The final completion time (FCT) of all requests within 10 s and average response time (RT) for each service chain (6 in total, numbered from 0 to 5) within the microservice system are shown in the Table 3.

Table 3. Comparison of simulation results for global edge collaboration and local edge collaboration.

Policy	FCT	RT (0)	RT (1)	RT (2)	RT (3)	RT (4)	RT (5)
GEC	10.16434 s	0.15847 s	0.12521 s	0.11785 s	0.09909 s	0.05105 s	0.04527 s
LEC (60 ms)	10.16233 s	0.15829 s	0.11415 s	0.09615 s	0.10799 s	0.04491 s	0.04435 s
LEC (100 ms)	10.20884 s	0.19946 s	0.12283 s	0.09949 s	0.12822 s	0.04469 s	0.05549 s
LEC (150 ms)	10.45002 s	0.19129 s	0.11871 s	0.13104 s	0.14047 s	0.04821 s	0.05785 s

It can be seen that when the cloud-edge network delay is 60 ms, the RT of each service chain under GEC is very close to that of the corresponding service chain under LEC. When the cloud-edge network latency increases to 100 ms and 150 ms, ServiceSim is able to simulate the change in response time due to the increase in network latency. Since the LEC policy sends a portion of the requests to the cloud for execution, overall, the response time of service chains increases. This phenomenon is more evident in the longer SC0 and SC3, further validating ServiceSim's accurate simulation of service invocation relationships.

Case 2: Study on Service Deployment Policies Under Different Traffic Preference Characteristics. In edge computing scenarios, the geographic location of the server and the mobility of end-users may cause the request sequence to exhibit certain spatial and temporal characteristics. In order to simulate the request sequence of these two features, as shown in Fig. 9, we divide the 32 edge nodes into four regions centered on the four routers in the second layer, and each region has a preference for a certain service chain, with blue, orange, gray, and brown indicating business services 0, 1, 2, and 3, respectively. Preference indicates the percentage of requests to a service chain in a certain time period.

- Spatial feature traffic scenario (SFT): As shown in Fig. 9(a), if Preference is 0.2, that is, the requests arriving in the four regions have 20% probability of being SC0, SC1, SC2, SC3, respectively, and the remaining 80% probability of being other requests.
- Temporal feature traffic scenario (TFT): This scenario is shown in Fig. 9(b), in this scenario, the user requests in the four regions are no longer differentiated, and all of them have a specific degree of preference for service chain 0. For example, if the Preference is 0.2, it means that the entire requests arriving at

the whole microservice system have a 20% probability of being for SC0, and the remaining 80% probability of being other requests.

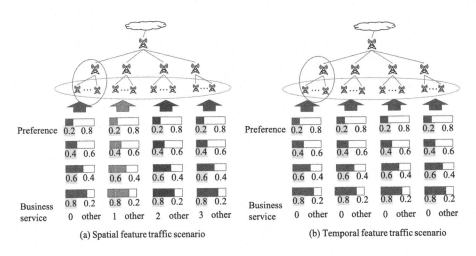

Fig. 9. Traffic scenarios with different characteristics.

In this case, the cloud edge network delay is set to 60 ms and the requests arrival rate of the microservice system is configured to be 600 r/s (each region is 150 r/s). The traffic distribution of each region is set according to the value of Preference for the two traffic scenarios mentioned above. We observe the impact of two service deployment methods, random deployment and simple deployment, on the response time of service chains under the GEC and LEC, respectively.

– Random deployment policy (RD): A total of 200 microservice instances are deployed, where the number of instances of each service is proportional to the number of times it is invoked by other services. These service instances are eventually deployed randomly on 32 edge nodes.
– Simple deployment policy (SD): A total of 200 microservice instances are deployed, where the number of instances of each service on each edge node is proportional to the volume of requests for the service.

We observe the response time of these service chains when adopting the four policies of GEC And RD (GEC-RD), GEC And SD (GEC-SD), LEC And RD (LEC-RD), and LEC And SD (LEC-SD), respectively.

Figure 10 shows the FCT of requests within 1 s under SFT and TFT scenarios. It can be seen that ServiceSim can simulate the effects of different service deployment policies. The FCT of the microservice system is smaller under the SD policy than the RD policy, regardless of the edge collaboration police. In addition, since each region in the TFT scenario has a preference for the same SC, the traffic distribution is more uneven compared to the SFT scenario.

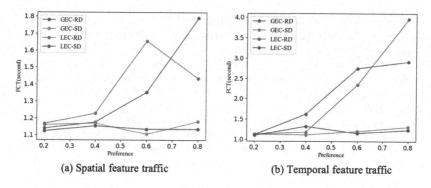

Fig. 10. Results under two different feature traffic scenarios.

The results of the two use cases show that ServiceSim can sensitively identify changes in end-user requests, changes in network and computing resources, and correctly verifies the effectiveness of the edge collaboration policies and microservice deployment policies.

5   Conclusion

In this paper, we propose ServiceSim, a modeling and simulation toolkit for microservice systems in cloud-edge environment. It extends CloudSim and can support the simulation of end-user requests, multi-level cloud-edge systems and microservice systems. The comparison experiments with real microservice system verify that ServiceSim can correctly reflect the distribution characteristics of end-user requests. The validation of edge collaboration and service deployment policies further illustrates that ServiceSim can capture the impact of different configuration policies on the microservice system in the cloud-edge environment. However, ServiceSim still has many shortcomings, and the simulation of system volatility factors such as the dynamic fluctuation characteristics of network and the system anomalous events will be further considered in the future.

Acknowledgements. Research in this paper is supported by the Key Research and Development Program of Heilongjiang Province (2022ZX01A11) and the National Natural Science Foundation of China (62372140, 61832014, 61832004).

References

1. Aslanpour, M.S., Toosi, A.N., Taheri, J., Gaire, R.: AutoScaleSim: a simulation toolkit for auto-scaling web applications in clouds. Simul. Model. Pract. Theory **108**, 102245 (2021)
2. Calheiros, R.N., Ranjan, R., Beloglazov, A., De Rose, C.A., Buyya, R.: CloudSim: a toolkit for modeling and simulation of cloud computing environments and evaluation of resource provisioning algorithms. Softw. Pract. Exper. **41**(1), 23–50 (2011)

3. Garg, S.K., Buyya, R.: NetworkCloudSim: modelling parallel applications in cloud simulations. In: 2011 Fourth IEEE International Conference on Utility and Cloud Computing, pp. 105–113. IEEE (2011)
4. Gupta, H., Vahid Dastjerdi, A., Ghosh, S.K., Buyya, R.: iFogSim: a toolkit for modeling and simulation of resource management techniques in the internet of things, edge and fog computing environments. Softw. Pract. Exper. **47**(9), 1275–1296 (2017)
5. He, Q., et al.: A game-theoretical approach for user allocation in edge computing environment. IEEE Trans. Parallel Distrib. Syst. **31**(3), 515–529 (2019)
6. Hu, P., Dhelim, S., Ning, H., Qiu, T.: Survey on fog computing: architecture, key technologies, applications and open issues. J. Netw. Comput. Appl. **98**, 27–42 (2017)
7. Hu, S., Shi, W., Li, G.: CEC: a containerized edge computing framework for dynamic resource provisioning. IEEE Trans. Mob. Comput. **22**, 3840–3854 (2022)
8. Khazaei, H., Mahmoudi, N., Barna, C., Litoiu, M.: Performance modeling of microservice platforms. IEEE Trans. Cloud Comput. **10**, 2848–2862 (2020)
9. Mahmud, R., Pallewatta, S., Goudarzi, M., Buyya, R.: IFogSim2: an extended IFogSim simulator for mobility, clustering, and microservice management in edge and fog computing environments. J. Syst. Softw. **190**, 111351 (2022)
10. Okegbile, S.D., Maharaj, B.T., Alfa, A.S.: A multi-user tasks offloading scheme for integrated edge-fog-cloud computing environments. IEEE Trans. Veh. Technol. **71**(7), 7487–7502 (2022)
11. Pallewatta, S., Kostakos, V., Buyya, R.: Microservices-based IoT application placement within heterogeneous and resource constrained fog computing environments. In: Proceedings of the 12th IEEE/ACM International Conference on Utility and Cloud Computing, pp. 71–81 (2019)
12. Pallewatta, S., Kostakos, V., Buyya, R.: Microservices-based IoT applications scheduling in edge and fog computing: a taxonomy and future directions. arXiv preprint arXiv:2207.05399 (2022)
13. Piraghaj, S.F., Dastjerdi, A.V., Calheiros, R.N., Buyya, R.: ContainerCloudSim: an environment for modeling and simulation of containers in cloud data centers. Softw. Pract. Exper. **47**(4), 505–521 (2017)
14. Porambage, P., Okwuibe, J., Liyanage, M., Ylianttila, M., Taleb, T.: Survey on multi-access edge computing for internet of things realization. IEEE Commun. Surv. Tutor. **20**(4), 2961–2991 (2018)
15. Son, J., Dastjerdi, A.V., Calheiros, R.N., Ji, X., Yoon, Y., Buyya, R.: CloudSimSDN: modeling and simulation of software-defined cloud data centers. In: 2015 15th IEEE/ACM International Symposium on Cluster, Cloud and Grid Computing, pp. 475–484. IEEE (2015)
16. Sonmez, C., Ozgovde, A., Ersoy, C.: EdgeCloudSim: an environment for performance evaluation of edge computing systems. Trans. Emerg. Telecommun. Technol. **29**(11), e3493 (2018)
17. Wickremasinghe, B., Calheiros, R.N., Buyya, R.: CloudAnalyst: a cloudSim-based visual modeller for analysing cloud computing environments and applications. In: 2010 24th IEEE International Conference on Advanced Information Networking and Applications, pp. 446–452. IEEE (2010)
18. Xiao, Z., et al.: Multi-objective parallel task offloading and content caching in D2D-aided MEC networks. IEEE Trans. Mob. Comput. **22**, 6599–6615 (2022)
19. Zhang, Y., Di, B., Wang, P., Lin, J., Song, L.: HetMEC: heterogeneous multi-layer mobile edge computing in the 6G era. IEEE Trans. Veh. Technol. **69**(4), 4388–4400 (2020)

Emerging Technologies and Approaches

2DPChain: Orchestrating Transactions in Order-Execute Blockchain to Exploit Intra-batch and Inter-batch Parallelism

Jianfeng Shi[1,3], Heng Wu[2,3,5], Wang Liu[2,3], Heran Gao[1,3], and Wenbo Zhang[2,3,4,5](✉)

[1] University of Chinese Academy of Sciences, Beijing, China
[2] University of Chinese Academy of Sciences, Nanjing, China
[3] Software Engineering Technology Research and Development Center (Institute of Software, Chinese Academy of Sciences), Beijing, China
[4] State Key Laboratory of Computer Science (Institute of Software, Chinese Academy of Sciences), Beijing, China
[5] Nanjing institute of software technology, Nanjing, China
zhangwenbo@otcaix.iscas.ac.cn

Abstract. The *order-execute* blockchains have two obvious features, namely batch processing and replicated state machine, which lead to two issues that degrade throughput. (1) Conflicting transactions within each batch degrade parallelism utilization, because conflicting transactions can only be executed serially. (2) Heterogeneous processing capabilities between nodes degrade parallelism utilization, because each node needs to execute each batch once. Therefore, we propose a collaboration-oriented parallelism enhancement architecture that is capable of exploiting intra-batch and inter-batch parallelism. The architecture is oriented towards parallel sub-batches, and includes a transaction management mechanism, a transaction packing mechanism and a parameter tuning and assignment mechanism. Experimental results show that our blockchain (**2DPChain**) effectively improves parallelism utilization and thus improves throughput compared to three related blockchains.

Keywords: Blockchain · Batch scheduling · Parallelism utilization

1 Introduction

Blockchain can be viewed as a decentralized database that support smart contract transactions (Txs). The *order-execute* transaction processing architecture is widely adopted by blockchains, such as Ethereum [17] and FISCO BCOS [2].

As shown in Fig. 1, the transaction processing in order-execute blockchains can be divided into 4 phases, i.e., ordering, packing, execution and consensus.

Feature 1: *Batch processing.* In each round, the blockchain node that obtains the packing right packs a batch of Txs from its own transaction pool (Txpool), executes them, and finally generates a block. Obviously, the blockchain transaction processing has the feature of online batch scheduling.

© The Author(s), under exclusive license to Springer Nature Switzerland AG 2023
F. Monti et al. (Eds.): ICSOC 2023, LNCS 14419, pp. 275–290, 2023.
https://doi.org/10.1007/978-3-031-48421-6_19

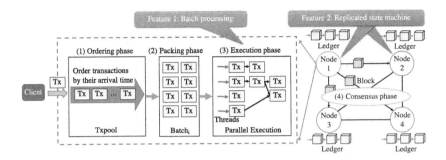

Fig. 1. Architecture of the order-execute blockchain.

In these blockchain systems applied to business scenarios, conflicts between Txs are common [10] [13] [11]. In Fig. 2(a), Tx_1 and Tx_2 indicate that *store1* issues 10 points to customers. Tx_3 means that a customer transfer 40 points to *store4* to pay his parking fee. Obviously, Tx_1 and Tx_2 can only be executed serially because there is a data conflict (i.e. *store1*) between them.

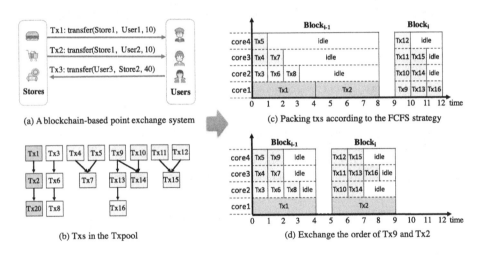

Fig. 2. The order of Txs affects the parallelism utilization during the execution phase.

Most blockchains use the first-come-first-served (FCFS) strategy to order and pack Txs [8]. Figure 2(b) shows the pending Txs and their conflicting relationships. Txs marked in red have a processing time of 4, while others have a processing time of 1. Assuming each block contains up to 8 Txs, Fig. 2(c) shows the blocks generated according to the FCFS strategy. The time taken by a node with 4-core CPU to process the blocks is 11. The parallelism utilization is 50%. However, if Tx_2 in $block_{i-1}$ is exchanged with Tx_9 in $block_i$, the processing time required is only 8. The parallelism utilization is improved to 68.75%.

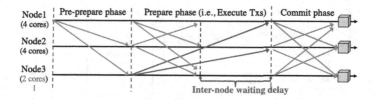

Fig. 3. Transaction flow of blockchains adopting PBFT consensus protocol.

Feature 2: *Replicated State Machine.* To prevent any node from tampering with the blockchain ledger, each node needs to maintain the same state. For each batch of Txs, each node will execute it to update its local state. Obviously, blockchain is a replicated state machine, which raises two issues. (1) The parallelism provided by nodes with strong processing capability may be wasted. As shown in Fig. 3, the nodes with 4-core CPU complete the execution of a batch of Txs earlier than the nodes with 2-core CPU. (2) Increasing the number of nodes cannot increase the transaction processing capability. The transaction processing capability of the blockchain is equal to that of the weakest node.

The above observations motivate us to enhance *order-execute* blockchains from two aspects. (1) How to make each batch of Txs fully utilize the parallelism provided by the multi-core processor. (2) How to enhance the nodes with weaker processing capabilities so that the parallelism provided by the nodes with stronger processing capabilities can be fully utilized.

Contributions. This paper makes the following contributions.

- We propose a collaboration-based parallelism enhancement architecture named 2DPChain, which enables two-dimensional parallelism, i.e., intra-batch parallelism and inter-batch parallelism.
- We propose three parallel-sub-batch-oriented mechanisms to improve parallelism utilization, namely a transaction management mechanism, a transaction packing mechanism, an adaptive parameter tuning and assignment mechanism.
- Using simulated datasets and real datasets, experimental results show that 2DPChain achieves higher parallelism utilization and thus higher throughput compared to three related blockchains.

The rest of the paper is organized as follows. Section 2 shows our system model. Section 3, 4 and 5 describe our methods. Section 6 shows the evaluation results. Section 7 summarizes the related work. Section 8 concludes the paper.

2   System Model

2.1   Concept Definition

- **Transaction (Tx):** A Tx usually consists of a series of operations that change the state of the blockchain ledger. For Tx_i, its processing time is pt_i, its read-operation set is $\rho(Tx_i)$, and its write-operation set is $\omega(Tx_i)$.

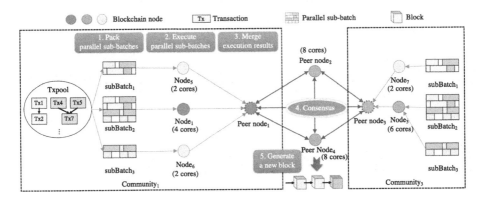

Fig. 4. System architecture of 2DPChain.

- **Conflict**: When there is an intersection between the read-write sets of two Txs (Tx_i and Tx_j), they are in conflict ($C_{ij} = 1$). Conflicting Txs cannot be executed in parallel at the same moment, because errors such as dirty reads and dirty writes may occur.

$$C_{ij} = \begin{cases} 1 \; if \; \rho(Tx_i) \cap \omega(Tx_j) \neq \emptyset \\ 1 \; if \; \omega(Tx_i) \cap \rho(Tx_j) \neq \emptyset \\ 1 \; if \; \omega(Tx_i) \cap \omega(Tx_j) \neq \emptyset \\ 0 \qquad otherwise \end{cases} \quad (1)$$

- **Batch**: A set of Txs, i.e. $batch_k = \{Tx_1, Tx_2, ...\}$.
- **Parallel Sub-batches**: A set of sub-batches that have no read-write set intersection with each other. They can be executed in parallel by different nodes without fear of conflicts. $batch_k$ consists of a set of parallel sub-batches.

$$batch_k = \{subBatch_1, subBatch_2, ...\} \quad (2)$$

$$\begin{aligned} if \quad & subBatch_m, subBatch_n \in batch_k \\ & \forall Tx_i \in subBatch_m \; \forall Tx_j \in subBatch_n, \; C_{ij} \neq 1 \end{aligned} \quad (3)$$

- **Block**: The basic unit for processing Txs, including the hash of the previous block, a set of parallel sub-batches and their merged execution results, etc.
- **Blockchain Node.** Each node receives Txs submitted by clients and stores them in its own Txpool, namely, $Txpool = \{Tx_1, Tx_2, ...\}$. The time taken by $node_j$ processing multiple sub-batches within $batch_k$ is nt_{jk}.
- **Peer Node.** Those nodes that participate in consensus on the new block.
- **Community.** Multiple nodes can join a weak peer node to form a community [6]. Each node executes one or more specified sub-batches, and return the execution result (i.e. a read-write set) to the peer node, augmenting the parallel processing capability of the weak peer node in a collaborative manner. We use cpt_{ik} to denote the time it takes for $community_i$ to finish processing $batch_k$.

$$cpt_{ik} = \max_{node_j \in community_i} nt_{jk} \quad (4)$$

- **Block Processing Time.** 2DPChain consists of multiple communities. To maintain the same state, each community needs to execute each batch once. The longest time taken to process $batch_k$ among all communities is bpt_k.

$$bpt_k = \max_{community_i \in communities} cpt_{ik} \tag{5}$$

2.2 Transaction Flow

2DPChain adopts PBFT (Practical Byzantine Fault Tolerance) as its consensus protocol. We will illustrate how 2DPChain processes Txs based on Fig. 4.

Stage 1: Pack Parallel Sub-batches. The peer node that obtains the packing right packs a set of parallel sub-batches from its own Txpool, and then broadcasts these parallel sub-batches to other peer nodes.

Stage 2: Execute Parallel Sub-batches. Each peer node distributes the received parallel sub-batches to other nodes belonging to the same community. When any node finishes executing the assigned sub-batches, it sends the read-write set of the assigned sub-batches to the peer node.

Stage 3: Merge Execution Results. For each peer node, after collecting all the execution results within its community, it can directly merge these results as the final result, because there are no conflicts between these sub-batches. Then, each peer node broadcasts its final execution result to other peer nodes.

Stage 4: Consensus. Each peer node compares its own final execution result with that of other peer nodes. In a blockchain with (3*f+1) peer nodes, if the final execution results generated by more than (2*f+1) peer nodes are consistent, the peer node broadcasts a commit message to other peer nodes.

Stage 5: Generate a New Block. If a peer node receives more than (2*f+1) commit messages, it will use the final execution result of the sub-batches to update its local state, and commit the new block to its local ledger.

2.3 Offline-Version Problem Formulation

The transaction processing in 2DPChain is actually to divide all pending Txs into multiple batches (i.e., batches = {$batch_1, batch_2, ...$}), and processing them in sequence. The goal of our paper is to maximize throughput (the average number of successfully processed Txs per second).

$$\textbf{2DPChain}: \max \text{ TPS} = \frac{n}{\sum_{batch_k \in batches} (bpt_k + bct_k)} \tag{6}$$

$$\textbf{s.t.} \sum_{batch_k \in batches} \sum_{subBatch_j \in batch_k} I_{ij} = 1 \qquad i = 1, \ldots n \tag{7}$$

$$\forall \text{batch}_k \in \text{batches}, \quad 0 < \sum_{\text{subBatch}_j \in \text{batch}_k} \sum_{i=1}^{n} I_{ij} \leq \text{blockSize} \qquad (8)$$

In objective function (6), n is the number of pending Txs, and bct_k is the consensus time on block$_k$. Const. (7) restricts each Tx to be assigned to only one sub batch. $I_{ij} \in \{0/1\}$ indicates whether Tx_i is packed into subBatch$_j$. Const. (8) limits the number of Txs within each block to be greater than 0 and not exceeding the block size.

3 A Transaction Management Mechanism for Parallel Sub-batches

3.1 Conflict Management Based on DAG

When a node starts, a DAG (Directed Acyclic Graph) is initialized for its Txpool. In the DAG, each vertex represents a Tx, and each edge indicates that the two Txs connected by it are in conflict. A Tx with in-degree equal to 0 is called a *ready Tx*. A Tx containing a shared variable v is called an *exit Tx* of v if it does not have a child Tx containing v.

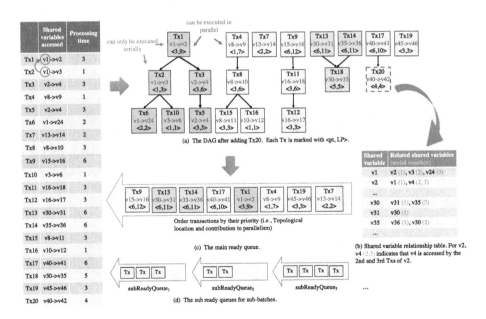

Fig. 5. Manage transaction in the Txpool through a DAG, a shared-variable relationship table and two-level ordered queues.

For a new Tx, add it to the DAG as a vertex, then find all exit Txs in Txpool that conflict with it, finally establish directed edges from these conflicting exit Txs to it. For example, in Fig. 5(a), when Tx$_{20}$ reaches the Txpool, the shared variables it accesses (i.e. $v40$ and $v42$) are first extracted through static analysis, and then the conflicting exit Txs that access these shared variables in the DAG are found (i.e. Tx_{17}), finally establish a directed edge from Tx_{17} to Tx_{20}.

3.2 Ready Transaction Management Based on Two-Level Ordered Queues

Ready Txs have no dependencies on each other, so they can be executed in parallel. However, when packing a ready Tx into a sub-batch, the ready Tx may conflict with a Tx in another sub-batch, i.e., the ready Tx is not suitable for packing into the current sub-batch. We call such a Tx an *inappropriate Tx*. For example, suppose Tx_1 has been packed into subBatch$_1$, and now you need to pack a Tx into subBatch$_2$. If Tx_2 is packed, due to a conflict between Tx_2 and Tx_1, Tx_2 can only be abandoned.

A large number of inappropriate Txs will increase the overhead of the packing phase. Therefore, 2DPChain adopt two-level ready queues, i.e., a main ready queue and multiple sub-ready queues.

- The main ready queue is responsible for recording new ready Txs that do not currently conflict with Txs in any of the sub-batches.
- Each sub-ready queue corresponds to a sub batch. A sub-ready queue records the ready Txs that conflict with a Tx in its corresponding sub-batch. When a ready Tx packed into a sub-batch is removed from the DAG, the released ready Txs will be directly added to the sub-ready queue corresponding to the sub batch.

  Ready Txs in any ready queue are ordered by their priority. The priority definition for Tx_i is similar to that in [15], which considers its topological position in the DAG (LP_i) and its ability to release ready Txs after being packed (CPD_i).

$$\text{priority}_i = LP_i + \alpha CPD_i \tag{9}$$

3.3 Conflict Prediction Based on Shared-Variable Relationship Table

In Fig. 5, if Tx_{13} is packed into subBatch$_1$ and Tx_{14} is packed into subBatch$_2$, Tx_{18} cannot be packed into any sub-batch because it conflicts with the Txs in both sub-batches. We call such a Tx a *cross-sub-batch Tx*.

A large number of cross-sub-batch Txs will make it more difficult to pack a batch Txs that can fully utilize parallelism. Therefore, 2DPChain introduces a shared-variable relationship table, which records the shared variables related to each shared variable.

When a Tx is added to the DAG, its shared variables are added to the shared-variable relationship table. In Fig. 5(b), the shared variables related to $v30$ include $v31$ and $v35$. If Tx_{13} is packed into subBatch$_1$, since Tx_{14} accesses $v35$, Tx_{14} will not be packed into another sub-batch, which avoids the generation of cross-sub-batch Txs (i.e., Tx_{18}).

When a Tx is removed from the DAG, its shared variables will be removed from the shared-variable relationship table.

The pseudo code of Algorithm 1 implements the above content.

Algorithm 1. Add a new Tx to the Txpool

Input: Tx_{new}: A new transaction;
Output: $\emptyset$;
 1: conflictingExitTxs = getConflictingExitTxsFromDAG(Tx_{new});
 2: **for** each $Tx_{conflicting} \in$ conflictingExitTxs **do**
 3:    addEdge($Tx_{conflicting}$, Tx_{new});
 4:    $Tx_{conflicting}$.outDegree += 1;
 5:    Tx_{new}.inDegree += 1;
 6: **end for**
 7: **if** Tx_{new}.inDegree == 0 **then**
 8:    insertIntoReadyQueue(Tx_{new});
 9: **end if**
10: updateSharedVariableRelationshipTable(Tx_{new});

---

4   A Transaction Packing Mechanism for Parallel Sub-batches

4.1   Problem Model Based on 2D Multi-bin Packing Problem

In order to make each sub-batch fully exploit parallelism during execution, the generation problem of parallel sub-batches can be abstracted as *a variable-sized two-dimensional multi-bin packing problem*. As shown in Fig. 6(d), Each sub-batch is treated as a rectangular bin. A block contains multiple bins. Each Tx is treated as a rectangular piece with width = 1 and length = Tx.pt.

(1) In each bin, each row represents a CPU core, and these rows can execute Txs in parallel. Therefore, the Txs executed at the same moment cannot conflict.

(2) The width of bin_i is equal to NPT_i (Number of Parallel Threads), and the length of bin_i is variable.

(3) There are no conflicting Txs between any two sub-batches. We equip each sub-batch with a pool *sharedVarsPool* that contains the shared variables accessed by the Txs within the sub-batch.

$$\text{sharedVarsPool}_i \bigcap \text{sharedVarsPool}_j = \emptyset \qquad (10)$$

Determining how to pack a set of parallel sub-batches to maximize parallelism is equivalent to determining how to make the lengths of these bins consistent while minimizing vacancies in these bins.

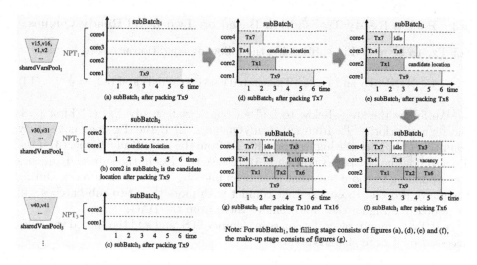

Fig. 6. Example of packing Txs for parallel sub-batches.

4.2 Select a Candidate Location Based on Load Balancing

For any bin, Txs are placed from left to right. Each row $core_k^i$ in bin_i maintains a variable APT_k^i (Accumulated Processing Time), which is the total time spent by $core_k^i$ executing Txs. For example, in Fig. 6(e), $APT_3^1 = 4$.

The row with the smallest APT is responsible for accommodating the next ready Tx to be packed. RT (Ready Time) indicates the smallest APT.

$$RT = \min_{i\in[1,\text{NPSB}]}\{\min_{k\in[1,\text{NPT}_i]}\{APT_k^i \mid k \notin \text{ITS}\}\} \qquad (11)$$

where NPSB is the number of parallel sub-batches. ITS (Idle Thread Set) is used to keep track of idle rows that have no executable Txs at this moment.

However, there may be multiple bins, each with at least one row with APT equal to RT. A static selection strategy will result in some sub-batches not having enough appropriate Txs. Therefore, we select the best candidate location $core_d^z$ (i.e., the row $core_d$ in bin_z) by the following load balancing algorithm.

$$core_d^z = \arg \max_{z\in[1,\text{NPSB}],d\in[1,\text{NPT}_z]}\{\frac{\text{NRT}_z}{\text{NPT}_z} + \beta\text{NPT}_z + \gamma\frac{1}{d}\} \qquad (12)$$

where β and γ are coefficients, and NRT_z denotes the number of rows with $APT = RT$ in bin_z.

In Fig. 6(a), after Tx_9 is packed into $subBatch_1$, the next candidate location is $core_1^2$ instead of $core_2^1$. APT for each row in ITS needs to be extended to RT. For rows with APT no greater than RT, the last Tx on each of them needs to be removed from the DAG.

4.3   Pack a Ready Transaction Based on Two-Level Ready Queues

For Tx_r to be placed in $subBatch_z$, the following condition needs to be met.

$$\forall i \in [1, \text{NPSB}] \text{ and } i \neq z, \ Tx_r.\text{sharedVars} \bigcap \text{sharedVarsPool}_i = \emptyset \qquad (13)$$

We follow the steps below to find an appropriate ready Tx. (1) First pack the highest-priority Tx from $subReadyQueue_z$. (2) If the Tx does not satisfy condition (13), pack the highest-priority Tx from the main ready queue. (3) If the Tx also does not satisfy condition (13), release the Txs in the sub ready queues corresponding to those bins that have been filled by Txs, and then retry. During the above process, those Txs that conflict with more than two sub-batches will be added to an ignore set, and remove them from the DAG.
- If Tx_r is found, place Tx_r on $core_d^z$, empty ITS, and add the shared variables accessed by Tx_r to $sharedVarsPool_z$.

$$\text{sharedVarsPool}_z \cup = Tx_r.\text{sharedVars} \qquad (14)$$

Based on the shared-variable relationship table, the first p related shared variables of each shared variable of Tx_r will also be added to $sharedVarsPool_z$.
- If Tx_r is not found, add $core_d^z$ to ITS. In Fig. 6(e), when $time = 2$, $RT = APT_4^1 = 2$. There is no appropriate ready Txs in the DAG at this moment, so add $core_4^1$ to ITS, and recompute RT. $RT = APT_2^1 = 3$, thus $core_2^1$ is selected to place the next ready Tx. Repeat the above steps until the number of packed Txs reaches $blockSize$. We call the above process the filling stage.

4.4   Align All Sub-Batches

After the filling stage, as shown on the right side of Fig. 6(f), the lengths of the rows in each bin may not be aligned, and the lengths of these bins may also not be aligned, resulting in many vacancies. Therefore, we pack a few more ready Txs to fill these vacancies. We call this process the make-up stage.

ET is used to represent the maximum value among all APTs.

$$\text{ET} = \max_{i \in [1, \text{NPSB}]} \{ \max_{k \in [1, \text{NPT}_i]} \text{APT}_k^i \} \qquad (15)$$

When packing a ready tx, the following condition will be added.

$$Tx_r.\text{pt} <= \text{ET} - \text{APT}_d^z \qquad (16)$$

As shown in Fig. 6(g), after the filling stage and the make-up stage, we obtain a set of parallel sub-batches that can maximize parallelism utilization. Finally, the Txs in the ignore set will be re-added to the DAG.

5   An Adaptive Parameter Tuning and Assignment Mechanism for Parallel Sub-batches

5.1   An Adaptive Parameter Negotiation Method

There are two parameters for parallel sub-batches, namely the number of parallel sub-batches (NPSB) and the number of parallel threads of each sub-batch (NPT). As shown in Fig. 7, (1) when the blockchain network starts or when a new node joins the network, each community will broadcast a message (the number of CPU cores per node it contains). (2) In each message, nodes are listed in descending order by the number of CPU cores. (3) Find the minimum number of CPU cores per layer as the number of parallel threads in the corresponding sub-batch. (4) Determine the number of parallel sub-batches based on the fact that the cumulative number of parallel threads in all sub-batches cannot exceed the cumulative number of CPU cores in the weakest community. In Fig. 7, the number of CPU cores in the weakest community is 8, so NPSB=3.

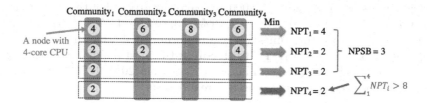

Fig. 7. Negotiate NPSB and NPT between communities.

5.2   A Greedy-Based Assignment Method for Parallel Sub-Batches

Each community uses the following steps to assign the received sub-batches to its nodes. (1) The community sorts its nodes in descending order by their number of CPU cores. (2) The community sorts sub-batches in descending order by their number of parallel threads. (3) Each sub-batch traverses each node in turn. If the number of remaining cores in a node is greater than or equal to the number of parallel threads of the sub-batch, the sub-batch is assigned to the node.

5.3   Analysis of Solutions for Malicious Behavior

2DPChain may suffer from two types of malicious behavior. (1) A node falsely reports its processing capability. Each node will record the waiting time for receiving execution results from other nodes and rate them. (2) There is a conflict between sub-batches packed by the node with the packing right. When other nodes execute these sub-batches, they will verify that there is an intersection between sub-batches based on their read-write sets. In the future, we will study reputation-based node scoring methods to address these malicious behaviors.

6   Experimental Evaluation

6.1   Baseline Blockchains

- *FISCO BCOS v2.7.2* [2]: A typical order-execute blockchain that employs the FCFS strategy to pack Txs, and supports each node to execute Txs in parallel using the multi-core processor. However, it does not support collaborative execution between nodes.
- *DiPETrans* [6]: A leader-follower-based blockchain that divides independent Txs within a block into multiple groups, and distributes them to followers to execute concurrently. Txs can only be executed serially on each follower.
- *DiPETrans-parallel:* An enhanced version of DiPETrans that we implemented, where Txs can be executed in parallel on each follower.

6.2   Datasets

- *Simulated dataset:* We generate multiple datasets by varying the conflict rate (CR) of Txs. Each contains 100,000 Txs, and the processing-time distribution of these Txs is $[10\% \rightarrow 1, 20\% \rightarrow 2, 40\% \rightarrow 3, 20\% \rightarrow 4, 10\% \rightarrow 10]$. Conflicts and different processing times follow a uniform distribution in each dataset.
- *Real dataset:* **Tether USDT Stablecoin** is the most popular ERC-20 application on Ethereum. For its transaction logs from 2019 to 2023, we extract the first 100,000 entries per year as a real dataset.

6.3   Overall Performance

Our environment has 4 communities, i.e., [8], [6,2], [4,4] and [4,2,2]. For FISCO BCOS, the strongest node in each community serves as the peer node, while the other nodes are observer nodes that only synchronize blocks. The block size of each blockchain is set to 1000 Txs.

We send the simulated datasets to 2DPChain, FISCO BCOS, DiPETrans, and DiPETrans-parallel at a transaction arrival rate (TAR) of 4,000 Txs/s. As shown in Fig. 8, 2DPChain achieves higher throughput (TPS) than other blockchains under various conflict rates. For example, when CR=40%, 2DPChain improves throughput by 38.61% over FISCO BCOS, 134.64% over DiPETrans, and 22.25% over DiPETrans-parallel.

For an experiment under CR=40% and TAR=4,000 Txs/s, Fig. 9 shows the first 20 blocks of 2DPChain. Each block achieves almost 100% parallelism utilization (PU), which shows the effectiveness of our approaches. As shown in Fig. 10, 2DPChain takes more time to import Txs (i.e., order Txs), but effectively reduces the time to execute them.

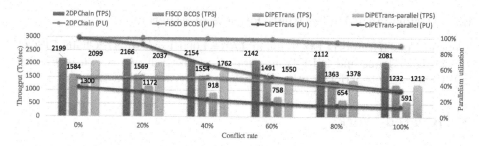

Fig. 8. Throughput and parallelism utilization under different conflict rates.

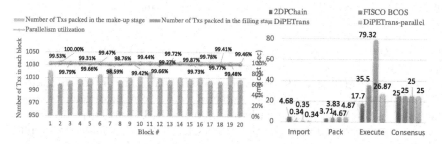

Fig. 9. Number of Txs packed in two stages.

Fig. 10. Runtime breakdown.

6.4 Scalability Evaluation

We evaluate the scalability of these blockchains by varying the number of 2-core-CPU nodes in each community. As shown in Fig. 11, 2DPChain can achieve better scalability than DiPETrans, because 2DPChain schedules Txs from a global perspective, while DiPETrans only schedules intra-block Txs. However, as the number of nodes in each community increases, the growth rate of 2DPChain's throughput decreases, as the complexity of the packing phase increases.

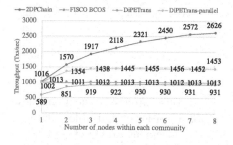

Fig. 11. Scalability comparison.

Fig. 12. Throughput under real datasets.

6.5   Performance Under Real Datasets of Ethereum

We send 5 real datasets of Ethereum at TAR=4,000 Txs/s to 2DPChain, FISCO BCOS, DiPETrans and DiPETrans-parallel, respectively. As shown in Fig. 12, 2DPChain still outperforms other blockchains in terms of throughput.

7   Related Work

According to the order of the ordering phase and the execution phase, blockchains can be divided into *order-execute* blockchains (e.g., Ethereum [17], FISCO BCOS [2] and ChainMaker [1]) and *execute-order* blockchains (e.g., Hyperledger Fabric [4] and XuperChain [16]).

- *Execute-order blockchains.* Hyperledger Fabric adopts MVOCC to support parallel execution of Txs. It can add execution nodes to enhance its transaction processing capability. However, it checks for transaction conflicts after the ordering phase, and aborts the conflicting Txs. To reduce conflicts, Fabric++ [14] uses reordering and early abort methods, FabricSharp [12] uses a fine-grained OCC-based method, and FabricCRDT [9] uses conflict-free replicated datatypes.
- *Order-execute blockchains.* In order to deterministically concurrently execute Txs within a block, studies such as ParBlockchain [3] and OptSmart [5] use a dependency graph. DiPETrans [6] uses a cluster of machines that form a community to execute or validate Txs. Each community consists of a leader and multiple follower. The leader divides independent Txs within a block into different groups through static analysis, and distributes them to followers to execute concurrently. SChain [7] can exploit intra-block concurrency by dispatching Txs within a block to multiple executors, and inter-block concurrency by using the pipeline technique.

In short, the aforementioned studies on order-execute blockchains mainly focus on scheduling intra-block Txs, so the optimization effect is limited. Different from them, we orchestrate the global pending Txs, so the scheduling space is larger. In addition, we also take into account the heterogeneous processing capabilities among blockchain nodes.

8   Conclusion

Conflicts between transactions and heterogeneous processing capabilities between nodes degrade the parallelism utilization in order-execute blockchains. We propose a collaboration-based parallelism enhancement architecture called 2DPChain, which allows multiple poorly performing nodes to form a single strong performing node (i.e., a community). In 2DPChain, a block contains a set of parallel sub-batches, which can be executed by multiple nodes in parallel. At the same time, each sub-batch can fully utilize the parallelism provided by the multi-core processor of the corresponding node. Therefore, 2DPChain enables two-dimensional parallelism, i.e., intra-batch parallelism and inter-batch parallelism. Experimental results show that 2DPChain effectively improves parallelism utilization and throughput compared to three related blockchains.

Acknowledgments. This work is supported by the Provincial Key Research and Development Program of Shandong, China (No. 2021CXGC010101), the National Natural Science Foundation of China (No. 61872344 and No. 61972386).

References

1. ChainMaker (2022). https://docs.chainmaker.org.cn
2. FISCO BCOS (2022). https://fisco-bcos-documentation.readthedocs.io
3. Amiri, M.J., Agrawal, D., El Abbadi, A.: Parblockchain: leveraging transaction parallelism in permissioned blockchain systems. In: 39th International Conference on Distributed Computing Systems (ICDCS), pp. 1337–1347. IEEE (2019)
4. Androulaki, E., et al.: Hyperledger fabric: a distributed operating system for permissioned blockchains. In: Proceedings of the Thirteenth EuroSys Conference, pp. 1–15 (2018)
5. Anjana, P.S.: Efficient parallel execution of block transactions in blockchain. In: Proceedings of the 22nd International Middleware Conference: Doctoral Symposium, pp. 8–11 (2021)
6. Baheti, S., Anjana, P.S., Peri, S., Simmhan, Y.: Dipetrans: a framework for distributed parallel execution of transactions of blocks in blockchains. Concurr. Comput. Pract. Exp. **34**(10), e6804 (2022)
7. Chen, Z., et al.: Schain: a scalable consortium blockchain exploiting intra-and inter-block concurrency. Proc. VLDB Endow. **14**(12), 2799–2802 (2021)
8. Goel, S., Singh, A., Garg, R., Verma, M., Jayachandran, P.: Resource fairness and prioritization of transactions in permissioned blockchain systems. In: Proceedings of the 19th International Middleware Conference Industry, pp. 46–53 (2018)
9. Nasirifard, P., Mayer, R., Jacobsen, H.A.: FabricCRDT: a conflict-free replicated datatypes approach to permissioned blockchains. In: Proceedings of the 20th International Middleware Conference, pp. 110–122 (2019)
10. Pîrlea, G., Kumar, A., Sergey, I.: Practical smart contract sharding with ownership and commutativity analysis. In: Proceedings of the 42nd ACM SIGPLAN International Conference on Programming Language Design and Implementation, pp. 1327–1341 (2021)
11. Ponnapalli, S., et al.: RainBlock: faster transaction processing in public blockchains. In: USENIX Annual Technical Conference, pp. 333–347 (2021)
12. Ruan, P., Loghin, D., Ta, Q.T., Zhang, M., Chen, G., Ooi, B.C.: A transactional perspective on execute-order-validate blockchains. In: Proceedings of 2020 ACM SIGMOD International Conference on Management of Data, pp. 543–557 (2020)
13. Saraph, V., Herlihy, M.: An empirical study of speculative concurrency in Ethereum smart contracts. In: International Conference on Blockchain Economics, Security and Protocols (Tokenomics 2019) (2019)
14. Sharma, A., Schuhknecht, F.M., Agrawal, D., Dittrich, J.: Blurring the lines between blockchains and database systems: the case of hyperledger fabric. In: Proceedings of the 2019 International Conference on Management of Data (2019)

15. Shi, J., Wu, H., Luo, D., Gao, H., Zhang, W.: InstantChain: enhancing order-execute blockchain systems for latency-sensitive applications. In: International Conference on Database Systems for Advanced Applications (2023)
16. Wei, X., Junyi, S., Qi, Z., Fu, C.: XuperChain: a blockchain system that supports smart contracts parallelization. In: 2020 IEEE International Conference on Smart Internet of Things (SmartIoT), pp. 309–313. IEEE (2020)
17. Wood, G., et al.: Ethereum: a secure decentralised generalised transaction ledger. Ethereum Proj. Yellow Pap. **151**(2014), 1–32 (2014)

A Dynamical Model for the Nonlinear Features of Value-Driven Service Ecosystem Evolution

Xinyue Zhou[1], Jianmao Xiao[2,3], Xiao Xue[1], Shizhan Chen[1], Hongyue Wu[1], and Zhiyong Feng[1(✉)]

[1] College of Intelligence and Computing, Tianjin University, 300350 Tianjin, China
{zhouxinyue,jzxuexiao,shizhan,hongyue.wu,zyfeng}@tju.edu.cn
[2] School of Software, Jiangxi Normal University, 330022 Nanchang, China
jm_xiao@jxnu.edu.cn
[3] Jiangxi Provincial Engineering Research Center of Blockchain Data Security and Governance, 330022 Nanchang, China

Abstract. As the full integration of human-cyber-physical has become mainstream, various services are interconnected to meet the ever-changing demands of users, forming service ecosystems. Service ecosystems constantly evolve driven by value and present many nonlinear responses, where inadvertent perturbations may lead to significant changes. This paper proposes a nonlinear dynamical model of value-driven service ecosystem evolution inspired by the energy flow of natural ecosystems, thereby explaining stability changes based on nonlinear features from the perspective of ecosystems. The model considers the nonlinear features, including interdependence and mutation of services and demands, and time delay due to service development. Further, we use stability and bifurcation theories to study the critical conditions under which parameter changes lead to phase transitions. In addition, numerical simulations are conducted to verify the effectiveness of the model and the correctness of the phase transition conditions. Through this method, service ecosystem managers can accurately predict the inflection point of the system from stable to unstable. Our method provides a novel way for the evaluation and governance of service ecosystems to have better universality and interpretability than current data-based mining methods and time series models based on neural networks.

Keywords: Service Ecosystem · Nonlinear Dynamical Model · Phase Transition · Time Delay · Numerical Simulation

This work was supported in part by the National Natural Science Foundation of China under Grants No.61832014, No.62032016 and No.62102281, the Jiangxi Provincial Natural Science Foundation under Grant No.20224BAB212015, the Foundation of Jiangxi Educational Committee under Grant No. GJJ210338. Zhiyong Feng is the corresponding author.

F. Monti et al. (Eds.): ICSOC 2023, LNCS 14419, pp. 291–306, 2023.
https://doi.org/10.1007/978-3-031-48421-6_20

1   Introduction

In recent years, human society, information space, and the physical world have been fully integrated with the development of information technology. Service ecosystems have become new organizational forms that have created huge economic and social value. The operation logic of value-driven service ecosystems is shown in Fig. 1. The demand side is personalized demands emerging from the evolving user social network. The supply side is service resources that evolve and integrate dynamically under the maintenance of service providers and operators. Value is the intermediary of transactions. Services are continuously matched with demands, thus gaining revenue. Service providers and operators develop, reuse, update, and innovate services to improve the service market for more value. Such a value circulation can facilitate the realignment of social networks and contribute to the evolution of service networks.

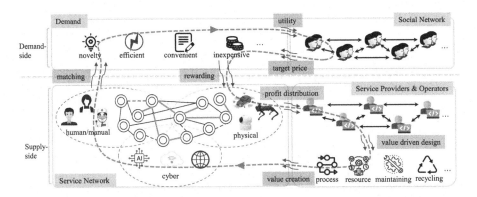

Fig. 1. Operation Logic of value-driven service ecosystem evolution.

Service ecosystems are complex systems that encompass natural ecosystems, economic systems, and information systems. Modeling and predicting service ecosystem evolution is very important and challenging. Meynhardt et al. [11] concluded nine system principles of value co-creation and the dynamics of service ecosystem evolution. Among them, nonlinearity is important to the global behavior of the systems and should be mainly considered [15]. Nonlinear perturbations may have insignificant effects for a short time, but explode at a critical point and have a huge impact on ecosystems, which makes service ecosystems difficult to control. However, due to the complexity of the service ecosystem, current data-based mining methods and time series models based on neural networks generally have low universality and interpretability. In addition, some works on service ecosystem evolution are based on computational experiments with multi-agent simulations. Their results cannot theoretically explain the conditions under which special phenomena emerge. In response, researchers spend a lot of time on tuning parameters.

This paper considers system dynamics approaches to directly model value-driven service ecosystems, thereby mining an efficient and interpretable evolution analysis method. Inspired by predator models in natural ecosystems, this paper proposes a dynamical model to analyze the nonlinear features, which are the most important features of the service ecosystem evolution, from a macroscopic perspective. Theoretical analysis and numerical simulation experiments promote the understanding of the service ecosystem evolution mechanism, thus providing an analysis and evaluation method for the governance of service ecosystems to ensure their health and sustainability. The contributions are summarized as follows:

- This paper points out the fact that value chains of supply and demand in service ecosystems are isomorphic to energy flows of predators and prey in natural ecosystems, and points out the obvious nonlinear features. Then, this paper proposes a dynamics model constructed for the service ecosystem evolution based on the Leslie-Gower model [8].
- We analyze the critical conditions for system stability and Hopf bifurcation. Especially when the time delay reaches the threshold, a periodic solution appears from the gradually stable positive equilibrium of the system. We theoretically show that reducing time delay due to service development is beneficial for the stability of the service ecosystem.
- Numerical simulations verify the effectiveness of the model and the correctness of the critical condition of the system phase transition.

2   Related Work

Service ecosystems contain multiple stakeholders and complex internal structures. Some researchers study service ecosystem evolution from the perspective of dynamic service networks. Huang et al. [5] studied the static structure of service ecosystems and proposed dynamic metrics for ecosystem evolution. Liu et al. [10] proposed a framework for identifying the evolutionary patterns of service ecosystems based on the service community. A systemic perspective asserts that studying a certain level in isolation is incomplete [11]. Some researchers model the service ecosystem evolution from the perspective of an ecosystem. Lim et al. [9] study the effects of developer dynamics on fitness in an evolutionary ecosystem model of the App Store. They also point out predator behaviors in the App ecosystem. Jia et al. [6] proposed a service population evolution model and a service community succession model of the Internet of Service based on ecosystem theory. Xue et al. [17] proposed a value entropy model linking the system operation state to the value creation efficiency. These works do not consider the important impact of the delay of service supply and have limited prediction ability and interpretability for critical points, which makes it hard to predict sudden collapses.

3   Model

3.1   Overall

Previous research on supply and demand matching often regards demand as the active side, which is due to the following considerations: whether to consume is decided by users, so the demand side holds the dominant power. It's microscopic and a representation. In fact, the service side has a stronger drive for survival and makes the best effort to capture demands, which is the essence and foundation of service ecosystem evolution. Inspired by natural ecosystems, we found that the matching of supply and demand in service ecosystems has similarities with the predation behavior in natural ecosystems.

We treat demands as prey and services as predators. Table 1 shows the comparison of evolution mechanisms between demand and service in service ecosystems and prey and predator in natural ecosystems in detail, including growth, death, etc. We also mapped the service ecosystem and the natural ecosystem as a whole, as shown in Fig. 2. In a service ecosystem, services constantly seek to match demand and gain profit. And services are developed or upgraded according to demand, thus generating a time delay. The demand population is restricted by the number of services and the environment's carrying capacity. In a natural ecosystem, predators prey on prey and obtain energy, which promotes the growth and development of the predator population. The predator population is constrained by the prey population and predation ability. The prey population depends on the number of predators and the environment's carrying capacity. The process of services matching the demands is abstracted as predators preying on prey. Value streams from demands to services are portrayed as biological energy transferred from prey to predators.

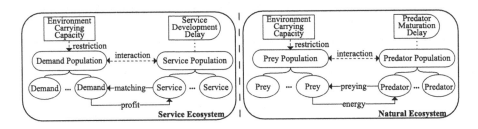

Fig. 2. Mapping of service ecosystems to natural ecosystems

Driven by value, the nonlinear features of service ecosystems are reflected in three main aspects: **1) supply and demand affect each other.** The increase in demand may attract an explosion of services. Reduced demand can lead to the death of services. **2) Mutation in service and demand.** Services and demands are evolutionary. The matching rate between supply and demand is constantly changing as well. **3) Time delay due to service development.** Service development and production are time-consuming, resulting in delays.

Table 1. Evolution mechanism of natural ecosystems and service ecosystems

Mechanism	Nature Ecosystem	Service Ecosystem
– –	*Prey*	*Demand*
Birth/Growth	Prey increases exponentially when resources are abundant and there are no predators.	Ecosystems gradually show trends of demand explosion when the supply decreases. For example, medicines and medical services are in shortage during the epidemic influenced by consumer psychology such as hoarding and panic.
Death	Prey die naturally and die when they are captured by predators. The prey then disappears in the ecosystem and turns into a source of survival energy for the predators.	Demands are time-limited. Demands that have not been satisfied for a long time will disappear from the system. If a demand is processed by a service in time, it will disappear and convert into the service's profit.
Competition	When prey density exceeds environmental carrying capacity, they will compete for resources and slow down growth.	When demand density is too high, some users will choose to avoid competition and delay the transaction, thus slowing down demand growth.
Mutation	Prey mutation evolves new abilities to avoid predation, reducing the predation rate of predators.	Demand mutation refers to the new demand derived from the original demand that is not in the system. Due to the lack of suitable supply, the matching rate of supply and demand in the system decreases.
– –	*Predator*	*Service*
Birth/Growth	Predators grow and reproduce based on their prey for energy. Exponential growth occurs when prey is abundant.	Services gain profit from demands, then optimize facilities, increase volume, and develop new services to match more demands. There may be a bullwhip effect [16] due to over-optimism about demand. A small increase in demand may lead to the emergence of a large number of services
Death	Predators die mainly because of a lack of prey.	Services die mainly because of a lack of demand. Even cloud services are deployed on demand. Service density is also constantly changing with demand. It's just easier to change
Competition	Predators compete for prey and fewer natural resources, such as water and habitat.	Service compete for demand and less social resources, such as computing resources and human resources.
Mutation	Predator mutation causes predators to evolve new abilities to better hunt and increase the rate of predation.	Service mutation refers to the development of new services that are not in the original system according to new demands or the development strategies of service providers, so as to increase the matching rate.
Time Delay	Juvenile predators have no ability to prey. There is a time delay for predator maturation.	Services under development can't match demand, thus generating a time delay for trading

However, demands are time-sensitive. If the service development time exceeds the time deadline of the demand, the demand no longer needs this service capability.

Based on these, we improve the modified Leslie-Gower model [8] to model the evolution of a service ecosystem. The density of demand and service in the service ecosystem is denoted by D and S, respectively. They are comprehensive reflections of the prosperity of demand and service. A delay term τ is added to the model to represent the service development time delay. The symbol p represents the probability that service and demand exactly match after they meet, and has the value range $(0, 1)$. It is mainly affected by mutation and the density of demand and service. The full model can be expressed as

$$\begin{cases} \frac{dD}{dt} = D\left(b_1 - d_1 - aD - \frac{pcS(t-\tau)}{1+pchD}\right) = y_1, \\ \frac{dS}{dt} = S\left(b_2 - d_2 - \frac{S}{\rho+kD}\right) = y_2, \\ \frac{dp}{dt} = p\left(\frac{S}{D} - vp\right) = y_3, \end{cases} \quad (1)$$

where all parameters are positive.

3.2   Demand Growth Model

Assuming that the growth of demand conforms to the logistic growth model. The change in demand density over time can be expressed as $\frac{dD}{dt} = D(b_1 - d_1 - aD)$, where b_1 and d_1 is the birth rate and death rate, respectively. a is the demand competition coefficient that is the inverse of the carrying capacity of the environment. Since services take time to process demand, the matching capability of service to demand is not linear with demand density. Draw on functional response in ecology [4], assuming that each service can match the demand quantity x in time t, the time for the service to handle the demand is h. Use c to represent the efficiency of supply and demand meeting. Then we can be obtained $x = Dpc(t - hx)$, i.e. $\frac{x}{t} = \frac{pcD}{1+pchD}$, where p represents the probability of service and demand match successfully. The delay term expresses that the number of services matching the demand at time t depends on the density of services at time $t - \tau$. Finally, the demand growth model is shown as y_1 in model (1).

3.3   Service Growth Model

Assuming that the growth of service conforms to the logistic growth model. The service growth model is expressed as $\frac{dS}{dt} = S\left(b_2 - d_2 - \frac{S}{C}\right)$, where b_2 is the birth rate, d_2 is the death rate, and C is the carrying capacity of the environment for services. The carrying capacity C is proportional to the density of demand [1]. In addition, the benefits that services derive from demand need to be stripped of costs. Finally, the service growth model is shown as y_2 in model (1), where k is the value conversion coefficient, which represents the value conversion ability between service and demand in the service ecosystem, ρ is the protection of the environment for the service.

3.4   Matching Probability Model

Assuming that the variation of the matching probability p with time t is described by the sigmoid function $p = \frac{1}{1+e^{-t}}$, i.e., $\frac{dp}{dt} = p(1-p)$. When demand increases(decreases), the price may increase(decrease), and the user's desire to trade may decrease(increase). Therefore, the probability p is closely related to the total amount of service and demand, which decreases with the increase of demands and increases with the increase of services. At the same time, there are continuous changes in services and demand. Mutations can bring a sudden no-match. Thus, p is related to the mutation coefficient of the new service and the new demand. We use $m_1(m_2)$ to denote the mutation coefficient of the new demand(service) relative to the original demand(service). The change in matching probability p over time can be expressed as

$$\frac{dp}{dt} = \frac{S}{D}p\left(1 - \frac{m_1 b_1 D}{m_2 b_2 S}p\right) = p\left(\frac{S}{D} - \frac{m_1 b_1}{m_2 b_2}p\right).$$

Let $v = \frac{m_1 b_1}{m_2 b_2}$, which is a non-scalar parameter that represents the ratio of demand variation to service variation intensity. Finally, the matching probability model is shown as y_3 in the model (1).

We take ride-hailing services as an example. At the time t, the demand density D is equal to the sum of the users who are in the car plus the potential demand for the ride-hailing divided by the unit area. The service density S is the total number of cars divided by the unit area. The parameter c represents that a car C encounters c potential demands at time t. But not all of these c demands can be matched with the car C. These c demands have different requirements for the quality, price, and destination of ride-hailing services. Likewise, different cars(drivers) have different demand preferences. The parameter p is used to describe the probability of matching supply and demand from a macro perspective. At the micro level, it describes how many demands in these c demands that can match the car C. Mutations are changes in requirements and the car's(driver's) preferences. The time delay can be mapped to the user's waiting time.

4   Stability and Bifurcation

4.1   Positive Equilibria

Equilibria mean that D, S, and p remain constant over time. We can get two equilibria containing 0: $E_1 = \left(\frac{b_1 - d_1}{a}, 0, 0\right)$, $E_2 = \left(\frac{b_1 - d_1}{a}, (b_2 - d_2)\left(\rho + \frac{k(b_1 - d_1)}{a}\right), 0\right)$. In addition, we get zero to three positive equilibria $E^* = (D^*, S^*, p^*)$, where D^* is the positive real roots of the equation

$$f(D) = D^3 + q_2 D^2 + q_1 D + q_0 = 0, \tag{2}$$

where

$$q = -achk(b_2 - d_2), q_0 q = -cp^2(b_2 - d_2)^2,$$
$$q_1 q = v(b_1 - d_1) - 2ck\rho(b_2 - d_2)^2 + ch\rho(b_1 - d_1)(b_2 - d_2),$$
$$q_2 q = chk(b_1 - d_1)(b_2 - d_2) - av - ach\rho(b_2 - d_2) - ck^2(b_2 - d_2)^2,$$

and $S^* = (b_2 - d_2)(\rho + kD^*)$, $p^* = \frac{S^*}{vD^*}$. Based on the root distribution characteristics of cubic equation in one unknown summarized in Lemma 3.3 [14], the distribution of roots of Eq. (2) is shown in the following lemma.

Lemma 1. *For the polynomial Eq. (2),*
i)Eq. (2) has no positive real roots, if one of the following holds: a)$q_0 \geq 0, q_1 \geq 0$, and $q_2 \geq 0$; b)$q_0 \geq 0$, and $\Delta = q_2{}^2 - 3q_1 \leq 0$.
ii)Eq. (2) has positive real roots, if one of the following holds: a)$q_0 \leq 0$; b)$q_0 \geq 0, \Delta = q_2^2 - 3q_1 \geq 0, D_0^* = \frac{-q_2 + \sqrt{\Delta}}{3} \geq 0$, and $f(D_0^*) \leq 0$.

In the following, we focus on the system features near positive equilibrium E^*.

4.2 Stability and Hopf Bifurcation Depends on Time Delay

This subsection discusses the stability condition of the system and Hopf bifurcation depending on the time delay τ. Linearizing system (1) at the equilibrium point E^*, we can obtain the characteristic equation

$$\begin{vmatrix} \lambda - a_{11} a_{12}e^{-\lambda\tau} & a_{13} \\ -a_{21} & \lambda - a_{22} & 0 \\ a_{31} & -a_{32} & \lambda - a_{33} \end{vmatrix} = 0, \tag{3}$$

where

$$a_{11} = b_1 - d_1 - 2aD^* - \frac{p^*cS^*}{(1 + p^*chD^*)^2}, a_{12} = \frac{p^*cD^*}{1 + p^*chD^*}, a_{13} = \frac{cS^*D^*}{(1 + p^*chD^*)^2},$$
$$a_{21} = (b_2 - d_2)^2 k, a_{22} = -(b_2 - d_2), a_{31} = \frac{S^*p^*}{D^{*2}}, a_{32} = \frac{p^*}{D^*}, a_{33} = -vp^*.$$

After calculation, the following equation can be obtained,

$$\lambda^3 + A_2\lambda^2 + A_1\lambda + A_0 + (B_1\lambda + B_0)e^{-\lambda\tau} = 0, \tag{4}$$

which is a third-degree transcendental polynomial, where

$$A_0 = a_{21}a_{32}a_{13} - a_{11}a_{22}a_{33} + a_{13}a_{31}a_{22}, A_1 = a_{11}a_{22} + a_{11}a_{33} + a_{22}a_{33} - a_{13}a_{31},$$
$$A_2 = -(a_{11} + a_{22} + a_{33}), B_0 = -a_{12}a_{21}a_{33}, B_1 = a_{12}a_{21}.$$

Based on nonlinear system theory, a positive equilibrium point is asymptotically stable if all the roots of Eq. (4) have negative real parts [7].
    Case1. For $\tau = 0$, Eq. (4) can be simplified to

$$\lambda^3 + A_2\lambda^2 + (A_1 + B_1)\lambda + A_0 + B_0 = 0. \tag{5}$$

Analyzing the characteristic polynomial by Routh-Hurwitz criterion [12], we can get the following lemma.

Lemma 2. *The system (1) is locally asymptotically stable at the positive equilibrium if the following hypotheses hold:*

$$A_2 > 0, A_0 + B_0 > 0, (A_1 + B_1)A_2 - (A_0 + B_0) > 0.$$

Case2. For $\tau > 0$, we consider the third-degree transcendental polynomial Eq. (4). Applying the Hopf bifurcation existence theorem [3], we obtain:

Lemma 3. *System (1) undergoes a Hopf bifurcation depend on τ near equilibrium E^*, if all the following conditions hold:*
i)Eq. (4) has a pair of simple pure imaginary eigenvalues λ_0 and $\overline{\lambda_0}$;
ii) all the remaining eigenvalues λ_j for any integer m, inequality $\lambda_j \neq m\lambda_0$ holds;
*iii)*Re $\left(\lambda'(\tau_j^{(k)}) \right) \neq 0.$

We assume that $i\omega(\omega > 0)$ is a pure imaginary root of Eq. (4). After substitution by Euler's formula, we obtain

$$i\omega^3 - A_2\omega^2 + A_1 i\omega + (B_1 i\omega + B_0)(\cos \omega\tau - i \sin \omega\tau) = 0.$$

Separating the real and imaginary parts, we have

$$-\omega^3 + A_1\omega = B_0 \sin \omega\tau - B_1\omega \cos \omega\tau, \ A_2\omega^2 - A_0 = B_0 \cos \omega\tau + B_1\omega \sin \omega\tau.$$
$$(6)$$

The trigonometric terms can be eliminated by squaring the two formulas and adding them together. Then, we get

$$(\omega^3 - A_1\omega)^2 + (A_2\omega^2 - A_0)^2 = B_0^2 + B_1^2\omega^2.$$

Let

$$h(\omega) = \omega^6 + C_2\omega^4 + C_1\omega^2 + C_0 = 0, \tag{7}$$

where

$$C_0 = A_0^2 - B_0^2, C_1 = A_1^2 - 2A_0A_2 - B_1^2, C_2 = A_2^2 - 2A_1.$$

Let $x = \omega^2$, Eq. 7 becomes a cubic equation in x:

$$h(x) = x^3 + C_2x^2 + C_1x + C_0 = 0. \tag{8}$$

Replacing C_0, C_1, C_2 and $h(x)$ for the q_0, q_1, q_2 and $f(D)$ respectively in Lemma 1, the conditions for the existence of positive real roots in Eq. (8) can be obtained. Assuming that Eq. (8) has positive real roots, without loss of generality, we suppose that Eq. (8) has three positive roots $x_j(j = 1, 2, 3)$, correspondingly, $\omega_j(j = 1, 2, 3)$ is the three positive roots of Eq.(7). Substituting ω_j into Eq. (6) and solving for τ, we get

$$\sin \omega_j \tau = \frac{(A_2 B_1 - B_0)\omega_j^3 + (B_0 A_1 - A_0 B_1)\omega_j}{B_0^2 + B_1^2 \omega_j^2},$$

$$\cos \omega_j \tau = \frac{B_1 \omega_j^4 + (A_2 B_0 - A_1 B_1)\omega_j^2 - A_0 B_0}{B_0^2 + B_1^2 \omega_j^2}.$$

Then

$$\tau_j^{(k)} = \begin{cases} \dfrac{1}{\omega_j}(\arccos \cos \omega_j \tau + 2\pi k), \sin \omega_j \tau \geq 0, \\ \dfrac{1}{\omega_j}(2\pi - \arccos \cos \omega_j \tau + 2\pi k), \sin \omega_j \tau < 0, \end{cases}$$

where $j = 1, 2, 3$ and $k = 0, 1, 2, ...$, thus $\pm i\omega_j$ is a pair of pure imaginary roots of Eq. (4) with $\tau = \tau_j^{(k)}$. Let $\lambda(\tau) = \alpha(\tau) + i\omega(\tau)(\omega > 0)$ be the root of Eq. (4), then $\alpha(\tau_j^{(k)}) = 0$ and $\omega(\tau_j^{(k)}) = \omega_j$ are satisfied near $\tau = \tau_j^{(k)}$. We define

$$\tau_0 = \tau_{j_0}^{(0)} = \min_{1 \leq j \leq 3} \left\{ \tau_j^{(0)} \right\}, \omega_0 = \omega_{j_0}, x_0 = x_{j_0}. \tag{9}$$

Here, we get the stability conclusion of positive equilibria by corollary 2.3 and 2.4 [13], which are about the zero-point characteristics of transcendental equations.

Theorem 1. τ_0 is defined by (9), if system (1) is locally asymptotically stable at the positive equilibrium E^*:

i)If Eq. (8) has no positive real roots, then the roots of the characteristic equation Eq. (4) with $\tau \in [0, +\infty)$ have negative real parts, thus system (1) is asymptotically stable at E^* with $\tau \in [0, +\infty)$;

ii)If Eq. (8) has positive real roots, then the roots of the characteristic equation Eq. (4) with $\tau \in [0, \tau_0)$ have negative real parts, thus system (1) is asymptotically stable at E^* with $\tau \in [0, \tau_0)$.

Then, we have the following lemma.

Lemma 4. Suppose $h'(\omega_j^2) \neq 0$, then

i)$\lambda(\tau_j^{(k)}) = i\omega(\tau_j^{(k)})$ is a simple root of Eq. (4);

ii)Re$\left(\lambda'(\tau_j^{(k)})\right) \neq 0$, and the sign of Re$\left(\lambda'(\tau_j^{(k)})\right)$ depends on $h'(\omega_j^2)$.

The proof is omitted for space reasons. Combined with Theorem 1, we get the following conclusions:

Theorem 2. $\tau_j^{(k)}$, τ_0 is defined by (6) and (9), system (1) undergoes a Hopf bifurcation at $\tau = \tau_j^{(k)}$ if the following hypotheses holds:

i)Eq. (8) has positive real roots;

ii)$h'(\omega_j^2) \neq 0$.

4.3 Hopf Bifurcation Depends on Other Parameters

Based on the Hopf bifurcation existence theorem [3], we know that the characteristic equation has a pair of conjugate pure imaginary roots when the system undergoes a Hopf bifurcation. If the characteristic equation Eq. (5) has a pair of conjugate pure imaginary roots, Eq. (5) can be written as $(\lambda + \mu_1)(\lambda^2 + \mu_2) = 0$, where $\mu_1 > 0$ and $\mu_2 > 0$. Then we can get

$$\begin{cases} \mu_1 = A_2, \\ \mu_2 = A_1 + B_1, \\ \mu_1\mu_2 = A_0 + B_0. \end{cases}$$

Thus we can obtain the conditions under which a Hopf bifurcation of the system occurs.

Lemma 5. *Eq. (5) has a pair of conjugate pure imaginary roots if the following hypotheses hold:*

$$A_2 > 0, A_1 + B_1 > 0, (A_1 + B_1)A_2 = A_0 + B_0.$$

Combining lemma 2, it can be concluded that holding $A_2 > 0$, $A_0 + B_0 > 0$ and $A_1 + B_1 > 0$, the system changes from stable to unstable when the parameters keep changing to make $(A_1 + B_1)A_2 \leq (A_0 + B_0)$. Periodic solutions appear at $(A_1 + B_1)A_2 = (A_0 + B_0)$. It also needs to verify the transversal condition. Here, we will analyze the competition coefficient a as an example. Using the similar approach as in the previous Subsect. 4.2, we can obtain if $a_{22}a_{33} - (A_1 + B_1 + (a_{22} + a_{33})A_2) \neq 0$, then $\mathrm{Re}\,(\lambda'(a)) \neq 0$. The proof is omitted for space reasons.

5 Numerical Simulations

We show specific examples and numerical simulations. We verify the stability conditions of the system and the Hopf bifurcation conditions related to the time delay τ and the competition coefficient a. The parameter values for these examples are shown in Table 2. These parameters are estimated based on our experience.

Table 2. Parameter settings of examples

	b_1	d_1	b_2	d_2	a	c	h	ρ	k	m_1	m_2
1	0.9	0.5	0.6	0.3	0.1	100	0.5	0.1	0.4	0.1	0.2
2	0.9	0.1	0.48	0.3	0.1	76	0.06	0.09	0.4	0.2	0.8
3	0.95	0.45	0.65	0.32	0.01	25	0.3	0.27	0.2	0.05	0.12
4	0.89	0.56	0.44	0.278	0.1735	393	0.33	0.078	0.36	0.026	0.26

5.1 System Stability

Two examples are presented to verify the stability conditions of the positive equilibrium point. The first is for stability, which parameter values are shown in the first line in Table 2. According to Lemma 2 in Sect. 4.2, the A_2, $A_0 + B_0$ and $(A_1 + B_1)A_2 - (A_0 + B_0)$ on $E^*(1.3643, 0.1937, 0.1893)$ are about 0.3338, 0.0048, and 0.0149, respectively. They're all greater than zero. Thus E^* is a stable equilibrium point. The results of the numerical simulations are shown in Fig. 3. It can be seen that D, S, and p converge to the equilibrium point E^* as time varies. The second example is for an unstable equilibrium point. The settings of the parameters are shown in the second line in Table 2. The stability conditions on $E^*(1.0783, 0.0938, 0.1856)$ are about 0.0445, 0.0045, and -0.0033. The positive equilibrium point is unstable. As shown in Fig. 4, the system will be attracted to the equilibrium near 0, which will cause the ecosystem to collapse.

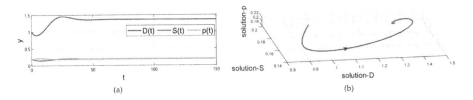

Fig. 3. Waveform plots and portrait diagram with values in the first line in Table 2 and $\tau = 0, D_0 = 1, S_0 = 0.2, p_0 = 0.18$.

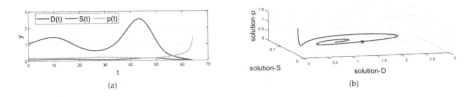

Fig. 4. Waveform plots and portrait diagram with parameters in the second line in Table 2 and $\tau = 0, D_0 = 1, S_0 = 0.2, p_0 = 0.18$.

5.2 Hopf Bifurcation Depends on Time Delay

We use an example to validate the Hopf Bifurcation conditions depending on the time delay τ. The settings of parameters are shown in the third line in Table 2. After calculation, we obtain that the positive equilibrium point E^* is approximately (27.8662, 1.9283, 0.1136). When $\tau = 0$, the A_2, $A_0 + B_0$ and $(A_1+B_1)A_2-(A_0+B_0)$ on E^* are about 0.4655, 0.0063, and 0.0488, respectively.

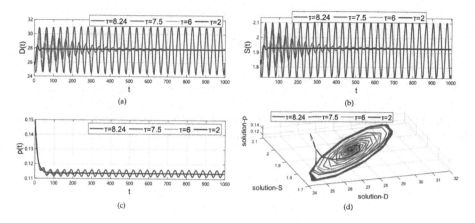

Fig. 5. Waveform plots and portrait diagram for Hopf bifurcation depending on the time delay τ with parameters in the third line in Table 2 and $\tau_0 \approx 8.2341, D_0 = 26, S_0 = 2, p_0 = 0.15$.

Thus, E^* is asymptotically stable. According to Eq. (7) we can get $\omega_0 \approx 0.1747$ and further we can get $\tau_0 \approx 8.2341$. We compute the transversal condition and get $h'(\omega_0^2) \approx 0.00014 > 0$. Therefore, according to Theorem 1 and Theorem 2, the system is asymptotically stable at E^* with $\tau \in [0, 8.2341)$ and undergoes a Hopf bifurcation at $\tau \approx 8.2341$. We selected four different values of τ for numerical simulations. The results are shown in Fig. 5. When $\tau = 2$, it converges to near the equilibrium point in a short time. As the time delay increases, the system fluctuates more and more. When $\tau = 7.5 < \tau_0$, the system starts with big fluctuations but eventually stabilizes around the equilibrium point. When $\tau = 8.24 > \tau_0$, the system will not converge to the equilibrium point and will continue to fluctuate periodically.

Such periodic fluctuations are dangerous. A slight perturbation may cause the system to collapse. Recurring changes in demand density and service density can lead to unstable supply and demand relationships, which may result in a waste of social resources. For example, if users wait too long for ride-hailing services, they may cancel and re-book frequently which brings chaos. To some extent, this explains theoretically why the e-commerce and service ecosystem can continue to grow and prosper steadily after the efficiency of logistics systems has increased and agile development has become popular in the information age.

5.3   Hopf Bifurcation Depends on Competition Coefficient

We verify the bifurcation condition depends on the competition coefficient a. The parameter settings of the system are shown in the fourth line in Table 2. Using the method in 4.3, after calculation, $a \approx 0.1735$ is a solution that makes the equation $(A_1 + B_1)A_2 = A_0 + B_0$ hold as well as $A_2 > 0, A_1 + B_1 > 0$. Since the value of the positive equilibrium depends on a, the equilibrium changes as

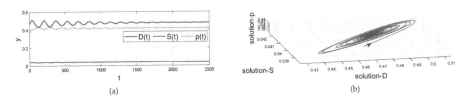

Fig. 6. Waveform plots and portrait diagram before bifurcation with values in the fourth line in Table 2 and $a = 0.1730, \tau = 0, D_0 = 0.47, S_0 = 0.04, p_0 = 0.35$.

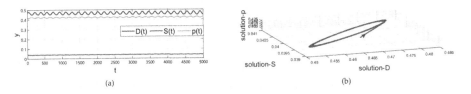

Fig. 7. Waveform plots and portrait diagram during bifurcation with values in the fourth line in Table 2 and $a = 0.1735, \tau = 0, D_0 = 0.47, S_0 = 0.04, p_0 = 0.4$.

a changes, unlike the example in 5.2. We choose values 0.1730, 0.1735 of a for numerical simulations.

When $a = 0.1730$, the stability criteria on the positive equilibrium point $E^*(0.4777, 0.0405, 0.4191)$ is about 0.0912, 0.00016, and 0.00003, respectively. The system gradually converges to E^*. The numerical simulation results are shown in Fig. 6. At this point, $\text{Re}\,(\lambda'(a)) \approx 0.0341 > 0$. This means that as the eigenvalues of the characteristic equation of the system increase as a increases, the system may change from stable to unstable. When $a = 0.1735$, the stability criteria on $E^*(0.4667, 0.0399, 0.4222)$ are about 0.0887, 0.00011, and 0.000001. E^* is close to the bifurcation condition. Periodic solutions appear. The numerical simulation results are shown in Fig. 7. At this point, $\text{Re}\,(\lambda'(a)) \approx 0.0345 > 0$. Based on the previous theoretical analysis, the system is undergoing a bifurcation.

According to the model, the competition coefficient is the reciprocal of the carrying capacity of the environment. When the competition factor of demand is too high, part of the demand can't be shown due to the restrictions of the market environment, resulting in fluctuations and instability. For example of ride-hailing services, during the pandemic, social environment and policy restrictions on people's demand for ride-hailing services. Similar examples include the network throughput capacity on user demand and resource environment carrying capacity on human economic activities [2], etc. Expansion of the carrying capacity of the environment for demand is beneficial for the stable development of the system.

6   Conclusion

This paper proposes a method that uses differential equations to model demand, service, and supply-demand matching probabilities in service ecosystems. We apply nonlinear system dynamics theory and numerical simulations to analyze and validate the evolutionary mechanisms of service ecosystems. Our model provides a strong basis for assessing the evolutionary direction, stability, and sustainability of service ecosystems. Our model is easily extensible. In the future, we'll refine our model for specific services. We can incorporate more influencing factors, such as group behavior of species and invasion of new species into the model.

References

1. Aziz-Alaoui, M., Okiye, M.D.: Boundedness and global stability for a predator-prey model with modified Leslie-Gower and Holling-type ii schemes. Appl. Math. Lett. **16**(7), 1069–1075 (2003)
2. Bao, H., et al.: Resources and environmental pressure, carrying capacity, and governance: a case study of Yangtze river economic belt. Sustainability **12**(4), 1576 (2020)
3. Hassard, B.D., Kazarinoff, N., Wan, Y-H.: Theory and applications of HOPF bifurcation, vol. 41. CUP Archive (1981)
4. Holling, C.S.: Some characteristics of simple types of predation and parasitism1. Can. Entomol. **91**(7), 385–398 (1959). https://doi.org/10.4039/Ent91385-7
5. Huang, K., Fan, Y., Tan, W.: An empirical study of programmable web: A network analysis on a service-mashup system. In: 2012 IEEE 19th International Conference on Web Services, pp. 552–559. IEEE (2012)
6. Jia, Z., Huang, S., Fan, Y.: Research on the synecological model and dynamic evolution mechanism of service internet. In: 2020 IEEE International Conference on Services Computing (SCC), pp. 12–19. IEEE (2020)
7. Lefschetz, S., Salle, J.P.L.: Differential—difference equations. In: International Symposium on Nonlinear Differential Equations and Nonlinear Mechanics, pp. 155–171. Elsevier (1963)
8. Leslie, P., Gower, J.: The properties of a stochastic model for the predator-prey type of interaction between two species. Biometrika **47**(3/4), 219–234 (1960)
9. Lim, S.L., Bentley, P.J., Ishikawa, F.: The effects of developer dynamics on fitness in an evolutionary ecosystem model of the app store. IEEE Trans. Evol. Comput. **20**(4), 529–545 (2015)
10. Liu, M., Tu, Z., Xu, H., Xu, X., Wang, Z.: Community-based service ecosystem evolution analysis. Service Oriented Computing and Applications, pp. 1–14 (2022)
11. Meynhardt, T., Chandler, J.D., Strathoff, P.: Systemic principles of value co-creation: synergetics of value and service ecosystems. J. Bus. Res. **69**(8), 2981–2989 (2016)
12. Routh, E.J.: A Treatise on the Stability of a Given State of Motion. Macmillan and Company, New York (1877)
13. Ruan, S., Wei, J.: On the zeros of transcendental functions with applications to stability of delay differential equations with two delays (2003)
14. Tipsri, S., Chinviriyasit, W.: The effect of time delay on the dynamics of an SEIR model with nonlinear incidence. Chaos, Solitons Fractals **75**, 153–172 (2015)

15. Tzafestas, S.G.: Energy, Information, Feedback. Adaptation and Self-organization. Springer, Cham (2018). https://doi.org/10.1007/978-3-319-66999-1
16. Wang, X., Disney, S.M.: The bullwhip effect: progress, trends and directions. Eur. J. Oper. Res. **250**(3), 691–701 (2016)
17. Xue, X., Chen, Z., Wang, S., Feng, Z., Duan, Y., Zhou, Z.: Value entropy: a systematic evaluation model of service ecosystem evolution. IEEE Trans. Serv. Comput. **15**, 1760–1763 (2020)

A Middleware for Hybrid Blockchain Applications: Towards Fast, Affordable, and Accountable Integration

Olzhas Yessenbayev[1] , Marco Comuzzi[1(✉)] , Giovanni Meroni[2] ,
and Dung Chi Duy Nguyen[1]

[1] Ulsan National Institute of Science and Technology, Ulsan, Korea
{yess,mcomuzzi,int2k}@unist.ac.kr
[2] Technical University of Denmark, Kgs. Lyngby, Denmark
giom@dtu.dk

Abstract. Hybrid blockchain architectures combine centralized applications, like enterprise systems, with (public) blockchain to implement additional functionality, such as tamper-proof record keeping. To reduce the latency and cost of using a public blockchain, these systems may rely on batching of transactions or general-state channel networks. While reducing costs, the former increase the latency. With the latter, only major state updates are recorded on-chain, while most transactions history remains only on the channels. This paper describes a novel solution that combines the benefits of both approaches to decrease the latency and cost of hybrid blockchain applications. We propose to combine a local blockchain that runs on a centralized server to provide near-immediate state update confirmation, with a batching mechanism sending transactions to a public blockchain for record-keeping at a most convenient time. We also introduce a dispute mechanism promoting the prompt delivery of correct batches to the public blockchain by the application provider, thereby deterring malicious behaviours. The solution is motivated by a fintech use case, for which we also show the implementation of a prototype and an experimental evaluation of the latency and cost savings.

Keywords: Blockchain · Ethereum · gas price · latency ·
meta-transaction delegation

1 Introduction

Blockchains, as transparent and open databases, enable immutable records traceable to the original signer; through smart contracts, they can provide automated rule enforcement [1]. Originally developed for decentralized peer-to-peer applications, blockchains also enable the so-called *hybrid blockchain architectures*, where users interact with traditional centralized applications augmented with blockchain [2]. Specifically, the use of public blockchains presents intriguing scenarios in enterprise applications. For instance, a corporate enterprise

F. Monti et al. (Eds.): ICSOC 2023, LNCS 14419, pp. 307–322, 2023.
https://doi.org/10.1007/978-3-031-48421-6_21

resource planning (ERP) system paired with the Ethereum blockchain can provide tamper-proof record keeping and digitized asset tracing. Platforms like Provenance leverage this to prove product authenticity on public blockchains [3], while MedRec employs the Ethereum blockchain to offer secure medical records, thus enhancing healthcare data interoperability [4].

The architectural limitations of public blockchains, such as latency from a few seconds to several hours [5] and volatile transaction costs depending on network congestion and transaction complexity [6], still limit the enterprise-wide adoption of hybrid architectures. To address these issues, batching and general state channel networks have emerged as viable solutions. Batching involves sending multiple transactions at once, instead of individually. In this way, the fixed per-transaction costs [7] can be reduced. However, latency could increase, since the transactions are not processed until the whole batch is sent. General-state channel networks allow near-instant interactions between participants by simulating smart contract state transitions [8] until the final state is posted on the public blockchain. However, most of the transaction history is recorded off-chain. Therefore, this option may not suit hybrid blockchain applications, where the transaction history often serves as a comprehensive, tamper-proof record for traceability and auditing purposes.

In this paper, we present a novel solution that combines the strengths of the two approaches described above. We propose a middleware system that can be integrated with a centralized application to provide reliable and immutable record-keeping on a public blockchain, limiting the application latency and costs. The system consists of two key components: (i) a local private blockchain to instantly simulate state transitions and (ii) an asynchronous process batch-transferring local transactions to the public blockchain network. A *target* smart contract used for record-keeping on the public blockchain is replicated on a local private blockchain, enabling near-instantaneous transaction confirmation. The transactions are then cost-efficiently batch-sent to a public blockchain network for permanent and immutable record-keeping. By maintaining the transaction order within batches, the proposed approach guarantees consistent execution across both networks. We also introduce a *dispute* mechanism that creates an incentive for the application provider to eventually send all the correct batches to the public blockchain, thus preventing opportunistic or generally malicious behaviours. The proposed approach is inspired by the needs of a real-life fintech company in South Korea providing a flexible salary payment service that uses a public blockchain for transparent record-keeping. Besides describing this use case, we also experimentally evaluate the proposed approach in terms of cost reduction as a function of the batch size, and latency improvement.

The remainder of the paper is organized as follows. Section 2 introduces the use case and the requirements, while Sect. 3 presents our solution. Section 4 discusses the implementation and the experimental evaluation. Section 5 compares our solution with existing literature. Finally, Sect. 6 draws the conclusions and outlines future work.

2 Problem Definition

Section 2.1 introduces the fintech use case that inspired the development of the proposed solution, whereas Sect. 2.2 extrapolates more general requirements that the proposed solution must address.

2.1 A Fintech Motivating Case Study

GivingDays Inc.[1] is a financial intermediary providing a flexible payment service (Thankspay) enabling employees of partner companies to request salary advances through their application. The advances are immediately paid by GivingDays (that is, earlier than the scheduled pay-day) and charged to the partner company later.

While managing funds purely in cryptocurrency is infeasibile, the ThanksPay service can leverage public blockchain to ensure traceability, transparency, and asset reusability. Through private key encryption, blockchain can allow to publicly verify that each salary advance request genuinely originates from a worker, and is not forged arbitrarily by the ThanksPay service to maliciously charge partners. This eliminates the need for laborious server audits. Smart contracts also enable automated and transparent compliance with salary withdrawal regulations. Finally, the open nature of public blockchains allows to extend the service to other use-cases, such as flexible loans.

2.2 Requirements

Inspired by the Thankspay use case, we identified a set of requirements that must be addressed by a more general system that provides transparent record-keeping by adopting a hybrid blockchain architecture.

R1: Minimize application latency: The latency of public blockchain is usually high and unpredictable, which might jeopardize an application whose logic relies on blockchain as a database. For instance, the Ethereum latency is 15–20 seconds for simple cases and significantly higher for complex transactions.

R2: Minimize transaction fees: As the number of transactions to be recorded grows, the costs of facilitating them also increase. Moreover, transaction fees on public blockchains like Ethereum might be extremely volatile, posing additional challenges for a record-keeping system.

R3: Maintain full transaction history: Record-keeping systems must demonstrate an unalterable record of every transaction. This requires each transaction to go through rules-checking and storage on the public blockchain. Therefore, posting only periodic hash updates would not be sufficient.

R4: Guarantee transaction order and inclusion: Reordering or excluding user transactions can alter the state of the blockchain. If the correct ordering is not enforced, the service owner can exploit this for its own benefit.

---

[1] https://www.thankspay.co.kr/.

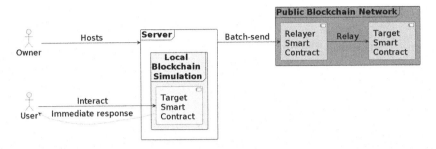

Fig. 1. Overview of the system

R5: Provide a balanced approach to user self-custody: It would be infeasible to expect each user to own a cryptowallet to fund and manage transactions. On the other hand, centralizing the entire process within a backend service recording all the transactions on behalf of the users would nullify the trust brought by blockchain technology [2].

3   Solution Design

We propose a middleware solution functioning as an intermediary between users and the public blockchain. The static system components are outlined in Sect. 3.1, with a use-case scenario discussed in Sect. 3.2. Economic incentives ensuring the service owner's adherence to the batch-process (i.e. the dispute mechanism) are explained in Sect. 3.3.

3.1   System Architecture

A high-level overview of the proposed middleware solution is sketched in Fig. 1. It involves the following entities:

- **Owner**: the host of the service (e.g., GivingDays hosting the ThanksPay service in our motivating use case), which deploys smart contracts on the local and the public blockchains.
- **Users**: the end-users of the owner's service (e.g., the workers and partner companies in the motivating use case).

User actions are recorded as invocations of a *Target smart contract* deployed at a *public blockchain network*, representing the specific business application logic (i.e., logic of the Thankspay service in the motivating use case, determining, for instance, when workers can receive their salary in advance). To facilitate the user interactions with it, the owner instantiates a *local private blockchain* and deploys in it a replica of the target smart contract for the lifetime of the application. The local private blockchan instantly processes user invocations, enabling any business logic dependencies on the target smart contract state to be immediately fulfilled. Besides hosting the target smart contract, the public blockchain network also hosts a *Relayer smart contract*, responsible for batch-transferring transaction invocations from the local blockchain to the public blockchain's Target smart contract.

Users sign what are known as meta-transactions [2], transactions signed by a user's private key but sent by a third-party service provider. This technique allows users to interact with smart contracts without having to interact with the Ethereum blockchain, addressing **R5**.

The meta-transactions are immediately executed on the local blockchain for instant feedback (i.e., satisfying **R1**). When sufficient local transactions are accumulated, the server batch-transfers them to the public network, combining reduced per-transaction invocation costs with the possibility of strategically selecting the best time to send a batch to minimize transaction costs (addressing **R2** and **R3**). The users' signed messages contain a batch identifier and a relative position within the batch, guaranteeing the same order of transaction execution. By leaving a hash-trace of which transactions were executed inside of a public blockchain, we enable users to open and win monetary disputes against transaction exclusion from malicious owners, thus addressing **R4**.

To ensure state consistency between the local and the public blockchains, the *Target smart contract* follows constraints similar to the ones of general state channel contracts [9]:

1. **Limited access**: they should only be invoked by authorized users. In the local blockchain, this is ensured by giving access only to the users of the service. On the public blockchain, all calls to the target smart contract are routed through the Relayer contract.
2. **Insulation from external contracts**: they should not depend on external contract states, allowing the application state to be accurately predicted in advance, before on-chain execution.
3. **No global clock dependencies**: they should ban references to `block.timestamp`, given the unpredictability of when a transaction will be executed on the public blockchain.
4. **Modifying references to the senders of transactions**: in a meta-transaction executed via a relayer contract, `msg.sender` refers to the initiating address (i.e., the Relayer), not the original user. Therefore, the sender's identity needs to be included in the relayed transactions for the target smart contract to identify the user actually sending a transaction.

The latter can be addressed by passing the deciphered user address to the *Target smart contract* when invoked by the Relayer smart contract. This is done in an implementation-specific way (we discuss how we address this in Ethereum in Sect. 4).

3.2 System In-Use View

The system usage involves two stages: i) local execution of meta-transactions, which users sign and exchange with the owner and ii) an asynchronous process batch-transferring these to the public blockchain.

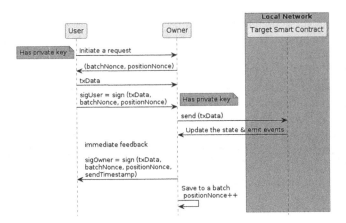

Fig. 2. Message exchange

Local Execution of Meta-Transactions. Upon user registration, a unique private key is created locally within a user's applications. This private key can be used to produce a unique digital signature against a given message, ensuring that the signed data has not been tampered with (integrity of the message) and that the true signer's public account can be recovered (identity of the user). Users employ the private key to sign the digest (hash) of meta-transactions. In particular, the digest is computed from the following data:

(a) txData: a byte-encoded representation of the selected blockchain function (e.g., requestSalaryAdvance) and specified parameters (e.g., amount).
(b) batchNonce: a per-batch nonce to prevent malicious replay attacks.
(c) positionNonce: a transaction's position in the batch to prevent reordering and maintain execution order integrity.

To exchange these meta-transactions with the owner and obtain the owner's commitment to including the transaction into a batch, users follow the process outlined in Fig. 2:

1. Users *initiate a request* to the owner, who responds with (batchNonce, positionNonce).
2. Users generate txData and their signature, sigUser, and send these to the owner.
3. The owner then *sends* the txData to the local network, which simulates the transaction, *updates the state*, and emits the necessary events for *immediate feedback* to the users. The owner also sends their signature (sigOwner) over the same parameters (with the addition of sendTimestamp, the timestamp by which the transaction is meant to be sent).

The sigOwner acts as proof of the owner's commitment to include the transaction into the next batch destined for the public network (important for the

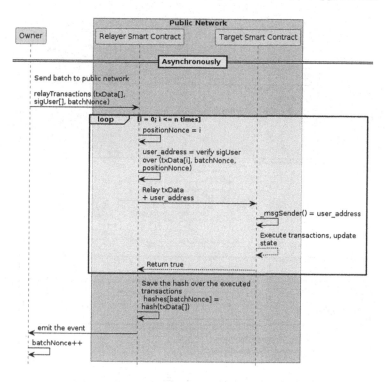

Fig. 3. Asynchronous sending

dispute procedure in Sect. 3.3). Until then, the users should assume the transaction has not yet been processed.

The owner can only process new transactions after the current one completes or times out. If a user fails to provide the necessary `txData` and `sigUser` within a specified timeout, the transaction is rejected and its `positionNonce` can be reused for the next transaction.

Asynchronous Batch-Transfer Process. Once enough transactions are collected, the owner (see Fig. 3) *sends a batch to public network* through the Relayer smart contract. The `relayTransactions` function iterates through the meta-transactions. For each set of (`positionNonce`, `batchNonce`, `txData[i]`), the `verify` function decodes a user's public address from the message hash composed of these parameters and the given `sigUser[i]`. Any alteration to the message hash or signature will result in a different public address than the original one, preserving the integrity of the signed message and authenticating the signer's identity. The Relayer smart contract then relays `txData` to the target smart contract, together with the original user's public address. The target smart contract *executes the transaction* and *updates its state* (and corresponding digital assets) accordingly, on the behalf of the original user.

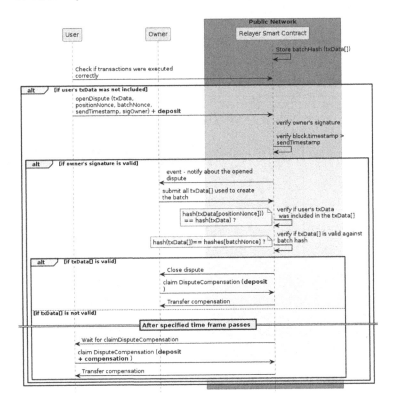

Fig. 4. Dispute procedure

Upon the completion of all transactions in the batch, the Relayer calculates and *saves the hash* over the executed transactions (`txData[]`), providing a reference for maintaining a consistent transaction execution order across batches. Afterwards, the smart contract *emits the event* signifying successful processing; the owner increments the nonce associated with the batch (`batchNonce`) off-chain, allowing for the processing of the next batch of transactions.

The signature verification coupled with user address relaying to the receiving target smart contract enables users to maintain unique and persistent on-chain identities in meta-transactions. The finalization of transaction batches and the storage of their associated hashes provide a traceable reference for maintaining accountability in the system, as detailed in the next section.

3.3 Maintaining Accountability of Meta-Transactions

A malicious owner can potentially disrupt the system by (i) not including certain local transactions in a batch sent to the public blockchain or (ii) modifying the order of execution of the transactions. In the Thankspay service scenario, this may be driven by financial objectives to manipulate the workers' account balances and forge undue settlement.

To address this issue, we introduce a dispute procedure fully managed by the public Relayer smart contract that allows for the monetary punishment of any owner misconduct (see Fig. 4)q. This mechanism requires the users to make a deposit of amount of cryptocurrency X to open a dispute, discouraging frivolous claims. If the owner does not address a dispute within a specified timeframe, the user can claim a compensation of X + Y, disincentivizing the owners from any wrongdoing. To enforce compensation payouts for successful disputes, the Relayer smart contract is required to have sufficient funding to continue operating.

Implementing the dispute mechanism requires the following:

1. *Proof of the owner's commitment to include the transaction.* The owner is required to sign a user's transactions, with the addition of a `sendTimestamp`, as part of the feedback to the user (see Sect. 3.2). This signature, as `sigOwner`, ensures that transactions are committed for inclusion in the batch. Conversely, without this signature, the transactions are not "confirmed" from a users' perspective. If a transaction is signed by the owner and not sent to the public blockchain, the user can use these signatures as proof of commitment on the public blockchain that has not been fulfilled.
2. *Trace of transaction execution.* To leave an efficient trace of executed transactions in `relayTransactions` without storing the entire array, all `txData[]` in a batch are hashed together and stored in a mapping (`batchId =>` `batchHash`).

The `sendTimestamp` is added to determine if the owner's promised timestamp has passed by comparing it to `block.timestamp`, therefore preventing premature disputes.

If the user is satisfied with the transaction execution, the process is concluded. If not, the user can initiate the dispute, which unfolds as follows (3.3):

(a) The user opens the dispute by invoking `openDispute` with the owner's signature as proof of commitment and the specified parameters (`txData + nonceId + batchId + sendTimestamp`). If *the owner's signature is valid* for these parameters, and `sendTimestamp > block.timestamp`, the dispute is successfully opened, and a corresponding event *notifies about the opened dispute* is emitted.
(b) The owner may close the dispute if they can provide evidence that the user's transaction was included and executed correctly. The owner *submits all* `txData[]` *used to create the batch* at a given `batchNonce` and calculates its hash. They win the dispute if the `txData` at `nonceId` matches the user's data, **and** the hash of the array `txData[]` corresponds to the recorded `batchHash` for that `batchNonce`.
(c) If the owner fails to resolve the dispute *after the specified timeframe passes*, the user is eligible to claim compensation.

Overall, this process safeguards against fraud. `sigOwner` only works for the given (`txData, positionNonce, batchNonce, sendTimestamp`) combination, deterring users from fabricating commitments. The hashing of all `txData[]` on-chain also prevents false inclusion of a user's `txData` in the owner's proof, if it was not genuinely executed.

4 Implementation and Evaluation

The prototype implementation[2] of the Thankspay service is detailed in Sect. 4.1, with an experimental evaluation presented in Sect. 4.2.

4.1 Thankspay Service Implementation

Target Smart Contract. The Thankspay target smart contract is implemented as an Ethereum ERC-20 token, called *ThanksPaySalaryToken*, customized to manage salary advances, debt tracking, and settlements. The salary advances are implemented through "minting" and "burning" of the tokens. On a designated salary day, partner companies mint new tokens equivalent to the workers' salaries, replenishing balances and offsetting previous advances. As workers request salary advances, these tokens are burned, reducing the worker's balance and increasing the debt of the partner company, as tracked by the `partnerDebt` mapping. The debt is settled off-chain by transferring real funds to Thankspay, which is then reflected on-chain via the `settlePartnerDebt` function. The ERC-20 standard provides pre-defined functions and events for token management, making the solution more generalizable to other use-cases; token-burning functionality is inherited from `ERC20Burnable`. To minimize on-chain data, worker salaries are stored off-chain and passed as arrays of integers when required.

To allow the Relayer to pass the user address to the Target smart contract, we attach the user's address (authenticated from `msgHash` and `sigUser`) to the end of the relayed call data as `contractAddr.call(abi.encodePacked (txArray[i], msgSender))`. Secondly, within the target smart contract, we substitute all references to `msg.sender` with `_msgSender()` from the ERC2771 Context [10]. This function interprets the tail-end of the call data as the sender's address, identifying the original user.

Relayer Smart Contract. We set both the deposit (X) and compensation (Y) values for `openDispute` to 0.1 ETH, with a dispute resolution time of one day. Disputes are managed within a mapping, `userAddress => disputes`. To ensure sufficient funds for dispute resolution, the smart contract is required to maintain a minimum balance of 0.5 ETH to continue operating (enough to cover five disputes), enforced by adding a modifier `onlyIfFunded` to the `relayTransactions` function.

---

[2] Available at: https://github.com/olzh-yess/A-Middleware-for-Hybrid-Blockchain-Applications.

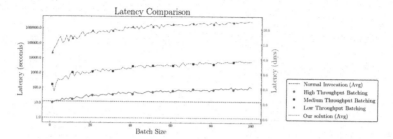

Fig. 5. Latency comparison

Initially, the owner deploys the contract with 0.5 ETH and can add more funds through the `fund` function. User deposits also contribute to the contract's balance and could potentially be used to resolve earlier disputes. This approach is justified, since successful dispute resolution results in a net loss of funds (0.2 ETH), implying that the owner would need to replenish the contract's balance to maintain the required minimum. This method is cost-effective as checking the smart contract balance consumes only 38 gas units, significantly less than the 2000 gas units needed to allocate and read a dedicated variable for tracking the owner's funds.

4.2   Experimental Evaluation

We implemented a server prototype using NestJS with a WebSocket connection for real-time client-server message exchange. A persistent Ganache simulation and the Sepolia test network served as local and public blockchains, respectively. Simulated transactions are stored in SQLite database for easy batch-transferring.

We set up a typical workflow (deploying the target contract, enrolling partner companies, enrolling workers, processing salary advances, increasing chargeable balances, and resetting withdrawable balances on salary day) on the Thankspay service prototype. Then, we evaluated (i) the transaction confirmation latency and (ii) the cost (gas) savings. We compare our solution with two baselines: one in which transactions are sent to the public blockchain as soon as generated by the users, and one in which standard batching of transactions is used (but without local blockchain simulation to speed-up the confirmation). For the standard batching, we consider batch sizes from 1 to 100.

Latency Savings. We define confirmation latency for the three considered scenarios as follows:

- **Public blockchain without batching**: Transactions are submitted directly to the Sepolia test network. To account for unpredictable network latency, we report average values from 10 tests for each smart contract function invocation, spaced at one-hour intervals.

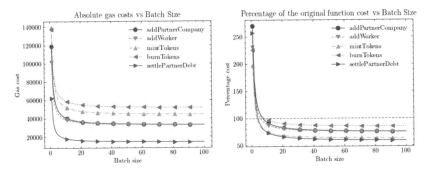

Fig. 6. Gas costs

- **Public blockchain with standard batching**: Transactions are reflected in the smart contract states only after an entire batch is completed and submitted to the public network. Consequently, latency comprises the public network latency and the rate at which new transactions are generated. For the latter, we consider three hypothetical throughput conditions: (a) *high* - an average of 100,000 transactions per day (approximately 70 per minute), similar to Uniswap [11]; (b) *medium* - an average of 1 transaction per minute; (c) *low* - a scenario inspired by the ThanksPay service, with 3.35 transactions per day based on a scenario with five partner companies with an average of 100 employees, 20% of whom request their salary ahead of time each month.
- **Our proposed approach**: latency consists of the time required for users to sign and settle the results on a local network, as well as to get the owner's signature. We evaluated the average confirmation latency using the same settings as the solution described above without batching. The confirmation times on the public blockchain are expected to be similar to those associated with standard batching, as they are contingent on the time taken to generate a full batch.

Figure 5 shows the results obtained. Our solution (0.1 s) is on average significantly faster than the baseline without batching (11 s). Note that the real Ethereum network may have latency up to four times higher than the Sepolia network [12]. The confirmation latency on the batching solutions is several orders of magnitude worse, especially for medium and low throughput scenarios.

Gas Cost Savings. We examine (see Fig. 6) gas costs of individual function invocations for batch transfers of varying sizes. Batching can notably reduce per-transaction *invocation* costs (e.g. miner fees and transaction verification), while not affecting the smart contract *execution* costs. Consequently, less complex functions, where invocation costs form a greater share of the total expense, benefit more from batching.

We can observe that gas reductions ranging from 15% to 45% can be achieved by setting batch sizes between 40 and 50, depending on the specific function.

Increasing batch size further might be impractical, as the gas price reduction flatlines. Different timing policies of the batch-transfer can even further increase its efficiency (extensively explored in [7]).

Dispute Procedure Costs. As disputes are expected to be opened infrequently, our primary focus is minimizing the amount of smart contract state stored for dispute resolution within the `relayTransactions` function. The only state-altering code instruction for disputes is saving the hash-trace of transaction execution for a given `batchNonce`, which adds a fixed per-batch additional cost of 30K gas units. In a batch of 40 transactions, this equates to a mere 750 gas units per transaction, a relatively low cost considering that the costs per transaction range from 20K to 100K gas units. Since it does not modify smart contract state, checking if the smart contract balance is higher than 0.5 ETH before the function invocation only adds negligible 38 gas units.

The remaining costs related to disputes are opening a dispute (149,623 gas units), closing a dispute (71,473) and claiming compensation costs (49,688).

5   Related Work

The blockchain's architectural scalability can be achieved by altering its fundamental architecture (Level-1 or L1), or by introducing cheaper side-chains anchored to the native one (Level-2 or L2).

One approach to L1 scaling involves increasing transaction count per block or accelerating block generation frequency. This, however, faces the "blockchain trilemma" [13] - a trade-off between security, scalability, and decentralization. For instance, reducing block time could undermine consensus mechanism if new blocks cannot promptly reach all nodes. However, increasing the block size might preclude less powerful nodes from processing new blocks, threatening decentralization. This is illustrated by Binance Smart Chain's lower fees, but reliance on only 21 validator nodes [14].

L2 sidechains address the blockchain trilemma by processing a significant portion of transactions on smaller, faster blockchains with lower fees, while interacting with the main L1 chain when needed [15]. L2 sidechains ensure that the data is reliable, consistent, and unaltered by posting periodic updates, state hashes, or cryptographic proofs on the L1 chain. Although L2 sidechains inherit L1-level security for data integrity, they are still vulnerable to data availability attacks due to the smaller number of nodes and the off-chain nature of L2 transactions.

Batching services aim to reduce L1 gas fees by packing multiple meta-transactions within a single invocation, reducing the fixed per-transaction overhead costs. Meta-transactions encapsulate a user's desired action, the target smart contract address, along with unique signatures verifying the senders' identity; they are then batch-sent to the public network on the users' behalf by a central relayer and executed by a specially deployed dispatcher smart contract after appropriate verification [16]. Different batching policies have been explored

Table 1. Comparison with different solutions

Requirement	Our Solution	Metatransaction Batching/Relaying	General-State Channel Networks
	✓	✗	✓
R1: Minimize application latency	Instant feedback with local blockchain simulation	Increased per-transaction latency for a batch to accumulate	Low-latency transactions through off-chain processing
	✓	✓	✓
R2: Minimize transaction fees	Batching and select-ing periods with lower gas fees	Reduced fees through batching transactions	Significantly reduced fees with only set-tling the final state
	✓	✓	✗
R3: Maintain full transaction history	Full transfer of transactions to the public blockchain	Full transfer of transactions to the public blockchain	Only the final state is settled on-chain
	✓	✗	✓
R4: Guarantee transaction order and inclusion	Nonce values and dispute resolution mechanism	Can maintain order within a batch, but may not guarantee transaction inclusion by a batcher	On-chain dispute process by publish-ing signatures of the state
	✓	?	?
R5: Provide a bal-anced approach to user self-custody	Multisignature wal-lets provide conve-nience and security	Varying degrees of user custody and traditional meth-ods depending on implementation	Often complex and may require higher technical expertise, less user-friendly

in iBatch [7], while MultiCall [17] has explored hash-based authentication to decrease the costs of verification. The EIP-4337 [18] is a successful proposal to enable meta-transactions in Ethereum.

Channel networks enable the participants to exchange simulated transac-tions off-chain, settling the final agreed-upon state on-chain. Examples are Bit-coin's Lighting Network [19] and Ethereum's Raiden [20]. General-state channel networks extend this idea to arbitrarily complex smart contracts [8]. In this approach, most of the transaction history is not recorded on the main chain; additionally, the parties need to be online to authorize new state transitions. While channels imply that multiple parties exchange simulated transactions among themselves based on self-enforcing signature authorizations, a local pri-vate blockchain can also be instantiated on the server of one party. Such a use-case has been explored in [21] for auctions.

To conclude, Tab. 1 qualitatively compares the proposed solution with the batching and general-state channel networks approaches while addressing the requirements elicited in Sect. 2.

6 Conclusion

This study presented a novel middleware solution that streamlines integration of public blockchains in hybrid architectures. By combining a local blockchain with asynchronous batch-transfers to a public blockchain, we ensure instant feedback and reduced costs. The effectiveness of the solution was confirmed by reduced latency and gas cost achieved by the Thankspay service prototype compared to two baseline cases. The solution also includes a dispute resolution mechanism enforcing accountability for the operator of the service.

At present, to ensure consistency between local and public blockchains, the owner can process only one transaction at a time. For instance, if we locally process a transaction with a higher positionNonce *before* a lower one is completed, it will be executed *after* the lower one on the public blockchain, leading to inconsistencies. In the future work, we plan to address this limitation, as well as to further enhance the dispute resolution mechanism and to test the system in more complex scenarios.

References

1. Tai, S., Eberhardt, J., Klems, M.: Not ACID, not base, but salt. Closer **2017**, 755–764 (2017)
2. Wöhrer, M., Zdun, U.: Architectural design decisions for blockchain-based applications. In: ICBC 2021, pp. 1–5. IEEE (2021)
3. Ltd, P.P.: Blockchain: The solution for supply chain transparency, November 2015
4. Azaria, A., Ekblaw, A., Vieira, T., Lippman, A.: MedRec: using blockchain for medical data access and permission management. In: OBD 2016, pp. 25–30. IEEE (2016)
5. Spain, M., Foley, S., Gramoli, V.: The impact of Ethereum throughput and fees on transaction latency during ICOS. In: Tokenomics 2019, Schloss Dagstuhl-Leibniz-Zentrum für Informatik (2020)
6. Donmez, A., Karaivanov, A.: Transaction fee economics in the Ethereum blockchain. Econ. Inq. **60**(1), 265–292 (2022)
7. Wang, Y., Zhang, Q., Li, K., Tang, Y., Chen, J., Luo, X., Chen, T.: iBatch: saving Ethereum fees via secure and cost-effective batching of smart-contract invocations. ESEC/FSE **2021**, 566–577 (2021)
8. Dziembowski, S., Faust, S., Hostáková, K.: General state channel networks. SIGSAC **2018**, 949–966 (2018)
9. McCorry, P., Buckland, C., Bakshi, S., Wüst, K., Miller, A.: You sank my battleship! A case study to evaluate state channels as a scaling solution for cryptocurrencies. In: Bracciali, A., Clark, J., Pintore, F., Rønne, P.B., Sala, M. (eds.) FC 2019. LNCS, vol. 11599, pp. 35–49. Springer, Cham (2020). https://doi.org/10.1007/978-3-030-43725-1_4
10. Sandford, R., et al.: ERC-2771: secure protocol for native meta transactions, July 2020
11. Chong, N.: As Ethereum Defi craze continues, Uniswap is processing over 100,000 transactions a day, November 2020
12. Zhang, L., Lee, B., Ye, Y., Qiao, Y.: Evaluation of Ethereum end-to-end transaction latency. In: NTMS 2021, pp. 1–5. IEEE (2021)

13. Abadi, J., Brunnermeier, M.: Blockchain economics. Technical report, National Bureau of Economic Research (2018)
14. Jia, Y., Xu, C., Wu, Z., Feng, Z., Chen, Y., Yang, S.: Measuring decentralization in emerging public blockchains. In: IWCMC 2022, pp. 137–141. IEEE (2022)
15. Sguanci, C., Spatafora, R., Vergani, A.M.: Layer 2 blockchain scaling: a survey. arXiv preprint arXiv:2107.10881 (2021)
16. Seres, I.A.: On blockchain metatransactions. In: ICBC 2020, pp. 178–187. IEEE (2020)
17. Hughes, W., Magnusson, T., Russo, A., Schneider, G.: Cheap and secure metatransactions on the blockchain using hash-based authorisation and preferred batchers, p. 100125. Research and Applications, Blockchain (2022)
18. Buterin, V., Weiss, Y., Gazso, K., Patel, N., Tirosh, D., Nacson, S., Hess, T.: ERC-4337: Account abstraction using alt mempool [draft], September 2021
19. Poon, J., Dryja, T.: The bitcoin lightning network: scalable off-chain instant payments (2016)
20. : Raiden network. https://raiden.network/ Accessed 15 Jun 2023
21. Desai, H., Kantarcioglu, M., Kagal, L.: A hybrid blockchain architecture for privacy-enabled and accountable auctions. In: ICBC 2019, pp. 34–43. IEEE (2019)

An AI Chatbot for Explaining Deep Reinforcement Learning Decisions of Service-Oriented Systems

Andreas Metzger(✉)⬤, Jone Bartel, and Jan Laufer

paluno – The Ruhr Institute for Software Technology, University of Duisburg-Essen, Essen, Germany
{andreas.metzger,jone.bartel,jan.laufer}@paluno.uni-due.de

Abstract. Deep Reinforcement Learning (Deep RL) is increasingly used to cope with the open-world assumption in service-oriented systems. Deep RL was successfully applied to problems such as dynamic service composition, job scheduling, and service adaptation. While Deep RL offers many benefits, understanding the decision-making of Deep RL is challenging because the action-selection policy that underlies its decision-making essentially appears as a black box. Yet, understanding the decision-making of Deep RL is key to help service developers perform debugging, support service providers to comply with relevant legal frameworks, and facilitate service users to build trust. We introduce Chat4XAI to provide natural-language explanations of the decision-making of Deep RL. Compared with visual explanations, the reported benefits of natural-language explanations include better understandability for non-technical users, increased user acceptance, and more efficient explanations. Chat4XAI leverages modern AI chatbot technology and dedicated prompt engineering. Compared to earlier work on natural-language explanations using classical software-based dialogue systems, using an AI chatbot eliminates the need for eliciting and defining potential questions and answers up-front. We prototypically realize Chat4XAI using OpenAI's ChatGPT API and evaluate the fidelity and stability of its explanations using an adaptive service exemplar.

Keywords: chatbot · explainable AI · reinforcement learning · service engineering · service adaptation

1 Introduction

Reinforcement Learning (RL) is increasingly used to cope with the open-world assumption of service-oriented systems, as it helps to address the design-time uncertainty during service and systems engineering [1,27]. In general, RL aims to learn an optimal action selection policy, which is used to decide on which action to execute in any given environment state [42]. In a service-oriented system, RL can learn suitable actions via the system's interactions with its initially

F. Monti et al. (Eds.): ICSOC 2023, LNCS 14419, pp. 323–338, 2023.
https://doi.org/10.1007/978-3-031-48421-6_22

unknown environment and thereby can make use of information only available at runtime [35]. RL helped successfully address various problems in service-oriented systems, including dynamic service composition [38], task/job scheduling [12,14, 44], resource management [13], and service adaptation [33].

Need for Explainability. Recent research on using RL for realizing service-oriented systems leverages Deep RL algorithms, which represent their action-selection policy as a deep artificial neural network (e.g., [9,12,20,29]). Benefits of Deep RL include that environment states are not limited to elements of finite or discrete sets, and that the used artificial neural networks can generalize well over unseen environment states.

However, one key shortcoming of Deep RL is that the learned action-selection policy is not represented explicitly, but is hidden in the parameterization of the artificial neural network. As the action-selection policy underlies RL's decision-making, the decision-making of Deep RL thus essentially appears as a black box [37]. This means that we require techniques to explain and interpret the internal workings of such black-box systems and how their decisions are made [3, 10,28,30].

Explaining the decision-making of Deep RL can help service developers debug the reward function by understanding why Deep RL took certain decisions. The successful application of Deep RL depends on how well the learning problem, and in particular the reward function, is defined [5]. Further, explainability can facilitate regulatory compliance [30]. For example, in the EU, service providers must ensure that their services comply with the relevant legal frameworks, such as the General Data Protection Regulation and the forthcoming AI Act. Third, explanations facilitate service users to build trust. They can understand how the service arrived at its results and thus can accept its results or not [30].

Problem Statement. Two major types of explanation formats can be distinguished [2,22,30]: (*i*) visual explanations, including graphical user interfaces, charts, data visualization, or heatmaps, and (*ii*) verbal explanations, which, for instance, may take the form of a natural-language dialogue between the explainer and explainee. The chosen presentation method has a direct effect on user comprehension and, therefore, on the success of the explanation [22]. Compared with visual explanations, the benefits of verbal explanations reported in the literature [2,23] include (1) better understandability for people with diverse backgrounds as well as non-technical users, (2) increased user acceptance, and (3) more efficient explanations.

While the literature on using Deep RL for service-oriented systems provides extensive and systematic evaluations of the performance of Deep RL [9,12,20,29], the problem of how to explain the decision-making of Deep RL using natural language was not yet addressed. In the broader area of explainable AI (XAI), approaches for providing natural-language explanations for machine learning exist [18,19,22,34]. However, these XAI approaches focus on supervised learning and not on RL. Also, they are all built using classical software-based dialogue systems [32], which require the additional engineering step of eliciting and defining potential questions and answers up-front.

Contributions. We introduce Chat4XAI, which leverages the capabilities of a modern AI chatbot powered by a large language model to provide natural-language explanations about the decision-making of Deep RL. AI chatbots are intriguing in that they provide answers to any question posed to them. However, as a downside of this flexibility, the underlying large language model may hallucinate, i.e., generate nonsensical text unfaithful to the provided source input [16]. This means AI chatbots may deliver explanations that do not faithfully explain the decision-making of RL, i.e., the explanations may exhibit low *fidelity* [10]. In addition, AI chatbots may provide different explanations for the very same question asked, i.e., the explanations may exhibit low *stability* [39].

To deliver natural-language explanations with high fidelity and high stability, Chat4XAI uses dedicated prompt engineering for the AI chatbot and careful selection of the hyper-parameters of the underlying large language model. Prompt engineering helps increase the correctness of the answers by providing a set of targeted, initial questions (a.k.a. prompts) before the actual question [41,43].

We prototypically realize and evaluate Chat4XAI using OpenAI's ChatGPT Completion API. We evaluate the fidelity and stability of the explanations delivered by Chat4XAI using an adaptive cloud service exemplar realized using Double DQN as Deep RL algorithm. We assess Chat4XAI for different prompting strategies, open and closed questions, as well as different hyper-parameter settings. To contextualize the performance of Chat4XAI, we compare Chat4XAI's explanations with the results of our earlier user study that assessed how well human software engineers were able to understand the decision-making of Deep RL using visual explanations [26].

Paper Structure. Section 2 provides background and a running example. Section 3 describes the conceptual architecture and proof-of-concept implementation of Chat4XAI. Section 4 provides the experiment design and results. Section 5 discusses limitations and future enhancements. Section 6 relates Chat4XAI to existing work.

2   Background and Exemplar

Deep RL in a Nutshell. In general, RL aims at learning an optimal action selection policy π for a given environment by interacting with this environment, typically at discrete timesteps [42]. Upon executing an action $a \in A$ in a state $s \in S$ at timestep t, the environment transitions to the next state s' and awards a specific numeric reward $R(s, a)$. The action selection policy π maps states S to a probability distribution over the set of possible actions A, i.e., $\pi : S \times A \to [0, 1]$ with $\pi = \text{Prob}(a|s)$. An optimal policy π is a policy that optimizes the cumulative reward received. We focus on providing insights into the decision-making of *value-based Deep RL* algorithms. In value-based Deep RL, the action selection policy π depends on a learned action-value function, also called Q function, $Q(s, a)$. The action-value function gives the expected cumulative reward when executing action a in state s. Value-based *Deep* RL uses an artificial neural network to approximate $Q(s, a)$.

XRL-DINE. Chat4XAI leverages the XRL-DINE technique from our earlier work [6]. XRL-DINE generates different types of so-called *Decomposed Interestingness Elements* (DINEs), which provide insights into different aspects of Deep RL's decision-making. In the original approach in [6], DINEs are visualized in the XRL-DINE graphical user interface. Here, we use the information of the DINEs as input to Chat4XAI. XRL-DINE combines and enhances the following two explanation techniques.

Reward Decomposition [17] splits the reward function $R(s, a)$ into k sub-functions $R_1(s, a), \ldots, R_k(s, a)$, called *reward channels*, which reflect a different aspect of the learning goal. For each of the reward sub-functions a separate action-value-function $Q_i(s, a)$, is learned. To select a concrete action a in state s, an aggregated action-value-function $Q(s, a)$ is computed: $\forall a \in A :$ $Q(s, a) = \sum_{i=1,\ldots,k} Q_i(s, a)$. Trade-offs in decision making become observable via the reward channels, and made explicit via the "Reward Channel Dominance" DINE.

Interestingness Elements [40] facilitate identifying situations where the decision-making of Deep RL is uncertain and thus helps select interesting timesteps for explanation. To determine the uncertainty of a decision for state s, the evenness $e(s)$ of the probability distribution over actions $a \in A$ is calculated. XRL-DINE approximates the probability distribution as $\hat{\pi}(s, a) = Q_k^+(s, a) / \sum_{a' \in A} Q_k^+(s, a')$ with $Q_k^+(s, a) = Q_k(s, a) - \max(0, \min_{a \in A} Q_k(s, a))$. An evenness of $e(s) = 1$ indicates maximum uncertainty. If at least one of the reward channels is uncertain (determined by a user-defined threshold) and the aggregated action does not correspond to the action that the sub-agent would choose, these actions are reported via the "Uncertain Action" DINE.

SWIM Exemplar. To demonstrate the use of Chat4XAI and to serve as basis for our experiments, we introduce the SWIM exemplar used in our previous work on XRL-DINE [6]. SWIM simulates an adaptive multi-tier webshop, where the goal of adaptation is to maximize a given utility function in the presence of varying workloads [31].

SWIM's action space consists of (1) adding/removing web servers, and (2) changing the proportion of requests for which optional, computationally intensive recommendations are generated (so called "dimmer"). SWIM's state space S is determined by different monitoring metrics, including (1) the request arrival rate (i.e., "workload"), (2) the average throughput, and (3) response time. While both types of adaptations have an impact on user satisfaction (due to their influence on throughput and response time), adaptations of type (1) have an impact on costs (due to the costs of more/fewer servers), and adaptations of type (2) have an impact on revenue (due to recommendations leading to potential further purchases in the webshop). The reward function R aims to balance conflicting QoS goals via the weights $a, b,$ and c (see [6] for rationales):
$$R_{\text{total}} = a \cdot R_{\text{user\_satisfaction}} + b \cdot R_{\text{revenue}} + c \cdot R_{\text{costs}}$$
The information of the DINEs is encoded in JSON format, an open-standard data interchange format using human-readable text, and thus can serve as input to the AI chatbot. The below JSON snippet illustrates a "Reward Channel

Dominance" DINE giving the relative contributions of the reward channels to the overall decision.

```
"reward_channel_dominance":
  "Add Web Server":{"U.Satisf.": 0.35, "Revenue": 2.61, "Cost": 1.19},
  "Decrease Dimmer":{"U.Satisf.": 0.13, "Revenue": 0.0, "Cost": 1.51}, ...
```

The next JSON snippet illustrates an "Uncertain Action" DINE, indicating the alternative actions proposed by the reward channels *Cost* and *Revenue* that have a probability of being chosen that is very close to the probability of the action actually been chosen.

```
"uncertain_actions": [["Cost", "Remove Server"],["Revenue","Add Server"]]
```

3   Chat4XAI Architecture and Realization

Figure 1 shows the main conceptual components of Chat4XAI and how they may be embedded to realize an explainable service-oriented system. The numbers depict the control and data flow among these components. The *Question Analyzer* takes the question received via the Explanation Interface ①, determines the timestep(s) to which the question refers ②, identifies the question type ③ and uses this information to request the matching DINEs from *XRL-DINE* ④. The *Prompt Generator* takes the question ①, its type ③, the matching DINEs ④, and a description of the main system concepts ⑥ to generate a series of prompts for the AI chatbot ⑦. The final response from the AI chatbot ⑧ is then sent back as explanation via the Explanation Interface ⑨.

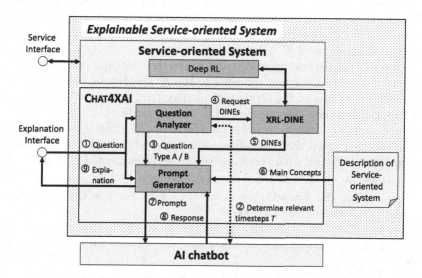

Fig. 1. Chat4XAI conceptual architecture and embedding into service-oriented system

Question Analyzer Component. This component classifies a given question into one of two question types: *Question Type A* concerns a *single* decision, i.e., it covers the decision taken at a single timestep. One example is to ask why Deep RL decided for adaptation "X" rather than "Y" at timestep t. *Question Type B* concerns a sequence of decisions, i.e., it covers the decision trajectory of several timesteps. One example is to ask how often, along the concerned timesteps t_k to t_l, Deep RL was uncertain in its decisions.

We classify the questions for two reasons. First, while state-of-the-art AI chatbots are capable of *directly* answering natural-language questions (zero-shot prompting), the quality of the answers can be increased via prompt engineering, i.e., by providing a set of instructions before the actual question [41,43]. Differentiating two types of questions allows for a more targeted prompt engineering. Second, AI chatbots typically limit the cumulative length of questions and answers per conversation. Depending on the question type, we can more precisely select the DINEs that are requested from XRL-DINE and forwarded to the Prompt Generator.

To identify the question type, we ask the AI chatbot to provide us with a list T of all relevant timesteps mentioned in the question. Then, by counting the size of T we can identify whether it is a question of Type A ($|T| = 1$) or Type B ($|T| > 1$). Note that in the case of $|T| = 0$, one may use a default set of timesteps; e.g., the 20 most recent ones, i.e., $T = (t_{now-19}, \ldots, t_{now})$.

Prompt Generator Component. The description of the service-oriented system given to this component provides relevant concepts, including domain-specific terms, the different actions available, and the learning goals. These concepts provide relevant service-specific knowledge to the AI chatbot, as the DINEs also refer to these concepts. Potential sources for such a description include WSDL specifications (in particular the documentation, types, and interface sections giving a logical description of the service) and WS-Agreement (providing the QoS goals in terms of SLA terms).

The Prompt Generator generates and issues the following prompts:

Prompt 1 provides relevant concepts to the AI chatbot by providing it with the textual description of the service-oriented system, introduced by the text `The following scenario description will be available...`

Prompt 2 provides the context for the answers to be given by the AI chatbot. It gives the type of data that will follow after this prompt (which depends on the question type) together with the name of the service-oriented system to allow the AI chatbot to connect to the description given in Prompt 1:

- *Question Type A:* `You will be given the state for a single timestep of <name> as JSON enclosed in ***:`
- *Question Type B:* `You will be given a trajectory of timesteps for <name> as JSON enclosed in ***:`

Prompt 3 provides the actual DINEs in JSON format enclosed in *** to mark the boundaries between the DINEs and the final question in Prompt 4.

Prompt 4 provides the actual question.

Typically, an explainee will ask open questions (i.e., without any fixed set of answers to choose from) and expect an answer in concrete terms. Directly asking open Type B questions turned out to be too challenging for the AI chatbot. We thus employ "chain of thought" prompt engineering, in which the AI chatbot is given smaller subtasks leading up to the final result. In a first prompt, we ask the AI chatbot to provide us with a list of relevant timesteps; e.g., the ones where Deep RL is uncertain. In a second prompt, we then ask the AI chatbot concrete questions about these relevant timesteps; e.g., to count these.

Proof-of-Concept Realization. We developed our proof-of-concept realization of Chat4XAI in Python using the OpenAI ChatGPT Completion API. We are using GPT 3.5 turbo as a large language model, which offers fast generation of responses, and is capable of providing in-depth answers. The following hyper-parameters are considered in our realization and experiments:

- n gives how many responses to generate.
- *max_token* limits the length of the answer. The OpenAI API imposes two constraints on the overall length of a request, i.e., a sequence of prompts and responses. First, there is an overall token limit of $4,096$ tokens (ca. $3,000$ words) per request. Second, there is a limit of $90,000$ tokens per minute. *max_token* helps to set a trade-off between these two constraints.
- *temperature* controls text generation behavior. Temperature $\in [0,2]$ controls the randomness of the text, with a higher temperature resulting in more "creative" text but with a higher risk of hallucinations. A temperature of 0 leads to deterministic text generation behavior.
- *Top_p sampling* is an alternative to temperature. Instead of considering all possible tokens, only a subset of tokens is considered whose cumulative probability adds up to top_p $\in [0,1]$.

Example Explanations. Table 1 gives examples of explanations (slightly edited for readability) for the SWIM exemplar.

Table 1. Example explanations generated by Chat4XAI for the SWIM exemplar

Question	Explanation
(EQ1) Why did Deep RL chose the action "Add Web Server" instead of "Decrease Dimer" at timestep t_{12}?	Based on the information provided, Deep RL chose the action "Add Web Server" instead of "Decrease Dimer" because the action "Add Web Server" has a higher positive impact on the goals "Revenue" and "User Satisfaction" compared to the action "Decrease Dimmer".
(EQ2) Which goal would the service-oriented system achieve when choosing action "Remove Server" instead of performing no adaptation at timestep t_{13}?	If Deep RL selects "Remove Server" instead of performing no adaptation at timestep t_{13}, the service-oriented system would achieve the goal of decreasing "Cost". The "Remove Server" action has the highest reward for the "Cost" goal compared to all other actions. However, Deep RL has chosen no adaptation because it has a higher positive impact on the "User Satisfaction" goal.

The explanation for EQ1 indicates that the aggregated decision is to execute "Add Web Server" because it has the highest relative reward with the "Revenue" reward channel contributing most to the aggregated decision. During debugging, software engineers can evaluate whether this strategy is what they expected, or whether they rather expected the dimmer value to be lowered at the expense of "Revenue". The explanation for EQ2 indicates why the overall decision is to perform "No Adaptation", instead of choosing the possible alternative action "Remove Server". If such a decision is not expected, this may indicate that the reward function has to be re-engineered to provide stronger rewards for the respective state to choose "Remove Server" over "No Adaptation".

4   Experiments

We perform a set of controlled experiments to evaluate the fidelity and stability of Chat4XAI's explanations. We contextualize the capabilities of Chat4XAI against the results of an empirical user study from our earlier work [26]. The user study involved 54 software engineers from academia (82%) and industry (8%), 87% of which held an academic degree in software engineering or related fields. It assessed how well software engineers were able to understand the decision-making of Deep RL by using DINEs in visual form. To compare the results, we use the same system exemplar (SWIM, as introduced in Sect. 2), the same realization of system's adaptation logic (Double DQN with Experience Replay), and the same 21 timesteps to be explained. Also, we ask Chat4XAI the same questions that were posed to the software engineers in the user study.

To facilitate reproducibility, relevant background and supplementary material is available from https://git.uni-due.de/rl4sas/chat4xai.

4.1   Experiment Setup

Metrics. We use the following metrics from the explainable AI literature [10,39]:

Fidelity expresses how well the explanations reflect the behavior of the black-box model. As we use AI chatbots to generate explanations, Chat4XAI exhibits the risk of hallucination, i.e., producing answers not corresponding to the learned Deep RL decision-making policy. We quantify fidelity by measuring the rate of correct explanations for m given questions. Let $x_i = 1$ mean correct explanation, and 0 otherwise, then fidelity is computed as $\sum x_i / m$.

Stability gives the degree to which the same explanation is generated for the same input. Explanations of Chat4XAI for the same input may vary because the AI chatbot may produce non-deterministic results depending on the chosen hyper-parameter settings. We measure stability as $1 - \sigma$, with σ being the standard deviation of fidelity across several experiment repetitions for the same input and configuration of independent variables.

To compare the performance of Chat4XAI with the performance of software engineers using XRL-DINE, we selected the following metric from [26]:

Effectiveness quantifies the performance of software engineers by measuring the rate of correctly answered questions among n participants. Let $c_i = 1$

mean correct explanation, and 0 otherwise, then the effectiveness is computed as $\sum c_i / n$.

Independent Variables. To analyze the performance of Chat4XAI, we varied the following three main independent variables.

Prompting: We analyze the performance depending on whether (i) zero-shot prompting or (ii) prompt engineering is used. This indicates how much Chat4XAI's performance is impacted by prompt engineering, resp. how robust the approach would be independent of any specific prompt engineering.

Question Form: We analyze the performance of Chat4XAI in providing explanations for open questions (which would be the typical scenario in a practical setting) and closed questions (like in the user study from [26]).

Hyper-parameters: We consider different concrete settings of temperature and top_p. We vary temperature $\in \{0, 0.2, 0.5, 1\}$. For each temperature, we vary top_p $\in \{1, 0.8, 0.5\}$ and report the aggregated results per temperature. We use 54 repetitions to get the same number of explanations as in the user study. We split these 54 repetitions into three clusters of 18 repetitions, with each cluster having a different top_p setting. To efficiently execute the experiment, we set $n = 18$, i.e., retrieve 18 answers per prompt. Also, we set $max\_token = 350$, delivering a good trade-off between length of answers and throughput.

Questions to be Explained. To assess the performance of Chat4XAI, we have to choose concrete questions that are posed to the AI chatbot to retrieve explanations. As we are interested in comparing the performance of Chat4XAI with that of software engineers from the empirical user study in [26], we use the same set of questions that were formulated there. Study participants were asked eight closed questions and were provided with several single-choice answers for each question. These questions are shown in Table 2.

Table 2. Questions for which explanations should be given[2]

Type A Questions Focussing on a single timestep	Type B Questions Covering a sequence of timesteps
Q2: At timestep 10, **which** action did the service choose?	Q1: For timesteps 22,575—22,596, **how many** adaptations were executed by the service?
Q4: At timestamp 8, **why** did the service choose the adaptation „Decrease Dimmer" instead of „Add Server"?	
Q5: At timestamp 15, **why** did the service choose "No Adaptation" instead of „Add Server"?	Q3: For timesteps 22,575—22,596, **how often** is the service uncertain when making a decision?
Q6: At timestamp 13, **which** QoS goal would the service achieve when selecting „Remove Server" instead of „No Adaptation"?	Q8: For timesteps 22,575—22,596, **what** is the main QoS goal that the service wants to achieve?
Q7: At timestamp 9, **which** QoS goal would the service achieve when selecting „Add Server"instead of „Remove Server"?	

---

[2] Questions are numbered in the order they were asked user study participants. Question text adapted from [26] and edited for clarity.

4.2 Experiment Results

Table 3 presents the results concerning the fidelity and stability of Chat4XAI as well as the effectiveness of software engineers from the user study.

Table 3. Experiment Results

Question Nbr	Question Type	Fidelity of Chat4XAI												Effective-ness of Software Engineers
		Closed Questions								Open Questions				
		Zero-shot Prompting				Prompt Engineering				Prompt Engineering				
		Temperature =				Temperature =				Temperature =				
		0,0	0,2	0,5	1,0	0,0	0,2	0,5	1,0	0,0	0,2	0,5	1,0	
Q1	A	0%	6%	4%	6%	100%	100%	85%	61%	100%	89%	69%	67%	65%
Q2	B	100%	100%	100%	100%	100%	100%	100%	100%	100%	100%	100%	100%	91%
Q3	A	100%	100%	100%	98%	100%	100%	100%	100%	100%	98%	100%	98%	94%
Q4	B	33%	96%	78%	50%	100%	100%	98%	96%	100%	98%	78%	78%	61%
Q5	B	100%	100%	100%	100%	100%	100%	100%	100%	100%	100%	100%	96%	63%
Q6	B	0%	0%	0%	0%	100%	100%	100%	100%	100%	100%	69%	56%	80%
Q7	B	0%	0%	0%	0%	100%	100%	94%	87%	100%	100%	100%	96%	69%
Q8	A	0%	0%	0%	0%	100%	100%	98%	87%	100%	65%	41%	35%	83%
	Average	42%	50%	48%	44%	100%	100%	97%	91%	100%	94%	82%	78%	
		46%				97%				88%				76%
		Stability of Chat4XAI												StdDev
		51%	50%	50%	50%	100%	100%	83%	72%	100%	76%	62%	59%	
		50%				89%				74%				44%

As expected Chat4XAI with prompt engineering outperforms Chat4XAI with zero-shot prompting. For closed questions, zero-shot prompting only achieves an average fidelity of 48% with an average stability of 50%. Prompt engineering achieves an average fidelity of 97% with an average stability of 85%, because the underlying large language model has been provided with better information about the scope and nature of answers expected via initial prompts.

Indeed, prompt engineering together with low-temperature settings can lead to a fidelity of 100% with a stability of 100%, because the underlying large language model gives deterministic answers. Here, increasing the temperature leads to a lower fidelity and lower stability, as the chance of wrong answers being created from an already strong baseline of correct explanations increases.

Interestingly, when considering zero-shot prompting, a temperature larger than 0 leads to a higher fidelity albeit with the same low stability. The higher temperature and the resulting more "creative" answers from the AI chatbot appear to increase the chance of providing a correct explanation as we start from a very weak baseline of correct explanations.

Finally, as one might expect, providing correct explanations for the open questions is more challenging. Except for temperature = 0, the fidelity for open questions is generally lower than for closed questions (88% vs. 97% on average) and also exhibits a lower stability (74% vs. 89% on average), indicating a higher randomness of answers.

Comparing the fidelity of Chat4XAI with the effectiveness of software engineers, Chat4XAI was able to outperform the software engineers in 8 out of the 12 experiment configurations and was able to answer all eight questions correctly

(100% fidelity) in 3 configurations. According to [26], only 33% of the software engineers were able to answer all eight questions correctly.

Validity Risks. Concerning internal validity, we addressed the risk that results for Chat4XAI may have been achieved by chance. To this end, we carefully controlled experimental variables. In addition, we repeated the experiment multiple times to account for the typical stochastic effects and thus variance of machine learning models [36]. While we chose metrics for Chat4XAI and the user study that allow numerically comparing them, semantically they are not fully comparable. To do so would require complementing the Chat4XAI results by user studies that assess how well explainees could use the natural-language explanations to understand Deep RL decision making.

Concerning external validity, we chose a concrete service exemplar (SWIM) together with real-world workload traces and an actual subset of the interactions between Deep RL and the service environment. Still, our experiments cover only one concrete problem in service-oriented systems (i.e., service adaptation) and use only one concrete service-oriented system exemplar. We cover different styles of questions ("what/which", "why", "how many") reflecting various insights into the decision-making of Deep RL. Yet, we limited the questions to the ones from the user study in [26] to compare the performance of Chat4XAI with that of software engineers. While we designed Chat4XAI to be as generic as possible and thus applicable to different problems in service-oriented systems, experimental results are limited with respect to generalizability.

5   Current Limitations and Potential Enhancements

Multi-round Question Answering. Currently, Chat4XAI generates a natural-language explanation for a given question. Enhancing Chat4XAI to also allow for follow-up questions thus appears as a natural next step. An interesting further direction for such multi-round question answering is to follow the metaphor of the Socratic dialogue. A Socratic dialogue may take the form of a cooperative argumentative dialogue between the explainer and explainee, where the explainer initiates the dialogue by asking questions to stimulate ideas by the explainee [43]. This may especially help non-technical users to come up with concrete questions concerning the decision-making of Deep RL.

Coping with Missing Insights. Once an explainee is provided with the powerful natural-language interface of an AI chatbot, the explainee may ask questions concerning the decision-making of Deep RL for which the underlying explainable AI technique (here: XRL-DINE) does not provide the required insights. One may check whether the answer given by the AI chatbot is backed by actual insights and inform the explainee accordingly. Here, work on explainable large language models may be leveraged [45]. Even more intriguing would be to use the AI chatbot to directly derive the actual explanations from the Deep RL policy without resorting to an external explanation technique such as XRL-DINE.

Protecting Sensitive Information. AI chatbots and thus Chat4XAI may be tricked into revealing information that should not be given away [11,24]. One open question thus is how to leverage AI chatbots for explainable service-oriented systems while protecting sensitive information of the service provider [7].

Explanations for Policy-Based Deep RL. We focused on value-based Deep RL, which represents the action-value function $Q(s, a)$ as an artificial neural network (see Sect. 2). Another important class of Deep RL is policy-based Deep RL. Policy-based Deep RL directly uses and optimizes a parameterized stochastic action selection policy $\pi_\theta(s, a)$ in the form of a deep artificial neural network, and thus does not make use of an action-value function $Q(s, a)$. In comparison to value-based Deep RL, policy-based Deep RL has the important advantage that it can naturally cope with concept drifts [25,35]. As the underlying XRL-DINE technique requires access to the action-value function $Q(s, a)$ to compute the DINEs, Chat4XAI currently works for value-based Deep RL only.

6   Related Work

As introduced in Sect. 1, RL – and recently Deep RL – was successfully applied to different problems in service-oriented systems [12–14,33,38,44]. While existing papers provide extensive and systematic evaluations of the performance of Deep RL for service-oriented systems, they did not yet address the problem of how to explain the decision-making of Deep RL using natural language.

There exists related work on natural-language explanations in the general area of explainable AI (XAI), which can be grouped into two main areas.

Requirements Elicitation. Jentzsch et al. perform an empirical study to elicit user expectations towards chatbots for XAI [15]. Results indicate that questions of users differ concerning the question form (open vs. closed), the level of abstraction, and the temporal scope (e.g., past, current or future outcomes). Kuzba and Biecek elicit typical questions a human would ask a chatbot [18]. From around 600 collected dialogues, they distill the 12 most common types of questions. Liao et al. construct a corpus of questions via literature review, as well as expert reviews and interviews [19]. The resulting corpus contains 73 types of questions in 10 categories. Gao et al. introduce a chatbot-based explanation framework built using IBM Watson Assistant [8]. Similar to Kuzba and Biecek, they use this framework to understand what users would like to know about AI and elicit concrete user requests about AI-generated results.

All these works provide interesting insights into what questions may be asked, but are limited to supervised learning. Also, in contrast to these works, Chat4XAI does not require the up-front elicitation and fine-grained classification of questions. Chat4XAI works with only two types of questions because more specific aspects are handled naturally by the underlying powerful large language model.

Design and Realization. Carneiro et al. suggest combining a chatbot with an explainable model serving as a less complex surrogate than the actual black-box prediction model [4]. They use natural language understanding to extract structured information from user questions concerning the user intent and the entity concerned with the question. Nguyen et al. leverage classical conversational agent architectures for question-answer dialogues [34]. They (1) construct a question phrase bank, (2) establish a mapping between questions and explainable AI techniques, and (3) use template-based natural language generation to create explanations. Malandri et al. consider the knowledge and experience of the users when generating explanations [22]. They explicitly introduce "clarification" as a further dialogue type on top of an earlier explanation framework [21]. Their user study indicates that different user groups perceive explanations differently, that all user groups prefer textual explanations over graphical ones, and that clarifications can enhance the usefulness of explanations.

All these works provide evidence for the benefits of using natural-language explanations. However, they do not deliver explanations for Deep RL. Also, they are all built using classical dialogue systems and natural language processing, and thus do not leverage the capabilities of modern large language models.

7   Conclusion

We took a first step towards natural-language explanations of Deep RL used for realizing service-oriented systems. We introduced Chat4XAI, an explainable AI technique powered by modern AI chatbot technology built on top of large language models. We performed a proof-of-concept implementation for Chat4XAI using ChatGPT. Experimental results suggest that Chat4XAI can provide explanations with high fidelity and stability.

In future work, we will work on the potential enhancements of Chat4XAI described above. We will also extend our experiments to other service-oriented system exemplars, which cover additional problems, such as service composition.

Acknowledgments. We cordially thank the anonymous reviewers and Xhulja Shahini for their constructive comments. Research leading to these results received funding from the EU's Horizon Europe R&I programme under grant 101070455 (DynaBIC).

References

1. Baresi, L., Nitto, E.D., Ghezzi, C.: Toward open-world software: issue and challenges. Computer **39**(10), 36–43 (2006)
2. Cambria, E., Malandri, L., Mercorio, F., Mezzanzanica, M., Nobani, N.: A survey on XAI and natural language explanations. Inf. Process. Manag. **60**(1), 103111 (2023)
3. Camilli, M., Mirandola, R., Scandurra, P.: XSA: explainable self-adaptation. In: 37th International Conference on Automated Software Engineering (ASE 2022). ACM (2022)
4. Carneiro, D., Veloso, P., Guimarães, M., Baptista, J., Sousa, M.: A conversational interface for interacting with machine learning models. In: 4th International Workshop on eXplainable and Responsible AI and Law. CEUR Workshop Proceedings, vol. 3168. CEUR-WS.org (2021)

5. Dewey, D.: Reinforcement learning and the reward engineering principle. In: 2014 AAAI Spring Symposia, Stanford University, Palo Alto, California, USA, 24-26 March 2014. AAAI Press (2014)

6. Feit, F., Metzger, A., Pohl, K.: Explaining online reinforcement learning decisions of self-adaptive systems. In: International Conference on Autonomic Computing and Self-Organizing Systems, ACSOS 2022. IEEE (2022)

7. Følstad, A., et al.: Future directions for chatbot research: an interdisciplinary research agenda. Computing **103**(12), 2915–2942 (2021)

8. Gao, M., Liu, X., Xu, A., Akkiraju, R.: Chat-XAI: a new chatbot to explain artificial intelligence. In: Arai, K. (ed.) IntelliSys 2021. LNNS, vol. 296, pp. 125–134. Springer, Cham (2022). https://doi.org/10.1007/978-3-030-82199-9_9

9. Ghanadbashi, S., Safavifar, Z., Taebi, F., Golpayegani, F.: Handling uncertainty in self-adaptive systems: an ontology-based reinforcement learning model. J. Reliable Intell. Environ. (2023)

10. Guidotti, R., Monreale, A., Ruggieri, S., Turini, F., Giannotti, F., Pedreschi, D.: A survey of methods for explaining black box models. ACM Comput. Surv. **51**(5), 1–42 (2019)

11. Hasal, M., Nowaková, J., Saghair, K.A., Abdulla, H.M.D., Snásel, V., Ogiela, L.: Chatbots: security, privacy, data protection, and social aspects. Concurr. Comput. Pract. Exp. **33**(19), e6426 (2021)

12. Huang, V., Wang, C., Ma, H., Chen, G., Christopher, K.: Cost-aware dynamic multi-workflow scheduling in cloud data center using evolutionary reinforcement learning. In: Troya, J., Medjahed, B., Piattini, M., Yao, L., Fernandez, P., Ruiz-Cortes, A. (eds.) Service-Oriented Computing. Lecture Notes in Computer Science, vol. 13740, pp. 449–464. Springer, Cham (2022). https://doi.org/10.1007/978-3-031-20984-0_32

13. Iftikhar, S., et al.: AI-based fog and edge computing: a systematic review, taxonomy and future directions. Internet Things **21**, 100674 (2023)

14. Jamil, B., Ijaz, H., Shojafar, M., Munir, K., Buyya, R.: Resource allocation and task scheduling in fog computing and internet of everything environments: a taxonomy, review, and future directions. ACM Comput. Surv. **54**(11s), 1–38 (2022)

15. Jentzsch, S.F., Höhn, S., Hochgeschwender, N.: Conversational interfaces for explainable AI: a human-centred approach. In: Calvaresi, D., Najjar, A., Schumacher, M., Främling, K. (eds.) EXTRAAMAS 2019. LNCS (LNAI), vol. 11763, pp. 77–92. Springer, Cham (2019). https://doi.org/10.1007/978-3-030-30391-4_5

16. Ji, Z., et al.: Survey of hallucination in natural language generation. ACM Comput. Surv. **55**(12), 1–38 (2023)

17. Juozapaitis, Z., Koul, A., Fern, A., Erwig, M., Doshi-Velez, F.: Explainable reinforcement learning via reward decomposition. In: IJCAI/ECAI Workshop on Explainable Artificial Intelligence (2019)

18. Kuźba, M., Biecek, P.: What would you ask the machine learning model? identification of user needs for model explanations based on human-model conversations. In: Koprinska, I., et al. (eds.) ECML PKDD 2020. CCIS, vol. 1323, pp. 447–459. Springer, Cham (2020). https://doi.org/10.1007/978-3-030-65965-3_30

19. Liao, Q.V., Gruen, D.M., Miller, S.: Questioning the AI: informing design practices for explainable AI user experiences. In: Conference on Human Factors in Computing Systems (CHI '20). ACM (2020)

20. Ma, W., Xu, H.: Skyline-enhanced deep reinforcement learning approach for energy-efficient and QoS-guaranteed multi-cloud service composition. Appl. Sci. **13**(11), 6826 (2023)

21. Madumal, P., Miller, T., Sonenberg, L., Vetere, F.: A grounded interaction protocol for explainable artificial intelligence. In: 18th International Conference on Autonomous Agents and MultiAgent Systems, AAMAS19. International Foundation for Autonomous Agents and Multiagent Systems (2019)

22. Malandri, L., Mercorio, F., Mezzanzanica, M., Nobani, N.: ConvXAI: a system for multimodal interaction with any black-box explainer. Cogn. Comput. **15**(2), 613–644 (2023)

23. Mariotti, E., Alonso, J.M., Gatt, A.: Towards harnessing natural language generation to explain black-box models. In: 2nd Workshop on Interactive Natural Language Technology for Explainable Artificial Intelligence. ACL (2020)

24. Maslej, P., et al.: The AI index 2023 annual report. Technical report, AI Index Steering Committee, Institute for Human-Centered AI, Stanford University (2023)

25. Metzger, A., Kley, T., Rothweiler, A., Pohl, K.: Automatically reconciling the trade-off between prediction accuracy and earliness in prescriptive business process monitoring. Inf. Syst. **118**, 102254 (2023)

26. Metzger, A., Laufer, J., Feit, F., Pohl, K.: A user study on explainable online reinforcement learning for adaptive systems. CoRR **abs/2307.04098** (2023)

27. Metzger, A., Quinton, C., Mann, Z.Á., Baresi, L., Pohl, K.: Realizing self-adaptive systems via online reinforcement learning and feature-model-guided exploration. Computing (2022)

28. Miller, T.: Explanation in artificial intelligence: insights from the social sciences. Artif. Intell. **267**, 1–38 (2019)

29. Mo, R., Xu, X., Zhang, X., Qi, L., Liu, Q.: Computation offloading and resource management for energy and cost trade-offs with deep reinforcement learning in mobile edge computing. In: Hacid, H., Kao, O., Mecella, M., Moha, N., Paik, H. (eds.) ICSOC 2021. LNCS, vol. 13121, pp. 563–577. Springer, Cham (2021). https://doi.org/10.1007/978-3-030-91431-8_35

30. Mohseni, S., Zarei, N., Ragan, E.D.: A multidisciplinary survey and framework for design and evaluation of explainable AI systems. ACM Trans. Interact. Intell. Syst. **11**(3–4), 1–45 (2021)

31. Moreno, G.A., Schmerl, B.R., Garlan, D.: SWIM: an exemplar for evaluation and comparison of self-adaptation approaches for web applications. In: 13th International Conference on Software Engineering for Adaptive and Self-Managing Systems, SEAMS@ICSE 2018. ACM (2018)

32. Motger, Q., Franch, X., Marco, J.: Software-based dialogue systems: survey, taxonomy, and challenges. ACM Comput. Surv. **55**(5), 1–42 (2023)

33. Mutanu, L., Kotonya, G.: State of runtime adaptation in service-oriented systems: what, where, when, how and right. IET Softw. **13**(1), 14–24 (2019)

34. Nguyen, V.B., Schlötterer, J., Seifert, C.: Explaining machine learning models in natural conversations: towards a conversational XAI agent. CoRR **abs/2209.02552** (2022)

35. Palm, A., Metzger, A., Pohl, K.: Online reinforcement learning for self-adaptive information systems. In: Dustdar, S., Yu, E., Salinesi, C., Rieu, D., Pant, V. (eds.) CAiSE 2020. LNCS, vol. 12127, pp. 169–184. Springer, Cham (2020). https://doi.org/10.1007/978-3-030-49435-3_11

36. Pham, H.V., et al.: Problems and opportunities in training deep learning software systems: an analysis of variance. In: 35th International Conference on Automated Software Engineering (ASE 2020). IEEE (2020)

37. Puiutta, E., Veith, E.M.S.P.: Explainable reinforcement learning: a survey. In: Holzinger, A., Kieseberg, P., Tjoa, A.M., Weippl, E. (eds.) CD-MAKE 2020. LNCS,

vol. 12279, pp. 77–95. Springer, Cham (2020). https://doi.org/10.1007/978-3-030-57321-8_5

38. Razian, M.R., Fathian, M., Bahsoon, R., Toosi, A.N., Buyya, R.: Service composition in dynamic environments: a systematic review and future directions. J. Syst. Softw. **188**, 111290 (2022)

39. Robnik-Šikonja, M., Bohanec, M.: Perturbation-based explanations of prediction models. In: Zhou, J., Chen, F. (eds.) Human and Machine Learning. HIS, pp. 159–175. Springer, Cham (2018). https://doi.org/10.1007/978-3-319-90403-0_9

40. Sequeira, P., Gervasio, M.T.: Interestingness elements for explainable reinforcement learning: understanding agents' capabilities and limitations. Artif. Intell. **288**, 103367 (2020)

41. Strobelt, H., et al.: Interactive and visual prompt engineering for ad-hoc task adaptation with large language models. IEEE Trans. Vis. Comput. Graph. **29**(1), 1146–1156 (2023)

42. Sutton, R.S., Barto, A.G.: Reinforcement Learning: An Introduction. MIT Press, Cambridge (2018)

43. White, J., et al.: A prompt pattern catalog to enhance prompt engineering with chatgpt. CoRR **abs/2302.11382** (2023)

44. Yu, Z., et al.: DeepSCJD: an online deep learning-based model for secure collaborative job dispatching in edge computing. In: Troya, J., Medjahed, B., Piattini, M., Yao, L., Fernandez, P., Ruiz-Cortes, A. (eds.) Service-Oriented Computing. Lecture Notes in Computer Science, vol. 13740, pp. 481–497. Springer, Cham (2022). https://doi.org/10.1007/978-3-031-20984-0_34

45. Zhao, H., et al.: Explainability for large language models: a survey. CoRR **abs/2309.01029** (2023)

BEAR: Revolutionizing Service Domain Knowledge Graph Construction with LLM

Shuang Yu, Tao Huang, Mingyi Liu, and Zhongjie Wang[✉]

Faculty of Computing, Harbin Institute of Technology, Harbin, China
yushuang@hit.edu.cn,22s103254@stu.hit.edu.cn{liumy,rainy}@hit.edu.cn

Abstract. Knowledge graph (KG), as a novel knowledge storage approach, has been widely used in various domains. In the service computing community, researchers tried to harness the enormous potential of KG to tackle domain-specific tasks. However, the lack of an openly available service domain KG limits the in-depth exploration of KGs in domain-specific applications. Building a service domain KG primarily faces two challenges: first, the diversity and complexity of service domain knowledge, and second, the dispersion of domain knowledge and the lack of annotated data. These challenges discouraged costly investment in large, high-quality domain-specific KGs by researchers. In this paper, we present the construction of a service domain KG called BEAR. We design a comprehensive service domain knowledge ontology to automatically generate the prompts for the Large Language Model (LLM) and employ LLM to implement a zero-shot method to extract high-quality knowledge. A series of experiments are conducted to demonstrate the feasibility of graph construction process and showcase the richness of content available from BEAR. Currently, BEAR includes $133,906$ nodes, $169,159$ relations, and about $424,000$ factual knowledge as attributes, which is available through **github.com/HTXone/BEAR**.

Keywords: Service domain knowledge graph · Service domain ontology · Knowledge graph construction · Large language model

1 Introduction

Knowledge graphs (KGs) are widely applied in knowledge-driven intelligent applications. The service computing community also acknowledges the immense potential of KGs, which allows providers to effectively manage resources, understand customer requirements, and enhance customer satisfaction by enabling personalized recommendations, semantic search, and other applications with interpretability and reasoning capabilities for more automated and intelligent service interactions [5, 7].

The benefits of introducing KGs are not always apparent due to the paradigms of utilization. Researchers typically employ two paradigms when applying KGs in service computing tasks: one involves utilizing open, general KGs [6, 7], and the other focuses on organizing data into KG formats tailored to

F. Monti et al. (Eds.): ICSOC 2023, LNCS 14419, pp. 339–346, 2023.
https://doi.org/10.1007/978-3-031-48421-6_23

specific service domains [3,12]. But neither of these two paradigms has truly leveraged the powerful capabilities of KGs. Thus, a large-scale, high-quality service-oriented KG is urgently needed in the current service computing community, which will promote application and algorithm innovation in the service computing community.

As a specific domain KG, service domain KG faces two major challenges during its construction:

1. **Diversity and complexity.** Constructing a service domain KG involves encompassing knowledge from various fields, each with its distinct terms and concepts that interrelate within the service computing community. Furthermore, the knowledge within the service domain exhibits unique characteristics, adding complexity to the construction of the service domain KG.
2. **Insufficient data source.** The lack of data is reflected in two aspects. Firstly, there is a severe shortage of annotated data in the service computing domain, and the labeling cost is also high due to the typically complex, heterogeneous nature of service data. Secondly, service-related knowledge data is highly scattered, making it challenging to gather enough sources and quickly organize their relationships.

To address the pressing requirements for an open service domain KG within the service computing community, we construct a service domain KG called **BEAR** in this paper. On the one hand, BEAR addresses the first challenge by providing a relatively comprehensive ontology and using this ontology to guide and standardize the construction process of the service domain KG. On the other hand, BEAR utilizes the exceptional semantic understanding and reasoning capabilities of LLM to address the second challenge.

The main contributions of this paper can be summarized as follows:

1. **Introducing a new open KG in the service computing community**: We have developed a comprehensive ontology specifically designed for the service computing field. Using this ontology, we have created a large-scale service domain KG comprising over **130,000** entities, **160,000** relations, and **4,240,000** factual knowledge[1].
2. **Novel approach for service domain KG construction**: We have devised a novel zero-shot framework for constructing KGs. This framework facilitates the extraction of knowledge based on ontology, enabling the acquisition of high-quality knowledge without the need for label training.

2 Related Works

2.1 Knowledge Graph in Service Computing

In the top venues of service computing, there has been a notable surge in the utilization of KGs in recent years, while few of them focus on constructing a service domain KG.

---

[1] The download address is github.com/HTXone/BEAR.

There are two main paradigms in the service domain community for utilizing KGs. The first paradigm involves applying general KGs to service computing tasks [6,7]. This paradigm suffers from coarse granularity and broad, weakly relevant content in general KGs when applied to the service domain. The second paradigm organizes original data into the form of a KG for each specific task [3, 12]. This paradigm repeatedly constructs small-scale service domain KGs for each task/dataset, which can be time-consuming, labor-intensive, and limited to the knowledge derived from the original input data without any additional information.

2.2   Specific Domain Knowledge Graph Construction Methods

With the development of knowledge-based research, in other specific domains, more and more domain KG construction methods have been proposed [1]. For the construction of service domain KGs, the real challenge lies in data collection, annotation, and how to limit the scope of knowledge effectively. The emergence of LLMs greatly reduces the amount of data annotation required and improves the quality of data extraction. Wei et al. [11] confirmed the feasibility and effectiveness of taking named entity recognition (NER) and relation extraction (RE) by using ChatGPT to solve the problem of missing annotation data. In this paper, the KG construction process will build upon this finding.

3   Ontology for Service Domain Knowledge

KG can be divided into two parts: concept layer and data layer, and ontology is the main content of the concept layer [8]. Ontology is essential in domain KGs due to the diversity and complexity of concepts within a domain. It provides a common framework for organizing and categorizing diverse concepts, allowing for efficient knowledge retrieval, integration, and reasoning.

> **RQ1:** What characteristics should be included in the service domain ontology?

IBM has introduced the concept of service science, which combines service, science, management, and engineering (SSME) [2]. Services in SSME encompass all non-tangible products or constructs that are typically consumed during production and offer additional value in terms of convenience, pleasure, time-saving, comfort, or health benefits [9]. Based on this description and further research [10], the main characteristics of the service domain can be summarized as follows:

1. **Behavioral nature of services**: The service provider performs a series of behaviors to the service consumer to realize the service value.
2. **Service participants**: Services require the participation of both service providers and consumers who interact with each other to realize the value transfer of service.

3. **Supporting resources for services**: Services do not exist in physical entities, but can be realized by relying on resources with physical entities.
4. **Value of services**: The service realizes some kind of value conversion during its execution, typically with the service provider delivering the service value to the service consumer, and these values can be assessed by some indicators within the industry.
5. **Goal of services**: The goal of services is an attribute related to the service value, and the value of services is measured by evaluating whether the goal of services is realized.
6. **Constraints on services**: In the real world, there are some provider-centric constraints that have an influence on the operation of services.

> *RQ2: What elements should service domain ontology contain and how do they reflect the characteristics of service domain ontology?*

In the original research on service computing, the concept of the service model focused on four elements: people, resources, shared information, and behavior [10]. However, as service computing has evolved and tackled real-world problems, these four elements no longer fully capture the breadth of the service field. To better characterize the knowledge in the service domain, we have re-summarized and organized the ontology. The definitions of the main entity classes are provided in Table 1. Currently, we have defined 24 entity classes and 68 relations in the service domain ontology[2]

4   Knowledge Extraction with LLM

In the service field, there is a shortage of annotated datasets, and creating such datasets usually requires a considerable amount of manual work. Additionally, gathering enough information poses a challenge due to the complex and dispersed nature of knowledge from various fields. To overcome the challenge of limited data sources in the service domain knowledge, we propose a knowledge extraction method based on LLM shown in Fig. 1.

> *RQ3: How to effectively obtain knowledge from unannotated data sources with LLM?*

In order to obtain sufficient knowledge, a KG construction framework that supports knowledge extraction from structured and text data is developed to fit most storage methods of real-world knowledge. For the structured data, the knowledge extraction is performed by the traditional approach: aligning the data concept with the ontology concept and then importing them into the KG [4].

---

[2] Full ontology is in https://github.com/HTXone/BEAR.

Table 1. Ontology element definition. Noted each element has rich relations that are not listed in this table.

Element	Introduction	Example
Organization	Service participant act as service providers or as service consumers. Service providers are responsible for releasing and maintaining the service, while service consumers are responsible for using it.	Google Company
Product	Product(resource) hosting services, as the tangible carrier of the service, the participants of the service realize the value exchange of the service through the carrier.	Google Translation Software
Business	Interactions between service participants, describes a certain predetermined interoperability behavior adopted by both service participants for a certain value exchange.	Text Translation Service
Document	Information exchanged within the service, valuable information records generated during the service, or description records of the elements of the service itself.	Google Translation Patent
People	Form organization, participate in the business, key figures appearing in the organization or service, perform a certain service on behalf of the organization or exert influence on the organization in real events.	Larry Page
Environment	The objective conditions on which organizations and businesses exist, which restrict the development of organization or execution of services.	Privacy Policy
Field	Abstract types related to organization or business, is the location of an organization or service, used to distinguish and compare similar services.	Internet
Service Value	Service value realized through business, in the business model, it usually means using funds to purchase a certain service.	Marketing Value

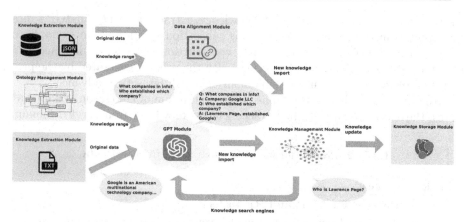

Fig. 1. Service domain knowledge extraction framework of BEAR

To extract knowledge and construct KG from text data, the system employs the prompt automatically generated from the service domain ontology through the expected knowledge scope, knowledge samples, response formats, and predefined prompt templates, and then engages in multiple rounds of question-and-answer interactions with ChatGPT[3] to extract the desired knowledge content and update the KG. Table 2 shows the template for prompts.

---

[3] https://chat.openai.com/.

In certain scenarios, ChatGPT might generate knowledge that extends beyond the predefined concepts of the ontology. This supplementary knowledge is stored as factual information attributes linked to relevant nodes within the KG.

> *RQ4: How to query the hidden knowledge outside the data source with LLM?*

To address the issues of wide range of knowledge involved in the service domain and the dispersed nature of knowledge across various corners of the Internet, and extract knowledge that may not be directly available in the data source but is publicly accessible, we employ the ontology to generate a query prompt that covers multiple aspects of the node information as shown in Table 2 to supplement knowledge in case of insufficient information.

Due to the validity threats associated with ChatGPT, we set a configurable parameter to determine that the search method can be applied when the node is pointed to by the specific number of edges.

5   Experiment and Result

As the effectiveness experiment of knowledge extraction using ChatGPT has been proved in the reference [11], in this subsection we provide an example to indicate that the ChatGPT based KG construction process we designed can obtain correct service domain knowledge with the prompt generated by the proposed ontology and without large manually labeled datasets in advance.

We use the first three paragraphs of the description of Google on Wikipedia[4] to test the effect of ChatGPT in extracting facts/knowledge from service domain.

Table 2. Prompt for knowledge extraction from text data

Role	Content
	Prompt for NER and RE tasks
system	As a knowledge extraction model, your task is to extract entities and their corresponding attributes and relationships from the given information.
user	Please perform the named entity recognition task on the given information now. information:{Text information that waiting for knowledge extraction}
user	Please extract the {entity class} entity in the above information, and return the results in the specified format. Result example: —Entity Type—Entity Name— —{sample entity class}—{sample entity name}—

---

[4] https://en.wikipedia.org/wiki/Google.

The prompt declared in Sect. 4 is used to question Google information. Figure 2[5] shows the knowledge extract result.

To further obtain knowledge outside the given information, we use the prompt declared in Sect. 4 to question Amazon information to test the feasibility of the knowledge search method. Figure 3[6] shows the knowledge search result.

In the final result, we get 186 entities and 230 relations where 116 entities and 147 relations are obtained by the search method. Through verification, the answers from ChatGPT are all correct.

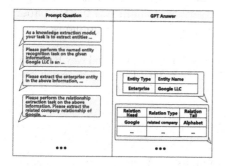

Fig. 2. Knowledge extraction of Google   **Fig. 3.** Knowledge search of Amazon

6   BEAR Overview

We gather data sources for BEAR from various content channels, including online application stores like Google Store, enterprise online data such as WikiData, and online news reports. The complete list of data sources is available on GitHub and is regularly updated. In BEAR, there are 133, 906 entities and 169, 159 relationships. To effectively use the information from LLM, we retain the knowledge not included in the ontology as the node attribute, and get 424, 184 attribute triples from this type of knowledge.

7   Threat of Validity

As a generative model, GPT3.5 (ChatGPT) may provide unintended answers. To address this issue, we include example samples in the generated prompt, which helps to standardize the generation of answers. We also implement rule checks to ensure that only samples meeting the desired format are included in the KG.

It should be noted that the LLMs are evolving rapidly, and at the time of writing this paper, GPT4 is already available. The more efficient LLM will greatly improve the accuracy of knowledge extraction.

---

[5] Full answer in https://github.com/HTXone/BEAR.
[6] Full answer in https://github.com/HTXone/BEAR.

8   Conclusion

In response to the urgent need of the service computing community for a large-scale, pre-constructed, high-quality domain KG, this paper constructs an open-access service domain KG called BEAR. Currently, BEAR contains $133,906$ entities, $169,159$ relationships, and over $420,000$ domain facts/knowledge stored in entity attributes. The use of ontology-based prompts and LLM's zero-shot learning ability greatly reduces the annotation cost in the entire process. In addition, LLM can also be used to retrieve/infer potential factual knowledge. Furthermore, the method of constructing the service domain KG in this paper can also provide a reference for the construction of KG in other domains.

Acknowledgment. This research is partially supported by the National Key Research and Development Program of China (No.2021YFB3300700), the Key Research and Development Program of Heilongjiang Province (No.2022ZX01A11).

References

1. Abu-Salih, B.: Domain-specific knowledge graphs: a survey. J. Netw. Comput. Appl. **185**, 103076 (2021)
2. Bishop, K., Bolan, G., et al.: Succeeding through service innovation: a service perspective for education, research, business and government (2008)
3. Gao, Z., Fan, Y., et al.: Service recommendation from the evolution of composition patterns. In: SCC 2017, pp. 108–115 (2017)
4. Hao, X., et al.: Construction and application of a knowledge graph. Rem. Sens. **13**(13), 2511 (2021)
5. Hu, S., Tu, Z., et al.: A poi-sensitive knowledge graph based service recommendation method. In: SCC 2019, pp. 197–201 (2019)
6. Huang, B., Dong, H., Bouguettaya, A.: Conflict detection in IoT-based smart homes. In: ICWS 2021, pp. 303–313 (2021)
7. Mezni, H.: Temporal knowledge graph embedding for effective service recommendation. IEEE Trans. Serv. Comput. **15**(5), 3077–3088 (2021)
8. Paulheim, H.: Knowledge graph refinement: a survey of approaches and evaluation methods. Sem. Web **8**(3), 489–508 (2017)
9. Quinn, J.B., Baruch, J.J., et al.: Technology in services. Sci. Am. **257**(6), 50–59 (1987)
10. Wang, Z., Xu, X.: Ontology-based service component model for interoperability of service systems. In: IESA 2008, pp. 367–380 (2008)
11. Wei, X., Cui, X., et al.: Zero-shot information extraction via chatting with ChatGPT. arXiv preprint arXiv:2302.10205 (2023)
12. Zhang, M., Zhao, J., et al.: A knowledge graph based approach for mobile application recommendation. In: ICSOC 2020, pp. 355–369 (2020)

Dependency-Aware Resource Allocation
for Serverless Functions at the Edge

Luciano Baresi[1], Giovanni Quattrocchi[1(✉)], and Inacio Gaspar Ticongolo[1,2]

[1] Dipartimento di Elettronica, Informazione e Bioingegneria, Politecnico di Milano,
Milano, Italy
{luciano.baresi,giovanni.quattrocchi,inaciogaspar.ticongolo}@polimi.it
[2] Departamento de Matematica e Informatica, Universidade Eduardo Mondlane,
Maputo, Mozambique

Abstract. Serverless computing allows developers to break their code
into small components, known as functions. Being lightweight and mod-
ular, serverless functions have been increasingly employed in edge computing, where quick responses and adaptability are key to meeting strict
latency requirements. In particular, edge nodes are intrinsically resource-
constrained, and efficient resource allocation strategies are crucial for
optimizing their usage. Different approaches exist in the literature, but
they often overlook the dependencies among functions, that is, how and
when functions invoke other functions, and obtain suboptimal results.
This paper presents NEPTUNE⁺, a dependency-aware resource (CPU
cores) allocation solution for serverless functions deployed on edge infrastructures. The approach extends NEPTUNE, an existing framework for
managing edge infrastructures, with a new theoretical model and control
algorithm that take function dependencies into account. We evaluated
NEPTUNE⁺ by using three applications and it is able to allocate up to
42% fewer cores compared to NEPTUNE.

Keywords: serverless · edge computing · function dependencies ·
resource allocation

1 Introduction

Complex[1] applications are increasingly built as sets of independent components,
like microservices [4], to foster agility and speed during both development and
runtime management. This high degree of modularization allows for independent
management, but complicates communication among components and affects
their performance. Understanding the logical dependencies among components
becomes then essential for the efficient management of these systems [11].

---

[1] The work presented in this paper is partially supported by project ICTD4Dev,
funded by AICS, and by project EMELIOT, funded by the MUR under the PRIN
2020 program (Contract 2020W3A5FY).

Serverless computing is imposing as a new family of such highly modularized architectural paradigms [17]. It promotes the creation of applications as collections of "small" functions [18], which are usually executed in lightweight containers to ensure their fast and efficient management [6]. Serverless functions are designed to be independently developed, deployed, and automatically scaled by a service provider. This high degree of flexibility allows for fast re-configuration and scaling in response to changes in the system workload and contributes to the overall agility of the system.

Given these characteristics, serverless functions have been increasingly employed in edge computing [17]. In this context, applications are often constrained by strict latency requirements. The inherent agility and ability to rapidly scale individual components allow serverless platforms to quickly adapt to workload fluctuations, facilitate the prompt execution of functions, and allow the system to meet latency requirements more effectively [22]. However, it is essential to acknowledge that serverless functions can depend on other functions, which can significantly impact their performance and management [10].

In the last few years, serverless computing has been widely studied as means to improve the management of applications deployed on edge infrastructures [13]. Some approaches tackle the intelligent placement of edge functions on resource-limited nodes [6,9]; others focus on optimizing resource allocation [20]. Yet, these approaches often overlook function dependencies, a crucial factor for performance modeling [23].

This paper introduces NEPTUNE$^+$, a solution that focuses on resource allocation for serverless functions deployed on edge infrastructures. NEPTUNE$^+$ extends NEPTUNE, our previously developed edge framework [2], which allows for the smart placement and allocation of serverless functions, but it does not consider function dependencies. NEPTUNE$^+$ extends the theoretical model behind NEPTUNE by proposing i) a new formalization of the problem that encodes function dependencies as an annotated Direct Acyclic Graph (DAG), and ii) a novel control algorithm that exploits the function dependency graph to save resources. To the best of our knowledge, this is the first work that specifically focuses on resource allocation for serverless functions with dependencies. This distinguishes our work from existing studies, which primarily concentrate on function placement rather than on resource allocation. This work focuses on edge computing, where resource-constrained devices necessitate optimized resource allocation for effective computation. However, it can also be adopted in cloud computing scenarios to minimize resource consumption and thereby reduce operational expenses.

A comprehensive empirical evaluation compared NEPTUNE and NEPTUNE$^+$ by means of three benchmark applications. Obtained results show that NEPTUNE$^+$ allocates up to 42% fewer cores than NEPTUNE, with comparable performance in terms of response times.

The rest of the paper is organized as follows. Section 2 introduces NEPTUNE and highlights its limitations. Section 3 describes our solution, the new problem formulation, and control algorithm. Section 4 presents the evaluation and discusses obtained results. Section 5 surveys the related work, and Sect. 6 concludes the paper.

2 NEPTUNE in a Nutshell

Serverless computing is the driver of a significant paradigm shift that frees developers from infrastructure management [18], and some approaches [7,23] explored this paradigm for deploying and managing applications on edge infrastructures. To our best knowledge, only NEPTUNE [2] provides a comprehensive and holistic management approach that considers network partitioning, placement, request routing, and combined dynamic allocation of memory, CPUs and GPUs.

NEPTUNE requires the code of the functions to deploy, a threshold (service level agreement or SLA) on its response time, and the identification of the memory required for proper execution. The management exploits a three-level hierarchy: topology, community, and node. The global network *topology* is split into a set of independent *communities*. Each community is composed of edge *nodes* (or servers) that are close to each other, that is, their network inter-delays are smaller than a set threshold. Each community is managed by a dedicated controller that takes into account user mobility, workload provenance, and memory requirements for each function. This controller exploits an optimization problem based on Mixed-Integer Programming to calculate the best placement of function instances and a set of routing policies that minimize network latency. Function placement implies deciding how many function instances are needed for each used function and the best node to host each of them. Since each node cannot always host all the instances and handle all the incoming workload, NEPTUNE uses routing policies to compute the request fraction to be routed to other nodes. The same formulation is used to first handle the workload that can be accelerated through GPUs, and then, the remaining workload is assigned to CPUs.

Whereas GPUs and memory are entirely managed by the community controller, the node level controller oversees the proper execution of requests on CPUs, and ensures that each function instance is provisioned with enough cores to execute within the given SLA. A lightweight Proportional Integral (PI) controller is attached to each function instance f_i with the goal of keeping the response time close to a given set point:

$$sp_i = \alpha * SLA_i \tag{1}$$

where α is a scaling parameter ($0 < \alpha \leq 1$). The more α is close to 1, the more the response time is kept close to SLA, with a risk for potential violations. Conversely, if α is significantly lower than 1, the controller ensures better performance, but more resources are needed. Therefore, α represents a tunable trade-off between performance and resource utilization.

2.1 Limitations

NEPTUNE does not consider function dependencies, which can lead to inefficient resource allocation. Let us consider, for example, the application in Fig. 1. This

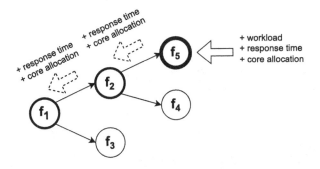

Fig. 1. Example application with function dependencies.

application consists of five functions, f_1, f_2, f_3, f_4, f_5, with their dependencies outlined in a directed acyclic graph (DAG): f_1 depends on f_2 and f_3, while f_2 depends on f_4 and f_5.

If we assume that function f_5 is supposed to manage a workload spike, its response time suddenly increases, and its local node level controller is prompted to augment allocated cores. While f_5's controller stabilizes the situation and brings the response time closer to the set point, the response times of f_2, and then of f_1, also grow, given their dependency on f_5.

The inefficiency of NEPTUNE lies in the behavior of the controllers associated with f_2 and f_1: higher response times, due to the slow responses from f_5, imply increasing the cores allocated to f_1 and f_2. This reaction is redundant, as the issue does not stem from either f_2 or f_1, but the bottleneck is f_5. Instead of allocating extra cores to f_2 and f_1, these resources would have been better utilized to speed up f_5.

This is why NEPTUNE must be improved/extended to address this limitation and fix redundant allocations: CPU cores must be allocated efficiently even in the presence of dependent serverless functions. Unlike CPUs, GPUs are statically allocated each time NEPTUNE determines a new placement. Therefore, they do not face the same issue of inefficient allocation.

3 NEPTUNE⁺

NEPTUNE⁺ extends NEPTUNE with a new theoretical model and control algorithm to efficiently allocate resources to serverless functions with dependencies. In particular, NEPTUNE⁺ aims to improve the allocation of CPUs cores at the node level in light of the limitations described in Sect. 2.1, while it inherits from NEPTUNE its placement strategy that minimizes network delays and the management of GPUs and memory.

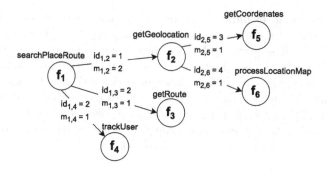

Fig. 2. Example of annotated DAG.

3.1 Theoretical Model

Let F be a set of serverless functions whose dependencies are encoded as a DAG, where nodes are function instances and edges are function invocations. This DAG is assumed to be either manually defined by the user or automatically generated by means of network or log analysis techniques [14].

We do not consider invocation cycles (i.e., we employed DAGs for modeling dependencies), in line with the recommendations against their use, as suggested by Fontana et al. [12]. A cycle denotes a situation where a function indirectly relies on its own output to commence execution, forming an untenable loop. This could lead to an endless cycle of executions or deadlock scenarios that are unmanageable cost-wise on real serverless platforms [21].

NEPTUNE$^+$ considers the response time rt_i of a function $f_i \in F$ as follows:

$$rt_i = lrt_i + ert_i \tag{2}$$

where lrt_i is the *local* response time spent for executing its code, that is, the set of instructions that implements the function without considering external calls to other functions, and ert_i is the *external* response time, that is, the time spent for invoking other functions. The external response time depends on the type of dependency between f_i and another function f_j. First, the invocation could be either *sequential* or *parallel*. In the former case, the invocation is synchronous, that is, other invocations must wait for its completion. The latter allows a function to be executed in parallel with some other invocations. More formally, each edge in the DAG is annotated with an identifier $id_{i,j}$. If two edges $E_{i,j}$ and $E_{i,k}$, which represent the invocations of f_j and f_k, respectively, in f_i, have different identifiers, the invocations are executed sequentially. If they are annotated with the same value, they are called in parallel.[2] Moreover, each edge is also annotated with a *multiplier* $m_{i,j}$, which denotes how many times such invocation is executed within the same function call [23].

---

[2] Note that our approach allows a function f_i to invoke another function f_j both in sequential and parallel mode by having multiple, properly annotated, edges between i and j (as in *multigraphs* [1]). Here, we do not focus on such edge cases to keep our formalization as simple as possible.

Figure 2 shows an example annotated DAG with 6 functions. Function f_1 (*searchPlaceRoute*) sequentially calls function f_2 (*getGeolocation*), thus $id_{1,2}$ is unique. This call is performed twice during its execution (i.e., $m_{1,2} = 2$)– for example, to get the coordinates of the user and of the destination location, respectively. Moreover, *searchPlaceRoute* invokes *getRoute* (f_3) and *trackUser* (f_4) in parallel (i.e., $id_{1,3} = id_{1,4} = 2$), each function executed once (i.e., $m_{1,3} = m_{1,4} = 1$). Finally, *getGeolocation* sequentially invokes *getCoordinates* (f_5) and *processLocationMap* (f_6), each once, since the edge identifiers are unique.

The external response time is defined as follows:

$$ert_i = \sum_{j \in S} m_{i,j} * rt_j + \sum_{P \in \bar{P}} max(m_{i,j} * rt_j, \ \forall j \in P) \tag{3}$$

where S is the set of functions sequentially invoked by f_i , $\bar{P}$ is the set of the subsets of functions that f_i invokes in parallel, and P represents each subset (i.e., a group of parallel invocations). In essence, the external response time is the sum of all sequential invocations plus the sum of all the longest response times of each parallel group times the number of times each dependency is called (i.e., $m_{i,j}$).

In NEPTUNE$^+$, function instances can receive requests from users (i.e., direct invocations) and/or from other functions (i.e., external invocations). More formally, the total amount of requests r_i^w received by f_i in a time window w is defined as follows:

$$r_i^w = r_{users \to f_i}^w + \sum_{j \in E_*, i} m_{j,i} * r_j^w \tag{4}$$

where $r_{users \to f_i}^w$ is the total amount of direct invocations of f_i in w and E_*, i is the set of source nodes i(i.e., a function f_j) having an edge directed to node f_i.

3.2   Control Algorithm

While NEPTUNE's node controllers consider each function independently, NEPTUNE$^+$ adapts the control strategy by considering the dependency DAG. The control algorithm we employ distinguishes between *entrypoint* and *externally invoked* functions. The former can be invoked by users, that is, $r_{users \to f_i}^w > 0$ for some w, whereas the latter are *only* called by other functions in the DAG[3].

NEPTUNE$^+$ allows users to define an SLA for each entrypoint function f_i. If f_i is only called by users and not by other functions, such an input is mandatory, whereas it is optional if f_i is also invoked by other functions (as a consequence of a direct invocation of another entrypoint).

NEPTUNE$^+$ inherits from NEPTUNE its PI controllers, which compute resource allocations without synchronizing with one another. The main difference between the two approaches is that NEPTUNE monitors and controls

---

[3] Note that an invocation is *external* with respect to the execution environment of the invoked function (as for the use of "external" in *external response time*).

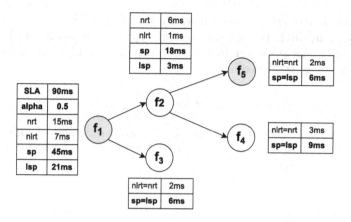

Fig. 3. Example of local set point computation.

the response rt_i of each function f_i without discriminating between local and external response times; NEPTUNE$^+$ focuses on the local response time lrt_i. The intuition behind this design is that rt_i is affected by the response times of other functions (external invocations), which results in the problems described in Sect. 2.1. In contrast, lrt_i depends solely on the resource allocation of f_i and allows for a more fine-grained and optimized control strategy.

Since NEPTUNE$^+$ exploits lrt_i, it cannot simply reuse Eq. 1 to define the *local set points* of the PI controllers, since SLA_i is defined as an upper bound of the *total* response rt_i. Thus, NEPTUNE$^+$ computes, at design time, the local set points lsp_i of each function f_i by considering: i) the user-defined SLAs for entrypoint functions, ii) the dependencies among functions, and iii) the *weight* of each function within the DAG. Intuitively, higher weights correspond to higher set points since such functions are considered more complex compared to others.

In particular, the weight of a function f_i is calculated by using the *nominal response time* nrt_i and the *nominal local response time* $nlrt_i$: nrt_i and $nlrt_i$ are modeled, respectively, by using the formulas used to calculate rt_i (Eq. 2) and lrt_i (Eq. 3). However, whereas rt_i and lrt_i are measured at runtime under user-generated workloads, nrt_i and $nlrt_i$ are measured during a profiling phase while considering the system in a quiescent state (i.e., without saturation or request queue). Each function is profiled with a static core allocation (e.g., 1 core) and by sending one request at a time, waiting for the previous to finish. To avoid considering cold starts, the measurement starts after a warm-up period. These two metrics are used to understand the complexity of functions and their dependencies in a "controlled" state and are used to properly compute set points.

To explain how we calculate local set points, we employ the same application described in Sect. 2 and Fig. 3 shows the main calculations. Functions f_1 and f_5 are depicted in light gray and are the two entrypoints of the application. For the sake of simplicity, we consider all the dependencies as sequential and with all multipliers $m_{i,j}$ equal to 1. Thus, we do not report the DAG annotations.

Let f_i be an entrypoint function with a user-defined SLA_i, and a set point sp_i defined as in Eq. 1. In the example, only f_1 has a user-defined SLA that is equal to 90 ms. Since α is set to 0.5, the set point sp_1 is equal to 45 ms. The local set point lsp_i is defined as:

$$lsp_i = sp_i * \frac{nlrt_i}{nrt_i} \tag{5}$$

Thus, it follows that, in the example, the local set point of function f_1 is equal to 21 ms. Moreover, for each function f_j that is invoked by f_i, the set point sp_j is then defined as:

$$sp_j = \frac{sp_i}{m_{i,j}} * \frac{nrt_j}{nrt_i} \tag{6}$$

The setpoint sp_i is used to compute the local set point of f_i and the set points sp_j of all the dependencies. Given that sp_j is intended to consider a single invocation, the calculation is divided by $m_{i,j}$.

In the example, the dependencies of f_1 are f_2 and f_3. This means that, ideally, the sum of the local response time of f_1 and the (total) response times of f_2 and f_3 should be equal to set point sp_1. Since f_3 has no dependencies, its nominal response time nrt_3 is equal to its nominal local response time $nlrt_3$. Intuitively, since nrt_3 is around 3 times lower than $nlrt_1$, the set point of f_3 (6 ms) is roughly 3 times lower than the local set point of f_1 (21 ms). Instead, f_2 depends on f_4 and f_5, and its set point sp_2 is set to 18 ms with a nominal response time nrt_2 equal to 6 ms. This means, in turn, that the sum of the local response time of f_2 and the response times of f_4 and f_5 should be kept equal to 18 ms.

Recursively, the local set points of each dependency are calculated by using Eq. 5. For example, the set point sp_2 is used to calculate the local set point of f_2 (3 ms) along with the set points of f_4 (6 ms) and f_5 (9 ms). Note that the case of a function without dependencies is the base case of the recursive procedure, and its set point is equal to its local set point, such as for f_3, f_4, and f_5. Finally, to further optimize the resource allocation, the set points of parallel dependencies (i.e., edges with the same source node and identifiers) are calculated as in Eq. 6. However, after the calculation, the set point of each dependency is set to be equal to the maximum of the parallel group. This means that even though siblings could complete execution faster, they are slowed down with higher set points to match the slowest function of the parallel group. This strategy does not affect the overall response time of the application and allows for saving resources.

Proportional-Integral Control. After the previous steps, each function is provided with a local set point lsp_i. As in NEPTUNE, each function f_i is equipped with a PI controller. In NEPTUNE$^+$, the controller for a function f_i monitors only the local response time lrt_i and allocates cores to meet lsp_i. Without any synchronization and thanks to the computations above, if all the controllers are able to meet their local set points, user-defined SLAs are fulfilled. The control algorithm we used, adapted from NEPTUNE, is reported in Algorithm 1.

Algorithm 1. Core allocation

1: $lrt_i \leftarrow getLocalResponseTime(f_i)$
2: $err \leftarrow lsp_i^{-1} - lrt_i^{-1}$
3: $P \leftarrow gain_P * err$
4: $I \leftarrow I + gain_I * err$
5: $cores \leftarrow P + I$
6: $cores \leftarrow min(cores_{MAX}, max(cores_{MIN}, cores))$
7: $allocateCores(f_i, cores)$

The procedure is invoked at every control period for each function instance f_i. The local response time (obtained at line 1) and the local set point are used to compute error err. The higher the error is, the higher the mismatch between the local set point and the actual measured local response time (line 2) is. The proportional contribution (P) is equal to the proportional gain $gain_P$ multiplied by err (line 3). The integral contribution (I) is the sum of the previous actions and the error times the integral gain $gain_I$ (line 4). Both $gain_P$ and $gain_I$ are tuning parameters of the controller and can be set using different well-known heuristics [5]. The core allocation is computed as the sum of P and I (line 5) properly scaled according to the allowed minimum ($cores_{MIN}$) and maximum ($cores_{MAX}$) amount of cores (line 6). The allocation is enacted at line 7.

4   Evaluation

To evaluate NEPTUNE$^+$, we compared it against NEPTUNE. A comprehensive comparison of NEPTUNE against industrial competitors (i.e., K3S, Knative, and OpenFaaS) is reported in our previous work [2] and demonstrated the advantages of NEPTUNE over these industrial solutions.

We ran all the experiments on a MacBook Pro equipped with 4 cores and 16GB of RAM and running macOS Ventura (version 13.2.1). To test the two systems, we relied on an existing simulator called RAS (Resource Allocation Simulator) [3]. RAS was originally used to evaluate the performance of the control algorithms of NEPTUNE against industrial approaches (i.e., Amazon Web Services, Google Cloud Platform, and Microsoft Azure). We extended the simulator[4] in two ways: i) we adapted the code to support function dependencies, and ii) we implemented the novel theoretical model and control algorithm.

The tests used three different applications. The first two are benchmarks widely used in the literature [16], namely *hotel reservation*[5] and *sockshop*[6]). The first is a serverless application that mimics a hotel reservation website, whereas the second is an online e-commerce application that exploits a microservice architecture that we converted to serverless functions [2]. *Hotel reservation* includes four functions (2 entrypoints), and it is characterized by a DAG with an average

---

[4] Source code available at https://github.com/deib-polimi/RAS/tree/dependencies.
[5] https://github.com/vhive-serverless/vSwarm/tree/main/benchmarks/hotel-app.
[6] https://github.com/microservices-demo/microservices-demo.

out-degree of 3 edges, an average in-degree of 1 edge, and all the dependencies have type *sequential*. *Sockshop* includes 7 functions (5 entrypoints) with an average *out − degree* of 6 edges, an average *in − degree* of 1 edge, and one third of the dependencies have type *sequencial* and two thirds have type *parallel*. We also created a more complex application (*complex*), by synthesizing a DAG of 25 functions (6 entrypoints), with an average out-degree of 2 edges, an average in-degree of 1 edge, and roughly balanced sequential and parallel dependencies. We repeated each experiment 10 times. In each test, we simulated executions of 20 minutes each, and for each function, we collected the average (μ) and the standard deviation (σ) of three metrics: response time (RT) in milliseconds, core allocation (C) in millicores, and percentage of SLA violations (V).

The tests employed workloads similar to the ones used to evaluate NEPTUNE in [2,3]. In particular, each entrypoint function was stimulated with either a *ramp* or a step *workload*. We employed ramps that start from 10 requests and added one request every second up to 100 (as in [2]) and randomly generated steps that varied the workload every 50 s in a range between 20 and 120 requests. We also simulated bottlenecks by changing the random step to a number of requests that ranges between 800 and 6000.

For NEPTUNE we set an SLA for each function, whereas for NEPTUNE$^+$ we only set them for entrypoints, since our approach is able to automatically calculate the set points for all the other functions. For *sock-shop*, we employed the same SLAs reported in the original NEPTUNE paper [2]. For *hotel reservation* and *complex application*, we set the SLAs to double their nominal response times. The nominal response times of *hotel reservation* were obtained by profiling each function, while for *complex application* we generated them randomly.

We configured both NEPTUNE and NEPTUNE$^+$ the same way. We employed a value for α equal to 0.5 for each function with an SLA as in [2]. We derived the values of $gain_P$ and $gain_I$ through manual tuning (again, as in [2]). To be sure that the simulator was aligned with realistic results and that our modifications did not affect its accuracy, we executed a preliminary experiment. We simulated the same tests on NEPTUNE as those reported in [2] with application *sockshop* (i.e., same workload and configuration). We collected the results and compared them against those reported in the paper. We observed that on average the differences were minimal: 0.3% for response times and 4.3% for core allocation.

4.1 Performance Without Bottlenecks

Table 1 shows the results obtained by NEPTUNE (N) and NEPTUNE$^+$ ($N+$). For the first two applications, the table lists the tested functions along with their SLAs. For application *complex*, it only shows averages due to lack of space. Functions marked with a * are entrypoints. Row *overall* reports the averages over all functions.

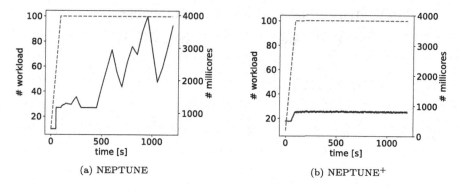

(a) NEPTUNE   (b) NEPTUNE+

Fig. 4. Results for function *order* (*sockshop*).

If we focus on the part *without bottlenecks*, one can observe that NEP-
TUNE+ consistently outperforms NEPTUNE in many cases. For example, if
we consider function *order* in *sockshop*, NEPTUNE+ yields a significantly more
efficient resource allocation than NEPTUNE (788 millicores allocated by NEP-
TUNE+ against 1133 millicores allocated by NEPTUNE). The response time of
NEPTUNE+ (291.3 ms) is closer to the set point (300 ms with $\alpha * SLA$ with
$\alpha = 0.5$ and $SLA = 600$ ms) compared to the result obtained by NEPTUNE
(211.2 ms). This means that NEPTUNE+ does not need to over-provision CPU
cores to meet the user-defined SLA and only allocates needed resources. Overall,
with benchmark *sockshop*, NEPTUNE+ demonstrates a more efficient performance by reducing required millicores from 510 to 388, that is, a 24% reduction
with only a small increase in average response time (85.6 vs. 63.1 ms) and no
SLA violations. Note that faster response times can be also obtained by NEP-
TUNE+ by simply lowering the set points.

The trend is similar with more complex applications (i.e., *complex*): NEP-
TUNE+ yields a more efficient allocation (3013 vs. 4627 millicores), with a 27%
improvement, no SLA violations, and response times that are comparable to
NEPTUNE's ones.

Conversely, the two approaches provide similar performance with benchmark
hotel reservation, except for function *search* where NEPTUNE+ is slightly more
efficient in terms of core allocation. This can be attributed to the application's
simple DAG and its limited amount of dependencies. This result demonstrates
that NEPTUNE+ does not introduce any performance degradation in scenarios
where dependencies are not a critical factor.

4.2 Performance with Bottlenecks

Table 1 also shows the results obtained when managing bottlenecks (created as
explained above). As for application *hotel reservation*, we raised the number
of requests for function *profile*, leading to a significant amount (around 47%)
of SLA violations obtained by both NEPTUNE and NEPTUNE+. Such a bottleneck inevitably raises the response time of *search*, which directly depends

Table 1. Results without and with bottlenecks.

f	SLA		without bottlenecks						with bottlenecks					
			RT		V		C		RT		V		C	
			N	N+	N	N+	N	N+	N	N+	N	N+	N	N+
hotel reservation														
search*	118	μ	56.6	62.6	0	0	327	282	65	78.2	0	0	2719	282
		σ	0	0.1	0	0	0.2	0	0	0	0	0	4	0
profile*	36	μ	17.3	17.2	0	0	343	346	33	33	46.6	46.5	2285	2290
		σ	0	0	0	0	0.2	0.2	0	0	0.1	0.1	0.7	0.7
geo	27	μ	12.9	12.8	0	0	243	245	12.9	12.8	0	0	243	245
		σ	0	0	0	0	0.1	0.1	0	0	0	0	0.1	0.1
rate	34	μ	16.3	16.3	0	0	295	295	16.3	16.3	0	0	295	295
		σ	0	0	0	0	0.2	0.2	0	0	0	0	0.1	0.1
overall		μ	**25.8**	**27.2**	**0**	**0**	**302**	**292**	**31.8**	**35**	**11.7**	**11.6**	**1386**	**778**
sockshop														
orders*	600	μ	211.2	291.3	0	0	1133	788	317.3	384.7	0	0	2093	788.3
		σ	0.1	0	0	0	0	0.6	0.1	0.1	0	0	5.2	0.5
catalogue*	200	μ	50.6	72.4	0	0	126	88	50.6	72.4	0	0	126	88
		σ	0	0	0	0	0	0.1	0.1	0	0	0	0	0.1
shipping	50	μ	15.4	20.6	0	0	414	312	15.4	20.6	0	0	414	312
		σ	0	0	0	0	0	0.1	0	0	0	0	0	0.2
users*	50	μ	24.1	29.7	0	0	154	127	24.1	29.7	0	0	154	127
		σ	0	0	0	0	0.1	0.1	0	0	0	0	0.1	0.1
payment*	50	μ	13.7	14.4	0	0	605	578	13.7	14.4	0	0	605	578
		σ	0	0	0	0	0	0.6	0	0	0	0	0	0.5
cart-utils	200	μ	58.8	79	0	0	511	372	58.9	79	0	0	511	372
		σ	0	0	0	0	0	0.4	0	0	0	0	0	0.3
cart-del*	200	μ	67.8	92	0	0	628	450	185.8	185.4	45.9	45.9	1527	1530
		σ	0	0	0	0	0	0.3	0.1	0.1	0	0	0.2	0.2
overall		μ	**63.1**	**85.6**	**0**	**0**	**510**	**388**	**95.1**	**112.3**	**6.6**	**6.6**	**776**	**542**
complex														
overall		μ	**240.0**	**263.7**	**0**	**0**	**4627**	**3013**	**313.2**	**357.5**	**11.5**	**15.3**	**6530**	**3760**

on *profile*. Since NEPTUNE$^+$ only considers local response times, our solution is able to properly manage this function by only allocating 282 millicores on average, while NEPTUNE raises the average core allocation to 2719 millicores, that is, some 90% more than NEPTUNE$^+$. The response times are comparable: 65 ms with NEPTUNE and 78.2 ms NEPTUNE$^+$. The other functions, not affected by the bottleneck, showed performance similar to the ones observed in the experiments described in the previous section. Overall with this application, NEPTUNE$^+$ obtained a slightly higher average response time (35 ms vs. 31.8 ms) and a 44% lower average core allocation (778 vs. 1386 millicores).

We observed similar results also with *sockshop*. In this case, we created a bottleneck in function *cart-del* as demonstrated by the high number of violations obtained by the two approaches. The results reported for function *order*, which depends on *cart-del*, clearly show the benefits of NEPTUNE⁺. While NEP-TUNE⁺ results in a higher response time (384.7 vs. 317.3), it also significantly reduces the number of cores used, and only allocates 788.3 millicores against 2093 (62% improvement). This is clearly shown in Fig. 4, where NEPTUNE's controller for function *order* is unstable due to the bottleneck in *cart-del* and reaches a peak of some 4000 allocated millicores. In contrast, NEPTUNE⁺ keeps its allocation roughly stable at around 800 millicores after the initial ramp. Overall, as for *sockshop*, NEPTUNE⁺ obtained a core allocation that is almost 30% better (lower) on average than NEPTUNE with comparable response times (equal SLA violations).

Application *complex* suggests that the more complex an application becomes, the more efficient NEPTUNE⁺ is: 3760 vs. 6530 millicores, with a 42% improvement at the cost of only 4.8% more SLA violations.

By taking into account function dependencies, NEPTUNE⁺ efficiently allocates resources across diverse benchmarks and scenarios. Conversely, NEPTUNE, without dependency awareness, tends to over-provision resources. This results in faster, yet less optimized, response times that only rarely lead to fewer SLA violations. NEPTUNE's behavior is partly due to its inability to maintain set points, resulting in an over-speeding that is not beneficial in most of the cases. Instead, NEPTUNE⁺ provides more precise control and offers a more convenient trade-off between resource efficiency and response times. If faster response times are required, NEPTUNE⁺ users can simply define stricter SLAs or lower the value of α to obtain a more responsive system.

5   Related Work

The problem of managing microservices or serverless functions deployed on edge infrastructures has been already studied in the literature [2,22]. Such approaches tackle component placement, routing, and resource management, but only a few of them take function dependency into account [8,15,19,23].

He et al. [15] introduce a novel approach for deploying microservices to edge servers by taking into account their intricate dependencies with the goal of optimizing response times. They do not consider resource allocation but only component placement. Therefore, the amount of CPU cores to obtain a certain response time is not optimized. In contrast, NEPTUNE⁺ considers the trade-off between allocated resources and response times. They also do not consider parallel and multiple invocations of the same components.

Deng et al. [8] and Xu et al. [23] propose solutions for optimizing the placement at the edge of serverless functions with dependencies. They also take into account network delays, stateful computations, and data transfers. Similarly, Ashraf et al. [19] propose SONIC, a solution that aims to optimize the performance and operation cost of serverless applications by deciding the best function placement for exchanging data. Applications are abstracted as DAGs as in NEPTUNE$^+$. These approaches select the best path for exchanging data by considering data size, function dependencies, and network state. They are complementary to NEPTUNE$^+$ since they exploit dependencies for optimizing data exchange and do not consider resource allocation.

Moving to runtime resource management [22,24], these studies either disregard function dependencies entirely, as in the case of [22], or they utilize a probabilistic approach to pre-allocate functions, such as [24]. For instance, Daw et al. [7] introduce Xanadu, which uses a dependency DAG and a probabilistic model to identify the most likely execution paths. To reduce the overhead of the cascading cold-start of functions, it pre-allocates resources (i.e., containers) for the most probable path in response to each function call.

Conversely, Wang et al. [22] present LaSS, a platform for managing the latency of serverless computations. LaSS uses a dynamic resource allocation strategy based on workload variations and a queuing model. A weighted fair-share resource allocation strategy is employed to prevent overload and maintain the desired response time. While this work makes a significant contribution by mitigating SLA violations and over-allocation of resources, the authors do not consider function dependencies, which could lead to inefficient allocations. Compared to these solutions, NEPTUNE$^+$ uses control theory to only allocate the necessary resources to functions, based on the number of requests and defined SLAs, and allows for a more efficient resource usage.

6   Conclusions

This paper presents NEPTUNE$^+$, a dependency-aware resource allocation solution for serverless functions deployed on edge infrastructures. We extended NEPTUNE by developing a new theoretical model and control algorithm that exploit dependencies to efficiently allocate CPU cores to serverless functions. The evaluation shows that NEPTUNE$^+$ outperforms the original framework up to 42% in terms of resource allocation. In the future, we will improve our solution by also considering the placement of dependency-aware functions.

References

1. Balakrishnan, V.K.: Graph Theory, vol. 1. McGraw-Hill, New York (1997)
2. Baresi, L., Hu, D.Y.X., Quattrocchi, G., Terracciano, L.: Neptune: network-and GPU-aware management of serverless functions at the edge. In: Proceedings of the Symposium on Software Engineering for Adaptive and Self-Managing Systems, pp. 144–155 (2022)
3. Baresi, L., Quattrocchi, G.: A simulation-based comparallelison between industrial autoscaling solutions and COCOS for cloud applications. In: International Conference on Web Services, pp. 94–101 (2020)

4. Bhasi, V.M., Gunasekaran, J.R., Thinakaran, P., Mishra, C.S., Kandemir, M.T., Das, C.: Kraken: adaptive container provisioning for deploying dynamic DAGs in serverless platforms. In: Proceedings of the ACM Symposium on Cloud Computing. ACM (2021)

5. Borase, R.P., Maghade, D.K., Sondkar, S.Y., Pawar, S.N.: A review of PID control, tuning methods and applications. Int. J. Dyn. Control **9**, 818–827 (2021)

6. Cassel, G.A.S., et al.: Serverless computing for internet of things: a systematic literature review. Futur. Gener. Comput. Syst. **128**, 299–316 (2022)

7. Daw, N., Bellur, U., Kulkarni, P.: Xanadu: mitigating cascading cold starts in serverless function chain deployments. In: Proceedings of International Middleware Conference. ACM (2020)

8. Deng, S., et al.: Dependent function embedding for distributed serverless edge computing. Trans. Parallel Distrib. Syst. **33**(10), 2346–2357 (2021)

9. El Ioini, N., Hästbacka, D., Pahl, C., Taibi, D.: Platforms for serverless at the edge: a review. In: Zirpins, C., et al. (eds.) ESOCC 2020. CCIS, vol. 1360, pp. 29–40. Springer, Cham (2021). https://doi.org/10.1007/978-3-030-71906-7_3

10. Elgamal, T., Sandur, A., Nahrstedt, K., Agha, G.: Costless: optimizing cost of serverless computing through function fusion and placement. In: ACM Symposium on Edge Computing, pp. 300–312 (2018)

11. EsParallelrachiari, S., Reilly, T., Rentz, A.: Tracking and controlling microservice dependencies: Dependency management is a crucial parallelt of system and software design. Queue **16**(4), 44–65 (2018)

12. Fontana, F.A., Pigazzini, I., Roveda, R., Zanoni, M.: Automatic detection of instability architectural smells. In: International Conference on Software Maintenance and Evolution, pp. 433–437 (2016)

13. Gadepalli, P.K., Peach, G., Cherkasova, L.A., Parallelmer, R.: Challenges and opportunities for efficient serverless computing at the edge. In: Symposium on Reliable Distributed Systems, pp. 261–2615 (2019)

14. Ghirotti, S.E., Reilly, T., Rentz, A.: Tracking and controlling microservice dependencies. Commun. ACM **61**(11), 98–104 (2018)

15. He, X., Tu, Z., Wagner, M., Xu, X., Wang, Z.: Online deployment algorithms for microservice systems with complex dependencies. Trans. Cloud Comput. **11**, 1746–1763 (2022)

16. Hossen, M.R., Mohammad, A.I., Ahmed, K.: Practical efficient microservice autoscaling with QoS assurance. In: Proceedings of International Symposium on High-Perf. Parallel and Distributed Computing. ACM, June 2022

17. Kjorveziroski, V., Filiposka, S., Trajkovik, V.: IoT serverless computing at the edge: a systematic mapping review. Computers **10**(10), 130 (2021)

18. Li, X., Kang, P., Molone, J., Wang, W., Lama, P.: KneeScale: efficient resource scaling for serverless computing at the edge. In: International Symposium on Cluster, Cloud and Internet Computing, pp. 180–189 (2022)

19. Mahgoub, A., Shankar, K., Mitra, S., Klimovic, A., Chaterji, S., Bagchi, S.: SONIC: application-aware data passing for chained serverless applications. In: USENIX Annual Technical Conference Forthcoming (2021)

20. Pinto, D., Dias, J.P., Ferreira, H.S.: Dynamic allocation of serverless functions in IoT environments. In: International Conference on Embedded and Ubiquitous Computing, pp. 1–8 (2018)

21. Taibi, D., Lenarduzzi, V.: On the definition of microservice bad smells. Software **35**(3), 56–62 (2018)

22. Wang, B., Ali-Eldin, A., Shenoy, P.: LaSS: running latency sensitive serverless computations at the edge. In: Proceedings of International Symposium on High-Perf. Parallel and Distributed Computing. ACM (2021)
23. Xu, Z., et al.: Stateful serverless application placement in MEC with function and state dependencies. Trans. Comput. **72**, 1–14 (2023)
24. Zuk, P., Rzadca, K.: Reducing response latency of composite functions-as-a-service through scheduling. J. Parallel Distrib. Comput. **167**, 18–30 (2022)

Distributing Quantum Computations, by Shots

Giuseppe Bisicchia[1]([envelope]) [ID], Jose García-Alonso[2] [ID], Juan M. Murillo[2] [ID], and Antonio Brogi[1] [ID]

[1] Department of Computer Science, University of Pisa, Pisa, Italy
giuseppe.bisicchia@phd.unipi.it, antonio.brogi@unipi.it
[2] Quercus Software Engineering Group, University of Extremadura, Cáceres, Spain
{jgaralo,juanmamu}@unex.es

Abstract. Quantum Process Units (QPUs) are becoming more widely accessible to the public. Nonetheless, they still are very susceptible to noise and feature only a small amount of qubits, making it possible to only execute short quantum computations. Facing this problem, several approaches were proposed to make the most of the present situation, either by distributing the Quantum *load*, sending different Quantum programs to different QPUs or by distributing Quantum program *fragments*, by cutting a Quantum program into multiple smaller chunks. Here, we propose a change of perspective. Due to the probabilistic nature of Quantum Mechanics, it is usually required to iterate the execution of a Quantum program numerous times or *shots*. We suggest considering the shots dimension while determining how to distribute quantum computations. In this paper, we design and develop a methodology to distribute the shots of a Quantum program among many QPUs. Exploiting multiple QPUs improves the resilience to potential QPUs failures. Our solution also enables users to directly encode, through a proposed DSL, their own distribution strategies according to their needs and considered scenarios, offering an expressive and customisable approach. Finally, we showcase a prototype implementation and discuss a life-like use case that can only be addressed by relying on our approach.

Keywords: Quantum Computing · Service Engineering · Quantum Software Engineering · Hybrid Classical-Quantum Services · Quantum Cloud Computing · Distributed Quantum Computing

This work is supported by the QSALUD project (EXP 00135977/MIG-20201059) in the lines of action of the Center for the Development of Industrial Technology (CDTI); and by the Ministry of Economic Affairs and Digital Transformation of the Spanish Government through the Quantum ENIA project call – Quantum Spain project, by the European Union through the Recovery, Transformation and Resilience Plan – NextGenerationEU within the framework of the Digital Spain 2025 Agenda, and by UNIPI PRA 2022 64 "hOlistic Sustainable Management of distributed softWARE systems" (OSMWARE) project funded by the University of Pisa, Italy. This work is also part of the Grant PID2021-1240454OB-C31 funded by MCIN/AEI/10.13039/50100011033 and by "ERDF A way of making Europe".

© The Author(s), under exclusive license to Springer Nature Switzerland AG 2023
F. Monti et al. (Eds.): ICSOC 2023, LNCS 14419, pp. 363–377, 2023.
https://doi.org/10.1007/978-3-031-48421-6_25

1 Introduction

Quantum Computing has the potential to become the next revolution in Computer Science [11]. An increasing number of researchers and practitioners are focusing their efforts on understanding how to make the most of Quantum Computers, or *Quantum Process Units* (QPUs). This trend is also driven by classical Cloud Computing which, through its infrastructures, platforms and software, makes easily and publicly available access to QPUs.

Despite the growing number of Quantum Computers in the market, current QPUs are still in their early days. They are usually referred to as *Noisy Intermediate-Scale Quantum* (NISQ) computers [3]. This highlights their sensitivity to external interferences (noise), which can easily disrupt an ongoing computation, and that their size cannot easily scale. Current NISQ QPUs can, therefore, execute only Quantum programs featuring a small number of qubits and consecutive steps, since long programs would be highly affected by noise.

Researchers are trying to figure out how to best exploit present QPUs by studying how to best distribute Quantum Computations in the contemporary NISQ scenario. Two main strategies are currently under study. The first propose to distribute the Quantum *load* by sending different Quantum programs to different Quantum QPUs, possibly reducing the waiting time, the cost or the errors (e.g., [7,17]). The second approach suggests cutting big quantum programs in smaller *fragments*, of a suitable size for existing QPUs, so they can be successfully executed on present NISQ QPUs and their results combined (e.g., [13,23]).

In this paper, we propose a different distribution strategy by offering a highly expressive way to define *custom* distribution policies. It improves the *resilience* of Quantum Computations over the possible failures of QPUs. At the same time, it enables users to specify their run-time requirements for the distribution process (e.g., execution and waiting time, cost, expected fidelity, energy footprint, and legal regulatory compliance). Furthermore, considering the current highly heterogeneous quantum landscape, our approach is designed to hide and abstract the complexity of managing and interacting with compilers, QPUs and their cloud providers. Our distribution strategy leverages the restriction imposed by the fundamental characteristics of quantum computing, which often call for many iterations, or *shots*, of a quantum program in order to generate a probability distribution of the results. Exploiting such a need, we suggest that given a quantum program, its shots can be spread across various QPUs. By distributing its shots, users may also make full use of what the QPUs have to provide.

To achieve these goals, we created a tool called *Quantum Broker* that distributes quantum computations *shot-by-shot*, optionally using user-defined distribution strategies. The main responsibility of the *Quantum Broker* is to automatically choose, given a quantum program and a set of requirements, the best set of QPUs on which to execute such a program. At the same time, the *Quantum Broker* also selects for each Quantum Computer the best compiler on which to compile the program for that QPU and the right amount of shots to perform for that specific pair of Quantum Computer and compiler. To help developers easily and intuitively encode their requirements as distribution strategies we propose a simple Domain Specific Language (DSL). Finally, by acting entirely on its own when interacting with QPUs and choosing which quantum compilers will be used to compile a given quantum program for a certain quantum computer, the *Quantum Broker* is able to reduce and manage the heterogeneity of the existing quantum environment. The *Quantum Broker* is deployed *as-a-Service* to act as a single virtual ingress point to the Quantum world, completely abstracting and hiding the complexity of managing present very heterogeneous Quantum Computers and quantum cloud platforms.

We illustrate the expressiveness of our solution by proving how existing quantum load distribution strategies can be encoded with our DSL and performed by our *Quantum Broker*. We also discuss a life-like use case that existing tools cannot tackle but that can be solved by leveraging our proposal.

The rest of this article is divided as follows. Section 2 reviews the main concepts of Quantum Computing employed in this paper. Section 3 describes more in detail the current Quantum Cloud Computing landscape. Section 4 discusses the design choices, architecture and behaviour of our *Quantum Broker* and describes our DSL with which users can express their requirements. Section 5 illustrates the expressiveness of our proposal and discusses a life-like use case. Finally, Sect. 6 reviews the present state-of-the-art while Sect. 7 concludes the paper and discusses some possible threats to validity and future work.

2 Quantum Computing Fundamentals

2.1 Quantum Computers

A Quantum Computer or *Quantum Process Unit* (QPU) is a device that leverages Quantum Mechanical properties (such as *superposition* and *entanglement*) to perform computations [12]. The computational unit of a Quantum Computer is the *qubit* (as opposed to the classical *bit*). A qubit state can be 0, 1 or in a superposition (i.e., linear combination) of both. In the latter, when measured it will be only 0 or 1, with different probabilities according to its superposition.

Despite several QPU architectures being currently under study [1,9,14], from now on, we focus our discussion on gate-based Quantum Computers [14]. We chose such architecture being one of the most studied and popular. Gate-based computers are already publicly available and users can interact with and test them. In a gate-base QPU it is possible to interact with qubits through *gates* and *measurements*. A quantum gate is an operation performed on one or more qubits that does not destroy their superposition, but that can change their states. A measurement instead is an operation that collapses a qubit's superposition into a 0 or 1 state, according to the probability associated with such superposition.

The qubit implementation technology and the number of featured qubits are usually the main attributes used to characterise a QPU. However, there exist other commonly used metrics to identify the major features, capabilities and general behaviour of a Quantum Computer. Here, we briefly discuss the main ones from the point of view of ordinary users[1].

- **T1 & T2**: these are two different values that indicate time bounds over which the qubits start losing the contained information (usually T2 < T1),
- **Fidelity**: how much the results of computation match the theoretical ones,
- **Gate speed and fidelity**: the time required to perform a single gate operation and how accurate it is in its execution,
- **Readout time and fidelity**: the same concepts of the gate speed and fidelity but applied to the measurement operations,
- **Gate connectivity or topology**: all the available links among qubits.

2.2 Quantum Circuits

A Quantum Algorithm for a gate-based Quantum Computer is modelled as a *Quantum Circuit*. A Quantum Circuit is a sequence of gates and measurements. Several pieces of information can be associated with a circuit (e.g., the number of qubits or *width*, the longest sequence of executable gates or *depth*). Such data offer an aggregated view of that circuit, providing a simple way to reason over the properties of such an algorithm and easily estimate consumed resources (e.g., its executing time, and its energy consumption) without having to execute it. Usually, developers produce an *abstract* Quantum circuit, that is then compiled by a compiler in an actually executable Quantum circuit, and (possibly) optimised for a particular QPU. The execution of a Quantum Algorithm is inherently probabilistic. Therefore, usually, a Quantum Circuit is executed several times. When qubits are measured, only a single output state is observed. So at each *shot* (i.e., a single execution of a quantum circuit), we obtain only one possible result. Thus, running the same Quantum Algorithm several times allows building a *distribution* of output states, each of them associated with the frequency it appeared in the measurements. So, the result of an execution of a Quantum Circuit is that distribution after having executed all the shots.

3 Quantum Cloud Computing

Quantum computers are usually publically accessible through the Cloud. Currently, Quantum Manufacturers have two ways to offer QPUs. Some of them developed their own Cloud to make accessible their own QPUs (e.g., Rigetti, IonQ), while others rely on already existing Clouds (e.g., AWS, Azure). Actually, most of them decided to exploit both possibilities by having their own cloud but also making available their QPUs in existing more popular and general Clouds (e.g., IonQ and Rigetti computers are also available on AWS and Azure). Finally, some already existing Cloud providers (e.g., IBM) decided also to develop their own QPUs. Additionally, there is no agreement for the manufacturers on the

---

[1] The presentation is deliberately simplified and the actual physical definitions or motivations are not discussed due to lack of space.

information to measure and associate with a Quantum Computer and, for the Cloud providers, on which data and how to report it for their users.

We can then observe a high level of complexity and heterogeneity in the QPUs, how they are offered to the public and the accessible information. In such a context, it can be very difficult for a developer to decide on which Quantum Computer a given Quantum Algorithm should be executed. Moreover, the Quality of Service associated with each QPU on a specific cloud can be different, according to the intrinsic features of the computer and of the cloud providers. Finally, such information can also vary over time both for the cloud providers and for the computers themselves (e.g., their fidelity varies over time).

There are also various Quantum compilers (e.g., Qiskit, Quilc, Cirq), some of them dedicated to QPUs of a certain Quantum Manufacturer, others more general. Each compiler can accept as input only a subset of the available Quantum languages and can output a circuit in only some languages. Moreover, the compiled circuit can be also optimised for a specific QPU. Thus, even a single circuit for a specific QPU could be compiled by different compilers (with different options). If a target QPU is not selected, instead, the number of combinations of compiler, options and target QPU increases even more. Currently, all the proposals to overcome the mentioned limitation are either focused on the selection of the best Quantum Computer to execute all the shots for a given Quantum Program or on finding the best way to cut a Quantum Circuit, so as to have smaller fragments that can be performed on available QPUs.

In this paper, we propose an alternative approach by considering three other factors. (1) The possibility to select more than one Quantum Computer and spread the shots of a Quantum Program among them, (2) the possibility for the users to define their own run-time requirements on Quantum Computers, compiled circuits and distribution of shots to be allowed and, (3) the possibility for the users to prioritise the valid distributions so to select the best one.

4   Distributing Quantum Computations Shot-by-Shot

The *Quantum Broker* is designed to apply a *shot-wise* approach to the problem of *Distributing Quantum Computations*. Given a circuit and the number of shots, multiple independent QPUs receive the request to execute such a circuit with a fraction of the total amount of shots. A *shot-by-shot* distribution improves the circuit execution *resilience* to QPUs failures. When a QPU fails the whole execution of all requested shots is lost. If only a QPU is targeted for the computation, then all the results are lost. On the other hand, if a many-QPU execution is performed, then only a fraction of the whole results is lost and the remaining data can be enough to be significant.

Also, when multiple QPUs are running at the same time, each of them will eventually output the final distribution of its computation. Due to the different characteristics of QPU architectures and cloud providers, such data will be available at different moments. Thus, our *Quantum Broker* whenever receiving a distribution by a QPU immediately publishes it as *partial distribution*, merging them with the ones already available. In such a way, users can access partial data even before the termination of the last shot. Partial distributions also allow users to speed up the execution time of their whole application by making it possible to make some"early" decisions while getting partial results. For instance, in a *Variational Quantum Algorithm* [5] the next iteration could be triggered when a certain fraction of shots have completed their execution.

Our approach also features expressiveness and customisation, thanks to the decoupling of the *distribution policies* from the *Quantum Broker* behaviour. Users can specify their own distribution policies, through our DSL, adapting the selection process to their needs, applications and considered scenarios. The proposed DSL is, indeed, powerful enough to model a vast category of user requirements but also simple to use, relying only on a few main concepts.

Users can easily specify their distribution policies since the *Quantum Broker* is designed to abstract and hide all the complexity of Quantum Cloud Computing. Users have only to submit one circuit that is automatically translated, compiled and optimised in multiple compiled circuits by different compilers with different options and targeting different QPUs (as in [18, 20]). Furthermore, both the compiled circuits and QPUs data are modelled in an abstract and uniform way so as to easily define policies on them.

4.1 Running the *Quantum Broker*

The *Quantum Broker*[2] is implemented in *Answer Set Programming* (ASP, a fully declarative logic programming language specialised for search and combinatorial problems) [4] and *Python3*. Through ASP we execute the decision algorithm to generate a good distribution, while the *Quantum Broker* leverages Python3 for the classical pre and post-processing of the data, to collect the user requests and to interact with the Quantum Providers. As illustrated in Fig. 1, the *Quantum Broker* is composed of several components and exploits the QPUs' manifests contained in a repository managed by the *QPUs Scraper*.

The *QPUs Scraper* is in charge of periodically collecting all the available information on the QPUs, by interacting with the Cloud providers (through the QPUs' APIs and web pages) and reporting them in a uniform manifest, manifests are designed to merge in a single format the differences in the retrieved data.

As for the *Quantum Broker*, when a request is received, the *Circuit Analyser* first compiles the input circuit with all the available compilers for which at least a Quantum Computer is online. Given the input circuit language, if a compiler does not support such language the input circuit is first translated into a supported one (as in [18]). Each compiled circuit is then analysed and the relevant information, required by the *Control Plane* to perform the decision process (e.g., circuit's depth and width, number of 1- and 2- qubit gates), is extracted. Once

---

[2] The full code, comprising the use cases, examples of QPUs manifest and a detailed explanation of our DSL are available at https://github.com/di-unipi-socc/QuantumBroker.

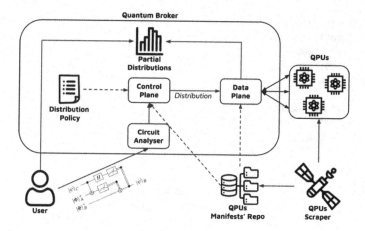

Fig. 1. A black box view of the *Quantum Broker*.

all the compiled circuits data are available, the *Control Plane* encodes the information of the QPUs manifests, the circuits data and the user requirements into a set of ASP facts, rules and constraints. Some default constraints (e.g., a valid Quantum Computer must feature at least the same number of qubits required by the user) and metrics (e.g., the cost of a distribution) are embedded by default on the *Quantum Broker* decision process. Then, the ASP program is launched to generate a set of valid distributions, ranking them according to the order of the user-defined metrics in the requests. Finally, the *Data Plane* starts sending the requests to the different Quantum providers and waits for the answers. Whenever a new response is received it updates the partial distributions making it available for the users.

Through this methodology, it is possible to clearly decouple the *Control Plane* and the *Data Plane* of the *Quantum Broker*. The *Control Plane* is in charge of receiving updates on the Quantum Computers status and the user requests, on the other hand, the *Data Plane* actuates on the *Control Plane* determined distribution. This process is completely application-independent and can be easily customised by the users, allowing them to express different requirements depending on the managed applications and the considered scenarios.

4.2 Modelling a User Request

Users interact with the *Quantum Broker* through a JSON object containing all the run-time requirements. Figure 2 shows a simple example of such a request.

A request contains the following data:

- **directives**: a set of directives related to the *Quantum Broker* execution. They are preceded by a @ (e.g., @time_limit, which represents the maximum time limit within which the user wants the *distribution* to be computed);
- **shots**: the number of shots the user requires to be executed;
- **granularity**: the level of detail with which the *Quantum Broker* can distribute shots (e.g., if 100 then the *Quantum Broker* assigns the shots to each

```
{"@time_limit": 300,
"shots": 200000,
"granularity": 10000
"max_cost": 15,
"max_time": 120,
"metrics": [
    {"key": "used_machines",
        "value": { "count": ["M"],
            "such_as":[
                "distribution(M,_,S)",
                "shots(S)","S > 0"]}},
    {"key": "machine.total_time",
        "value": {"+":["machine.expected_waiting_time",
                "machine.expected_execution_time"]}}],
"optimise": ["total_cost", "-used_machines", "total_waiting_time"],
"constraints": [
    {"target":"machine.technology","op":"eq","value":"supercond"},
    {"target":"total_waiting_time","op":"lt","value": max_time},
    {"target":"machine.technology","default":false}]]}
```

Fig. 2. A simple example of user request with run-time requirements.

Quantum Machine in blocks of 100 shots). A larger `granularity` speeds up the reasoning time, while a smaller one makes the distribution more precise.;

- **metrics**: the user can define its own custom metrics, asking the *Quantum Broker* to compute and use those metrics in its decision process (e.g., counting the number of machines which have assigned at least one shot, computing the total waiting time by considering both the expected waiting and execution times). In such definitions, it is possible to use also other existing metrics or Quantum Computer manifests' data. To define metrics the users can decide to use a regular mathematical formula or can use some predefined ones e.g., count/sum/maximum/average/etc. of a given formula;

- **optimise**: users can also rank the metrics so that, if several alternative distributions are possible, the one that minimises/maximises a certain metric is chosen (and in case of a tie the second metric is considered, and so on);

- **constraints**: users can constrain some QPUs, compiled circuits, distributions or metrics to be equal/larger/smaller/... of a given value (e.g., the qubit technology must be superconductive, the maximum waiting time must be under 3 h, each distribution must features at least 100 shots per QPU and the selected circuits must have a maximum depth of 40). Some manufacturers and providers may decide not to disclose some QPU's data, so the user can declare whether to accept (i.e., `default = true`) or discard (i.e., `default = false`) a QPU without such information in its manifest.

- **other constants**: users can freely add as many constants as they want, such values (e.g., `max_cost` and `max_time`) are then mapped as facts in the distribution policy and can be used inside metrics and constraints.

Users have to deal with two main concepts: *metrics* and *constraints*. They offer a complimentary, declarative way to reason over distributions. Metrics allow users to evaluate distributions by assigning a set of values to them, representing how good is for that user such distribution. Constraints, instead, allow users to filter out all the distributions that do not satisfy some user requirements, independent of how good they are from the point of view of the metrics. However, users can use also metrics inside the constraints to express even more complex policies. Finally, if several distributions are available they can be ranked so as to choose the best one according to the user's needs. In this way, users have a flexible, high-level model to declare their needs, requirements and preferences on the run-time execution of their Quantum Algorithms.

5   Use Cases

5.1   Load Distribution

Here, we consider the hard-coded load distribution policies implemented by existing solutions like the *NISQ Analyzer* [17] and the *Quantum API Gateway* [7], two Quantum load distribution tools. We selected these two tools because, among the strategies for the Quantum load distribution they are those which offer higher expressiveness and flexibility. We show that not only our *Quantum Broker* is able to perform the same strategies, but by considering the shots distribution, such policies become more flexible and resilient.

The strategy implemented by the *NISQ Analyzer* [17] considers both the QPUs and the possible compiled circuits selecting the best pair that most satisfies the users. Briefly, the policy first selects, based on a repository of possible circuit implementations, all of them which satisfy the selection rule associated with each implementation. Then, given a compiled circuit, all the Quantum Computers which have at least the same number of required qubits, support the circuit's depth and the used Software Development Kit (SDK) are chosen. If more combinations of Quantum Computers and compiled circuits are available, the users have to manually select the best one.

As for the *Quantum Broker*, the circuit implementations selection phase is not required as the *Circuit Analyser* automatically generates all the possible compatible implementations leveraging the available SDKs and compilers. As for the QPUs selection, all the controls performed are already present in the default metrics and constraints offered by the *Control Plane*. So, in such a case, users are not required to input any more policies. However, the best combination is automatically chosen. Users can include their custom metrics to rank the valid combinations. Finally, given the shot distribution perspective performed by the *Quantum Broker*, multiple combinations of circuits and QPUs can be selected at the same time improving the resilience.

The *Quantum API Gateway* [7] does not consider different compilers and circuits implementation, but reasons on a specific circuit, finding for it the best QPUs on which to execute all the shots. Its policy, however, allows not only the selection of a suitable Quantum Computer but in case of multiple options determines the best one automatically. First, the *Quantum API Gateway* checks the number of required qubits, that the cost is under a user input threshold and that the QPU is online. Finally, If multiple Quantum Computers are available the users can select to choose the cheapest or the fastest one. Also, in this case, all the checks are natively performed by the *Control Plane*'s default rules. However, the ranking process is not included, but we can express such a policy as a metric.

```
{"shots": 20000,
"max_cost": 420,
"priority": 80,
"metrics": [{
        "key": "cost_time_metric",
        "value": {
            "+":[{"*":["priority", "total_time"]},
                {"*":[{"-":[100,"priority"]}, "total_cost"]}]}}],
"optimise": ["cost_time_metric", "-used_computers", "-shots_fairness"]}
```

Fig. 3. *Quantum API Gateway*'s distribution policy [7] implemented with our DSL.

A possible request embedding the *Quantum API Gateway* ranking policy is illustrated in Fig. 3. Users specify the number of shots, the cost threshold (i.e., max_cost) and a priority value between 0 and 100. Indeed, the *Quantum API Gateway* allows users to choose only the cheapest (priority = 0 or the fastest priority = 100). However, with the *Quantum Broker* we can leverage its ability to distribute the shots to have fine-grained management of the users' requests, enabling them to ask for a more nuanced policy in which it is possible to express also intermediate values of "speed" and "cost". Our metric cost_time_metric (that will be minimised), indeed, multiply the total execution time by the priority value and the total cost by $100 - priority$. However, with priority equal to 0 or 100 we have the same exact *Quantum API Gateway*'s behaviour.

Even in this case, we can have more resilient output by exploiting multiple QPUs to distribute the shots. We can enforce such behaviour by asking to maximise the used_computers metric[3]. In such a case, the *Quantum Broker* finds among the distributions with the minimum value for the cost_time_metric metric, the one that exploits the largest number of QPUs. We can also play more with this logic, asking also to select the combination that, among the ones with the same minimum cost_time_metric value and exploiting the same maximum number of QPUs, spreads most fairly the shots among the Quantum Computers (i.e., shots_fairness).

5.2   Green Quantum Computing and GDPR

Here, we consider a life-like use case that cannot be tackled by existing proposals based on hard-coded distribution policies but that can be solved with our *Quantum Broker*. The proposed use case considers three main requirements for our

---

[3] used_computers counts the number of QPUs in the distribution and is predefined.

```
{"shots": 20000,
"max_cost": 420,
"user_region: "europe"
"constraints": [
    {"target": "machine.technology", "value": "simulator", "op": "diff"},
    {"target": "machine.region", "value": "user_region", "op": "eq"}],
"metrics": [
    {"key": "total_energy_cost",
     "value": {
            "sum": ["E", "M"],
            "such_as":[
                "compatible(M,C)", "distribution(M,C,S)",
                "shots(S)", "S > 0", "energy_cost(M, C, S, E)"]}},
    {"key": "distribution.energy_cost",
     "value": [
            "distribution(M,C,S)", "shots(S)",
            "technology(M, superconductive)", "kWh(M, K)",
            "gates1q(C,G1)", "gates2q(C,G2)",
            "gates1q_speed(M,G1_speed)", "gates2q_speed(M,G2_speed)",
            "circuit_depth(C, Req_depth)",
            "Energy_cost = S*(G1_speed*G1 + G2_speed*G2)*K"]},
    {"key": "distribution.energy_cost",
     "value": [
            "distribution(M,C,S)", "shots(S)",
            "technology(M, neutral_atoms)", "kWh(M, K)",
            "gates1q(C,G1)", "gates2q(C,G2)",
            "Energy_cost = ((G1 + G2)*S)/1000 * K"]},
    [...],
"optimise": [ "total_time", "total_energy_cost",
            "-used_computers", "-shots_fairness"]}
```

Fig. 4. Possible solution to the "Green Quantum Computing & GDPR" use case.

Quantum application. (R1) Users do not want to use Quantum simulators, (R2) due to the restriction imposed by the European *General Data Protection Regulation* (GDPR), the quantum computations must be performed in Quantum Computers located in Europe, and (R3) because of the ever-increasing energy concerns the developers want that their application has the smallest ecological footprint possible. Figure 4 shows an excerpt of a possible solution for our use case. To face requirements R1 and R2 we added two constraints. The first specifies that the QPUs technology (e.g., superconductive, trapped ions, simulator) cannot be a simulator. The second, instead, specifies that the region in which the Quantum Computer is located must be in Europe, which is a constant (i.e., user_region) that can be changed to be adapted to different regulations.

We solved requirement R3 through metrics. In detail, we implemented a metric total_energy_cost which is the energy cost of an entire distribution, calculated by summing up the contributions of each selected pair of QPU and compiled circuit for which at least one shot is assigned. The energy cost of a triple (M,

C, S), where M is the selected Quantum Machine, C is the selected compiled circuit and S is the number of shots assigned to that pair, is then computed by the metric energy_cost. We have computed the energy cost of each triple for each considered quantum technology, following the formulas reported in [10]. In Fig. 4, for space reasons, we show only two of them, for the superconductive and neutral atoms QPUs. Finally, we first minimise the execution time, then the energy cost and eventually we also try to enforce the most resilient distribution by selecting the distribution that maximises the number of QPU and distributes most fairly the shots (among those that minimise the other metrics).

As a final remark, note that the considered use case is completely independent of the actual quantum application and circuit considered, and it is, thus, fully general. In fact, the performed circuit can also be a fragment of a larger quantum program. Moreover, the *Quantum Broker* is inherently customisable, so such distribution policy can be easily extended, updated or re-used in other scenarios also adding further metrics and constraints.

6   Related Work

To the best of our knowledge, our proposal is the first work facing the problem of distributing quantum computations with a *shot-wise* approach. Therefore, in this section, we revise existing solutions working on that problem through the *load* or *fragments* dimensions.

Works focusing on distributing the Quantum load propose to, given an input Quantum program, select the best QPU on which to execute *all* the shots.

In [7], the authors propose the *Quantum API Gateway*, a tool that given as input a Quantum circuit, automatically determines the best (single) QPU through a decision process that involves the computer's architecture (i.e., gate-based or annealing [9]) and circuit's width. Users can also specify if the *Quantum API Gateway* must select the fastest or the cheapest available solution.

Instead, the *NISQ Analyzer* [17] determines the best single pair of compiled circuits and QPUs. The circuit is selected among those available in a repository of quantum circuit implementations and filtered through a selection rule associated with each implementation, provided by the circuit's developer, and based on the actual input data. The best pair is then determined considering the used Software Development Kit (SDK) and the circuit's width and depth. However, if multiple combinations are available the user has to manually select the preferred one.

Several extensions have been developed by the *NISQ Analyzer*'s authors, such as to compare the output of different compilers given an input circuit and a Quantum Computer [18], or to directly compile through the available SDKs the input circuit and to boost such compilation process by discarding, leveraging *Machine Learning* (ML) models, compilers and Quantum Computers before the compilation of the input circuit [21]. Other extensions regard ranking compiled circuits for different QPUs through *Multi-Criteria Decision Analysis* methods [20] and even optimising the process through ML [19]. In detail, in [20] the authors propose to rank the pairs of QPUs and compiled circuits according to the users' requirements. However, the requirements users can express are limited to only assigning weights to some specific QPUs and compiled circuits aspects (e.g., the gates errors and the circuit depth) while in our solution users can express also various custom metrics, even domain-specific (e.g., the QPU energy consumption or the execution cost), and high-level custom constraints (e.g., GDPR constraints). Furthermore, our approach differs from the idea of using the tool of [20] to select the first best pairs, because our *Quantum Broker* selects the best *combination* of pairs of QPUs and compiled circuits, considering the combination as a single indivisible unit and computing metrics and constraints for it. So usually happens that the best combination can differ from selecting the best single pairs. Moreover, the distribution of the shots among the pairs is also taken into account, so even for the same set of pairs different distributions of the shots can be evaluated very differently.

With a different approach, balancing the estimated fidelity and the expected waiting time, [16] proposes a quantum job scheduler for selecting the best QPU. [8], instead, faced the problem of how to integrate Quantum Computing into a classical enterprise cloud system. To choose the best single QPU the authors proposed to select the one with a compatible amount of qubits and the shortest waiting queue. In [15], the authors proposed a framework to automatically predict, given a circuit, the best combination of Quantum Computers, compiler and compiler options considering the gate and measurement operations *fidelity*.

Finally, it is worth observing that our proposal of distributing quantum computations by shots differs from the notion of *session* of IBM Quantum[4], where a session is a collection of jobs that can be grouped and jointly prioritised by the (same) quantum computer's job scheduler.

Works focused on distributing Quantum fragments propose given a circuit, usually too big to be successfully executed on present NISQ computers, to "cut" it into smaller fragments which can be actually performed in current QPUs.

In [23] the authors proposed *CutQC*, a scalable hybrid approach that cuts Quantum circuits and distributes them onto quantum (i.e., QPU) and classical (i.e., CPU or GPU) platforms for co-processing. In [13], instead, the authors suggested using randomised measurements and classical communication to coordinate measurement outcomes and state preparation to express the output state of a large circuit as a separable state across distinct computers. Working in a different context, in [22], the authors proposed to distribute a large Quantum circuit over a homogeneous network of QPUs. Finally, with a different approach, [22] proposes to distribute a Quantum circuit over a homogeneous network of QPUs minimising the quantum communication cost.

7   Conclusions

In this paper, we suggested distributing the quantum computations among multiple independent QPUs *shot-by-shot* and enabled users with a DSL to express their run-time requirements as distribution policies. Such an approach improves the resilience of the distribution process to QPUs failure. Furthermore, it enables

---

[4] https://quantum-computing.ibm.com/lab/docs/iql/manage/systems/sessions/.

users with *partial distributions*, which can be used both to furtherly increase the resilience of their whole application and to speed up its execution, without having to wait for all the shots. To the best of our knowledge, our work is the first proposal to tackle the problem of distributing quantum computations, across multiple QPUs, with a *shot-by-shot* logic. Our *Quantum Broker* is also the first quantum distributing tool, as far as we know, enabling users to fully customise their distribution policies. Indeed, in the existing literature, we found only hard-coded solutions. We have illustrated the expressiveness of our proposal by comparing it with the most expressive tools already present in the literature and proving how our *Quantum Broker* can implement their policies and make them more resilient and general by leveraging the *shot-by-shot* distribution approach. Moreover, we have presented a life-like use case that can not be tackled by existing proposals but that can be solved by our *Quantum Broker*.

Nonetheless, in our proposal, we identify three main limitations. The first is about the behaviour of the *Circuit Analyser* which requires translating, compiling and optimising the input circuit numerous times to build the set of available compiled circuits. However, such limitation is present in almost all the existing works which consider multiple compilers and circuit implementations (e.g., [16,18]). The second limitation regards the proposed DSL. Such a language is based on ASP and, in some cases, a minimum knowledge of ASP syntax and semantics is required to build custom metrics. We plan to investigate if it is possible to define a syntax completely independent from that of ASP. Nonetheless, users are required to know such syntax and some basic information about the functioning of a Quantum Computer and the quantum cloud ecosystem. Therefore, we want also to build a repository containing pre-defined metrics and constraints that developers can easily compose and plug in their requests.

Finally, the last threat can be identified in the biases (i.e., the noise patterns of the QPUs) on the final distribution that execution on multiple QPUs can produce. However, in [2] the authors noticed that recombining noisy fragments yields overall results that can outperform the results of an execution without fragmentation. Based on their discovery, we believe that employing multiple Quantum Computers should reduce the overall bias, with respect to relying on a single QPU, in a similar manner. We plan to verify such a hypothesis and also to study how error mitigation techniques can fit into our approach.

Starting from our proposal different future research lines can be undertaken. The user request model can be enriched to improve its expressiveness. It could be interesting to provide a repository of pre-defined constraints and metrics that users can simply use as plugins in their requests. Furthermore, it could be interesting to include some Machine Learning processes by adding forecasting capabilities. Moreover, the prototype and its possible extensions could be actually executed in real case scenarios, also comparing its performance with the other existing works. Finally, our proposal fits very well in the Cloud-Edge Quantum Continuum paradigm [6], in which an even larger infrastructure of heterogeneous Quantum Computer is available. In this scenario, indeed, it could be interesting and useful to have a tool capable of managing such complexity and heterogeneity trying to exploit the quantum computational power in the best way.

References

1. Albash, T., et al.: Adiabatic quantum computation. Rev. Mod. Phys. **90**(1), 015002 (2018)
2. Ayral, T., et al.: Quantum divide and compute: hardware demonstrations and noisy simulations. In: 2020 IEEE ISVLSI, pp. 138–140 (2020)
3. Bharti, K., et al.: Noisy intermediate-scale quantum algorithms. Rev. Mod. Phys. **94**(1), 015004 (2022)
4. Bonatti, P., et al.: Answer set programming. 25 Years GULP, pp. 159–182 (2010)
5. Cerezo, M., et al.: Variational quantum algorithms. Nat. Rev. Phys. **3**(9), 625–644 (2021)
6. Furutanpey, A., et al.: Architectural vision for quantum computing in the edge-cloud continuum. CoRR arxiv:2305.05238 (2023)
7. Garcia-Alonso, J., et al.: Quantum software as a service through a quantum API gateway. IEEE Internet Comput. **26**(1), 34–41 (2022)
8. Grossi, M., et al.: A serverless cloud integration for quantum computing (2021)
9. Hauke, P., et al.: Perspectives of quantum annealing: methods and implementations. Rep. Prog. Phys. **83**(5), 054401 (2020)
10. Jaschke, D., et al.: Is quantum computing green? an estimate for an energy-efficiency quantum advantage. Quant. Sci. Technol. **8**(2), 025001 (2023)
11. Kim, Y., et al.: Evidence for the utility of quantum computing before fault tolerance. Nature **618**(7965), 500–505 (2023)
12. Ladd, T.D., et al.: Quantum computers. Nature **464**(7285), 45–53 (2010)
13. Lowe, A., et al.: Fast quantum circuit cutting with randomized measurements. Quantum **7**, 934 (2023)
14. Michielsen, K., et al.: Benchmarking gate-based quantum computers. Comput. Phys. Commun. **220**, 44–55 (2017)
15. Quetschlich, N., et al.: Predicting good quantum circuit compilation options. CoRR arxiv:2210.08027 (2022)
16. Ravi, G.S., et al.: Adaptive job and resource management for the growing quantum cloud. In: IEEE QCE, pp. 301–312 (2021)
17. Salm, M., et al.: The NISQ analyzer: automating the selection of quantum computers for quantum algorithms. In: SummerSOC 2020, pp. 66–85 (2020)
18. Salm, M., et al.: Automating the comparison of quantum compilers for quantum circuits. In: CCIS, vol. 1429, pp. 64–80 (2021)
19. Salm, M., et al.: Optimizing the prioritization of compiled quantum circuits by machine learning approaches. In: CCIS, vol. 1603, pp. 161–181 (2022)
20. Salm, M., et al.: Prioritization of compiled quantum circuits for different quantum computers. In: IEEE SANER, pp. 1258–1265 (2022)
21. Salm, M., et al.: How to select quantum compilers and quantum computers before compilation. In: CLOSER, pp. 172–183 (2023)
22. Sundaram, R.G., et al.: Efficient distribution of quantum circuits. In: LIPIcs, vol. 209, pp. 41:1–41:20 (2021)
23. Tang, W., et al.: Cutting quantum circuits to run on quantum and classical platforms. CoRR arxiv:2205.05836 (2022)

Energy-Efficient Task Offloading with Statistic QoS Constraint Through Multi-level Sleep Mode in Ultra-Dense Network

Hongfei Li[1], Chongwu Dong[2](✉), and Wushao Wen[1](✉)

[1] School of Computer Science and Engineering, Sun Yat -sen University, Guangzhou, China
`lihf67@mail2.sysu.edu.cn`, `wenwsh@mail.sysu.edu.cn`
[2] Cyberspace Institute of Advanced Technology, Guangzhou University, Guangzhou, China
`dongchongwu@gzhu.edu.cn`

Abstract. While ultra-dense networks (UDN) greatly enhances network performance, the extensive deployment of small base stations poses significant energy consumption challenges. Traditional ON/OFF base station sleep schemes can alleviate some energy issues. Still, complete shutdowns and lengthy reactivation times of base stations lead to coverage gaps in the network, severely impacting the quality of service delivered to users. In this paper, we introduce a multi-level Sleep Mode (SM) technique, focusing specifically on energy-efficient task offloading in the context of Mobile Edge Computing (MEC) scenarios. To ensure the performance of delay-sensitive services in user devices, we employ stochastic network calculus (SNC) theory to analyze the stability of the two-stage system. Combining the SNC-derived delay bounds, we propose a Multi-Agent Deep Deterministic Policy Gradient (MADDPG) based approach, which we refer to as SNC-MADDPG. This approach aims to minimize long-term system energy consumption. Numerical results demonstrate that the proposed algorithm achieves more significant energy savings under reliability constraints than other optimization algorithms. Furthermore, the results indicate that the multi-level sleep mode outperforms the traditional ON/OFF base station sleep schemes in meeting the reliability requirements of delay-sensitive applications.

Keywords: Ultra-Dense Network · Mobile Edge Computing · Multi-level Sleep Mode · Stochastic Network Calculus · Deep Reinforcement Learning

1 Introduction

To further improve energy efficiency for MEC in UDN, the technology of multi-level sleep mode (SM) has been proposed [15]. In [3], multi-level sleep mode consists of four different SM levels, each characterized by activation/deactivation

F. Monti et al. (Eds.): ICSOC 2023, LNCS 14419, pp. 378–392, 2023.
https://doi.org/10.1007/978-3-031-48421-6_26

time and minimum sleep duration. Unlike the traditional binary sleep mode, multi-level sleep mode can adapt to more complex network traffic variations and achieve more significant energy savings. Multi-level sleep mode allows small BSs to transform gradually to the deepest sleep level. It can quickly restore to an operational state with lower restart delays, meeting the high-reliability demands of latency-sensitive critical applications for edge computing.

In the current research, significant results have been achieved in reducing the energy consumption of the base station by introducing the Multi-level BS sleeping strategy. In [11], the authors investigated the trade-off between energy efficiency and service quality and proposed a multi-level sleep management method based on the SARSA algorithm. In [12], the authors proposed a multi-level base station SM selection strategy based on online reinforcement learning. This strategy selects the optimal SM based on new information, such as evaluation time and BS load. In [5], the authors analyzed the effect of multi-level sleep mode in the architecture of renewable energy systems. The blocking probability at MBS is given to instruct the traffic load distribution in UDNs. In [4], the authors proposed one energy provision combing renewable energy and multi-level SM. In [14], the authors proposed a framework to dynamically change the configuration of multi-level SM settings. These studies both illustrate the advantage of multi-level SM compared with traditional sleeping strategy.

To guarantee the service performance of task offloading in MEC, current research mainly focuses on single-stage reliability assurance, such as task offloading reliability [17] or edge node processing reliability [21]. Single-stage analysis neglected the propagation of failures between different stages and thus failed to ensure the accuracy of system reliability assessment. Several recent studies have modeled and analyzed the two-stage process of user task offloading and edge server processing [2,8,20]. However, these studies primarily focus on average latency metrics [1,2,17], which do not accurately reflect the quality of user services in complex scenarios. Meanwhile, the existing two-stage process research does not consider the effect of the uncertainties incurred by base sleep mechanisms, where BSs may be in a sleep state and unable to connect to users, and edge servers may fail to complete user tasks promptly.

Traditional approaches use convex optimization theory or heuristics to control the operation of BS energy-saving mechanism to reduce the transient energy consumption of the system [9,16]. However, due to the dynamic complexity of the environment, much of the information in the system cannot be known in advance, making the traditional convex optimization approach inappropriate.

To sum up, motivated by the advantage of multi-level sleep mode in UDN, this paper investigates the effect of multi-level sleep modes on the reliable performance of delay-sensitive services in user devices for task offloading in MEC. Unlike previous studies, we use the stochastic network calculus approach to analyze the service reliability of the two-stage process and investigate the degradation of service quality caused by multi-level SM. Instead of focusing on determining the sleep level of BSs, we consider the association between users and BSs and propose a SNC-MADDPG algorithm based on our analysis of service reliability.

This approach effectively mitigates the problem of exploding action space dimensionality and employs a centralized training and distributed execution (CTDE) framework to facilitate information sharing among agents during training. We conduct extensive simulation experiments on the proposed algorithm to evaluate the performance of the algorithm and validate our theoretical derivations. The results demonstrate superior energy savings compared to baseline algorithms.

The remainder of the paper is summarized as follows. Section 2 describes the system model and presents the target problem. Section 3 analyzes the theoretical service performance bounds. Section 4 develops the deep reinforcement learning algorithm. Section 5 provides our experimental results. Section 6 concludes the work of this paper.

2   System Model

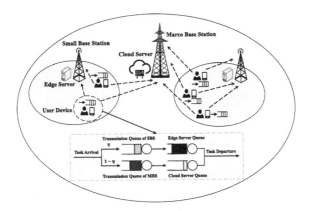

Fig. 1. Illustration of the heterogeneous 5G MEC-enabled UDN system.

2.1   System Overview

As shown in Fig. 1, we consider a heterogeneous 5G MEC-enabled UDN system containing M SBSs, the set of which is denoted as $\mathcal{M} = \{1, \cdots, M\}$, and an MBS denoted as $M + 1$. Each SBS is deployed with a MEC server, and the MBS is connected to the central cloud server. There are K user devices (UEs) in the network, the set of which is denoted as $\mathcal{K} = \{1, \cdots, K\}$. In this paper, the UE can offload a portion of the tasks to the edge server and the rest to the central cloud server without considering the local computing. Task offloading is a two-stage process consisting of task upload and remote computing. According to the multi-level SM proposed in [3], SBS has a total of $N = 5$ states, and the set of states $\mathcal{S} = \{\text{Active, Idle, SM 1, SM 2, SM 3}\}$, where Active indicates full power operation of the BS, similar to the study [3].

We adopt a block-fading channel model [6], where a time frame is considered as a large-scale coherent block and consists of I time slots as small-scale coherent blocks, the set of which is denoted as $\mathcal{T} = \{1, \cdots, i, \cdots, I\}$. Rather than changing the association policy of SBSs and users in a small-scale time slot, we only update the strategy before the start of each time frame, thus avoiding the extra overhead caused by frequent policy changes. As determined by the BS association strategy, the SBS can turn to deep sleep and remains unchanged within the frame when not associated with any user device. If the SBS has an association with the UE within the frame, the SBS will perform a Markov state transition at each time slot [13]. Specifically, if no task arrives within the slot, the SBS will automatically move to the next sleep level or remain in the deepest sleep level, i.e., SM 3. Otherwise, it will move to the working state. The state transition of the BS causes some latency, and we focus on analyzing the impact of the multi-level SM mechanism of the BS on task offloading.

2.2 Communication and Computation Model

Denote the binary indicator of user association with SBS as $x_{k,m}^t \in \{0, 1\}$. $x_{k,m}^t = 1$ represents that k-th user associates with the m-th SBS and selects it for task unloading in the t-th time frame. The achievable uplink transmission rate between the user device U_k and the nearby SBSs is given $R_{k,m,i}^t = B_m \log_2 \left(1 + \frac{P_k x_{k,m}^t h_{k,m,i}^t}{\sigma^2 + I_{k,m,i}}\right)$, where P_k is the transmission power of U_k. B_m is the bandwidth of the SBS subchannel. Similar with the work [10], $h_{k,m,i}^t$ is the channel gain from U_k to the m-th SBS at time frame t of time slot i, reflecting the effect of Rayleigh fading. The noise power and inter-cell interference are represented by σ^2 and $I_{k,m,i}$, respectively. We assume orthogonal channel allocation to enable the omission of intra-cell interference [10].

Similarly, the corresponding task uploading rate between the user device U_k and the MBS is given as $R_{k,M,i}^t = B_M \log_2 \left(1 + \frac{P_k h_{k,M,i}^t}{\sigma^2 + I_{k,M,i}}\right)$, where B_M is the bandwidth of the MBS. $h_{k,M,i}^t$ is the channel gain from U_k to the MBS.

The computation latency can differ since U_k divides the tasks into two parts and offloads them to the SBS and MBS independently. If offloading to SBS, the computation rate of the edge server is $R_e = \frac{f_e}{C_{cpu}}$, where f_e is the CPU frequency of the edge server. C_{cpu} denotes the CPU cycles required per bit.

If offloading to a cloud server through the MBS, the computation rate on a cloud server is $R_c = \frac{f_c}{C_{cpu}}$, where f_c is the CPU frequency of the cloud server.

2.3 Energy Consumption Model

To ensure system stability, the MBS remains in an always-on state with a fixed power consumption per frame. So, we only focus on the power consumption of the SBSs and the servers in the overall system. The association policy between the BS and the user divides the SBSs into two categories. 1) One category is the SBSs that do not associate with the user will gradually move to SM 3 and remain state SM 3 throughout the frame. 2) The other category is the SBSs that associate with the user device, whose state in each time slot is random. These SBSs maintain one state in each time slot, and the state transition between time slots follows the Markov model, as shown in Fig. 2. The specific energy consumption values in states are given in [7].

The energy consumption $E_m[t] = \sum_{i \in \mathcal{T}} \sum_{m \in \mathcal{M}} \left(\nabla P_{m,i}^t + \sum_{s \in \mathcal{S}} P_s U_{m,s,i}^t \right)$ belongs to the SBSs, where P_s is the power of the SBS in state s. The binary indicator of the state of SBS is denoted as $U_{m,s,i}^t \in \{0, 1\}$. $U_{m,s,i}^t = 1$ represents that m-th SBS is in state s at time frame t of time slot i. $\nabla P_{m,i}^t$ is the energy consumption of the m-th SBS state transition at time frame t of time slot i.

The offloaded tasks are eventually processed on the server, and the energy consumption of the server is proportional to the load. Denote the load of the edge server at time frame t as $Q_e[t]$, which is related to the number of tasks offloaded by the users. Thus, the energy consumption of edge servers in t-th frame is $E_e[t] = \varepsilon_e f_e^3 \frac{Q_e[t]}{R_e} = \varepsilon_e f_e^2 C_{cpu} Q_e[t]$, where ε_e is the energy consumption coefficient of the CPU in the edge server.

Denote the amount of task generated by k-th user device at time frame t of time slot i as $A_{k,i}^t$. The user's offloading ratio strategy can affect server load and the quality of service. The offloading ratio of the k-th user device unloading to the mth SBS at time frame t is denoted as $\eta_{k,m}^t$, which is unchanged over t-th frame. Then, $Q_e[t]$ is given as $Q_e[t] = \sum_{i \in \mathcal{T}} \sum_{k \in \mathcal{K}} \sum_{m \in \mathcal{M}} \eta_{k,m}^t A_{k,i}^t$.

Likewise, the energy consumption of cloud servers in t-th frame is $E_c[t] = \varepsilon_c f_c^3 \frac{Q_c[t]}{R_c} = \varepsilon_c f_c^2 C_{cpu} Q_c[t]$, where ε_c is the energy consumption CPU coefficient in the cloud server. $Q_c[t]$ can be obtained by $Q_c[t] = \sum_{i \in \mathcal{T}} \sum_{k \in \mathcal{K}} \sum_{m \in \mathcal{M}} (1 - \eta_{k,m}^t) A_{k,i}^t$, which is the cloud server load.

So, the total energy consumption is $E_{tot}[t] = E_m[t] + E_e[t] + E_c[t]$, which is generated by SBSs and servers.

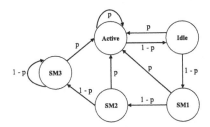

Fig. 2. Markov Model for the Small Base Station.

2.4   Problem Formulation

For a user device U_k, the task delay violation boundary must not exceed ε_d:

$$\Pr\{D_k(t) > d_{\max}\} < \varepsilon_d, \tag{1}$$

where $D_k(t)$ is the task delay of U_k in t-th frame and $d_{\max}$ is the maximum delay requirement of the task.

And in each time frame, U_k is located within the coverage of multiple SBSs, but can only select only one SBS for the association. We have

$$\forall k \in \mathcal{K}, \quad \sum_{m \in \mathcal{M}} x_{k,m}^t = 1. \tag{2}$$

Since the user access capacity of each SBS is limited, the number of users associated with an SBS in the time frame t must not exceed its maximum capacity. We have

$$\forall m \in \mathcal{M}, \quad \sum_{k \in \mathcal{K}} x_{k,m}^t \leq C_m, \tag{3}$$

where C_m is the maximum user-associated capacity of the m-th SBS.

In this paper, our goal is to minimize the long-term system energy consumption while satisfying the task delay violation reliability, and the problem is formulated as

$$\mathbf{P1}: \quad \min_{\{x_{k,m}^t\}, \{\eta_{k,m}^t\}} \lim_{T \to \infty} \frac{1}{T} \sum_{t=1}^{T} E_{tot}[t] \tag{4}$$

$$\text{s.t.}(1), (2), (3)$$

3 Stochastic Delay Analysis

In this section, we perform a comparative analysis of the QoS for BSs with and without the sleep strategy while investigating the end-to-end delay bounds. To simplify the analysis, we assume that the task arrival process for all user devices follows a compound Poisson process with a parameter λ for each time slot, and the length of each task remains fixed at a value L. Then, using the SNC theory, we derive the probability of a task delay violation under different scenarios.

3.1 Delay Analysis for Offloading to MBS

Task offloading consists of two phases: task upload to the MBS and central cloud server computation. To maintain the system's stability, the MBS is always on without running the energy-efficient mechanism, which indicates that there is no BS state transition delay in the task latency. So, $D_k = d_{\text{queue}} + d_{\text{off}} + d_{\text{com}}$.

For device U_k, assuming association with m-th SBS at a certain frame, then the task arrival process to the MBS throughout the frame is denoted as $A_k^1(t) = \sum_{i=1}^{I} A_{k,i}^1 (1 - \eta_k)$, and the task departure process to the MBS is denoted as $A_k^{1*}(t)$, where t denotes the length of the time frame.

The phase of U_k uploading tasks to the MBS has the corresponding stochastic arrival curve $\alpha_k^1(t)$ and the boundary function $f_k^1(x)$, i.e., $A_k^1(t) \sim \langle f_k^1, \alpha_k^1 \rangle$. Then based on the SNC theory [19], we can obtain the stochastic arrival curve (SAC) and bound function as $\alpha_k^1(t) = \frac{1}{\theta t} \log E\left[e^{\theta A_k^1(t)}\right] t$ and $f_k^1(x) = e^{-\theta x}$.

Moreover, the service process of task upload throughout the t-th frame is denoted as $S_k^1(t) = \sum_{i=1}^I R_{k,M,i}$, which is related to the channel capacity of the wireless link. Then, the corresponding stochastic service curve (SSC) $\beta_k^1(t)$ and the boundary function $g_k^1(x)$, i.e., $S_k^1(t) \sim \langle g_k^1, \beta_k^1 \rangle$, can be calculated as $\beta_k^1(t) = \frac{1}{-\theta t} \log E \left[e^{-\theta S_k^1(t)} \right] t$, and $g_k^1(x) = e^{-\theta x}$.

According to the characterization of output traffic [19], the task departure process to the MBS $A_k^{1*}(t)$, i.e., task arrival process to the cloud server from the device U_k, has the corresponding random arrival curve $\alpha_k^{1*}(t)$ and boundary function $f_k^{1*}(x)$, i.e., $A_k^{1*}(t) \sim \langle f_k^{1*}, \alpha_k^{1*} \rangle$, which is given as $\alpha_k^{1*}(t) = \alpha_k^1 \oslash \beta_k^1(t)$ and $f_k^{1*}(x) = f_k^1(x) \otimes g_k^1(x)$.

For the cloud server, its arrival process $A_c(t)$ is the aggregation of all devices' departure processes from the MBS, saying that $A_c(t) = \sum_{k \in \mathcal{K}} A_k^{1*}(t)$.

According to the aggregation nature of SNC, the stochastic arrival curve (SAC) and bound function to the cloud server is $\alpha_c(t) = \sum_{k \in \mathcal{K}} \alpha_i^{1*}(t)$ and $f_c(x) = f_1^{1*} \otimes \cdots \otimes f_K^{1*}(x)$.

The whole arrival traffic except U_k to the cloud server can be considered as a background arrival traffic $\alpha_{bg}(t)$ for target device U_k with the corresponding boundary function $f_{bg}(x)$, which is given as $\alpha_{bg}(t) = \alpha_c(t) - \alpha_k^{1*}(t)$ and $f_{bg}(x) = f_1^{1*} \otimes \cdots \otimes f_{k-1}^{1*} \otimes f_{k+1}^{1*} \otimes \cdots \otimes f_K^{1*}(x)$.

The cloud server has a deterministic service curve $\beta_c(t) = R_c t$. The service process provided by the central cloud server for target device U_k is denoted as $S_k^2(t)$. Then based on the theory of Leftover Service [19], the corresponding SSC β_k^2 and boundary function g_k^2, i.e., $S_k^2(t) \sim \langle g_k^2, \beta_k^2 \rangle$, can be derived as $\beta_k^2(t) = (\beta_c - \alpha_{bg})(t)$ and $g_k^2(x) = f_{bg}(x)$.

In summary, the equivalent stochastic service curve $\beta_k(t)$ and delay boundary $g_k(x)$ service of the whole service process for target device U_k can be calculated as $\beta_k(t) = \beta_k^1 \otimes \beta_k^2(t) = \beta_k^1 \otimes (\beta_c - \alpha_{bg})(t)$ and $g_k(x) = g_k^1 \otimes g_k^2 = g_k^1 \otimes f_{bg}(x)$.

As a result, the time delay boundary of target device U_k for offloading to MBS in the tandem network is given by

$$\Pr\{D_k(t) > d_{\max}\} \leq \left[f_k^1 \otimes g_k \left(\inf_{0 \leq s \leq t} \{ \beta_k(t - s + d_{\max}) - \alpha_k^1(t - s) \} \right) \right]_1 \quad (5)$$
$$\leq \left[f_k^1 \otimes g_k \left(\beta_k^1 \otimes \beta_k^2(d_{\max}) \right) \right]_1,$$

where $[\cdot]^+$ denotes $\max\{0, \cdot\}$.

3.2 Delay Analysis for Offloading to SBS

The process of offloading tasks to SBS and MBS follows a similar procedure. However, two key differences deserve attention: task size and the inclusion of BS sleep mode in SBSs. Specifically, the task arrival process to the m-th SBS associated with U_k at a certain frame is simplified as $A_k^1(t) = \sum_{i=1}^I \eta_k A_{k,i}^1$.

Since the BS may be in different states, resulting in uncertainty in the state transition delay d_{trans}, to further analyze the effect of the

BS state on the task delay, we derive the stationary distribution $\boldsymbol{\pi} = [\pi_{Active} \ \pi_{Idle} \ \pi_{SM1} \ \pi_{SM2} \ \pi_{SM3}] = [\pi_0 \ \pi_1 \ \pi_2 \ \pi_3 \ \pi_4]$.

The Markov model in Fig. 2 is not the same in each large time frame due to the different association strategies between the BS and the user. The transition probability p of the SBS can be derived from the user association and offloading ratio, and it is transferred to the next sleep level only when no user task arrives in the small time slot. For the m-th SBS in t-th frame, its task arrival process obeys the Poisson process with parameter $\lambda_m^t = \sum_{k \in \mathcal{K}} \eta_{k,m}^t \lambda_k$. Thus, the transition probability for the m-th SBS in t-th frame is denoted as p_m^t, which can be $p_m^t = 1 - e^{-\lambda_m^t \tau}$, where τ is the duration of a small time slot.

We drop the indices t and m to simplify the expressions in the following. Then according to the Markov model, the stationary distribution can be

$$\forall j \in [0, N-1], \quad \pi_j = \sum_{i=0}^{N-1} \pi_i P_{i,j}, \quad \sum_{j=0}^{N-1} \pi_j = 1, \quad (6)$$

where $P_{i,j}$ is the probability of transition from state i to j.

Once we have the stationary distribution $\boldsymbol{\pi}$, we seek to determine the reactivation delay for user devices transitioning from sleep state to active state, as this is a critical factor affecting service reliability. Due to the uncertainty of the state within each time slot, the transition delay is a random variable. Let d_j denote the delay for transitioning from the sleep state j to the active state, with specific values given in [3]. Using the stationary distribution $\boldsymbol{\pi}$, we can calculate the average state transition delay within each time slot, just as $d_{\text{trans}} = \sum_{j=0}^{N-1} \pi_j d_j$.

The task arrival process to the edge server is the sum of the departure process from the SBS and the edge provides a deterministic service curve $\beta_e(t) = R_c(t)$ for the uploaded tasks. Similar to (5), the time delay boundary is given by

$$\Pr\{D_k(t) > d_{\max} - d_{\text{trans}}\} \le \left[f_k^1 \otimes g_k \left(\beta_k^1 \otimes \beta_k^2 (d_{\max} - d_{\text{trans}})\right)\right]_1. \quad (7)$$

So far, the time delay boundary of target device U_k for offloading to SBS is obtained. Therefore, the optimization problem is formulated as **P2**:

$$\mathbf{P2}: \min_{\{x_{k,m}^t\}, \{\eta_{k,m}^t\}} \lim_{T \to \infty} \frac{1}{T} \sum_{t=1}^{T} E_{tot}[t] \quad (8)$$
$$\text{s.t.} (2), (3), (5), (7)$$

4 Algorithm

In this section, the original optimization problem in the last section first needs to be transformed into the MDP (Markov decision process) form and then solved using the MADDPG approach.

4.1 MADDPG Problem Formulation

We consider task offloading in a network based on the BS sleep mode. In general, two factors affect the sleep of a BS: one is the BS association policy, i.e., a BS not associated with any user device will gradually shift to the deepest level; the other is the possibility of the BS shifting to the next sleep level, and the triggering of this sleep depends on the arrival of the task in each time slot.

The main goal of this work is to find a BS association strategy that minimizes the cumulative system energy consumption and a task offloading ratio strategy while satisfying the user device latency. Furthermore, given the dynamic and complex nature of such a system, traditional single-agent reinforcement learning methods may struggle to cope with challenges such as action space dimension explosion and policy learning difficulty. To achieve the goal of energy consumption minimization, we formulate the optimization problem as a multi-agent MDP, which is specified by a five-tuple $\{\mathcal{S}, \mathcal{A}, \mathcal{P}, \mathcal{R}, \gamma\}$. $\mathcal{S}$ is the state space and $\mathcal{A}$ is the action space. $\mathcal{P}$ represents the state transition probability. $\mathcal{R}$ is the reward function, and $\gamma \in [0, 1]$ denotes the reward discount factor.

We present a MADDPG-based solution for BS association and task offloading to minimize the penalty for user device delay violation probability and maximize the reward for energy consumption utility. Each user device acts as an agent, and the agents are in a complex relationship of cooperation and mutual competition to achieve the desired goal. At each stage, the agent learns the best policy in the decision problem by observing and interacting with the environment, and we use the sum of the penalty for task delay violation and the energy consumption utility as the system reward. To implement the MADDPG approach, we define the state space, action space, and reward function at each large time frame as follows:

State Space. The state refers to the specific environmental situation observed by each agent. The set state should be able to fully reflect the current observation of the environment by the agent and contain important information for strategy training. Therefore, the state space of the Agent k can be expressed as

$$s_k(t) = \{\chi(t), \alpha_k(t-1), \beta_k(t-1)\}. \tag{9}$$

where $\chi(t) = \{\chi_1(t), \chi_2(t), .., \chi_M(t)\}$ represents the BS association at the beginning of time frame t. If the current small BS m is associated with the user device, then $\chi_m(t) = 1$, otherwise $\chi_m(t) = 0$. $\alpha_k(t-1)$ and $\beta_k(t-1)$ represents the BS association policy and the offload ratio policy of the user device k at the last time frame, respectively. Given the local observations of all agents, the global state space is derived by $S(t) = \{s_1(t), s_2(t), ..., s_K(t)\}$.

Action Space. The action space contains all possible decisions (BS association and offloading ratio) made by the agent. In this paper, the agent's action is represented as

$$a_k(t) = \{\alpha_k(t), \beta_k(t)\}. \tag{10}$$

To solve the dimensional problem and improve the training efficiency, this paper discretizes the action space. Specifically, the unloading ratios are sliced, i.e., there are three types of unloading ratios $\{\frac{1}{3}, \frac{2}{3}, 1\}$, instead of outputting a continuous value. Therefore, the global state space is $A(t) = \{a_1(t), a_2(t), ..., a_K(t)\}$.

Reward Function. The reward should accurately reflect the quality of the agent's actions. The main goal of Eq. (8) is to maximize the long-term system energy reward while satisfying the user device delay constraint. Since many active BSs can lead to increased system power consumption, it is possible to reduce power consumption by putting BSs into a sleep state. Meanwhile, to satisfy the service reliability requirements of user device tasks, a corresponding penalty is given if the latency constraint is not satisfied. Therefore, we set the reward as follows

$$r_k(t) = (1 - w)U_e(t) + wU_d(t)$$
$$= (1 - w)(E_{max} - E_{tot}(t)) - w(P_k^{mbs}(t) + P_k^{sbs}(t)) \tag{11}$$

where w is the weight. w can be set higher if the quality of service is more important. Conversely, if the system is more inclined to save energy, w can be decreased. $U_e(t)$ represents the energy consumption utility, and E_{max} denotes all energy consumption when all SBSs are turned on. $U_d(t)$ denotes the delay violation penalty, and $P_k^{mbs}(t)$ and $P_k^{sbs}(t)$ denote the penalty terms for not satisfying the reliability of offloading to the MBS and SBS, respectively.

Then, the overall reward of the system is expressed as $R(t) = \sum_{k \in \mathcal{K}} r_k(t)$

4.2 Stochastic Network Calculus-Driven MADDPG Algorithm

Since the service reliability derived from the SNC theory largely affects the selection of agent actions and the system energy consumption, we propose an algorithm called stochastic network calculus-driven MADDPG (SNC-MADDPG) that can reduce the system energy consumption as much as possible while satisfying the user device delay constraint.

MADDPG is an Actor-Critic based algorithm, where each agent has two networks, i.e., a policy network and an evaluation network, with parameters of ϑ_k and θ_k, respectively, and the network structure is a deep neural network (DNN). The agent makes the appropriate decision based on its observed state, and the critic is responsible for evaluating the actions taken by the agent in the current state. To address the limitation of Q-learning, which requires the use of the same information during both training and application, MADDPG uses a centralized training decentralized execution framework, which allows the critic to use additional information (global state and action strategies of other agents) for learning during training, and local information for decision making during execution. In addition, in order to improve the stability of the training, each agent also has a target-policy network and a target-evaluation network with parameters ϑ_k' and θ_k', respectively. Thus, the main framework of the algorithm consists of the four DNNs. To improve the training efficiency, a technique called experience replay pool is introduced, which stores a large amount of training

---

Algorithm 1. SNC-MADDPG for BS Association and Task Offloading

---

1: **Initialization:** each agent's replay buffer $\mathcal{D}$, the parameters of policy network ϑ_k and evaluation network θ_k, the parameters of target-policy network ϑ'_k and target-evaluation network θ'_k.

2: **for** episode $= 1,2,\ldots$ **do**

3:    Initialize the state space $S(t)$.

4:    **for** $t = 1,2,\ldots$ **do**

5:       Each agent selects action $a_k(t) = \mu_k(s_k(t))$ + random noise ζ.

6:       All SBSs set their status of association with user devices according to the joint action $A(t)$.

7:       Each agent obtain the reward $r_k(t)$ and the next state $s'_k(t) \leftarrow s_k(t)$.

8:       Save the tuples $(s_k(t), a_k(t), R(t), s'_k(t))$ in $\mathcal{D}$.

9:       **for** agent $k = 1,2,\ldots,$K **do**

10:          Sample a random mini-batch of B tuples $\{\mathbf{s}_j, \mathbf{a}_j, r_j, \mathbf{s}'_j\}$ from $\mathcal{D}$

11:          Update evaluation network parameters with (13).

12:          Update policy network parameters with (12).

13:       **end for**

14:       Update target-policy network and target-evaluation network for each agent in (14).

15:    **end for**

16: **end for**

---

data. During each training iteration, a random subset of data is sampled from the pool. This approach helps break the correlation between the data, resulting in improved training performance.

The SNC-MADDPG approach for the optimization problem is summarized in **Algorithm 1**. During training, for each UE, a random mini-batch of $\{\mathbf{s}_j, \mathbf{a}_j, r_j, \mathbf{s}'_j\}$ of size B is sampled from the replay buffer $\mathcal{D}$. Suppose the parameter set of the corresponding deterministic strategy is given by $\mu = \{\mu_{\vartheta_1}, \ldots, \mu_{\vartheta_K}\}$. The policy network for agent k is updated using the gradient approach as follows:

$$\nabla_{\vartheta_k} J(\mu_k) = \tfrac{1}{B}\sum_{j=1}^{B} \nabla_{\vartheta_k}\mu_k\left(s_k^j\right)\nabla_a Q_k^\theta\left(\mathbf{s}_j, a_1^j, a_k, \ldots, a_K^j\right)\Big|_{a_k = \mu_k(s_k^j)} \tag{12}$$

where j denotes the index of the sample, and the Q-function is denoted as $Q_k^\theta\left(\mathbf{s}_j, a_1^j, \ldots, a_k, \ldots, a_K^j\right)$. Then, the parameters of the policy network are $\vartheta_k = \vartheta_k - \xi_a \nabla_{\vartheta_k} J(\mu_k)$, where ξ_a denotes the learning rate. The evaluation network updates the weights by minimizing the mean square error loss, which can be represented as

$$L(\theta_k) = \frac{1}{B}\sum_{j=1}^{B}\left[y_j - Q_k^\theta(\mathbf{s}_j, \mathbf{a}_j)\right]^2$$

$$y = r_k + \gamma Q_k^{\theta'}(\mathbf{s}'_j, \mathbf{a}'_j), \tag{13}$$

where γ is denoted as the discount factor and $\mathbf{a}'_j$ is the target actions. Therefore, the parameters of the evaluation network are updated as $\theta_k = \theta_k - \xi_c \nabla_{\theta_k} L(\theta_k)$, where ξ_c denotes the learning rate. On the other hand, the target network uses soft update to update the parameters, and the parameters ϑ'_k and θ'_k of the target policy network and target evaluation network of each UE Agent are updated as

$$\vartheta'_k = \tau\vartheta_k + (1-\tau)\vartheta'_k$$
$$\theta'_k = \tau\theta_k + (1-\tau)\theta'_k \tag{14}$$

where τ denotes the updating rate.

5   Simulation Results

5.1   Experimental Setup

In this section, we conduct simulation experiments to evaluate the effectiveness of the algorithm. Specifically, considering a heterogeneous network, there is one MBS, $M = 6$ SBSs, and $K = 10$ user devices randomly distributed within the coverage of the MBS and SBSs. The core cloud is connected to the MBS, and the computational frequency of the server is 14 GHz. While each SBS is connected to an edge server, and the computational frequency of the edge server is 2.5 GHz. On the timescale, a large time frame contains $n = 100$ slots, and the length of the slots is $\tau = 0.02$ sec. For the time delay constraint, the time delay threshold d_{max} = 0.2 sec and the violation probability $\epsilon_d = 0.05$ indicate that the reliability is expected to be at least 95%. The bandwidth of the SBS and the MBS is 6MHz and 2MHz, respectively. The CPU cycles per bit is set as 800. The White Gaussian noise is set as -70dBm. The energy consumption coefficient of the edge server and the cloud server is 10^{-27} and 10^{-29}. The length for each task is set as 0.23 Mbits. The task arrival rate of each UE is set as 0.3 packets/slot.

5.2   Comparing Methods

To evaluate the performance of the proposed algorithm, we compare it with the following four benchmark algorithms: (1) Binary sleep mode algorithm (BiSM): In a large time frame, if no task arrives in the current time, the SBS with user association is directly transferred to the next sleep mode, and then to the Active mode when a task arrives next time. Binary sleep mode is widely used in previous studies [6,18]. (2) Without base station sleep mode (NoSM): For the base station without user association, it will gradually enter into deepest sleep mode to save energy; for the base station with user association, it will not make any state transfer throughout the large time frame and maintain the Active state. (3) Only offload to SBSs policy (OnlySBS): All user devices' offloading decisions are only related to SBSs and will not be offloaded to the MBS.

In this section, we analyze the training performance as well as the convergence of the proposed algorithm. Figure 3a shows the system reward with training time, at 0–500 episodes, the rewards increase sharply after a period of small fluctuations and finally level off at 800 episodes. Figure 3b and Fig. 3c show the change in delay penalty and energy score during training. From Fig. 3b and Fig. 3d, we can see that the penalty for delay violation consistently decreases

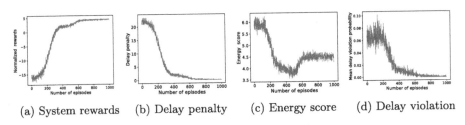

(a) System rewards   (b) Delay penalty   (c) Energy score   (d) Delay violation

Fig. 3. Training curves of SNC-MADDPG.

from 0 to 500 episodes, indicating a gradual decrease in the probability of delay violation resulting from the agent's decision. Finally, the probability tends to be 0, confirming the satisfaction of service reliability for all user devices. From Fig. 3c, it can be seen that the system energy consumption is sacrificed for the delay constraint in the early stage, but after 500 episodes, the agent's decision is more biased towards the system energy saving under the premise that the user's decision does not violate the reliability, which makes the energy score rebound a lot, which also shows the effectiveness of the multiple sleep mechanism for energy saving.

Figure 4b and Fig. 4b show the variation of delay penalty and the energy score of different algorithms when $M = 5$, respectively. From Fig. 4a, we can find that the binary sleep mode algorithm can not satisfy user latency reliability, compared with other strategies. This is because the binary sleep mode can be more in deep sleep level and potentially more energy efficient. Besides, the activation time and reactivation time also increase in the binary sleep mode, which will affect the user delay constraints. From Fig. 4b, we can see that the energy value of the binary sleep mode algorithm does not outperform the multi-level sleep mode algorithm, which may be because the binary sleep mode algorithm does not reduce the delay penalty, and thus cannot learn the optimal base station association and task offloading strategies.

Figure 4c shows the relationship between the system rewards and the task reach rate λ for different algorithms. As the task reach rate increases, more energy needs to be consumed by the edge server or cloud server, leading to a decrease in rewards for all algorithms. Also, it can be seen that the proposed

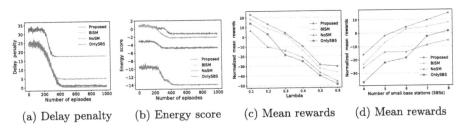

(a) Delay penalty   (b) Energy score   (c) Mean rewards   (d) Mean rewards

Fig. 4. Training curves of SNC-MADDPG.

algorithm can guarantee that the system rewards are always higher than the other algorithms.

Fig. 4d shows the relationship between system rewards and the number of small base stations M for different algorithms. As the number of SBSs increases, the choice of base station access points for user devices increases, and the number of SBSs not associated with user devices increases, which can be more energy efficient and increase the system rewards. Compared with the other four learning methods, our proposed method achieves the maximum total system reward for any number of SBSs.

6   Conclusion

In this paper, we investigate the joint optimization problem of base station power saving and edge computing in B5G heterogeneous networks. Based on the multi-level base station sleep mode technique, we address the BS association problem and analyze the uncertainties incurred by the multi-level sleep mode. Besides, to ensure the performance of delay-sensitive services in user devices, we apply stochastic network theory to analyze the delay of the two-stage process and use the derived conclusions to construct the model of service reliability for delay-sensitive services in UDN. We then formulate the problem of minimizing the system energy consumption as a Markov decision process model and propose an algorithm called SNC-MADDPG to address these challenges. The algorithm uses the framework of CTDE, where each user acts as an agent, to learn the optimal base station association and task offloading strategies. Extensive simulation results show that our proposed algorithm effectively satisfies stringent service reliability requirements.

Acknowledgments. This research was funded by National Natural Science Foundation of China (Grant No. U1711264).

References

1. Chen, X., Yao, Z., Chen, Z., Min, G., Zheng, X., Rong, C.: Load balancing for multi-edge collaboration in wireless metropolitan area networks: a two-stage decision-making approach. IEEE Internet of Things J. **10**, 17124–17136 (2023)
2. Chu, W., Jia, X., Yu, Z., Lui, J.C., Lin, Y.: Joint service caching, resource allocation and task offloading for MEC-based networks: a multi-layer optimization approach. IEEE Trans. Mobile Comput. (2023)
3. El Amine, A., Chaiban, J.P., Hassan, H.A.H., Dini, P., Nuaymi, L., Achkar, R.: Energy optimization with multi-sleeping control in 5G heterogeneous networks using reinforcement learning. IEEE Trans. Netw. Service Manag. **19**, 4310–4322 (2022)
4. Israr, A., Yang, Q., Israr, A.: Emission-aware sustainable energy provision for 5g and b5g mobile networks. IEEE Trans. Sustain. Comput. (2023). https://doi.org/10.1109/TSUSC.2023.3271789

5. Israr, A., Yang, Q., Israr, A.: Renewable energy provision and energy-efficient operational management for sustainable 5G infrastructures. IEEE Trans. Netw. Service Manag. **20**, 2678–2710 (2023)
6. Kim, S., Son, J., Shim, B.: Energy-efficient ultra-dense network using LSTM-based deep neural networks. IEEE Trans. Wireless Commun. **20**(7), 4702–4715 (2021)
7. Lähdekorpi, P., Hronec, M., Jolma, P., Moilanen, J.: Energy efficiency of 5G mobile networks with base station sleep modes. In: 2017 IEEE Conference on Standards for Communications and Networking (CSCN), pp. 163–168. IEEE (2017)
8. Li, X., Li, C., Liu, X., Chen, G., Dong, Z.Y.: Two-stage community energy trading under end-edge-cloud orchestration. IEEE Internet Things J. **10**(3), 1961–1972 (2023)
9. Liao, Y., Friderikos, V.: Optimal deployment and operation of robotic aerial 6G small cells with grasping end effectors. IEEE Trans. Veh. Technol. (2023)
10. Liu, S., Cheng, P., Chen, Z., Xiang, W., Vucetic, B., Li, Y.: Contextual user-centric task offloading for mobile edge computing in ultra-dense network. IEEE Trans. Mobile Comput. **22**, 5092–5108 (2022)
11. Malta, S., Pinto, P., FernÃaindez-Veiga, M.: Using reinforcement learning to reduce energy consumption of ultra-dense networks with 5g use cases requirements. IEEE Access **11**, 5417–5428 (2023)
12. Masoudi, M., Khafagy, M.G., Soroush, E., Giacomelli, D., Morosi, S., Cavdar, C.: Reinforcement learning for traffic-adaptive sleep mode management in 5G networks. In: 2020 IEEE 31st Annual International Symposium on Personal, Indoor and Mobile Radio Communications, pp. 1–6 (2020)
13. Masoudi, M., Soroush, E., Zander, J., Cavdar, C.: Digital twin assisted risk-aware sleep mode management using deep q-networks. IEEE Trans. Veh. Technol. **72**(1), 1224–1239 (2023)
14. Renga, D., Umar, Z., Meo, M.: Trading off delay and energy saving through advanced sleep modes in 5G RANs. IEEE Trans. Wireless Commun. (2023)
15. Salahdine, F., Opadere, J., Liu, Q., Han, T., Zhang, N., Wu, S.: A survey on sleep mode techniques for ultra-dense networks in 5G and beyond. Comput. Netw. **201**, 108567 (2021)
16. Tan, X., Xiong, K., Gao, B., Fan, P., Letaief, K.B.: Energy-efficient base station switching-off with guaranteed cooperative profit gain of mobile network operators. IEEE Trans. Green Commun. Netw. **7**, 1250–1266 (2023)
17. Wei, Z., Li, B., Zhang, R., Cheng, X., Yang, L.: Many-to-many task offloading in vehicular fog computing: a multi-agent deep reinforcement learning approach. IEEE Trans. Mobile Comput. (2023)
18. Wu, Q., Chen, X., Zhou, Z., Chen, L., Zhang, J.: Deep reinforcement learning with spatio-temporal traffic forecasting for data-driven base station sleep control. IEEE/ACM Trans. Netw. **29**(2), 935–948 (2021)
19. Liu, Y., Jiang, Y.: Stochastic Network Calculus. Springer, London (2008). https://doi.org/10.1007/978-1-84800-127-5
20. Zhou, X., et al.: Edge-enabled two-stage scheduling based on deep reinforcement learning for internet of everything. IEEE Internet Things J. **10**(4), 3295–3304 (2023)
21. Zhou, Z., et al.: Learning-based URLLC-aware task offloading for internet of health things. IEEE J. Sel. Areas Commun. **39**(2), 396–410 (2021)

Enhancing Blockchain Performance via On-chain and Off-chain Collaboration

Wuhui Chen[1], Zhaoxian Yang[1], Jianting Zhang[2(✉)], Junyuan Liang[1], Qilin Sun[1], and Fan Zhou[1]

[1] Sun Yat-sen University, Guangzhou, China
{chenwuh,isszf}@mail.sysu.edu.cn,
{yangzhx9,liangjy53,sunqilin}@mail2.sysu.edu.cn
[2] Purdue University, West Lafayette, USA
zhan4674@purdue.edu

Abstract. Transactions concurrent execution is one of the most promising solutions to enhance throughput for blockchain systems. Traditional concurrent execution schemes include on-chain concurrency and off-chain concurrency. However, they either increase hardware requirements to nodes or bring extra overheads for transaction verification, compromising the decentralization and security properties of blockchains. In this paper, we propose a new concurrent execution scheme that integrates off-chain execution into the on-chain concurrent execution scheme, by which a blockchain system can enhance performance without compromising security and decentralization. To achieve this, we first propose a consistent information scheduling mechanism. This mechanism divides scheduling information of transactions based on the execution-related information, improving the efficiency of scheduling information transmission and execution between on-chain and off-chain nodes. Then, to achieve secure and efficient collaboration between on-chain and off-chain nodes, our scheme proposes a secure collaboration validation mechanism without additional security assumptions. Finally, we implement our prototype based on Tendermint and compare it with the serial execution scheme in the blockchain. The experimental results show that our scheme can achieve a maximum throughput improvement of 2.6×, 11.2× less execution time, and 2.1× less verification time.

Keywords: Blockchain · concurrent computing · off-chain computing

1 Introduction

Blockchain is a distributed ledger where participants jointly maintain a consistent state without trusting each other, and it has been applied to many fields, such as the financial sector, healthcare and wellness application scenarios. To achieve this, blockchain relies on a consensus protocol, e.g., Proof-of-Work [1] and Byzantine Fault Tolerance (BFT) [2]. A consensus protocol works in two

F. Monti et al. (Eds.): ICSOC 2023, LNCS 14419, pp. 393–408, 2023.
https://doi.org/10.1007/978-3-031-48421-6_27

stages: first, a block proposer creates a new block consisting of a list of transactions and broadcasts it to the network; then, the other nodes verify the received block and execute and commit it to their local ledgers if the block is valid. To achieve strict consistency, traditional blockchain systems execute transactions of a block in a serial way. Such a serial execution scheme, however, significantly limits the capability of processing transactions, leading to poor system performance [3].

To enable concurrent execution, many recent works [4–11] propose various concurrent execution schemes for blockchain systems. In summary, there are two types of concurrent execution schemes: on-chain and off-chain concurrent schemes. In on-chain solutions [4–7], a block proposer divides transactions of a block into several sets based on their data dependencies, by which other nodes can utilize their multi-core feature to execute these sets of transactions in parallel. Obviously, this solution can improve system performance by adding more transactions into a block and dividing more transaction sets. However, the on-chain solution still requires each node to execute all transactions. For some nodes with limited computation resources, they cannot execute transactions efficiently when a block becomes larger, and thus slow the consensus process. To address this problem, off-chain solutions [8–11] try to offload some transactions (e.g., computation-intensive transactions) into off-chain. Specifically, in an off-chain scheme, there are some off-chain nodes that are responsible for executing a set of transactions but do not participate in on-chain consensus. The on-chain nodes, therefore, can get the execution results from the off-chain nodes for consensus without executing these computation-intensive transactions. This prevents resource-limited nodes from slowing the consensus process. However, it introduces new security problems and requires additional costs. To ensure the trustworthiness of off-chain results, various schemes are proposed, such as leveraging the hardware Trusted Execution Environments [11], assuming new security models [8,9], and relying on cryptographic proofs [12]. However, all these off-chain methods either introduce new security problems or extra overheads [13,14], sacrificing the security and performance of blockchains. In this work, we propose a new on-chain and off-chain collaboration scheme to implement a high-performance blockchain system. In a nutshell, our collaboration scheme has on-chain validation for a portion of the transactions and off-chain validation for another portion, allowing on-chain nodes and off-chain nodes to collaborate in executing transactions efficiently and ensuring system security. Transaction processing in our scheme consists of two stages: first, a block proposer creates a block with separate portions of transactions (i.e., scheduling information); then, on-chain and off-chain nodes collaboratively execute and verify transactions based on the separate transactions. However, designing such a two-stage collaborative verification is non-trivial. Specifically, since our scheme involves both on-chain concurrency and off-chain concurrency, it faces two main challenges: 1) how does the block proposer effectively generate, partition, and distribute scheduling information, and 2) how to achieve efficient and secure collaboration between on-chain and off-chain nodes?

To solve the above challenges, first, we propose a new information scheduling mechanism. We introduce a so-called *versioning information* in the scheduling relationship and perform finer-grained slicing and allocation of transactions. This ensures consistency of the node states on the blockchain and improves the efficiency of subgraph transmission and execution, thereby enhancing the system's performance. Furthermore, this mechanism can effectively balance the computational overhead among on-chain nodes by which nodes with limited resources will not slow the consensus process. Then, for the second challenge, we propose a mechanism named *secure collaboration validation mechanism* without any additional security assumptions. Specifically, we divide the on-chain nodes into groups flexibly based on the trust assumptions and ensure that each group of on-chain nodes has at least one honest node. The at-least-one honest node setting guarantees the correct execution in each group.

The contributions of this work can be summarized as follows:

- We propose a scheme for collaborative execution on-chain and off-chain, reducing the validation burden on on-chain nodes. On-chain nodes only need to validate a portion of the transactions, improving system performance while ensuring security.
- Building upon the on-chain and off-chain scheme, we design an information scheduling mechanism and a secure collaboration validation mechanism to enhance the security and efficiency of the system.
- We implement our prototype based on Tendermint [15]. Compared with the serial execution scheme, experimental results show that our concurrent execution scheme can improve throughput by $2.6\times$ and achieve $11.2\times$ less execution time and $2.1\times$ less validation time.

2   Related Work and Motivation

A blockchain is a distributed ledger. To ensure a consistent state for nodes, a consensus protocol is used in blockchain systems. Informally, a consensus protocol in blockchain systems is a repeated two-phase activity. Specifically, in the first stage, there is a block proposer creating a new block and broadcasting it to the network. In the second stage, other nodes (or called validators) check the validity of the new block. They then execute and commit transactions of the block into their local ledgers. This two-phase activity will repeat continuously as new transactions are created and received by nodes of the blockchain system. As a result, the ledger grows as a chain consisting of blocks. To ensure a consistent state, traditional blockchain systems adopt a *serial execution scheme* when performing a consensus [16], i.e., a block proposer first orders transactions in a new block and serially execute them, and then other nodes serially execute transactions in the same transaction order. However, such a serial execution scheme cannot utilize the multi-core features in modern computers and thus leads to poor system performance [4–6].

On-chain Concurrent Execution . To enhance performance of blockchains, many recent works propose on-chain concurrent execution solutions [4, 6, 7, 17, 18]. The main idea is to introduce a concurrent scheduling algorithm in the first stage of consensus by which the block proposer can generate a dependency graph that is used for validators to execute transactions concurrently. For instance, Dickerson et al. [4] propose the use of abstract lock mechanisms to prevent resource contention and allow miners and validators to execute transactions in parallel. Miners generate deterministic fork-join programs, enabling consistent parallel execution by validators. Jin et al. [7] takes a two-stage approach to accelerate contract execution between the master node and validation nodes. They design a TDG (Transaction Dependency Graph) to maintain consistency between the master node and validation nodes. Garamvölgyi et al. [6] propose Optimistic Concurrency Control with Deterministic Aborts (OCC-DA), which makes it possible to use OCC scheduling in public blockchain settings The above on-chain concurrent execution solutions allow nodes to utilize their multi-core hardware to execute transactions efficiently. However, a node still needs to execute all transactions. When transactions are computation-intensive (e.g., smart contract transactions [19]), the improvement of throughput is limited. Besides, the existence of hotspot accounts (i.e., data are accessed frequently) can lead to high data contention, and thus nodes still need to execute transactions serially.

Off-chain Concurrent Execution . To better execute computation-intensive transactions and hotspot account transactions concurrently, other works [8–11, 20, 21], propose an off-chain concurrent execution scheme. Its main idea is to offload some transactions into off-chain nodes by which on-chain nodes and off-chain nodes can execute disjoint sets of transactions in parallel. On-chain nodes, in this case, can directly use execution results from off-chain nodes for consensus. However, since on-chain nodes do not execute locally, the results computed by off-chain nodes may not be trusted. Therefore, additional measures need to be taken to ensure the trustworthiness of the off-chain results, which incurs extra costs. Arbitrum [8] introduces a so-called challenge mechanism to ensure the correctness of off-chain executions. Specifically, the mechanism allows users or nodes to challenge the execution results from off-chain nodes for a period of time before a transaction can eventually be committed. Such a challenge period, however, increases the confirmation of transactions. Some other works [10, 12] adopt zero-knowledge proof techniques to provide verifiable execution results, where off-chain nodes must perform a highly-cost computation for generating a proof. Ekiden [11] and Fastkitten [22] rely on a hardware Trusted Execution Environment (TEEs) to assist on-chain nodes in verifying execution results from off-chain nodes. However, many recent works [13] report TEEs are vulnerable to some attacks.

Motivation. The existing concurrent execution solutions, unfortunately, have their intrinsic limitations. While on-chain concurrent execution solutions cannot parallelize computation-intensive and hotspot account transactions well, the existing off-chain concurrent execution solutions either introduce non-negligible overheads or security risks [9]. In this work, we will present a new concurrent execution scheme to enhance the performance of blockchains without sacrificing the security property.

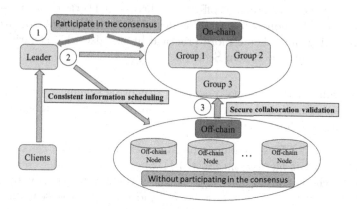

Fig. 1. System overview

3   Scheme Overview

In this section, we will present an overview of our scheme, followed by its challenges.

3.1   System Overview and Trust Assumptions

System Overview. Figure 1 presents an overview of our scheme, consisting of three node types.

- *Clients.* Clients are the users of the blockchain system. Their state data is maintained by the blockchain ledger, and they request to modify the state data by sending transactions to the blockchain network.
- *On-chain nodes.* On-chain nodes run consensus protocol to maintain the blockchain ledger jointly. An on-chain node can either be a (i) block proposer (also called leader), who is responsible for generating new blocks, or (ii) block validator, who verifies new blocks.
- *Off-chain nodes.* Off-chain nodes work as service nodes that help on-chain nodes commit transactions. They do not participate in consensus directly but execute transactions based on the scheduling information received from block proposers.

Trust Assumptions. We assume a partially synchronous network, where nodes can receive messages from honest nodes within an unknown time-bound [23]. Under the partial synchrony network, we assume our system consists of $n = 3f + 1$ on-chain nodes, where f nodes are Byzantine nodes. The Byzantine nodes can behave maliciously by intentionally delaying messages or sending incorrect messages. Different from previous off-chain schemes [9,11] that assume some off-chain nodes must be honest, off-chain nodes in our scheme could be arbitrarily malicious, making our scheme more practical in a real-world scenario. We will show how we can achieve this in Sect. 4.2.

Workflow. Similar to previous concurrent execution schemes, we adopt a two-stage consensus. Figure 1 shows the transaction processing in our scheme, which mainly includes the following steps:

- Steps ①and ②: First, leaders separates transactions via a *consistent information scheduling mechanism* (Sect. 4.1). Specifically, a leader creates a block with a batch of transactions and executes them concurrently to generate scheduling information. After that, the leader divides the scheduling information into several parts that will be sent to specific on-chain nodes and off-chain nodes for executions.
- Steps ③: Then, on-chain nodes and off-chain nodes collaboratively verify and execute the received transaction parts via a *secure collaboration validation mechanism* (Sect. 4.2).

3.2   Challenges

However, designing an on-chain and off-chain collaborative execution scheme is non-trivial and faces the following challenges.

Challenge A: In our scheme, similar to the previous on-chain concurrent execution schemes, the leader will collect a batch of transactions and execute them concurrently, generating scheduling information and dividing it into three parts, which are then sent to the nodes both on-chain and off-chain. However, unlike previous work, in our scheme, on-chain nodes do not need to validate all transactions. The leader sends the scheduling information to both on-chain validators and off-chain nodes. Therefore, the challenge in the design of the scheme lies in how to generate, partition, and distribute the scheduling information to ensure consistency.

Challenge B: Different from previous on-chain concurrent execution solutions, we also assign off-chain nodes to assist in executing transactions. As a result, the on-chain nodes need to combine the results from both themselves and off-chain nodes to determine the correctness of the results and update the state. This introduces a new challenge in the coordination between on-chain and off-chain nodes. Therefore, in our scheme, ensuring secure and efficient collaboration between on-chain and off-chain nodes is another challenge.

4   On-chain and Off-chain Collaborative Execution Scheme

In this section, we will detail our on-chain and off-chain collaborative execution scheme. First, we propose a consistent information scheduling mechanism, which, even if some transactions are delegated to off-chain validation, still ensures the consistency of on-chain nodes and enables more efficient partitioning, providing the system with better concurrency and reducing the amount of data that needs to be transmitted by on-chain nodes. After that, we present a secure collaboration validation mechanism. By dividing on-chain nodes into groups and introducing a new challenge approach, our scheme reaps a secure and efficient collaboration between on-chain and off-chain nodes without any additional security assumptions on off-chain nodes.

4.1   Consistent Information Scheduling Mechanism

The first stage of processing transactions in our scheme is to ask leaders to generate scheduling information for transactions so that both on-chain nodes and off-chain nodes can execute transactions concurrently in the second stage. The key to generating scheduling information is the Transaction Scheduling Information Graph (TSIG).

TSIG Structures . Figure 2 shows an example of a TSIG. Specifically, a TSIG is a directed acyclic graph consisting of the following elements: i) Tx_i, where $i = 1, 2, ..., n$, $i \in N$, represents the transaction id; ii) Directed edges, represent the execution order of transactions, where arrows point to the transactions that are executed later; iii) $E_{i,j}$, represents the information passed from Tx_i to Tx_j, which can be any relevant information; 4. S_i, where $i = 1, 2, 3$, indicates the subgraph to which the scheduling information belongs.

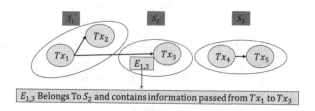

Fig. 2. Transaction scheduling information graph

The leader ensures conflict-free execution of resources by using a locking mechanism. Whether a transaction is executed depends on whether it has acquired the lock. However, the locking mechanism introduces some randomness, as the order of execution may vary even for the same batch of transactions.

To enable the other nodes to know the order in which the leader executes transactions, the leader needs to provide scheduling information, i.e., the dependency relationship between transactions. To maintain consistency when utilizing the off-chain results, we propose a *versioning information* method to ensure consistency. Specifically, in addition to the account values, we include additional version information in $E_{i,j}$, representing the version of an account in this batch of transactions. When an account is updated, the on-chain nodes can compare the version number returned by the off-chain nodes with the version number of the account they executed. The results with the higher version number indicate that its state is more up-to-date; thus, the results with the higher version number are selected for updating.

A TSIG provides the dependent relationships among transactions, along with some intermediate states (i.e., $E_{i,j}$). To allow independent validation of transactions within each subgroup, we need to partition the TSIG into subgraphs and allow each subgraph to run independently. If there are dependencies between transactions in different subgraphs, such as $E_{1,3}$ in Fig. 2, then the dependency needs to be included in S_2 so that S_2 can execute Tx_3 without executing Tx_1, as the execution result of Tx_1 is already known. However, there are no dependencies between S_2 and S_3. Clearly, we only need to transmit the topological relationship of the subgraphs, as the dependency information $E_{i,j}$ can be generated internally and does not rely on other subgraphs.

Different partitioning ways result in different sizes of the transmitted information and also lead to variations in the computation time required for each subgroup. In our scheme, the leader records the execution time of each transaction and the size of the data to be transmitted between transactions. We use $t(Tx_i)$ to represent the execution time of Tx_i and W_{ij} to represent the size of the message transmitted from Tx_i to Tx_j. After concurrent execution, we sort W_{ij} in descending order and set one-third of the total execution time as the threshold. We then add transactions to the subgroup in descending order of W_{ij} until the computation threshold is reached. By following this approach, we minimize the amount of information that needs to be transmitted between subgroups and achieve a more balanced distribution of computation load among the subgroups.

Illustrative Example: In Fig. 2, we assume Tx_1 is a transaction involving accounts *Alice* and *Bob*; Tx_2 is a transaction involving account *Alice*; Tx_3 is a transaction involving account *Bob*, Tx_4 and Tx_5 are both transactions involving *Tom*. It is given that Tx_1 is executed before Tx_2 and Tx_3, and Tx_4 is executed before Tx_5. Three directed edges are present in the graph and contain relevant information, namely $E_{1,2}$, $E_{1,3}$, and $E_{4,5}$. We sort the sizes of $E_{i,j}$ in descending order, assuming $E_{1,2}$, $E_{4,5}$, and $E_{1,3}$ in that order. We set the threshold to be $1/3$ of the total execution time.

During the process of generating subgraphs, we first split the larger edge, $E_{1,2}$, which involves Tx_1 and Tx_2. Assuming that the sum of the execution time of the two transactions exceeds the threshold, we consider them as a single subgroup. Next, we proceed with the second subgraph. We then examine $E_{4,5}$, which involves Tx_4 and Tx_5. If their total execution time exceeds the threshold, we separate them into another subgraph. Since we need to create three subgraphs in total, we do not need to perform any further checks. The transactions involved in $E_{1,3}$ will be assigned to the last subgraph. However, Tx_1 is already present in another subgraph. Therefore, we need to keep $E_{1,3}$ in the last subgraph. In this way, we generate the TSIG as shown in Fig. 2.

4.2 Secure Collaboration Validation Mechanism

The second stage of processing transactions in our scheme is that on-chain nodes and off-chain nodes collaboratively execute transactions and verify the execution results. The key is to ensure secure and efficient collaboration between on-chain and off-chain nodes.

Corresponding to the division of transaction subgraphs, our scheme also divides on-chain nodes into groups, by which on-chain nodes only need to execute part of subgraphs but not all transactions. If a group of nodes in the on-chain groups consists entirely of malicious nodes, it can compromise the security of the system. Specifically, these malicious nodes can collude to manipulate the off-chain nodes into returning incorrect results for a specific subgraph.

Illustrative Example: Figure 3 shows an example where malicious on-chain and off-chain nodes collude to manipulate the execution result and eventually compromise the correctness of the ledger. As shown in Fig. 3, there are two subgraphs, S_1 and S_2, two on-chain groups, G_1 and G_2, and multiple off-chain nodes. All nodes in G_1 are malicious, while all nodes in G_2 are honest. G_1 is assigned to execute S_1 and receives the result of S_2 returned by off-chain nodes. Because all the nodes in G_1 are malicious, they can manipulate the execution result of S_1 in a malicious manner. G_2 executes another subgraph and receives an erroneous off-chain result about S_1. Since G_2 does not execute S_1 but directly relies on the off-chain results, the malicious nodes can successfully modify the result of the S_1 without being detected by the on-chain nodes.

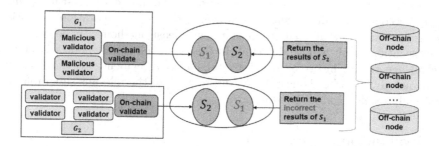

Fig. 3. An example of collusion between on-chain and off-chain nodes

To ensure the security of the system, we propose an *at-least-one honesty* mechanism. Specifically, we guarantee that there is at least one honest node involved in the computation of each subgraph. Recall from the trust assumptions in Sect. 3, where are $n = 3f + 1$ on-chain nodes in our system, where f is the number of byzantine nodes. Therefore, in our scheme, we divide the nodes into three groups, each of which consists of f nodes and the leader (thus, $(f+1)$ nodes in each group). However, we emphasize the number of groups in our scheme can be adjusted to accommodate different trust models and requirements. For example, we can allow *group overlap* where on-chain nodes can join multiple groups at the same time.

Groups are responsible for executing different subgraphs. The group size of $(f + 1)$ ensures that each subgraph has at least one honest node involved in its computation. By having at least one honest node in the group responsible for computing a particular subgraph, we can detect malicious behavior when the result of a subgraph is tampered with off-chain. When honest on-chain nodes detect malicious behavior from a node, they no longer rely on the off-chain results returned by that node. Instead, they calculate the remaining subgraphs to update their local state. After calculating the remaining subgraphs, they can compare their own computed results with the off-chain results to identify which ones are incorrect. They can then issue challenges to punish the malicious node.

By grouping the transactions in this way, our scheme prevents the malicious leader from succeeding. If the TSIG sent by the leader contains incorrect $E_{i,j}$ values, the honest on-chain nodes, having access to all the TSIGs, will compare the computed $E_{i,j}$ values after executing the transactions. If they find any discrepancies, they will roll back to executing all the transactions themselves and issue challenges to punish the malicious leader.

Security Proof: We prove that our scheme can satisfy consistency, i.e., any two honest nodes store the same prefix ledger.

Theorem 1 (Consistency). *Our on-chain and off-chain collaborative execution scheme guarantees consistency.*

Proof. If malicious nodes want to compromise consistency among honest nodes, they need to output inconsistent execution results to different honest nodes during the second stage of consensus. However, since our collaboration validation mechanism ensures that each group contains at least one honest node, an incorrect execution result will be detected. In this case, the honest node will launch a challenge to the incorrect result by broadcasting evidence to the network. Consequently, all other honest nodes will re-execute the relevant subgraph and eventually reach a consistent state.

5   Evaluation

Implementation. We implement a prototype system for our scheme in Golang. Additionally, we leverage Tendermint [15] consensus to implement our scheme. Tendermint is a project that can be used to securely and consistently replicate applications across multiple machines [24]. Building upon Tendermint, we establish P2P connections between on-chain and off-chain nodes using the HTTP protocol for information transmission, which enables collaboration between on-chain and off-chain nodes. In order to make a comparison, we will compare our scheme with the serial execution scheme. To ensure a fair comparison, we also implement batch transaction execution for the serial execution scheme.

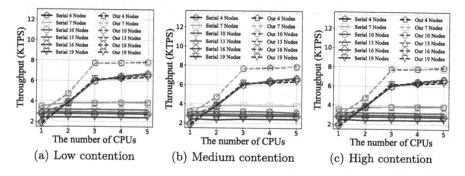

Fig. 4. Comparison of throughput under different CPUs

Dataset. In order to evaluate the performance of our scheme, we have implemented SmallBank in Golang, a commonly used OLTP benchmark that has also been applied in blockchain networks to simulate contract transactions [7]. Additionally, we have used the Zipfian distribution to simulate the access frequency of contracts in the real world and adjusted the skew parameter to simulate transaction conflicts. The skew parameter ranges from 0 to 1, where a higher value indicates a higher conflict rate.

Setup. We conduct all experiments on one machine with an Intel Xeon Gold 5320 Processor and 128 GB RAM to reveal the performance improvement of our scheme, which is fairly common in a series of related works [4,5,7]. To impose finer resource constraints on each node, we package the required resources for each node into a docker image. By instantiating each image, we create independent containers that represent individual nodes. To enable communication between these container nodes, we set up a subnet on the machine and use the tc command in Linux to restrict communication between nodes. We add a qdisc to each node's communication interface and use the Token Bucket Filter (TBF) as the queuing algorithm. The token generation rate is set to an average of 1Gbps, with a peak rate of 1.5Gbps. The maximum burst transmission size is 64KB, and the minimum transmission size is 1540 bytes. We introduce a delay of 50ms to simulate the communication process between distributed machines. Additionally, we use docker-compose to orchestrate each container node, limiting their CPU and memory resources and ensuring that the nodes are on the same subnet for communication. We repeat each experiment three times and calculate the average of the results.

Metrics. We use the following metrics to measure the performance of the system. 1) Transaction throughput, measured in transactions per second (TPS), represents the throughput of confirmed transactions. 2) Confirmation latency refers to the time delay from when a transaction is sent from the client to when it is confirmed by the nodes in the system. 3) Transaction execution time is the time it takes for the leader in the system to execute a batch of transactions upon receiving them. 4) Transaction verification time is when the other validators in the system validate the transactions in a block sent by the leader.

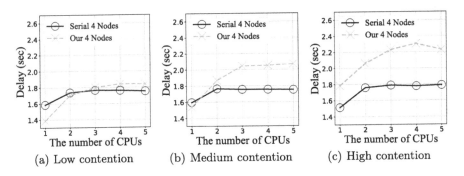

(a) Low contention   (b) Medium contention   (c) High contention

Fig. 5. Comparison of delay under different CPUs with 4 nodes

In the experiment, we set the number of on-chain nodes to be 4, 7, 10, 13, 16, and 19, respectively, and an off-chain node, of which the resource allocation is consistent with on-chain nodes. To evaluate the performance, we measured the system's throughput with different CPU numbers per node, ranging from 1 to 5, under different conflict rates, shown in Fig. 4. We simulated low, medium, and high conflict rate scenarios by setting the skew parameter to 0.1, 0.5, and 0.9, respectively. We find that as the number of nodes in the system increased, the throughput gradually decreased for both our scheme and the serial execution scheme. With increasing nodes, the communication overhead in the system significantly increased. The complexity of network communication implemented by Tendermint is $O(n^3)$, which leads to a decrease in system throughput.

Although batch transaction execution is being implemented in the serial scheme, the conflict rate does not affect it. Whether the conflict rate is low, medium, or high, the throughput and latency of batch processing remain largely unaffected. On the other hand, our scheme's throughput is generally unaffected, but the latency increases linearly with the increase in conflict rate, as shown in Fig. 5, which measures the latency of the system when the nodes number is 4, and the CPUs number ranges from 1 to 5, under different conflict rates. This is mainly because our scheme needs to transmit subgraphs, and if the conflict rate is high, the amount of information that needs to be transmitted among subgraphs increases due to the increased dependencies among them. In contrast, batch processing executed in a serial manner is not affected because it does not require the transmission of additional information and can simply be executed based on the order of transactions.

The performance of the serial execution scheme is not significantly affected by the number of CPUs. As the number of CPUs increases, the throughput of serial execution remains relatively constant. However, in our scheme, we can observe an increase in throughput as the number of CPUs increases. This is because the serial batch processing scheme cannot leverage the performance of multiple cores, and all transactions need to be executed sequentially, our scheme can take advantage of multiple cores, resulting in improved system performance with an increasing number of CPUs. As the number of CPUs reaches 3, the growth gradually slows down, indicating that the parallel performance is approaching its limit. However, as the number of CPUs increases, the throughput of the scheme increases, but the latency also increases. Because with increased throughput, there are more transactions that need to be transmitted between nodes, which consumes more network bandwidth and leads to higher system latency.

To further demonstrate how our scheme can reduce the computational burden on on-chain nodes, we increased the complexity of each transaction execution and measured the time cost for the leader to execute and the validators to verify. We increased the computational complexity of each transaction by calculating the SHA256 hash 100 times on a 1000-byte length input before execution. We conducted experiments using 7 nodes, shown in Fig. 6.

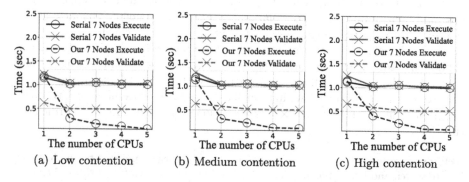

Fig. 6. Comparison of execution time and validation time under different CPUs with 4 nodes

When the CPU is limited to 1, our scheme reduces verification time compared to serial execution by nearly half. This illustrates that even with limited CPU resources, we are able to reduce the computational burden on the on-chain nodes by approximately 2 times. The execution time of the leader in our scheme and the serial execution scheme is very close, indicating that they have similar computational loads. The leader scheme has the additional burden of transmitting subgraphs to off-chain nodes. We have utilized Go's goroutines to asynchronously send the subgraphs to off-chain nodes without affecting the leader computation.

With the increasing number of CPUs, the execution time of the leader in our scheme has been dramatically reduced, as the leader can fully utilize the multi-core CPUs. However, validators only have slight improvement. This is because the leader execution is based on lock mechanisms, which fully leverage the multi-core CPU, while the validators need to execute based on the dependency relationships in the TSIG. The validators need first to perform a topological sort on received subgraphs and then sequentially execute transactions with dependency relationships. Independent transactions can be executed in parallel. Increasing the number of CPUs can speed up the execution of independent transactions, but the number of independent transactions is still relatively small compared to transactions with dependencies. Therefore, the increase in CPU does not significantly impact reducing validation time.

In addition, as the conflict rate increases, the validators require more time for validation. With an increasing conflict rate, there are fewer independent transactions in the subgraph, and more transactions have dependencies. This prevents the validation nodes from effectively utilizing multi-core CPU, resulting in an increased validation burden on the on-chain nodes. However, overall, the validation time is still reduced by a factor of two compared to batch serial execution.

6   Conclusion

In this paper, we aim to improve the performance of blockchain systems. We propose an on-chain and off-chain collaborative execution scheme. This new execution scheme integrates off-chain execution into the on-chain concurrent execution scheme, enhancing the performance of blockchain systems significantly without introducing any security assumptions on off-chain nodes. We implement our prototype based on Tendermint and compare it with the serial execution scheme. The experimental results show that our scheme can achieve a maximum throughput improvement of $2.6\times$, $11.2\times$ less execution time, and $2.1\times$ less verification time.

Acknowlegements. The work described in this paper was supported by the National Key Research and Development Plan(2022YFF0903100), the National Natural Science Foundation of China (62172453), the National Natural Science Foundation of Guangdong province(2022A1515010154), the Major Key Project of PCL(PCL2021A06), and the Pearl River Talent Recruitment Program (No. 2019QN01X130).

References

1. Wang, X., Muppirala, V.V., Yang, L., Kannan, S., Viswanath, P.: Securing parallel-chain protocols under variable mining power. In: Proceedings of the 2021 ACM SIGSAC Conference on Computer and Communications Security, pp. 1700–1721 (2021)
2. Duan, S., Zhang, H.: Foundations of dynamic bft. In: 2022 IEEE Symposium on Security and Privacy (SP), pp. 1317–1334. IEEE (2022)

3. Zhang, J., Hong, Z., Qiu, X., Zhan, Y., Guo, S., Chen, W.: Dynamic sharding: a trade-off between security and scalability. In: Blockchain Scalability, pp. 193–221. Springer, Heidelberg (2023). https://doi.org/10.1007/978-981-99-1059-5_8
4. Dickerson, T., Gazzillo, P., Herlihy, M., Koskinen, E.: Adding concurrency to smart contracts. In: Proceedings of the ACM Symposium on Principles of Distributed Computing, pp. 303–312 (2017)
5. Anjana, P.S., Kumari, S., Peri, S., Rathor, S., Somani, A.: An efficient framework for optimistic concurrent execution of smart contracts. In: 2019 27th Euromicro International Conference on Parallel, Distributed and Network-Based Processing (PDP), pp. 83–92. IEEE (2019)
6. Garamvölgyi, P., Liu, Y., Zhou, D., Long, F., Wu, M.: Utilizing parallelism in smart contracts on decentralized blockchains by taming application-inherent conflicts. In: Proceedings of the 44th International Conference on Software Engineering, pp. 2315–2326 (2022)
7. Jin, C., Pang, S., Qi, X., Zhang, Z., Zhou, A.: A high performance concurrency protocol for smart contracts of permissioned blockchain. IEEE Trans. Knowl. Data Eng. 34(11), 5070–5083 (2021)
8. Kalodner, H., Goldfeder, S., Chen, X., Weinberg, S.M., Felten, E.W.: Arbitrum: scalable, private smart contracts. In: 27th USENIX Security Symposium (USENIX Security 2018), pp. 1353–1370 (2018)
9. Wüst, K., Matetic, S., Egli, S., Kostiainen, K., Capkun, S.: ACE: asynchronous and concurrent execution of complex smart contracts. In: Proceedings of the 2020 ACM SIGSAC Conference on Computer and Communications Security, pp. 587–600 (2020)
10. Kang, H., Dai, T., Jean-Louis, N., Tao, S., Gu, X.: Fabzk: supporting privacy-preserving, auditable smart contracts in hyperledger fabric. In: 2019 49th Annual IEEE/IFIP International Conference on Dependable Systems and Networks (DSN), pp. 543–555. IEEE (2019)
11. Cheng, R., et al.: Ekiden: a platform for confidentiality-preserving, trustworthy, and performant smart contracts. In: 2019 IEEE European Symposium on Security and Privacy (EuroS&P), pp. 185–200. IEEE (2019)
12. Xie, T., et al.: zkbridge: trustless cross-chain bridges made practical. In: Proceedings of the 2022 ACM SIGSAC Conference on Computer and Communications Security, pp. 3003–3017 (2022)
13. Van Bulck, J., et al.: Foreshadow: extracting the keys to the intel SGX kingdom with transient out-of-order execution. In: 27th USENIX Security Symposium (USENIX Security 2018), pp. 991–1008 (2018)
14. Cai, Z., et al.: Benzene: scaling blockchain with cooperation-based sharding. IEEE Trans. Parallel Distrib. Syst. 34(2), 639–654 (2022)
15. Cason, D., Fynn, E., Milosevic, N., Milosevic, Z., Buchman, E., Pedone, F.: The design, architecture and performance of the tendermint blockchain network. In: 2021 40th International Symposium on Reliable Distributed Systems (SRDS), pp. 23–33. IEEE (2021)
16. Zhang, R., Zhang, D., Wang, Q., Wu, S., Xie, J., Preneel, B.: Nc-max: breaking the security-performance tradeoff in nakamoto consensus. Cryptology ePrint Archive (2020)
17. Reijsbergen, D., Dinh, T.T.A.: On exploiting transaction concurrency to speed up blockchains. In: 2020 IEEE 40th International Conference on Distributed Computing Systems (ICDCS), pp. 1044–1054. IEEE (2020)

18. Bartoletti, M., Galletta, L., Murgia, M.: A true concurrent model of smart contracts executions. In: Bliudze, S., Bocchi, L. (eds.) COORDINATION 2020. LNCS, vol. 12134, pp. 243–260. Springer, Cham (2020). https://doi.org/10.1007/978-3-030-50029-0_16

19. Klems, M., Eberhardt, J., Tai, S., Härtlein, S., Buchholz, S., Tidjani, A.: Trustless intermediation in blockchain-based decentralized service marketplaces. In: Maximilien, M., Vallecillo, A., Wang, J., Oriol, M. (eds.) ICSOC 2017. LNCS, vol. 10601, pp. 731–739. Springer, Cham (2017). https://doi.org/10.1007/978-3-319-69035-3_53

20. Sariboz, E., Kolachala, K., Panwar, G., Vishwanathan, R., Misra, S.: Off-chain execution and verification of computationally intensive smart contracts. In: 2021 IEEE International Conference on Blockchain and Cryptocurrency (ICBC), pp. 1–3. IEEE (2021)

21. Kim, Y., Jeong, S., Jezek, K., Burgstaller, B., Scholz, B.: An off-the-chain execution environment for scalable testing and profiling of smart contracts. In: 2021 USENIX Annual Technical Conference (USENIX ATC 21), pp. 565–579 (2021)

22. Das, P., et al.: Fastkitten: practical smart contracts on bitcoin. In: USENIX Security Symposium, pp. 801–818 (2019)

23. Dwork, C., Lynch, N., Stockmeyer, L.: Consensus in the presence of partial synchrony. J. ACM (JACM) 35(2), 288–323 (1988)

24. Zhang, J., Chen, W., Luo, S., Gong, T., Hong, Z., Kate, A.: Front-running attack in distributed sharded ledgers and fair cross-shard consensus. arXiv preprint arXiv:2306.06299 (2023)

Author Index

F. Monti et al. (Eds.): ICSOC 2023, LNCS 14419, pp. 409–411, 2023.
https://doi.org/10.1007/978-3-031-48421-6